Lecture Notes in Artificial Intelligence 667

Subseries of Lecture Notes in Computer Science
Edited by J. Siekmann

Lecture Notes in Computer Science

Edited by G. Goos and J. Hartmanis

Lecture Notes in Artificial Intelligence   607

Subseries of Lecture Notes in Computer Science
Edited by J. Siekmann

Lecture Notes in Computer Science
Edited by G. Goos and J. Hartmanis

Pavel B. Brazdil (Ed.)

Machine Learning: ECML-93

European Conference on Machine Learning
Vienna, Austria, April 5-7, 1993
Proceedings

Springer-Verlag

Berlin Heidelberg New York
London Paris Tokyo
Hong Kong Barcelona
Budapest

Series Editor

Jörg Siekmann
University of Saarland
German Research Center for Artificial Intelligence (DFKI)
Stuhlsatzenhausweg 3, W-6600 Saarbrücken 11, FRG

Volume Editor

Pavel B. Brazdil
LIACC-CIUP
Rua Campo Alegre 823, P-4100 Porto, Portugal

CR Subject Classification (1991): I.2.6

ISBN 3-540-56602-3 Springer-Verlag Berlin Heidelberg New York
ISBN 0-387-56602-3 Springer-Verlag New York Berlin Heidelberg

Typesetting: Camera ready by author/editor
Printing and binding: Druckhaus Beltz, Hemsbach/Bergstr.
45/3140-543210 - Printed on acid-free paper

Foreword

The European Conference on Machine Learning 1993 (ECML-93) continued with the tradition of earlier EWSLs *(European Working Sessions on Learning)*. The aim of these conferences is to provide a platform for presenting the latest results in the area of machine learning. Although ECML-93 is the first conference under this name, it can be considered as the sixth meeting of this kind in Europe.

The scientific programme included the presentation of invited talks, selected papers, and the presentation of ongoing work in poster sessions. The ECML-93 programme was complemented by several workshops on specific topics. The proceedings contain papers related to all these activities.

The first chapter of the proceedings contains two invited papers. The first one accompanies the invited talk of *Ross Quinlan* from the University of Sydney. The second one is by *Stephen Muggleton* giving an overview of the area of *Inductive Logic Programming (ILP)* that has become a very active area indeed. The paper of *Derek Sleeman* accompanying his invited lecture is available on request from the author. This paper covers some European research projects in the area of ML and their significance for the future development of ML.

The reader may be interested to note that the call for papers was very successful, resulting in 69 submissions. In order to maintain a good standard of the conference, all submissions were reviewed by at least two members of the programme committee or their close colleagues. Of course, only some of the submitted papers could actually be accepted.

The second chapter of the proceedings contains 18 scientific papers that have been accepted for the main sessions of the conference. It includes both long papers and some short ones which describe the results of ongoing work.

The third chapter contains 18 shorter position papers. In order not to make the proceedings too bulky, all the papers in this chapter have been condensed.

The final chapter of this book includes three overview papers related to the ECML-93 workshops / panels supplied by the organizers. As the workshops were organized independently of the main conference, this volume does not include any of the papers presented by its participants.

Organization of ECML-93

All matters related to the programme were coordinated by the Programme Chair who had the support of the ECML-93 Programme Committee. It included the following members of the ML or AI community:

Francesco Bergadano (Italy)
Ivan Bratko (Slovenia)
Pavel Brazdil (Portugal)
Ken de Jong (USA)
Luc de Raedt (Belgium)
Jean-Gabriel Ganascia (France)
Antonios Kakas (Cyprus)
Yves Kodratoff (France)
Nada Lavrac (Slovenia)
Ramón L. de Mantaras (Spain)

Katharina Morik (Germany)
Igor Mozetic (Austria)
Stephen Muggleton (UK)
Lorenza Saitta (Italy)
Jude Shavlik (USA)
Derek Sleeman (UK)
Maarten van Someren (Netherlands)
Walter Van de Velde (Belgium)
Rüdiger Wirth (Germany)

Several members of the Programme Committee have taken up an active role in the organization of ECML-93 workshops, and also invested a great deal of effort into reviewing papers. I wish to express my gratitude to all the people involved for this work.

ECML-93 was organized by the

Department of Medical Cybernetics and Artificial Intelligence,
University of Vienna

in cooperation with the

Austrian Research Institute for Artificial Intelligence.

Igor Mozetic and Gerhard Widmer have acted in the role of Local Chairs.

ECML-93 was supported by the following organizations:

Commission of the European Communities,
Vienna Convention Bureau,
Austrian Federal Ministry of Science and Research,
Austrian Society for Cybernetic Studies (OeSGK),
Austrian Society for Artificial Intelligence (OeGAI),
European Coordinating Committee for Artificial Intelligence (ECCAI).

The official patrons of ECML-93 were:

Austrian Federal Minister of Science and Research, Dr. Erhard Busek,
Mayor of Vienna, Dr. Helmut Zilk,
Rector of the University of Vienna, Prof. Dr. Alfred Ebenbauer.

I would like to thank, on behalf of all participants, all the sponsors and patrons who supported this venue.

I appreciate also the effort of the following members of the ML community who were solicited to help and accepted the task of reviewing papers:

E. Aimeur,	Attilio Giordana,	I. Moulinier,
C. Tsatsarakis,	Matjaz Gams,	R. Ochlmann,
Siegfried Bell,	Bill Gasarch,	Erich Prem,
Y. Bennani,	Nicolas Graner,	Anke Rieger,
Gilles Bisson,	S. Grolimund,	G. Ramalho,
Marko Bohanec,	Daniele Gunetti,	M. Rissakis,
Maurice Bruynooghe,	Achim G. Hoffmann,	Céline Rouveirol,
Karine Causse,	Klaus P. Jantke,	Sunil Sharma,
Fengru Chen,	Aram Karalic,	Ashwin Sriniwasan,
Bojan Cestnik,	Jörg-Uwe Kietz,	Irene Stahl,
V. Corruble,	Volker Klingspor,	Joachim Stender,
Marc Denecker,	Igor Kononenko	Birgit Tausend,
Saso Dzeroski,	Miroslav Kubát,	Luís Torgo,
Peter Edwards,	B. Leroux,	Tanja Urbancic,
Werner Emde,	Stan Matwin,	Gilles Venturini,
M.C. D'Erceville,	Mabel Mosli,	Gerhard Widmer.
		Stefan Weber.

Finally I wish all those who have acquired a copy of these proceeding many interesting insights into machine learning! Personally I believe that everyone's effort was well justified!

Porto, February 1993

Pavel B. Brazdil
Programme Chair of ECML-93

Contents

Chapter 1:

Invited Papers

FOIL: A Midterm Report

J. R. Quinlan and R. M. Cameron-Jones

Basser Department of Computer Science
University of Sydney
Sydney Australia 2006
quinlan@cs.su.oz.au, mcj@cs.su.oz.au

Abstract: FOIL is a learning system that constructs Horn clause programs from examples. This paper summarises the development of FOIL from 1989 up to early 1993 and evaluates its effectiveness on a non-trivial sequence of learning tasks taken from a Prolog programming text. Although many of these tasks are handled reasonably well, the experiment highlights some weaknesses of the current implementation. Areas for further research are identified.

1. Introduction

The principal differences between zeroth-order and first-order supervised learning systems are the form of the training data and the way that a learned theory is expressed. Data for zeroth-order learning programs such as ASSISTANT [Cestnik, Kononenko and Bratko, 1986], CART [Breiman, Friedman, Olshen and Stone, 1984], CN2 [Clark and Niblett, 1987] and C4.5 [Quinlan, 1992] comprise preclassified cases, each described by its values for a fixed collection of attributes. These systems develop theories, in the form of decision trees or production rules, that relate a case's class to its attribute values. In contrast, the input to first-order learners (usually) contains ground assertions about a number of multi-argument predicates or relations and the learned theory consists of a logic program, restricted to Horn clauses or something similar, that predicts when a vector of arguments will satisfy a designated predicate.

Early first-order learning systems such as MIS [Shapiro, 1983] and MARVIN [Sammut and Banerji, 1986] were based on the notion of first-order proof. A partial theory was modified when it was insufficient to prove a known fact or able to (mis)prove a known fiction. The dependence on finding proofs meant that systems like these were relatively slow, most of the time being consumed in theorem-proving mode, so that they were able to analyse only small training sets. Later systems such as FOIL [Quinlan, 1990, 1991] and GOLEM [Muggleton and Feng, 1990] abandoned proof-based algorithms for more efficient methods; GOLEM uses Plotkin's *relative least general generalisation* to form clauses while FOIL uses a divide-and-cover strategy adapted from zeroth-order learning. These approaches have proved to be more efficient and robust, enabling larger training sets to be analysed to learn more complex programs. Later systems such as CHAM [Kijsirikul, Numao and Shimura, 1991], FOCL [Pazzani, Brunk and Silverstein, 1991; Pazzani and Kibler, 1992] ILE [Rouveirol, 1991] and FORTE [Richards and Mooney, 1991] often contain elements of both proof-based and empirical approaches.

This paper examines FOIL, summarising its development over the last four years. After outlining its key features, we describe an experiment designed to evaluate its program-writing ability, using problems that human Prolog students are expected to be able to master. Not surprisingly, FOIL has difficulty with some of the problems. We discuss FOIL's shortcomings and what they tell us about the research that will be needed to extend it into a useful logic programming tool.

2. FOIL

In a nutshell, FOIL is a system for learning function-free Horn clause definitions of a relation in terms of itself and other relations. The program is actually slightly more flexible since it can learn several relations in sequence, allows negated literals in the definitions (using standard Prolog semantics), and can employ certain constants in the definitions it produces.

FOIL's input consists of information about the relations, one of which (the *target relation*) is to be defined by a Horn clause program. For each relation it is given a set of tuples of constants that belong to the relation. For the target relation it might also be given tuples that are known not to belong to the relation; alternatively, the closed world assumption may be invoked to state that no tuples, other than those specified, belong to the target relation. Tuples known to be in the target relation will be referred to as ⊕ tuples and those not in the relation as ⊖ tuples. The learning task is then to find a set of clauses for the target relation that accounts for all the ⊕ tuples while not covering any of the ⊖ tuples.

The basic approach used by FOIL is an AQ-like covering algorithm [Michalski, Mozetič, Hong and Lavrač, 1986]. It starts with a *training set* containing all ⊕ and ⊖ tuples, constructs a function-free Horn clause to 'explain' some of the ⊕ tuples, removes the covered ⊕ tuples from the training set, and continues with the search for the next clause. When clauses covering all the ⊕ tuples have been found, they are reviewed to eliminate any redundant clauses and reordered so that any recursive clauses come after the non-recursive base cases.

Perfect definitions that exactly match the data are not always possible, particularly in real-world situations where incorrect values and missing tuples are to be expected. To get around this problem, FOIL uses encoding-length heuristics to limit the complexity of clauses and programs. The final clauses may cover most (rather than all) of the $\oplus$ tuples while covering few (rather than none) of the $\ominus$ tuples. See [Quinlan, 1990] for details.

2.1 Finding a Clause

FOIL starts with the left-hand side of the clause and specialises it by adding literals to the right-hand side, stopping when no $\ominus$ tuples are covered by the clause or when encoding-length heuristics indicate that the clause is too complex. As new variables are introduced by the added literals, the size of the tuples in the training set increases so that each tuple represents a possible binding for all variables that appear in the partially-developed clause.

If the target relation R has k arguments, the process of finding one clause for the definition of R can be summarised as follows:

- Initialise the clause to

$$R(V_1, V_2, ..., V_k) \leftarrow$$

  and a local training set T to the $\oplus$ tuples not covered by any previous clause and all the $\ominus$ tuples.

- While T contains $\ominus$ tuples and is not too complex:
  - Find a literal L to add to the right-hand side of the clause.
  - Form a new training set T':
    * for each tuple t in T, and
    * for each binding b of any new variables introduced by literal L,
      · if the tuple $t.b$ (obtained by concatenating t and b) satisfies L, then add $t.b$ to T' with the same label ($\oplus$ or $\ominus$) as t.
  - Replace T by T'.

- Prune the clause by removing any unnecessary literals.

Although FOIL incorporates a simple backup mechanism, the clause-building process is essentially a greedy search; once a literal is added to a clause, alternative literals are usually not investigated.

The key question is how to determine appropriate literals to append to the developing clause. FOIL uses two criteria: a literal must either help to exclude unwanted $\ominus$ tuples from the training set, or must introduce new variables that may be needed for future literals. Literals of the first kind are called *gainful* while *determinate* literals are included primarily because they introduce new variables.

2.2 Choosing Gainful Literals

Consider the partially developed clause

$$R(V_1, V_2, ..., V_k) \leftarrow L_1, L_2, ..., L_{m-1}$$

containing variables $V_1, V_2, ..., V_x$. Each tuple in the training set T looks like $\langle c_1, c_2, ..., c_x \rangle$ for some constants $\{c_j\}$, and represents a ground instance of the variables in the clause. Now, consider what happens when a literal L_m of the form

$$P(V_{i_1}, V_{i_2}, ..., V_{i_p})$$

is added to the right-hand side. If the literal contains one or more new variables, the arity of the new training set will increase; let x' denote the number of variables in the new clause. Then, each tuple in the new training set T' will be of the form $\langle d_1, d_2, ..., d_{x'} \rangle$ for constants $\{d_j\}$, and will have the following properties:

- $\langle d_1, d_2, ..., d_x \rangle$ is a tuple in T, and

- $\langle d_{i_1}, d_{i_2}, ..., d_{i_p} \rangle$ is in the relation P.

That is, each tuple in T' is an extension of one of the tuples in T, and the ground instance that it represents satisfies the literal. Every tuple in T thus gives rise to zero or more tuples in T' with the $\oplus$ or $\ominus$ label of a tuple in T' being copied from its ancestor tuple in T.

Let T_+ denote the number of $\oplus$ tuples in T and T'_+ the number in T'. The effect of adding a literal L_m can be assessed from an information perspective as follows. The information conveyed by the knowledge that a tuple in T has label $\oplus$ is given by

$$I(T) = -log_2(T_+ \, / \, |T|)$$

and similarly for $I(T')$. If $I(T')$ is less than $I(T)$ we have 'gained' information by adding the literal L_m to the clause; if s of the tuples in T have extensions in T', the total information gained about the $\oplus$ tuples in T is

$$gain(L_m) = s \times (I(T) - I(T')).$$

FOIL explores the space of possible literals that might be added to a clause at each step, looking for the one with greatest positive gain.

The form of the gain metric allows significant pruning of the literal space, so that FOIL can usually rule out large subspaces without having to examine any literals in them. If a potential literal contains new variables, it is possible to compute the maximum gain that could be obtained by replacing some or all of them with existing variables. When the maximum gain is below that of some literal already considered, the literals resulting from such replacements do not need to be investigated.

Another form of pruning involves literals that use the target relation itself. Since we do not want FOIL to produce non-executable programs that fail due to infinite recursive looping, recursive definitions must be screened carefully. Recursive literals that could lead to problems are barred from consideration, as described below.

2.3 Determinate Literals

Some clauses in reasonable definitions will inevitably contain literals with zero gain. Suppose, for instance, that all objects have a value for some property D, and the literal $D(X, Y)$ defines the value Y for object X. Since this literal represents a one-to-one mapping from X to Y, each tuple in T will give rise to exactly one tuple in T' and so the gain of the literal will always be zero. We could also imagine a literal $P(X, Y)$ that, for any value of X, supplied several possible values for Y. Such a literal might even have negative gain.

If X is a previously defined variable and Y a new variable, there is an important difference between adding literals $D(X, Y)$ and $P(X, Y)$ to a clause; the first will produce a new training set of exactly the same size, while the second may exclude some $\oplus$ tuples or may cause the number of tuples in the training set to grow. This is the key insight underlying *determinate* literals, an idea inspired by GOLEM's *determinate terms* [Muggleton and Feng, 1990]: the value of each new variable is forced or determined by the values of existing variables.

More precisely, suppose that we have an incomplete clause

$$R(V_1, V_2, ..., V_k) \leftarrow L_1, L_2, ..., L_{m-1}$$

with an associated training set T as before. A literal L_m is determinate with respect to this partial clause if L_m contains one or more new variables and there is exactly one extension of each $\oplus$ tuple in T, and no more than one extension of each $\ominus$ tuple, that satisfies L_m. The idea is that, if L_m is added to the clause, no $\oplus$ tuple will be eliminated and the new training set T' will be no larger than T.

FOIL notes determinate literals found while searching for gainful literals as above. The maximum possible gain is given by a literal that excludes all $\ominus$ tuples and no $\oplus$ tuples; in the notation used before, this gain is $T_+ \times I(T)$. Unless a literal is found whose gain is close to ($\geq 80\%$ of) the maximum possible gain, FOIL adds *all* determinate literals to the clause and tries again. This may seem rather extravagant, since it is unlikely that all these literals will be useful. However, FOIL incorporates clause-refining mechanisms that remove unnecessary literals as each clause is completed, so there is no ultimate penalty for this all-in approach. Since no $\oplus$ tuples are eliminated and the training set does not grow, the only computational cost is associated with the introduction of new variables and the corresponding increase in the space of subsequent possible literals. It is precisely the enlargement of this space that the addition of determinate literals is intended to achieve.

There is a potential runaway situation in which determinate literals found at one cycle give rise to further determinate literals at the next *ad infinitum*. To circumvent this problem, FOIL borrows another idea from GOLEM. The *depth* of a variable is determined by its first occurrence in the clause. All variables in the left-hand side of the clause have depth 0; a variable that first occurs in some literal has depth one greater than the greatest depth of any previously-occurring variable in that literal. By placing an upper limit on the depth of any variable introduced by a determinate literal, we rule out indefinite runaway. This limit does reduce the class of learnable programs. However, the stringent requirement that a determinate literal must be uniquely satisfied by *all* $\oplus$ tuples means that this runaway situation is unlikely and FOIL's default depth limit of 5 is rarely reached.

2.4 Further Literal Forms

We are now moving into areas covered by recent extensions to FOIL. The first of these concerns the kinds of literals that can appear in the right-hand side of a clause.

Early versions of FOIL considered literals of the forms

- $P(W_1, W_2, ..., W_p)$, $\neg P(W_1, W_2, ..., W_p)$
  where P is a relation and the W_i's are variables, at least one of which must have occurred already in the clause; and

- $V_i = V_j$, $V_i \neq V_j$
  that compare the values of existing variables.

Two further forms have now been added.

In the first of these, certain constants can be identified as *theory* constants that

can appear explicitly in a definition. Examples might include a constant []
representing the null list in list-processing tasks, or the integers 0 and 1 in tasks
that involve the natural numbers. For such a theory constant c, FOIL will also
consider literals of the forms

$$V_i = c, \quad V_i \neq c$$

where V_i is a variable of the appropriate type that appears earlier in the clause.
This minor addition is equivalent to declaring a special relation is-c for each such
constant c; in fact, the extension is implemented in this way.

The second extension is more substantial. Relations encountered in the real
world are not limited to discrete information but commonly include numeric
fields as well. We could imagine simple relations such as

atomic-weight(E,W)

that provides the (numeric) atomic weight W of each element E, or

quote(C,B,S)

detailing the buy and sell prices for a commodity C. As a first step towards being
able to exploit numeric information like this, FOIL now includes literal types

$$V_i > k, \quad V_i \leq k, \quad V_i > V_j, \quad V_i \leq V_j$$

that allow an existing variable V_i with numeric values to be compared against a
threshold k found by FOIL or against another variable V_j of the same type. Such
an extension falls a long way short of Prolog facilities that allow a continuous
value for V_i to be computed in the clause; however, it does permit bound numeric
values to be used in conditions on the right-hand side of a clause.

2.5 Managing Recursion

Recursive theories are expressive and hence powerful, so that the ability to learn
recursive programs is one of the principal advantages of first-order systems like
GOLEM and FOIL. The increase in expressiveness, however, is counterbalanced
by the care that must be taken to avoid nonsensical recursion.

As an illustration, consider the task of learning a program for multiplication of
non-negative integers in terms of addition and decrement. We might have three
relations:

mult(A,B,C)	meaning	$C = A \times B$
plus(A,B,C)		$C = A + B$
dec(A,B)		$B = A - 1$.

A suitable definition for multiply is

$$\text{mult}(A,B,C) \leftarrow A{=}0,\ C{=}0$$
$$\text{mult}(A,B,C) \leftarrow \text{dec}(A,D),\ \text{plus}(B,E,C),\ \text{mult}(D,B,E)$$

where the last clause captures the identity

$$A \times B = B + (A - 1) \times B.$$

This definition seems intuitively to be well-behaved in the sense that it will always terminate. On the other hand, a simpler definition

$$\text{mult}(A,B,C) \leftarrow \text{mult}(B,A,C)$$

will clearly lead to an infinite recursive loop. How does FOIL, which is biased towards finding simpler definitions, eschew the latter in favour of the former? The short answer is that, as a clause is being developed, recursive literals must satisfy certain criteria for inclusion in the right-hand side. In particular, a recursive literal on the right-hand side must be judged to be less than the head of the clause in some ordering of literals.

The earliest version of FOIL used a method based on discovering an ordering of the constants appearing in tuples. This method guaranteed that a single clause could not lead to a recursive loop by calling itself directly. The order discovery was removed in following releases, which relied on the user specifying the constants of each type in an appropriate order. Order discovery mechanisms have been reinstated in the most recent versions and the method of ordering recursive literals has been generalised so that the guarantee now applies to sets of clauses for a single relation, not just to a single clause. The following is meant to give an informal sketch of the idea, with a complete discussion available in [Cameron-Jones and Quinlan, 1993].

Returning to the multiply example above, we see that the clause for the general case

$$\text{mult}(A,B,C) \leftarrow \text{dec}(A,D),\ \text{plus}(B,E,C),\ \text{mult}(D,B,E)$$

cannot lead to infinite recursion since the literal $\text{dec}(A,D)$ guarantees that D is always less than A; $\text{mult}(D,B,E)$ is thus less than $\text{mult}(A,B,C)$ in an intuitive ordering of mult literals. FOIL assumes that some relations provided for a task will behave like dec in establishing an ordering of their arguments and attempts to identify them. For every relation R and every pair of arguments A, B of R that are of the same type Q, FOIL asks:

Are there orderings of the constants of type Q that are consistent with the hypothesis that $A < B$?

When answers to all these questions have been determined, FOIL establishes a single definitive ordering of the constants of type Q so that the number of such inequalities is maximised.

The now-fixed ordering of constants of each type allows us to determine rankings among pairs of variables in an incomplete clause. If such a clause contains variables $V_1, V_2, ..., V_x$ and the training set consists of tuples of constants $\langle d_{a1}, d_{a2}, ..., d_{ax} \rangle$, $a = 1, 2, ..., |T|$, then $V_i < V_j$ if they belong to the same type and d_{ai} always comes before d_{aj} in the constant ordering for that type.

The inequalities among pairs of variables can be extended to an ordering of literals involving a predicate R and variables. In broad terms, if $W_1, W_2, ...$ denote variables in $V_1, V_2, ..., V_x$, then

$$R(W_1, W_2, ..., W_k) < R(V_1, V_2, ..., V_k) \text{ if}$$
$$W_\alpha < V_\alpha, \text{ or}$$
$$W_\alpha = V_\alpha \text{ and } W_\beta < V_\beta, \text{ or}$$
$$W_\alpha = V_\alpha \text{ and } W_\beta = V_\beta \text{ and } W_\gamma < V_\gamma, \text{ or } ...$$

Here α, β, γ etc. denote argument positions that, together with the ordering of variables in the clause, specify a particular ordering of the literals involving R.

Suppose now that we have an incomplete definition for relation R that consists of zero or more completed clauses and a partial clause. A recursive literal $R(W_1, W_2, ..., W_k)$ can be added to the right-hand side of the developing clause only when there are values of α, β etc. as above so that

- this literal is less than the left-hand side of the clause, and
- the same is true for all recursive literals in the completed clauses.

This may sound complex but its implementation is simple and efficient. The restriction on recursive literals in the right-hand side of clauses prevents infinite recursive loops due to a definition of R calling itself directly, yet does not exclude even complex recursive definitions such as that for Ackermann's function:

```
Ack(A,B,C) ← A=0, dec(C,B)
Ack(A,B,C) ← B=0, dec(A,D), Ack(D,E,C), dec(E,B)
Ack(A,B,C) ← dec(A,D), dec(B,E), Ack(A,E,F), Ack(D,F,C)
```

In this case, the ordering of literals found by FOIL is

$$Ack(W_1, W_2, W_3) < Ack(V_1, V_2, V_3) \text{ if}$$
$$W_1 < V_1, \text{ or}$$
$$W_1 = V_1 \text{ and } W_2 < V_2.$$

In the definition above, dec(A,D) gives D<A in the second and third clauses, and dec(B,E) in the third clause gives E<B, so all recursive literals in these clauses are less than the heads of the clauses. Consequently, this definition can be guaranteed to terminate when invoked with ground instances of A and B.

2.6 Improved Definitions

Programs like FOIL that depend on greedy search will occasionally follow unprofitable paths leading to poor definitions or no definitions at all. FOIL's backup mechanism is designed to ameliorate the latter condition by restarting search at saved backup points. The problem of poor definitions is much more difficult to circumvent.

From its earliest version, FOIL has incorporated post-processing of definitions in which unnecessary literals are excised from finished clauses and redundant clauses are removed from complete definitions. When there are numerous superfluous literals, clause pruning can consume a noticeable amount of time; a recent extension is a fast heuristic pruning method that reverts to the slow-but-sure algorithm in the event of failure.

The most recent versions have two additional mechanisms for producing better clauses. It sometimes happens that, when the possible literals to be added to a clause are being considered, one literal L would complete the clause but another literal of higher gain is selected instead. The search can meander along in this way, leading eventually to a clause that is inferior to the one that would have been produced if L had been chosen. FOIL now remembers the best complete clause that could have been obtained by a different choice of literal at any point. When the clause is complete, the system checks to see whether the remembered clause is at least as good as the final clause and, if so, uses the remembered clause instead. This extension, which requires hardly any additional computation, is responsible for much improved definitions in some tasks.

We have also observed cases in which a non-recursive literal L, chosen to complete a clause, involves only variables that appear in the left-hand side of the clause. Such a literal could clearly have appeared at the beginning of the right-hand side. If the right-hand side contains literals other than L, they may have had the effect of making the clause too specific. To circumvent this possibility, the clause is regrown starting with the single literal L on the right-hand side.

The final polishing involves reordering the clauses. After all clauses making up a definition have been sifted as above to remove redundancies, all non-recursive "base case" clauses are moved to the front so that they appear before any recursive clauses.

3. An Experiment

Many evaluations of learning systems involve a limited amount of background information – just that required for the task at hand – and sometimes carefully chosen training examples as well. Such experiments can demonstrate the feasibility of certain types of learning, but do not address the usefulness of the learning system in practical applications, where there is usually a large amount of irrelevant information and where training examples come from a neutral, unbiased source.

As a step towards a more pragmatic evaluation, we started with Ivan Bratko's well-known text *Prolog Programming for Artificial Intelligence* [Bratko, 1986]. Chapter 3 of this book introduces several programs for manipulating lists and includes a set of student exercises. We conducted trials to see whether FOIL could learn the expository programs and exercises in the same order as they appear in the book, omitting only the last two exercises that were quite different from the others. (One of them, canget, deals with lists specific to the monkey and bananas problem; the other, flatten, uses structured lists.) A brief summary of the problems attempted is:

member(E,L)	E is an element of list L
conc(L1,L2,L3)	appending L1 to L2 gives list L3
member1(E,L)	as for member with conc available
last(E,L)	E is the last element of L
last1(E,L)	ditto, but without using conc
del(E,L1,L2)	deleting an occurrence of E from L1 gives L2
member2(E,L)	as for member with del available
insert(E,L1,L2)	inserting E somewhere in L1 gives L2
sublist(L1,L2)	L1 is a sublist of L2
permutation(L1,L2)	L2 is a permutation of list L1
even/oddlength(L)	L has an even/odd number of elements (both relations to be defined)
reverse(L1,L2)	L2 is the reverse of list L1
palindrome(L)	list L is a palindrome
palindrome1(L)	as above, but not using reverse
shift(L1,L2)	rotating elements of L1 to the left gives L2
translate(L1,L2)	L2 is the results of translating L1 using an element-to-element mapping
subset(S1,S2)	S2 is a subset of set S1
dividelist(L1,L2,L3)	L2 contains the odd-numbered elements of L1, L3 contains the even-numbered elements of L1

We included the additional relation components(L,H,T), meaning list L has head H and tail T, that corresponds to Prolog's built-in [H|T] notation for lists. For each program, all relations encountered previously were available as background knowledge so that there were many irrelevant relations to confuse FOIL's search.

We also attempted to assemble training examples in an unbiased manner. The trials were repeated for two universes, defined as

- U3, the 40 lists containing up to three elements (where each element is in the set {1,2,3}); and

- U4, the 341 similar lists containing up to four elements from {1,2,3,4}.

In a trial, FOIL was given all ⊕ tuples over the relevant universe for each relation. In U3, for example, the 142 ⊕ tuples for conc include ⟨[], [13], [13]⟩ and ⟨[32], [2], [322]⟩ but not ⟨[322], [13], [32213]⟩ since, in the last case, one of the lists contains more than three elements. Two relations in the book are defined over restricted subclasses of lists, sets in the case of subset and lists without repetitions in the case of permutation. All other relations are defined over all lists. The ⊖ tuples for the relation being learned are generally the complement of the ⊕ tuples. However, for the second universe U4, some relations would then have an enormous number of such tuples – about $341^3 \approx 40$ million for conc – so we used the FOIL option that selects a random sample of ⊖ tuples to keep them down to about 90,000. The relations affected were conc and dividelist (where we used 0.2% of ⊖ tuples), del and insert (20%), translate (40%), and sublist, permutation, reverse and shift (80%).

FOIL was allowed 1500 seconds on a DECstation 5000/240 for each problem. As the book had not introduced negation at this stage, negated literals were barred from definitions. All FOIL's other options had their default values, including the default memory limit of 100,000 tuples on any training set.

The outcomes of this experiment are summarised in Table 3.1. In the *result* column, a √ means that a correct definition was obtained (often, but not always, the same as the program in the book). The notation *restricted* indicates that the definition was correct for the universe over which the examples were defined, but would give incorrect results for lists of arbitrary length. A common problem with the restricted definitions is an incorrect base case that relies on fortuitous properties of the limited domain. For instance, the definition of reverse found in universe U3 was

```
reverse(A,B) ← A=B, conc(A,C,D), sublist(A,C)
reverse(A,B) ← components(A,C,D), reverse(D,E), conc(F,D,A), conc(E,F,B)
```

The second (recursive) clause is correct. However, the odd-looking base case exploits the fact that all lists in U3 have length at most 3; if A is a sublist of C and the result of conc'ing A to C has length at most 3, this ensures that A has length 0 or 1. Of course, the first clause is correct for such short lists A.

Task		Tuples		Result	Time
		$\oplus$	$\ominus$		(secs)
member	U3	75	45	√	0.1
	U4	880	484	√	0.9
conc	U3	142	63,858	√	28
	U4	1593	79,300	√	34
member1	U3	75	45	√	1.7
	U4	880	484	√	1.7
last	U3	39	81	restricted	0.2
	U4	340	1024	√	2.7
last1	U3	39	81	√	0.1
	U4	340	1024	√	1.9
del	U3	81	4719	√	422
	U4	1024	92,640	time limit	> 1500
insert	U3	81	4719	√	2.1
	U4	1024	92,640	√	56
member2	U3	75	45	√	0.1
	U4	880	484	√	0.9
sublist	U3	202	1398	√	1.8
	U4	2913	90,697	√	94
permutation	U3	52	204	√	1.6
	U4	749	3476	√	337
even/oddlength	U3	10/30	30/10	unsound mutual recursion	0.1
	U4	273/68	68/273	unsound mutual recursion	63
reverse	U3	40	1560	restricted	9.3
	U4	341	92,796	restricted	220
palindrome	U3	16	24	√	0.1
	U4	41	300	√	0.9
palindrome1	U3	16	24	restricted	928
	U4	41	300	restricted	212
shift	U3	39	1561	√	4.2
	U4	340	92,787	√	253
translate	U3	40	3120	time limit	> 1500
	U4	341	92,573	time limit	> 1500
subset	U3	27	37	restricted	0.2
	U4	81	175	restricted	19
dividelist	U3	40	63,960	restricted	182
	U4	341	79,302	erroneous	901

Table 3.1: results on learning programs

One definition produced by FOIL, dividelist in universe U4, was actually in error, even when only lists in the restricted universe are considered. FOIL relies on $\ominus$ tuples to show up over-generalisations. For this task, the training set included only 0.2% of the $\ominus$ tuples, none of which happened to reveal that the clause was defective. This underlines the heuristic nature of any learning from incomplete information.

Apart from running out of time, the other problem occurred in the task that required definitions of both evenlength and oddlength. The definitions found for U3 were

> evenlength(A) $\leftarrow$ del(B,C,A), oddlength(C)
> oddlength(A) $\leftarrow$ components(A,B,C), evenlength(C).

Each definition is correct in itself but, together, they lead to recursive looping since C is longer than A in the definition of evenlength but shorter in oddlength. This highlights the fine print in FOIL's guarantee of recursive soundness; an individual definition will not lead to problems, but two definitions invoking each other might.

4. Discussion

The results of this experiment can only be described as mixed. It is encouraging to see that FOIL can find correct definitions for many of the small programs, but less encouraging when we remember that students are expected to be able to produce all of them as a matter of course.

In particular, the fact that later definitions tend to be restricted (if they are found at all) highlights FOIL's sensitivity to irrelevant information. For example, when all the superfluous relations were removed, a correct definition of subset

> subset(A,B) $\leftarrow$ B=[]
> subset(A,B) $\leftarrow$ components(A,C,D), components(B,C,E), subset(D,E)
> subset(A,B) $\leftarrow$ components(A,C,D), subset(D,B)

was found from U4 in only 0.5 seconds.

Another cause for concern is that recursive definitions require near-complete sets of $\oplus$ tuples. If we consider the simplest task, member in universe U3, it is interesting to observe the effect of deleting a single $\oplus$ tuple without changing the $\ominus$ tuples (corresponding to an item of missing information, but no mis-information). If the tuple is of the form $\langle X, Y \rangle$ where X is an element and Y is a list, then:

- There is no effect if Y is of length 3.

- If Y is of length 1 or 2, at least one recursive continuation is affected. FOIL still finds a correct definition but adds an extra clause to cover the apparent "special case".

When 25% of the $\oplus$ tuples were deleted at random, the resulting definition was still "correct" but contained three superfluous clauses.

The tasks in this experiment have the property that each can be defined by a Horn clause program without the use of negated literals. Even when negated literals are allowed, the definition language used by FOIL is too weak to capture some ideas. As an illustration, the first-order expression

$$(\forall x \text{ likes}(x, y)) \supset \text{happy}(y)$$

cannot be written as a Prolog definition without the use of a cut or the establishment of an ancillary concept. Similarly, a program to recognise sentences of the language $a^*b^*c^*$ requires an extra concept such as sequence-of(Seq,Elt); a Prolog programmer would see this immediately and define the subsidiary predicate. FOIL cannot invent new relations of this kind, and can only apply negation to individual literals. Consequently, there are some quite simple concepts for which FOIL cannot find general definitions, no matter how many examples it is given.

5. Conclusion

As the title of this paper suggests, FOIL is still under development. In its current form it is an experimental vehicle for exploring ideas in learning, not a practical tool for constructing substantial logic programs. In the same way, ID3 circa 1978 was an experimental program that required a lot more work before a practical tool, C4.5, was obtained.

Several shortcomings of the system were mentioned in the previous section. Generalising slightly, we can identify the following features that will be required by any robust system for learning recursive logic programs:

- *Construction of new predicates:* Logic programmers make frequent use of predicates that do not appear in the problem statement. This is sometimes required to express the program in Horn clause form, but more frequently because ancillary predicates make the program simpler and more efficient. FOIL has no facilities for inventing new predicates, but the promising research of Muggleton and Buntine [1988], Kietz and Morik [1993] and others suggests that such facilities may be able to be grafted on.

- *Strategy for constructing programs:* Human logic programmers are taught to get the simplest base case first, then to develop the general recursive case. This kind of strategic approach is missing from FOIL, which just attempts to bite off as many $\oplus$ tuples as possible in each clause. This super-greedy strategy can lead to problems of the kind illustrated by the reverse example. Instead of the simple base case

  reverse(A,B) $\leftarrow$ A=[], B=[]

  FOIL greedily tries to extend this to include single-element lists, leading to the restricted definition of section 3.

- *Selective use of relations:* At the moment, any learning task can be made harder for FOIL simply by including more and more irrelevant relations, thereby increasing the number of literals that must be examined at each step. We hypothesise that any practical system for learning logic programs must employ a characterisation of each remembered relation, so that a relation is only considered when there is a prior reason to believe that it may be of use.

- *Incomplete training sets:* It seems unlikely that near-complete sets of $\oplus$ tuples will be available when constructing recursive definitions for relations in the context of real-world problems. Practical training sets will be small and, in problems involving synthesis of a novel theory, the given tuples will not be helpfully selected with the form of the final definition in mind. While FOIL can currently learn non-recursive definitions from sparse training cases, it has difficulty with recursive theories under these conditions.

- *Extended treatment of numeric fields:* Not many first-order systems seem to have addressed the issue of using continuous-valued information. FOIL's use of numeric fields is limited to thresholding and comparisons of known values rather than computing new values. Since many practical Prolog programs involve computation, learning systems that are intended to generate these programs must somehow come to grips with computational clauses.

With the inclusion of theory constants and tests on numeric values, FOIL can now express any theory derivable by zeroth-order learning systems such as C4.5. We have carried out some initial tests running FOIL on zeroth-order attribute-value data in which there is a single relation with one argument for each attribute. Since FOIL explores a strictly larger hypothesis space than these systems, it is not surprising that FOIL is slower. It will be interesting to see whether the increased search results in more accurate theories than those learned by zeroth-order systems.

The current version of FOIL is always available by anonymous ftp from 129.78.8.1, file name pub/foilN.sh for some integer N.

Acknowledgements

This research was supported by a grant from the Australian Research Council and by a research agreement with Digital Equipment Corporation.

References

1. Bratko, I. (1986). *Prolog Programming for Artificial Intelligence.* Wokingham, UK: Addison-Wesley.

2. Breiman, L., Friedman, J.H., Olshen, R.A. and Stone, C.J. (1984). *Classification and Regression Trees.* Belmont: Wadsworth International.

3. Cameron-Jones, R.M., and Quinlan, J.R. (1993). Avoiding pitfalls when learning recursive theories (draft). Available by anonymous ftp from 129.78.8.1, file pub/recurse.tex.

4. Cestnik, B., Kononenko, I. and Bratko, I. (1987). ASSISTANT 86: a knowledge elicitation tool for sophisticated users. In Bratko and Lavrač (Eds.) *Progress in Machine Learning.* Wilmslow: Sigma Press.

5. Clark, P and Niblett, T. (1987). Induction in noisy domains. In Bratko and Lavrač (Eds.) *Progress in Machine Learning.* Wilmslow: Sigma Press.

6. Kietz, J. and Morik, K. (1993). A polynomial approach to the constructive induction of structural knowledge. *Machine Learning,* to appear.

7. Kijsirikul, B., Numao, M. and Shimura, M. (1991). Efficient learning of logic programs with non-determinate, non-discriminating literals. *Proceedings Eighth International Workshop on Machine Learning,* Evanston, Illinois, 417-421.

8. Michalski, R.S., Mozetič, I., Hong, J. and Lavrač, N. (1986). The multipurpose incremental learning system AQ15 and its testing application to three medical domains. *Proceedings Fifth National Conference on Artificial Intelligence,* Philadelphia, 1041-1045.

9. Muggleton, S., and Buntine, W. (1988). Machine invention of first-order predicates by inverting resolution. *Proceedings Fifth International Conference Machine Learning,* Ann Arbor, 339-352.

10. Muggleton, S., and Feng, C. (1990). Efficient induction of logic programs. *Proceedings First Conference on Algorithmic Learning Theory,* Tokyo.

11. Pazzani, M.J., Brunk, C.A. and Silverstein, G. (1991). A knowledge-intensive approach to learning relational concepts. *Proceedings Eighth*

International Workshop on Machine Learning, Evanston, Illinois, 432-436.

12. Pazzani, M.J. and Kibler, D. (1992). The utility of knowledge in inductive learning. *Machine Learning 9*, 1, 57-94.

13. Quinlan, J.R. (1990). Learning logical definitions from relations. *Machine Learning 5*, 239-266.

14. Quinlan, J.R. (1991). Determinate literals in inductive logic programming. *Proceedings Twelfth International Joint Conference on Artificial Intelligence*, Sydney, 746-750.

15. Quinlan, J.R. (1992). *C4.5: Programs for Machine Learning*. San Mateo: Morgan Kaufmann.

16. Richards, B.L. and Mooney, R.J. (1991). First-order theory revision. *Proceedings Eighth International Workshop on Machine Learning*, Evanston, Illinois, 447-451.

17. Rouveirol, C. (1991). Completeness for induction procedures. *Proceedings Eighth International Workshop on Machine Learning*, Evanston, Illinois, 452-456.

18. Sammut, C.A., and Banerji, R.B. (1986). Learning concepts by asking questions. In R.S. Michalski, J.G. Carbonell and T.M. Mitchell (Eds.) *Machine Learning: An Artificial Intelligence Approach* (Vol 2). Los Altos: Morgan Kaufmann.

19. Shapiro, E.Y. (1983). *Algorithmic Program Debugging*. Cambridge, MA: MIT Press.

Inductive Logic Programming: derivations, successes and shortcomings

Stephen Muggleton
Oxford University Computing Laboratory,
11 Keble Road,
Oxford,
OX1 3QD,
United Kingdom.

Abstract

Inductive Logic Programming (ILP) is a research area which investigates the construction of quantified definite clause theories from examples and background knowledge. ILP systems have been applied successfully in a number of real-world domains. These include the learning of structure-activity rules for drug design, finite-element mesh design rules, rules for primary-secondary prediction of protein structure and fault diagnosis rules for satellites. There is a well established tradition of learning-in-the-limit results in ILP. Recently some results within Valiant's PAC-learning framework have also been demonstrated for ILP systems. In this paper it is argued that algorithms can be directly *derived* from the formal specifications of ILP. This provides a common basis for Inverse Resolution, Explanation-Based Learning, Abduction and Relative Least General Generalisation. A new general-purpose, efficient approach to predicate invention is demonstrated. ILP is underconstrained by its logical specification. Therefore a brief overview of extra-logical constraints used in ILP systems is given. Some present limitations and research directions for the field are identified.

1 Introduction

The framework for Inductive Logic Programming (ILP) [37, 38] is one of the most general within the field of Machine Learning. ILP systems construct concept definitions (logic programs) from examples and a logical domain theory (background knowledge). This goes beyond the more established *empirical learning* framework [32, 48, 5, 6] because of the use of a quantified relational logic together with background knowledge. It goes beyond the *explanation-based learning* framework [33, 11] due to the lack of insistence on complete and correct background knowledge.

The use of a relational logic formalism has allowed successful application of ILP systems in a number of domains in which the concepts to be learned cannot easily be described in an attribute-value language. These applications include structure-activity prediction for drug design [25, 57], protein secondary-structure prediction [42], and finite element mesh design [12]. It is worth comparing these results with existing *scientific discovery* systems in machine learning. By normal scientific standards it does not make sense to call BACON's [27] and AM's [29] achievements scientific/mathematical discovery since they did not produce new knowledge refereed and published in the journals of their subject area. The above applications of drug design and protein folding *did* produce machine-derived new knowledge, published in top scientific journals. There are very few other examples within AI where this has been achieved.

The generality of the ILP approach has allowed many exciting new types of application domain. In addition to the above real-world application areas ILP systems such as MIS [55], Marvin [54], CIGOL [44], ML-SMART [3], FOIL [50], Golem [41], ITOU [52], RDT [24], CLINT [9], FOCL [46], SIERES [61] and LINUS [14] are all capable of synthesising logic programs containing recursion. They can also deal with domains containing explicit representation of time [16] and learn grammar rules for natural language processing [60].

Learning-in-the-limit results are well-established in the ILP literature both for full-clausal logic [47] and definite clause logic [1, 9]. However, these results tell one little about the efficiency of learning. In contrast, Valiant's [59] PAC (Probably-Approximately-Correct) framework is aimed at providing complexity results for machine learning algorithms. However, Haussler's [21] negative PAC result concerning existentially quantified formulae seemed initially to exclude the possibility of PAC results for quantified logic. The situation has been improved by recent positive results in significant sized subsets of definite clause logic. Namely, single constrained Horn clauses [45] and k-clause ij-determinate logic programs [15]. Recent results by Kietz [23] indicate that every proper superset of the k-clause ij-determinate language is not PAC learnable. This seems to indicate a ceiling to extensions of present approaches.

As the ILP applications areas show, Horn clause logic is a powerful representation language for concept learning. It also has a clear model-theoretic semantics which is inherited from Logic Programming [30]. However, with the generality of the approach come problems with searching a large hypothesis space. A clear logical framework helps in deriving efficient algorithms for constraining and searching this space. In Section 2 the formal definitions of ILP are used to derive existing specific-general and general-specific algorithms. Additionally, in Section 2.5 a new method for carrying out predicate invention is derived in this way. In Section 3 extralogical constraints used within existing ILP systems are discussed. In Section 4 some of the shortcomings of existing ILP systems are discussed and potential remedies suggested.

2 Formal logical setting for ILP

One might ask why ILP should need a very formal definition of its logical setting? After all, Machine Learning research has progressed quite happily without much formal apparatus. Surely formalisation is time-consuming and impedes progress in implementing systems? This paper argues the opposite. Without formalisation it is not clear what one is trying to achieve in an implementation. Techniques from one implementation cannot be transferred easily to another. However, this section will demonstrate a more direct and immediate advantage. That is, if a small number of formulae are used to define the high level properties of a learning system it is often possible to manipulate these formulae algebraically to derive a complete and correct algorithm which satisfies them.

2.1 The setting

The usual context for ILP is as follows. The learning agent is provided with background knowledge B, positive examples E^+ and negative examples E^- and constructs an hypothesis H. B, E^+ E^- and H are each logic programs. A logic program is a set of definite clauses each having the form

$$h \leftarrow b_1, b_2, \ldots$$

where h is an atom and $b_1, b_2, \ldots$ is a set of atoms. Usually E^+ and E^- contain only ground clauses, with empty bodies. The following symbols are used below: $\wedge$ (logical and), $\vee$ (logical or), $\vdash$ (logically proves), $\square$ (Falsity). The conditions for construction of H are

Necessity: $B \not\vdash E^+$

Sufficiency: $B \wedge H \vdash E^+$

Weak consistency: $B \wedge H \not\vdash \square$

Strong consistency: $B \wedge H \wedge E^- \not\vdash \square$

Note that *strong consistency* is not required for systems that deal with noise (eg. Golem, FOIL and LINUS). The four conditions above capture *all* the logical requirements of an ILP system. Both *Necessity* and *Consistency* can be checked using a theorem prover. Given that all formulae involved are Horn clauses, the theorem prover used need be nothing more than a Prolog interpreter, with some minor alterations, such as iterative deepening, to ensure logical completeness.

2.2 Deriving algorithms from the specification of ILP

The *sufficiency* condition captures the notion of generalising examples relative to background knowledge. A theorem prover cannot be directly applied to derive H from B and E^+. However, by simple application of the Deduction Theorem the *sufficiency* condition can be rewritten as follows.

Sufficiency*: $B \wedge \overline{E^+} \vdash \overline{H}$

This simple alteration has a very profound effect. The negation of the hypothesis can now be deductively derived from the negation of the examples together with the background knowledge. This is true no matter what form the examples take and what form the hypothesis takes. So, in order to understand the implications of *sufficiency** better, in the following sections it is shown how different algorithms, for different purposes can be derived from this relation.

2.3 Single example clause, single hypothesis clause

This problem has been studied extensively by researchers investigating both EBL [33, 11], Inverse Resolution [54, 1, 44, 37, 52, 9] and Abduction [26, 31]. For simplicity, let us assume that both the example and the hypothesised clause are definite clauses. Thus

$$E^+ = h \leftarrow b_1, b_2, \ldots = h \vee \overline{b_1} \vee \overline{b_2} \ldots$$
$$H = h' \leftarrow b'_1, b'_2, \ldots = h' \vee \overline{b'_1} \vee \overline{b'_2} \ldots$$

Now substituting these into *sufficiency** gives

$$B \wedge \overline{(h \vee \overline{b_1} \vee \overline{b_2} \ldots)} \quad \vdash \quad \overline{(h' \vee \overline{b'_1} \vee \overline{b'_2} \ldots)}$$
$$B \wedge \overline{h} \wedge b_1 \wedge b_2 \ldots \quad \vdash \quad \overline{h'} \wedge b'_1 \wedge b'_2 \ldots$$

Note that $\overline{h}, \overline{h'}, b_i$ and b'_i are all ground skolemised literals. Suppose we use $B \wedge \overline{E^+}$ to generate *all* ground unit clause consequences. When negated, the resulting (possibly infinite[1]) clause is a unique, most specific solution for all hypotheses which fit the *sufficiency* condition. All such clauses entail this clause. Thus the entire hypothesis space can be generated by dropping literals, variabilising terms or inverting implication [28, 39, 22]. No matter what control method is used for searching this space (general-specific or specific-general), all algorithms within EBL and Inverse Resolution are based on the above relationship. This is shown in detail for Inverse Resolution in [37].

What happens when more than one negative literal is a ground consequence of $B \wedge \overline{E^+}$? In the general case, the most specific clause will then be $h'_1 \vee h'_2, \ldots \vee \overline{b'_1}, \vee \overline{b'_2} \ldots$. If the hypothesis is required to be a definite clause, the set of most-specific solutions is

$$h'_1 \leftarrow b'_1, b'_2, \ldots$$
$$h'_2 \leftarrow b'_1, b'_2, \ldots$$
$$\ldots$$

h'_1 and h'_2 may not have the same predicate symbol as h in the example. This set of most specific clauses, representing a set of hypothesis spaces, can be seen

---

[1]Specific-general ILP algorithms such as CLINT [9] Golem [41] use contrained subsets of definite clause logic to ensure finiteness of the most-specific clause.

as the basis for abduction, theory revision [51] and multiple predicate learning [10].

Example 1 *Let*

$$B = \left\{ \begin{array}{l} haswings(X) \leftarrow bird(X) \\ bird(X) \leftarrow vulture(X) \end{array} \right.$$

$$E^+ = haswings(tweety) \leftarrow$$

The ground unit consequences of $B \wedge \overline{E^+}$ *are*

$$C = \overline{bird(tweety)} \wedge \overline{vulture(tweety)} \wedge \overline{haswings(tweety)}$$

This leads to 3 most-specific starting clauses.

$$H = \left\{ \begin{array}{l} bird(tweety) \leftarrow \\ vulture(tweety) \leftarrow \\ haswings(tweety) \leftarrow \end{array} \right.$$

If any one of these clauses is added to B *then* E^+ *becomes a consequence of the new theory.*

2.4 Multiple examples, single hypothesis clause

This problem is faced in general-specific learning algorithms such as MIS [55], FOIL [50], RDT [24] as well as specific-general algorithms such as Golem [41]. Let us assume that $E^+ = e_1 \wedge e_2 \wedge \ldots$ is a set of ground atoms. Suppose C denotes the set of unit consequences of $B \wedge \overline{E^+}$. From *sufficiency** it is clear that

$$B \wedge \overline{E^+} \vdash \overline{E^+} \wedge C$$

Substituting for E^+ and rearranging gives

$$B \wedge \overline{E^+} \vdash (\overline{e_1} \vee \overline{e_2} \vee \ldots) \wedge C$$
$$B \wedge \overline{E^+} \vdash (\overline{e_1} \wedge C) \vee (\overline{e_2} \wedge C) \vee \ldots$$

Therefore $H = (e_1 \vee \overline{C}) \wedge (e_2 \vee \overline{C}) \wedge \ldots$, which is a set of clauses. Since the solution must be a single clause, systems such as Golem construct the most specific clause which subsumes all these clauses. General-specific algorithms search the set of clauses which subsume subsets of these clauses, starting from the empty clause. If the hypothesis is a set of two or more clauses, then again each clause in this set subsumes the set of most-specific clauses above. FOIL assumes explicit pre-construction of the ground atoms in C to speed subsumption testing.

Example 2 *Let*

$$B = \left\{ \begin{array}{l} father(harry, john) \leftarrow \\ father(john, fred) \leftarrow \\ uncle(harry, jill) \leftarrow \end{array} \right.$$

$$E^+ = \left\{ \begin{array}{l} parent(harry, john) \leftarrow \\ parent(john, fred) \leftarrow \end{array} \right.$$

The ground unit consequences of $B \wedge \overline{E^+}$ are

$$C = father(harry, john) \wedge father(john, fred) \wedge uncle(harry, jill)$$

This leads to the following most specific clauses

$$e_1 \vee \overline{C} = parent(harry, john) \leftarrow \quad father(harry, john), father(john, fred),$$
$$uncle(harry, jill)$$
$$e_2 \vee \overline{C} = parent(john, fred) \leftarrow \quad father(harry, john), father(john, fred),$$
$$uncle(harry, jill)$$

The least general generalisation is then

$$lgg(e_1 \vee \overline{C}, e_2 \vee \overline{C}) = parent(A, B) \leftarrow father(A, B), father(C, D)$$

2.5 Single example, multiple clause hypothesis (predicate invention)

The *sufficiency** condition can be used for any form of hypothesis construction. Thus it should be possible to derive how *predicate invention* (introduction of new predicates) is carried out with this relationship. Let us first define predicate invention more formally. If P is a logic program then the set of all predicate symbols found in the heads of clauses of P is called the definitional vocabulary of P or $V(P)$. ILP has the following three definitional vocabularies.

Observational vocabulary: $\mathcal{O} = V(E^+ \cup E^-)$

Theoretical vocabulary: $\mathcal{T} = V(B) - \mathcal{O}$

Invented vocabulary: $\mathcal{I} = V(H) - (\mathcal{T} \cup \mathcal{O})$

An ILP system is said to carry out *predicate invention* whenever $\mathcal{I} \neq \emptyset$.

Most specific predicate invention can be carried out using the rule of And-introduction (conversely Or-introduction [22]). These logical equivalences are as follows.

And-introduction: $X \equiv (X \wedge Y) \vee (X \wedge \overline{Y})$

Or-introduction: $X \equiv (X \vee Y) \wedge (X \vee \overline{Y})$

Note that the predicate symbols in Y can be chosen arbitrarily and may be quite distinct from those in X. Now letting C be the set of all unit consequences of $B \wedge \overline{E^+}$ and using And-introduction gives

$$B \wedge \overline{E^+} \vdash C$$
$$B \wedge \overline{E^+} \vdash (p \wedge C) \vee (\overline{p} \wedge C)$$

where p is a ground atom whose predicate symbol is not in $(\mathcal{T} \cup \mathcal{O})$. Thus H is any set of clauses which entails $(\overline{p} \vee \overline{C}) \wedge (p \vee \overline{C})$. This can be viewed as the introduction of a clause head (p) and a calling atom from the body of a clause $(\overline{p})$. All methods of predicate invention, such as those using the W-operator [44], construct clauses which entail the above forms of clauses. However, there is an infinite set of atoms p which could be And-introduced in this way. Each of these represents the invention of a different predicate. In [40] it is shown how these invented predicate can be arranged in a partially-ordered lattice of utility with a unique top ($\top$) and bottom ($\bot$) element. Within this lattice invented predicates are unique up to renaming of the predicate symbol and re-ordering of arguments. This provides for a unique p, which is an instance of $\bot$ to be introduced which simply contains the set of all ground terms in C. Clauses can then be generalised through the relative clause refinement lattice by dropping arguments from p or generalising $C \vee p$ and $C \vee \overline{p}$.

Example 3 *The following example involves inventing 'lessthan' in learning to find the minimum element of a list. Let*

$$B \quad = min(X, [X]) \leftarrow$$
$$E^+ \quad = min(2, [3, 2]) \leftarrow$$

The ground unit consequences of $B \wedge \overline{E^+}$ are

$$\overline{min(2, [3, 2])} \wedge min(2, [2]) \wedge min(3, [3])$$

Let $p = p1(2, 3, [2], [3], [3, 2])$. This leads to the following 2 most-specific starting clauses for predicate invention.

$$H = \left\{ \begin{array}{l} min(2, [3, 2]) \leftarrow min(2, [2]), min(3, [3]), p1(2, 3, [2], [3], [3, 2]) \\ p1(2, 3, [2], [3], [3, 2]); min(2, [3, 2]) \leftarrow min(2, [2]), min(3, [3]) \end{array} \right.$$

Generalising and renaming the predicate symbol gives

$$H' = \left\{ \begin{array}{l} min(Y, [Y|Z]) \leftarrow min(X, Z), lessthan(Y, X) \\ lessthan(2, 3) \leftarrow \end{array} \right.$$

3 Extralogical constraints in ILP

In the previous section only the logical constraints used in ILP systems were discussed. It was shown that these can be usefully manipulated to derive the skeleton of an ILP system. However, in order to ensure efficiency, it is usually found necessary to employ extra-logical constraints within ILP systems. This is done in two complementary ways: statistical confirmation and language restrictions (bias). Confirmation theory fits a graded preference surface to the hypothesis space, while language restrictions reduce the size of the hypothesis space. In the following two subsections ILP developments in these areas are discussed.

3.1 Statistical confirmation

Philosophy of Science uses the notion of a confirmation function [19] to give a grading of preferred hypotheses. A confirmation function is a total function that maps elements of the hypothesis space onto a subset of the real numbers. Within ILP confirmation functions based on concepts from Algorithmic Complexity Theory and Minimal Description Length Theory have been developed [36, 50, 43, 8]. Confirmation functions based on Bayesian statistical analysis have also been found useful in handling noise in ILP real-world domains [13].

In [56] the authors explore the use of upper and lower bound estimates of a confirmation function to guide multi-layered predicate invention. The resulting algorithm is a non-backtracking version of an $A*$ search. This approach is effective for guiding "deep" predicate invention, with multiple layers.

3.2 Language restrictions (bias)

Recent results in PAC-learning [45, 15, 23] show that reducing the size of the target language often makes ILP learning more tractable. The main restrictions are on the introduction of existentially quantified variables in the bodies of definite clauses. CLINT [9] places a finite limit on the number of such variables that are allowed to be introduced. Golem [41] requires that the quantification of such variables is limited to Hilbert ϵ^* quantification (exists at most one) and that these "determinate" variables be introduced into the clause body in a fixed number of at most i layers. FOIL [49] has since also made use of the determinate restriction introduced first in Golem.

An alternative approach to language restriction involves the provision of declarative templates which describe the form hypotheses must take. For instance, the algorithm may be told the hypothesis takes the form

$$Q(S1) \leftarrow P1(S1), preceding\_state(S1, S0), P2(S0)$$

where $Q, P1, P2$ can be instantiated with any predicate symbols from the background knowledge. This approach is sometimes referred to as "rule-models" [24], but can also be viewed as learning by analogies expressed as higher-order logic

Restriction	Systems	Problematic Domains
Ground background knowledge	FOIL, Golem	Qualitative, chess, natural language
Non-numerical data	ITOU, FOIL, Golem, SIERES, CLINT, RDT	Meshes, drugs
Determinacy	Golem, FOIL, LINUS	Qualitative, chess meshes
Search myopia	FOIL, FOCL	List&number theory,
Efficiency of learning	ITOU, CLINT	Proteins, chess, satellites

Figure 1: Restrictions that have led to problems in real-world applications

defaults [18, 20, 9]. This has led to some interest within ILP in being able to learn higher-order predicates [17].

Related to the idea of rule-models is the use of mode and type declarations in MIS, Golem, SIERES, FOIL and LINUS. A general scheme of using mode declarations is under development by the author in the ILP system Progol. The mode declarations for Progol take the following form.

$$mode(1, append(+list, +list, -list))$$
$$mode(*, append(-list, -list, +list))$$

The first mode states that append will succeed once (1) when the first two arguments are instantiated with lists and on return the third argument will be instantiated by a list. Types such as 'list' are user-defined as monadic background predicates. The second declaration states that append will succeed finitely many times (*) with the third argument instantiated as a list. The specified limit on the degree of indeterminacy of the call can be any counting number or '*'.

In [7, 2] the concept of "rule-models" is further generalised to that of an hypothesis space language specified by a set of grammar rules. This approach provides a general purpose "declarative bias" and is reminiscent of earlier work on "determinations" [53]. Although determinations in their present form are restricted to propositional logic learning, they have been proved to have a dramatic effect on reducing learning complexity [53].

4 Shortcomings of ILP systems

Despite the rapid development of the ILP research area there is some way to go before ILP could deliver a technology that would be used widely by working scientists and engineers. Figure 1 lists restrictions that certain ILP systems have that have led to awkwardness in applying them to real-world applications. The domains referred to cryptically in the table are, in alphabetical order, the following

Chess. Learning endgame strategies [35].

Drugs. Structure-activity prediction [25].

List&number theory. Quick-sort, multiply, etc. [41].

Meshes. Rules for Finite Element Mesh design [12].

Natural language. Grammar acquisition [60].

Proteins. Secondary-structure prediction [42].

Qualitative. Learning qualitative models [4].

Satellites. Temporal fault diagnosis. [16].

In the following subsections some approaches to avoiding these restrictions will be sketched. The problems encountered in applications will be explained and some remedies suggested.

4.1 Ground background knowledge

Golem and FOIL require all background knowledge to be given extensionally in tabular form. This is acceptable and very efficient when the number of ground instances required is small. In domains such as qualitative model construction, chess and natural language this is not feasible. Effective learning algorithms need to be able to call a Prolog interpreter to derive ground atoms from intensionally-coded specifications of background predicates. To do so they should only derive background atoms that are relevant to the examples. CLINT, ITOU and LINUS all achieve these aims to varying degrees.

4.2 Non-numerical data

The mesh domain involves predicting the number of sections that an edge of a CAD object should be broken into for efficient finite-element analysis. The rules developed by Golem thus have the following form.

$$mesh(Obj, 8) \leftarrow connected(Obj, Obj1), \ldots$$

However with a small number of examples it is hard to get enough examples in which the prediction is an exact number, such as 8. Instead we would like the rules to predict an interval such as

$$mesh(Obj, X) \leftarrow 7 \leq X \leq 9, connected(Obj, Obj1), \ldots$$

This kind of construction is not handled elegantly by existing systems. In statistics this problem of numerical prediction is known as regression. Many efficient statistical algorithms exist for handling numerical data. ILP system designers might do well to look at smoothly integrating such approaches into their systems. Recent work on introducing linear inequalities into inductively constructed definite clauses [34] provides an elegant logical framework for this problem.

4.3 Determinacy

The ij-determinate restriction is both powerful and widely used. However, it is very unnatural for many domains. Consider the following chess strategy clause.

$$won(Position, black) \leftarrow move(Position, Position1), \ldots$$

Clearly there will usually be many valid substitutions for Position1. This problem comes up whenever the objects in the domain represent nodes in a connected graph. This is precisely the kind of problem in which ILP algorithms should be more easily applied than attribute-value systems. Kietz's result [23] indicates that there may not be any general PAC solution to learning non-determinate logic programs.

4.4 Search myopia

This problem is an inherent weakness of heuristically-guided general-specific clause construction systems such as FOIL and FOCL. Consider the following recursive clause for multiplication.

$$mult(A, B, C) \leftarrow succ(A, D), mult(D, B, E), plus(E, B, C).$$

The original FOIL [50] could not learn this clause because with a partially developed clause, none of the atoms in the body make a distinction between positive and negative instances. Only the entire set of three atoms together have a non-zero "gain". FOIL2 [49] overcame this problem by introducing all zero-gain determinate literals at the beginning. This gives FOIL2 a mixed general-specific and specific-general control strategy. However, the problem now simply recedes to non-determinate clauses with the same property. For instance, consider the following clause concerning graphs.

$$threeloop(Node) \leftarrow edge(Node, Node1), edge(Node1, Node2),$$
$$edge(Node2, Node)$$

When FOIL2 tries to construct this clause, each 'edge' literal will again have zero gain. Since the atoms are nondeterminate FOIL2 will fail. This form of myopia is not encountered by specific-general algorithms such as CLINT which start with all relevant literals and prune out unnecessary ones.

4.5 Efficiency of learning

One of the most demanding problems for ILP system developers is that of efficiency. Many interesting real-world problems, such as the protein prediction problem, involve thousands or even millions of examples. Scaling ILP systems to deal with such large databases is a non-trivial task. It may be that methods such as "windowing", successfully applied in ID3, could be incorporated into ILP systems.

5 Conclusion and future directions

Inductive Logic Programming is a fast-growing research area. The last few years have seen the area of quantified logic learning develop from a theoretical backwater into a mainstream applied research area. Many of the problems encountered on the way can make use of solutions developed in Machine Learning, Statistics and Logic Programming.

It should be clear from Section 2 that logical theorem-proving is at the heart of all ILP methods. For this reason it must be worth asking whether the technology of Prolog interpreters is sufficient for all purposes. Reconsider Example 1 in Section 2.3. Implementing a general system that carried out the inference in this example would require a full-clausal theorem prover. Is it worth going to this more computationally expensive thechnique? Luc de Raedt has recently started investigating the new generation of efficient full-clausal theorem-provers such as that described by Stickel [58]. Stickel's theorem prover compiles full clauses into a set of definite clauses. These definite clauses are then executed by a Prolog interpreter using iterative deepening. This technique maintains most of Prolog's efficiency while allowing full theorem proving. Full theorem proving is also useful for implementing constraint checking in ILP systems [9]. Learning full-clausal theories is a largely unexplored and exciting new area for ILP.

ILP research has many issues to deal with and many directions to go. By maintaining strong connections between theory, implementations and applications, ILP has the potential to develop into a powerful and widely-used technology.

Acknowledgements.
The author would like to thank Luc de Raedt for helpful and interesting discussions on the topics in this paper. This work was supported by the Esprit Basic Research Action ILP, project 6020.

References

[1] R.B. Banerji. Learning in the limit in a growing language. In *IJCAI-87*, pages 280–282, San Mateo, CA, 1987. Morgan-Kaufmann.

[2] F. Bergadano. Towards an inductive logic programming language. Technical report, University of Torino, Torino, Italy, 1992.

[3] F. Bergadano and A. Giordana. Guiding induction with domain theories. In Y. Kodratoff and R. Michalski, editors, *Machine learning: an artificial intelligence approach*, volume 3, pages 474–492. Morgan Kaufmann, San Mateo, CA, 1990.

[4] I. Bratko, S. Muggleton, and A. Varsek. Learning qualitative models of dynamic systems. In *Proceedings of the Eighth International Machine Learning Workshop*, San Mateo, Ca, 1991. Morgan-Kaufmann.

[5] B. Cestnik, I. Kononenko, and I. Bratko. Assistant 86: a knowledge-elicitation tool for sophisticated users. In *Progress in machine learning*, pages 31–45, Wilmslow, England, 1987. Sigma.

[6] P. Clark and T. Niblett. The CN2 algorithm. *Machine Learning*, 3(4):261–283, 1989.

[7] W. Cohen. Compiling prior knowledge into an explicit bias. In D. Sleeman and P. Edwards, editors, *Proceedings of the Ninth International Workshop on Machine Learning*, pages 102–110. Morgan Kaufmann, San Mateo: CA, 1992.

[8] D. Conklin and I. Witten. Complexity-based induction. Technical report, Dept. of Computing and Information Science, Queen's University, Kingston, Ontario, Canada, 1992.

[9] L. de Raedt. Interactive concept-learning and constructive induction by analogy. *Machine Learning*, 8:107–150, 1992.

[10] L. de Raedt, N. Lavrac, and S. Dzeroski. Multiple predicate learning. CW 65, Dept. of Computer Science, Katholieke Universiteit Leuven, Leuven, Belgium, 1992.

[11] G. DeJong. Generalisations based on explanations. In *IJCAI-81*, pages 67–69, San Mateo, CA, 1981. Morgan-Kaufmann.

[12] B. Dolsak and S. Muggleton. The application of Inductive Logic Programming to finite element mesh design. In S. Muggleton, editor, *Inductive Logic Programming*, London, 1992. Academic Press.

[13] S. Dzeroski. *Handling noise in Inductive Logic Programming*. PhD thesis, :University of Ljubljana, 1991.

[14] S. Dzeroski and N. Lavrac. Refinement graphs for FOIL and LINUS. In S. Muggleton, editor, *Inductive Logic Programming*. Academic Press, London, 1992.

[15] S. Dzeroski, S. Muggleton, and S. Russell. PAC-learnability of determinate logic programs. In *COLT 92: Proceedings of the Conference on Learning Theory*, San Mateo, CA, 1992. Morgan-Kaufmann.

[16] C. Feng. Inducing temporal fault dignostic rules from a qualitative model. In S. Muggleton, editor, *Inductive Logic Programming*. Academic Press, London, 1992.

[17] C. Feng and S. Muggleton. Towards inductive generalisation in higher order logic. In D. Sleeman and P. Edwards, editors, *Proceedings of the Ninth International Workshop on Machine Learning*, pages 154–162. Morgan Kaufmann, San Mateo: CA, 1992.

[18] D. Gentner. Structure-mapping: a theoretical framework for analogy. *Cognitive Science*, 7:155–170, 1983.

[19] D. Gillies. Confirmation theory and machine learning. In *Proceedings of the Second Inductive Learning Workshop*, Tokyo, 1992. ICOT TM-1182.

[20] M. Harao. Analogical reasoning based on higher-order unification. In *Proceedings of the First International Conference on Algorithmic Learning Theory*, Tokyo, 1990. Ohmsha.

[21] D. Haussler. Applying Valiant's learning framework to AI concept-learning problems. In Y. Kodratoff and R. Michalski, editors, *Machine learning: an artificial intelligence approach*, volume 3, pages 641–669. Morgan Kaufman, San Mateo, CA, 1990.

[22] P. Idestam-Almquist. Generalization under implication: Expansion of clauses for linear roots. Technical report, Dept. of Computer and Systems Sciences, Stockholm University, 1992.

[23] J-U Kietz. Some lower bounds for the computational complexity of inductive logic programming. In *Proceedings of the European Conference on Machine Learning*, Berlin, 1993. Springer-Verlag.

[24] J-U. Kietz and S. Wrobel. Controlling the complexity of learning in logic through syntactic and task-oriented models. In S. Muggleton, editor, *Inductive Logic Programming*. Academic Press, London, 1992.

[25] R. King, S. Muggleton R. Lewis, and M. Sternberg. Drug design by machine learning: The use of inductive logic programming to model the structure-activity relationships of trimethoprim analogues binding to dihydrofolate reductase. *Proceedings of the National Academy of Sciences*, 89(23), 1992.

[26] R. Kowalski. Logic Programming in Artificial Intelligence. In *IJCAI-91: proceedings of the twelfth international joint conference on artificial intelligence*, pages 596–603, San Mateo, CA, 1991. Morgan-Kaufmann.

[27] P. Langley, G.L Bradshaw, and H. Simon. Rediscovering chemistry with the Bacon system. In R. Michalski, J. Carbonnel, and T. Mitchell, editors, *Machine Learning: An Artificial Intelligence Approach*, pages 307–330. Tioga, Palo Alto, CA, 1983.

[28] S. Lapointe and S. Matwin. Sub-unification: a tool for efficient induction of recursive programs. In *Proceedings of the Ninth International Machine Learning Conference*, Los Altos, 1992. Morgan Kaufmann.

[29] D.B. Lenat. On automated scientific theory formation: a case study using the AM program. In J.E. Hayes and D. Michie, editors, *Machine Intelligence 9*. Horwood, New York, 1981.

[30] J.W. Lloyd. *Foundations of Logic Programming*. Springer-Verlag, Berlin, 1984.

[31] A. Kakas P. Mancarella. Generalized stable models: a semantics for abduction. In L. Aiello, E. Sandewall, G. Hagert, and B. Gustavsson, editors, *ECAI-90: proceedings of the ninth European conference on artificial intelligence*, pages 385–391, London, 1990. Pitman.

[32] R. Michalski, I. Mozetic, J. Hong, and N. Lavrac. The AQ15 inductive learning system: an overview and experiments. In *Proceedings of IMAL 1986*, Orsay, 1986. Université de Paris-Sud.

[33] T.M. Mitchell, R.M. Keller, and S.T. Kedar-Cabelli. Explanation-based generalization: A unifying view. *Machine Learning*, 1(1):47–80, 1986.

[34] F. Mizoguchi and H. Ohwada. Constraint-directed generalization for learning spatial relations. In *Proceedings of the Second Inductive Learning Workshop*, Tokyo, 1992. ICOT TM-1182.

[35] E. Morales. Learning chess patterns. In S. Muggleton, editor, *Inductive Logic Programming*. Academic Press, London, 1992.

[36] S. Muggleton. A strategy for constructing new predicates in first order logic. In *Proceedings of the Third European Working Session on Learning*, pages 123–130. Pitman, 1988.

[37] S. Muggleton. Inductive Logic Programming. *New Generation Computing*, 8(4):295–318, 1991.

[38] S. Muggleton. *Inductive Logic Programming*. Academic Press, 1992.

[39] S. Muggleton. Inverting implication. *Artificial Intelligence Journal*, 1993. (to appear).

[40] S. Muggleton. Predicate invention and utility. *Journal of Experimental and Theoretical Artificial Intelligence*, 1993. (to appear).

[41] S. Muggleton and C. Feng. Efficient induction of logic programs. In S. Muggleton, editor, *Inductive Logic Programming*, London, 1992. Academic Press.

[42] S. Muggleton, R. King, and M. Sternberg. Protein secondary structure prediction using logic-based machine learning. *Protein Engineering*, 5(7):647–657, 1992.

[43] S. Muggleton, A. Srinivasan, and M. Bain. Compression, significance and accuracy. In *Proceedings of the Ninth International Machine Learning Conference*, San Mateo, CA, 1992. Morgan-Kaufmann.

[44] S.H. Muggleton and W. Buntine. Machine invention of first-order predicates by inverting resolution. In *Proceedings of the Fifth International Conference on Machine Learning*, pages 339–352. Kaufmann, 1988.

[45] D. Page and A. Frisch. Generalization and learnability: A study of constrained atoms. In S. Muggleton, editor, *Inductive Logic Programming*. Academic Press, London, 1992.

[46] M. Pazzani, C. Brunk, and G. Silverstein. An information-based approach to integrating empirical and explanation-based learning. In S. Muggleton, editor, *Inductive Logic Programming*. Academic Press, London, 1992.

[47] G.D. Plotkin. *Automatic Methods of Inductive Inference*. PhD thesis, Edinburgh University, August 1971.

[48] J.R. Quinlan. Generating production rules from decision trees. In *Proceedings of the Tenth International Conference on Artificial Intelligence*, pages 304–307, San Mateo, CA:, 1987. Morgan-Kaufmann.

[49] J.R. Quinlan. Determinate literals in inductive logic programming. In *IJCAI-91: Proceedings of the Twelfth International Joint Conference on Artificial Intelligence*, pages 746–750, San Mateo, CA:, 1991. Morgan-Kaufmann.

[50] R. Quinlan. Learning logical definitions from relations. *Machine Learning*, 5:239–266, 1990.

[51] B. Richards. *An operator-based approach to first-order theory revision*. PhD thesis, University of Austin, Texas, 1992.

[52] C. Rouveirol. Extensions of inversion of resolution applied to theory completion. In S. Muggleton, editor, *Inductive Logic Programming*. Academic Press, London, 1992.

[53] S. Russell. Tree-structured bias. In *Proceedings of the Eighth National Conference on Artificial Intelligence*, San Mateo, CA, 1988. Morgan-Kaufmann.

[54] C. Sammut and R.B Banerji. Learning concepts by asking questions. In R. Michalski, J. Carbonnel, and T. Mitchell, editors, *Machine Learning: An Artificial Intelligence Approach. Vol. 2*, pages 167–192. Morgan-Kaufmann, San Mateo, CA, 1986.

[55] E.Y. Shapiro. *Algorithmic program debugging*. MIT Press, 1983.

[56] A. Srinivasan, S. Muggleton, and M. Bain. Distinguishing exceptions from noise in non-monotonic learning. In S. Muggleton, editor, *Proceedings of the Second Inductive Logic Programming Workshop.* ICOT TM-1182, Tokyo, 1992.

[57] M. Sternberg, R. Lewis, R. King, and S. Muggleton. Modelling the structure and function of enzymes by machine learning. *Proceedings of the Royal Society of Chemistry: Faraday Discussions,* 93:269–280, 1992.

[58] M. Stickel. A Prolog technology theorem prover: implementation by an extended prolog compiler. *Journal of Automated Reasoning,* 4(4):353–380, 1988.

[59] L. Valiant. A theory of the learnable. *Communications of the ACM,* 27(11):1134–1142, 1984.

[60] R. Wirth. Learning by failure to prove. In *EWSL-88,* pages 237–251, London, 1988. Pitman.

[61] R. Wirth and P. O'Rorke. Constraints for predicate invention. In S. Muggleton, editor, *Inductive Logic Programming,* London, 1992. Academic Press.

Chapter 2:

Research Papers

Two Methods for Improving Inductive Logic Programming Systems

Irene Stahl[1], Birgit Tausend[1] and Rüdiger Wirth[2]

[1] Fakultät Informatik, Universität Stuttgart, Breitwiesenstr. 20-22,
D-7000 Stuttgart 80
[2] Research Institute for Applied Knowledge Processing, P. O. Box 2060, D-7900 Ulm

Abstract. In this paper we describe two methods for improving systems that induce disjunctive Horn clause definitions. The first method is the well-known use of argument types during induction. Our novel contribution is an algorithm for extracting type information from the example set mechanically.

The second method provides a set of clause heads partitioning the example set in disjuncts according to structural properties. Those heads can be used in top-down inductive inference systems as starting point of the general-to-specific search and reduce the resulting space of clause bodies.

1 Introduction

Inductive inference of Horn clause definitions from ground facts faces the problem of a very large, in general infinite hypothesis space. No matter whether it is searched from general to specific (top-down) or from specific to general (bottom-up) there are problems with inefficiency or even intractability.

One simple way to reduce the space of possible clauses is the use of *argument types* for predicates. Clauses that contain a variable occurring at argument positions with conflicting types need not be considered. Due to its simple and efficient realizability typing has been employed from the very beginning of inductive inference in first order logic, e.g. in Shapiro's Model Inferece System MIS [Sha83]. However, all systems using argument types require user-supplied type declarations.

We show that the argument types of a predicate can be determined automatically from its example set. The problem is an instance of the general inductive inference problem and can be solved deterministically.

Apart from reducing the space of possible clauses, argument types can be used to discover structural commonalities among the examples. We propose a method for determining a set of clause heads that partitions the example set according to structural properties.

For top-down approaches to inductive inference, the knowledge about those heads helps in inducing *disjunctive definitions*, i.e. definitions consisting of more than one clause. Systems performing a general-to-specific search like MIS [Sha83] and FOIL [Qui90] start their search for each single clause with the *most general form* of the target predicate as clause head and then successively add body literals or instantiate variables with complex terms. In doing so they look both for *discriminating* and *characterizing* information at the same time. The size of the search space can be reduced by *seperating these two tasks into subtasks.*

Most of the discriminating information is structural, e.g. the difference between base case and recursive case of a predicate. The method we propose first learns discriminating information by partitioning the example set according to structural properties. These structural properties are expressed as predicates which form the heads of clauses covering a disjunct. In the second step we induce clauses characterizing each disjunct by specialising the clause heads derived in step one. This technique provides two advantages: the search is started with less general heads and the structure of the terms in the head yield powerful constraints for the search, which for instance can be employed during predicate invention [WO91].

Both methods have been incorporated in an experimental implementation called INDICO (INduction of DIsjunctive COncepts). This implementation has been used to measure the improved efficiency against MIS [Sha83], FOIL [Qui90] and CHAM [Kij92].

This paper is organized as follows. First, we discuss the algorithm for determining the type restrictions. Secondly, the method for computing clause heads for the target predicate is described. In the following section we give an overview of our experimental system INDICO. Finally, we present some experimental results obtained with INDICO and conclude.

2 Determining the Argument Types

Determining argument types can be viewed as inductive inference of Horn clause definitions from facts. Given the sets E and N of ground facts, the positive and negative examples, a logic program B as background knowledge and mode declarations [Sha83] for each predicate in E, N and B, the task of inductive inference is to find a logic program P such that $B \cup P \vdash_{SLD} E$ and $B \cup P \nvdash_{SLD} N$. P is an extension of the given theory B such that all examples in E, but none in N, are covered by the extended theory. As we restrict our algorithms to positive examples, we consider only the set E. Furthermore, we assume that E contains only examples for one target predicate p/n. However, the generalisation of our algorithms to the case that E contains examples of different predicates is straightforward.

For describing argument types of a predicate p/n we use the following notation:

$$type\_restriction(p(X_1, ..., X_n), \{type_1(X_1), ..., type_n(X_n)\})$$

where each $type_i(X_i)$ is defined by a set of Horn clauses, each satisfying the following syntactic rules:

- the head literal is of the form $type_i(T)$, where T is a term.

- every body literal is of the form $p(X)$, where X is a variable and p is either a type $type_l$ or a predicate in the background knowledge B_{type}. We restricted B_{type} to the standard definitions of *atom*, *number* and *atomic*.
- every variable occurs exactly once in the head and once in the body of the clause.

Example 1. If the example set is $\{append([], [], []), append([1, a, 2], [3], [1, a, 2, 3]),$ $append([p], [], [p])$ ..... $\}$, then the corresponding type restriction is

$$type\_restriction(append(X, Y, Z), \{t_1(X), t_1(Y), t_1(Z)\}).$$
$$t_1([]).$$
$$t_1([X|Y]) \leftarrow atomic(X), t_1(Y).$$

The type t_1 defines recursive lists of atomic terms with the empty list $[]$ as base case.

The rules restrict type definitions within our framework to *regular unary logic (RUL) programs* [YS91]. As the extensions of predicates defined by RUL-programs are regular sets, inclusion and equivalence of different types can easily be checked. This is an important precondition for the use of argument types during induction.

B_{type} need not be restricted to *atom*, *number* and *atomic*, but may be extended by further unary predicates expressing semantic restrictions as e.g. *odd_number*. However, there must be an effective method that, given a set of terms, returns the unique most specific predicate p within B_{type} that is valid for all terms in the set, and fails if none exists. Therefore, the extensions of the predicates in B_{type} have to constitute a complete lattice with respect to set union and intersection. Allowing arbitrary unary or n-ary ($n > 1$) predicates in B_{type} leads to non-regular types. For those, inclusion and equivalence may be undecidable.

For each argument position i of the target predicate, the starting point of our algorithm is the set of i-th arguments of the examples. Let A be this set for a position i and set

$$E_A = \{type_A(T)|T \in A\}.$$

Then the task of the algorithm for determining the argument types is to find a set of clauses P_{type_A} such that

$$B_{type} \cup P_{type_A} \vdash E_A.$$

Thus determining argument types is a special case of inducing Horn clause definitions from positive examples. Both the background knowledge B_{type} and the form of the target clauses P_{type_A} are strongly restricted.

In principle both bottom-up and top-down induction approaches can be used. Because of the ease of control, we decided to proceed top-down. Figure 1 shows our deterministic algorithm for determining argument types. It proceeds in two steps.

Input: set A of argument terms
Algorithm: $argument\_type(A)$

(1) Determine heads:
    $A_0 := \{T \in A \mid T \text{ atomic}\}$
    $A_f := \{T \in A \mid T = f(T_1, ..., T_m), m \geq 1\}$ for each f occurring in A
    Heads: for each A_f a head $H_f = t_A(lgg(A_f))$
    where lgg is the least general generalisation [Plo70]

(2) Top-down induction of bodies:
    for each Head H_f
        for each $V \in vars(H_f)$
            if $\exists\, p \in B_{type}$ such that $p(V\sigma) \;\forall H_f\sigma \in A_f$
            then add $p(V)$ to the body of H_f
            else if $t_x(V\sigma) \;\forall H_f\sigma \in A_f$ where $t_x = t_A$ or t_x calls t_A
                then add $t_x(V)$ to the body of H_f
                else $A' = \{V\sigma \mid H_f\sigma \in A_f\}$
                    add $t_{A'}(V)$ to the body of H_f
                    call $argument\_type(A')$

Output: t_A

Fig. 1. Top-down algorithm for determining argument types

The first step determines clause heads for the target argument type t_A. The set A is partitioned according to different functors, and for each partition its least general generalisation lgg [Plo70] is taken as head argument of t_A. The second step induces clause bodies defining t_A by searching for type restrictions for the variables in each clause head H_f of t_A. First, the background knowledge B_{type} is checked. If a predicate p is valid for all instantiations of V in A, and p is the most specific predicate in B_{type} fulfilling this condition, $p(V)$ is added as body literal. Else, the same is tested for predicates t_x, where t_x calls t_A directly or via intermediate predicates t_z, or $x = A$. In the last case, t_A is defined recursively.

If none of those applies, a literal $t_{A'}(V)$ is added to the body of H_f and the algorithm is called recursively on the set A' of all instantiations of V in A_f.

Example 2. Let the set of argument terms occurring at an argument position in E be $A = \{not(and([a])), not(and([x, y])), not(and([u, v, w]))\} = A_{not}$. The clause head determined for A_{not} is

$$(1) \quad t_A(lgg(A_{not})) = t_A(not(and([X|Y]))).$$

A type restriction for both variables X and Y is to be found. As $atom(X)$ is true for the instantiations a, x and u of X in A_{not}, it is added to the body of (1) yielding

$$(1') \quad t_A(not(and([X|Y]))) \leftarrow atom(X).$$

For the instantiations of Y, neither *atom*, *number*, *atomic* nor a predicate t_x calling t_A is true. Therefore, a new literal $t_{A'}(Y)$ is added to the body of (1') resulting in

$$(1'') \ t_A(not(and([X|Y]))) \leftarrow atom(X), t_{A'}(Y).$$

The algorithm is called recursively with the set $A' = \{[], [y], [v, w]\}$ of Y's instantiations. A' contains the atomic term $[]$ and the 2-place functor $[\_|\_]$. Therefore we get two sets $A'_0 = \{[]\}$ and $A'_{[\_|\_]} = \{[y], [v, w]\}$ and, accordingly, two heads

$$(2) \ t_{A'}([]).$$
$$(3) \ t_{A'}([H|T]).$$

As (2) does not contain any variable, it is complete. For H and T further restrictions have to be determined. As above, H is restricted by the condition $atom(H)$ yielding

$$(3') \ t_{A'}([H|T]) \leftarrow atom(H).$$

For the instantiations $[]$ and $[w]$ of T in $A'_{[\_|\_]}$ the predicate $t_{A'}(T)$ defined by (2) and (3') is valid such that we get a recursive definition of $t_{A'}$. This completes the argument type definition for A:

$$(1'') \ t_A(not(and([X|Y]))) \leftarrow atom(X), t_{A'}(Y).$$
$$(2) \ \ t_{A'}([]).$$
$$(3'') \ t_{A'}([H|T]) \leftarrow atom(H), t_{A'}(T).$$

Because of the small number of possible body literals the search space is small even for complex types, e.g. types containing more than one recursion like binary trees or types recurring over several steps.

A problem is how to induce type restrictions for predicates in the background knowledge. As usually no examples are supplied, our method is not applicable. In our experimental system, we chose the simplest solution and required those types to be given or learnt incrementally. However, there are alternative methods for computing the types of given programs, e.g. [Kluz87].

3 Determining Clause Heads

The algorithm in this section determines a set of clause heads partitioning the examples according to structural properties. In general, the least general generalisation [Plo70] of each subset of the example set is a candidate for being clause head of a disjunctive clause. As it is intractable to consider each subset and the corresponding clause head, we restrict our algorithm to subsets with the same argument structure and try to construct clause heads from them.

Given the set E of positive examples for a predicate p/n, a mode declaration for p/n [Sha83] and the type restriction

$$type\_restriction(p(X_1, ..., X_n), \{type_1(X_1), .., type_n(X_n)\})$$

together with complete definitions of each $type_i$, our algorithm proceeds in three steps. First, it partitions the example set according to the type restriction by clustering examples with the same structure at an argument position. The least general generalisations of those partitions are refined further in the second step. The last step implements a subsumption-based reduction of the set of clause heads.

3.1 Determining Clause Heads According to the Type Restriction

The first step of the algorithm partitions the example set according to the different structures described in the type restriction. Different structures at a single argument position i correspond to different proofs of the ith argument being of $type_i$. To distinguish the different structures at position i, the proof structures for $type_i$ have to be considered.

Let C_i be the clauses defining $type_i$. A set $S_i \subseteq C_i$ corresponds to a proof structure *iff*

- at least one clause $D \in S_i$ has $type_i$ as head predicate
- for each $D \in S_i$, if D calls $type_j$ then S_i contains at least one clause with $type_j$ as head predicate.

That is, S_i must conform the subgoal hierarchy of $type_i$. As $S_i \subseteq C_i$, $2^{|C_i|}$ is an upper bound for the number of possible proof structures. For each proof structure S_i we define

$$E_{i,S_i} = \{e \in E \mid \text{the proof } (C_i \cup B_{type} \vdash type_i(e_i)), \text{ where } e_i \text{ is the ith}$$
$$\text{argument of } e, \text{ uses all and only the clauses in } S_i$$
$$\text{apart from those in } B_{type}\}.$$

The sets E_{i,S_i} contain examples with the same structure at the i-th argument position. For complex types, there may be a large number of those sets and accordingly a large number of clause heads. However, it might be the case that the heads for different sets E_{i,S_i} coincide, as our example will show.

Example 3. Let the example set for merging two sorted lists of numbers in one be $E = \{$ $merge([], [], [])$,
$merge([6], [], [6])$,
$merge([], [7], [7])$,
$merge([1], [2, 4], [1, 2, 4])$,
$merge([6, 8], [5], [5, 6, 8])$ $\}$.
The type restriction our algorithm determines is

$$type\_restriction(merge(X, Y, Z), \{t_1(X), t_1(Y), t_1(Z)\})$$

with t_1 being defined as

$$C_i = \{ \ 1 \ t_1([]).$$
$$2 \ t_1([A|B]) \leftarrow number(A), t_1(B). \ \}$$

For $i = 1, 2, 3$ there are two possiblities for S_i, namely $\{1\}$ and $\{1, 2\}$. The nonempty sets E_{i,S_i} are

$$
\begin{aligned}
E_{1,\{1\}} &= \{merge([], [], []), merge([], [7], [7])\} \\
E_{2,\{1\}} &= \{merge([], [], []), merge([6], [], [6])\} \\
E_{3,\{1\}} &= \{merge([], [], [])\} \\
E_{1,\{1,2\}} &= \{merge([1], [2, 4], [1, 2, 4]), merge([6, 8], [5], [5, 6, 8]), merge([6], [], [6])\} \\
E_{2,\{1,2\}} &= \{merge([1], [2, 4], [1, 2, 4]), merge([6, 8], [5], [5, 6, 8]), merge([], [7], [7])\} \\
E_{3,\{1,2\}} &= \{merge([1], [2, 4], [1, 2, 4]), merge([6, 8], [5], [5, 6, 8]), merge([6], [], [6]), \\
&\qquad merge([], [7], [7])\}
\end{aligned}
$$

Base cases of structured argument terms correspond to proofs that use exactly one clause in C_i, e.g. the empty list $[]$ is a base case of t_1 in our example as the proof of $t_1([])$ needs only clause 1. For singleton sets S_i E_{i,S_i} contains examples with base cases at argument position i. We define the set of all base examples as

$$
E_{bases} = \bigcup_{i \in \{1,..,n\}} E_{i,S_i} \text{ for } S_i \subseteq C_i \text{ such that } |S_i| = 1
$$

With those definitions the first set of clause heads is defined as

$$
H = H_{bases} \cup H_{structured}
$$

where

$$
H_{bases} = \bigcup_{i \in \{1,..,n\}} \{lgg(E_{i,S_i}) \mid S_i \subseteq C_i \wedge |S_i| = 1 \wedge E_{i,S_i} \neq \phi\}
$$

and

$$
H_{structured} = \bigcup_{i \in \{1,..,n\}} \{lgg(E_{i,S_i} - E_{bases}) \mid S_i \subseteq C_i \wedge |S_i| \geq 2 \wedge E_{i,S_i} \neq \phi\}
$$

Example 4. Continuing the previous example, we get the following clause heads:

$$
\begin{array}{l|l|l}
H_{bases} & i = 1 & lgg(\{merge([], [], []), merge([], [7], [7])\}) = merge([], L, L) \\
S_i = \{1\} & i = 2 & lgg(\{merge([], [], []), merge([6], [], [6])\}) = merge(L, [], L) \\
& i = 3 & lgg(\{merge([], [], [])\}) = merge([], [], [])
\end{array}
$$

$$
\begin{array}{l|l|l}
H_{structured} & i = 1 & lgg(\{merge([1], [2, 4], [1, 2, 4]), merge([6, 8], [5], [5, 6, 8])\}) \\
& & = merge([A|B], [C|D], [E, F|G]) \\
S_i = \{1, 2\} & i = 2 & lgg(\{merge([1], [2, 4], [1, 2, 4]), merge([6, 8], [5], [5, 6, 8])\}) \\
& & = merge([A|B], [C|D], [E, F|G]) \\
& i = 3 & lgg(\{merge([1], [2, 4], [1, 2, 4]), merge([6, 8], [5], [5, 6, 8])\}) \\
& & = merge([A|B], [C|D], [E, F|G])
\end{array}
$$

3.2 Refining the Set of Clause Heads

Though the set of clause heads determined in the previous step partitions the examples according to their overall structure, further refinements are possible. A useful refinement is the search for equal structures at different argument positions. This is done by unifying terms within a clause head. In order to restrict the possible unifications we use Wirth and O'Rorke's heuristic of *critical variables* [WO91].

Definition 1. Let H be a clause head with variables V_H. The *critical variables* Vc_H of H are all input variables that occur in H only once and all output variables that do not occur as input variables

Critical terms are all terms in H that contain only critical variables and no atoms except for the base cases of structured types.

E.g., given $merge(+, +, -)$ as mode declaration, the critical input terms of $merge([A|B], [C|D], [A|E])$ are $\{B, C, D, [C|D]\}$ and the only critical output term is E.

Figure 2 shows the algorithm for refining the set of clause heads. Given a clause head h and a pair of critical terms of the same type within h, the algorithm tests whether the head h' resulting from unifying the terms covers some examples. If this is the case, the least general generalisation of that examples is taken as a further head, and the algorithm is recursively applied to it. The algorithm stops if no further heads result from the unifications.

Input: H as determined in step 1, E
Output: $\bigcup_{h \in H} c\_heads(h)$
  Algorithm: $c\_heads(T)$
  $result := \{T\}$
  for each pair of critical terms X, Y of the same type do
    $T_0 = T|_{X \text{ and } Y \text{ unified}}$
    if T_0 covers examples $E_1 \subseteq E$
    then $result := result \cup c\_heads(lgg(E_1))$
  Return: $result$

Fig. 2. Algorithm for refining clause heads

E.g. unifying the critical terms A and E in $merge([A|B], [C|D], [E, F|G])$ yields a more specific head $merge([A|B], [C|D], [A, F|G])$ covering examples like $merge([1, 2], [4], [1, 2, 4])$. Extending this branch by unifying C and F, we get $merge([A|B], [C|D], [A, C|G])$, and at last $merge([A], [C|D], [A, C|D])$ by unifying D and G. As this head contains no more critical terms, the algorithm stops on this branch.

Figure 3 shows the clause heads our algorithm determines starting with the head $merge([A|B], [C|D], [E, F|G])$ according to the example set we gave. If different examples are given, the algorithm may result in further heads indicated by the dashed lines. The example shows that the resulting set of clause heads is generally redundant and can be minimized.

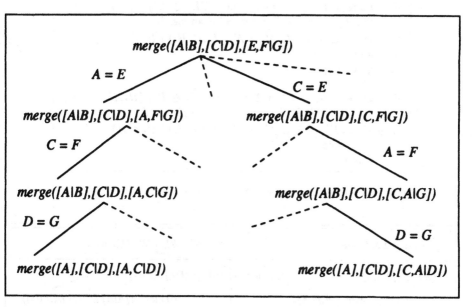

Fig. 3. Non-base clause heads for *merge*

3.3 Minimizing the Set of Clause Heads

The set of clause heads determined in the previous step is redundant in two ways. It contains both heads that are too general and heads that are too specific. The aim of this step is to remove redundant heads. For that aim, we developed a simple heuristical subsumption-based method. Let G be the graph spanned by θ-subsumption on the set H of clause heads, i.e.

$$G = (H, A) \text{ where } A = \{(H_i, H_j) \in H \times H \mid H_i \neq H_j \land \exists \sigma \ H_j\sigma = H_i\}.$$

The first step of our method removes all redundant heads starting with the most general ones in G. The second step eliminates the redundant heads starting with the most specific ones in the remaining graph. Figure 4 shows the algorithm more formally.

Example 5. The clause heads determined for merge yield the graph in figure 5 according to θ-subsumption.

In step 1 of our algorithm head (4) is removed as a most general redundant head. In the reduced graph there are no more most general redundant heads,

```
Input: G = (H, A), example set E
Algorithm:
H' := H, A' := A
Step 1:
if     there is H_i ∈ H' such that ¬(∃H_j ∈ H')((H_i, H_j) ∈ A')
       and H' − {H_i} still covers all examples in E
then H' := H' − {H_i}, A' := A' − {(H_j, H_i) | H_j ∈ H}
       go to step 1
else  go to step 2
Step 2:
if     there is H_i ∈ H' such that ¬(∃H_j ∈ H')((H_j, H_i) ∈ A')
       and H' − {H_i} still covers all examples in E
then H' := H' − {H_i}, A' := A' − {(H_i, H_j) | H_j ∈ H}
       go to step 2
else  return H'
```

Fig. 4. Algorithm for optimizing the set of clause heads

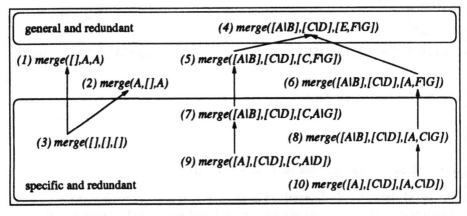

Fig. 5. Optimizing the clause heads for *merge*

and the algorithm proceeds to step 2. This step removes successively the most specific redundant heads (3), (9), (10), (7) and (8). The remaining set H' consists of the heads (1), (2),(5) and (6).

Our method worked surprisingly well on our examples. However, there are simple counterexamples where it removes heads necessary for the subsequent learning process. E.g. the first head in the set $\{min(X, [X]),\ min(X, [Y|R])\}$ is removed though it is a necessary base case. The method should be adapted to recognize and retain base cases of that kind.

The most similar approach to our partitioning algorithm is the method of Arimura, Shinohara and Otsuki [ASO91]. Given a set of positive examples, it produces a non-redundant set of clause heads covering the example set. In contrast to our algorithm, it works in polynomial time. However, it is restricted on producing at most two different clause heads for the example set. The extension of the method to arbitrary many heads is not straightforward and may lead to exponential running times.

In the following section we show how the optimized set of clause heads is employed during top-down induction in our system INDICO.

4 Overview of INDICO

The setting for our sytem INDICO is as follows: Given a set E of positive examples for a functional predicate p/n, a mode declaration for p/n [Sha83] and a logic program B as background knowledge, the learning task is to find a set of clauses P such that $B \cup P$ computes the correct output for each of the examples in E.

INDICO proceeds in three steps. First, it determines the argument types of the target predicate by means of our algorithm described in section 2. Then, it computes the minimized set of clause heads using the second algorithm we discussed in this paper. This set of clause heads is taken as possibly overgeneral PROLOG-program for the target predicate. In the third step, INDICO locates overgeneral clauses within the preliminary program and specialises them by adding literals, including newly invented ones, to their bodies.

Note that any other top-down inductive learner could use the clause heads INDICO determined. For example, FOIL could be supplied with the head showing the largest information gain [Qui90] on the example set as starting point of its search.

The method INDICO employs for inducing clause bodies is discussed in detail in [STW91]. As we restricted INDICO to positive examples as input only, the crucial problem during the third step is how overgeneralisation can be detected in the absence of negative examples. In [STW91] we describe a method for constructing negative examples *without* the completeness restriction on positive examples that must hold for the application of the closed world assumption. This method is suitable only for a restricted class of functional predicates. However, the restriction on functional predicates is not necessary for applying the algorithms described in section 2 and 3.

The negative examples are used for localizing overgeneral clauses and specialising them by adding a literal to their body. The body literals can be background predicates, the target predicate itself and newly invented predicates. The search space is strongly constrained by type restrictions, restrictions on data flow, correctness conditions and a heuristic measure combined with beam search. In doing so, ideas from MIS [Sha83], CHAM [Kij92], and SIERES [WO91] have been used.

5 Experimental Results

INDICO has been tested on several examples including logic programs operating on lists like *append, merge, split, reverse, partition* and *sort*. For each of those, it performed well in detecting the main structural distinctions in the example set.

A more complex class of example programs is a set of logic programs operating on ordered binary trees. Binary trees are represented as lists [*left_subtree*, *root*, *right_subtree*], where *root* is a number and *left_-* and *right_subtree* are binary trees. The empty tree is [].

INDICO has been able to induce definitions for inserting an element in an ordered binary tree in the appropriate position and, as a more difficult example, for retracting an element from the tree such that the ordering is maintained. This may require rotations in the tree, as illustrated in figure 6. For retracting

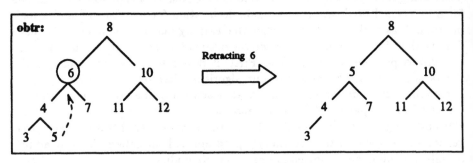

Fig. 6. Retracting an element from an ordered binary tree

an element from a tree INDICO discovered the main disjunctive cases in the example set as far as structure is concerned: the two cases that the left or right subtree of the element to be deleted is empty, the case that both subtrees of the element are not empty and a suitable element for replacing the retracted element has to be found in the tree, and the two recursive cases where the element to be deleted is not the root of the actual tree, but has to be deleted in the left or right subtree.

Given this partitioning of the 21 examples we supplied for *obtr*, INDICO induces the following definition:

```
obtr(A,[[],A,[B,C,D]],[B,C,D]).
obtr(A,[[B,C,D],A,[]],[B,C,D]).
obtr(A,[[],A,[]],[]).
obtr(A,[B,A,C],[D,E,C]) :-          newp0([[A,B,C],D,[]],D,[A,B,C]).
        newp0(B,E,D).                newp0([[],A,[]],A,[]).
obtr(A,[B,C,D],[B,C,E]) :-          newp0([A,B,C],D,[A,B,E]) :-
        obtr(A,D,E).[1]                     newp0(C,D,E).
obtr(A,[B,C,D],[E,C,D]) :-
        obtr(A,B,E).[1]
```

---

[1] The definition of the recursive cases does not check whether A is contained in the left or in the right subtree. As obtr fails if the element to be deleted does not occur in the tree, this is merely a difference in efficiency.

For the case that both subtrees of the element to be deleted are not empty, INDICO *invented* a new predicate which locates a suitable element for replacing the element to be deleted and performs the rotation.

Our examples show that the algorithm is reasonable efficient and powerful in inducing Horn clause definitions in structured domains.

		♯ examples		♯ tested	background
		pos.	neg.	hypotheses	knowledge
append	CHAM	39	365	142	none
	FOIL	261	8991	1018	*components, null, list*
	MIS	$1 + 28^2$	—	144	none
	INDICO	13	$(1)^3$	$6 / 5^4$	none
reverse	CHAM	16	256	167	*addlast*
	FOIL	65	4225	299	*components, null, list append*
	MIS	$1 + 5$	—	66	*addlast* induced
	INDICO	$11 + 8$	(1)	3 / 6	*addlast* invented
isort	CHAM	23	17	325	*part, append, component*
	FOIL	16	256	201	*insert, null, component*
	MIS	$1 + 6$	—	56	$<$, *insert* induced
	INDICO	$11 + 8$	(1)	5 / 6	$<$, *insert* invented

Table 1. Test results

At last, we want to compare our system INDICO with MIS [Sha83], FOIL [Qui90] and CHAM [Kij92] running on similar tasks in order to measure the improved efficiency resulting from our problem reduction approach. The selection of these tasks was a difficult problem since all systems differ quite strongly in the predicates they are able to learn. Therefore we restricted our tests on three list-manipulating predicates, namely *append*, *reverse* and *sort*. Those tests are of course far from being representative for the different behaviour of the systems, but they give some idea of it.

Another problem with the tests was which evaluation criteria to chose. As running times are meaningless – especially since FOIL is C-encoded and the rest in QUINTUSPROLOG – we took the number of examples needed, the background knowledge B supplied and the number of hypotheses generated and tested.

Each system was supplied the examples provided by its authors. We assumed those to be the best-suited for the learning task. E.g. due to the *information gain*

---

[2] $x + y$ means that the system was given x examples and asked y membership- or existential queries

[3] Parenthesized numbers of negative examples refer to the examples INDICO constructs from positive examples as described in [STW91].

[4] Here, x/y means that INDICO generated x clause heads and, for the selected set of clause heads, y different body hypotheses.

heuristic, FOIL [Qui90] needs more examples than MIS [Sha83]. Concerning the number of examples, INDICO ranges between MIS and CHAM. It does not need as carefully chosen examples as MIS. However, they must not be as arbitrary as for FOIL. For each disjunct, at least two examples must be given, and the examples should be simple. That is, the learning behaviour of INDICO deteriorates if e.g. *append* is exemplified only for lists with a length above 1000.

For MIS, FOIL and CHAM the number of hypotheses is exactly the number of clauses that have been searched. For INDICO, both the number of clause heads the system generated and the number of body hypotheses are listed. However, we do not list the amount of search INDICO performs for determining argument types, as MIS, FOIL and CHAM employ user-supplied type declarations.

The results of our experiments are illustrated in table 1. Note that there is a difference between MIS and INDICO in inferring the necessary background knowledge as e.g. for *isort* or *reverse*. MIS asks the oracle which predicates it may use for constructing a clause body and, if not yet defined, induces their definition. INDICO proceeds differently: it does not know which predicates to use for constructing a clause body. It realizes the point at which a new predicate is needed and extends its vocabulary at that point. Unlike MIS, the user does not have to supply the system with examples for the new predicate.

The results in table 1 show that the problem reduction method is successfully applicable to the problem of inductive inference. Due to the constraints resulting from the clause heads, INDICO searches the fewest hypotheses and is additionally capable of inventing new predicates if the existing background knowledge is not sufficient. Furthermore, the amount of work for determining the clause heads is small and so there is a real increase in overall efficiency. If the other systems integrated the structural constraints from the partitioning of the example set, they would have much less hypotheses to generate and test.

6 Conclusions

The current implementation of our algorithm shows that reducing the problem of top-down inductive inference to the simpler subproblems of determining clause heads and clause bodies improves the efficiency of top-down inductive learners considerably. The constraints emerging from the clause heads and the type restrictions can be exploited during the induction of the clause bodies and help systems in finding definitions more efficiently or, for complex definitions, even in finding them at all.

In our system INDICO we use the algorithm for determining clause heads as a real alternative to the covering approach, as the optimized set of clause heads is taken as complete but possibly overgeneral program for the target predicate. It would be interesting to integrate it with a greedy algorithm for inducing clauses, e.g. FOIL, and investigate the resulting improvement in efficiency and power.

References

[ASO91] Arimura, H., Shinohara, T., Otsuki, S. (1991): *Polynomial Time Inference of Unions of Tree Pattern Languages* in Proc. of the 2nd Workshop on Algorithmic Learning Theory, Tokyo

[Kij92] Kijsirikul, B., Numao, M., Shimura, M. (1992): *Efficient Learning of Logic Programs with Non-determinate, Non-dicriminating Literals* in S. Muggleton (ed): Inductive Logic Programming, Academic Press

[Kluz87] Kluzniak, F. (1987): *Type Synthesis for Ground Prolog*, in J. L. Lasses (ed): Logic Programming, Proc. of the 4th International Conference , MIT-Press

[Plo70] Plotkin, G. D. (1970): A Note on Inductive Generalisation in: B. Meltzer, D. Mitchie (eds): *Machine Intelligence 5*, Edinburgh University Press.

[Qui90] Quinlan, J. R. (1990): Learning Logical Definitions from Relations, *Machine Learning 5*, 239 – 266.

[Sha83] Shapiro, E. Y. (1983): Algorithmic Program Debugging, MIT Press, Cambridge, Mass.

[Sta91] Stahl, I. (1991): Induktion von disjunktiven Konzepten, *Diplomarbeit Nr. 807*, Universität Stuttgart, Fakultät Informatik.

[STW91] Stahl, I., Tausend, B., Wirth, R. (1991): General-to-specific Learning of Horn Clauses from Positive Examples, in *Proc. of the CompEuro92*, The Hague, NL

[WO91] Wirth, R., O'Rorke, P. (1991): Constraints on Predicate Invention, *Proc. of the 8th International Workshop on ML*, Chicago, Morgan Kaufmann.

[YS91] Yardeni, E., Shapiro, E. (1991): A Type System for Logic Programs, *Journal of Logic Programming 10*.

Generalization under Implication by using Or-Introduction

Peter Idestam-Almquist

Department of Computer and Systems Sciences
Stockholm University
Electrum 230, 164 40 Kista, SWEDEN

Abstract. In the area of inductive learning, generalization is a main operation. Already in the early 1970's Plotkin described algorithms for computation of least general generalizations of clauses under θ-subsumption. However, there is a type of generalizations, called roots of clauses, that is not possible to find by generalization under θ-subsumption. This incompleteness is important, since almost all inductive learners that use clausal representation perform generalization under θ-subsumption. In this paper a technique to eliminate this incompleteness, by reducing generalization under implication to generalization under θ-subsumption, is presented. The technique is conceptually simple and is based on an inference rule from natural deduction, called or-introduction. The technique is proved to be sound and complete, but unfortunately it suffers from complexity problems.

1 Introduction

In recent years there has been a rising interest in clausal representation of knowledge in machine learning. Generalization is a main operation for inductive algorithms, and the usual definition of induction is based on logical implication [13]. However, almost all inductive learners that use clausal representation, for example CIGOL [10], GOLEM [11], LFP2 [19], ITOU [16], perform generalizations under θ-subsumption, instead of generalization under implication. The reason is that there are well-known and reasonably efficient algorithms to compute least general generalizations under θ-subsumption [14].

The derivation rule used together with clausal representation, in logic programming and automatic theorem proving, is resolution. Resolution is refutation complete, but not derivation complete [15]. Therefore by inverting resolution [10, 8, 17, 5] we have not obtained a complete generalization procedure.

There is a type of generalizations of self-recursive clauses, called roots of clauses (see section 2.3), that is not possible to find by generalization under θ-subsumption or by inverse resolution. Consequently we need to add a new inference rule to make it possible to find such generalizations. In natural deduction there is an inference rule called *or-introduction* [18]. This rule has inspired us to develop an algorithm to reduced generalization under implication to generalization under θ-subsumption. After such a reduction the well-known algorithms for least general generalizations under θ-subsumption can be used to compute least general generalizations under implication. Our technique for reduction of generalization is proven to be sound and complete, but unfortunately it suffers from complexity problems.

Recently the problem of generalization under implication has also been studied by Muggleton [9] and Lapointe and Matwin [6]. Lapointe and Matwin describe an efficient method to find two particular types of roots of clauses. But these two types of roots only cover a fraction of all possible self-recursive clauses. Muggleton consider the general problem of inverting implication, and gives a theoretical comparison between implication and resolution. However, the algorithms he presents are restricted to a subclass of self-recursive clauses, namely single-recursive clauses.

We assume the reader to be familiar with the basic notions in logic programming [7] or automatic theorem proving [2]. In particular we shall adopt the notation in [7]. In section 2, a necessary background for our learning problem, generalization of clauses, is given. In section 3, our technique for reduction of generalization by or-introduction, is presented. Finally in section 4, related work and contributions are discussed.

2 Preliminaries

The basic definitions and terminology of generalization of clauses will be given in this section. It includes generalization under θ-subsumption, generalization under implication, and powers and roots of clauses. These notions will also be related to each other.

2.1 Generalization under θ-subsumption

As already mentioned in the introduction, least general generalization under θ-subsumption is the most common form of generalization of clauses. The following definitions are taken from [14], but the terminology is adapted to inductive logic programming.

Definition 1. A clause C θ-subsumes a clause C, denoted $C \preceq D$, if and only if there exists a substitution θ such that $C\theta \subseteq D$.

Example 1. The clause $C = (p(x) \leftarrow p(f(x)), p(y))$ θ-subsumes the clause $D = (p(a) \leftarrow p(f(a)), q(c))$, since $C\{x/a, y/f(a)\} \subseteq D$.

Definition 2. A clause C is a *least general generalization under θ-subsumption* (LGGθ) of a set of clauses $\{C_1, \ldots, C_n\}$, denoted $C = lgg_{\preceq}\{C_1, \ldots, C_n\}$, if and only if:

1. $C \preceq C_1, \ldots, C \preceq C_n$, and
2. for each clause D, such that $D \preceq C_1, \ldots, D \preceq C_n$, then also $D \preceq C$.

Example 2. Let $C = (p(a) \leftarrow q(a), q(f(a)))$ and $D = (p(b) \leftarrow q(f(b)))$ be clauses. Then both clauses $E = (p(x) \leftarrow q(f(x)))$ and $F = (p(x) \leftarrow q(y), q(f(x)))$ are LGGθs of C and D, which shows that LGGθs are not unique.

2.2 Generalization under Implication

We agree with Niblett [12] that there is no reason why the straight forward notion of implication, instaed of θ-subsumption, should not be used as a basis for generalization.

Definition 3. A clause C *implies* a clause D, denoted $C \Rightarrow D$, if and only if every model of C is a model of D ($C \models D$).

It is easy to see that if a clause C θ-subsumes a clause D then C implies D. But the converse does not hold which is shown by the following example.

Example 3. Let $C = (p(x) \leftarrow p(f(x)))$ and $D = (p(x) \leftarrow p(f(f(x))))$ be clauses. Then $C \Rightarrow D$, but C does not θ-subsume D.

Definition 4. A clause C is a *least general generalization under implication* (LGGI) of a set of clauses $\{C_1, \ldots, C_n\}$, denoted $C = lgg_\Rightarrow\{C_1, \ldots, C_n\}$, if and only if:

1. $C \Rightarrow C_1, \ldots, C \Rightarrow C_n$, and
2. for each clause D such that $D \Rightarrow C_1, \ldots, D \Rightarrow C_n$, then also $D \Rightarrow C$.

Example 4. Let $C = (p(a) \leftarrow p(f(a)), p(c))$, and $D = (p(b) \leftarrow p(f(f(b))), p(c))$ be clauses. Then for the clause $E = (p(x) \leftarrow p(f(y)), p(a))$, we have $E = lgg_\preceq\{C, D\}$, and for the clause $F = (p(x) \leftarrow p(f(x)), p(a))$, we have $F = lgg_\Rightarrow\{C, D\}$.

This example illustrates that LGGθs sometimes are over-generalizations (not least general with respect to implication), since $E \Rightarrow F$ but the converse does not hold.

2.3 Nth Powers and Nth Roots of Clauses

In [9] Muggleton introduces the notion of powers and roots of clauses, for a type of specialization and generalization of self-recursive clauses, where the clauses are resolved with themselves. The definitions of nth powers and nth roots of clauses are based on a function $\mathcal{L}$.

Definition 5. Let T be a clausal theory. Then, the *function* $\mathcal{L}$ is recursively defined as:

1. $\mathcal{L}^1(T) = T$, and
2. $\mathcal{L}^n(T) = \{R \mid C \in T, D \in \mathcal{L}^{n-1}(T)$ and R is a resolvent of C and $D\}$ $(n > 1)$.

The *resolution closure* $\mathcal{L}^*(T) = \mathcal{L}^1(T) \cup \mathcal{L}^2(T) \cup \ldots$

Definition 6. A clause D is an *nth power* of a clause C if and only if D is a variant of a clause in $\mathcal{L}^n(\{C\})$ $(n \geq 1)$. We also say that C is an *nth root* of D.

Example 5. Let $C = (p(x) \leftarrow p(f(x)), p(a))$ be a clause. Then $D = (p(x) \leftarrow p(f(f(x))), p(a))$ is a second power of C, and $E = (p(x) \leftarrow p(f(f(f(x)))), p(a))$ is a third power of C. The clause $F = (p(x) \leftarrow p(f(f(x))), p(f(a)), p(a))$ is also a third power of C.

Note that E and F are not equivalent in any way. The difference between E and F is due to that the resolving literals in the resolution of C and D are not the same. Thus, this example illustrates that powers and roots of clauses are not unique.

It might be the case that a clause C implies a clause D, C does not θ-subsume D, and C is not a root of D. For this relationship we define indirect powers and indirect roots.

Definition 7. A clause D is an *indirect nth power* of a clause if and only if there exists a clause E such that $E \preceq D$ and E is an nth power of C. We also say that C is an *indirect nth root* of D.

Example 6. Let $C = (p(x) \leftarrow p(f(x)))$ and $D = (p(g(a)) \leftarrow p(f(f(g(a)))), p(b), q(c))$ be clauses. Then there exists a clause $E = (p(x) \leftarrow p(f(f(x))))$ such that E is a second power of C and $E \preceq D$. Consequently D is an indirect second power of C, and C is an indirect second root of D.

Note that a root of a clause is also, by definition, an indirect root of that clause. Important to point out is also that all generalizations of clauses under implication are indirect roots of these clauses.

3 Reduction of Generalization by Or-introduction

Our main idea is to reduce generalization under implication to generalization under θ-subsumption (reduction of generalization) by or-introduction. First we present our idea, then we infer the notion of expansion of clauses, which covers this idea. Last in this section, we prove soundness and completeness of our technique for reduction of generalization.

3.1 The Main Idea

As mentioned in the introduction, our technique for reduction of generalization makes use of the sound natural deduction rule called or-introduction. This rule says that if we have a formula E, then we can derive a new formula $E \vee F$, where F is any formula. Let D be a disjunction, then we can derive $D \vee (A \wedge \neg A)$ by or-introduction. This formula can be rewritten to $(D \vee A) \wedge (D \vee \neg A)$. Thus in clausal form we can derive a set of clauses $\{(D \cup \{A\}), (D \cup \{\neg A\})\}$, where A is an atom, from a clause D. It is of interest because we have found that if a clause C is a second root of a clause D, then there exists an atom A such that $C \preceq (D \cup \{A\})$ and $C \preceq (D \cup \{\neg A\})$. Consider the following example.

Example 7. Let $D = (p(x) \leftarrow p(f(f(x))))$ be a clause. Then $C = (p(x) \leftarrow p(f(x)))$ is a second root of D, and we have $C \Rightarrow D$ but C does not θ-subsume D. Let $A = p(f(x))$, then by or-introduction of the contradiction $(A \wedge \neg A)$ we obtain the clauses $(D \cup \{A\}) = (p(x), p(f(x)) \leftarrow p(f(f(x))))$ and $(D \cup \{\neg A\}) = (p(x) \leftarrow p(f(x)), p(f(f(x))))$. Then we have $C\{x/f(x)\} \subseteq (D \cup \{A\})$ and $C \subseteq (D \cup \{\neg A\})$. Consequently, $C \preceq (D \cup \{A\})$ and $C \preceq (D \cup \{\neg A\})$.

Our technique for reduction of generalization works just as well for nth roots as for second roots. But then we have to or-introduce $n - 1$ contradictions, instead of only one. For finding a third root we or-introduce two contradictions. Let D be a clause and A and B atoms. Then by or-introduction we can get $D \vee (A \wedge \neg A) \vee (B \wedge \neg B)$, which in clausal form is a set of four clauses $\{(D \cup \{A, B\}), (D \cup \{A, \neg B\}), (D \cup \{\neg A, B\}), (D \cup \{\neg A, \neg B\})\}$. If C is a third root of D and we have chosen the right atoms A and B, then we will have $C \preceq (D \cup \{A, B\})$, $C \preceq (D \cup \{A, \neg B\})$, $C \preceq (D \cup \{\neg A, B\})$ and $C \preceq (D \cup \{\neg A, \neg B\})$. That our technique works for nth roots, and even for indirect nth roots, is indicated by the following example.

Example 8. Let $D = (p(a) \leftarrow p(f(f(f(a)))))$ be a clause. Then the clause $C = (p(x) \leftarrow p(f(x)))$ is an indirect third root of D, and we have $C \Rightarrow D$ but C does not θ-subsume D. Let $A = p(f(a))$ and $B = p(f(f(a)))$, then by or-introduction we obtain the clauses:

$$D_1 = (D \cup \{A, B\}) = (p(a), p(f(a)), p(f(f(a))) \leftarrow p(f(f(f(a))))),$$
$$D_2 = (D \cup \{A, \neg B\}) = (p(a), p(f(a)) \leftarrow p(f(f(a))), p(f(f(f(a))))),$$
$$D_3 = (D \cup \{\neg A, B\}) = (p(a), p(f(f(a))) \leftarrow p(f(a)), p(f(f(f(a))))),$$
$$D_4 = (D \cup \{\neg A, \neg B\}) = (p(a) \leftarrow p(f(a)), p(f(f(a))), p(f(f(f(a))))).$$

Then we have $C\{x/f(f(a))\} \subseteq D_1$, $C\{x/f(a)\} \subseteq D_2$, $C\{x/a\} \subseteq D_3$ and $C\{x/a\} \subseteq D_4$, and thus C θ-subsumes all the clauses D_1, D_2, D_3 and D_4.

3.2 Expansion of Clauses

In the previous subsection it was illustrated how a reduction of generalization can be achieved by replacing a clause by a set of clauses. Here we will show how this set of clauses equivalently can be described by a single clause, which also is an expansion of the original clause. We start by describing our idea of or-introduction more formally.

Definition 8. Let Ω be a set of atoms, and $\{\Omega_1, \Omega_2\}$ a partition of Ω, where $\Omega_2 = \{A_1, \ldots, A_n\}$. Then $\Sigma = \Omega_1 \cup \{\neg A_1, \ldots, \neg A_n\}$ is a *sign assignment* of Ω.

Definition 9. Let D be a clause and Ω a set of atoms. Then a set of clauses *or-introduced* from D with Ω, denoted $\{D \pm \Omega\}$, is the set of clauses $\{C \cup \Sigma \mid \Sigma$ is a sign assignment of $\Omega\}$.

Example 9. Let $D = (p(a) \leftarrow p(f(f(f(a)))))$ be a clause, and $\Omega = \{p(f(a)), p(f(f(a)))\}$ a set of atoms. Then $\{D \pm \Omega\} = \{D_1, D_2, D_3, D_4\}$, where D_1, D_2, D_3 and D_4 are the same as in example 8.

By definition 2, if a clause C θ-subsumes every clause in a set of clauses, then C will also θ-subsume the LGGθ of the set of clauses. This leads us to our definition of expansion of clauses.

Definition 10. Let $\{D \pm \Omega\}$ be a set of clauses or-introduced from D with Ω. Then $E = lgg_{\preceq}\{D \pm \Omega\}$ is an *expansion* of D by Ω.

Example 10. Let D and Ω be as in example 9. Then the expansion of D by Ω is $E = lgg_{\preceq}\{D \pm \Omega\} = (p(a), p(x) \leftarrow p(f(x)), p(f(f(f(a)))))$. Hence, the third root $C = (p(x) \leftarrow p(f(x)))$ of D, which does not θ-subsume D, θ-subsumes the expansion E of D.

Expansion can be regarded as a transformation technique, since the expansion of a clause C is logically equivalent to the clause C. More important is that there always exists an expansion of a clause C such that every generalization under implication of C is reduced to a generalization under θ-subsumption. Both these results are proved in the next subsection.

Algorithm 1 Expansion of clauses
Input: a non-tautological clause D.
Output: a clause E such that $E \Leftrightarrow D$, and $C \preceq E$ for every indirect root C of D $(C \Rightarrow D)$.
1. Find the desirable set of atoms Ω.
2. Compute the expansion $E = lgg_{\preceq}\{D \pm \Omega\}$.

The algorithm is non-deterministic, since we have not described how the set of atoms Ω can be found. In [4] a technique to find such a set of atoms for single-recursive clauses is described, and it is not hard to extend this technique to cover arbitrary clauses. But in this paper we are satisfied with an indeterministic version of the algorithm, since it will turn out that the second part of the algorithm is computationally intractable anyway.

3.3 Soundness and Completeness

Soundness and completeness of our expansion technique of clauses, which reduces generalization under implication to generalization under θ-subsumtion, are guaranteed by the following theorems. Theorem 12 and corollary 13 are taken from [9], and use the function $\mathcal{L}$ which is defined in section 2.3.

Theorem 11 Soundness of expansion of clauses. *Let C be a clause and Ω a set of atoms. Then $lgg_{\preceq}\{C \pm \Omega\} \Leftrightarrow C$.*

Proof. Let $E = lgg_{\preceq}\{C \pm \Omega\}$. Then for each $D \in \{C \pm \Omega\}$ we have $E \preceq D$ and thus $E \Rightarrow \{C \pm \Omega\}$. We also have $\{C \pm \Omega\} \vdash C$ (by resolution). Consequently $E \Rightarrow C$. Each literal $L_i \in C$ is included in every clause in $\{C \pm \Omega\}$, and since $lgg_{\preceq}(L_i, L_i) = L_i$ we have $C \subseteq lgg_{\preceq}\{C \pm \Omega\}$, and thus $C \preceq E$. Consequently $C \Rightarrow E$, and thus $E \Leftrightarrow C$.

Theorem 12 Subsumption theorem. *Let T be a set of clauses and C a non-tautological clause. Then $T \models C$ if and only if there exists a clause $D \in \mathcal{L}^*(T)$ such that $D \preceq C$.*

Proof. A proof can be found in [1].

Corollary 13 Implication between clauses using resolution. *Let C be a clause and D a non-tautological clause. Then $C \Rightarrow D$ $(C \models D)$ if and only if there exists a clause $E \in \mathcal{L}^*(\{C\})$ such that $E \preceq D$.*

Proof. Follows directly as a special case of theorem 12.

Lemma 14 Completeness of or-introduction for roots of clauses. *Let C be a clause an D_n an nth power of C. Then there exists a set of atoms Ω_n such that $C \preceq (D_n \cup \Sigma_n)$ for each sign assignment Σ_n of Ω_n.*

Proof. The proof is by mathematical induction on n.

Base step (n=1): D_1 is a first power of C, that is $D_1 = C$. Consequently, $C \preceq (D_1 \cup \Sigma_1)$ for each sign assignment Σ_1 of any set of atoms Ω_1.

Induction hypothesis (n=k): If D_k is a kth power of C then there exists a set of atoms Ω_k such that $C \preceq (D_k \cup \Sigma_k)$ for each sign assignment Σ_k of Ω_k.

Induction step (n=k+1): Let $C = \{A\} \cup \Gamma$ and $D_k = \{B\} \cup \Lambda$, such that $A\theta_A = \overline{B}\theta_B$, where $\theta_A \cup \theta_B$ is an mgu for $\{A, \overline{B}\}$. Then a $(k+1)$th power of C will be $D_{k+1} = \Gamma\theta_A \cup \Lambda\theta_B$. Let $\Omega_{k+1} = \Omega_k\theta_B \cup \{A\theta_A\}$ if $A\theta_A$ is an atom, or $\Omega_{k+1} = \Omega_k\theta_B \cup \{\overline{A}\theta_A\}$ if $\overline{A}\theta_A$ is an atom. Then we distinguish between two different cases. A sign assignment Σ_{k+1} of Ω_{k+1} could be either:

1. $\Sigma_{k+1} = \Sigma_k\theta_B \cup \{A\theta_A\}$, where Σ_k is a sign assignment of Ω_k, or
2. $\Sigma_{k+1} = \Sigma_k\theta_B \cup \{B\theta_B\}$ (since $A\theta_A = \overline{B}\theta_B$), where Σ_k is a sign assignment of Ω_k.

Case 1: $D_{k+1} \cup \Sigma_{k+1} = \Gamma\theta_A \cup \Lambda\theta_B \cup \{A\theta_A\} \cup \Sigma_k\theta_B$, and thus $C\theta_A \subseteq (D_{k+1} \cup \Sigma_{k+1})$. Consequently $C \preceq (D_{k+1} \cup \Sigma_{k+1})$, which completes the proof for case 1.

Case 2: $D_{k+1} \cup \Sigma_{k+1} = \Gamma\theta_A \cup \Lambda\theta_B \cup \{B\theta_B\} \cup \Sigma_k\theta_B$, and thus $(D \cup \Sigma_k)\theta_B \subseteq (D_{k+1} \cup \Sigma_{k+1})$. Consequently $(D \cup \Sigma_k) \preceq (D_{k+1} \cup \Sigma_{k+1})$. By the induction hypothesis $C \preceq (D \cup \Sigma_k)$, and thus $C \preceq (D_{k+1} \cup \Sigma_{k+1})$ (since $\preceq$ is transitive), which completes the proof for case 2.

Theorem 15 Completeness of expansion of clauses. *Let C and D be non-tautological clauses such that $C \Rightarrow D$. Then there exists a set of atoms Ω such that $C \preceq lgg_{\preceq}\{D \pm \Omega\}$.*

Proof. By corollary 13, there exists a clause D_n such that D_n is an nth power of C and $D_n \preceq D$. Hence there exists a substitution θ such that $D_n\theta \subseteq D$. By lemma 14, there exists a set of literals Ω_n such that $C \preceq (D_n \cup \Sigma_n)$ for each sign assignment Σ_n of Ω_n. Then let $\Omega = \Omega_n\theta$, and thus $(D_n \cup \Sigma_n) \preceq (D \cup \Sigma)$ for each sign assignment Σ of Ω, where $\Sigma = \Sigma_n\theta$. Consequently $C \preceq (D \cup \Sigma)$ for each sign assignment Σ of Ω (since $\preceq$ is transitive). Then by definition 2, we have $C \preceq lgg_{\preceq}\{D \pm \Omega\}$.

4 Concluding Remarks

Almost all inductive learners that use clausal representation perform generalizations under θ-subsumption. But generalizations of a certain type, roots of clauses, are not possible to find by generalization under θ-subsumption. To eliminate this incompleteness, we have presented a technique to expand clauses so that, generalization under implication are reduced to generalization under θ-subsumption. The expansion technique has been proved to be sound and complete. It is also conceptually simple.

Recently two other approaches to the problem of generalization under implication have been presented, one by Muggleton [9] and one by Lapointe and Matwin [6]. The algorithms described in [9] are non-deterministic and restricted to single-recursive clauses. In [6] it is described how two particular types of recursive clauses, which they call purely recursive and left recursive, efficiently can be learned. However, these two types of clauses only cover a fraction of all possible self-recursive clauses.

In a recent work by Idestam-Almquist [3], which is a development of the work in [6], the class of efficiently learnable clauses is extended to cover most single-recursive clauses. By the technique he presents, the generalizations are also guaranteed to be minimally general with respect to implication.

As we have shown our expansion technique of clauses is sound and complete, which is our main contribution. Now finally we will discuss its main disadvantage, its computational complexity. The complexity of the second part of the algorithm is terrible. The or-introduced set of clauses grows exponentially with the cardinality of the set of atoms used in the or-introduction. As noted in [11] the size of an $LGG\theta$ may also grow exponentially with the number of input clauses. We recommend that an $LGG\theta$ of two clauses is reduced, by removing all redundant literals, before the next input clause is taken into account. By that the size explosion can be handled, but the time complexity problem of our technique still remains.

A question for future research is to investigate if there is a way to reduce the complexity, of the presented technique, by using some approximative and more efficient computation of $LGG\theta$s. Another direction for future research is to further extend the class of efficiently learnable clauses by the technique based on the work in [6].

Acknowledgement

This work was partially supported by NUTEK, the Swedish National Board for Technical and Industrial Development under the contract 9001734, and is a part of the work in the ESPRIT BRA ILP project 6020. The author would also like to thank Douglas Busch for inspiring discussions, and Carl-Gustaf Jansson and Fredrik Kilander for help with writing the final version of this paper.

References

1. M. Bain and S. Muggleton. Non-monotonic learning. *Machine Intelligence*, 12, 1991.
2. Jean H. Gallier. *Logic for Computer Science: Foundations of Automatic Theorem Proving*. John Wiley & Sons, 1987.
3. P. Idestam-Almquist. Generalization under implication by recursive anti-unification. Submitted to the International Workshop on Inductive Logic Programming 1993.
4. P. Idestam-Almquist. Generalization under implication. Technical report, Department of Computer and Systems Sciences, Stockholm University, 1992. Report 92-020-SYSLAB.
5. P. Idestam-Almquist. Learning missing clauses by inverse resolution. In *Proceedings of the International Conference on Fifth Generation Computer Systems 1992*, Ohmsha, Tokyo, 1992.
6. Stéphane Lapointe and Stan Matwin. Sub-unification: A tool for efficient induction of recursive programs. In *Proceedings of the Ninth International Conference on Machine Learning*. Morgan Kaufmann, 1992.
7. J. W. Lloyd. *Foundations of Logic Programming*. Springer-Verlag, 1987. Second edition.
8. Stephen Muggleton. Inductive logic programming. *New Generation Computing*, 8(4):295–318, 1991.
9. Stephen Muggleton. Inverting implication. In Stephen Muggleton, editor, *Proceedings of the International Workshop on Inductive Logic Programming*, 1992.
10. Stephen Muggleton and Wray Buntine. Machine invention of first-order predicates by inverting resolution. In *Proceedings of the Fifth International Conference on Machine Learning*. Morgan Kaufmann, 1988.
11. Stephen Muggleton and C. Feng. Efficient induction of logic programs. In *Proceedings of the First Conference on Algorithmic Learning Theory*, Tokyo, 1990. Ohmsha Publishers.
12. Tim Niblett. A study of generalization in logic programs. In *Proceedings of the Third European Working Session on Learning*. Pitman, 1988.
13. Nilsson and Genesereth. *Logic Foundations of Artificial Intelligence*. Morgan Kaufmann, 1987.
14. G. D. Plotkin. *Automatic Methods of Inductive Inference*. PhD thesis, Edinburgh University, 1971.
15. J. Robinson. A machine-oriented logic based on the resolution principle. *Journal of the ACM*, 12(1), 1965.
16. Céline Rouveirol. Extensions of inversion of resolution applied to theory completion. In Stephen Muggleton, editor, *Inductive Logic Programming*. Academic Press, San Diego, CA, 1992.
17. Céline Rouveirol and Jean François Puget. Beyond inversion of resolution. In *Proceedings of the Seventh International Conference on Machine Learning*. Morgan Kaufmann, 1990.
18. Richmond H. Thomason. *Symbolic Logic—An Introduction*. McMillan Publishers, 1970.
19. Ruediger Wirth. Completing logic programs by inverse resolution. In *Proceedings of the Fourth Working Session on Learning*. Pitman, 1989.

On the proper definition of minimality in specialization and theory revision

Stefan Wrobel

GMD (German National Research Center for Computer Science)
FIT.KI, Pf. 1316
W-5205 St. Augustin 1
wrobel@gmdzi.gmd.de

Abstract. A central operation in an incremental learning system is the specialization of an incorrect theory in order exclude incorrect inferences. In this paper, we discuss what properties are to be required from such theory revision operations. In particular, we examine what it should mean for a revision to be minimal. As a surprising result, the seemingly most natural criterion, requiring revisions to produce maximally general correct specializations, leads to a number of serious problems. We therefore propose an alternative interpretation of minimality based on the notion of base revision from theory contraction work, and formally define it as a set of base revision postulates. We then present a revision operator (MBR) that meets these postulates, and shown that it produces the maximally general correct revision satisfying the postulates, i.e., the revisions produced by MBR are indeed minimal in our sense. The operator is implemented and used in KRT, the knowledge revision tool of the MOBAL system.

1 Introduction

An incremental learning system receives a sequence of positive and negative examples from its environment, and always maintains one current hypothesis that is updated after each new input. Two possible cases can arise: If the new input is a positive example (true statement) not covered by the current hypothesis, the hypothesis needs to be *generalized* so that this input can then be explained by the hypothesis. If the new input is a negative example (incorrect statement) erroneously covered by the system's current hypothesis, the system must *specialize* its hypothesis so that the incorrect inference is not produced any more. Ideally, the system should change its current hypothesis *minimally* in order to keep as much as possible of the knowledge it already had.

In this paper, we are concerned with the specialization problem for incremental learning systems that maintain a *first-order theory* as their current hypothesis, i.e., the system learns not only a single clause for one concept, but a set of clauses for a set of interrelated concepts. For single clauses or rules, there is a good understanding of what it means to modify them minimally in order to exclude a negative example — the system should simply perform a minimal specialization (in the logical sense) on the clause. The situation is more difficult when multiple-clause, multiple concept theories are used as the system's hypothesis, since here, we must not only modify individual clauses, but first decide which clauses to modify. Clearly, in this setting the system should also revise its current hypothesis minimally, but what is the exact definition of minimality in this case? To answer this question Machine Learning can benefit from existing work on *theory revision*, specifically from work on the logic of theory change [Gär88].

In this paper, we for the first time explicitly examine the proper definition of minimality to be used when revising a first-order theory in an incremental learning system. In particular, we will take issue with the hypothesis that minimal revision means minimal specialization of a theory, as has been argued in [MB92]. By relating specialization to work on theory contraction, we will show that such revisions correspond to contraction operations on closed theories, which have very undesirable properties from a computational point of view. We instead propose a more adequate notion of minimality by adapting the well-known set of Gärdenfors postulates for closed theory revision [Gär88] to revisions of theories in an incremental learning system.

We then present the MBR (for "minimal base revision") operator for revision of clausal first-order theories that is shown to meet the revised set of postulates, and is fully implemented in KRT, the knowledge revision tool of the MOBAL system [MWKEss]. It has been successfully used for revision of a set of telecommunication access control rules when faced with a number of incorrect access assignments in an application developed in cooperation with Alcatel Alsthom Recherche, Paris [SMAU93]. In contrast to algorithms previously proposed by [MB92] and [Lin91], our method correctly computes the set of all possible minimal changes to the original knowledge base, and can ensure that lost inferences are recovered when removed statements are re-added to the theory. By using an exception set notation, our method also shows that the use of non-monotonically interpreted predicates, as advocated in [MB92, Lin91], is an unnecessary complexity for minimal theory specialization.

The paper is organized as follows. In the next section (2), we will introduce basic definitions and notations to be used in the rest of the paper. In section 3, we will define the minimal specialization (mgcs) hypothesis, and point out its negative properties by relating to work on closed theory contraction. In section 4, we will present our alternative interpretation of minimality in revision by defining a set of postulates that any revision operation must satisfy if it is to avoid the problems of minimal specialization. In section 5, we then present an operator that implements our notion of minimality, and show that this operator meets our postulates, and actually produces the most general correct revisions that meet the postulates, i.e., is indeed minimal in this sense. Section 6 discusses some related work, and section 7 contains summary and conclusions.

2 Basic definitions

In the following, we will denote with Γ the current knowledge base (inductive hypothesis) of the learning system, where Γ is meant to be a first-order theory in the standard logical syntax as defined eg. in [Men87][1]. We will further assume that standard first-order derivability is used as a consequence operation, denoted by $\vdash$[2], and let $Cn(\Gamma)$ denote the closure of Γ under $\vdash$. If $\Gamma_2 = Cn(\Gamma_1)$, Γ_1 is called a *base* of Γ_2; if $Cn(\Gamma) = \Gamma$, Γ is called *closed*. As a simple example, consider the knowledge base

$$\Gamma_1 = \{p(a), \forall x : p(x) \rightarrow q(x)\}.$$

Assuming that the underlying alphabet contains the predicate symbols p and q, no function symbols, and the constants a and b, we find that

$$\Gamma_2 := Cn(\Gamma_1) = \{p(a), \forall x : p(x) \rightarrow q(x), q(a), p(a) \vee p(b), p(a) \vee \neg p(b), \ldots\}.$$

Γ_1 is a base of Γ_2, and Γ_2 is a closed theory. Finally, by a substitution we mean a possibly empty set of pairs $\sigma = \{v_1/t_1, \ldots, v_n/t_n\}$, where all the v_i are variable symbols and pairwise different, and the t_i are terms. The application of a substitution to a statement s, denoted $s\sigma$, is the statement obtained by replacing in s each occurrence of v_i with t_i for all i.

To more formally define the problem of specializing a theory against a negative example, note that in the general case, this negative example can be any statement about the world that the system currently believes, and is now told to be wrong. Therefore, if we define a *fact* to be a (not necessarily ground)[3] positive or negated atom, we can formally define the specialization or revision problem as follows.

Definition 1 (Revision) Given *a theory Γ and a set of facts $F = \{f_1, \ldots, f_n\}$,* **find** *a revised theory $\Gamma \overset{.}{-} F$ ("Γ minus F") such that*

$$Cn(\Gamma \overset{.}{-} F) \cap F = \emptyset.$$

If $F = \{f\}$ is a singleton set we will write $\Gamma \overset{.}{-} f$ instead of $\Gamma \overset{.}{-} \{f\}$.

For simplicity of notation, in the following we will give all results for the singleton set case; as pointed at the end of section 5, they all carry over to the case of multiple simultaneous revisions by performing the obvious modifications on definitions and theorems.

Below, we will also need the generalization/specialization relationship on theories, which as usual we define with respect to derivability.

Definition 2 (Generality) *A theory Γ_1 is said to be* more general *than a theory Γ_2, written $\Gamma_1 \geq_g \Gamma_2$ iff*

$$\Gamma_1 \vdash \Gamma_2.$$

By the definition of Cn, this is equivalent to $\Gamma_1 \geq_g \Gamma_2 \Leftrightarrow Cn(\Gamma_1) \supseteq Cn(\Gamma_2)$.

---

[1] We use $\rightarrow$ instead of $\Rightarrow$ to denote implication, however.

[2] We will usually write $\Gamma \vdash S$ instead of "$\Gamma \vdash s$ for all $s \in S$.

[3] If nonground, variables are assumed to be universally quantified.

3   Minimal specialization and theory contraction

Since the definition of the revision task seriously underconstrains the operator $\hat{-}$, the question we must consider is which further properties to require from the revision result $\Gamma \hat{-} f$. Above, we already pointed out that in general, we want our revisions to be minimal in some sense. In this section, we will examine a seemingly natural instantiation of the notion of minimality that has been proposed in a recent paper by Muggleton and Bain [MB92], who define minimal revisions as *minimal specializations* of a theory. In particular, they define the notion of a maximally general correct specialization as follows.

Definition 3 (mcgs) *Let f be an incorrect statement derived by a theory Γ. A maximally general correct specialization (mgcs) of Γ with respect to f is any theory Γ' such that*

  1. $\Gamma \geq_g \Gamma'$
  2. $\Gamma' \not\vdash f$
  3. For all Γ'': If $\Gamma \geq_g \Gamma'' >_g \Gamma'$, then $\Gamma'' \vdash f$.

In other words, a *mgcs* is any theory that is a specialization of the original theory, and does not have any correct supersets, i.e., supersets that do not imply the fact to be removed. We will often refer to the *mgcs* simply as the *minimal specialization* of Γ with respect to f.

To evaluate the properties of this notion of minimal revision, we can draw upon some well-known results from work on closed theory contraction [Gär88, Neb89]. As we will see, maximally general correct specializations are a special case of the operations examined there. In the next section, we will briefly summarize some important results, following the exposition in [Neb89, ch. 6].

3.1   Closed theory contraction

The goal of work on closed theory contraction was a knowledge-level examination of theory change operations. Consequently, in this work, it is generally assumed that the theories under consideration are *closed*. Theory contraction then refers to the same task that we have called theory revision above. One of the best-known results from theory contraction work is the set of *Gärdenfors postulates*, which are a set of minimal constraints claimed to be necessary for every sensible revision operation. The six major postulates are summarized in table 1, for a closed theory Γ and a fact f to be removed. These postulates are mostly unspectacular and describe reasonable properties one would expect from a revised theory. Postulate 1 simply requires the revised theory to be closed, which if necessary can be ensured by applying Cn. Postulate 2 is more interesting, as it requires the revised theory to be a subset of the original theory, thus ruling out revision operations that generalize some part of the theory. Postulates 3 and 4 simply capture the definition of the revision task, requiring the operation to leave the theory alone if f was not in the theory, and requiring it to effectively

---

1. $\Gamma \dot{-} f$ is a closed theory (*closure*).
2. $\Gamma \dot{-} f \subseteq \Gamma$ (*inclusion*).
3. If $f \notin \Gamma$, then $\Gamma \dot{-} f = \Gamma$ (*vacuity*).
4. If $f \notin Cn(\emptyset)$, then $f \notin \Gamma \dot{-} f$ (*success*).
5. If $Cn(f) = Cn(g)$, then $\Gamma \dot{-} f = \Gamma \dot{-} g$ (*preservation*).
6. $\Gamma \subseteq Cn(\Gamma \dot{-} f \cup \{f\})$ (*recovery*).

Table 1. The main Gärdenfors postulates for closed theory contraction

remove f if f is not a tautology (which is always the case if f is a fact). Postulate 5 requires the preservation of semantic equivalence.

The final postulate, recovery, is the most interesting one from the standpoint of machine learning, as it addresses a likely scenario for an incremental learning system. The recovery postulate requires that if we modify a theory to exclude an inference f, and later find out that f was true after all, we should be able to obtain at least the same set of inferences again that we used to have before removing f in the first place. It thus acts as a lower bound on the revisions we may perform, and excludes for instance the trivial empty theory as a revision result.

Interestingly, as pointed out in [Neb89], all possible revision operations that meet the above postulates can be defined with respect to the set of maximal correct subsets of a closed theory.

Definition 4 (Maximal correct subsets) *If Γ is a theory, and f a statement to be removed, the family of maximal subsets of Γ not implying f, denoted $\Gamma \downarrow f$ (pronounced "Γ down f" or "Γ less f") is defined by:*

$$\Gamma \downarrow f := \{\Gamma' \subseteq \Gamma | f \notin Cn(\Gamma') \text{ and for all } \Gamma'' : \text{if } \Gamma' \subset \Gamma'' \subseteq \Gamma \text{ then } f \in Cn(\Gamma'')\}.$$

As an example, consider the closed theory Γ_2 from the example in section 2 above, i.e.,

$$\Gamma_2 = \{p(a), \forall x : p(x) \rightarrow q(x), q(a), p(a) \vee p(b), p(a) \vee \neg p(b), \ldots\}.$$

If we want to remove $q(a)$ from this theory, some of the maximally correct subsets are:

$$\Gamma_2 \downarrow q(a) = \left\{ \begin{array}{l} \{p(a), p(a) \vee p(b), p(a) \vee \neg p(b), \ldots\} \\ \{\forall x : p(x) \rightarrow q(x), p(a) \vee p(b), \ldots\} \\ \{\forall x : p(x) \rightarrow q(x), p(a) \vee \neg p(b), \ldots\} \\ \ldots \end{array} \right\}$$

The following theorem (first shown in [AGM85]) allows us to express any revision operation on closed theories that meets the Gärdenfors postulates in one common form.

Theorem 1 $\dot{-}$ *is a revision operation that meets the Gärdenfors postulates 1–6 if and only if there is a selection function* $\gamma : \Gamma \downarrow f \mapsto \gamma(\Gamma \downarrow f) \subseteq \Gamma \downarrow f$ *such that*

$$\Gamma \dot{-} f = \begin{cases} \bigcap \gamma(\Gamma \downarrow f) & \text{if } f \notin Cn(\emptyset) \\ \Gamma & \text{otherwise.} \end{cases}$$

In other words, any revision operation meeting postulates 1 through 6 can be defined by specifying a function γ that returns a subset of $\Gamma \downarrow f$, the set of all maximally correct subsets of Γ, and computing the intersection of these sets. Depending on the size of the set returned by γ, the resulting operations are given different names:

Definition 5 (Partial meet, full meet, maxi-choice contractions) *All revision operations of the form defined in theorem 1 are called* partial meet contractions. *If γ returns a singleton, the operation is called a* maxi-choice contraction, *if γ simply returns $\Gamma \downarrow f$, the operation is called* full-meet contraction.

3.2 Mgcs as maxi-choice contractions

Returning to minimal specializations resp. maximally general correct specializations (mgcs), we can see that they correspond precisely to the maxi-choice contractions on a closed theory as defined above.

Theorem 2 *Given a (not necessarily closed) theory Γ, and statement to be removed f, the mgcs of Γ with respect to f are exactly the results of all possible maxi-choice contractions on $Cn(\Gamma)$, i.e., the members of the set $Cn(\Gamma) \downarrow f$.*

Proof. The proof follows trivially from definition 4, according to which $Cn(\Gamma) \downarrow f =$

$$\{\Gamma' \subseteq Cn(\Gamma) | f \notin Cn(\Gamma') \text{ and for all } \Gamma'' : \text{if } \Gamma' \subset \Gamma'' \subseteq Cn(\Gamma) \text{ then } x \in Cn(\Gamma'')\},$$

which is a reformulation of the definition of *mgcs*. $\square$

This correspondence, unfortunately, means that minimal specializations inherit all the known undesirable properties of maxi-choice contractions as revision operations, as pointed out by [Neb89] and others:

Nonfinite representation. Since minimal specialization revisions are equivalent to maxi-choice operations on closed theories, they also produce closed theories. In general, it is impossible to determine whether a closed theory has a finite axiomatization, which is a necessary prerequisite for the use of minimal specialization for practical theory revision.

Loss of reason maintenance. An operation on the closure of a theory does not take into account which statements were derived from which others. For instance, if from Γ_1 (section 2), we were to remove $p(a)$ by minimal specialization, one of the possible minimal specializations would be

$$mgcs(\Gamma_1, p(a)) = Cn(\Gamma_1) \downarrow p(a)$$
$$= \{\{\forall x : p(x) \rightarrow q(x), q(a), p(a) \vee p(b), \ldots\}, \ldots\},$$

i.e., we would remove the antecedent $p(a)$, but keep statements that were derived from it such as $q(a)$.

Besserwissers. Last, for a maxi-choice contraction $\dot{-}$, we know (theorem 6.2 from [Neb89] foll. [AM82]) that for any proposition g:

either $g \in Cn(\Gamma \dot{-} f \cup \neg f)$, or $\neg g \in Cn(\Gamma \dot{-} f \cup \neg f)$.

This means that if a learning system finds out that instead of f, as currently believed, $\neg f$ is true, and uses minimal specialization to remove f before adding $\neg f$, the system will have miraculously completed its theory, which is certainly not desirable[4].

4 Minimal base revisions

We can thus conclude that an interpretation of minimal revisions as minimal specializations, or *mgcs* in the terminology of [MB92], is not an advantageous strategy, since it is an operation that can be performed only on closed theories, resulting in the drawbacks enumerated above. Based on the base contraction postulates in [Neb89], we have therefore developed a revised set of revision postulates that applies to revision operations on non-closed first-order theories; these postulates are shown in table 2.

---

1. $\Gamma \dot{-} f \subseteq \Gamma \cup \{g' | \exists g \in \Gamma$ such that $g \geq_g g'\}$ (*minimal syntactic distance*).
2. $Cn(\Gamma \dot{-} f) \subseteq Cn(\Gamma)$ (*inclusion*).
3. If $f \notin Cn(\Gamma)$, then $\Gamma \dot{-} f = \Gamma$ (*vacuity*).
4. If $f \notin Cn(\emptyset)$, then $f \notin Cn(\Gamma \dot{-} f)$ (*success*).
5. If $Cn(f) = Cn(g)$, then $Cn(\Gamma \dot{-} f) = Cn(\Gamma \dot{-} g)$ (*preservation*).
6. $Cn(\Gamma) \subseteq Cn(\Gamma \dot{-} f \cup \{f\})$ (*recovery*).

Table 2. Revised set of postulates for revision of theory bases

The most important difference between the closed theory postulates and the ones defined here is the first postulate, which together with the recovery postulate, expresses a new notion of minimal revision for theory bases. According to

---

[4] The term besserwisser is due to [Gär88].

the first postulate, a revision is minimal if the new theory contains only statements that had been in the old theory, and perhaps other statements that are specializations of statements in the original theory. Note that minimal specialization revisions in general do not meet this new first postulate, as their results will contain elements from the closure of Γ that were not originally in Γ nor are specializations of single statements in Γ.

If we assume that our theories are in clausal form, as we will from now on, we can define $\geq_g$ for individual clauses simply as θ-subsumption [Plo70]:

$$f \geq_g f' \text{ iff there is a substitution } \theta \text{ such that } f\theta \subseteq f'.$$

This definition ensures that indeed the revised knowledge base is syntactically close to the original knowledge base, since new clauses must be derived by substitution or added literals from existing clauses.

5 A minimal base revision operator

To show that the above set of revised postulates indeed allows useful theory revision operations, we will now present a revision operator for clausal theories that meets all of these postulates. This operator, which we will call MBR, for *minimal base revision*, and denote by $\doteq$, has been implemented and is used in KRT, the knowledge revision tool of the MOBAL system [MWKEss], to perform knowledge revision. In order to define $\doteq$, we need to define the *derivation tree* of a fact in a theory. As usual, we will assume that $\vdash$ is implemented as refutation proofs by resolution.

Definition 6 (Derivation) *Let Γ be a theory, and $f \in Cn(\Gamma)$ a factual query finitely refutable from Γ by resolution. The derivation of f in Γ, $\Delta(f, \Gamma)$, is the pair*

$$\Delta(f, \Gamma) := (f, S),$$

where S, the supports of f, is the following set of triples:

$$S := \{(C, \sigma, A) | \exists C \in \Gamma \wedge \exists g_1, \ldots, g_n \in Cn(\Gamma) : \ C \text{ resolves with} \\ \{g_1, \ldots, g_n\} \text{ using substitution } \sigma \text{ to produce } f\}.$$

A, the antecedents of S, are recursively defined as follows:

$$A := \{\Delta(g_1, \Gamma), \ldots, \Delta(g_n, \Gamma)\}.$$

Wherever Γ is clear from context, we will simply write $\Delta(f)$ instead of $\Delta(f, \Gamma)$.

Since different refutation proofs of f may share the same clauses and substitutions, the (C, σ, A) triples representing clause applications may repeat in a derivation structure, meaning that a derivation is best understood as a directed acyclic graph. In the following, we will assume that for any inferences f to be removed, $\Delta(f, \Gamma)$ is finite, which may not be the case in theories with function symbols. From a derivation, a standard *proof tree* can be obtained by beginning at the root, choosing one of its supports, and then repeating this recursively for the derivation subtrees rooted at the antecedents of this supports. By varying the choices in all possible ways, the set of all proof trees can be obtained. As an example of a derivation, consider the theory

$$\Gamma_1 = \{p(a), \forall x : p(x) \rightarrow q(x)\}.$$

defined in section 2. Dropping the quantification symbol, and using capitalized variables instead, this theory is written as

$$\Gamma_1 = \{p(a), p(X) \rightarrow q(X)\}.$$

Let us assume that q(a) is to be removed from this theory. There is only one way of proving q(a), so

$$\Delta(q(a), \Gamma_1) = (q(a),$$
$$\{(p(X) \rightarrow q(X), \{X/a\},$$
$$\{(p(a),$$
$$\{(p(a), \emptyset, \emptyset)\}) \}) \}),$$

Using this definition of a derivation, we can define the clause application set of a theory Γ with respect to a fact f.

Definition 7 (Application set) *Let Γ be a theory and $f \in Cn(\Gamma)$ a fact. We define the* clause application set *of Γ with respect to f as:*

$$\Pi(f, \Gamma) := \{(C, \sigma) | \exists S = (C, \sigma, A) \text{ somewhere in } \Delta(f, \Gamma)\}.$$

Instead of $(C, \emptyset)$ (where $\emptyset$ in this context is the empty substitution), we often simply write C in $\Pi(f, \Gamma)$.

In our example, the clause application set is

$$\Pi(q(a), \Gamma_1) = \{(p(a), \emptyset), (p(X) \rightarrow q(X), \{X/a\})\},$$

and we define for later use abbreviations for the two nonempty subsets of this application set:

$$P_1 := \{(p(a), \emptyset)\}$$
$$P_2 := \{(p(X) \rightarrow q(X), \{X/a\})\}$$

These application sets are needed so that each clause application in the proof of an offending fact can be individually kept or removed; otherwise, we would unnecessarily overspecialize in cases where one rule is used several times. Consequently, below we will define a version of $\Gamma \downarrow f$ that can work on application sets instead of on theories. First, however, we need to define substitution and instance sets.

Definition 8 (Substitution and Instance sets) *Let C be a clause in a theory Γ, with variables $\text{vars}(C) = \{X_1, \ldots, X_n\}$, let $f \in Cn(\Gamma)$ be a fact, and $P \subseteq \Pi(f, \Gamma)$. The substitution set of C with respect to P is defined as follows. We say that one substitution is more general than another, $\sigma_1 \geq_g \sigma_2$, iff there is a substitution θ such that $\sigma_1\theta = \sigma_2$. Let*

$$\Sigma_0(C, P) := \{\sigma | (C, \sigma) \in P\}$$

denote all substitutions used with C in P. Then

$$\Sigma(C, P) \subseteq \Sigma_0(C, P)$$

is any set such that:

- *for any $\sigma \in \Sigma_0(C, P)$, there is a $\sigma' \in \Sigma(C, P)$ such that $\sigma' \geq_g \sigma$.*
- *for no $\sigma \in \Sigma(C, P)$, there is a $\sigma' \in \Sigma(C, P)$ such that $\sigma' \geq_g \sigma$.*

For non-ground clauses ($n \geq 1$), the instance set of C with respect to P is defined as

$$I(C, P) := \{(X_1, \ldots, X_n)\sigma | \sigma \in \Sigma(C, P)\}.$$

We should note that the construction of $\Sigma(C, P)$ ensures that there are no redundant substitutions in this set. Continuing with our example, we see that

$$\Sigma(p(a), P_1) = \{\emptyset\}$$
$$\Sigma(p(X) \rightarrow q(X), P_2) = \{\{X/a\}\}$$
$$\Sigma(p(a), P_2) = \Sigma(p(X) \rightarrow q(X), P_1) = \emptyset$$
$$I(p(X) \rightarrow q(X), P_1) = \emptyset$$
$$I(p(X) \rightarrow q(X), P_2) = \{(a)\}.$$

We can now define which theory corresponds to an application set:

Definition 9 (Corresponding theory) *Let Γ be a theory and $f \in Cn(\Gamma)$ a fact, and $P \subseteq \Pi(f, \Gamma)$. If we define the clauses occurring in P as*

$$C(P) := \{C | (C, \sigma) \in P\},$$

we can define the theory corresponding to P as:

$$\Gamma_\Pi(P) := (\Gamma \backslash C(P))$$
$$\cup \{\text{vars}(C) \notin I(C, P) \diamond C \mid C \in C(P) \text{ and } C \text{ nonground}\}$$
$$\cup \{C\sigma | (C, \sigma) \in P\}.$$

Here, $L_0 \diamond C$ is a shorthand notation for the addition of a premise, i.e., if C is a clause of the form $L_1 \& \cdots \& L_n \rightarrow L_{n+1}$, then

$$L_0 \diamond C := L_0 \& L_1 \& \cdots \& L_n \rightarrow L_{n+1}.$$

$\text{vars}(C)$ denotes the tuple of variables of the clause.

We can now define the promised version of $\Gamma \downarrow f$ that can work on application sets instead of on theories.

Definition 10 (Maximal application, Minimal removal sets) *Let Γ be a theory, and f a fact to be removed. The* set of maximal application sets *of Γ with respect to f is defined as:*

$$\Gamma \downarrow_\Pi f := \Pi(f, \Gamma) \downarrow f := \{P \subseteq \Pi(f, \Gamma) | f \notin Cn(\Gamma_\Pi(P)) \text{ and for all } P' :$$
$$\text{if } P \subset P' \subseteq \Pi(f, \Gamma) \text{ then } f \in Cn(\Gamma_\Pi(P'))\}.$$

The complement of $\Gamma \downarrow_\Pi f$ is called the set of minimal removal sets, *and defined by*

$$\overline{\Gamma \downarrow_\Pi f} := \overline{\Pi(f, \Gamma) \downarrow f} := \{\Pi(f, \Gamma) \backslash P | P \in \Gamma \downarrow_\Pi f\}.$$

In our example, there are two maximal correct application subsets, which are each others complement, so

$$\Gamma_1 \downarrow_\Pi q(a) = \overline{\Gamma_1 \downarrow_\Pi q(a)} = \{P_1, P_2\}.$$

As our last preliminary, we now define sets of clauses that are added to a theory to replace any clause, or more precisely, any application of a clause, that needs to be removed.

Definition 11 (Add set) *For a clause C with variables* vars$(C) = \{X_1, \ldots, X_n\}$, *$n \geq 1$, in a theory Γ, a fact f to be removed, and $P \subseteq \Pi(f, \Gamma)$ such that $C \in C(P)$, i.e. occurs in P, define*

$$add(C, f, P) := \{(X_1, \ldots, X_n) \notin I(C, P) \diamond C\} \cup \{(f \diamond C)\sigma | \sigma \in \Sigma(C, P)\}^5.$$

If $n = 0$, i.e., C is ground, $\Sigma(C, P) = \{\emptyset\}$, so we define

$$add(C, f, P) := \{f \diamond C\}.$$

This definition assumes that set membership ($\in$) is a predefined predicate that is properly handled by the proof procedure with sets of both ground and non-ground tuples, i.e. as if $\in$ were defined by

$$(T_1, \ldots, T_n) \in S \text{ iff there exists } T \in S \text{ and a substitution } \sigma \text{ so that}$$
$$T\sigma = (T_1, \ldots, T_n).$$

For instance, $(a) \in \{(b)\}$ will evaluate to false, whereas $(f(a)) \in \{(f(X))\}$ will evaluate to true[6]. In our example, the add sets for our two statements in Γ_1 would be:

$$add(p(a), q(a), P_1) = \{q(a) \rightarrow p(a)\},$$
$$add(p(X) \rightarrow q(X), q(a), P_2)$$
$$= \{(X) \notin \{(a)\}\& \ p(X) \rightarrow q(X), q(a)\& \ p(a) \rightarrow q(a)\}$$
$$= \{(X) \notin \{(a)\}\& \ p(X) \rightarrow q(X)\}.$$

We can now define the minimal base revision (MBR) operator $\dot{-}$.

---

[5] Instead of the set of $(f \diamond C)\sigma$, it would be possible to simply use $(f\sigma \diamond C)$, but this would produce redundancy in the revised theory.

[6] For unary tuples, we usually omit the parentheses. In KRT/MOBAL, the exception sets are represented in an equivalent, but syntactically slightly different form called a *support set* [Wro88]. In this paper, we will stick with the form as just defined for simplicity.

Definition 12 (MBR operator $\hat{-}$) *Let Γ be a knowledge base, f be a fact to be removed, and γ a selection function on $\Gamma \downarrow_\Pi f$. If $\hat{P} := \gamma(\Gamma \downarrow_\Pi f)$ denotes the chosen maximally correct application subset of $\Pi(f, \Gamma)$, and $\overline{P} := \Pi(f, \Gamma) \backslash \hat{P}$ its complement, we can define the* minimal base revision (MBR) *operator $\hat{-}$ as follows:*

$$\Gamma \hat{-} f := \begin{cases} \Gamma \backslash C(\overline{P}) \;\; \cup \;\; \bigcup_{C \in C(\overline{P})} add(C, f, \overline{P}) & \text{if } f \in Cn(\Gamma) \\ \Gamma & \text{otherwise.} \end{cases}$$

The above definition assumes that we are given some choice function γ that returns a single element from $\Gamma \downarrow_\Pi f$. For the purposes of this paper, we may simply assume that γ is implemented by user queries, and that $\Gamma \downarrow_\Pi f$ is computed by a top-down search through the subset lattice of Γ. We should point out, however, that $\Gamma \downarrow_\Pi f$ (or rather, its complement) can be computed efficiently with a recursive procedure based on the derivation tree of the fact to be removed. In [Wro93], we describe this procedure in detail, and also develop a two-tiered confidence model on the basis of which γ can be defined. The implementation of $\hat{-}$ in KRT/MOBAL in addition uses a confidence-ranked beam search to ensure bounded computation times for $\Gamma \downarrow_\Pi f$.

In the above example, the MBR operation would produce the following results. If the first element of $\Gamma_1 \downarrow_\Pi q(a)$, P_1, were chosen by γ, we would have to remove P_2, so the resulting new theory would be

$$\begin{aligned} \Gamma_1 \hat{-} q(a) &= \{p(a), (X) \notin \{(a)\} \& \ p(X) \rightarrow q(X), q(a) \& \ p(a) \rightarrow q(a)\}; \\ &= \{p(a), (X) \notin \{(a)\} \& \ p(X) \rightarrow q(X)\}; \end{aligned}$$

if the second element, P_2 were chosen, we would remove P_1, resulting in

$$\Gamma_1 \hat{-} q(a) = \{q(a) \rightarrow p(a), p(X) \rightarrow q(X)\}.$$

As another example involving a non-ground fact to be removed, consider the theory (shown in rule form with capitalized variables for readability)

$$\Gamma_3 = \left\{ \begin{array}{l} f1 : p(X) \\ r1 : p(X) \rightarrow q(X) \\ r2 : q(X) \rightarrow r(X) \end{array} \right\}$$

from which we want to remove q(f(Y)). In this example, we see that the minimal removal sets are

$$\overline{\Gamma_3 \downarrow_\Pi q(f(Y))} = \{\{(r1, \{X/f(Y)\})\}, \{(f1, \{X/f(Y)\})\}\}.$$

The two theories that result from these choices are:

$$\Gamma_3 \hat{-} q(f(Y)) = \left\{ \begin{array}{ll} f1 : & p(X) \\ r11 : & X \notin \{f(Y)\} \& \ p(X) \rightarrow q(X) \\ [r12 : & q(f(Y)) \& \ p(f(Y)) \rightarrow q(f(Y))] \\ r2 : & q(X) \rightarrow r(X) \end{array} \right\}$$

where $r12$ is a tautology and would be omitted, and

$$\Gamma_3 \dot{-} q(f(Y)) = \left\{ \begin{array}{l} f11 : X \notin \{f(Y)\} \rightarrow p(X) \\ f12 : q(f(Y)) \rightarrow p(f(Y)) \\ r1 : \quad p(X) \rightarrow q(X) \\ r2 : \quad q(X) \rightarrow r(X) \end{array} \right\}$$

respectively. To see why the revision operator must consider individual clause applications in deciding about minimal removal sets, consider the example of

$$\Gamma_4 = \left\{ \begin{array}{l} p(X) \\ p(a)\& \, p(b) \rightarrow r(a) \end{array} \right\}$$

from which we want to remove $r(a)$. If we choose to modify $p(X)$ (or rather, one or more of its applications), $\dot{-}$ will correctly produce either one of

$$\left\{ \begin{array}{l} (X) \notin \{(a)\} \rightarrow p(X) \\ r(a) \rightarrow p(a) \\ p(a)\& \, p(b) \rightarrow r(a) \end{array} \right\} \text{ or } \left\{ \begin{array}{l} (X) \notin \{(b)\} \rightarrow p(X) \\ r(a) \rightarrow p(b) \\ p(a)\& \, p(b) \rightarrow r(a) \end{array} \right\}$$

whereas a revision operation not based on individual clause applications would have to produce the overly specific

$$\left\{ \begin{array}{l} (X) \notin \{(a), (b)\} \rightarrow p(X) \\ r(a) \rightarrow p(a) \\ r(a) \rightarrow p(b) \\ p(a)\& \, p(b) \rightarrow r(a) \end{array} \right\}$$

We now prove that indeed $\dot{-}$ meets the set of postulates for base revision operations defined in table 2.

Theorem 3 $\dot{-}$ *is a theory revision operation that meets the base revision postulates (1) through (6) from table 2.*

Proof. We show each postulate individually. For the exceptional case where $f \notin Cn(\Gamma)$, the postulates are trivially true, so in the following we will assume $f \in Cn(\Gamma)$.

(1). Since $\Gamma \backslash C(\overline{P}) \subseteq \Gamma$ anyway, we only need to show that for any removed clause $C \in C(\overline{P})$, $add(C, f, \overline{P})$ only contains statements that are θ-subsumed by elements of Γ. Looking at the definition of add, we see that new statements are defined by adding literals to and/or instantiating existing statements, so this is indeed true.

(2). True as an immediate consequence of (1).

(3). True by definition of $\dot{-}$.

(4). By the definition of $\Gamma \downarrow_\Pi f$, f is not derivable from the theories corresponding to its members. It thus remains to verify that this is not changed by the
additional statements from *add*. This is easy to see, because the additional premises added to removed statements ensure that all substitutions which could be
used to prove f are excluded; the other additional statements can be used only
if f is present.

(5). Trivially true since for factual queries, $Cn(f) = Cn(g)$ implies $f = g$.

(6). We can easily show that $\Gamma \subseteq Cn(\Gamma \dot{-} f \cup \{f\})$. For non-removed statements,
this is trivially true. For each nonground removed statement C, we find that

$$
\begin{aligned}
& Cn(add(C, f, \overline{P}) \cup \{f\}) \\
&= Cn(\{(X_1, \ldots, X_n) \notin I(C, \overline{P}) \diamond C\} \cup \{(f \diamond C)\sigma | \sigma \in \Sigma(C, \overline{P})\} \cup \{f\}) \\
&= Cn(\{(X_1, \ldots, X_n) \notin I(C, \overline{P}) \diamond C\} \cup \{C\sigma | \sigma \in \Sigma(C, \overline{P})\}) \\
&= Cn(C),
\end{aligned}
$$

and similarly for ground statements. $\qquad\square$

The reader may be curious how $\dot{-}$ relates to the closed theory contraction
operations defined above, and in particular, whether using a singleton choice
function γ will not produce the same besserwisser effect that we criticized for
minimal specialization revisions. Indeed this is not the case, since on the level
of closed theories, this singleton choice actually corresponds to a set of subsets
of the closed theory, as shown by the following theorem, the proof of which can
be found in [Wro93].

Theorem 4 *For a theory Γ and a fact f, $\dot{-}$ is equivalent to a partial meet
contraction on the theory $\Gamma' := \Gamma_\Pi(\Pi(f, \Gamma))$, i.e., the theory that results when all
clauses are split into their individual applications (cf. definition 9). In particular,
given a selection function γ,*

$$
Cn(\Gamma' \dot{-} f) = \begin{cases} \bigcap \gamma_{Cn}(Cn(\Gamma') \downarrow f) & \text{if } f \notin Cn(\emptyset) \\ Cn(\Gamma) & \text{otherwise} \end{cases},
$$

where

$$
\gamma_{Cn}(Cn(\Gamma') \downarrow f) := \{B \in (Cn(\Gamma') \downarrow f) \mid \exists C \in \Gamma_\Pi(\gamma(\Gamma \downarrow_\Pi f)) \text{such that } C \subseteq B\}.
$$

Knowing that $\dot{-}$ meets the set of revision postulates from table 2, the remaining open question is whether it truly captures the essence of minimality as
expressed by these postulates, i.e., whether it produces the maximally general
base revisions consistent with these postulates. Indeed this is the case.

Theorem 5 (Minimality) *Let $\dot{-}'$ any base revision operation that also meets
the base revision postulates. Then for any theory Γ, and any fact f,*

$$
\Gamma \dot{-} f \geq_g \Gamma \dot{-}' f.
$$

Proof. By postulate (1), $\Gamma \hat{\underline{}}' f$ must consist of a subset of Γ, plus perhaps some added statements. With a proper selection function, we can make $\hat{\underline{}}$ choose the same subset. As for the added statements, we know they must be specializations of existing statements. We thus must only show that $add(C, f, \overline{P})$, where $\overline{P} = \overline{\gamma(\Gamma \downarrow_\Pi f)}$, is a minimal specialization of C to complete the proof. So assume that there is a statement C' such that $C \geq_g C' >_g add(C, f, \overline{P})$. That is, there must be some substitution (inference) possible with both C and C' that is not admitted by $add(C, f, \overline{P})$. Since $add(C, f, \overline{P})$ excludes precisely the substitutions mentioned in the minimal removal set $\overline{P}$, however, we know that none of them may be readmitted without rederiving f again. Thus C' is not a correct specialization of C. □

We conclude by pointing out that $\hat{\underline{}}$ can very simply be extended to multiple parallel revisions. So let $F = \{f_1, \ldots, f_n\}$ a set of facts to be removed. If we define

$$\Delta(F, \Gamma) := (\Delta(f_n, \Gamma), \ldots, \Delta(f_n, \Gamma),$$

and replace f by F in all other definitions, we see that all of the methods still apply, and that all proofs still carry through as the reader will be able to verify.

6 Related work

The approach presented here is an elaboration of the knowledge revision method used in the knowledge acquisition and machine learning system BLIP, a predecessor of MOBAL. As described in [Wro88, Wro89], BLIP already used exception sets to produce minimal specializations of individual rules. As in MOBAL, these exception sets were represented as support sets, a simple form of which was first proposed in [EHR83]. In other respects, BLIP was seriously lacking in contrast to the method described here that is used by KRT/MOBAL. In particular, the computation of removal sets was incomplete in many cases, and no formal characterization was available. Furthermore, BLIP could not work on multiple revisions at the same time, and could not ensure recovery (postulate 6).

In section 3, we already discussed the problems of the minimal specialization hypothesis that was proposed in [MB92]. In the same paper, the authors also present a specialization algorithm based on the introduction of non-monotonically interpreted premises with new predicates. Thus, for example, if the substitutions $\{\{X/a\}, \{X/b\}\}$ were to be excluded from $p(X) \rightarrow q(X)$, the algorithm of Muggleton and Bain would produce the theory

$$p(X) \wedge not(c1(X)) \rightarrow q(X); c1(a); c1(b),$$

where $c1$ is a new predicate, and *not* is interpreted as negation by failure. As can easily be seen, this is a notational variant of the exception set method used to specialize clauses used in BLIP and KRT/MOBAL. Thus, the introduction of non-monotonically interpreted predicates just adds unnecessary complexity, as it is not necessary for correct minimal specialization of clauses. The algorithm of [MB92] always selects to modify those clauses that have directly resolved with the fact that is to be removed. Nonetheless, contrary to what is implied in [MB92], this is insufficient to guarantee minimal specialization, as can be seen by considering our example theory Γ_3. In this example, when modifying the clause $r1$ that resolved with $q(f(Y))$, we necessarily lose the inference $r(f(Y))$ that was possible with the original theory. Nonetheless, this fact cannot be used to derive $q(f(Y))$, so it would be in a minimal specialization.

Our method of using exception lists to specialize individual clauses has also been adopted in the algorithm proposed in [Lin91]. This paper also introduces the important notion of learning in a growing language: specialization operations should be such that when a new constant is added to the language anything provable about the new constant with the original theory should also be provable from the specialization. As Ling points out, the exception methods ensures that this is the case. He also points to an important problem that was also recognized in [Wro88, Wro89]: if exclusion is used as the only specialization operator on individual clauses, we may build up long (possibly infinite) exception lists. In KRT, this problem is addressed through a user specified *plausibility criterion* that defines when further specialization is necessary to get rid of an overly long exception list. KRT then applies a number of specialization operators that specialize further, essentially by introducing new premise literals on existing variables of the clause (cf. [Wro88, Wro89]). Ling instead uses a *complete* set of refinement operators, i.e., capable of producing all specializations of a clause, and simply replaces a clause by all of its specializations. This guarantees minimal specialization and thus identification in the limit, but brings with it the undesirable properties of minimal specializations as spelled out in section 3.

MIS [Sha83] was one of the first first-order learning systems to include theory revision. In MIS, however, minimality of revision was not a concern, since subsequent generalization steps were relied upon to fix up a theory that had become overspecialized. Nonetheless, the MIS approach is highly relevant to the work presented here, since its backtracing algorithm offers a way of determining with a minimum number of user queries which possible revision to choose, i.e., it offers one particular way of implementing γ, the choice function among minimal revisions. As pointed out above (but not described in this paper), KRT uses a different method of implementing γ that relies on a two-tiered model of confidence in statements, and proposes to the user the revision that would entail a minimal loss of confidence. Evidently, this could easily combined with a backtracing strategy. The backtracing strategy of MIS is also used in the interactive learning programs MARVIN [SB86] and CLINT [DeR91] to recover from overgeneralizations that lead to incorrectly covered negative examples.

7 Conclusion

In this paper, we have discussed the question of what properties are to be required from the results of theory revision operations, i.e., operations that specialize the current hypothesis of a learning system in order to remove an erroneously covered inference. In particular, we have examined how the notion of minimality (or "Occam's razor") should be interpreted in this context. As a surprising result, it has turned out that a most natural restriction from the standpoint of Machine Learning, namely the use of minimal specializations, has very undesirable properties: because it leads to closed theories, loses any notion of reason maintenance, and when removing a statement to add its negation, results in complete theories. We have therefore developed an alternative notion of minimality, and formalized this notion in the form of a set of base revision postulates derived from similar postulates by Gärdenfors [Gär88] and Nebel [Neb89]. As the perhaps central contribution of the paper, we have described a minimal base revision operator MBR ($"\dot{-}"$) that produces revisions meeting all of the revision postulates; moreover, it produces the maximally general correct revisions meeting the postulates, and is thus really minimal in our alternative sense.

In precisely specifying how to perform minimal base contractions, the work described here can be used as a basis for approaching a number of interesting questions of a larger scope in theory revision in incremental learning systems. The first one concerns the role of the recovery postulate, which we have adopted from Gärdenfors' theory change work. While it is a desirable property for a revision algorithm to be able to give a recovery guarantee to a user, it is nonetheless not clear in what circumstances a learning system (or a user) would want to actually make use of it, since it adds clauses to the theory that are largely uninteresting as long as the removed fact is not added back in. A second question concerns the question of when to perform minimal specialization in the sense as defined here, and when to perform non-minimal specialization, eg. in order to obtain a more succinct theory. The plausibility criterion currently used in KRT is only a rudimentary answer to this problem. Last, and certainly not least, is the open question of whether there is something to be gained by combining specialization and generalizing revisions into one general and theory revision operation, as argued by [Emd89]. Such an operation would most likely be driven mainly not by criteria such as completeness or correctness, but by "scientific" notions about the structural qualities of a good theory.

Acknowledgements

This work has been supported partially by the European Community ESPRIT program in projects MLT (Machine Learning Toolbox) and ILP (Inductive Logic Programming). I want to thank all colleagues at GMD and at the University of Dortmund for interesting discussions and suggestions, and Katharina Morik and Tim Niblett for reading and commenting on an earlier draft. The MOBAL system, including KRT, is available via anonymous FTP from ftp.gmd.de, directory pub/gmd/mlt, for non-commercial academic use.

References

[AGM85]   C. E. Alchourrón, P. Gärdenfors, and D. Makinson. On the logic of theory change: Partial meet contraction and revision functions. *The Journal of*

Symbolic Logic, 50:510 – 530, 1985.

[AM82]   C. E. Alchourrón and D. Makinson. On the logic of theory change: contraction functions and their associated revision functions. Theoria, 48:14 – 37, 1982.

[DeR91]   Luc DeRaedt. Interactive Concept-Learning. PhD thesis, Kath. Univ. Leuven, Leuven, Belgium, February 1991.

[EHR83]   Werner Emde, Christopher U. Habel, and Claus-Rainer Rollinger. The discovery of the equator or concept driven learning. In IJCAI-83, pages 455 – 458, San Mateo, CA, 1983. Morgan Kaufman.

[Emd89]   Werner Emde. An inference engine for representing multiple theories. In Katharina Morik, editor, Knowledge Representation and Organization in Machine Learning, pages 148–176. Springer Verlag, Berlin, New York, 1989.

[Gär88]   Peter Gärdenfors. Knowledge in Flux — Modeling the Dynamics of Epistemic States. MIT Press, Cambridge, MA, 1988.

[Lin91]   Charles Ling. Non-monotonic specialization. In Proc. Inductive Logic Programming Workshop, Portugal, 1991.

[MB92]   Stephen Muggleton and Michael Bain. Non-monotonic learning. In Stephen Muggleton, editor, Inductive Logic Programming. Academic Press, London, New York, 1992.

[Men87]   Elliot Mendelson. Introduction to Mathematical Logic. Wadsworth & Brooks, Belmont, CA, third edition, 1987.

[MWKEss]   K. Morik, S. Wrobel, J.U. Kietz, and Werner Emde. Knowledge Acquisition and Machine Learning: Theory, Methods, and Applications. Academic Press, London, New York, in press. To appear.

[Neb89]   Bernhard Nebel. Reasoning and Revision in Hybrid Representation Systems. Springer Verlag, Berlin, New York, 1989. Doctoral Dissertation.

[Plo70]   Gordon D. Plotkin. A note on inductive generalization. In B. Meltzer and D. Michie, editors, Machine Intelligence 5, chapter 8, pages 153 – 163. Edinburgh Univ. Press, Edinburgh, 1970.

[SB86]   Claude Sammut and Ranan B. Banerji. Learning concepts by asking questions. In R.S. Michalski, J.G. Carbonell, and T.M. Mitchell, editors, Machine Learning — An Artificial Intelligence Approach, volume II, chapter 7, pages 167 – 191. Morgan Kaufman, San Mateo, CA, 1986.

[Sha83]   Ehud Y. Shapiro. Algorithmic Program Debugging. ACM Distinguished Doctoral Dissertations. The MIT Press, Cambridge, Mass., 1983.

[SMAU93]   E. Sommer, K. Morik, J-M. André, and M. Uszynski. What online machine learning can do for knowledge acquisition — a case study. To appear, 1993.

[Wro88]   Stefan Wrobel. Automatic representation adjustment in an observational discovery system. In D. Sleeman, editor, Proc. of the 3rd Europ. Working Session on Learning, pages 253 – 262, London, 1988. Pitman.

[Wro89]   Stefan Wrobel. Demand-driven concept formation. In Katharina Morik, editor, Knowledge Representation and Organization in Machine Learning, pages 289–319. Springer Verlag, Berlin, New York, 1989.

[Wro93]   Stefan Wrobel. Representation adjustment by demand-driven concept formation. in preparation, 1993.

Predicate Invention
in Inductive Data Engineering

Peter A. Flach

ITK

Institute for Language Technology and Artificial Intelligence
Tilburg University, PObox 90153, 5000 LE Tilburg, the Netherlands
☎ +31 13 663119, fax +31 13 663069
flach@kub.nl

Abstract. By *inductive data engineering* we mean the (interactive) process of restructuring a knowledge base by means of induction. In this paper we describe INDEX, a system that constructs decompositions of database relations by inducing attribute dependencies. The system employs heuristics to locate exceptions to dependencies satisfied by most of the data, and to avoid the generation of dependencies for which the data don't provide enough support. The system is implemented in a deductive database framework, and can be viewed as an Inductive Logic Programming system with predicate invention capabilities.

1. Motivation and Scope

The application of Machine Learning techniques to databases is a subject that is receiving increasing amounts of attention (Piatetsky-Shapiro & Frawley, 1991). Databases typically contain large quantities of extensional data, while for applications like query answering and data modeling intensional data is needed. Machine Learning techniques such as Inductive Logic Programming or ILP (Muggleton, 1992) can generate intensional predicate definitions from extensional data.

In this paper, we are describing inductive techniques to obtain predicate definitions that can be used to restructure a knowledge base in a more meaningful way. What is meaningful and what is not can be partly determined by means of heuristics, but some user interaction is typically required. We use the term *inductive data engineering* to denote the interactive process of restructuring a knowledge base by means of induction.

We will introduce the main ideas by means of an example. Fig. 1 shows a fragment of a train schedule, listing the direction, departure time, and first stop of the trains leaving between 8:00 and 10:00. While such a schedule is useful from a traveler's point of view, a database designer would object to storing the schedule in a database as is: the schedule appears to be unstructured, yet contains a lot of redundancy. Instead, she would decompose

Part of this work was carried out under Esprit Basic Research Action 6020 (Inductive Logic Programming). Many thanks to Luc De Raedt, Nada Lavrac and Saso Dzeroski for stimulating discussions and helpful comments on an earlier draft. Saso also conducted the experiment with mFOIL.

```
% train(Direction,Hour,Minutes,FirstStop).
train(utrecht,8,8,den-bosch).
train(tilburg,8,10,tilburg).
train(maastricht,8,10,weert).
train(utrecht,8,13,eindhoven-bkln).
train(tilburg,8,17,eindhoven-bkln).
train(utrecht,8,25,den-bosch).
train(utrecht,8,31,utrecht).
train(utrecht,8,43,eindhoven-bkln).
train(tilburg,8,47,eindhoven-bkln).
train(utrecht,9,8,den-bosch).
train(tilburg,9,10,tilburg).
train(maastricht,9,10,weert).
train(utrecht,9,13,eindhoven-bkln).
train(tilburg,9,17,eindhoven-bkln).
train(utrecht,9,25,den-bosch).
train(utrecht,9,43,eindhoven-bkln).
train(tilburg,9,47,eindhoven-bkln).
```

Fig. 1. A train schedule.

the data into more primitive relations, and define the complete schedule as a view or intensional relation. The reader is encouraged to try to find a meaningful decomposition for herself before reading on.

Usually, the design of a database schema is based on a conceptual model of the universe of discourse, and precedes the creation of the database. Central to the research reported on in this paper is the idea, that part of a database schema can be derived from the data itself, by analysing the regularities displayed by the data. This process is inherently inductive, since we are deriving general rules (predicate definitions, integrity constraints) from specific data (instances of a database relation). We have implemented a system called INDEX that is able, with some help of the user, to construct the knowledge base in fig. 2.

The restructured knowledge base contains predicates not present in the data. Thus, INDEX is capable of *predicate invention*. This is achieved by inducing *integrity constraints* that indicate that introducing a new predicate could be meaningful. E.g., the distinction between fast and slow trains is made on the basis of a *functional dependency* from direction to first stop, which holds for fast and slow trains separately. Also, the introduction of the predicates fast_stop1 and slow_stop1 is justified by this dependency.

The plan of the paper is as follows. In the next section, we introduce some terminology and notation. In the two sections that follow, the main steps of our algorithm are described: the search for specific integrity constraints (section 3), and the construction

```
train(A,B,C,D) :-
     regulartrain(A,B,C,D) ; irregulartrain(A,B,C,D).
regulartrain(A,B,C,D) :-
     hour(B),
     regulartrain1(A,C,D).
regulartrain1(A,B,C) :-
     fasttrain(A,B,C) ; slowtrain(A,B,C).
fasttrain(A,B,C) :-
     fasttrain1(A,B),
     fast_stop1(A,C).
slowtrain(A,B,C) :-
     slowtrain1(A,B),
     slow_stop1(A,C).
```

```
% hour(Hour).                          % irregulartrain(Dir,Hour,Mins,Stop1).
hour(8).                               irregulartrain(utrecht,8,31,utrecht).
hour(9).
% fast_stop1(Dir,Stop1).              % slow_stop1(Dir,Stop1).
fast_stop1(tilburg,tilburg).          slow_stop1(tilburg,eindhoven-bkln).
fast_stop1(maastricht,weert).         slow_stop1(utrecht,eindhoven-bkln).
fast_stop1(utrecht,den-bosch).
% fasttrain1(Dir,Mins).               % slowtrain1(Dir,Mins).
fasttrain1(maastricht,10).            slowtrain1(tilburg,17).
fasttrain1(tilburg,10).               slowtrain1(tilburg,47).
fasttrain1(utrecht,8).                slowtrain1(utrecht,13).
fasttrain1(utrecht,25).               slowtrain1(utrecht,43).
```

Fig. 2. The restructured knowledge base for train schedules.

of decompositions that are justified by the induced constraints (section 4). In section 5, we describe the heuristics employed by INDEX to be able to deal with constraints with a limited number of exceptions, and to avoid the generation of constraints that are too specific. In section 6, we relate INDEX to other ILP systems. The concluding section contains some ideas for future work.

2.   Preliminaries

Our terminology and notation will be mainly drawn from the fields of Logic Programming (Lloyd, 1987) and Deductive Databases (Minker, 1988). If r is an n-ary predicate, then an *extensional relation* is a set of ground facts $r(a_1, ..., a_n)$. An *intensional relation* or *predicate definition* of a predicate p is a set of definite clauses with p in the head. A (*deductive*) *database* is a collection of intensional and extensional relations. In addition, it will be convenient to denote argument positions of predicates by *attributes*, as customary in the theory of relational databases (Maier, 1983).

Our aim is to reformulate an extensional relation as an intensional relation, defined in terms of newly introduced, more compact extensional relations. This process is referred to as *decomposition*, and it is done on the basis of integrity constraints. In general, an integrity constraint is a logical formula expressing knowledge about the database, without being part of any predicate definition. In this paper, we will only consider constraints on a single extensional relation, and we will use the following, more restricted definition. If R is an extensional relation, an *integrity constraint on R* is a logical formula containing only the predicate of R, and possibly directly evaluable predicates like = and <. An integrity constraint on R is satisfied by R if R constitutes a Herbrand model of the constraint. For instance, C<60:-train(A,B,C,D) is a constraint satisfied by the relation in fig. 1.

Attribute dependencies constitute a class of integrity constraints of particular interest, because they signal that the relation can be decomposed into smaller relations containing less redundancy. In this paper, we consider two types of attribute dependencies, namely functional and multivalued dependencies. A *functional dependency* (fd) is an integrity constraint like D1=D2:-train(A,B1,C,D1),train(A,B2,C,D2), stating that if two trains have the same direction and leave at the same number of minutes after the hour, they will have the same first stop. Given the attributes direction, minutes and stop1, this fd will be written as [direction,minutes]-->[stop1]. It states that the value of the attribute stop1 can be derived from the values of the attributes direction and minute. The attributes found on the lefthand side are called *antecedent attributes*, those on the righthand side *consequent attributes*.

Multivalued dependencies (mvds) generalise functional dependencies by associating a *set* of possible values of the consequent attribute to each combination of possible values for the antecedent attributes. For instance, if a relation describes describes events that occur weekly, the mvd [day]->->[date] holds: given the day of week, we can determine the set of dates on which the event occurs. E.g., if the Computer Science course occurs on Monday, October 5, and the AI course occurs on Monday, September 28, then the AI course also occurs on Monday, October 5 (and, by symmetry, the Computer Science course also occurs on Monday, September 28). Logically, this can be expressed as

event(Day,Date1,E2):-event(Day,Date1,E1),event(Day,Date2,E2)

Fds and mvds both describe the same phenomenon: that the consequent attribute(s) can be removed from the relation, and stored in a separate relation containing only the attributes in the dependency. The only difference is, that in the case of fds the antecedent attributes form a key in the second relation. We call this a decomposition of the relation; it will be the subject of section 4. In the next section, we describe how attribute dependencies can be induced from an extensional relation.

3. Induction of Attribute Dependencies

In (Flach, 1990) we adressed the following problem: given an extensional relation, find all fds and mvds satisfied by it. Briefly, the approach is to order the set of dependencies by generality (implication) and to search this set in a top-down fashion, much in the spirit of Shapiro's Model Inference System (1981). To illustrate, for the train relation a most general fd would be [] --> [direction] (all trains go in the same direction). This fd is contradicted by many pairs of facts, e.g. train (utrecht, 8, 8, den-bosch) and train (tilburg, 8, 10, tilburg). It can be specialised by adding attributes to the antecedent. Note that the fd [hour] --> [direction] is contradicted by the same pair of facts: by analysing the contradicting facts, we can avoid constructing this specialisation.

By disabling the heuristics employed by INDEX, the system will find the most general dependencies satisfied by a relation. For the train schedule in fig. 1, these are

```
[minutes]->->[hour]
[stop1]->->[hour]
[stop1,minutes]-->[direction]
[minutes,direction]-->[stop1]
```

The first two mvds are specialisations of the mvd [] ->-> [hour], expressing that trains run every hour. There is only one fact that causes contradiction of this mvd, and that is train (utrecht, 8, 31, utrecht). In other words, had this fact not been in the relation, then the mvd would have been satisfied. As we will see later, INDEX is able to recognise that a dependency is 'almost' satisfied, and to locate the exception(s).

The fourth fd is a specialisation of [direction] --> [stop1]. This dependency is contradicted by many pairs of facts, but the relation can be divided into two subrelations of approximately equal size, which both satisfy the fd (fast trains and slow trains). Since several such divisions are possible, some user interaction is required to choose a meaningful one, but INDEX is able to discover that the fd is interesting in this respect.

The heuristics used by INDEX to decide whether a dependency is almost satisfied, or whether it can lead to a useful partition of the relation, are described in section 5. In the next section, we show how dependencies can be used to decompose a relation, thereby introducing new predicates.

4. Introducing New Predicates by Decomposition

A *decomposition* of a relation R is a set of relations, such that R can be reconstructed from

```
% train1(Dir,Mins,Stop1).              % stop1hour(Stop1,Hour).
train1(maastricht,10,weert).           stop1hour(weert,8).
train1(tilburg,10,tilburg).            stop1hour(weert,9).
train1(tilburg,17,eindhoven-bkln).     stop1hour(tilburg,8).
train1(tilburg,47,eindhoven-bkln).     stop1hour(tilburg,9).
train1(utrecht,8,den-bosch).           stop1hour(eindhoven-bkln,8).
train1(utrecht,13,eindhoven-bkln).     stop1hour(eindhoven-bkln,9).
train1(utrecht,25,den-bosch).          stop1hour(den-bosch,8).
train1(utrecht,31,utrecht).            stop1hour(den-bosch,9).
train1(utrecht,43,eindhoven-bkln).     stop1hour(utrecht,8).
```

Fig. 3. A horizontal decomposition.

this set by a *composition function*. If the composition function is the join operation, the decomposition is called *horizontal*. Every attribute dependency induces a unique horizontal decomposition. A *vertical* decomposition is a partition of R into subsets, with set-theoretical union as composition function. An attribute dependency induces a vertical decomposition if the dependency is satisfied by every subrelation. In general, a dependency induces many vertical decompositions, even if we are interested in *minimal* decompositions (that are not finer partitions than other decompositions induced by the same dependency). Choosing a meaningful vertical decomposition requires domain knowledge, and is done in INDEX with the help of an oracle.

Both horizontal and vertical decompositions introduce new extensional relations, with new predicates. The composition function then serves as an intensional definition of the original relation. Thus, decompositions 'intensionalise' existing relations in terms of new, extensional relations. This will be illustrated below.

We will first consider horizontal decompositions, induced by non-violated dependencies. E.g., the mvd [stop1]->->[hour] says that we can remove the attribute hour from the train relation, and store it in a separate relation with the stop1 attribute. This results in the decomposition in fig. 3. The composition function is a join over the attribute stop1. This can be expressed as a logical formula:

train(A,B,C,D):-train1(A,C,D),stop1hour(D,B)

Given an extensional relation and a dependency satisfied by it, INDEX automatically constructs the horizontal decomposition and the clause expressing the join (querying the user to name the new predicates).

A vertical decomposition is induced if the dependency is violated by the relation. Formally, given a relation R and a logical formula F representing a dependency, a pair of facts $\langle f_1 f_2 \rangle$ is called *F-conflicting* if it satisfies the body of F by means of a substitution θ, while $H\theta$ is false, where H denotes the head of F. F-conflicting tuples are separated in the

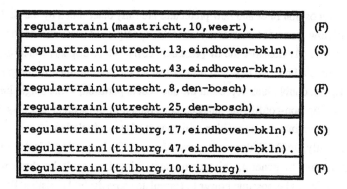

Fig. 4. A non-minimal decomposition.

first two steps of the following procedure. In the third step, blocks are combined to form a minimal decomposition.

1. Partition R into subsets with equal values for the antecedent attributes; call this the *antecedent partition*.

2. In each block B, define $f_1 \approx_B f_2$ if $<f_1, f_2>$ is not F-conflicting; $\approx_B$ is an equivalence relation. Refine each block of the antecedent partition into $\approx_B$-equivalence classes. Let m be the maximum number of equivalence classes constructed for a class.

3. We have now constructed a non-minimal vertical decomposition. To obtain a minimal decomposition, we combine as many blocks with different antecedent values as possible. This can be done in many ways, and we assume an oracle to guide this process. Note that this minimal decomposition consists of m relations.

We will illustrate this procedure by two examples. First, we consider the mvd `[]->->[hour]`, that is almost satisfied by the train relation. Since this dependency doesn't have antecedent attributes, the first step of the procedure is superfluous. The second step of the algorithm will result in two blocks ($m=2$), one containing the exceptional fact `train(utrecht,8,31,utrecht)`, and the other containing the rest. This is the unique minimal decomposition, and no user interaction is required (apart from naming the new relations). The composition rule is the disjunctive clause

`train(A,B,C,D):-regulartrain(A,B,C,D) ; irregulartrain(A,B,C,D)`

which can be written as two separate clauses, if preferred. Since `regulartrain` now satisfies the constraint `[]->->[hour]`, we can horizontally decompose it and obtain the rule `regulartrain(A,B,C,D):-hour(B),regulartrain1(A,C,D)` (note that both composition rules and new predicates are fully determined by the decomposition).

We now consider a more elaborate example of vertical decomposition of regulartrain1. Consider the fd [direction]-->[stop1], which is not satisfied by regulartrain1. INDEX will now construct the non-minimal decomposition in fig. 4. In this figure, double lines represent the antecedent partition, while single lines represent the division into non-conflicting subsets, constructed in the second step. Again, we have $m=2$, and any minimal decomposition will consist of two subrelations.

Currently, INDEX does not provide any help in putting blocks together in a meaningful way. In general, this seems something that can't be done without user interaction. It might be possible hower to formulate some useful heuristics. For instance, in fig. 4 all slow trains (marked (S)) have the value eindhoven-bkln for the consequent attribute, while fast trains have different values.

We end this section with a brief analysis of the complexity of the decomposition algorithm. Step 1 is accomplished by sorting the facts on the values of the antecedent attributes, requiring $O(af \log f)$ comparisons (a is the number of antecedent attributes, f is the number of facts in the relation). Likewise, step 2 is of complexity $O(f_B \log f_B)$, where f_B is the number of facts in block B. Finally, the number of queries to the user is $n_B * m$ in the worst case (n_B is the number of blocks in the antecedent partition).

5. Heuristics

Satisfied dependencies induce horizontal decompositions, while dependencies that are not satisfied induce vertical decompositions. Many dependencies however induce uninteresting decompositions. Thus, we need heuristics for predicting whether a dependency induces a meaningful decomposition.

In INDEX, two heuristics are used: satisfaction and confirmation. *Satisfaction* estimates the extent to which a dependency is satisfied (1 means no contradiction). It is abstractly calculated as follows:

$$Sat = 1 - weighted\ fraction\ of\ deviating\ facts \qquad (1)$$

In order to estimate the fraction of deviating facts, the two-step partitioning procedure of the previous section is executed. For each block of the antecedent partition, the largest block resulting from the second step is taken to represent non-deviating facts. If the sum of the sizes of these largest blocks is N_n, then the fraction of deviating facts is $(N_R - N_n)/N_R$, where N_R is the total number of facts. This fraction is weighted with $m-1$ (recall that m is the maximum number of blocks constructed in the second step for a block of the antecedent partition; if $m=1$, the dependency is satisfied). This weight is added because minimal decompositions consist of m blocks, and decompositions with fewer blocks are preferred.

This gives the following formula:

$$Sat = 1 - (m-1) * \frac{N_R - N_n}{N_R} \tag{2}$$

For instance, for the dependency [] ->-> [hour] on the relation train, we have $N_R=17, N_n=16$, and $m=2$, which gives $Sat=0.94$. This value indicates that the dependency is almost satisfied. The fd [direction] --> [stop1] on the relation regulartrain1 gets the value 0.63 ($N_R=8, N_n=5$, $m=2$). This indicates a vertical decomposition into two subrelations of similar size. Thus, Sat can be used in two ways: with a lower bound (e.g. 0.8), one selects dependencies that are almost satisfied. With an interval around 0.5, one selects dependencies that are likely to result in an evenly-sized decomposition.

In order to avoid generating very specific dependencies (with many antecedent attributes), a confirmation measure is used. If a dependency is very specific, then the blocks in the antecedent partition will be small. *Confirmation* is defined as the average block size in the antecedent partition:

$$Conf = \frac{N_R}{n_B} \tag{3}$$

where n_B is the number of blocks in the antecedent partition. Putting a lower bound on *Conf* (typically 2.5) avoids too specific dependencies.

In practice, putting $Sat \geq 0.8$ for tracing exceptions, $0.3 \leq Sat \leq 0.7$ for vertical decompositions, and $Conf \geq 2.5$ worked well in the train example. For the train relations, the following dependencies were found:

[] --> [hour]	$Sat=0.53$	$Conf=8.5$
[] ->-> [hour]	$Sat=0.94$	$Conf=8.5$

For the regulartrain1 relation, the dependencies found by INDEX were

[direction] --> [stop1]	$Sat=0.63$	$Conf=2.7$
[direction] ->-> [stop1]	$Sat=0.63$	$Conf=2.7$

As was to be expected, user interaction is still required to choose the preferred dependency for vertical decomposition. For instance, choosing [] --> [hour] means splitting the relation according to the hour (an even partition), while choosing the mvd [] ->-> [hour] means splitting the relation into general cases and exceptions. In the second case, there is not a real choice involved since both the fd and the mvd lead to the same decomposition (as is already suggested by the equal Sat values).

It should be noted that these heuristics are computationally expensive, since they require almost the same amount of work involved in constructing a vertical decomposition. Currently, the applicability of static data analysis (for instance, correlation between attribute values) is investigated.

6. Related Work

We presented INDEX as a tool for inductive data engineering. However, since INDEX operates in the framework of Deductive Databases, it can also be viewed as an ILP system. If we use E to denote the ground facts of the initial relation, B to denote the ground facts in the new relations obtained by decomposition, and H to denote the corresponding composition rules, then we have $B \wedge H \models E$. ILP systems typically aim at constructing H from B and E. INDEX extends this by constructing B and H from E[1].

To illustrate the relation between INDEX and other ILP systems, we reformulated the train problem as an ILP problem, using the ground facts in fig. 2 as background knowledge B, and the ground facts in fig. 1 as examples E. We then applied mFOIL (Dzeroski & Bratko, 1992), a descendant of FOIL (Quinlan, 1990), to the problem[2]. mFOIL induced the following set of rules:

```
train(A,B,C,D):-fast_stop1(A,D),fasttrain1(A,C).
train(A,B,C,D):-slow_stop1(A,D),slowtrain1(A,C).
train(A,B,C,D):-irregulartrain(D,B,C,A).
```

There are two minor differences with the rules induced by INDEX. Firstly, the hour literal is missing in the body of the first two clauses. Since mFOIL requires variables to be typed, and 8 and 9 are the known hours, this literal is redundant. Secondly, the first and fourth argument of `irregulartrain` are swapped in the third clause, which is explained by the fact that the only example for this clause has the same value for these arguments.

The most salient feature of INDEX as an ILP system is the invention of new predicates, a capability shared with CIGOL (Muggleton & Buntine, 1988), LFP2 (Wirth, 1989) and BLIP (Wrobel, 1989). The main difference with these systems is that in INDEX introduces new predicates indirectly, as a result of constructing integrity constraints.

INDEX is able to identify exceptions to dependencies that are 'almost' satisfied. Thus, it is related to the Closed World Specialisation technique of (Bain & Muggleton, 1991). This is demonstrated clearly by the composition rule that distinguishes between regular and irregular trains. Given the extensional definitions of `train`, `regulartrain` and `irregulartrain`, the implication in this rule is in fact an equivalence, and we may also write

```
regulartrain(A,B,C,D):-train(A,B,C,D),¬irregulartrain(A,B,C,D)
```

Interpreting ¬ as negation as failure, this represents a default rule with exceptions.

INDEX is also related to De Raedt's Clausal Discovery Engine (De Raedt 1992),

---

[1] This change of perspective prohibits a more extensive evaluation of INDEX relative to other ILP systems.
[2] We also applied GOLEM (Muggleton & Feng, 1990) to the problem, but the result was a set of specific rules that didn't cover all the examples.

which induces a clausal integrity theory from a Datalog database. Both systems apply refinement operators to search the space of possible integrity constraints in a top-down fashion. However, in De Raedt's system inducing constraints (such as 'nobody can be both a father and a mother') is an end in itself, while in our framework, it is a means to achieve knowledge base reformulation. Another method to induce functional dependencies is described in (Ziarko, 1991). Ziarko's method does not extend to multivalued dependencies. Finally, we note that there is a strong relation between attribute dependencies and determinations (Russell, 1989).

The increased power of INDEX as an ILP system comes at a price. First of all, some user interaction is required to choose the most meaningful dependencies used for decomposition. In the present context, we think this is inevitable: invented predicates require semantic and pragmatic justification, which seems beyond the capabilities of an inductive system. Secondly, the language for composition rules employed by INDEX is limited in expressive power: it disallows existentially quantified variables in the body of clauses.

7. Conclusion

Inductive data engineering aims at automating part of the database design process by means of inductive methods. INDEX is a system for inductive data engineering, that achieves relation decomposition through the induction of attribute dependencies. As such, it is related to other approaches to the induction of integrity constraints (Ziarko, 1991; De Raedt, 1992), and to the general problem of knowledge discovery in databases (Piatetsky-Shapiro & Frawley, 1991). The search for meaningful decompositions is guided by heuristics, that are able to locate exceptions to dependencies and to find decompositions into two subrelations of approximately equal size, while avoiding the generation of dependencies that are too specific. Since INDEX operates in the framework of Deductive Databases, it can be seen as an ILP system with predicate invention capabilities.

INDEX is a research prototype, implemented in some 1000 lines of Quintus Prolog code. We are currently working on a reimplementation that can handle more substantial decomposition problems. Also, we are working on heuristics that are easier to compute, by employing static analysis of the attribute values occurring in the given tuples. Future work includes methods for constraining the search by domain knowledge, thereby alleviating the amount of user interaction needed. Furthermore, the restriction that composition rules exclude existentially quantified variables should be relaxed. A possible approach is to search for dependencies between attributes of different relations. Another approach would be the introduction of derived attributes.

References

M. BAIN & S. MUGGLETON (1991), 'Non-monotonic learning'. In *Machine Intelligence 12*, J.E. Hayes, D. Michie & E. Tyugu (eds.), pp. 105-119, Oxford University Press, Oxford.

L. DE RAEDT (1992), 'A clausal discovery engine'. In *Proc. ECAI Workshop on Logical approaches to Machine Learning*, C. Rouveirol (ed.).

S. DZEROSKI & I. BRATKO (1992), 'Handling noise in inductive logic programming'. In Proc. Second International Workshop on Inductive Logic Programming, ICOT TM-1182, Tokyo.

P.A. FLACH (1990), 'Inductive characterisation of database relations'. In *Proc. International Symposium on Methodologies for Intelligent Systems*, Z.W. Ras, M. Zemankowa & M.L. Emrich (eds.), pp. 371-378, North-Holland, Amsterdam. Full version appeared as ITK Research Report no. 23.

J.W. LLOYD (1987), *Foundations of Logic Programming*, second edition, Springer-Verlag, Berlin.

D. MAIER (1983), *The theory of relational databases*, Computer Science Press, Rockville.

J. MINKER (1988), *Foundations of Deductive Databases and Logic Programming*, Morgan Kaufmann, Los Altos.

S. MUGGLETON & W. BUNTINE (1988), 'Machine invention of first-order predicates by inverting resolution'. In *Proc. Fifth International Conference on Machine Learning*, J. Laird (ed.), pp. 339-352, Morgan Kaufmann, San Mateo.

S. MUGGLETON & C. FENG (1990), 'Efficient induction of logic programs'. In *Proc. First Conference on Algorithmic Learning Theory*, Ohmsha, Tokyo.

S. MUGGLETON, ed. (1992), *Inductive Logic Programming*, Academic Press.

G. PIATETSKY-SHAPIRO & W.J. FRAWLEY, eds. (1991), *Knowledge discovery in databases*, MIT Press.

J.R. QUINLAN (1990), 'Learning logical definitions from relations', *Machine Learning 5*:3, 239-266.

S. RUSSELL (1989), *The use of knowledge in analogy and induction*, Pitman, London.

E.Y. SHAPIRO (1981), *Inductive inference of theories from facts*, Techn. rep. 192, Comp. Sc. Dep., Yale University.

R. WIRTH (1989), 'Completing logic programs by inverse resolution'. In *Proc. Fourth European Working Session on Learning*, K. Morik (ed.), pp. 239-250, Pitman, London.

S. WROBEL (1989), 'Demand-driven concept formation'. In *Knowledge representation and organization in Machine Learning*, K. Morik (ed.), pp. 289-319, LNAI 347, Springer-Verlag, Berlin.

W. ZIARKO (1991), 'The discovery, analysis, and representation of data dependencies in databases'. In (Piatetsky-Shapiro & Frawley, 1991).

Subsumption and Refinement in Model Inference

Patrick R. J. van der Laag[1,2] and Shan-Hwei Nienhuys-Cheng[1]

[1] Department of Computer Science, Erasmus University of Rotterdam,
P.O. Box 1738, 3000 DR Rotterdam, the Netherlands
[2] Tinbergen Institute

Abstract. In his famous Model Inference System, Shapiro [10] uses so-called refinement operators to replace too general hypotheses by logically weaker ones. One of these refinement operators works in the search space of reduced first order sentences. In this article we show that this operator is not complete for reduced sentences, as he claims. We investigate the relations between subsumption and refinement as well as the role of a complexity measure. We present an inverse reduction algorithm which is used in a new refinement operator. This operator is complete for reduced sentences. Finally, we will relate our new refinement operator with its dual, a generalization operator, and its possible application in model inference using inverse resolution.

1 Introduction

In 1981, Shapiro [10] has introduced the notion of model inference. It has since then drawn a lot of attention in the world of inductive learning using logic. Even now the new operation of inverse resolution [5] is in fashion, people still discuss and use his ideas of inference and learning problems [1, 3, 7]. Given a sequence of positive and negative examples of an unknown concept, his incremental Model Inference System tries to find a theory (finite set of hypotheses) that can infer all given positive examples and none of the negative examples. The system essentially uses two techniques: if the theory is too strong (a negative example can be inferred from it) the backtracing algorithm locates a guilty hypothesis and refutes it; if the theory is too weak (a positive example can not be inferred) then refinements (specializations), found by a refinement operator, of the thrown away hypotheses are added. In the limit, a theory will be found that is neither too strong nor too weak.

In this article we will discuss Shapiro's *refinement operator* ρ_0. This operator is defined for *reduced* sentences in a first order language where sentences and refinements of them are restricted by some complexity measure size. The notion of reduced sentences, related to *subsumption*, is introduced by Plotkin [8].

The strength of Shapiro's model inference algorithm is its theoretical approach, the formal description of the operators used in it and their properties. One of these properties is the completeness of a refinement operator for a subset of a first order language, i.e., every sentence in the subset can be derived from the empty sentence by repeatedly applying the refinement operator. We will show that, exactly because of theoretical reasons, the refinement operator ρ_0 is not complete for reduced sentences, as Shapiro claims. To understand the problems, we should know more about the concepts of subsumption and size. Also, we will show that the definition of size which Shapiro has adopted from Reynolds [9] is inadequate for the theories he tries to build. We will introduce another kind of complexity measure.

Due to special properties of subsumption, we will show that the technique of *inverse reduction* is needed for certain problems. An algorithm for inverse reduction finds non-reduced clauses that are equivalent to a given reduced sentence. With this new technique and the new complexity measure we can change the ρ_0-operator into a refinement operator that is complete for reduced sentences.

Our refinement operator can derive exactly one representative of every equivalence class under subsumption, namely the reduced sentence in it (this sentence can be reached by different sentences since the subsumption ordering is a lattice, not a tree). The space of all reduced sentences is much smaller than the space of all sentences in a first order logic. Therefore, considering reduced sentences only is more efficient than considering all sentences.

Some of the results of a working report [12] are included in this article.

The article is divided in the following sections. In Sect. 2 we concentrate on some properties of subsumption which are important in proving the (in-)correctness of refinement operators. In Sect. 3 we introduce some terminology adopted from Shapiro and we show the incompleteness of ρ_0 with examples. Also, we discuss the complexity measure rsize and its shortcomings when related to subsumption. In Sect. 4 we define a new refinement operator and a new complexity measure. In Sect. 5 we compare our new refinement operator with another refinement operator [2] that is complete for first order sentences. In Sect. 6 we look at refinements in a wider framework. We relate refinement operators to their duals, generalization operators, and these generalization operators to inverse resolution and model inference. These relations will also be a subject for future research.

2   Subsumption, Reduction and Inverse Reduction

Let $\mathcal{L}$ be a language of first order logic. In this language we use P, Q, R,... for predicate symbols, f, g, h,... for function symbols, a, b, c,... for constants, and x, y, z,... for variables. Throughout this article, constants are treated as functions with arity zero. Atoms are denoted by A, B,.... A literal is an atom or the negation of an atom, and is denoted by L, M,.... Every sentence in $\mathcal{L}$ is a set of literals:

$$\{A_1, \ldots, A_m, \neg B_1, \ldots, \neg B_n\}$$

where $\neg B_j$ is the negation of the atom B_j. A sentence represents the disjunction of its literals, where all variables in it are universally quantified over the whole sentence. Sentences can also be written in the following form:

$$\{A_1, \ldots, A_m\} \leftarrow \{B_1, \ldots, B_n\}$$

Sentences are denoted by p, $q, \ldots$, and substitutions by θ, σ, τ. All these symbols may have subscripts. A Horn sentence requires $m \leq 1$. The results in this article are described for the set of first order sentences but hold for the set of Horn sentences as well.

2.1 Subsumption and Reduction

The notions of subsumption and reduction originate from Plotkin [8], and are defined as follows:

Definition 1. A sentence p *subsumes* a sentence q $(p \succeq q)$ iff there exists a substitution θ such that $p\theta \subseteq q$.

A sentence p *properly subsumes* a sentence q $(p \succ q)$ iff p subsumes q but q does not subsume p.

Two sentences p and q are called (*subsume*) *equivalent* $(p \sim q)$ iff p subsumes q and q subsumes p. This is an equivalence relation which defines a partition on sentences. Every set of equivalent sentences is called a (*subsume*) *equivalence class*.

A sentence p is called *reduced* if $p' \subseteq p$ together with $p \sim p'$ implies $p = p'$.

Example 1. The reduced sentence $\{P(x, y)\}$ is equivalent to $\{P(x, y), P(x, z)\}$ which is (therefore) not reduced.

If q is not reduced, we can reduce q to a sentence $p \subset q$ $(p \subseteq q$ and $p \neq q)$ such that p is reduced and $p \sim q$. An algorithm to reduce sentences to their smallest equivalent subset is presented by Plotkin [8].

Subsumption is weaker than logical implication [6]. If a sentence p subsumes a sentence q then p logically implies q but not the other way around. $p = \{P(f(x))\} \leftarrow \{P(x)\}$ logically implies $q = \{P(f(f(y)))\} \leftarrow \{P(y)\}$, but p does not subsume q. In the rest of this article, we investigate the ordering induced by subsumption. We will define an operator that, given a reduced representative of an equivalence class under subsumption, yields reduced repesentatives that are subsumed by it. However, sentences that are logically implied but not subsumed will not be found.

It is proved by Plotkin [8] that if two equivalent sentences both are reduced then they are equal up to renaming variables, i.e., they are alphabetical variants.

Throughout this paper alphabetical variants are considered identical. We can therefore speak of one reduced representative of every equivalence class.

Subsumption has some unexpected properties. For example, substitutions do not always preserve equivalence, and subsets of reduced sentences need not be reduced.

Let $p = \{P(x,y)\}$, $q = \{P(x,y), P(x,z)\}$, $r = \{P(x,y), P(x,z), P(y,z)\}$, and $\theta = \{x/z\}$. Then $p \subset q \subset r$, $p \sim q$, $p\theta = \{P(z,y)\}$ and $q\theta = \{P(z,y), P(z,z)\}$. $\{P(z,z)\}$ is the reduced equivalent of $q\theta$, and $p\theta$ is not equivalent to $q\theta$. Also, $q \subseteq r$, where r is reduced and q is not.

The ordering induced by subsumption is a quasi ordering because $x \succeq x$ (reflexivity), and if $x \succeq y$ and $y \succeq z$ then $x \succeq z$ (transitivity). The empty sentence ($\square$) is the maximal element in this ordering.

In a (learning) system that uses a search space of logic formulae, it often is a waste of time and memory to examine more than one sentence of an equivalence class. Since for any two sentences p and q if $p \sim q$ then $p \vdash r$ iff $q \vdash r$, using reduced sentences as a representative of an equivalence class might lead to more efficient (learning) systems.

However, operations such as substitutions on equivalent sentences can lead to non-equivalent sentences. To overcome this problem we want to build a simple algorithm to reverse the process of reduction. We need the following lemma and theorem for this algorithm.

Lemma 2. *Let p be a sentence. If $p\theta = p$, then for some natural number k, $L\theta^k = L$, for all literals L in p.*

Proof. θ must be injective: if $L_1\theta = L_2\theta$ for different $L_1, L_2 \in p$ then θ would decrease the number of literals in p, i.e., $|p\theta| < |p|$. For every literal L in p consider the following sequence

$$L, L\theta, L\theta^2, L\theta^3, \ldots$$

Since $p = p\theta = p\theta^2 = \cdots$ and since p is finite, not all $L\theta^i$ can be different. Then for some i, j, $i < j$, we have $L\theta^i = L\theta^j$. Because θ is injective, this implies $L\theta^{j-i} = L$.
For every L, let $n(L)$ be the smallest number such that $L\theta^{n(L)} = L$. Then $L\theta^i = L$ if i is a multiple of $n(L)$. Let k be the least common multiple of all $n(L)$. Then $L\theta^k = L$ for all $L \in p$. $\square$

Lemma 3. *Let p be a reduced sentence, and $p \subseteq q$ such that $p \sim q$. Then there exists a substitution θ such that $q\theta = p$ and $L\theta = L$ for all literals $L \in p$.*

Proof. Since q subsumes p, for some σ, $q\sigma \subseteq p$, this implies $p\sigma \subseteq p$. If $q\sigma \subset p$, then also $p\sigma \subset p$ and p would not be reduced, and we conclude that $p\sigma = p$. By Lemma 2, we know that for some k, $L\sigma^k = L$ for all $L \in p$. Define $\theta = \sigma^k$. $\square$

2.2 Inverse Reduction

Given a reduced sentence, an inverse reduction algorithm finds equivalent sentences. An inverse reduction algorithm is needed in Sect. 4 to define a complete refinement operator, ρ_r. Also, it shows the kind of sentences that are in the same equivalence class under subsumption.

Let p be a reduced sentence and m a given positive integer. We want to find all sentences that are equivalent to p and contain less than or exactly m literals. For every sentence q' such that $p \sim q'$, an alphabetic variant q of q' exists such that $q = p \cup r$. For example $p = \{P(x, x)\}$ is equivalent to $q' = \{P(u, u), P(u, v)\}$ which is an alphabetic variant of $q = \{P(x, x), P(x, y)\}$ that contains p. Therefore we only have to find equivalent sentences that contain p. By Lemma 3 we know that for every such sentence q a substitution θ exists, such that $q\theta = p$ and $L\theta = L$ for all literals $L \in p$. This implies that q can be reduced to p via θ, where θ is defined only on variables not occuring in p. The following example gives an idea which sentences are to be found.

Example 2. Let $p = \{P(x, x)\}$, and let $m = 3$. All possible q's such that $q \sim p$ and $|q| = 2$ are of the form $\{P(x, x), M_1\}$ where M_1 could be $P(y, z)$, $P(x, y)$, $P(y, x)$ or $P(y, y)$.
For $|q| = 3$, we get $q = \{P(x, x), M_1, M_2\}$ where some of the possible M_1, M_2 and corresponding θ are

M_1	M_2	θ
$P(y, z)$	$P(x, y)$	$\{y/x, z/x\}$
$P(y, z)$	$P(y, x)$	$\{y/x, z/x\}$
$P(y, z)$	$P(y, w)$	$\{y/x, z/x, w/x\}$
$P(x, y)$	$P(y, x)$	$\{y/x\}$
$P(y, y)$	$P(z, z)$	$\{y/x, z/x\}$

To find all sentences that are equivalent to a sentence p, literals have to be added to p. Since for a certain substitution θ, all added literals have to be mapped onto a literal in p, only literals that are more general than literals in p have to be added.

Algorithm 1 *(Inverse Reduction) Let p be a reduced sentence and let $m \geq 0$ be given. The following algorithm finds all sentences equivalent to p with $\leq m$ literals.*

Let $l = 0$, if $|p| \leq m$ then output p
While $l < (m - |p|)$ do
    $l := l + 1$
    For every sequence $\{L_1, \ldots, L_l\}$,
    where every $L_i \in p$, but the L_i's are not necessarily distinct.
        Find all sets $r = \{M_1, \ldots, M_l\}$ such that $M_i\theta = L_i$ for all i,
        where every M_i contains at least one variable not occuring p
        and $\theta = \{x_1/t_1, \ldots, x_m/t_m\}$, $x_j \notin \text{var}(p)$ for all j;
        For every such r output $p \cup r$

3 Incorrectness of the Refinement Operator ρ_o

3.1 Refinement

The ideas we present in this article are based on the refinement operators used in Shapiro's Model Inference System [10], for which he has defined three concrete refinement operators ρ_0, ρ_1, and ρ_2. We therefore first give a brief description of model inference. Let a first order language $\mathcal{L}$, an observational language $\mathcal{L}_o$, and a hypotheses language $\mathcal{L}_h$, such that $\mathcal{L}_o \subseteq \mathcal{L}_h \subseteq \mathcal{L}$, be given. Let M be an unknown model defined on $\mathcal{L}$ and let $\mathcal{L}_o^M = \{\alpha \in \mathcal{L}_o | \alpha \text{ is true in } M\}$. Suppose that we can enumerate all the sentences in $\mathcal{L}_o$ by α_1, α_2,..., and that we can tell the truth value V_i of every α_i. From these facts $\langle \alpha_i, V_i \rangle$, we want to find a finite set of sentences T expressed in $\mathcal{L}_h$ such that $\mathcal{L}_o^M = \{\alpha \in \mathcal{L}_o | T \vdash \alpha\}$. Such a theory T is called a $\mathcal{L}_o$-complete axiomatization and it can be used to represent the model M.

Example 3. As an example, given a first order language $\mathcal{L}$, Shapiro's refinement operator ρ_2 uses $\mathcal{L}_o$ = the set of ground atoms in $\mathcal{L}$ and $\mathcal{L}_h$ = the set of atoms and context free transformations in $\mathcal{L}$, where context free transformations are sentences in the form $\{p(t_1,\ldots,t_n)\} \leftarrow \{p(x_1,\ldots,x_n)\}$ where all x_i's are distinct and occur in t_i.

If the language $\mathcal{L}$ contains the constant 0 (zero) and a function s (which can be interpreted as the successor function), then given some positive and negative examples like

$\langle plus(s(s(0)), s(0), s(s(s(0)))), true \rangle$ and
$\langle plus(s(0), 0, 0), false \rangle$,

the Model Inference System will find the hypotheses

$\{plus(x, 0, x)\} \leftarrow$, and
$\{plus(x, s(y), s(z))\} \leftarrow \{plus(x, y, z)\}$.

Following Shapiro, we assume some structural complexity measure *size*, which is a function from sentences of $\mathcal{L}$ to natural numbers, with the property that for every $n > 0$ the set of sentences of size n is finite. The following definitions are also his.

Definition 4. [10] A sentence q is a *refinement* of p if p (logically) implies q and $\text{size}(p) < \text{size}(q)$.

A *refinement operator* ρ is a mapping from sentences of $\mathcal{L}$ to subsets of their refinements, such that for any $p \in \mathcal{L}$ and any $n > 0$ the set of $\rho(p)(n)$, that is, the set $\rho(p)$ restricted to sentences of size $\leq n$, is computable.

If there is a chain $p = p_0, p_1, \ldots, p_n = q$ such that $p_i \in \rho(p_{i-1})$, then we call it a *finite total ρ-chain*. We use $\rho^*(p)$ to denote the set of all sentences that can be reached by a finite total ρ-chain from p.

We change Shapiro's definition of completeness to weakly completeness because we want to use the notion of completeness for a stronger concept.

Definition 5. Let S be a subset of $\mathcal{L}$ which includes the empty sentence $\square$. A refinement operator ρ over $\mathcal{L}$ is called *weakly complete* for S if $\rho^*(\square) = S$.

A refinement operator ρ is called *(strongly) complete* for S if for any two sentences $p, q \in S$ such that q is a refinement of p, $q \in \rho^*(p)$.

3.2 Definition of ρ_0

In the section where Shapiro presents the refinement operator ρ_0, he claims that ρ_0 is weakly complete for any first order language $\mathcal{L}$. On the other hand, he redefines 'a sentence' to mean 'a reduced representative of the equivalence class of this sentence' [10, p27]. We assume that his intention was to define a refinement operator which is weakly complete for the set of reduced sentences. Even in this situation, however, it is not.

Definition 6. [10] If $p\theta = q$ and $|p| = |q|$ then θ *does not decrease* p, i.e., by choosing the right indices, we have $p = \{L_1, \ldots, L_m\}$, $q = \{M_1, \ldots, M_m\}$ and $L_i\theta = M_i$ for all i.

A literal L is *more general than M with respect to p* if there is a substitution θ such that $L\theta = M$ and $p\theta = p$.

If L is any literal that contains as arguments only distinct variables that do not occur in p, then we call L *most general with respect to p*.

Let M be a literal that is not most general w.r.t. a sentence p. Then we can always find a literal L that is more general than M w.r.t. p and that is most general w.r.t. p. In fact, we just need to replace all arguments of M by distinct variables that are not in p.

Definition 7. [10] A literal L is *most general with respect to p such that $p \cup \{L\}$ is reduced* if for any M such that M is properly more general than L w.r.t. p, $p \cup \{M\}$ is not reduced.

Example 4. Let $p = \{P(x, y)\}$, and let $L_1 = Q(u)$, $L_2 = \neg P(u, v)$, $L_3 = P(u, v)$ and $L_4 = P(u, x)$.

Then L_1, L_2 and L_3 are most general literals with respect to p, since they contain only distinct variables as arguments that do not occur in p. As can be verified, L_4 is a most general literal with respect to p such that $p \cup \{L_4\}$ is reduced.

Definition 8. [10] Let p be a reduced sentence of $\mathcal{L}$. Then $q \in \rho_0(p)$ when exactly one of the following holds:

ρ_0^1: $q = p\theta$, where $\theta = \{x/y\}$ does not decrease p and both variables x and y occur in p.

ρ_0^2: $q = p\theta$, where $\theta = \{x/f(y_1, \ldots, y_n)\}$ does not decrease p, f is an n-place function symbol, x occurs in p and all y_i's are distinct variables not in p.

ρ_0^3: $q = p \cup \{L\}$, where L is a most general literal with respect to p for which $p \cup \{L\}$ is reduced.

Although the definition of the refinement operator uses the concept of size, these ρ_0^1, ρ_0^2 and ρ_0^3 are concretely defined without it. Hence, we can begin our discussion of the completeness of ρ_0 without worrying about size. In Sect. 3.4 we will relate refinement operators with size.

3.3 Incompleteness of ρ_0

In this subsection we will show that Shapiro's Lemma 5.15 and 5.16 [10] are not correct, and hence that ρ_0 is not (strongly) complete. Shapiro never uses the terminology of strong completeness of ρ_0, Lemma 5.15 and 5.16 together, however, would imply it. We will also show that his Theorem 5.14 is not correct, and hence that ρ_0 is not even weakly complete.

Lemma 5.15 of Shapiro [10]. *Let p and q be two reduced sentences such that $p\theta = q$ for some substitution θ that does not decrease p. Then there is a finite total ρ_0-chain from p to q.*

Proof. [10] This lemma is a generalization of Theorem 4 in Reynolds' paper [9]. Examination of the proof of this Theorem shows that it can be applied to p and $p\theta$ to obtain a finite total chain. □

Reynolds has proved this theorem for atoms. Indeed if we do not restrict ourselves to reduced sentences and consider only non-decreasing substitutions, then we can consider a sentence as a generalized atom.

Example 5. Consider the following chains of sentences $p = p_0, p_1, p_2, p_3, p_4 = q$ and $p = p_0, p_1', p_2', p_3', p_4 = q$. Since $p\theta = q$, and p and q are reduced, Shapiro claims that there is a finite total ρ_0-chain from p to q.

$$p = p_0 = \{P(a, w), P(x, b), P(c, y), P(z, d)\}, p_0 \text{ is reduced}$$
$$p_1 = \{P(a, b), P(x, b), P(c, y), P(z, d)\} \sim p_1' = \{P(a, b), P(c, y), P(z, d)\}$$
$$p_2 = \{P(a, b), P(c, b), P(c, y), P(z, d)\} \sim p_2' = \{P(a, b), P(c, b), P(z, d)\}$$
$$p_3 = \{P(a, b), P(c, b), P(c, d), P(z, d)\} \sim p_3' = \{P(a, b), P(c, b), P(c, d)\}$$
$$q = p_4 = \{P(a, b), P(c, b), P(c, d), P(a, d)\}, p_4 \text{ is reduced}$$

Here we are facing a dilemma, either we allow non-reduced sentences (p_1, p_2, p_3) or we reduce after substitution and hence allow decreasing substitutions (e.g., $p_1' \in \rho_0(p_0)$).

Lemma 9. *For some reduced sentences p and q such that $p\theta = q$, there is no finite total ρ_0-chain from p to q.*

Proof. Let $p = \{P(a, w), P(x, b), P(c, y), P(z, d)\}$, and let $q = \{P(a, b), P(c, b), P(c, d), P(a, d)\}$ as above. We prove that none of ρ_0^1, ρ_0^2 and ρ_0^3 is a candidate to generate the successor of p in a ρ_0-chain from p to q.

ρ_0^1: All variables of p have to be substituted by constants to achieve q and all constants a, b, c, d are to be substituted only once. Unification of variables causes that a variable occurs at least twice. Therefore unification of variables is not applicable to get the next element in the chain.

ρ_0^2: All substitutions by constants in the intended place lead to non-reduced sentences. Every other introduction of a function-symbol can not be removed and does not lead to q.

ρ_0^3: Increasing the number of literals is not applicable, since only non-decreasing substitutions are allowed. Once increased, this number can never be reduced again.

□

Lemma 5.16 of Shapiro [10]. *Let p and q be two reduced sentences such that $p \subseteq q$. Then there is a finite total ρ_0-chain from p to q.*

Proof (Outline of [10]). The proof is by induction on the number of literals in the difference set $q - p$. If some of the literals in this difference set are removed from q, it is assumed that the resulting sentence still is reduced. □

This assumption, if p and q are reduced sentences such that $p \subseteq q$ then every sentence r such that $p \subseteq r \subseteq q$ is also reduced, is falsified by the following example:

Example 6. Consider the reduced sentences
$$p = \{P(x), \neg Q(x, a)\},$$
$$q = \{P(x), \neg Q(x, a), \neg Q(y, z), \neg Q(z, y)\}.$$
Then
$$r = \{P(x), \neg Q(x, a), \neg Q(y, z)\}$$
fulfills $p \subseteq r \subseteq q$ and r is not reduced.

Lemma 10. *For some reduced sentences p and q such that $p \subseteq q$, there is no finite total ρ_0-chain from p to q.*

Proof (Outline). Consider the sentences p and q from the last example. The problem is to find a successor of p in a ρ_0-chain from p to q. Clearly, literals have to be added by ρ_0^3. Both literals in $q - p$ are most general with respect to p, but adding to p a literal of $q - p$ results in a non-reduced sentence. Formally, it can be proved that there is no candidate for a successor of p in a ρ_0-chain from p to q by the same technique as at Lemma 9. □

The problems of incompleteness are illustrated in Fig. 1. Non-reduced sentences are represented by filled circles, reduced sentences by open circles. Ovals represent equivalence classes under subsumption, and arrows represent a single ρ_0-application.

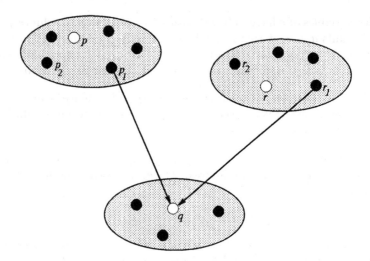

Fig. 1. Equivalence classes and refinements, a reduced sentence that can only be reached from non-reduced sentences

Shapiro's intention was that for every pair of reduced sentences p and q, satisfying $p \subseteq q$ or $p\theta = q$ where θ is non-decreasing, there is a chain of arrows from p to q where only reduced sentences are visited. Problems with ρ_0 arise when a reduced sentence (open circle) like q is only reachable from non-reduced sentences (filled circles) like p_1 and r_1.

Consider the following sentences:

$$p = \{P(x, y), P(y, z), P(z, x)\}$$
$$p_1 = \{P(u, w), P(w, v), P(x, y), P(y, z), P(z, x)\}$$
$$r = \{P(v, w), P(w, v)\}$$
$$r_1 = \{P(v, w), P(w, v), P(x, y), P(y, z)\}$$
$$q = \{P(v, w), P(w, v), P(x, y), P(y, z), P(z, x)\}$$

Both p and r properly subsume q, $p_1 \sim p$ and $r_1 \sim r$. If we apply the substitution $\{u/v\}$ to p_1 we get q. q can also be obtained from r_1 by adding $P(z, x)$, a most general literal w.r.t. r_1 such that $r_1 \cup \{P(z, x)\}$ is reduced.

It is proved in the working report [12] that there is no reduced sentence (open circle) such that q can be derived from it by ρ_0. Therefore, this sentence q is a counterexample of Shapiro's Theorem 5.14 which states that there is a ρ_0-chain from the empty sentence $\square$ to every reduced sentence.

3.4 The Incorrectness of Using rsize

Shapiro has defined a refinement as follows: 'We say that q is a refinement of p if p implies q and size$(q) >$ size(p)'. Although any complexity measure size that satisfies the requirement that for any fixed value k there are finitely many sentences of size $\leq k$ is allowed, in his concrete refinement operators Reynolds' [9] complexity measure (that we denote by rsize) for atoms is used. This complexity measure can be generalized to sentences by defining

rsize(p) = the number of symbol occurrences in p minus the number of distinct variables in p.

A nice property of Reynolds' rsize is that if an atomic sentence p subsumes an atomic sentence q ($q = p\theta$ for some substitution θ), then p properly subsumes q iff rsize(q) > rsize(p). The idea behind Shapiro's refinement operators is also to find properly subsumed sentences. If a sentence p properly subsumes a sentence q, he intends q to be reachable from p by a chain of refinements found by a refinement operator. Since size can only return integer values and refinements are required to be of strictly larger size, if size(q) − size(p) = l then the chain of refinements from p to q is guaranteed not to exceed length l. As we know, for any sentence p, for example $\{P(x)\}$, we can find an infinite chain of refinements, $\{P(f(x))\}, \{P(f(f(x)))\}, \ldots$. If, however, only sentences of size $\leq k$ are allowed, no chain can exceed length k.

Shapiro's refinement operator ρ_1 is defined for atomic sentences by ρ_0^1 and ρ_0^2. In the atomic case, increasing rsize coincides with proper specialization and vice versa. Also, there are only finitely many atoms of rsize $\leq k$. Therefore, restricting the search of refinements to atomic sentences of rsize $\leq k$ and restricting to refinements of increasing rsize, all atomic sentences of rsize $\leq k$ can be found by ρ_1.

When we study Shapiro's refinement operator ρ_0, some problems arise with the use of Reynolds' rsize and subsumption as ordering.

Consider the following sentences:

$$p = \{P(x, y), P(y, x)\}, \quad \text{rsize}(p) = 4$$
$$q_1 = \{P(a, y), P(y, a)\}, \quad \text{rsize}(q_1) = 5$$
$$q_2 = \{P(x, x)\}, \quad \text{rsize}(q_2) = 2$$

Then

rsize(p) < rsize(q_1) and p subsumes q_1 ($p\theta = q_1$ for $\theta = \{x/a\}$)
rsize(p) > rsize(q_2) and p subsumes q_2 ($p\theta = q_2$ for $\theta = \{y/x\}$)

Clearly, there is no direct relationship between subsumption and rsize.

To solve this problem, Shapiro restricts to so-called non-decreasing substitutions (the number of literals is not allowed to decrease). By this constraint, every sentence q found by applying the refinement operator ρ_0 to p satisfies rsize(p) < rsize(q). However, although p properly subsumes q_2, in this approach it is no longer possible to construct a chain of refinements from p to q_2 because rsize(p) > rsize(q). This also leads to incompleteness.

In Sect. 4.2 we will introduce a new complexity measure called newsize that avoids these problems.

4 A New Refinement Operator

When we define an equivalence relation on a set, it is usually required that the equivalence relation is compatible with the important operations on this set, i.e., operations on different members of the same equivalence class yield equivalent results. Unfortunately, this is not true for the equivalence relation defined by subsumption. Two subsumption equivalent sentences may not be equivalent after substitution. Therefore, if substitution is one of the operations, it is not enough to consider only the reduced representative of an equivalence class. This is an important reason why ρ_0 is not complete. Also, subsumption is not compatible with rsize, equivalent sentences may have a different rsize. Allowing non-decreasing substitutions only, guarantees that resulting sentences have a strictly larger rsize. However, if such a sentence is not reduced it will not be accepted. Even if reduction after a non-decresing substitution is allowed, its reduced equivalent can have a strictly smaller rsize and will not be regarded as a refinement.

In this section we will define a new refinement operator ρ_r which is complete for the set of all reduced sentences in $\mathcal{L}$. Although we will define a new complexity measure in Sect. 4.2, we are not going to use it explicitly in Sect. 4.1 when we define ρ_r.

4.1 A New Refinement Operator for Reduced Sentences

Before defining ρ_r, we revisit the problems and difficulties of Shapiro's ρ_0. For every two reduced sentences p and q such that p properly subsumes q, there should be ρ_r-chain from p to q.

o Consider the following two reduced sentences:

$$p = \{P(x), \neg Q(x, a)\}$$
$$q = \{P(x), \neg Q(x, a), \neg Q(y, z), \neg Q(z, y)\}$$

Here, p properly subsumes q since $p \subset q$. In Lemma 10 we have shown that there is no sentence r such that $r \in \rho_0(p)$ and $r \succeq q$. Adding to p one of the literals in $q - p$ results in a non-reduced sentence equivalent to p. Since q should be derivable from p, this suggests that sometimes more than one literal has to be added in one refinement step.

o Next, consider the following two reduced sentences:

$$p = \{P(x, y), P(y, x)\}$$
$$q = \{P(x, x)\}$$

Now, p properly subsumes q since $p\theta = q$ for $\theta = \{y/x\}$. Since $|p| > |q|$, we must allow decreasing substitutions.

In Sect. 2.2 we have presented an algorithm that generates all sentences p' with less than or equal to m literals that are equivalent to a given (reduced) sentence p. In the definition of ρ_r (ρ_r^1 and ρ_r^2) we will use $eq(p)$ to denote the set of all such p''s. Note that every sentence $p' \neq p$ in this set satisfies $p' = p \cup r$ for some set of literals r. Since $|r|$ can be larger than 1, we can use p' to solve the first problem presented above.

In one of the refinement steps of our new refinement operator (ρ_r^3), only one literal is added. For example, if $p = \{P(x, y)\}$, then $\neg P(u, v), Q(u)$ and $\neg Q(u)$ can be added to p. We first give a lemma to illustrate its use.

Lemma 11. *Let p be a sentence, and let L be a most general literal with respect to p, i.e., L has only distinct variables as arguments that do not occur in p. Then the following two conditions are equivalent:*

1. *p properly subsumes $q = p \cup \{L\}$*
2. *For any literal M in p, L differs from M in either predicate name or sign.*

Proof. $1 \Rightarrow 2$: Assume that 2 does not hold. Then there is an M in p such that M and L have the same predicate name and sign. Let θ be defined on variables of L only, such that $L\theta = M$. Then $q\theta = (p \cup \{L\})\theta = p$. This means that q also subsumes p. Therefore, $p \sim q$.

$2 \Rightarrow 1$: $p \subset q$, so clearly p subsumes q. Assume that also q subsumes p, then for some θ, $q\theta \subseteq p$. But then also $L\theta \in p$, and $L\theta$ and L must have the same predicate name and sign. □

It is easy to verify that, if p is reduced and L satisfies the conditions of Lemma 11, then $q = p \cup \{L\}$ is also reduced.

Definition 12. Let p be a reduced sentence. Then $q \in \rho_r(p)$ if q is reduced and one of the following conditions holds:

ρ_r^1: $p \succ q$ and there are $p' \in eq(p)$ and $q' \in eq(q)$ such that $q' = p'\theta$, where $\theta = \{x/y\}$ and both x and y occur in p'.

ρ_r^2: $p \succ q$ and there are $p' \in eq(p)$ and $q' \in eq(q)$ such that $q' = p'\theta$, where $\theta = \{x/f(y_1, \ldots, y_n)\}$, f is an n-place function symbol, x occurs in p', and all y_i's are distinct variables not occurring in p'.

ρ_r^3: $q = p \cup \{L\}$, where L is a most general literal such that for every literal $M \in p$, L differs from M in either predicate name or sign.

Theorem 13. *Let p and q be reduced sentences. If $p \succ q$, then there is a ρ_r-chain from p to q.*

Lemma 14. *Let $p, q \in \mathcal{L}$ be two reduced sentences such that p properly subsumes q and let $p' \in eq(p)$, $q' \in eq(q)$ satisfy $p'\theta = q'$. Then there is a $r \in \rho_r(p)$ such that r subsumes q.*

Proof. Let $p' = p_0, p_1, \ldots, p_n = q'$ be a chain of sentences such that $p_i = p_{i-1}\theta_{i-1}$, $0 < i \le n$, where every θ_i is a substitution as defined in ρ_r^1 or ρ_r^2. Reynolds [9, proof of Theorem 4] has shown how such a chain of substitutions can be constructed. Let p_k be the first p_i that is not equivalent to p. Since $p \succ q$ such a p_k exists. If we let r be the reduced equivalent of p_k, then $p_{k-1} \in eq(p)$, $p_k = p_{k-1}\theta_{k-1}$ and $r \in \rho_r(p)$. Also, since r subsumes p_k, $p_k\theta_k \cdots \theta_{n-1} = p_n = q'$, and $q' \sim q$, r subsumes q. □

The following example illustrates the proof of Lemma 14.

Example 7. Let $p = \{P(a, w), P(x, b), P(c, y), P(z, d)\}$ and
$q = \{P(a, b), P(c, b), P(c, d), P(a, d)\}$ as in the first example of Sect. 3.3. If $p' = p$ and $q' = q$ then $p'\theta = q'$ for $\theta = \{w/b, x/c, y/d, z/a\}$. θ can be split in $\theta_0 = \{w/b\}, \theta_1 = \{x/c)\}, \theta_2 = \{y/d\}$ and $\theta_3 = \{z/a\}$.

$$p_0 = p' = p$$
$$p_1 = p_0\theta_0 = \{P(a, b), P(x, b), P(c, y), P(z, d)\}$$

p_1 is not equivalent to p. The reduced equivalent r of p_1 is

$$r = \{P(a, b), P(c, y), P(z, d)\},$$

and r is a member of $\rho_r(p)$ that subsumes q.

Lemma 15. *Let $p, q \in \mathcal{L}$ be two reduced sentences such that p properly subsumes q and $p \subset q$. Then there is a refinement $r \in \rho_r(p)$ such that r subsumes q.*

Proof. Let s be a maximal subset of $q - p$ such that $p \cup s \sim p$. That means, for every literal M in $(q - p) - s$, p properly subsumes $p \cup s \cup \{M\}$. Let L be a most general literal with respect to $p \cup s$ such that $L\theta = M$ for one of those literals.

If $p \cup s \cup \{L\}$ is not equivalent to $p \cup s$, then, by Lemma 11, L differs from all literals in $p \cup s$ in either predicate name or sign. L also has this property with respect to p. Let $r = p \cup \{L\}$. Then $r \in \rho_r^3(p)$, and clearly r subsumes q.

Otherwise, $p' = p \cup s \cup \{L\}$ and $q' = p \cup s \cup \{M\}$ satisfies $p'\theta = q'$. Using Lemma 14 a sentence r can be found such that $r \in \rho_r(p)$ and r subsumes q'. Since $q' \subseteq q$, r also subsumes q. □

The following examples illustrate the proof of Lemma 15.

Example 8. Let $p = \{P(x)\}$ and $q = \{P(x), \neg Q(a, x)\}$.
The only subset s of $q - p$ such that $p \cup s \sim p$ is $\{\}$, the empty set. $M = \neg Q(a, x)$ is the only literal in $(q - p) - s$. $L = \neg Q(y, z)$ is most general w.r.t. p and $L\theta = M$ for $\theta = \{y/a, z/x\}$. $p \cup \{L\}$ is reduced and

$$r = \{P(x), \neg Q(y, z)\}$$

satisfies $r \in \rho_r(p)$ and r subsumes q.

Example 9. Let $p = \{P(x), \neg Q(x, a)\}$ and
$q = \{P(x), \neg Q(x, a), \neg Q(y, z), \neg Q(z, y)\}$.
$s = \{\neg Q(y, z)\}$ is a maximal subset of $q - p$ such that $p \cup s \sim p$. Taking $M = \neg Q(z, y)$ we get $L = \neg Q(u, v)$ as a most general literal with respect to $p \cup s$. $p' = p \cup s \cup \{L\}$ is equivalent to p and p' properly subsumes $q' = p \cup s \cup \{M\}$. By Lemma 14 we can find a refinement r of p that subsumes q.

In Lemma 14 we have $p' = \{P(x), \neg Q(x, a), \neg Q(y, z), \neg Q(u, v)\}$,
$q' = \{P(x), \neg Q(x, a), \neg Q(y, z), \neg Q(z, y)\}$ and $\theta = \{u/z, v/y\}$. θ can be split in $\theta_0 = \{u/z\}$ and $\theta_1 = \{v/y\}$. $p'\theta_0$ is not equivalent to p' so

$$r = \{P(x), \neg Q(x, a), \neg Q(y, z), \neg Q(z, v)\}$$

satisfies $r \in \rho_r^1(p)$ and r subsumes q.

Proof of Theorem 13. For every pair of reduced sentences p and q such that p properly subsumes q, $p\theta \subseteq q$ for some θ, let s be the reduced equivalent of $p\theta$.

If p properly subsumes s then p and s satisfy the conditions of Lemma 14. Otherwise, $s \in eq(p)$, and s and q satisfy the conditions of Lemma 15.

In both cases the first element r of a ρ_r-chain from p to q can be found. We can complete a ρ_r-chain from p to q by repeatedly finding the first element in a chain from r to q. In Lemma 18 in the next subsection we prove that this chain is of finite length. □

4.2 A New Complexity Measure

Shapiro has defined that q is a refinement of p if p implies q and size$(p) <$ size(q). If we consider atoms and rsize, then q is a refinement of p is equivalent to p properly subsumes q. Suppose that rsize can indeed be generalized to sentences or that there is another kind of size which satisfies this property, then the use of size has the following advantages: it can restrict the search space of sentences by discarding sentences of size$> k$; it prohibits infinite chains of refinements, by demanding size to increase no cycles will occur; also, it can be used to ease proofs of completeness and finiteness.

However, in concrete examples, Shapiro uses rsize. In Sect. 3, we have shown that if p subsumes q, then rsize(p) can be smaller as well as larger than rsize(q). In the latter situation, q is not even regarded as a refinement of p, so there surely is no chain from p to q. Shapiro uses non-decreasing substitutions to prevent rsize to decrease. An argument in favor of this approach is that if $p\theta = q$ then there is always a subset p' of p such that $p'\theta = q$ and θ is non-decreasing w.r.t. p'. Since p' also subsumes q, and assuming that p' can be derived from the empty sentence, q can still be derivable via p'. This gives two problems. Firstly, as we have shown before, non-decreasing substitutions are not compatible with reduced sentences. Secondly, suppose that we already have some background information about the theory to be inferred, say that we know that a given sentence p subsumes a sentence q that has to be found. Then it is much more efficient to search for a chain from p to q than from the empty sentence to q. What we want is strong completeness, and non-decreasing substitutions do not fit in this approach.

All complications seem to be caused by adapting the refinement operator to the definition of size. If we know that we are looking for properly subsumed sentences, why don't we define refinement concretely by proper subsumption? This prevents cycles to occur. Size is then only needed to restrict the search space to a finite number of sentences.

Definition 16. Given a sentence $p \in \mathcal{L}$:
newsize$(p) = ($maxsize$(p), |p|)$, where
maxsize$(p) = max\{$rsize$(L)|L \in p\}$ and $|p|$ is the number of literals in p.

It is easy to prove that if p subsumes q then maxsize$(p) \leq$ maxsize(q), from this it follows that if $p \sim q$ then maxsize$(p) =$ maxsize(q). Also, if maxsize$(p) >$

maxsize(q) then p cannot subsume q. Contrary to rsize, maxsize has a natural relationship with subsumption.

Since the number of literals of rsize $\leq k$ is finite, the number of sentences satisfying newsize(p) $\leq (k, m)$ (maxsize(p) $\leq k$ and $|p| \leq m$) is also finite.

We now redefine the notions of refinement and refinement operator in the context of subsumption.

Definition 17. A sentence q is called a *refinement* of a sentence p iff p properly subsumes q. A *refinement operator* is a mapping from sentences to a subset of their refinements, such that for any $p \in \mathcal{L}$ and any $k, m > 0$ the set of all $\rho(p)(k, m)$, that is the set $\rho(p)$ restricted to sentences q such that newsize(q) $\leq (k, m)$, is computable.

In this definition 'computability' is guaranteed if every sentence that is involved to compute $\rho(p)$ satisfies newsize $\leq (k, m)$. We should add this condition to the definition of ρ_r (i.e., p, q, p' and q' have a newsize $\leq (k, m)$). This also restricts the sentences to be generated by the inverse reduction algorithm to sentences with less than or equal to m literals. Notice that if p properly subsumes q and both p and q satisfy newsize $\leq (k, m)$, then every related sentence to find r in Lemma 14 and 15 satisfies newsize $\leq (k, m)$.

Since every element in a chain of refinements properly subsumes its successor and subsumption is transitive, a chain cannot contain cycles.

These observations together with the following lemma imply that ρ_r is a refinement operator, complete for reduced sentences.

Lemma 18. *Let $p_0, p_1, p_2 \ldots$ be a ρ_r-chain, where* newsize(p_i) $\leq (k, m)$ *for every p_i. Then this chain is of finite length.*

Proof. There are finitely many sentences such that newsize(p) $\leq (k, m)$, so there are finitely many different sentences in every ρ_r-chain. Since for every two reduced sentences $p, q \in \mathcal{L}$ such that $q \in \rho_r(p)$, $p \succ q$, no sentence can occur more than once in a ρ_r-chain. $\qquad\qquad\square$

The properties of newsize and its strong relation with subsumption as described above, are a motivation for adopting it as a complexity measure to restrict the search space of refinements.

Using these new definitions, ρ_r is a refinement operator and it behaves like Shapiro thought ρ_0 would do, it is complete for reduced sentences.

5   Comparison with Lairds' ρ_L

Laird [2] has also defined a refinement operator, ρ_L. He uses a different notation to define his refinement operator. Instead of sentences $C \leftarrow D$ where C and D are sets of atoms, Laird considers clauses of a language $\mathcal{L}_L$ where repetition of literals is allowed, substitutions are never decreasing, and also non-reduced clauses are allowed. The price we have to pay for this is the presence of many equivalent hypotheses in the search space.

Definition 19. [2] Let $p = C \leftarrow D$ be a clause in the language $\mathcal{L}_\mathrm{L}$. Then $q \in \rho_\mathrm{L}(p)$ when exactly one of the following holds:

1. $q = p\theta$, where $\theta = \{x/y\}$ and both variables x and y occur in p.
2. $q = p\theta$, where $\theta = \{x/t\}$ and t is a most general term, i.e., all variables in t are distinct and do not occur in p.
3. $q = C \vee L \leftarrow D$, where L is a most general atom.
4. $q = C \leftarrow D \wedge L$, where L is a most general atom.

In [11], Shapiro has included the Prolog-source of another general refinement operator that is similar to Laird's ρ_L. Like Laird's, this operator does not restrict the search space of hypotheses to reduced sentences (clauses).

Laird does not give a proof of completeness of his version of ρ_0, instead he refers to the proof of Shapiro's Theorem 5.14. Moreover, Laird does not mention the difference between his and Shapiro's operator. In the working report [12] a proof of the completeness of ρ_L can be found.

Let $\mathcal{L}_\mathrm{L}$ be a language that contains one constant a, one 1-place function f, and one 2-place predicate P. Suppose at some moment, $P(a, a) \leftarrow$ is a clause that has to be refined. The set of one-step refinements will contain $P(a, a) \vee P(x, y) \leftarrow$, equivalent to $P(a, a) \leftarrow$. All one-step refinements of this clause are $P(a, a) \vee P(x, x) \leftarrow$, $P(a, a) \vee P(a, y) \leftarrow$, $P(a, a) \vee P(x, a) \leftarrow$, $P(a, a) \vee P(x, y) \vee P(v, w) \leftarrow$, $P(a, a) \vee P(f(z), y) \leftarrow$, $P(a, a) \vee P(x, f(z)) \leftarrow$ and $P(a, a) \vee P(x, y) \leftarrow P(v, w)$. The first four of these seven refinements are all equivalent to $P(a, a) \leftarrow$. In the next refinement steps this number will increase even faster. In fact we have a gigantic search space which contains a lot of equivalent clauses. All these (equivalent) clauses are regarded as different, all are kept in memory, and are subjected to refinement separately.

Laird has pointed out that in an implementation of ρ_L, variants of clauses can be treated as identical, and one can avoid generating variants of the same clause in computing $\rho_\mathrm{L}(p)$. In this way repeated literals and sentences that are equal up to renaming variables are prohibited. None of the sentences in our example would be avoided in this way.

In our approach, only properly subsumed reduced sentences are refinements. Of every equivalence class at most one representative is refined. When we refine a reduced sentence, inverse reduction is used. The time-complexity of inverse reduction, to generate equivalent sentences that are refined, is not very attractive. These sentences, however, can be thrown away immediately after refinement. In Lairds' approach these non-reduced equivalent sentences will also be generated when application of ρ_L results in non-reduced sentences. They will be kept in memory seperately until they are refined. Since only one sentence is refined at a time, our memory requirements are much smaller Lairds'. We therefore think, that with 'interesting problems', i.e., theories with a high complexity (measure), the extra time needed to compute refinements can be compensated for by the much smaller memory requirements since every equivalence class under subsumption has only one representative. This is subject of future research.

6   Refinement in a Wider Framework

In this section we will briefly introduce the connections between Shapiro's model inference and inverse resolution. It is said that model inference and inverse resolution reach the same destination from opposite directions: The first uses specialization, the second generalization. First we will invert the specialization operator defined in this paper to obtain a generalization operator, then we will relate it to inverse resolution and model inference using generalization.

6.1   Generalization Operators

Our refinement operator ρ_r can easily be inverted to a generalization operator δ_r. Given a reduced sentence q, a reduced sentence $p \in \delta_r(q)$ if $q \in \rho_r(p)$.

In [3] Ling has described so-called abstraction operators for atoms and Horn clauses. These operators are similar to the inverted versions of Shapiro's ρ_1 and ρ_2. They are used in a system called SIM which is roughly a system that works like Shapiro's MIS the other way around. Starting with some positive examples as hypotheses, generalizations are found by applying an abstraction operator to hypotheses if the hypotheses are too weak. An advantage of this specific to general approach over Shapiro's general to specific approach is that in SIM the positive examples play a more important role in determining the target theory.

δ_r can be viewed as a theoretically interesting generalization operator for the domain of reduced first order sentences, for example in a system like MIS.

6.2   Inverse Resolution

Given a logic program, we can use it to derive its logical consequences by using resolution. To reverse this process, we ask ourselves the following question: Given some positive examples that cannot be derived from the given program, how can we extend this program so that the new examples can be derived from it?

One possible answer is using Ling's sytem SIM, as described in the last subsection. Another approach is inverse resolution. In inverse resolution operators are used that invert one or more resolution steps. One of these operators is the so-called V-operator [5]: given two sentences p and r, a V-operator finds different sentences q such that r is a resolvent (or instance of a resolvent) of p and q.

For example, let $\mathcal{L}$ be a language that contains the predicate $even$, a constant symbol 0, and a function s (successor). Given the sentences

$p = \{even(0)\} \leftarrow$, and
$r = \{even(s(s(0)))\} \leftarrow$,

a V-operator should be able to derive

$$q = \{even(s(s(x)))\} \leftarrow \{even(x)\}.$$

In general there are many solutions for q. These depend on many choices. Some of the choices are: which literal L_1 in p is resolved with a literal L_2 in q; and what are the substitutions θ_1 and θ_2^{-1} such that $L_2 = L_1\theta_1\theta_2^{-1}$. However, Muggleton [4] has shown that for every choice of L_1 and θ_1 there is a unique least general solution q^*. He notes that every solution q subsumes q^*. In order to determine (all or some) solutions q when q^* is found, δ_r, the inverse of ρ_r, might prove useful. In the example above, δ_r could be used to derive q from the most specific solution

$$q^* = \{even(s(s(0)))\} \leftarrow \{even(0)\}.$$

For more detail on most specific V-operators we refer to [4].

6.3   Model Inference and Generalization

Shapiro's Model Inference System is concerned with finding a theory that is consistent with the given examples. Starting from the most general theory, a refinement operator is used to replace too strong hypotheses by logically weaker ones. This process can also be reversed. We do not know any learning system that uses generalization operators and restricts the search space to reduced sentences. We are thinking of a MIS- (or SIM-)like system that works with reduced sentences only. Starting with positive examples as hypothese, a generalization operator like δ_r is used to generalize too weak hypotheses like in Ling's MIS [3].

When the target theory contains recursive predicates or when auxiliary predicates occur in it, literals have to be added to hypotheses. We think that a V-operator is very useful for this part of the system. Guided by the positive examples and the predicates in the background theory, only the least general solutions of this V-operator will be accepted as new hypotheses. Too weak solutions can be generalized by applying δ_r. The formulation of an inductive inference algorithm that operates in this way is a subject of future research.

7   Conclusions

In this article we showed by concrete examples that ρ_0 is not complete for reduced sentences. The reasons behind this incompleteness were given by analyzing the special properties of subsumption and a complexity measure size. We noticed that it is most important that refinements of a sentence are properly subsumed by it. Size is used only to limit the number of refinements. Therefore, we redefined the notion of a refinement operator. Also, we defined a new refinement operator ρ_r, complete for reduced sentences, and a new complexity measure to limit the search space of refinements. In the end, we related our new refinement operator to generalization operators such as δ_r and the V-operator used in inverse resolution. In the future, we hope to use these operators to solve the model inference problem by generalization.

Acknowledgements. We thank Cor Bioch for the suggestions that lead to the subject of this article. We thank Leon van der Torre and Arie de Bruin for the discussions and support. Also, we thank Mark Vermeer for reading and commenting this article.

References

1. M. Kirschenbaum and L.S. Sterling. Refinement strategies for inductive learning of simple prolog programs. In *Proceedings of IJCAI-91*, Sydney, Australia, 1991. Morgan Kaufmann.
2. P.D. Laird. *Learning from Good and Bad Data*. Kluwer Academic Publishers, 1988.
3. X. Ling. Inductive learning from good examples. In *Proceedings of IJCAI-91*, Sydney, Australia, 1991. Morgan Kaufmann.
4. S.H. Muggleton. Inductive logic programming. In *First Conference on Algorithmic Learning Theory*, Ohmsha, Tokyo, 1990. Invited paper.
5. S.H. Muggleton and W. Buntine. Machine invention of first-order predicates by inverting resolution. In *Proceedings of the Fifth International Conference on Machine Learning*, pages 339-352. Kaufmann, 1988.
6. T. Nibblet. A study of generalisation in logic programs. In *Proceedings of EWSL-88*, London, 1988. Pittman.
7. W.E. Nijenhuis and C. Witteveen. Constructive identification with Poole's default logic. Technical Report 90-96, Faculty of Technical Mathematics and Informatics, TU-Delft, 1990.
8. G.D. Plotkin. A Note on Inductive Generalization. In *Machine Intelligence 5*, pages 153-163. Edinburgh University Press, Edinburgh, 1970.
9. J.C. Reynolds. Transformational Systems and the Algebraic Structure of Atomic Formulas. In B. Meltzer and D. Mitchie, editor, *Machine Intelligence 5*, pages 135-153. Edinburgh University Press, Edinburgh, 1970.
10. E.Y. Shapiro. Inductive Inference of Theories from Facts. Technical Report 624, Department of Computer Science, Yale University, New Haven. CT., 1981.
11. E.Y. Shapiro. *Algorithmic program debugging*. MIT Press, 1983.
12. P.R.J. Van der Laag. A Most General Refinement Operator for Reduced Sentences. Technical Report EUR-CS-92-03, Erasmus University Rotterdam, Dept. of Computer Science, June 1992.

Some Lower Bounds for the Computational Complexity of Inductive Logic Programming

Jörg-Uwe Kietz

German National Research Center for Computer Science, I3-KI,
P.O.Box 1316, D-5205 St.Augustin, Germany

Abstract. The field of Inductive Logic Programming (ILP), which is concerned with the induction of Hornclauses from examples and background knowledge, has received increased attention over the last time. Recently, some positive results concerning the learnability of restricted logic programs have been published. In this paper we review these restrictions and prove some lower-bounds of the computational complexity of learning. In particular, we show that a learning algorithm for $i2$-determinate Hornclauses (with variable i) could be used to decide the PSPACE-complete problem of Finite State Automata Intersection, and that a learning algorithm for 12-nondeterminate Hornclauses could be used to decide the NP-complete problem of Boolean Clause Satisfiability (SAT). This also shows, that these Hornclauses are not PAC-learnable, unless RP = NP = PSPACE.
Keywords: Inductive Logic Programming, PAC-Learning.

1 Introduction

Most success within the field of Machine Learning has been achieved with systems learning in a propositional logic. Also the theory of learnability, e.g. PAC-learnability, was mostly concerned with propositional logic. But, despite their successes, propositional learning approaches suffer from the limited expressiveness of their hypothesis languages and the lack of background knowledge. Therefore, the field of Inductive Logic Programming (ILP), which is concerned with the induction of first-order Hornclauses from examples and background knowledge, has received increased attention recently [13, 2, 6, 7, 8, 9, 12, 14]. The problem tackled by these approaches can be described formally as follows.

Definition 1 Learning Problem.
Given:

- background knowledge B in a language LB
- positive and negative examples $E = E^+ \cup E^-$ in a language LE consistent with B ($B, E \not\models \Box$) and not a consequence of B ($B \not\models E$).
- a hypothesis language LH.

Find a hypothesis $h \in LH$ such that:

(I) $(B, h, E \not\models \Box)$, h is consistent with B and E.

(II) $(B, h \models E^+)$, h and B explain E^+.

(III) $(B, h \not\models E^-)$, h and B do not explain E^-.

The triple (LB, LE, LH) is called the *learning problem*. Deciding whether there exists such an $h \in LH$, is called the *consistency problem*. An algorithm which accepts any $B \in LB$ and $E \in LE$ as input and computes such an $h \in LH$ if it exists, or "no" if it does not exist is called a *learning algorithm* for (LB, LE, LH). If LB, LE and LH are subsets of first-order clauses, (LB, LE, LH) is called the ILP-problem and a learning algorithm for (LB, LE, LH) is called an ILP-algorithm.

As the ILP problem has been proven to be undecidable in the general case, where LE, LB and LH are first-order clauses [10], current research focuses on the identification of effective subclasses of first-order logic that are efficiently learnable. Recently, some positive results on the PAC-learnability of so called constrained Hornclauses [9] and a superset of them called ij-determinate Hornclauses (with fixed i and j) [3] have been obtained.

In this paper, we show that these hypothesis languages cannot be further extended without the loss of the PAC-learnability property. To prove non-PAC-learnability, we will use an adaptation of a theorem of Pitt and Valiant, also proven as theorem 6.2.1 in [1].

Corollary 2. *If a learning problem (LB, LE, LH) is PAC-learnable, then the consistency problem for (LB, LE, LH) is in RP, or turning it the other way around, if the consistency problem is not in RP, then (LB, LE, LH) is not PAC-learnable.*

In the following we will prove that the ILP problem for determinate Hornclauses is PSPACE-hard, and therefore $i2$-determinate Hornclauses are not PAC-learnable in general (where i is variable), unless RP = PSPACE. We will also show that the consistency problem for 12-nondeterminate Hornclauses is NP-hard, and therefore 12-nondeterminate Hornclauses are not PAC-learnable, unless RP = NP. But, first let us review the proposed restrictions of the ILP problem more formally.

2 Common Restrictions of the ILP Problem

The background knowledge used in ILP programs must always be restricted, otherwise the ILP problem inherits the undecidability of the deduction process. A common restriction in ILP programs (e.g.[7, 12]) is the restriction to ground background knowledge and ground unit clauses as examples.

Definition 3 Ground background knowledge. The backgound knowledge B is ground if it consists of ground unit clauses only. A clause is ground if it does not contain any variables.

One way to avoid such a restriction is the use of generative Hornclauses and a depth-bounded inference process to generate such finite ground background knowledge prior to learning (e.g. [6],[7]).

Definition 4 Generative Hornclause. A Hornclause is generative if every variable in the head also occurs in the body of the clause.

Another common restriction applied not only to B, but also to LH is the restriction to function-free clauses (e.g. [6, 12]).

Definition 5 Function-free clause. A clause is called function-free if all its arguments are either variables, or constants (function symbols of arity 0).

The restriction to function-free ground unit clauses as examples and function-free ground background knowledge enables us to use $\theta - subsumption$ as a complete inference procedure in the following way: The learning problem (ground B, ground unit E, LH) as defined in definition 1, is equivalent to the learning problem ($\{\}, E_{new}, LH$), where E_{new} is defined as $E_{new}^+ := \{e \leftarrow B \mid e \in E^+\}$, and $E_{new}^- := \{e \leftarrow B \mid e \in E^-\}$. Clearly, the examples are now ground Hornclauses. Between function-free Hornclauses θ-subsumption is a correct and complete inference procedure ($h \models h'$, iff $h\theta \subseteq h'$). This means the theorems 10 and 16 which use ground function-free Hornclauses as examples and θ-subsumption as inference relation also hold for ground unit clause examples and ground background knowledge together with implication as inference.

Function-free knowledge has another positive effect on deduction. It has been proven that inferring ground background knowledge can be done completely in time polynomial to the size of B if B consists only of function-free generative Hornclauses ([15]) and there is a fixed maximum arity of predicates in the background knowledge.

Definition 6 Bounded-arity background knowledge.
The language for background knowledge LB is of bounded arity if there exist an integer j, which is greater than the maximum arity of any of the predicates in B.

This bounded-arity restriction is also used by Page and Frisch [9] to prove the PAC-learnability of a special kind of hypothesis language LH called *constrained clauses*.

Definition 7 Constrained clause. A clause is constrained if all variables in the body also occur in the head.

Muggleton and Feng [7], have proposed a restriction of LH to ij-determinate Hornclauses.

Definition 8 Determinate Clauses and determinate depth of terms.
A Hornclause h is determinate with respect to the examples E and the background knowledge B if every term t in h is linked by a determinate linking-chain. A term occurring in the head is linked by a determinate linking-chain of

length 0. Let $h = \{A, \neg B_1, \ldots, \neg B_m, \neg B_{m+1}, \ldots, \neg B_n\}$ be ordered. The term t found in $\neg B_{m+1}$ is linked by a determinate linking-chain of length $d + 1$, if and only if all terms in $\{A, \neg B_1, \ldots, \neg B_m\}$ are linked by a determinate linking-chain of length at most d and for every substitution θ such that $A\theta \in E^+$ and $\{\{B_1\}, \ldots, \{B_m\}\}\theta \subseteq B$ there is a unique substitution δ whose domain is the variables in t such that $\{B_{m+1}\}\theta\delta \in B$. The determinate depth of a term is the minimum length of its determinate linking chains.

A clause with maximum determinate depth of terms i, and maximum arity of literals j, is called ij-determinate.

Muggleton and Feng have used this ij-determinate restriction to prove that the ILP-problem (ground background knowledge, ground unit clause examples, one ij-determinate Hornclause) is solvable in polynomial time [7].

Recently, it has been proven [3] that a k-disjunction of function-free non-recursive ij-determinate Hornclauses is PAC-learnable under simple distributions. This was proven by showing that this ILP-learning problem can be reduced to an equivalent only polynomially larger propositional learning problem, i.e., learning function-free ij-determinate Hornclauses from ground background knowledge and ground examples is no more powerful than learning in propositional logic. The remaining advantage is that this kind of representation is more compact and therefore potentially more user-friendly in the preparation of the input.

So far, there is no answer to the question wether the restriction to ij-determinate Hornclauses can be relaxed without the loss of polynomial computability of the ILP-problem. This paper gives a negative answer to this question by proving that the consistency problem for non depth-bounded determinate Hornclauses is PSPACE-hard and that the consistency problem for depth bounded non-determinate Hornclauses is NP-hard.

Definition 9 Linked Hornclause and depth of terms.
A Hornclause is linked if all its literals are linked. A literal is linked if at least one of its terms is linked. A term is linked with linking-chain of length 0 if it occurs in the head of the clause. A term in a literal is linked with a linking-chain of length $d + 1$, if another term in the same literal is linked with a linking-chain of length d. The depth of a term is the minimum length of its linking-chains.

A not determinate clause with maximum depth of terms i, and maximum arity of literals j, is called ij-nondeterminate.

Clearly, terms in nondeterminate clauses need not have a determinate linking-chain. If a term has a *determinate linking-chain*, this is also a (nondeterminate) *linking-chain*, but not vice versa. Therefore, the *determinate depth* of a term is always greater than or equal to the (nondeterminate) *depth* of a term.

3 Non-Learnability of Determinate Hornclauses

Theorem 10. *The consistency-problem for non depth bounded 2-determinate Hornclauses is PSPACE-Hard.*

We will prove this theorem, by reducing the following PSPACE-complete problem [4] to the consistency-problem (cf. Def. 1).

Definition 11 Finite State Automata Intersection. Given an alphabet Σ and a sequence $A_1 \ldots, A_n$ of deterministic finite state automata with input alphabet Σ, does there exist a word $w \in \Sigma^*$ accepted by each of the A_i, $1 \leq i \leq n$?

First let us recall some basics of deterministic finite state automata (DFA). A DFA A is formally described as a 5-tuple $(Q, \Sigma, \delta, s, F)$, where Q is the set of states, Σ is the input alphabet, $s \in Q$ is the initial state, $F \subseteq Q$ is the set of final states, and δ is the transition function mapping $Q \times \Sigma$ to Q. The transition function δ is extended to words on Σ^* as follows: $\hat{\delta}(q, \epsilon) = q$, $\hat{\delta}(q, wa) = \delta(\hat{\delta}(q, w), a)$ where ϵ is the empty word, $a \in \Sigma$, $w \in \Sigma^*$. A DFA is said to accept a word $x \in \Sigma^*$, iff $\hat{\delta}(s, x) \in F$.

Now, we are able to give a useful encoding of DFAs and words as 2-determinate Hornclauses.

Definition 12 Encoding of DFA's and words as Hornclauses. Let Γ be a function from $\Sigma^* \cup (Q, \Sigma, \delta, s, F)$ to Hornclauses defined as follows:
$$\Gamma_{word}(x_1 x_2 \ldots x_n) = h(Q_0) \leftarrow x_1(Q_0, Q_1), x_2(Q_1, Q_2), \ldots, x_n(Q_{n-1}, Q_n), f(Q_n)$$
$$\Gamma_{DFA}(A) = \{h(s)\} \cup \{\neg x(q, p) | x \in \Sigma, p, q \in Q, \delta(q, x) = p\} \cup \{\neg f(q) | q \in F\}$$

As is easily seen, DFAs are encoded as ground 2-determinate Hornclauses, i.e. they are suitable as examples. Words are encoded as non-ground 2-determinate Hornclauses, i.e. they are suitable as hypotheses. The usefulness of this encoding is shown by the following lemma.

Lemma 13. *A word is recognized by a DFA if and only if the encoding of the word θ-subsumes the encoding of the DFA.*

Proof. $\hat{\delta}(s, x) \in F \Rightarrow \Gamma(x) \leq_\theta \Gamma(A)$
Let $x = x_1 \ldots x_m$, then there exist a sequence of states (the computation of A on x) $q_0, \ldots, q_m$, such that $q_0 = s, q_m \in F$, and $\delta(q_{i-1}, x_i) = q_i$. Let θ be $\{Q_i/q_i\}$, for $0 \leq i \leq m$, from the definition of Γ it follows that $\Gamma(x)\theta \subseteq \Gamma(A)$.
$\Gamma(x) \leq_\theta \Gamma(A) \Rightarrow \hat{\delta}(s, x) \in F$
Let θ be $\{Q_i/q_i\}$, for $0 \leq i \leq m$, from the definition of Γ it follows that $q_0 = s, q_m \in F$, and $\delta(q_{i-1}, x_i) = q_i$, i.e. the sequence $q_0 \ldots, q_m$ is an accepting computation of x by A. □

Now we are able to prove that Γ is indeed an encoding of the DFA intersection problem in terms of the learning problem of determinate Hornclauses.

Lemma 14. *Let $A_1 \ldots, A_n$ be a sequence of deterministic finite state automata. There exists a nonempty word $x \in \Sigma^*$ accepted by each of the $A_1 \ldots, A_n$ if and only if there exists a linked determinate Hornclause consistent with the following set of positive and negative examples: $E^+ = \{\Gamma(A_i) | 1 \leq i \leq n\}$*
$E^- = \{h(s) \leftarrow f(s), x_1(s, q), \ldots, x_m(s, q), x_1(q, q), \ldots, x_m(q, q),$
$h(s) \leftarrow x_1(s, s), \ldots, x_m(s, s)\}, where \Sigma = \{x_1, \ldots, x_m\}$

Proof. "the if direction"

Let h be a linked determinate Hornclause consistent with the examples. As h is a generalization of all positive examples each of its literals are either of the form $h(X)$, $\neg f(X)$, or $\neg x(S1, S2)$, where $x \in \Sigma$. As h is a Hornclause $h(Q_0)$ is in h. As h is consistent with the second negative example it contains a literal $f(Q_n)$, and as h is consistent with the first negative example, the variable $f(Q_n)$ is only unifiable with the head variable Q_0 if this unification also unifies a second argument of an $\neg x(S1, S2)$ literal with the head variable. As h is linked the literal $f(Q_n)$ must be linked by a chain of $\neg x(S1, S2)$ literals. The Hornclause C_w consisting only of the head literal $h(Q_0)$, the final literal $f(Q_n)$, and the linking chain of $\neg x(S1, S2)$ literals is a generalization of h and therefore a generalization of all the positive examples. Using the argument above it is not a generalization of the negative examples. C_w is by construction the Γ encoding of a word. By Lemma 13 this word is accepted by each of the automata $A_1 \ldots, A_n$.

"the only if direction"

Let x be the non empty word accepted by all the $A_1, \ldots, A_n$. By Lemma 13 $\Gamma(x)$ is a generalization of E^+. $\Gamma(x)$ is not a generalization of the first negative example, as x is not empty. $\Gamma(x)$ is not a generalization of the second negative example as it contains a literal $\neg f(Q)$. Therefore $\Gamma(x)$ is a consistent generalization of the examples. Clearly, $\Gamma(x)$ is linked and determinate. $\qquad \square$

Corollary 15 Non PAC-learnability of determinate Hornclauses. *Using Corollary 2 and Theorem 10 we can conclude that determinate linked Hornclauses are not PAC-learnable, as long as the widely assumed $RP \neq PSPACE$ conjecture is true.*

4 Non Learnability of nondeterminate Hornclauses

Theorem 16. *Consistency of 12-nondeterminate Hornclauses is NP-hard.*

We will prove this theorem, by reducing the well known NP-complete SAT problem [4] to the consistency-problem as stated above. The reduction is inspired by a similar proof of Haussler [5] for *existentially quantified conjunctive expressions.*

Definition 17 SAT. Given a set $V = \{v_1, \ldots, v_n\}$ of Boolean variables and a set of clauses $C = \{C_1, \ldots, C_m\}$ over V, the question is whether there exists a truth assignment of V that satisfies the clauses in C.

Now, let us prove that a SAT instance is satisfiable iff a special learning problem is solvable. The idea is to construct positive examples, such that every generalisation consists of truth assignements to Boolean variables of the SAT problem and to construct the negative examples so that only hypotheses whose truth assignments satisfy the SAT problem are consistent with them.

Lemma 18. *The SAT instance (V, C) is satisfiable if and only if there exists a Hornclause consistent with $E = E^+ \cup E^-$ defined as follows:*

Define a set of $2n$ 1-place predicates $a_1 \ldots, a_{2n}$, each of which are mapped via Ψ to one of the $2n$ literals $v_1, \ldots, v_n, \bar{v}_1, \ldots, \bar{v}_n$. The positive examples are then coded as following: $E^+ = \{p(X) \leftarrow$
$p(X, X_1), a_1(X_1), \ldots, a_{i-1}(X_1), a_{i+1}(X_1), \ldots, a_{2n}(X_1),$
$p(X, X_2), a_1(X_2), \ldots, a_{n+i-1}(X_2), a_{n+i+1}(X_2), \ldots, a_{2n}(X_2)\ \}$, *for all* $i : 1 \leq i \leq n$
The negative example is coded as follows. $E^- = \{\{p(X)\} \cup \{\neg p(X, X_j), \neg a_i(X_j)\ |$
$\Psi(a_i) \notin C_j, 1 \leq i \leq 2n, 1 \leq j \leq m\}\}$

Proof. "the if direction"
Let h be a Hornclause that is consistent with the positive and negative examples. As h is a generalization of all positive examples, it is of the form

$$p(X) \leftarrow p(X, Y_k), a_1(Y_k), \ldots, a_{2n}(Y_k), k : 1 \leq k \leq 2^n$$

and for all $i : 1 \leq i \leq n$, at most one of $a_i(Y_k)$ or $a_{n+i}(Y_k)$ is in h. As h does not θ-subsume the negative example, there exists at least one k such that

$$h' = p(X) \leftarrow p(X, Y_k), a_1(Y_k), \ldots, a_{2n}(Y_k) h' \subseteq h$$

and there is no substitution $\theta = X/X, Y_k/X_j$ such that

$$h'\theta \subseteq \{\{p(X)\} \cup \{\neg p(X, X_j), \neg a_i(X_j)\ |\ \Psi(a_i) \notin C_j, 1 \leq i \leq 2n\}\}$$

This means for every $C_j \in C$, h' contains at least one literal $a_i(Y_k)$, such that $\Psi(a_i) \in C_j$. This means $\{\Psi(a_i)\ |\ a_i(Y_k) \in h'\}$ is a partial truth assignment for V that satisfies all clauses in C.
"the only if direction"
Assume, that (V, C) is satisfiable. Let L be the set of literals true in an assignment that satisfies (V, C) such that either v_i or $\neg v_i$ is in L, but not both. Let h be a Horn clause defined by

$$h = \{\{p(X)\} \cup \{\neg p(X, Y), \neg a_i(Y)\ |\ \Psi(a_i) \in L, 1 \leq i \leq 2n\}\}$$

h θ-subsumes all positive examples, as for every $i : 1 \leq i \leq n$ it contains either $a_i(X_1)$ or $a_{n+i}(X_1)$, but not both. We now prove by contradiction that h does not θ-subsume the negative example. If h θ-subsumes the negative example, there is an $\theta = \{X/X, Y/X_j\}$, such that

$$h\theta \subseteq \{\{p(X)\} \cup \{\neg p(X, X_j), \neg a_i(X_j)\ |\ \Psi(a_i) \notin C_j, 1 \leq i \leq 2n\}\}$$

But, this means that h contains only a_i, such that $\Psi(a_i)$ is not in C_j, which contradicts the assumption that L satisfies all clauses of C. $\square$

Corollary 19. *Using Corollary 2 and Theorem 16 we can conclude that 12-nondeterminate linked Hornclauses are not PAC-learnable, as long as the widely assumed $RP \neq NP$ conjecture is true.*

5 Conclusion

In this paper, we have proven some lower bounds of the computational complexity of learning within the ILP framework. These results show that large classes of Hornclauses cannot be learned by a complete and efficient learning algorithm. This includes e.g. CLINT's [2] languages greater equal L2, and the hypothesis space searched by the inverse resolution approaches e.g. [8, 14]. It also shows that fast heuristic search algorithms like FOIL [11] are necessarily incomplete, i.e they may not find a correct definition, even if one exists. Theorem 10 also shows that the extension of FOIL2 [12], which adds determinate literals if no good information gain can be achieved by a literal, could lead to an explosion of the size of the hypothesis exponential in the number of times this happens.

Acknowledgements: I would like to thank Katharina Morik and Bernhard Nebel for the discussions and suggestions they have provided to this work. I would also like to thank the DFKI for the research visit, they have supported. This work is partially supported by the European Community ESPRIT program under contract number P6020 "Inductive Logic Programming".

References

1. M. Anthony and N.Biggs. *Computational Learning Theory*. Cambridge University Press, 1992.
2. L. de Raedt and M. Bruynooghe. An overview of the interactive concept-learner and theory revisor clint. In S. Muggleton, editor, *Inductive Logic Programming*. Academic Press, 1992.
3. S. Džeroski, S. Muggleton, and S. Russell. Pac-learnability of determinate logic programs. In *Proc. of the 5th ACM Workshop on Computaional Learning Theory (COLT)*, 1992.
4. Michael R. Garey and David S. Johnson. *Computers and Intractability - A Guide to the Theory of NP-Completeness*. Freeman, San Francisco, Cal., 1979.
5. David Haussler. Learning conjunctive concepts in structural domains. *Machine Learning*, 4(1):7–40, 1989.
6. Jörg-Uwe Kietz and Stefan Wrobel. Controlling the complexity of learning through syntactic and task-oriented models. In S. Muggleton, editor, *Inductive Logic Programming*, pages 107–126. Academic Press, 1992.
7. Stephan Muggleton and Cao Feng. Efficient induction of logic programs. In S. Muggleton, editor, *Inductive Logic Programming*. Academic Press, 1992.
8. Stephen Muggleton and Wray Buntine. Machine invention of first-order predicates by inverting resolution. In *Proc. Fifth Intern. Conf. on Machine Learning*, Los Altos, CA, 1988. Morgan Kaufman.
9. C. D. Page and A. M. Frisch. Generalisation and learnability: a study in constained atoms. In S. Muggleton, editor, *Inductive Logic Programming*. Academic Press, 1992.
10. Gordon D. Plotkin. A further note on inductive generalization. In B. Meltzer and D. Michie, editors, *Machine Intelligence*, volume 6, chapter 8, pages 101–124. American Elsevier, 1971.

11. J. R. Quinlan. Learning logical definitions from relations. *Machine Learning*, 5(3):239 – 266, 1990.
12. J. R. Quinlan. Determinate literals in inductive logic programming. In *Proc. of the 12th IJCAI*, 1991.
13. Celine Rouveirol. Completness for inductive procedures. In *Proc. Eigth Intern. Workshop on Machine Learning*, pages 452–456, 1991.
14. Celine Rouveirol. Semantic model for induction of first order theories. In *Proc. 12th International Joint Conference on Artificial Intelligence*, 1991.
15. Stefan Wrobel. Higher-order concepts in a tractable knowledge representation. In K. Morik, editor, *GWAI-87 11th German Workshop on Artificial Intelligence*, Informatik-Fachberichte Nr. 152, pages 129 – 138, Berlin, New York, Tokyo, October 1987. Springer.

Improving Example-Guided Unfolding

Henrik Boström

Dept. of Computer and Systems Sciences
Stockholm University
Electrum 230, 164 40 Kista, SWEDEN
henke@dsv.su.se

Abstract. It has been observed that the addition of clauses learned by explanation-based generalization may degrade, rather than improve, the efficiency of a logic program. There are three reasons for the degradation: i) increased unification cost ii) increased inter-clause repetition of goal calls iii) increased redundancy. There have been several approaches to solve (or reduce) these problems. However, previous techniques that solve the redundancy problem do in fact increase the two first problems. Hence, the benefit of avoiding redundancy might be outweighed by the cost associated with these techniques. A solution to this problem is presented: the algorithm EGU II, which is a reformulation of one of the previous techniques (Example-Guided Unfolding). The algorithm is based upon the application of program transformation rules (definition, unfolding and folding) and is shown to preserve the equivalence of the domain theory. Experimental results are presented showing that the cost of avoiding redundancy is significantly reduced by EGU II, and that even when the redundancy problem is not present, the technique can be superior to adding clauses redundantly.

1 Introduction

The benefits of adding clauses learned by explanation-based generalization (EBG) [13, 9] to a logic program come from reordering effects and decreased path costs when the clauses are successfully applied (cf. [12]). However, it has been observed that the addition of learned clauses may degrade the efficiency of a program. There are three reasons for the degradation. First, the total time spent on unifying a particular goal with heads of clauses may increase when the number of clauses defining a predicate increases (the problem of increased unification cost). Second, the same goals are called repeatedly in different clauses to a greater extent after learning than before (the problem of increased inter-clause repetition of goal calls). Third, for some goal calls, the number of ways to succeed increases when learned clauses are added redundantly, and hence the number of times subsequent goals may be called increases (the redundancy problem). There have been a number of approaches to solve (or reduce) the three problems. These include techniques for reducing the number of goals called in different clauses [11, 20, 15], indexing of learned clauses [17] and techniques that avoid redundancy [1, 3]. However, none of the previous approaches addresses all three problems, and notably, the methods that avoid redundancy do in fact increase the two first problems.

In this work, we present EGU II, a reformulation of one of the algorithms that avoid redundancy, EGU (Example-Guided Unfolding) [1]. The new algorithm shows that redundancy can be avoided without increasing the two first problems. Moreover, the algorithm EGU II has been combined with a technique for organizing learned clauses efficiently [2], and this combination is the first approach to address all three problems.

In the next section, we give definitions of the three program transformation rules (definition, unfolding and folding) upon which the algorithm EGU II is based. In section three, we present the algorithm and show that it preserves the equivalence of the domain theory. In section four, we present experimental results from comparing the algorithm to both EGU and adding clauses redundantly. Finally, in section five we give concluding remarks and point out some future research directions.

2 Preliminaries

In the following we assume the reader to be familiar with the standard terminology in logic programming [10]. The following rules for transformation of a definite program (below referred to as P) are taken from [19], where formal definitions can be found as well as proofs of their equivalence preserving properties.

Rule 1. Definition
Add to P a clause C of the form $p(x_1, \ldots, x_n) \leftarrow A_1, \ldots, A_m$ where p is a predicate symbol not appearing in P, $x_1, \ldots, x_n$ are distinct variables and $A_1, \ldots, A_m$ are literals whose predicate symbols all appear in P.

Rule 2. Unfolding
Let C be a clause in P, A a goal in its body and $C_1, \ldots, C_n$ be all clauses in P whose heads are unifiable with A. Let $C_i'(1 \leq i \leq n)$ be the result of resolving C with C_i upon A. Then replace C with $C_1', \ldots, C_n'$.

Rule 3. Folding
Let C be a clause in P of the form $A \leftarrow A_1, \ldots, A_{i+1}, \ldots, A_{i+m}, \ldots, A_n$ and C_1 be a clause that previously have been introduced by the rule of definition of the form $B \leftarrow B_1, \ldots, B_m$. If there is a substitution θ such that $A_{i+1}, \ldots, A_{i+m} = B_1, \ldots, B_m \theta$ where θ substitutes distinct variables for the internal variables of C_1 and moreover those variables do not occur in $A, A_1, \ldots, A_i$ or $A_{i+m+1}, \ldots, A_n$, then replace C by the clause $A \leftarrow A_1, \ldots, A_i, B\theta, A_{i+m+1}, \ldots, A_n$.

3 Example-Guided Unfolding Revisited

In this section, we first review how the algorithm EGU works using an example. We point out in what way the problems of increased unification cost and increased inter-clause repetition of goal calls become more significant when using EGU compared to adding learned clauses redundantly to the program. We then present a solution to this problem: the algorithm EGU II. The algorithm is illustrated using the same example and is shown to preserve the equivalence of the domain theory.

3.1 The Algorithm EGU

The algorithm EGU is a reformulation of PROLOG-EBG [9] in terms of definition, unfolding and folding [1]. In contrast to the previous formulation, a learned clause is not supposed to be added redundantly but is derived while the domain theory is transformed.

Example [1] Let the domain theory be the simple english grammar shown in Figure 1 and the target concept be :-s(X,Y). Let the training example be represented by the training instance :-s([sue,loves,a,man],[]) and the training clauses: {(F1) nm([sue|X],X), (F2) tv([loves|X],X), (F3) d([a|X],X), (F4) n([man|X],X)}. Then there is a SLD-refutation of the training instance, given the domain theory and training clauses, for which the sequence of input clauses is $R1, R3, F1, R5, F2, R2, F3, F4$. Let the operationality criterion be defined by the following predicate symbols $\{d, n, nm, iv, tv\}$. Removing clauses defining operational predicates from the sequence results in $R1, R3, R5, R2$. This sequence is used by EGU to guide unfolding. It is done in the following way.[2]

The first clause in the sequence ($R1$) is selected and the first non-operational goal in its body is unfolded. Then $R1$ is replaced with the following clauses:
(R6) s(X,Z):- d(X,Y),n(Y,Y2),vp(Y2,Z).
(R7) s(X,Z):- nm(X,Y),vp(Y,Z).

The resolvent $R7$ of the selected clause $R1$ and the next clause in the sequence $R3$ is then selected. The first non-operational goal in $R7$ is unfolded, giving two clauses:
(R8) s(X,Z):- nm(X,Y),iv(Y,Z).
(R9) s(X,Z):- nm(X,Y),tv(Y,Y2),np(Y2,Z).

The resolvent $R9$ of the selected clause $R7$ and the next clause in the sequence $R5$ is then selected. The first non-operational goal in $R9$ is unfolded, giving two clauses:

---

[1] The standard Edinburgh syntax for logic programs is used [4].

[2] This example is somewhat simplified. In EGU the rules of definition and folding are used in addition to unfolding to overcome a problem associated with recursive domain theories. However, in non-recursive domain theories the application of these rules in the algorithm is superfluos.

```
(R10)  s(X,Z):- nm(X,Y),tv(Y,Y2),d(Y2,Y3),n(Y3,Z).
(R11)  s(X,Z):- nm(X,Y),tv(Y,Y2),nm(Y2,Z).
```

The resolvent R10 of the selected clause R9 and the last clause in the sequence R2 is then finally selected. This clause is placed first in the program. The resulting domain theory is shown in Figure 2.

It can be observed that the problems of increased unification cost and interclause repetition of goal calls have become more significant in comparison to adding the learned clause (R10) redundantly to the original domain theory. Instead of two clauses defining the target concept, there are four in the transformed domain theory. Moreover, the goal nm(X,Y) may in the worst case be called three times in the transformed theory (not including repetition within a clause), and only two times when adding the clause redundantly.

```
(R1)  s(X,Z):- np(X,Y),vp(Y,Z).
(R2)  np(X,Z):- d(X,Y),n(Y,Z).
(R3)  np(X,Y):- nm(X,Y).
(R4)  vp(X,Y):- iv(X,Y).
(R5)  vp(X,Z):- tv(X,Y),np(Y,Z).
```

Fig. 1. Original domain theory.

```
(R10)  s(X,Z):- nm(X,Y),tv(Y,Y2),d(Y2,Y3),n(Y3,Z).
(R6)   s(X,Z):- d(X,Y),n(Y,Y2),vp(Y2,Z).
(R8)   s(X,Z):- nm(X,Y),iv(Y,Z).
(R11)  s(X,Z):- nm(X,Y),tv(Y,Y2),nm(Y2,Z).
(R2)   np(X,Z):- d(X,Y),n(Y,Z).
(R3)   np(X,Y):- nm(X,Y).
(R4)   vp(X,Y):- iv(X,Y).
(R5)   vp(X,Z):- tv(X,Y),np(Y,Z).
```

Fig. 2. Domain theory after applying EGU.

3.2 The Algorithm EGU II

We first informally describe the algorithm EGU II, and illustrate it using the grammar example. Then we formally describe the algorithm, and show that the algorithm produces a program that is equivalent to the original domain theory.

Informal description of EGU II The problem of increased unification cost when using EGU is due to the unfolding of a goal that unifies with the head of more than one clause, since the clause in which the goal appears is replaced with more than one clause. Moreover, all goals that precede the goal in the original clause are repeated in the clauses that replace the original one, thus increasing the inter-clause repetition of goal calls. Note that this is a potential problem for all techniques that are based on unfolding (e.g. partial evaluation [16] and lazy partial evaluation [3]). This problem is solved by EGU II in the following way.

Instead of unfolding the first non-operational goal in a selected clause, which is done in EGU, a new predicate is defined, that is equivalent to the conjunction consisting of the first non-operational goal and the subsequent goals in the selected clause (definition). The first goal in the clause defining the new predicate is then unfolded, yielding a new set of clauses. The input sequence is then used to select one of these clauses, that is processed in the same way as the first clause. This process continues until one clause is finally selected after having iterated through the input sequence.

The body of each previously selected clause (except the last one) is then folded using the new definitions.

The finally selected clause is then resolved with the only clause calling a goal that unifies with the head of the selected clause. The selected clause is removed and the resolvent is then treated in the same way as the first clause. This process is iterated until the final resolvent is selected, which is then placed first in the program.

Finally, goals that unify with one clause only are unfolded (since this is guaranteed to improve efficiency).

Example revisited Let the domain theory, operationality criterion and the input sequence $(R1, R3, R5, R2)$ from the previous example be the input to EGU II.

The first clause in the sequence $(R1)$ is selected, and the first non-operational goal in its body is np(X,Y). A new predicate $(p1)$ is defined by the clause:
(R6) p1(X,Z):- np(X,Y),vp(Y,Z).

Unfolding upon the first goal in R6, gives two new clauses:
(R7) p1(X,Z):- d(X,Y2),n(Y2,Y),vp(Y,Z).
(R8) p1(X,Z):- nm(X,Y),vp(Y,Z).

Then R8 is selected since it is the resolvent of R6 and the next clause in the sequence $(R3)$. The first non-operational goal in R8 is vp(Y,Z) and a new

predicate ($p2$) is defined by the clause:
```
(R9)  p2(Y,Z):- vp(Y,Z).
```
Unfolding upon the first goal in $R9$, gives two new clauses:
```
(R10) p2(Y,Z):- iv(Y,Z).
(R11) p2(Y,Z):- tv(Y,Y2),np(Y2,Z).
```
Then $R11$ is selected since it is the resolvent of $R9$ and the next clause in the sequence ($R5$). The first non-operational goal in $R11$ is np(Y2,Z) and a new predicate ($p3$) is defined by the clause:
```
(R12) p3(Y2,Z):- np(Y2,Z).
```
Unfolding upon the first goal in $R12$, gives two new clauses:
```
(R13) p3(Y2,Z):- d(Y2,Y3),n(Y3,Z).
(R14) p3(Y2,Z):- nm(Y2,Z).
```
Then $R13$ is the finally selected clause since it is the resolvent of $R12$ and the last clause in the sequence ($R2$). In the second step of the algorithm, the body of $R1$ is folded using $R6$, the body of $R8$ is folded using $R9$, and the body of $R11$ is folded using $R12$. The transformed domain theory is shown in Figure 3.

```
(R1')  s(X,Z):- p1(X,Z).
(R2)   np(X,Z):- d(X,Y),n(Y,Z).
(R3)   np(X,Y):- nm(X,Y).
(R4)   vp(X,Y):- iv(X,Y).
(R5)   vp(X,Z):- tv(X,Y),np(Y,Z).
(R7)   p1(X,Z):- d(X,Y2),n(Y2,Y),vp(Y,Z).
(R8')  p1(X,Z):- nm(X,Y),p2(Y,Z).
(R10)  P2(Y,Z):- iv(Y,Z).
(R11') p2(Y,Z):- tv(Y,Y2),p3(Y2,Z).
(R13)  p3(Y2,Z):- d(Y2,Y3),n(Y3,Z).
(R14)  p3(Y2,Z):- nm(Y2,Z).
```

Fig. 3. Domain theory after the two first steps in EGU II.

In the third step of the algorithm, the selected clause ($R13$) is used to resolve upon the only goal that unifies with the head of the clause. By resolving upon the goal p3(Y2,Z) in $R11'$, the following clause is obtained:
```
(R15) p2(Y,Z):- tv(Y,Y2),d(Y2,Y3),n(Y3,Z).
```
The clause $R13$ is now redundant and is removed. The clause $R15$ is then used to resolve upon the goal p2(Y,Z) in $R8'$, resulting in the clause:
```
(R16) p1(X,Z):- nm(X, Y),tv(Y,Y2),d(Y2,Y3),n(Y3,Z).
```
The clause $R15$ is then removed. The clause $R16$ is then, before being removed, used to resolve upon the only goal that unifies with the head, and that is the goal in $R1'$, resulting in the finally selected clause, which is placed first in the program:
```
(R17) s(X,Z):- nm(X,Y),tv(Y,Y2),d(Y2,Y3),n(Y3,Z).
```
In the fourth step of the algorithm, all goals that can be reduced by one

clause only are unfolded. The final domain theory (after removing dead code cf. [6]) is shown in Figure 4. It can be observed that the problem of increased unification cost and increased inter-clause repetition of goal calls are not more significant in comparison to adding the clause $R17$ redundantly.

```
(R17)   s(X,Z):- nm(X,Y),tv(Y,Y2),d(Y2,Y3),n(Y3,Z).
(R1')   s(X,Z):- p1(X,Z).
(R2)    np(X,Z):- d(X,Y),n(Y,Z).
(R3)    np(X,Y):- nm(X,Y).
(R4)    vp(X,Y):- iv(X,Y).
(R5)    vp(X,Z):- tv(X,Y),np(Y,Z).
(R7)    p1(X,Z):- d(X,Y2),n(Y2,Y),vp(Y,Z).
(R8')   p1(X,Z):- nm(X,Y),p2(Y,Z).
(R10)   P2(Y,Z):- iv(Y,Z).
(R11'')p2(Y,Z):- tv(Y,Y2),nm(Y2,Z).
```

Fig. 4. Final domain theory after applying EGU II.

Algorithm EGU II
Input: a definite program P (domain theory), a definite unit goal $: -T$ (target concept), an operationality criterion O and a sequence of clauses $C_1, \ldots, C_m$ (proof of training example).
Output: a definite program P

Let $S_1 = C_1$.
FOR $i = 2$ TO m DO
    Let B_j be the first non-operational goal in the body of
    $S_{i-1} = H : -B_1, ..., B_n$, that unifies with the heads of the clauses
    $E_1, \ldots, E_p$.
    Let B'_j be defined by the clause $D_i = B'_j : -B_j, \ldots, B_n$ where the
    arguments of B'_j are all variables in $B_j, ..., B_n$ that appear in
    $H, B_1, \ldots, B_{j-1}$ (definition).
    Replace D_i with $R_1, \ldots, R_p$, where $R_k(1 \leq k \leq p)$ is the resolvent of
    D_i and E_k upon B_j (unfolding).
    Let S_i be the resolvent R_k of D_i and E_k such that $E_k = C_i$.
FOR $i = 1$ TO $m - 1$ DO
    Replace $S_i = H : -B_1, ..., B_n$ with a clause $S'_i = H : -B_1, \ldots, B_{j-1}, B'_j$
    using $D_{i+1} = B'_j : -B_j, \ldots, B_n$ (folding).
Let $C = S_m$.
FOR $i = 1$ TO $m - 1$ DO
    Let C' be the resolvent of C and the clause in P in which body
    there is a goal that unifies with the head of C.
    Remove C and let $C = C'$.
Place C first in P.
Unfold all goals that can be reduced by one clause only.

Correctness of EGU II The algorithm EGU II produces a new domain theory that is equivalent to the original domain theory with respect to a target concept T, i.e. an instance $T\theta$ follows from the original domain theory if and only if $T\theta$ follows from the transformed domain theory. To see this, we look at each step in the algorithm.

According to a theorem in [19], any program that is obtained by unfolding and folding, from a program P and a set of clauses introduced by the rule of definition D, is equivalent to $P \cup D$. Thus the program P' that is obtained after the two first steps in EGU II is equivalent to the original domain theory P together with the set of new definitions D. Hence, an instance $T\theta$ follows from P' if and only if it follows from $P \cup D$. Moreover, an instance of the target concept $T\theta$ follows from P if and only if it follows from $P \cup D$, since the predicates defined in D do not appear in P. Thus P' is equivalent to P with respect to a target concept T.

The third step in the algorithm does also preserve the equivalence of the domain theory with respect to a target concept as is shown by the following. Let P be a definite program (domain theory), T a unit goal (target concept) and C_1 a clause in P, in which there is a goal G with a different predicate symbol from T and that unifies with the head of another clause C_2 in P. If there is no other goal in P that unifies with the head of C_2, then P with respect to T is equivalent to the program obtained by adding the resolvent of C_1 and C_2 upon G to P, and removing C_2. This is the case since the resolvent follows logically from P and thus can be added, and C_2 cannot be used to reduce any other goal in P and not any instance of T and thus can be removed. The above conditions hold in the third step of the algorithm since each goal that is resolved upon only appears in one clause and has a different predicate symbol than T.

The fourth step in the algorithm preserves equivalence of the domain theory since it only involves unfolding (see [19]).

4   Experimental Results

The significance of the three problems that may degrade the efficiency of a program due to learned clauses are domain dependent. For example, if no predicates are declared as operational (e.g. the theorem proving domain in [14]) then the problem of increased inter-clause repetition of goal calls does not occur, since this problem only involves operational goals. If learned clauses are not invoked on other goals than on top level unit goals, then the redundancy problem is of no importance. However, if some goals are specified as operational or learned clauses are allowed to be invoked from other clauses (e.g. recursively), then these problems can be of major importance. Note that the redundancy problem can increase repetition of non-operational as well as operational goal calls.

In this section we present results from experiments with a domain theory for theorem proving in the MIU system [8]. The algorithm EGU II is compared to EGU [1] and to adding learned clauses redundantly (cf. PROLOG-EBG [9]). All three algorithms have been extended by a technique for organizing learned clauses efficiently, called CLORG [2]. The effect of disallowing learned clauses from being invoked recursively is also investigated. The algorithms have been implemented in SICStus PROLOG 2.1, and the experiments have been run on a Personal DECstation 5000 with 16 Mb PM.

The MIU System A theorem in the MIU system is a string $w \in m(u \cup i)*$, and there are four rules of inference: i) if wi is a theorem, then so is wiu ii) if mw is a theorem, then so is mww iii) if w_1iiiw_2 is a theorem then so is w_1uw_2 iv) if w_1uuw_2 is a theorem then so is w_1w_2. The problem of finding a sequence of rule applications from an axiom to a theorem can be solved by the program in the appendix.

The test examples in this experiment were produced by finding all strings that could be proved as theorems with not more than six rule applications given mi as an axiom (282 theorems). A subset of the test examples was used as a training set. In the experiment, the size of the subset varied from 10% to 100% of the test set. In Figure 5, it can be seen that the cost of using EGU is higher than the benefits of learning (when the size of the training set is less than 80%). The reason for this is the increased unification cost and inter-clause repetition of goal calls. In this domain it is certainly better to add clauses redundantly (organized efficiently) than to use EGU. However, redundancy can be eliminated at lower cost as is shown by EGU II. In fact, the resulting program is more efficient than the program obtained by adding clauses redundantly. This would not have been a surprise had the redundancy problem been significant (as in [1]), but this is not the case in this domain since the target concept is never backtracked into. This result can however be explained by the elimination of failure branches that is obtained when the domain theory is transformed. To show that the increase in efficiency was not caused by elimination of redundancy, we also present results from an experiment where learned clauses were not invoked recursively (Figure 6).

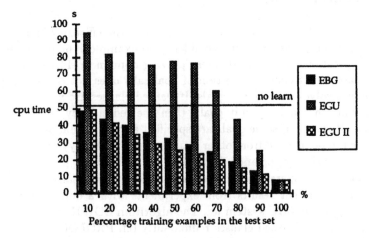

Fig. 5. Comparing three ways of transforming the MIU domain theory.

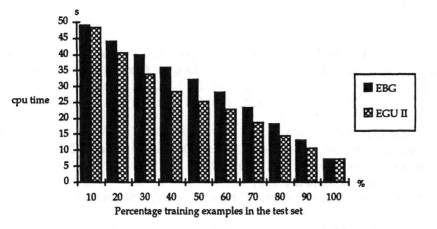

Fig. 6. Using EBG and EGU II when chaining of learned clauses is not allowed.

5 Concluding Remarks

There are three potential causes of the decreased efficiency of a logic program when adding clauses learned by EBG: i) increased unification cost ii) increased inter-clause repetition of goal calls iii) increased redundancy. None of the previous approaches for reducing these problems has addressed all three problems, and notably, the methods that avoid redundancy increase the two first problems.

We have presented a solution to this problem: EGU II, which is a reformulation of one of the previous algorithms that avoid redundancy (Example-Guided Unfolding). By the new algorithm it is shown how to avoid redundancy without increasing the two first problems. Moreover, the algorithm has been combined with a technique for organizing learned clauses efficiently, thus showing that all three problems can be addressed at a time.

Experimental results have been presented showing that the cost of avoiding redundancy by EGU may outweigh the benefits compared to adding clauses redundantly. However, this cost can be significantly reduced by the algorithm EGU II, as was shown by the experiments. The experiments also showed that even when the redundancy problem is not significant, it can be more beneficial to use EGU II than to add clauses redundantly.

There are several interesting directions for future research. One direction is to investigate under what conditions the algorithm is beneficial. These conditions include the distribution of problems, the cost of testing whether learned clauses are applicable, and the benefits when they are successfully applied.

Another question is the problem of generalizing number (e.g. [5, 18, 7]). A direction for future research is to investigate how clauses learned by methods for generalizing number can be incorporated without introducing redundancy.

Appendix

```
% The call solve(Axiom,Theorem,Length,[Axiom], Sequence) will find
% Sequence of length less or equal to Length from Axiom to Theorem.
% E.g. ?- solve([m,i],[m,i,u,i,u],s(s(0)),[[m,i]],Sequence).
%           Sequence = [add_u, double]

solve(State,State,_,_,□).
solve(State1,State2,s(Length),History,[Operator|Solution]):-
    successor(Operator,State1,State3),
    not_member(State3,History),
    solve(State3,State2,Length,[State3|History],Solution).

successor(add_u,L1,L2):-
    append(_,[i],L1),
    append(L1,[u],L2).
successor(double,[m|L1],[m|L2]):-
    append(L1,L1,L2).
successor(iii_to_u,L1,L2):-
    append(L3,[i,i,i|L4],L1),
    append(L3,[u|L4],L2).
successor(delete_uu,L1,L2):-
    append(L3,[u,u|L4],L1),
    append(L3,L4,L2).

append(□,L,L).
append([X|L1],L2,[X|L3]):-
    append(L1,L2,L3).

not_member(_,□).
not_member(X,[Y|L]):-
    X\==Y,
    not_member(X,L).

% Operationality criterion: operational(\==(_,_)).
```

References

1. Boström H., "Eliminating Redundancy in Explanation-Based Learning", *Machine Learning: Proceedings of the 9th International Conference*, Morgan Kaufmann, CA (1992) 37–42
2. Boström H., *Efficient Organization of Clauses Learned by Explanation-Based Generalization*, SYSLAB Report, Dept. of Computer and Systems Sciences, Stockholm University (1993)

3. Clark P. and Holte R., "Lazy Partial Evaluation: an Integration of Explanation-Based Generalization and Partial Evaluation", *Machine Learning: Proceedings of the 9th International Conference*, Morgan Kaufmann, CA (1992) 82–91

4. Clocksin W. F. and Mellish C. S., *Programming in Prolog*, Springer Verlag, Berlin Heidelberg (1981)

5. Cohen W. W., "Generalizing Number and Learning from Multiple Examples in Explanation-Based Learning", *Proceedings of the Fifth International Conference on Machine Learning*, Morgan Kaufmann, CA (1988) 256–269

6. Debray S. K., *Global Optimization of Logic Programs*, Ph.D. thesis, Stony Brook (1986)

7. Feldman R. and Subramanian D., "Example-Guided Optimization of Recursive Domain theories", *Proceedings of Conference on Artificial Intelligence Applications*, Miami Beach, Florida, IEEE (1991) 240–244

8. Hofstadter D. R., *Godel, Escher, Bach: an Eternal Golden Braid*, Penguin Books, New York (1980)

9. Kedar-Cabelli S. and McCarty L. T., "Explanation-based generalization as resolution theorem proving", *Proceedings of the Fourth International Machine Learning Workshop*, Morgan Kaufmann, CA (1987) 383–389

10. Lloyd J. W., *Foundations of Logic Programming*, Springer-Verlag (1987)

11. Minton S., *Learning Effective Search Control Knowledge: An Explanation-Based Approach* , Ph.D. thesis, Department of Computer Science, Carnegie-Mellon University, Pittsburgh, PA (1988)

12. Minton S., "Issues in the Design of Operator Composition Systems", *Proceedings of the Seventh International Conference on Machine Learning*, Morgan Kaufmann, CA (1990) 304–312

13. Mitchell, T. M., Keller R. M. and Kedar-Cabelli S. T., "Explanation-Based Generalization: A Unifying View", *Machine Learning* 1, (1986) 47–80

14. Mooney R., "The Effect of Rule Use on the Utility of Explanation-Based Learning", *Proceedings of the Eleventh International Joint Conference on Artificial Intelligence*, Morgan Kaufmann, CA (1989) 725–730

15. Sablon G., De Raedt L. and Bruynooghe M., "Generalizing Multiple Examples in Explanation Based Learning", *Proceedings of the International Workshop AII 2*, Reinhardsbrunn, GDR (1989) 177–183

16. Sahlin D., *An Automatic Partial Evaluator for Full Prolog*, Ph.D. thesis, Dept. of Tele-communication and Computer Systems, The Royal Institute of Technology, Stockholm (1991)

17. Samuelsson C. and Rayner M., "Quantitative Evaluation of Explanation–Based Learning as an Optimization Tool for a Large Scale Natural Language System", *Proceedings of the 12th International Joint Conference on Artificial Intelligence*, Morgan Kaufmann, CA (1992) 609–615

18. Shavlik J. W., "Acquiring Recursive Concepts with Explanation-Based Learning", *Proceedings of the Eleventh International Joint Conference on Artificial Intelligence*, Morgan Kaufmann, CA (1989) 688–693

19. Tamaki H. and Sato T., "Unfold/Fold Transformations of Logic Programs", *Proceedings of the Second International Logic Programming Conference*, Uppsala University, Uppsala, Sweden (1984) 127–138

20. Wogulis J. and Langley P., "Improving Efficiency by Learning Intermediate Concepts", *Proceedings of the Eleventh International Joint Conference on Artificial Intelligence*, Morgan Kaufmann, CA (1989) 657–662

Bayes and Pseudo-Bayes Estimates of Conditional Probabilities and Their Reliability

James Cussens

Centre for Logic and Probability in IT
King's College, Strand, London, WC2R 2LS, UK
Phone: +44 71 873 2291, Fax: +44 71 836 1799
email: j.cussens@uk.ac.kcl.cc.elm

Abstract. Various ways of estimating probabilities, mainly within the Bayesian framework, are discussed. Their relevance and application to machine learning is given, and their relative performance empirically evaluated. A method of accounting for noisy data is given and also applied. The reliability of estimates is measured by a significance measure, which is also empirically tested. We briefly discuss the use of likelihood ratio as a significance measure.

1 Introduction

The importance of conditional probability estimation in machine learning has been rightly stressed in, for example, [4]. Learning algorithms generally output rules of the form $C \leftarrow A$. An obvious measure of the quality of such a rule is simply $P(C|A) = p$, the probability that a randomly chosen example, given that it is covered by the rule, is correctly classified by the rule.[1] We will sometimes informally refer to p as the *probability of the rule* $C \leftarrow A$.

The exact value of p will generally be unknown—but it can be estimated. Standard Bayesian techniques for the estimation of probabilities are well known [13,25,15]. In recent years they have been used successfully in machine learning [4,5,9,8,16] using m-estimation. In this paper, we use, as well as standard Bayes estimates, *pseudo-Bayes* estimates of conditional probabilities, drawing heavily on the work of Bishop, Fienberg and Holland [2].

Given that we have an estimate for $P(C|A) = p$, it is useful to have a measure of the reliability of this estimate. This reliability is often termed the *significance* of the rule $C \leftarrow A$. A measure of significance is proposed in Sect. 7, and in Sect. 8.4, we map significance against estimate accuracy to check that it is an adequate measure of estimate reliability.

2 Bayesian Estimation of Probabilities

In the Bayesian approach to the estimation of an unknown quantity, for example the probability p, a *prior* distribution is selected which represents information

---

[1] Throughout this paper, $P(X)$ represents the probability that a randomly chosen example satisfies X.

concerning possible values of p. As we gather data relevant to the value of p, this distribution is updated via a continuous version of Bayes theorem to give a *posterior* distribution. We can then take the mean of this posterior distribution as a point estimate of p. To estimate a probability, the prior is invariably constrained to be a *beta distribution*, since this makes updating it extremely easy. Beta distributions are parameterised by two values r_0 and n_0 ($n_0 > r_0 > 0$) as follows:

$$f_{r_0, n_0}(x) = \begin{cases} \frac{(n_0-1)!}{(r_0-1)!(n_0-r_0-1)!} x^{r_0-1} (1-x)^{n_0-r_0-1} & \text{if } 0 \leq x \leq 1 \\ 0 & \text{elsewhere} \end{cases} \quad (1)$$

The mean of such a distribution is r_0/n_0. n_0 determines the spread or variance of the distribution, the distribution becoming flatter as n_0 decreases; consequently n_0 has been called a 'flattening constant' [10] or a 'smoothing constant' [2,23].

Assume our prior distribution is parameterised by r_0 and n_0. Suppose that out of n examples, the event whose probability we are attempting to estimate, occurs r times. The posterior distribution is then a beta distribution with parameters $r_1 = r_0 + r$ and $n_1 = n_0 + n$. The mean of this distribution is $\frac{r_1}{n_1} = \frac{r_0+r}{n_0+n}$ and we can use this to estimate the probability in question.

3 Choosing the Mean of the Prior Distribution

On the choice of mean for the prior distribution, I concur with the value used in m-estimation. If we are to estimate $P(C|A) = p$, we use $P(C)$ as the prior mean. This choice can be justified as follows.

Suppose the domain about which we are learning is finite and of size D. Hence the number of examples which satisfy A is $D.P(A)$. Identify A, C and $A \wedge C$ with the sets of examples which satisfy them. Prior to gathering any training data, we have no indication about which particular examples fall within A, hence we model this by supposing the members of A are chosen at random. We have $D.P(A)$ elements to chose, at random, from a finite domain where the proportion of elements in C is $P(C)$. Such a scenario is modelled by the *hypergeometric distribution*, so the mean number of elements of A which fall within C, i.e. the mean number in $A \wedge C$, will be $D.P(A).P(C)$ [11, p.139]. This means the mean value of $P(A \wedge C)$ is $D.P(A).P(C)/D = P(A).P(C)$ and finally the mean value of $P(C|A) = P(A \wedge C)/P(A)$ is $P(C)$.

Note, however, that $P(C)$ is generally not known—so it too must be estimated. Fortunately, since the whole of the training data can be used as a sample with which to estimate $P(C)$, we can get very reliable estimates of it. In this paper we use Laplace estimation (see below) to estimate $P(C)$.

4 Selecting the Prior Distribution

Recall that the prior distribution is fixed by the values of r_0 and n_0, and that the prior mean is given by r_0/n_0. So, from above, we have that $r_0/n_0 = P(C) \leftrightarrow r_0 = n_0.P(C)$. All that remains is to fix a value for n_0.

4.1 Bayesian Estimation

m-Estimation: Finding n_0 Experimentally In m-estimation [4,5,9,8,16], the value n_0 above is designated by m. Bayesian estimation is then done in the normal way, giving the usual estimate $(r + r_0)/(n + n_0)$ for p, where r and n are as above. With $r_0 = n_0.P(C)$ and $n_0 = m$, the estimate becomes

$$p_m = \frac{r + m.P(C)}{n + m} = \left(\frac{n}{n+m}\right)\left(\frac{r}{n}\right) + \left(\frac{m}{n+m}\right)P(C) \qquad (2)$$

The best value for m in a given domain is currently found experimentally— '...several different values for m should be applied. At the end, after measuring the performance of the induced classifiers, the value of the m which gives the best performance can be selected' [9]. Such an approach has been found to be very successful. The extra effort required to find the best m value is outweighed by better estimates once it is found and put to use.

As can be seen from (2), the value m 'controls the balance between relative frequency and prior probability' [9]. A high value of m indicates that we are very confident in our prior estimate for $P(C|A)$, namely $P(C)$. The variance of the prior distribution is then small. If noise is expected in the examples, m is set higher so that the (noisy) value for r/n plays less of a rôle in the final estimate.

Non-Experimentally Derived Values for n_0 Various non-experimentally derived values for n_0 have been discussed in the statistical literature, a list can be found in [10]. In this paper we use the a priori value $n_0 = 1$ and also the data-dependent value $n_0 = \sqrt{n}$. For the properties of these values see [2, p.407].

4.2 Pseudo-Bayes Estimation

Pseudo-Bayes estimation can be seen as a variety of Bayesian estimation where n_0 is strongly data-dependent, being a function of both r and n. This explains what is 'pseudo' about it. The prior distribution, determined by n_0, is no longer truly prior, since it contains relative frequency information from the training data. By the same argument, one can see $n_0 = \sqrt{n}$ as semi-pseudo-Bayes, since it depends on n; however, it is generally categorised as a plain Bayesian estimator.

There is an infinite family of pseudo-Bayes estimators, as described in [23]. Here, however, we consider only the one described in [2]. There, the value $\hat{K}$, which is the maximum likelihood estimator of the optimal flattening constant K, plays the rôle of n_0. It is defined as follows:

$$\hat{K} = \frac{\frac{r}{n}(1 - \frac{r}{n})}{(P(C) - \frac{r}{n})^2} = \frac{r(n - r)}{(n.P(C) - r)^2} \qquad (3)$$

The pseudo-Bayes estimator of p is hence given by

$$p^* = \frac{r + \hat{K}.P(C)}{n + \hat{K}} = \left(\frac{n}{n + \hat{K}}\right)\left(\frac{r}{n}\right) + \left(\frac{\hat{K}}{n + \hat{K}}\right)P(C) \qquad (4)$$

5 A Non-Bayesian Approach to Estimation

In all the experiments given below, we have that a set of training data consisting of N examples is drawn at random from the domain. n examples of this training data are in A, s are in C and r are in $A \wedge C$—so the rule $C \leftarrow A$ has training accuracy r/n. Assume the domain in question contains D examples in total. After the collection of training data, there are $D.P(A) - n$ examples left in the domain which are members of A. Clearly we do not know how many of these are also in C, otherwise our estimation problem would be solved. However, by assuming that the remaining members of A are distributed at random (which models our ignorance about A), we can easily calculate the *mean* number number which fall in C.

Our domain has $D - N$ members left from which to pick. The proportion left in C is $\frac{D.P(C)-s}{D-N}$ and we are to pick $D.P(A)-n$ examples at random. The number of these examples that are in C is governed by the hypergeometric distribution, since we are sampling examples without replacement from a finite domain. The mean number of new examples in A that are also in C is thus given by

$$(D.P(A) - n)\frac{D.P(C) - s}{D - N} \qquad (5)$$

We can now add in the original r examples, to get the mean number of examples in the domain which satisfy $A \wedge C$. Dividing by D, gives the mean value for $P(A \wedge C)$; and, finally, dividing by $P(A)$ gives the following mean value for $P(C|A)$.

$$\frac{(D.P(A) - n)(D.P(C) - s) + r(D - N)}{D(D - N)P(A)} \qquad (6)$$

This gives an alternative non-Bayesian way of estimating p and has been tested by the author empirically, giving generally poor results (Table 4). One big problem is that to get optimal estimates, the value of D had to be set far lower than the known sizes of domains.

The most likely explanation for the poor performance of (6) as an estimator, is that the modelling assumption that A is randomly distributed will generally not be appropriate. The choice of antecedents for learnt rules is, in fact, subject to considerable bias depending on a number of factors [20,7,14,24]. Incorporating such bias into the estimation of the probability of rules is an important research task, but is beyond the scope of this paper.

6 Accounting for Noise

6.1 Winkler and Franklin's Approach to Accounting for Noise in Bayesian Estimation

Rather than account for noise by increasing the value of n_0, we alter the method of updating the prior distribution. Winkler and Franklin [27] show how to account for noise using both alternatives. For both cases, Winkler and Franklin calculate approximations to the exact posterior distribution[2] and find that with both methods, the approximation is generally good.

We adopt the 'modified-updating' approach because it is consonant with the philosophy behind Bayesian inference. The presence of noise means that the observed values of empirical data are unreliable. Since empirical data affects estimation via the updating of the distribution, it is natural that noise be accounted for in the updating procedure. Prior distributions, on the other hand, are meant to represent prior knowledge.[3] There is no particular reason for this prior knowledge to be affected by the noise level in the training set. Another advantage of this approach is that the parameters that emerge have a natural interpretation in terms of reduced sample size, as we shall see below. The following approach is, with notational changes, that of Winkler, as given in [26].

We have, for the rule $C \leftarrow A$, a set of training examples with r 'successes' $(A \wedge C)$ and $n - r$ 'failures' $(A \wedge \neg C)$. Let the probability that a success is misclassified as a failure be ϕ and the probability that a failure is misclassified as a success be ψ. The maximum likelihood estimator of p (that value of p which makes r successes and $n - r$ failures most likely) is $\hat{p}$, where $\hat{p}_B = r/n$ and,

$$\hat{p} = \begin{cases} 0 & \text{if } r/n < \psi \\ (\hat{p}_B - \psi)/(1 - \phi - \psi) & \text{if } \psi \leq r/n \leq 1 - \phi \\ 1 & \text{if } r/n > 1 - \phi \end{cases} \quad (7)$$

Note that setting $\phi = \psi = 0$ (the noise-free case) entails $\hat{p} = \hat{p}_B = r/n$, as expected, since r/n, relative frequency, is the maximum likelihood estimator for p in the absence of noise.

Winkler shows that, as long as

$$\psi < r/n < 1 - \phi \quad (8)$$

we can set

$$n^* = \frac{n\hat{p}(1 - \hat{p})}{(\hat{p} + c_1)(1 - \hat{p} + c_2)} \quad (9)$$

and

$$r^* = n^*\hat{p} \quad (10)$$

where

$$c_1 = \frac{\psi}{1 - \phi - \psi}, \quad c_2 = \frac{\phi}{1 - \phi - \psi} \quad (11)$$

The observation of r successes from n examples with noise parameters ϕ and ψ, is then approximately[4] equivalent to having r^* successes out of n^* *noise-free* examples. We have, $n^* < n$, as long as the initial condition (8) is satisfied. So '[a]s anticipated, then, the noise leads to an effective reduction in sample size.' [26]. We can then view $1 - (n^*/n)$ as 'a rough measure of the proportion of information lost as a result of noise' [26].

---

[2] An *exact* posterior distribution in the presence of known amounts of noise is possible to calculate, but the calculations tend to be cumbersome [27].

[3] The qualities of pseudo-Bayes estimates show that it is sometimes worth 'cheating' in this respect!

[4] The approximation is particularly good when $\phi = \psi$, which is the case we will consider. See [27] for various graphs showing the precision of the approximation.

6.2 Accounting for Noise in Machine Learning

If noise accords to the *Classification Noise Process* model as described in [1], then Winkler and Franklin's method is directly applicable. In this model we assume that examples are generated by an oracle, and that the examples are subject to independent and random misclassification with some probability $\eta < 1/2$. This is clearly equivalent to the situation described above with $\phi = \psi = \eta$. Quinlan in [19] introduces $\eta \times 100\%$ noise by replacing, with probability η, the correct classification of an example by a random one. In this case the above is applicable with $\phi = \psi = \frac{1}{2}\eta$.

For the noisy data used in this paper, a measured amount of noise was introduced using the *Classification Noise Process*, so we set $\phi = \psi = \eta$. Such noise affects the observed value of r, whilst having no effect on the observed value of n (we have *classification noise* but no *description noise*—these two forms of noise are discussed in [21]). Also, since the noise was artificially introduced, the value η is known. We do not the address the issue of estimating unknown noise levels here—for a discussion of this issue see [1,22].

Rewriting the above equations for n^* and r^* in terms of r, n and η, gives the following:

$$n^* = n\frac{(r - \eta n)(n - r - \eta n)}{r(n - r)} \tag{12}$$

$$r^* = n^*\hat{p} = \frac{(r - \eta n)^2(n - r - \eta n)}{(1 - 2\eta)r(n - r)} \tag{13}$$

The above equations are only applicable if $\eta < r/n < 1 - \eta$, an inequality that does not always hold. However, it is clear that $n^* \to 0$ as $r/n \to 1 - \eta$, i.e. the amount of information lost due to noise tends to be total as r/n approaches $1 - \eta$. Hence for values of r/n such that $r/n \geq 1 - \eta$, we set n^* and subsequently r^* to zero.[5] In this case, all Bayesian and pseudo-Bayesian estimates equal the prior probability $P(C)$, reflecting the fact that we have gained no real information from the data.

To summarise, except for the cases mentioned immediately above, given $\eta \times 100\%$ noise and observing r successes out of n examples covered by the rule in question $(C \leftarrow A)$, we can estimate the probability $P(C|A)$ using Bayesian estimation with n^* and r^* as updating parameters.

7 The Reliability of Estimates

It is clearly desirable not only to have good estimates of probabilities, but also some measure of how good a given estimate is. We shall use the posterior distribution to find $P(|\text{estimate} - p| < t)$, which is the (posterior) probability that the estimate is within a certain distance (t) of the true probability. This value is found by integrating the posterior distribution between $(\text{estimate} - t)$ and

---

[5] The case when $r/n \leq \eta$ can be dealt with similarly, but is not of interest for machine learning.

(estimate $+t$).[6] We shall call $P(|$estimate $- p| < t)$ a *significance measure*. In our experiments, t was set to 0.025, since this gave convenient significance values.

8 Empirical Results

8.1 Experimental Procedure

The data used here is that used in [18]. There, the value of *HP Compression* as a significance measure was considered. Unfortunately we do not have space to examine this issue here.

Rules were learnt using Golem, an Inductive Logic Programming algorithm [17]. The learning domains were as follows

PROTEINS Prediction of protein secondary structure. We have rules which predict when a given residue is part of an α-helix.

DRUGS Modelling drug structure-activity relationships. Rules relate the structure of a drug to its chemical activity.

KRK Rules for characterising illegality in two Kings and a Rook chess endgames. We do estimation for the cases of 5%, 10% and 20% added noise.

The estimates used can be split into two groups. In the first group, estimation is undertaken without reference to testing data (Table 1) and in the second, testing data is used to find the best possible estimate (Table 2).

Table 1. Non-empirically derived estimators

p^*	Pseudo-Bayes estimation as given by (4).
$p_{n_0=1}$	Estimation by setting $n_0 = 1$. This approach is discussed in [2].
$p_{n_0=\sqrt{n}}$	Estimation by setting $n_0 = \sqrt{n}$. This approach is also discussed in [2].
p_L	Laplace estimation. This amounts to choosing the uniform distribution as a prior. Estimates are given by $(r + 1)/(n + 2)$.
$\hat{p}$	Training accuracy as an estimate. This is the same as fixing $n_0 = 0$. It is the maximum likelihood estimator.

In a given domain, the probability $P(C|A)$ for each rule $C \leftarrow A$ was estimated using all of the above estimates. The significance of each rule was also calculated for the Bayes/pseudo-Bayes estimates, as described above. Noise, for the Bayes/pseudo-Bayes estimates, was accounted for using Winkler's approach.

---

[6] In the empirical results that follow, this integration was done by a Numerical Analysis Group subroutine within a Fortran program. Indeed, all results are the output of various Fortran programs.

Table 2. Empirically derived estimators

p_m m-estimation. The best value for m was found using the testing data.
p_D Estimation using (6). The best value for D was found using the testing
   data.

Some Special Cases After we have accounted for noise, it sometimes occurs
that the values for n and r are reduced to zero (see above). In this case, $p_{n_0 = \sqrt{n}}$
and $\hat{p}$ are undefined. Since $n = 0$ is equivalent to having no training data, we
use the prior mean $P(C)$ as an estimate in these cases, and since this estimate
is based on effectively no training data, significance is set of zero.

From (3), we see that, $r/n = 1 \Rightarrow \hat{K} = 0$. Recall that $\hat{K}$ is used as a flattening
constant n_0 for a prior beta distribution, and that we must have $n_0 > 0$. In
this case, we consider what happens as $\hat{K} \to 0$ and $r/n \to 1$; we have that
$p^* \to r/n = 1$ and significance $\to 1$. So in this case, we set both estimate and
significance to 1. This seems the only consistent way of dealing with this case,
but it gives rise to anomalous behaviour. For example, if $r = n = 1$, p^* returns
an estimate of 1 with maximum significance! This reveals a clear weakness with
pseudo-Bayesian estimation as used in this paper.

There are two more special cases for pseudo-Bayes. If $r/n = P(C)$, then $\hat{K}$
becomes infinite. Similarly to above, we consider what happens as $\hat{K} \to \infty$ and
set p^* to $P(C)$ and significance to 1. Finally if $r = n = 0$, $\hat{K}$ is undefined. Now
$\hat{K} = 1$ when $n = 0$, but $r \neq 0$ so we set $\hat{K} = 1$ in this case, giving an estimate
of $P(C)$, as above.

8.2 Looking at Mean Squared Error

Our goal in estimation, since we are using posterior *means* as point estimates,
is to minimise $(\text{estimate} - p)^2$ (see [3, Appendix A5.6]). Since the value p is
unknown, this expression can not be evaluated. So, in the following, the true
probability value, p, for any rule is simply estimated by the *testing accuracy*
of that rule. In other words, we use relative frequency in the testing set as a
(second) estimator of p. Although, as our results show, relative frequency is a
poor estimator, we use testing accuracy since this is the standard method of
evaluating rule performance in machine learning.

For each domain and each choice of estimate, we found the mean value of
$(\text{estimate} - \text{training accuracy})^2$ over all the rules from a given domain. The results
for estimates which used only the training data are given in Table 3. Those for
empirically tunable estimates are given in Table 4, with the optimal parameter
values which gave these results. In both tables, the estimate with smallest mean
squared error is in **bold**.

We would like more domains on which to test the various estimates, but
there are already some significant results. If we exclude the Drugs domain (for
why, see below), $\hat{p}$ is always the worst estimator of all, and $p_{n_0 = \sqrt{n}}$ is always the
best from amongst those that take $P(C)$ into account. The probability of this

Table 3. Mean squared errors for p^*, $p_{n_0=1}$, $p_{n_0=\sqrt{n}}$, p_L and $\hat{p}$

	p^*	$p_{n_0=1}$	$p_{n_0=\sqrt{n}}$	p_L	$\hat{p}$
Proteins	7.491×10^{-2}	7.633×10^{-2}	$\mathbf{6.038 \times 10^{-2}}$	7.040×10^{-2}	8.269×10^{-2}
Drugs	3.204×10^{-3}	3.162×10^{-3}	7.079×10^{-3}	3.883×10^{-3}	$\mathbf{2.808 \times 10^{-3}}$
KRK (5%)	8.125×10^{-3}	9.758×10^{-3}	$\mathbf{7.813 \times 10^{-3}}$	9.920×10^{-3}	1.0876×10^{-2}
KRK (10%)	6.796×10^{-2}	6.458×10^{-2}	6.062×10^{-2}	$\mathbf{4.324 \times 10^{-2}}$	7.400×10^{-2}
KRK (20%)	3.464×10^{-2}	3.538×10^{-2}	$\mathbf{2.718 \times 10^{-2}}$	3.300×10^{-2}	4.982×10^{-2}

Table 4. Mean squared errors for p_m and p_D

	p_m	p_D
Proteins	2.703×10^{-2} $(m = 114)$	$\mathbf{2.610 \times 10^{-2}}$ $(D = 1 \times 10^5)$
Drugs	$\mathbf{2.808 \times 10^{-3}}$ $(m = 0)$	4.251×10^{-3} $(D = 1743)$
KRK (5%)	$\mathbf{8.545 \times 10^{-3}}$ $(m = 4)$	3.327×10^{-1} $(D = 998)$
KRK (10%)	6.144×10^{-2} $(m = 3)$	$\mathbf{4.216 \times 10^{-2}}$ $(D = 1000)$
KRK (20%)	$\mathbf{1.884 \times 10^{-2}}$ $(m = 10)$	2.831×10^{-2} $(D = 1001)$

occurring by chance is very small—these are significant results. (This could be proved rigourously using nonparametric rank-order statistical tests [12]). On the other hand, there is not enough evidence to say that p_m is superior to the other Bayes/pseudo-Bayes estimates, since it only the best estimate of this class three times out of five.

8.3 Domain Peculiarities

In the protein domain, the data used was unsatisfactory, since the training and testing sets had significantly different proportions of positive examples (residues which really were in α-helices). This means that estimates derived from training data could be expected to be unsuccessful on the given testing data. This probably explains why p_D performed well here, as opposed to most of the other domains.

The Drugs domain is remarkable in that many rules have 100% accuracy on training or test data, and frequently on both. This explains why $\hat{p}$ (equivalently m-estimation with $m = 0$) was the most successful on this domain, whilst being the worst estimator on all other domains. $p_{n_0=\sqrt{n}}$ did particularly badly on the Drugs domain. Since in the Drugs domain, the prior mean was exactly $1/2$, $p_{n_0=\sqrt{n}}$ is the unique constant risk minimax estimator [2, p.407]. This estimator has high expected error when the true value of the probability to be estimated is close to 0 or 1 (see [2, Fig. 12.4-1, p.416]) and this explains its poor performance in the Drugs domain.

The KRK (10%) domain is surprising since all estimators perform more badly there than on the KRK (20%) domain, and the optimal m value is smaller than on the KRK (5%) domain. Again p_D is most successful here, where all other estimators do badly. What has happened here is that Golem has generated a number of rules of low significance that have very large errors, thus increasing the total mean squared error considerably. If we cut out these rules, and look, for example, at only the 20 most significant rules for KRK(10%) and KRK(20%), we find that estimators have lower error on the KRK(10%) domain, as expected (see Fig. 1). Relative frequency ($\hat{p}$) performs badly in the KRK domains, since it cannot account for noise. The Bayes and pseudo-Bayes estimators react to noise by giving the prior mean, $P(C)$, greater weight. In contrast, relative frequency can take no account of $P(C)$.

8.4 Comparing Squared Error and Significance

In Fig. 1, we compare the performance of the four Bayes/pseudo-Bayes estimators p_m, $p_{n_0=1}$, p^* and $p_{n_0=\sqrt{n}}$ on the three KRK domains. We plot their mean squared errors over subsets of the rule base, as we progressively eliminate less significant rules. We will represent the number of rules left on the x-axis, and mean squared error on the y-axis, so the rightmost point for each estimator represents the mean squared error over all the rules. These graphs demonstrate a number of important points.

1. The significance measure is working as it should. Significant rules have lower mean squared error, whatever the particular estimator.
2. The value of m used in m-estimation has been chosen to be optimal over the whole rule set. Such a value of m is successful over the whole set because it has been chosen to be reasonably successful on even quite insignificant rules (rules where an estimate of the probability is unreliable). The graphs for 20% noise demonstrate this ably: the errors for less significant rules are all large with the exception of those estimated by $m = 10$. On significant rules, however, m-estimation is not always superior.
3. The nth most significant rule is often the same for all estimates, as can be seen by the similar shape of the graphs for each estimator.

Our significance measure is meant to give the probability that an estimate diverges from the true probability by a given amount. We now put this to the test by mapping significance against squared error for each rule in each domain. We also do a scatter diagram for the combined results of three KRK domains. That this diagram has the outline of the sort of curve we would expect for a single domain is evidence that noise is being accounted for properly within the three domains. Firstly we do all this for p^* (Fig. 2) and then for p_m (Fig. 3). In the combined KRK domain, the highest point has been omitted so as not to interfere with the KRK(10%) graph above.

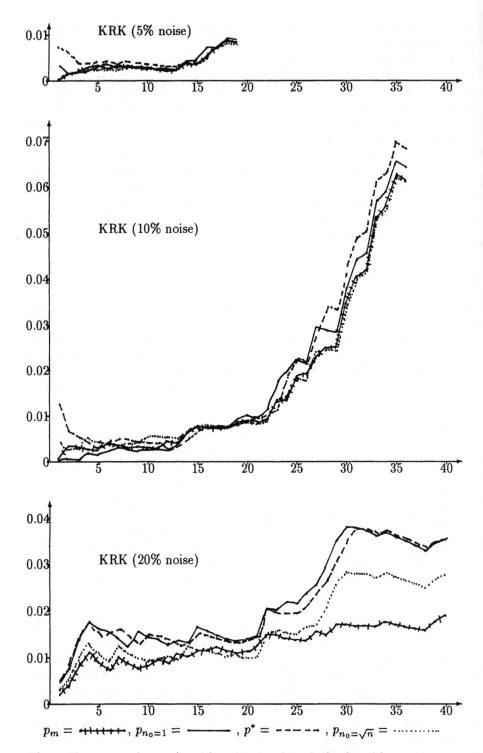

Fig. 1. Mean squared error (y-axis) against number of rules (x-axis)

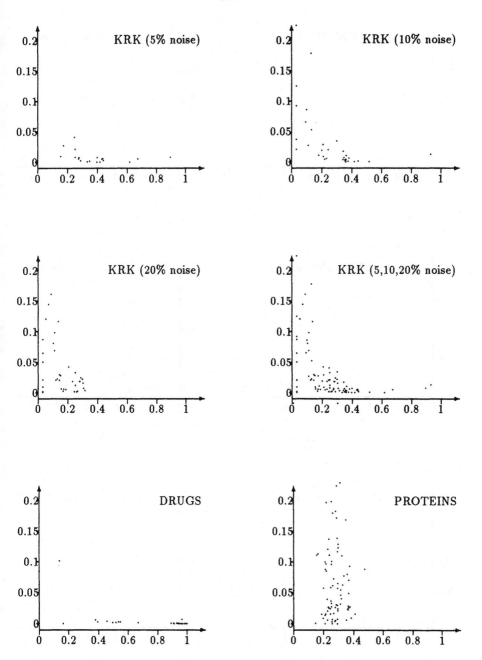

Fig. 2. Scatter diagrams of squared error (y-axis) against significance (x-axis) for p^*

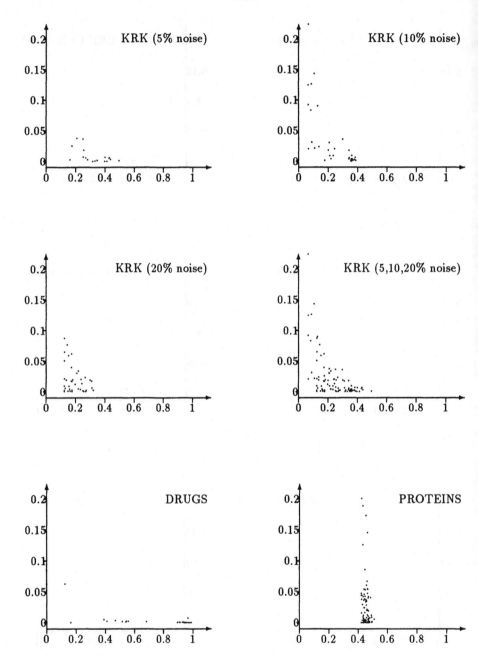

Fig. 3. Scatter diagrams of squared error (y-axis) against significance (x-axis) for p_m

In the Protein domain, training and testing sets are qualitatively different, so both measures give unimpressive results. In the Drugs domain, the data is highly concentrated around the x-axis, as expected.

Recall that the significance measure is $P(|\text{estimate} - p| < t)$ and we have $t = 0.025$. So significance is measuring $P(|\text{estimate}-p| < 0.025) = P((\text{estimate}-p)^2 < 6.25 \times 10^{-4})$. In Table 5 we give the number of points above and below 6.25×10^{-4} for several significance value intervals for the combined domain KRK(5%, 10%, 20%). We also give, in brackets, the values expected for that interval, to the nearest integer. For example, if there are 18 points with significance in the interval $[0.3, 0.4)$, we expect about $\frac{0.3+0.4}{2} \times 18 = 6.3$ points to be below 6.25×10^{-4} and 11.7 above.

Table 5. Number (expected number) of squared errors above and below 6.25×10^{-4}

Significance		0–0.1	0.1–0.2	0.2–0.3	0.3–0.4	0.4–0.5	0.5–0.6	0.6–0.7	0.7–0.8
p^*	$> 6.25 \times 10^{-4}$	21 (22)	19 (16)	24 (18)	15 (12)	4 (3)	0 (0)	1 (1)	1 (0)
	$\leq 6.25 \times 10^{-4}$	2 (1)	0 (3)	0 (6)	3 (6)	2 (3)	1 (1)	1 (1)	0 (1)
$p_{n_0=1}$	$> 6.25 \times 10^{-4}$	15 (15)	18 (16)	25 (19)	13 (10)	4 (4)	1 (1)	1 (0)	0 (0)
	$\leq 6.25 \times 10^{-4}$	1 (1)	1 (3)	0 (6)	2 (5)	4 (4)	1 (1)	0 (1)	0 (0)
$p_{n_0=\sqrt{n}}$	$> 6.25 \times 10^{-4}$	31 (31)	37 (35)	23 (17)	17 (14)	6 (5)	0 (0)	0 (0)	0 (0)
	$\leq 6.25 \times 10^{-4}$	2 (2)	4 (6)	0 (6)	4 (7)	3 (4)	0 (0)	0 (0)	0 (0)
p_m	$> 6.25 \times 10^{-4}$	11 (10)	29 (27)	23 (19)	14 (13)	5 (4)	0 (0)	0 (0)	0 (0)
	$\leq 6.25 \times 10^{-4}$	0 (1)	3 (5)	2 (6)	6 (7)	2 (3)	0 (0)	0 (0)	0 (0)

For all four estimators there is some correspondence between actual and expected values, but it appears that our significance measure is overestimating actual significance, since the expected number of points below 6.25×10^{-4} is nearly always higher than the actual number. m-estimation is the most successful estimator with respect to significance, presumably since it has the advantage of being empirically tunable. It is also notable that the expected number of good estimates was close to the actual number only when significance was very low.

9 Conclusions

The main problem with the above is that much more empirical testing of the various estimates and the significance measure needs to be carried out. However, it is already clear that Bayesian and pseudo-Bayesian estimation are superior to the standard maximum likelihood estimator ($\hat{p}$), especially in the presence of noise. This is because Bayesian estimation can use our prior estimate, $P(C)$, for $P(C|A)$. The success of estimation in the noisy KRK domains show that the proposed method of accounting for noise is working. Also, the results show the given measure of significance behaving roughly as it ought.

A Two Meanings of Significance

My intention here is to disentangle two related but different meanings of the term *significant* which appear to have become conflated in the literature.

Definition 1 *A rule is* significant$_1$ *if there is a high probability that its accuracy on testing data will be close to its training accuracy.*

Definition 2 *A rule is* significant$_2$ *if the distribution over classes of examples covered by the rule is appreciably different to the distribution over classes of examples in the domain as a whole.*

Estimates of a rule's probability are reliable when training accuracy is likely to be close to testing accuracy, so we have been measuring significance$_1$ in this paper. Significance$_2$ can be measured, for example, by likelihood ratio

$$LikelihoodRatio = 2n \left(r/n \log \left(\frac{r/n}{P(C)} \right) + (1 - r/n) \log \left(\frac{1 - r/n}{1 - P(C)} \right) \right) \quad (14)$$

which is used in [6]. It is also used in [18] to measure significance$_1$. Since it is not designed to measure significance$_1$, it is not surprising that it gives unimpressive results there.

Suppose our domain is the set of people who attended ECAI-92. Consider the three rules:

$$H_A = \text{native\_english\_speaker} \rightarrow \neg \text{multilingual}$$
$$H_B = \neg \text{native\_english\_speaker} \rightarrow \text{multilingual}$$
$$H_C = \text{brown\_eyes} \rightarrow \text{multilingual}$$

Let us assume that in a randomly chosen set of training examples, H_A and H_B get training accuracy 95% and H_C gets 90%—fairly realistic figures! Assume that the number of training examples is reasonably large; so all rules have reasonably good cover. This means that all will be significant$_1$. This agrees with what we know about the domain—we would expect all rules to be similarly accurate on any possible testing set. H_A is significant$_1$ because most native English speakers, at ECAI-92 as elsewhere, are monoglots. H_C is significant$_1$, because most brown-eyed people *at ECAI-92* are multilingual. However it is clear that although there is a correlation between brown eyes and multilingualism in this domain, it is of a rather uninteresting nature. H_C is significant$_1$ merely because it covers a reasonably large number of individuals in a domain where multilingualism is common. H_B, on the other hand, is significant$_1$ for rather more 'genuine' reasons and will be also somewhat *more* significant$_1$ than H_C, due to its higher training accuracy.

Turning to significance$_2$, we find that H_A is highly significant$_2$, H_B is moderately significant$_2$ and H_C is insignificant$_2$. Native English speakers have considerably poorer linguistic abilities than most other subsets of the domain, so H_A is amongst the best rules for predicting $\neg$multilingual. H_B is similarly a good rule, but $P(\text{multilingual} \mid \neg \text{native\_english\_speaker})$ is only slightly higher than $P(\text{multilingual} \mid \top)$, the probability of the default rule $\top \rightarrow \text{multilingual}$,[7] which

---

[7] which is maximally insignificant$_2$, but highly significant$_1$

decreases its significance$_2$. As for H_C, P(multilingual | brown_eyes) will be very close to P(multilingual | T), so H_C will be insignificant$_2$.

The above argues that the two significances are distinct, but for an important class of rules, high significance$_1$ and high significance$_2$ coincide. If a rule $C \leftarrow A$ has high training accuracy and high training cover ($r/n \approx 1$, n is big), we have

1. Estimates of the probability of the rule will be high.
2. Significance$_1$ will be high.
3. Significance$_2$ will be high, *as long as the relevant default rule ($C \leftarrow T$) has not also equally high training accuracy.*

This indicates that if we are looking for rules with 'a genuine correlation between attribute values and classes' as Clark and Niblett are in [6], we should focus on rules such as above. The question remains: which is the 'best' measure of 'genuine correlation', the probability estimate, significance$_1$ or significance$_2$?

Significance$_2$ (likelihood ratio) certainly can be used to find 'genuine correlation' as demonstrated by its successful employment in [6]. However, I feel that a *combination* of probability estimate and significance$_1$ measure has much to recommend it. For a rule $C \leftarrow A$, we can see the probability estimate as a 'best guess' at the extent of correlation between C and A. However, there is always the problem that even our best guess may be unreliable, so we can qualify the probability estimate with a significance$_1$ measure. We are only confident in those rules which have both high probability estimate and high significance$_1$.

Acknowledgements This work was funded by UK SERC grant GR/G 29854 for the Rule-Based Systems Project. Special thanks are due to Ashwin Srinivasan, who provided all of the necessary data, and to an anonymous reviewer for some helpful comments. Thanks are also due to Anthony Hunter, Donald Gillies, Stephen Muggleton and Dov Gabbay.

References

1. Dana Angluin and Philip Laird. Learning from noisy examples. *Machine Learning*, 2:343–370, 1988.
2. Yvonne M. M. Bishop, Stephen E. Fienberg, and Paul W. Holland. *Discrete Multivariate Analysis: Theory and Practice*. MIT Press, Cambridge, Mass., 1975.
3. George E. P. Box and George C. Tiao. *Bayesian Inference in Statistical Analysis*. Addison-Wesley, Reading, Mass., 1973.
4. Bojan Cestnik. Estimating probabilities: A crucial task in machine learning. In Aiello, editor, *ECAI-90*, pages 147–149. Pitman, 1990.
5. Bojan Cestnik and Ivan Bratko. On estimating probabilities in tree pruning. In Yves Kodratoff, editor, *Machine Learning—EWSL-91*, pages 138–150. Lecture Notes in Artificial Intelligence 482, Springer, 1991.
6. Peter Clark and Tim Niblett. The CN2 induction algorithm. *Machine Learning*, 3(4):261–283, 1989.
7. Luc de Raedt. *Interactive Theory Revision: An Inductive Logic Programming Approach*. Academic Press, London, 1992.

8. Sašo Džeroski and Ivan Bratko. Using the m-estimate in inductive logic programming. In *Logical Approaches to Machine Learning*, August 1992. ECAI-92 Workshop Notes.

9. Sašo Džeroski, Bojan Cestnik, and Igor Petrovski. The use of Bayesian probability estimates in rule induction. Turing Institute Research Memorandum TIRM-92-051, The Turing Institute, Glasgow, 1992.

10. Stephen E. Fienberg and Paul W. Holland. On the choice of flattening constant for estimating multinomial probabilities. *Journal of Multivariate Analysis*, 2:127–134, 1972.

11. Marek Fisz. *Probability Theory and Mathematical Statistics*. John Wiley, New York, third edition, 1963.

12. Jean Dickinson Gibbons. *Nonparametric Statistical Inference*. McGraw-Hill, New York, 1971.

13. I. J. Good. *The Estimation of Probabilities: An Essay on Modern Bayesian Techniques*. M. I. T. Press, Cambridge, Mass, 1965.

14. David Haussler. Quantifying inductive bias: AI learning algorithms and Valiant's learning framework. *Artificial Intelliegence*, 36:177–221, 1988.

15. Colin Howson and Peter Urbach. *Scientific Reasoning: The Bayesian Approach*. Open Court, La Salle, Illinois, 1989.

16. Nada Lavrač, Bojan Cestnik, and Sašo Džeroski. Search heuristics in empirical inductive logic programming. In *Logical Approaches to Machine Learning*, August 1992. ECAI-92 Workshop Notes.

17. Stephen Muggleton and Cao Feng. Efficient induction of logic programs. In *Proceedings of the First Conference on Algorithmic Learning Theory*, pages 473–491, Tokyo, 1990.

18. Stephen Muggleton, Ashwin Srinivasan, and Michael Bain. Compression, significance and accuracy. In *IML 92*, 1992.

19. J.R. Quinlan. Induction of decision trees. *Machine Learning*, 1:81–106, 1986.

20. Stuart J. Russell and Benjamin N. Grosof. Declarative bias: An overview. In D. Paul Benjamin, editor, *Change of Representation and Inductive Bias*, pages 267–308. Kluwer, Boston, 1990.

21. Cullen Schaffer. When does overfitting decrease prediction accuracy in induced decision trees and rule sets? In Yves Kodratoff, editor, *Machine Learning—EWSL-91*, pages 192–205. Lecture Notes in Artificial Intelligence 482, Springer, 1991.

22. Ashwin Srinivasan, Stephen Muggleton, and Michael Bain. The justification of logical theories. In Stephen Muggleton, editor, *Machine Intelligence 13*. Oxford University Press, 1993. To appear.

23. Michael Sutherland, Paul W. Holland, and Stephen E. Fienberg. Combining Bayes and frequency approaches to estimate a multinomial parameter. In Stephen E. Fienberg and Arnold Zellner, editors, *Studies in Bayesian Econometrics and Statistics*, pages 275–307. North-Holland, Amsterdam, 1974. volume 2.

24. Paul E. Utgoff. *Machine Learning of Inductive Bias*. Kluwer, Boston Mass., 1986.

25. Robert L. Winkler. *Introduction to Bayesian Inference and Decision*. Holt, Rhinehart and Winston, New York, 1972.

26. Robert L. Winkler. Information loss in noisy and dependent processes. In J. M. Bernardo, M. H. Groot, D. V. Lindley, and A. F. M. Smith, editors, *Bayesian Statistics*, volume 2, pages 559–570. North-Holland, 1985.

27. Robert L. Winkler and Leroy A. Franklin. Warner's randomized response model: A Bayesian approach. *Journal of the American Statistical Association*, 74(365):207–214, March 1979.

Induction of Recursive Bayesian Classifiers

Pat Langley

Learning Systems Department, Siemens Corporate Research
755 College Road East, Princeton, New Jersey 08540 USA

Abstract. In this paper, we review the induction of simple Bayesian classifiers, note some of their drawbacks, and describe a recursive algorithm that constructs a hierarchy of probabilistic concept descriptions. We posit that this approach should outperform the simpler scheme in domains that involve disjunctive concepts, since they violate the independence assumption on which the latter relies. To test this hypothesis, we report experimental studies with both natural and artificial domains. The results are mixed, but they are encouraging enough to recommend closer examination of recursive Bayesian classifiers in future work.

1. Introduction

In recent years, there has been growing interest in probabilistic methods for induction. Although much of the recent work in this area [e.g., 6] has focused on unsupervised learning, the approach applies equally well to supervised tasks. Such methods have long been used within the field of pattern recognition [4], but they have only recently received attention within the machine learning community [3, 7, 8, 9].

In this paper we review the most straightforward probabilistic approach to supervised learning – the induction of simple Bayesian classifiers. We also examine this method's apparent drawbacks and propose a revised algorithm that constructs a hierarchy of probabilistic summaries. We present an illustrative domain that this approach can handle but that the simpler scheme cannot, and we report experimental studies of the two algorithms on both natural and artificial induction tasks. Finally, we discuss work on related approaches and some directions for future research.

2. The induction of simple Bayesian classifiers

The most straightforward and widely tested method for probabilistic induction is known as the *simple Bayesian classifier*. This scheme represents each concept with a single probabilistic summary. In particular, each description has an associated class probability or base rate, $p(C_k)$, which specifies the prior probability that one will observe a member of class C_k. Each description also has an associated set of conditional probabilities, specifying a probability distribution for each attribute. In nominal domains, one typically stores a discrete distribution for each attribute in a description. Each $p(v_j|C_k)$ term specifies the probability of value v_j, given an instance of concept C_k. In numeric domains, one must represent a *continuous* probability distribution for each attribute. This requires that one assume some general form or model, and one usually selects the normal distribution. Conveniently, a given normal curve can be represented entirely in terms of its mean μ and variance σ^2. Moreover, the probability for a given numeric value v can be determined from the normal probability density function.

2.1 Prediction in Bayesian classifiers

To classify a new instance I, a Bayesian classifier applies Bayes' theorem to determine the probability of each description given the instance,

$$p(C_i|I) = \frac{p(C_i)p(I|C_i)}{p(I)} \quad .$$

However, since I is a conjunction of j values, one can expand this expression to

$$p(C_i|\bigwedge v_j) = \frac{p(C_i)p(\bigwedge v_j|C_i)}{\sum_k p(\bigwedge v_j|C_k)p(C_k)} \quad ,$$

where the denominator sums over all classes and where $p(\bigwedge v_j|C_i)$ is the probability of the instance I given the class C_i. After calculating these probabilities for each description, the algorithm assigns the instance to the class with the highest overall probability.

In order to make the above expression operational, one must still specify how to compute the term $p(\bigwedge v_j|C_k)$. Typically, one assumes independence of attributes, so that the classifier can calculate it using the equality

$$p(\bigwedge v_j|C_k) = \prod_j p(v_j|C_k),$$

where the values $p(v_j|C_k)$ represent the conditional probabilities stored with each class.

In some cases, the training data may produce a zero for some base rate or conditional probability. Since the classification decision involves multiplication, this overwhelms the effects of other factors. Clark and Niblett [3] avoid this problem by replacing zero entries with $p(C_i)/N$, where N is the number of training examples. The factor $1/N$ represents the belief that this entry has a near-zero value as a function of the size of the training set.

2.2 Learning in Bayesian classifiers

Learning in a Bayesian classifier is an almost trivial matter. The simplest implementation increments a count each time it encounters a new instance, along with a separate count for a class each time it observes an instance of that class. Together, these counts let the classifier estimate $p(C_k)$ for each class C_k. In addition, for each instance of a class that has a given nominal value, the algorithm updates a count for that class-value pair. Together with the second count, this lets the classifier estimate $p(v_j|C_k)$. For each numeric attribute, the method retains and revises two quantities, the sum and the sum of squares, which let it compute the mean and variance for a normal curve that it uses to find $p(v_j|C_k)$. In domains that can have missing attributes, it must include a fourth count for each class-attribute pair.

In contrast to many induction methods, which learn only when they make some error, a Bayesian classifier incorporates information from *every* instance that it encounters. Thus, the action taken by the learning component is entirely independent of whether the performance element makes the correct classification. The basic process can operate either incrementally or nonincrementally, since the order of training instances has no effect on learning. However, one can usefully view the Bayesian classifier as carrying out a hill-climbing search through the space of probabilistic concepts, in that it retains a single summary description at each point during processing. This makes the learning algorithm quite efficient.

2.3 Strengths and limitations of simple Bayesian classifiers

Bayesian classifiers should have advantages over many induction algorithms. For example, they should be inherently robust with respect to noise, due to their collection of class and conditional probabilities. Similarly, their statistical basis should also let them handle large numbers of irrelevant attributes. Langley, Iba, and Thompson [9] present an average-case analysis of these factors' effect on the algorithm's behavior for a specific class of target concepts.

However, the basic approach relies on an important assumption: that the instances in each class can be summarized by a single probabilistic description, and that these are sufficient to distinguish the classes from each other. If we represent each attribute value as a feature that may be present or absent, this is closely related to the assumption of linear separability in early work on neural networks. Other encodings lead to a more complex story, but the effect is nearly the same. Nevertheless, like perceptrons, Bayesian classifiers are typically limited to learning classes that occupy contiguous regions of the instance space.

Figure 1 shows an idealized, noise-free training set that illustrates this difficulty. The domain involves three classes of cells – one from **healthy** patients, another from patients with **lethargia**, and a third from patients with the disease **burpoma**. Four attributes describe the observed cells – the number of **nuclei**, the number of **tails**, the **color** of the cell body, and the **thickness** of the cell walls; each such attribute takes on one of two possible values. Running the 12 training cases in the figure through a simple Bayesian classifier produces one probabilistic summary for each class and, combined with Bayes' rule, these descriptions correctly classify all training instances from the **lethargia** and **burpoma** classes. However, it misclassifies two of the **healthy** cells as instances of **lethargia**. The basic problem is a representational one; the **healthy** cases

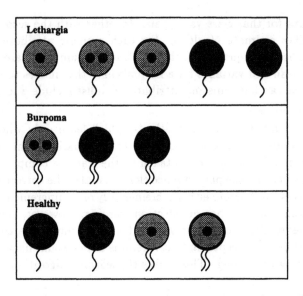

Figure 1. Training instances from an idealized cell domain, involving four attributes and three classes, that cannot be discriminated by a simple Bayesian classifier.

occupy two noncontiguous regions of the instance space, and one cannot represent such disjunctive situations with a single probabilistic summary for each class. In the remainder of the paper, we explore another extension that moves beyond the above representational limitation.

3. The formation of recursive Bayesian classifiers

The assumptions that underlie simple Bayesian classifiers are similar to those commonly made in curve fitting. The technique of linear regression posits that one can approximate the function in question by a single straight line, and this approach fares remarkably well on many tasks. However, in some domains one must resort to *piecewise* linear methods, which fit straight lines only to local portions of the overall curve.

One can apply a similar idea to supervised induction, identifying regions of the instance space in which the independence assumption holds and constructing a simple Bayesian classifier for each such region. One approach to determining such regions, which we will refer to as the RBC algorithm, groups instances by their associated class names, then uses probabilistic averaging to generate intensional descriptions for each cluster. Next, it uses these descriptions to reassign instances, producing a revised partition and summaries. In most situations, the resulting descriptions will not completely discriminate among the classes, so the revised partition and descriptions will differ from the original ones.

If a cluster contains instances from more than one class, this suggests that some refinement is necessary. Thus, the algorithm calls on itself recursively to further subdivide the data and form more specific concept descriptions for each subclass. This approach to partitioning makes less sense if one's goal is a monothetic hierarchy, in which case splitting on one of the predictive attributes is much more direct. Nor can one easily adapt this scheme to handle unsupervised training data, since it relies on class information to form partitions. On the other hand, it provides an elegant approach to generating polythetic hierarchies from supervised data.

Recall that, when used in isolation, a Bayesian classifier is severely limited in its representational ability, and thus in its ability to learn. The current approach should not suffer from such limitations because the hierarchy stores knowledge at multiple levels of abstraction. Subdivisions at lower levels overcome the representational drawbacks at a given level, letting the hierarchy as a whole represent complex concepts even though each level only describes simple ones.

Figure 2 depicts the concept hierarchy generated by RBC for the training data in Figure 1. As in a simple classifier, each node includes a base rate and a conditional probability for each attribute-value pair. In generating this tree, the algorithm first partitions the training instances into three clusters, one for each class, and then uses a Bayesian classifier to produce a probabilistic summary for each set. The resulting descriptions predict the correct class names for all instances of lethargia and burpoma, as well as for the second two healthy cases. However, it assigns the first two healthy cells to the lethargia class.

In response, RBC generates a revised partition based on these three groups of instances, then computes a revised probabilistic summary for each one. Because one of the clusters contains instances from two classes, it calls itself recursively on this subset of instances. Thus, the algorithm creates one partition for the five lethargia cases and another for the two healthy instances, after which it invokes the Bayesian classifier a second time to produce descriptions for each such cluster. This time the probabilistic summaries correctly predict the class associated with each instance, so RBC halts its construction process.

4. Comparative studies of Bayesian classifiers

We have presented intuitive arguments for the superiority of recursive Bayesian classifiers over their simpler cousins, and we have given an illustrative example in which the former outperforms the latter. However, it remains an empirical question whether the RBC algorithm fares better than a simple Bayesian classifier in general. To answer this question, we carried out experiments with both natural domains from the UCI repository and artificial ones designed to test specific hypotheses. For each study, we generated 20 training and test sets, randomly drawn from the domain in question; in each case, we report the average

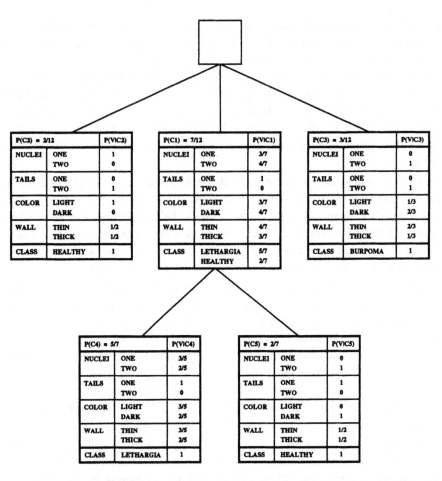

Figure 2. A probabilistic concept hierarchy generated by the RBC algorithm from the training instances in Figure 1. Each node contains a probabilistic summary, which the recursive classifier uses to sort instances and to make predictions.

accuracy of each algorithm on the test set after different numbers of training cases, along with 95% error bars for each point.

Figure 3 (a) presents the results of a comparative study on a domain that involves only nominal attributes. This data set [6] indicates votes ('yea' or 'nea') of the 435 members of the U.S. House of Representatives on 16 issues. The class name corresponds to the member's party, Democrat (267) or Republican (168). By the time they have seen 15 training cases, both algorithms have acquired probabilistic summaries that can predict a member's party with 90% accuracy, though the recursive method does noticeably worse early in the run. However, many induction algorithms produce similar results on this domain, making it useful mainly as an adequacy check. The most interesting result is that the simple Bayesian classifier performs as well as many more sophisticated methods.

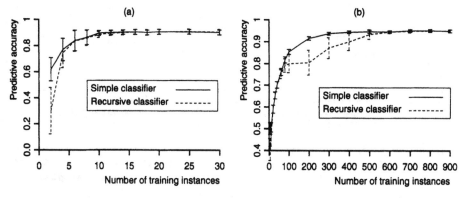

Figure 3. Learning curves for the simple Bayesian classifier and the recursive Bayesian classifier on (a) Congressional voting records and (b) splice junction data.

However, we find very similar effects in Figure 3 (b), which shows learning curves for a more complex domain, this one involving data on "splice junctions" in DNA sequences [12]. The domain includes three classes and some 60 nominal attributes, which specify the nucleotides that precede and follow the position to be classified. The rate of learning in this domain is much slower than for the voting records, but the asymptotic accuracy is slightly higher (95%). As before, the two algorithms reach the same level, but RBC requires more training cases than the simple classifier.

The pattern repeats in Figure 4 (a), which summarizes results on a domain that involves determining, based on nine numeric measures, whether or not a glass fragment came from a window. Again the asymptotic accuracy for both techniques hovers around 90%, with the recursive Bayesian classifier appearing to take slightly more training to reach this level, though the error bars overlap in this case. Analogous learning curves even emerge on the data for heart diseases (originally collected by R. Detrano), which involve two classes and 13 attributes, some numeric and some nominal. In this case the curves are statistically indistinguishable, though RBC's mean accuracy is consistently below that for the simple Bayesian classifier.

Naturally, these results are disappointing and deserve some explanation. Inspection of the induced knowledge structures for these domains reveal that RBC constructs probabilistic decision trees that are quite shallow, in many cases only two levels deep. This suggests that the domains used in our studies closely approximate the independence assumption, making the simple Bayesian classifier appropriate for them, and that other factors (such as noise) are responsible for both methods' imperfect asymptotic accuracies. This does not explain the depression in RBC's learning curve on the splice junction data, but it accounts for most of the observed phenomena.

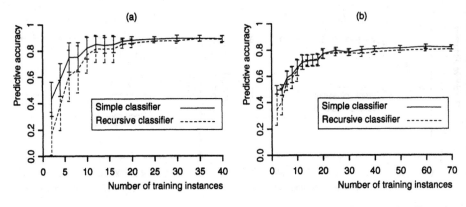

Figure 4. Learning curves for the simple Bayesian classifier and the recursive Bayesian classifier on (a) glass classification and (b) heart disease records.

This theory suggests that we should turn to artificial or synthetic domains to reveal the difference between the two learning algorithms. In response, we ran further comparative studies on a set of noise-free domains that involved two classes, three relevant Boolean attributes $(A, B,$ and $C)$, and three irrelevant Boolean attributes $(D, E,$ and $F)$. We varied the number of disjunctive terms in the target concept from one to four. In particular, we used the target concepts

$$(A \wedge B \wedge C)$$
$$(A \wedge B \wedge C) \vee (A \wedge \bar{B} \wedge \bar{C})$$
$$(A \wedge B \wedge C) \vee (A \wedge \bar{B} \wedge \bar{C}) \vee (\bar{A} \wedge \bar{B} \wedge C)$$
$$(A \wedge B \wedge C) \vee (A \wedge \bar{B} \wedge \bar{C}) \vee (\bar{A} \wedge \bar{B} \wedge C) \vee (\bar{A} \wedge B \wedge \bar{C})$$

which include increasing numbers of nonadjecent vertices of the cube defined by the three relevant features. In each case, adding a new disjunctive term introduces another noncontiguous region to the instance space.

Figure 5 presents the learning curves for both learning algorithms on the first two of these concepts. Each curve is averaged over 20 randomly selected training sets, with the test set including the entire space of 64 instances. As before, the error bars indicate 95% confidence intervals. As expected, the asymptotic accuracies of the simple and recursive Bayesian classifiers approach 100% on the first (conjunctive) domain, as shown in Figure 5 (a), but the more complex algorithm takes more training cases to reach this level, as we found in the natural domains. However, the results for the second (disjunctive) target concept in Figure 5 (b) are quite different. Again, the recursive algorithm starts off worse than its simpler counterpart, but at ten training instances, the learning curves cross over, with the asymptotic accuracy of RBC being significantly higher than that for the simple Bayesian classifier.

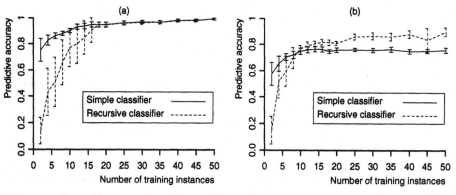

Figure 5. Learning curves for the simple Bayesian classifier and the recursive Bayesian classifier on artificial domains involving (a) a conjunctive target concept and (b) a two-disjunct concept.

The learning curves in Figure 6 provide additional evidence of the recursive scheme's superiority in disjunctive domains. Here we see the same pattern for the three-disjunct and four-disjunct concepts as we found in Figure 5 (b). The RBC algorithm's initial accuracy is lower than that for the simple Bayesian classifier, but crossovers occur between the fifth and tenth training instances, with the more sophisticated method outperforming its simpler counterpart after that point. These results support our original intuitions about the conditions under which RBC will outperform a scheme that relies on the independence assumption. However, the results of the simple Bayesian classifier on the four natural domains remains impressive, and one should by no means abandon it as a useful tool for inductive learning.

5. Related approaches to induction

The idea of organizing knowledge in a tree or hierarchy is far from new, going back to Feigenbaum's [5] EPAM. However, such early algorithms and their descendents, including Quinlan's C4.5 [11] and its relatives, use a single attribute to partition the instance space at each level of the tree. As others have noted, this 'monothetic' approach encounters difficulties when the decision boundaries for the target concept are not parallel to the axes of the instance space. In contrast, 'polythetic' approaches like perceptrons and simple Bayesian classifiers, which consider multiple attributes during a decision, are unaffected by this situation.

On the other hand, the recursive partitioning of the instance space into regions lets decision-tree algorithms deal with disjunctive concepts, which cause problems for perceptrons and simple Bayesian classifiers. A natural response is to combine the recursive structure of decision trees with the discriminating power of polythetic classifiers. Brieman, Friedman, Olshen, and Stone [1] have done some work along these lines, using linear threshold units at each node in the tree.

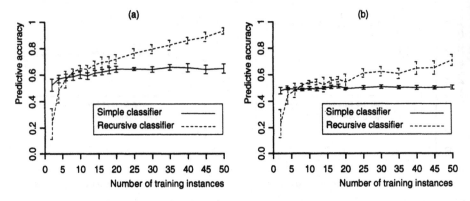

Figure 6. Learning curves for the simple Bayesian classifier and the recursive Bayesian classifier on artificial domains involving (a) a three-disjunct target concept and (b) a four-disjunct concept.

More recently, Utgoff and Brodley [13] have developed LMDT, an incremental method for inducing decision trees in which each nonterminal node specifies a linear machine. As in threshold units, such knowledge structures specify a set of weights for each class-attribute pair, but they operate competitively. The LMDT algorithm requires many passes through the training set, but otherwise it has many similarities to our approach. Sahami (personal communication, 1992) has developed a similar algorithm for inducing polythetic trees.

Fisher [6] has also dealt extensively with methods for organizing probabilistic concepts in a hierarchy. His COBWEB algorithm uses an identical representation and organization of knowledge, but there are also some important differences. COBWEB is unsupervised, attempting to maximize predictive accuracy across all attributes even if class names are present. Also, Fisher's incremental algorithm constructs complex trees that can be strongly affected by training order, which can produce knowledge structures that are difficult to understand.

In contrast, the RBC method is not subject to order effects and recurses only enough to discriminate the class names; thus, we predict that its trees will be more comprehensible than COBWEB's, though we have not tested this hypothesis. Moreover, Kononenko [7] has shown that a simple Bayesian classifier can explain its decisions as the sum of information gain over all attributes, and that physicians prefer such explanations to monothetic decision trees. Given that, in our experience, the RBC algorithm tends to build shallow trees, we expect that at least some domain experts will prefer them to normal monothetic decision trees as well.

Some researchers have explored other approaches to adapting Bayesian classifiers to disjunctive domains that violate the independence assumption. For example, Michie and Al Attar [10] describe a 'sequential Bayesian classifier' that inspects one attribute at a time during performance, selecting the most informative one at each step and halting when the probability of a class exceeds a maximum threshold or falls below a minimum. However, this method's behavior is equivalent to constructing a monothetic decision tree using a probabilistic evaluation function, thus losing the ability to consider evidence from multiple attributes simultaneously.

Kononenko [8] describes a quite different approach that explicitly tests for dependencies among attributes, creating new features based on the conjunctions of correlated values. This 'semi-naive Bayesian classifier' then uses the training data to compute conditional probabilities for these higher-order features, using them to classify test cases rather than the original ones. However, in an experimental comparasion of his algorithm and a simple Bayesian classifier, Kononenko found no differences on two medical domains and only very slight improvement on two others. These findings are consistent with our results on the robustness of the naive method in natural domains.

6. Directions for future research

Despite the promise of recursive Bayesian classifiers, much work remains before we can claim that they constitute a robust approach to induction. We have yet to identify any natural domains on which the method outperforms a simple Bayesian classifier, despite our intuitions about the former's superiority. Moreover, we must still examine the effect of other domain characteristics on the method's behavior. For instance, we should study the influence of both the number of relevant and irrelevant attributes, as well as the effect of class and attribute noise. We should also study the behavior of an incremental version developed by Schlimmer and Hermens (personal communication, 1992).

Some extensions will also be necessary. Like any hierarchical induction algorithm, RBC can overfit the data by constructing an overly detailed tree, and we should install a pruning scheme to counter this tendency. One simple technique would recurse only if the classifier at a given level exceeds a certain error rate. The current version also has difficulty with parity concepts, in which all attributes appear independent of the class name. In such cases, a revised system might resort to an arbitrary monothetic partition to overcome the bottleneck. Finally, future versions should use Cestnik's [2] m estimate, which he has shown improves accuracy over the relative frequencies currently used.

Despite these limitations, we believe that the RBC algorithm constitutes a promising extension to simple Bayesian classifiers which should be less sensitive to domains that violate the assumption of independence. We anticipate that further comparative studies, combined with theoretical analyses, will reveal the conditions under which this method outperforms both the simpler probabilistic algorithm from which it evolved and other techniques that rely on the induction of traditional decision trees.

Acknowledgements

Thanks to Stephanie Sage, Jeff Schlimmer, Carla Brodley, Kevin Thompson, and Wayne Iba for discussions that helped clarify our ideas, and to Nils Nilsson for his support and encouragement. The author carried out this work while at Stanford University and the Institute for the Study of Learning and Expertise.

References

1. Brieman, L., Friedman, J. H., Olshen, R. A., & Stone, C. J. (1984). *Classification and regression trees*. Belmont: Wadsworth.

2. Cestnik, G. (1990). Estimating probabilities: A crucial task for machine learning. *Proceedings of the Ninth European Conference on Artificial Intelligence* (pp. 147–149). Stockholm, Sweden.

3. Clark, P., & Niblett, T. (1989). The CN2 induction algorithm. *Machine Learning, 3*, 261–284.

4. Duda, R. O., & Hart, P. E. (1973). *Pattern classification and scene analysis*. New York: John Wiley & Sons.

5. Feigenbaum, E. A. (1963). The simulation of verbal learning behavior. In E. A. Feigenbaum & J. Feldman (Eds.), *Computers and thought*. New York: McGraw-Hill.

6. Fisher, D. H. (1987). Knowledge acquisition via incremental conceptual clustering. *Machine Learning, 2*, 139–172.

7. Kononenko, I. (1990). Comparison of inductive and naive Bayesian learning approaches to automatic knowledge acquisition. In B. Wielinga et al. (Eds.), *Current trends in knowledge acquisition*. Amsterdam: IOS Press.

8. Kononenko, I. (1991). Semi-naive Bayesian classifier. *Proceedings of the Sixth European Working Session on Learning* (pp. 206–219). Porto: Pittman.

9. Langley, P., Iba, W., & Thompson, K. (1992). An analysis of Bayesian classifiers. *Proceedings of the Tenth National Conference on Artificial Intelligence* (pp. 223–228). San Jose, CA: AAAI Press.

10. Miche, D., & Al Attar, A. (1991). Use of sequential Bayes with class probability trees. In J. E. Hayes-Michie, D. Michie, & E. Tyugu (Eds.), *Machine intelligence 12*. Oxford: Oxford University Press.

11. Quinlan, J. R. (1993). *C4.5: Programs for induction*. San Mateo, CA: Morgan Kaufmann.

12. Towell, G. G. (1991). *Symbolic knowledge and neural networks: Insertion, refinement, and extraction*. Dissertation, Department of Computer Science, University of Wisconsin, Madison.

13. Utgoff, P. E., & Brodley, C. E. (1990). An incremental method for finding multivariate splits for decision trees. *Proceedings of the Seventh International Conference on Machine Learning* (pp. 58–65). Austin, TX: Morgan Kaufmann.

Decision Tree Pruning as a Search in the State Space

Floriana Esposito, Donato Malerba*, Giovanni Semeraro

Dipartimento di Informatica, Università degli Studi di Bari
via G. Amendola 173, 70126 Bari, Italy

Abstract. This paper presents a study of one particular problem of decision tree induction, namely (post-)pruning, with the aim of finding a common framework for the plethora of pruning methods appeared in literature. Given a tree T_{max} to prune, a state space is defined as the set of all subtrees of T_{max} to which only one operator, called any-depth branch pruning operator, can be applied in several ways in order to move from one state to another. By introducing an evaluation function f defined on the set of subtrees, the problem of tree pruning can be cast as an optimization problem, and it is also possible to classify each post-pruning method according to both its search strategy and the kind of information exploited by f. Indeed, while some methods use only the training set in order to evaluate the accuracy of a decision tree, other methods exploit an additional pruning set that allows them to get less biased estimates of the predictive accuracy of a pruned tree. The introduction of the state space shows that very simple search strategies are used by the post-pruning methods considered. Finally, some empirical results allow theoretical observations on strengths and weaknesses of pruning methods to be better understood.

1 Introduction

Decision tree induction has been widely investigated both in the area of machine learning and in pattern recognition. In the vast literature concerning decision trees, at least two seminal works have to be cited: [1, 2]. They come from two schools which worked independently of each other on the same problem, and only at the end of the eighties some papers comparing methods and results from different schools and authors appeared in literature [3, 4, 5, 6]. In this paper we investigate one particular problem concerning decision tree induction, namely the determination of which nodes are leaves, with the aim of finding a common framework for the plethora of methods proposed by the two schools.

In fact, there are two different ways to cope with this problem: either deciding when to stop the growth of a tree or reducing the size of a fully expanded tree, T_{max}, by pruning some branches. Methods that control the growth of a decision tree during its development are called *pre-pruning* methods, while the others are called *post-pruning* methods [7]. The former methods suffer from the problem that the decision of arresting the growth of a branch is always based on local information. Consequently, a test that seems not to add any information on the distribution of the examples is always discarded by any pre-pruning method, even if it would be very useful when subsequently combined with some other tests. This problem is also present in some learning systems that learn Horn clauses and exploit information-based heuristics in order to choose the next literal to add [8]. For this reason, given enough data, it is generally preferred to grow a large tree and then to prune those branches that seem superfluous or even harmful with respect to predictive accuracy [9].

---

* Currently at the Department of Information and Computer Science, University of California, Irvine, CA 92717.

The variety of post-pruning (or simply pruning) methods proposed in literature does not encourage the comprehension of both the common and the individual aspects. In fact, while some methods proceed from the root towards the leaves of T_{max} when they examine the branches to prune (*top-down approach*), other methods follow the opposite direction, starting the analysis from the leaves and finishing with the root node (*bottom-up approach*). Furthermore, while some methods use only the *training set* in order to evaluate the accuracy of a decision tree, other methods exploit an additional *pruning set*, sometimes improperly called test set, that allows them to get less biased estimates of the predictive accuracy of a pruned tree.

In the next section, we introduce the state space as common framework for all the well-known pruning methods. By introducing an evaluation function defined on the set of states, the problem of tree pruning can be cast as the problem of searching the state with the highest value of *f*. In section 3 this framework is exploited in order to comparatively study different pruning methods so to emphasize their strengths and weaknesses. In this comparison, we will always refer to the same example of decision tree in order to show how the methods really work. Finally, some experimental results together with an explanation of the experimental method are presented in section 4.

2. The search space of pruning methods

Henceforth, we assume that the reader is familiar with some basic notions on decision trees. However, for the sake of clearness, we introduce some notations that we use throughout the paper. In particular, $\mathfrak{N}_T$ denotes the set of *non terminal* nodes of a tree T, while $\mathfrak{I}_T$ denotes the set of *leaves* of T. Moreover, T_t denotes the *branch* of T containing a node t and all its descendants.

Let $\mathfrak{T}$ be the set of all trees. Then the *operation of pruning a branch from a tree* T is a function π_T:

$$\pi_T : \mathfrak{N}_T \to \mathfrak{T}$$

such that each node $t \in \mathfrak{N}_T$ is associated with the tree $\pi_T(t)$ whose set of nodes is $T \setminus (T_t \setminus \{t\})$, where $\setminus$ denotes the set difference. Such tree is named *subtree of T with a pruned branch*. Note that it does not make sense to prune single node trees.

Given a tree $T \in \mathfrak{T}$ with n non-terminal nodes $(n = |\mathfrak{N}_T|)$, let $\pi_T(\mathfrak{N}_T)$ denote the set of the n subtrees of T with a single pruned branch. When $|\mathfrak{N}_T| = 0$, we set $\pi_T(\mathfrak{N}_T) = \varnothing$.

The branch pruning operation can be in turn applied to a tree $T' \in \pi_T(\mathfrak{N}_T)$, provided that $|\mathfrak{N}_{T'}| > 0$. Then it is possible to define recursively $\pi^i(\mathfrak{N}_T)$ as follows:

$$\pi^i(\mathfrak{N}_T) = \begin{cases} \{T\} & \text{if } i=0 \\ \pi_T(\mathfrak{N}_T) & \text{if } i=1 \\ \bigcup_{T' \in \pi^{i-1}(\mathfrak{N}_T)} \pi_{T'}(\mathfrak{N}_{T'}) & \text{if } i>1 \end{cases}$$

that is $\pi^i(\mathfrak{N}_T)$ represents the set of subtrees of T obtained by i subsequent branch pruning operations.

It is worthwhile to note that $\pi^{n+1}(\mathfrak{N}_T) = \varnothing$, since the operation of pruning a branch can be applied at most n times to a tree with n non-terminal nodes. Therefore the set of all possible subtrees of T, $\mathfrak{S}(T)$, is given by:

$$\mathbf{S}(T) = \bigcup_{i=0}^{n} \pi^i(\mathbf{R}_T)$$

The problem of post-pruning can be cast as a search in a *state space* [14], where *states* are trees in $\mathbf{S}(T)$ and branch pruning is the only *operator* that can be applied in several ways to each tree in $\mathbf{S}(T)$. This space can be represented like a directed acyclic graph whose vertices are just the elements in $\mathbf{S}(T)$ and for each pair $(T,T') \in \mathbf{S}(T) \times \mathbf{S}(T)$ there is an edge from T to T' if and only if $T' \in \pi_{T}(\mathbf{R}_T)$, that is T' is obtained by pruning only one branch of T. It should be noted that in this space we move from one state to another by pruning a branch of *any depth*. A matter of interest is also the space of *one depth* branch pruning in which there is an edge between every pair of trees $(T,T') \in \mathbf{S}(T) \times \mathbf{S}(T)$ if and only if T' is obtained from T by pruning a branch having a depth equal to one. Indeed, by inverting the direction of the edges, we get a space that coincides with the lattice $(\mathbf{S}(T), \leq)$ in which the order relationship is the tree inclusion.

For the sake of clearness, let us consider the decision tree depicted in Fig. 1. Then its corresponding lattice of the *one depth* branch pruning operations is that reported in Fig. 2 while the corresponding state space of the *any depth* branch pruning operations is shown in Fig. 3. In these spaces, each tree T_j^i is uniquely identified by a pair of indices, i and j, where i denotes the number of leaves of the tree while j discriminates among all the trees with the same number of leaves. Obviously, there exists only one tree with one node that can be obtained from T_{max} by means of the (multiple) application of the branch pruning operator, and such a tree is denoted by T_1^1. Moreover if $|\mathbf{T}_{Tmax}|$=M, there exists just one tree having M leaves, namely $T_1^M = T_{max}$. A further observation concerns the fact that in any state space there exists an edge from any $T_j^i \neq T_1^1$ to T_1^1 since T_1^1 can be obtained from T_j^i by applying the pruning operator to the root of T_j^i.

In order to define the *goal* of the search, a function f that estimates the goodness of a tree has to be introduced. It associates each tree in $\mathbf{S}(T)$ with a numerical value, namely:

$$f : \mathbf{S}(T) \to \mathbf{R}$$

where $\mathbf{R}$ is the set of real values. Therefore, the goal of the search is to find the vertex in the graph with the highest value for f, that is to find the *best* subtree of T_{max} with respect to f. In this way, the problem of pruning is cast as a problem of function optimization.

Independently of the adopted optimization method, it is necessary to establish the starting point for the search process. All the pruning methods in literature perform a *forward search*, since they start from T_{max} and go through the graph according to the direction of the edges, nevertheless, they adopt different strategies to generate the sequence of states to explore. We classify the pruning methods as follows:

- *Top-down methods* evaluate first the convenience of pruning the root and then its children, until leaves are considered
- *bottom-up methods*, that start their analysis from the leaves and climb up until the root is considered.

Such a classification does not exactly establish the order in which states are visited, yet. Indeed, T_{max} can have several leaves and it is not clear which leaf will be considered initially and which finally. Therefore, a traversal order for the nodes in a tree must be defined [10].

For instance, with reference to the state space in Fig. 3, a top-down method would first

168

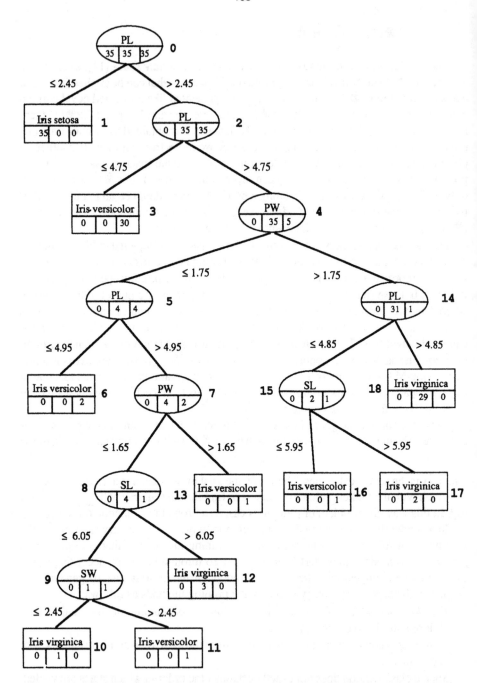

Fig. 1. An example of decision tree induced from a subset of 105 cases of the database "Iris Plants". Observations are classified according to values taken by four distinct continuous attributes: sepal length (SL), sepal width(SW), petal length (PL) and petal width (PW). The nodes of the tree are labelled with numbers assigned by a preorder traversal. Moreover, in each node the number of training instances belonging to each class (*iris setosa, iris virginica* and *iris versicolor*) is reported.

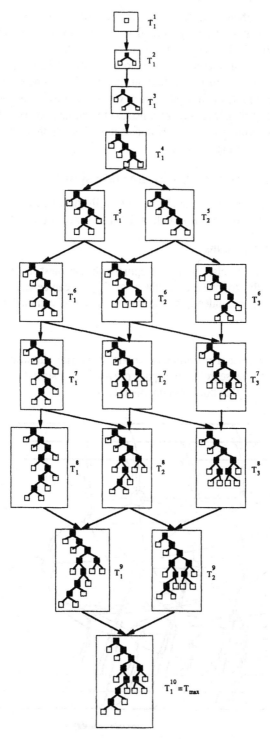

Fig. 2. The lattice of the one depth branch pruning operation for the tree in Fig. 1.

explore the state T_1^1, then T_1^2, then T_1^3, and eventually the state T_1^8 by following a pre-order traversal. Conversely, a bottom-up method would first consider the state T_2^9, then T_3^8, then T_3^7, and eventually T_1^1, by following a post-order traversal.

A further criterion to classify the methods presented in literature is the rationale underlying the definition of the evaluation function f. In some methods, f is based on statistical information drawn from the *training set* alone, while in other methods information coming from an additional *pruning set* is also exploited. The experimental results reported in [6] show that pruned trees are better according to both predictive accuracy and simplicity when a pruning set is used.

3 Tree pruning as a search in the state space

In this section, a comparative study of five well-known post-pruning methods with respect to the framework of the search in the state space is presented.

3.1 Reduced error pruning

This method, due to Quinlan [3], is conceptually the simplest and uses the pruning set in order to evaluate the goodness of a subtree of T_{max}. It can be easily framed as a search through the state space. Indeed, the evaluation function f can be defined as follows:

$$f(T) = -\sum_{t \in \mathcal{J}_T} e(t)$$

where $e(t)$ is the number of errors made by node t during the classification of the examples in the pruning set. The search in the space moves from a state T to a state $T' \in \pi_T(\mathcal{R}_T)$ if the inequality $f(T') \geq f(T)$ holds or equivalently if

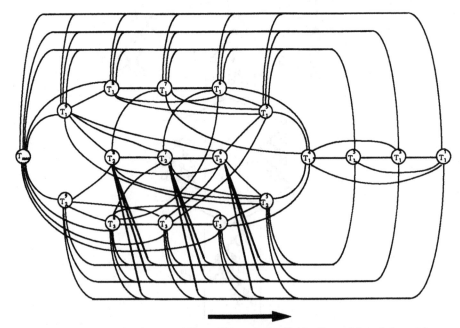

Fig. 3. State space for the tree in Fig. 1. Edges are implicitly directed from left to right.

$$\sum_{t\in \mathcal{J}_{T'}} e(t) \; < \; \sum_{t\in \mathcal{J}_{T}} e(t)$$

Table 1 summarizes the results obtained by applying the reduced error pruning method to the decision tree in Fig. 1 using an independent pruning set of 45 examples. Each non-terminal node is accompanied with the expected error rate for both the case in which the tree undergoes a pruning operation in that node and the case in which no pruning is performed (the corresponding number of classification errors made on the examples of the pruning set is reported in brackets). It is easy to see that, the reduced error pruning method prunes the nodes 9, 8, 7, 15 and 14 since each pruning operation does not increase the error rate of the decision tree. The path followed during the search in the state space is given by:

$$T_{max}, T_2^9, T_3^8, T_3^7, T_3^6, T_1^5.$$

Table 1: Error rates on the pruning set.

# node	error when pruned	error when not pruned
0	66.67% (30)	2.22% (1)
2	33.33% (15)	2.22% (1)
4	4.44% (2)	2.22% (1)
5	4.44% (2)	2.22% (1)
7	2.22% (1)	2.22% (1)
8	2.22% (1)	2.22% (1)
9	2.22% (1)	2.22% (1)
14	2.22% (1)	2.22% (1)
15	2.22% (1)	2.22% (1)

The generation of the states to be explored is made according to the order defined by *bottom-up* methods, therefore there is no choice of the best state to reach, starting from another state. This contrasts with the description of the same method reported in [6]. In fact, Mingers claims that among all the nodes, the one having the largest difference between the number of errors (on the pruning set) when the subtree is kept and the number of errors when the node is pruned must be chosen. This is equivalent to choosing, from all the states of the search space directly connected to the current state, the one with the best value for f. This variant introduces a hill-climbing search strategy instead of the uninformed bottom-up ordered search proposed by Quinlan, thus the guarantee of finding the *smallest version of the most accurate tree with respect to the pruning set* is lost [11].

The problems related to the method of reduced error pruning are basically two:
1) The use of a pruning set distinct from the training set is inadequate when a small number of observations are available
2) the parts of the original tree that correspond to special cases outside the test set may be lost after pruning. Therefore trees pruned via that pruning method may fail in correctly classifying exceptional cases.

At last, it is worthwhile to note that the computational complexity of the method is linear in the number of leaves or exponential in the depth of the tree. Indeed, in the case of a binary balanced tree of depth K, whose best subtree is just that consisting of the root alone, the method of the reduced error pruning will consider all the $2^K - 1$ internal nodes before obtaining the best tree.

3.2 Pessimistic error pruning

This pruning method, proposed by Quinlan [3] as well, is characterized by the fact that it avoids using an independent pruning set. The misclassification rate, estimated by means of the training set alone, results to be optimistic, thus it always happens that pruning operations based on the same data set produce trees that are larger than it is needed. That reason induced Quinlan to introduce the continuity correction for the binomial distribution that, in his opinion, should provide a more realistic estimate of the classification error rate. Let $N(t)$ be the number of training examples reaching the node $t \in T$ and $e(t)$ the number of them which are misclassified when t is (possibly transformed into) a leaf. Then the number of misclassifications with the continuity correction for the binomial distribution gives:

$$n'(t) = [e(t) + 1/2]$$

for a node t, and:

$$n'(T_t) = \Sigma\, e(s) + |\tilde{T}_t| / 2$$

for a subtree T_t.

It should be observed that, when the development of a tree goes on until all its leaves do not make errors on the training set, $e(s)=0$ for each $s \in \tilde{T}_t$. In that case $n'(T)$ only represents a measure of the tree complexity that associates each leaf with a cost equal to $1/2$. This is no longer true for partially pruned trees or when contradictions (equal observations belonging to distinct classes) occur in the training set.

When a subtree T_t makes fewer errors on the training set than the node t transformed into a leaf, that is $n'(t) \lesssim n'(T_t)$, the node t can be pruned. Nonetheless, $n'(T_t)$ is still an optimistic estimate, thus Quinlan weakens the condition that rules the pruning of a subtree T_t and requires that:

$$n'(t) \le n'(T_t) + SE(n'(T_t))$$

where

$$SE(n'(T_t)) = [n'(T_t) \cdot (N(t) - n'(T_t)) / N(t)]^{1/2}$$

is the standard error for the subtree T_t. The algorithm evaluates each node starting from the root of the tree and, if a subtree is chosen for pruning, its internal nodes are not examined. This top-down approach gives the pruning technique a high run speed.

Table 2 reports some data that are relevant for the application of the pessimistic error pruning to the example in Fig. 1. It can be easily seen that the first node to be pruned is node 4, therefore the resultant decision tree has only 3 leaves. In terms of state space, the method moved directly from T_{max} to T_1^3.

The evaluation function associated with each state is the following:

$$f(T) = -\underset{t \in \tilde{T}_T}{\Sigma}\, n'(t)$$

In fact, let T' be the arrival state of an edge outcoming from T such that it is obtained by pruning a node $t \in T$. Then it is easy to prove that:

$$f(T') - f(T) = n'(T_t) - n'(t)$$

that, as told above, is still an optimistic measure for deciding whether to move from a state to another one. This is the reason for which pruning is accomplished also when the following conditions hold:

$$- SE(n'(T_t)) \le f(T') - f(T) \Leftrightarrow f(T) - f(T') \le SE(n'(T_t)) \Leftrightarrow n'(T_t) + SE(n'(T_t)) \ge n'(t)$$

Moving from the state T to the state T' occurs when, during the generation of T', the above inequality becomes true. Therefore, there is no evaluation of the best pruning to perform among the possible ones, and the first pruning operation that turns out to be good is performed. The adopted strategy seems rather poor since the top-down approach to tree

Table 2: Results of the pessimistic error pruning for the tree in Fig. 1.

# node	n'(t)	n'(T$_t$)	SE(n'(T$_t$))	$|\mathbf{f}_{T_t}|$
0	70.5	5.0	2.18	10
2	35.5	4.5	2.04	9
4	5.5	4.0	1.89	8
5	5.5	2.5	1.31	5
7	2.5	2.0	1.15	4
8	1.5	1.5	1.15	3
9	1.5	1.0	0.7	2
14	1.5	1.5	1.19	3
15	1.5	1.0	0.81	2

pruning is not justified when there is no guarantee that all subtrees of a pruned branch T$_t$ should be pruned. By looking at data reported in Table 2 it is easy to note that pruning node 4 involves the elimination of the subtree T$_5$ too, which should not be pruned according to the same criterion. This method has a linear complexity in the number of leaves, and the worst case is that in which the tree has not to be pruned at all.

Lastly, the continuity correction, which has no theoretical justification, simply introduces a sort of tree complexity factor which is improperly compared to an error rate.

3.3 Minimum error pruning

Niblett and Bratko [12] proposed a bottom-up approach seeking a single tree that minimizes the expected error rate on an independent data set. In the following, we will refer to an improved version of the minimum error pruning reported in [13].

For a k-class problem, the expected probability of an observation that reaches a node t of belonging to the i-th class is the following:

$$p_i(t) = [n_i(t) + p_{ai} \cdot m] / [N(t) + m]$$

where

- $n_i(t)$ is the number of training examples in t classified into the i-th class
- p_{ai} is the *a priori* probability of the i-th class
- m is a parameter of the estimate method
- $N(t)$ is the number of training examples reaching t.

The parameter m determines the contribution of the *a priori* probability of the i-th class to the estimate of the conditional probability of the i-th class in a node t by means of the relative frequency $n_i(t) / N(t)$. For the sake of simplicity, m is assumed to be equal for all the classes. Cestnik and Bratko name $p_i(t)$ as *m-probability estimate*. When a new case reaching t is classified, the expected error rate is given by:

$$EER(t) = \min_i \{ 1 - p_i(t) \} = \min_i \{ [N(t) - n_i(t) + (1-p_{ai}) \cdot m]/[N(t)+m] \}$$

This formula is a generalization of the expected error rate computed by Niblett and Bratko [12]. Indeed, when m=k and p_{ai}=1/k, i=1,2,..., k, that is the a priori probability distribution is uniform and equal for all classes, we get:

$$EER(t) = \min_i \{ [N(t) - n_i(t) + k-1] / [N(t) + k] \}$$

which is the formula proposed in the earlier version of the method.

Table 3: Static and dynamic errors for each internal node of the tree in Fig. 1.

	m=1.0		m=3.0		m=10.0	
t	STE(t)	DE(t)	STE(t)	DE(t)	STE(t)	DE(t)
0	66.67%	4.44%	66.67%	9.12%	66.67%	18.59%
2	50.23%	5.73%	50.68%	11.05%	52.08%	20.48%
4	13.82%	8.42%	16.28%	14.79%	23.33%	25.28%
5	51.85%	24.31%	54.55%	39.69%	59.26%	53.41%
7	38.10%	25.00%	44.44%	39.58%	54.17%	52.69%
8	27.78%	23.33%	37.50%	40.00%	51.11%	55.01%
9	55.56%	33.33%	60.00%	50.00%	63.89%	60.61%
14	5.05%	4.44%	8.57%	9.73%	18.25%	20.86%
15	41.67%	25.93%	50.00%	43.33%	58.97%	57.24%

In the minimum error pruning method, the expected error rate for each non-terminal node $t \in \mathfrak{N}_T$ is computed. It is called *static error*, STE(t). Then the expected error rate when t is not pruned, called *dynamic* (or *backed-up*) *error*, DE(t), is computed. It is given by a weighted sum of the expected error rates of the children, where the weights are the probabilities that an observation will reach the corresponding child. For instance, by referring to the tree in Fig. 1, we have:

STE(4) = p_5·EER(5)+p_{14}·EER(14)

In the original method proposed by Niblett and Bratko, the weights p_i were estimated by the proportion of training examples reaching the *i*-th child. In this case, p_5=8/40 while p_{14}=32/40. Cestnik and Bratko suggest an *m*-probability estimate with m=2 for p_i, even though the same authors admit that *m* is chosen arbitrarily. However, in this case the *a priori* probability p_{ai} in the *m*-probability estimate refers to the *i*-th node of the tree and not to the *i*-th class. Since it is not clear how it can be computed, in the following we will consider the original proposal, which corresponds to an *m*-probability estimate for p_i with m=0.

In Table 3 values concerning the static error and the dynamic error for each internal node of the tree in Fig. 1 are reported. They have been computed with three distinct values of m: 1.0, 3.0 and 10.0. It is easy to see that when m=1.0 the original tree is not pruned at all, while for m=3.0 only nodes 8 and 14 are pruned and, finally, for m=10.0 nodes 8, 14 and 4 are pruned. Having obtained three distinct trees, the problem of choosing the best one raises. Cestnik and Bratko suggests the intervention of a domain expert who can choose the right value of *m* according to the level of noise in the data or even study the selection of produced trees. Alternatively, when no expert is available, the classification accuracy of the three trees can be evaluated on an independent data set and the smallest tree with the lowest error rate on the pruning set can be selected. In the above example, we get the best results for m=3.0, since the error rate on the pruning set is 2.22%.

The minimum error pruning method can be seen as a way of searching in the state space. In this case the evaluation function of a tree T can be defined as the dynamic error of the root of T. It can be proven that such an error equals the weighted sum of the static errors of all the leaves of the tree, where the weights are the proportion of the training examples in the leaves themselves. Formally, we can write:

$$f(T) = -\sum_{t \in \widetilde{\mathcal{I}}_T} N(t) \cdot STE(t)/N$$

where

- N is the total number of training examples
- $N(t)$ is the number of examples reaching t.

The search starts with T_{max} and a new state T_j^i is reached if $f(T_j^i) \geq f(T_{max})$. If T_j^i is obtained by pruning a node t in T_{max}, $T_j^i \in \pi_{T_{max}}(t)$, then the previous inequality can be equivalently written as:

$$STE(t) \leq DE(t)$$

which is the condition for pruning a node according to Niblett and Bratko's formulation of the method.

The order of visit of the states is defined *a priori* by the post-order traversal of the bottom-up approach. For instance, when m=3.0 the search path followed by the pruning method in the state space of Fig. 3 is given by: T_{max}, T_3^8, T_1^6. In this example T_1^6 has the highest value of f. Nevertheless, it is not clear if the minimum error pruning method always finds the maximum in the state space. It is also worthwhile to observe that, generally, the higher the m, the more severe the pruning. In fact, when m is infinity, it is $p_i(t) = p_{ai}$ and since p_{ai} is estimated as the percentage of examples of the i-th class in the training set, it happens that the tree reduced to a single leaf has the lowest expected error rate. In other words, when m is infinity the path gets to T_1^1. However this characteristic does not mean that a path corresponding to an m' > m is a continuation of the path corresponding to m. In fact the two paths may be completely different, as it is the case of the previous example when m'=10.0. This non-monotonicity property has a severe consequence on computational complexity: for every different value of m search must always start from T_{max}.

3.4 Error-Complexity Pruning

The pruning method proposed by Breiman *et al.* [1], the so called *error-complexity pruning*, is characterized by two phases:

1) selection of a family of subtrees of T_{max} according to some heuristics
2) choice of the best tree that belongs to the family by means of an accurate estimate of the actual error rate either on an independent test set or on validation sets.

The method is certainly the most complex among those presented in the paper, nevertheless its description in terms of search in the state space is greatly simplified. Indeed, the evaluation function for $T \in \mathcal{S}(T_{max})$ is given by:

$$f(T) = -\sum_{t \in \widetilde{\mathcal{I}}_T} e(t)/N$$

and a state $T' \in \pi_T(\mathcal{R}_T)$ is reached from a state T if it happens that:

$$\alpha_T = [f(T) - f(T')]/[|\widetilde{\mathcal{I}}_T| - |\widetilde{\mathcal{I}}_{T'}|] = \min_{T'' \in \pi_T(\mathcal{R}_T)} [f(T) - f(T'')]/[|\widetilde{\mathcal{I}}_T| - |\widetilde{\mathcal{I}}_{T''}|]$$

At each reached state, the next state that gives the lowest value of the ratio "apparent error rate increase" on "number of leaves decrease" is detected. The search goes on till the minimum tree T_1^1 is reached. When $T' = \pi_{T_t}(t)$ it can be proved that:

$$\alpha_{T'} = - [e(t) - e(T_t)]/[(|\tilde{T}_{T_t}|-1)/N]$$

thus a hill-climbing strategy is adopted to go from state T to state T', which minimizes $\alpha_{T'}$. Table 4 reports the values of $\alpha_{T'}$ for all the $T' \in \pi_{T_{max}}(\tilde{T}_{T_{max}})$, that is the ratio "error rate change" on "number of leaves change" for all the subtrees that can be obtained from T_{max} through one branch pruning operation. It is easy to note that α takes its lowest value in correspondence of nodes 8 and 14, and, since the intersection of T_8 and T_{14} is empty, the tree obtained by pruning both these nodes should be preferred to that obtained by pruning only one of the two nodes. Consequently, the following concept of *transient* state is introduced:

Let $T_{max} = T_m, T_{m-1}, ..., T_2, T_1, T_0 = T_1^1$ be the states followed by the search process and let α_{T_i} be the ratio "error rate change" on "number of leaves change" for a state T_i, then T_i is transient if $\alpha_{T_i} = \alpha_{T_{i-1}}$. At the end of the *hill climbing* search performed by the *error-complexity pruning* method, only the non-transient states in the path are taken into account to select the best tree.

Going on with the example in Fig. 1, Tables 5, 6 and 7 report the values of α for the states T_1^6, T_1^4, T_1^2 respectively. The complete path followed in the state space by the *error-complexity pruning* method is the following:

$$T_{max}, \mathbf{T_3^8}, T_1^6, \mathbf{T_1^5}, \mathbf{T_1^3}, \mathbf{T_1^2}, T_1^1$$

where transient states are reported in bold type.

The best subtree selected in the second phase by using the pruning set is T_1^6. This happens because its error rate on this set is 2.22%, that is equal to that of T_{max}, but less than that of T_1^3, T_1^2 and T_1^1. This result does not change if we consider the smallest tree with an error rate within one standard error of the

Table 4: Values of α for the state T_{max}.

t	e(t)	e(T_t)	$|\tilde{T}_{T_t}|$	α
0	70	0	10	0.074074
2	35	0	9	0.041666
4	5	0	8	0.006803
5	4	0	5	0.009524
7	2	0	4	0.006349
8	1	0	3	0.004762
9	1	0	2	0.009524
14	1	0	3	0.004762
15	1	0	2	0.009524

Table 5: Values of α for the state T_1^6.

t	e(t)	e(T_t)	$|\tilde{T}_{T_t}|$	α
0	70	2	6	0.129524
2	35	2	5	0.078571
4	5	2	4	0.009524
5	4	1	3	0.014286
7	2	1	2	0.009524

Table 6: Values of α for the state T_1^4.

t	e(t)	e(T_t)	$|\tilde{T}_{T_t}|$	α
0	70	5	3	0.309524
2	35	5	2	0.285714

Table 7: Values of α for the state T_1^2.

t	e(t)	e(T_t)	$|\tilde{T}_{T_t}|$	α
0	70	35	2	0.333333

minimum (1SE rule).

By comparing these results with those obtained by the *reduced error pruning* method, it turns out that the tree selected by the error complexity pruning method is not the best one with respect to the pruning set, since it would be possible to prune also node 7 with no error rate increase. By generalizing this result, we can state that this method detects the best subtree in a parametric family of pruned subtrees that might not contain the best tree in an absolute sense or a good one with respect to an evaluation criterion such as the error rate estimated on pruning sets or validation sets.

Finally, the computational complexity of the first phase of the method is the same of the reduced error pruning but the error rate estimate through validation sets requires the building of v auxiliary decision trees.

3.5 Iterative growing and pruning algorithm

Gelfand *et al.*[15] propose a different solution in which all the data set is exploited when growing and pruning a tree and furthermore a search of the optimally pruned tree is performed on the whole set of subtrees. These goals are reached by splitting the data set into two subsets and then by repeatedly growing and pruning a tree on different subsets. More in detail, a tree is grown by using the first subset, then it is pruned by using the second subset. At this point the role of the two subsets is exchanged, so the pruned tree is further grown by using the second subset and pruned with the first one (see Fig. 5).

The authors have also proved a theorem which guarantees the convergence of this iterative process and provides a stopping criterion. In particular they first prove that:

$$T^*_{k-1} \leq T^*_k \quad \forall k=1,2,\dots$$

where T^*_k is the optimally pruned tree of the k-th iteration (in each iteration a tree is grown by using one subset and then pruned by using the other one). Subsequently they prove that there exists a finite positive number K such that

$$T^*_k = T^*_K \quad \forall k \geq K$$

The proof of this theorem is constructive since it establishes that

$$K = \inf\{ k \geq 1 : |T^*_{k-1}| = |T^*_k| \}$$

where $|T|$ is the number of nodes in T. Thus the stopping criterion is the following:

$$|T^*_{k-1}| = |T^*_k|$$

When this equality holds for a given k, the tree T^*_k can be accepted as the optimally pruned tree for the entire data set.

The growing phase of this iterative algorithm is accomplished according to the usual recursive partition of the feature space implemented both in CART and in ID3. In their presentation, Gelfand *et al.* employed the GINI index of diversity as selection measure

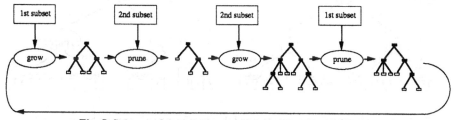

Fig. 5. Schema of the iterative growing and pruning algorithm.

[1] even if this choice does not affect the above theorem. Henceforth, we will use the *gain ratio* [5] to show how this method works.

As to the pruning algorithm proposed by Gelfand *et al.* , it should be noted that it is just the reduced error pruning by Quinlan. Indeed, the estimation of the error rate of each subtree is based on the alternative subset which plays the role of test set. Moreover, the introduction of a cost parameter α as in the error-complexity method, is only a matter of generality in the presentation, since the authors themselves seem to set $\alpha = 0$, thus bringing the evaluation of $R_\alpha(t)$ back to the simple estimation of the error rate on the test set.

A particular attention must be paid to splitting the entire data set into two disjoint sets, since they should be homogeneous as much as possible. In the opposite case, an attribute could show a sufficiently high information gain on the entire data set, but a low information gain in one subset, with the consequence that nodes with tests on that attribute are easily pruned. Such a consideration is also important to point out that the best tree found by this method is not necessarily a subtree of the tree T_{max} grown by using the entire data set.

In order to illustrate this method, the training data set has been split into two subsets: the first 52 examples in the first subset and the remaining 53 in the second one. The tree grown by using the first subset is depicted in Fig. 6a, while the results of the classification of the examples of the second subset are reported in Fig. 6b. According to the reduced error pruning the tree should not undergo any branch pruning operation, thus the second iteration starts just from T_0 and keeps on growing the tree on the second subset until T_1

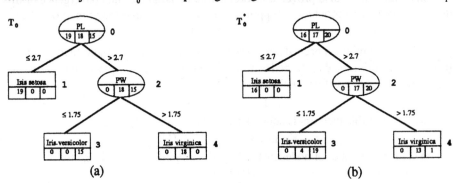

Fig. 6. First iteration: (a) grown tree and (b) classification of cases in the first subset.

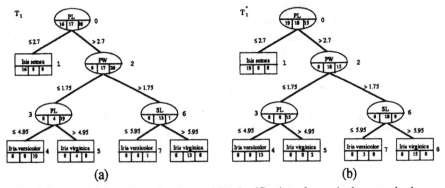

Fig. 7. Second iteration: (a) grown tree and (b) classification of cases in the second subset.

is obtained (see Fig. 7a). By classifying the examples in the second subset, we get the results given in Fig. 7b, therefore the optimally pruned subtree is again T_0. Since trees resulting from two consecutive iterations are exactly alike, the iterative process comes to an end and the final tree is just T_0.

Defining the iterative growing and pruning method in terms of search is more difficult than the other methods. The two phases, growing and pruning, can be individually seen in the framework of search. In particular, the construction of a tree can be cast as search in the (sometimes unlimited) space of all decision trees. However, since we are interested in pruning, we will not investigate this aspect further. As to pruning, we have already presented the reduced error pruning in terms of search in the state space, and those considerations are still valid for this method. In particular, the optimally pruned tree with respect to the pruning set is found. The only difference is that at each iteration the state space may change since the expanded tree may be different from that of the previous iteration. If T_k and T_k^* are the fully expanded tree and the optimally pruned tree of iteration k respectively, then

$$T_{k-1}^* \leq T_k \text{ and } T_k^* \leq T_{k+1} \quad \forall k=1,2,\ldots$$

therefore $\$(T_{k-1}^*) \subseteq \$(T_k)$ and $\$(T_k^*) \subseteq \$(T_{k+1})$. This means that the state space can change at each iteration but all subtrees of T_{k-1}^* are present in the two subsequent state spaces.

A further interesting theorem due to Gelfand *et al.* positively affects the computational complexity of this method. They prove that if a node is a leaf in two consecutive optimally pruned subtrees, T_{k-1}^* and T_k^*, then it will be a leaf in all subsequent optimally pruned subtrees, $T_i^* \quad \forall i \geq k$.

The authors exploit this result during the growing phase, since it is not necessary to split those leaves that satisfy this condition. In our opinion, such a theorem can be extensively exploited in the pruning phase, as well. Indeed, a consequence of this theorem is that it is not necessary to prune all those branches containing at least one leaf appearing in two consecutive optimally pruned subtrees. In other words, the state space for the pruning phase can be reduced by simply marking the ancestors of such leaves.

4 An empirical comparison of pruning methods

The need of making some experiments on some pruning methods arises from the fact that the experimental procedure designed by Mingers [6] to compare several pruning methods is not very fair. Indeed, the author splits each data set into three subsets, a training set (60% of the whole data set), a first test set (20%) and a second test set (20%). The first of these is used by some of the pruning methods, either when a final tree has to be selected from a given family of pruned trees (such as the new version of the minimum error pruning and the error complexity pruning), or in the actual pruning process (reduced error pruning). The second test set is used for measuring the accuracy (or conversely, the error rate) of the resultant trees. Thus, some methods will exploit additional information contained in the first subset to prune, while the others not. We believe that such an unfair experimental procedure may have affected the conclusions drawn out by Mingers in favor of those methods that exploit an independent set for pruning.

Another point concerns the use of the Analysis of Variance (ANOVA) to detect statistically significant differences between pruning methods or between splitting criteria and interactions between them. Unfortunately, the ANOVA test is based on the assumption that standard deviation is constant for all the experiments and this is not our case because we will compare the algorithms on different data sets. A paired two-tailed t-test for each experiment is the most appropriate way to compare pairs of error averages concerning the same data set.

Similar considerations have also been reported in [16], but they refer to the comparison of splitting rules for decision trees and not to pruning methods. We are also conscious that different pruning methods represents different biases, as already pointed out in [17]. Therefore, we will avoid to draw conclusions on which is the "best" method, but, following the main stream of the analytical comparison between methods followed in the paper, we will try to understand why in some cases a method works better than the others.

In our experimentation, each data set is still randomly divided into three subsets, according to the following criterion:
- *Growing* set (49%)
- *pruning* set (21%)
- *test* set (30%).

The union of the growing and pruning set is called *training* set, and its size is just 70% of the whole data set. The growing set contains the 70% of cases of the training set, while the pruning set the remaining 30%. Both the growing set and the training set are used to learn decision trees, that, for simplicity of naming, we will call *grown* tree and *trained* tree, respectively. The former is used by those methods that need an independent pruning set in order to prune a decision tree, namely reduced error pruning (REP), the new version of the minimum error pruning (MEP), and the error complexity pruning with either the 0SE rule (0SE) or the 1SE rule (1SE). The latter is used by those methods that exploit the training set only, such as pessimistic error pruning (PEP) and iterative growing and pruning algorithm (IGP). The evaluation of the error rate is always made on the test set.

For each data set considered, 20 experiments are made by randomly partitioning the data set into three subsets. Moreover, for each experiment two statistics are recorded:
- The number of leaves (size) of the resultant tree
- the error rate (e.r.) of the tree on the test set.

This is done both for the trees obtained by the different pruning methods (*pruned* trees) and for the grown and trained trees, so that a paired two-tail t-test can be used to evaluate the significance of the error rate difference between pruned trees as well as between each pruned tree and the grown/trained tree. Only the results of those methods that use a prune set will be compared with the results of the grown tree. This is done in order to understand if some results can be partially explained in terms of differences of the tree to prune.

As to the method of minimum error pruning we selected the same values of m used by Niblett and Bratko in their experimentation, that is 0.01, 0.5, 1, 2, 3, 4, 8, 12, 16, 32, 64, 128 and 999. The further partitioning of the training set into two equally sized subsets used by the iterative growing and pruning algorithm is done randomly, as well. However, each subset contains nearly the same proportion of cases per class of the training set, in order to satisfy the conditions presented in [15].

Another difference between our and Mingers' experimentation is that we consider only trees developed according to the gain-ratio (GR) selection measure [5]. Of course, this is a limit for our experimentation, since we cannot detect interesting interactions between the selection measures and the pruning methods. Future work will need a wider experimentation concerning also this aspect.

4.1 Iris data

This data set contains 150 examples, each of which described by 4 real valued attributes[1]. The examples belong to three different classes corresponding to three different species of iris plants. There are 50 examples per class, thus in each experiment the data set was partitioned as follows: 70 cases in the growing set, 30 cases in the pruning set, and 50 cases in the test set.

The mean and the standard deviation for each statistics concerning the various methods are reported in Table 8, while Table 9 shows the result of the comparison between the error rate of the pruned trees and that of the grown and trained trees (each entry contains the t value and the corresponding significance level). It is worthwhile to note that only the PEP method shows a statistically significant improvement with respect to the trained tree (the probability of error in rejecting the hypothesis that the two mean are equal is less than 0.005). For the other methods, tree pruning seems not to be really effective. On the contrary, if we compare their results with those obtained from the grown tree, we note that pruning tends to slightly increase the error rate.

By pairwise comparing the average error rates obtained by the different methods we can conclude that there is no statistically significant difference between the methods (see Table 10). This means that the best average error rate obtained by PEP is not much better than that of the other average error rates.

Table 8: Mean and standard error for both size and error rate of the resultant trees (iris data).

	REP		MEP		OSE		ISE		grown		PEP		IGP		trained	
	mean	s.d.	mean	s.d.	mean	s.d.	mean	s.d.	mean	s.d.	mean	s.d.	mean	s.d.	mean	s.d.
size	3.5	1.0	3.7	1.3018	3.7	1.3018	3.5	1.0513	6.05	1.5381	3.85	0.8127	3.45	0.8256	7.4	2.0365
e.r.	5.9	2.7891	5.9	2.7891	5.9	2.7891	5.8	2.8946	5.5	2.5026	5.0	3.6992	5.3	3.3888	6	3.4944

Table 9: t value and significance value for the paired two-tailed t-test (iris data)

	REP	MEP	OSE	ISE	PEP	IGP
grown	.809 (.43)	.847 (.41)	.847 (.41)	.616 (.55)	-	-
trained	-.165 (.87)	-.175 (.86)	-.175 (.86)	-.357 (.73)	-3.25 (.004)	-1.23 (.232)

Table 10: results of the paired two-tailed t-tests between methods (iris-data).

	MEP	OSE	ISE	PEP	IGP
REP	.0 (1.0)	.0 (1.0)	.438 (.67)	1.48 (.154)	.9 (.38)
MEP	-	.0 (1.0)	1.0 (.33)	1.53 (.14)	.946 (.36)
OSE		-	1.0 (.33)	1.528 (.14)	.946 (.36)
ISE			-	1.361 (.19)	.793 (.44)
PEP				-	-.459 (.65)

---

1. Real valued attributes are treated as described in [2].

Finally, there are at least other three points that are worthwhile to note. Firstly, the PEP has the highest average in the number of leaves of the pruned tree. It is possible that its positive bias when pruning is well suited for very regular data like this. Secondly, the IGP always finds the best tree in two steps, that is it needs to develop and prune a tree only twice. The IGP method globally shows good results and is generally able to improve the predictive accuracy of the classifier, but in some experiments it produced the highest error rate. This partly explains its highest standard deviation. In other words, the IGP method seems quite instable.

4.2 Glass data

This data set contains 214 examples, each of which described by 9 real valued attributes plus an identification number that we did not consider. There are 7 classes but no example is provided for the fourth class. In each experiment the data set was partitioned as follows: 105 cases for the growing set, 45 cases for the pruning set and 64 cases for the test set.

Table 11 shows the mean size and the average error rate of each method together with the corresponding standard deviations. By looking at Table 12 it can be seen that there is a statistically significant difference ($p<0.01$) between the error rates given by MEP, OSE and 1SE, and the error rate of the trained tree. Unfortunately, this difference is positive, meaning that these methods decreased the predictive accuracy of the trained decision tree. A similar result can also be observed for IGP at a .1 significance level. This time the PEP did not actually improve the error rate, as well as REP.

The high error rate of the trained tree show how difficult discovering regularities in this data set is.Perhaps the underlying model is quite complex while data is weak, thus the bias of some pruning methods may cause the very opposite problem of underfitting [17].

5 Conclusions

Determining the leaves of a decision tree is a critical problem of decision tree induction. It can be faced either by (post-)pruning a fully expanded tree or by stopping the growth of the tree itself (pre-pruning). The latter method is generally preferred to the former, since selection measures proposed for decision tree induction are not polythetic, that is the discriminant power of logical combinations of attribute-value pairs is not taken into account. Thus, pre-pruning may stop the growth of a tree because all attributes seem individually meaningless even if some combinations of them may be highly discriminant.

Table 11: Mean and standard error for both size and error rate of the resultant trees (glass data).

	REP		MEP		OSE		1SE		grown		PEP		IGP		trained	
	mean	s.d.	mean	s.d.	mean	s.d.	mean	s.d.	mean	s.d.	mean	s.d.	mean	s.d.	mean	s.d.
size	17.15	4.977	23.1	5.17	18.05	8.036	12.25	6.889	29.85	6.738	25.05	3.103	15.35	4.511	39.6	3.202
e.r.	37.301	6.356	38.752	4.138	39.454	5.142	41.407	6.541	37.265	6.614	34.219	5.409	37.266	6.215	34.295	6.301

Table 12: t value and significance value for the paired two-tailed t-test (glass data)

	REP	MEP	OSE	1SE	PEP	IGP
grown	.028 (.978)	1.171 (.256)	1.304 (.208)	2.11 (.0485)	-	-
trained	1.536 (.141)	2.89 (.0094)	2.974 (.008)	3.44 (.0027)	-0.087 (.93)	1.73 (.1002)

In this paper, a comparative study of six well-known post-pruning methods is presented, together with a unifying view of the tree pruning problem in terms of search in a state space. Given a tree T_{max} to prune, the corresponding state space is defined as the set of all subtrees of T_{max}, $\$(T_{max})$, and the branch pruning operation is the only operator defined on such a set. Each state of $\$(T_{max})$ is associated with the value taken by an evaluation function, f, that assesses the goodness of the tree. Therefore, the problem of pruning may be cast as the problem of visiting different states in $\$(T_{max})$ with the aim of maximizing f.

In the methods considered in the paper, states are always visited according to a pre-established order, depending on the kind of approach: bottom-up or top-down. While in the *reduced error pruning, pessimistic error pruning*, and *minimum error pruning*, a branch is pruned as soon as a better state is detected, in the *error complexity pruning* method, the best state among all the directly reachable states is selected according to an hill-climbing search strategy. This last method, together with the *minimum error pruning*, select a parametric family of subtrees of T_{max}, that will undergo a further evaluation process with the aim of detecting the best tree in the family. However, this two-phased selection, thought in order to reduce the computational complexity, has a main drawback: it does not guarantee that the best tree (or a good one) with respect to the predictive accuracy is in the family. A more in-depth analysis of these methods is provided in [11].

Another criterion to discriminate among post-pruning methods is the kind of information exploited by the evaluation function f. Indeed, in the pessimistic error pruning, only information coming from the training set is used, whereas all the other methods need an additional independent test set. A different consideration should be made for the minimum error pruning, since its original formulation used only information coming from the training set and in the newer version the use of an independent pruning set is only hypothesized. When predictive accuracy is estimated by means of cross-validation, the error-complexity pruning does not need a pruning set, as well.

In the paper, some preliminary results concerning a redesigned experimentation on pruning methods have been presented. The first data set contains strong data relative to the simple underlying model. Indeed, the average error rate of the grown tree was better than that of the trained tree. However, all the methods exploiting an independent data set tried to prune further, generally increasing the error rate of the resultant tree. The method that gave a statistically significant improvement on the predictive accuracy is the pessimistic error pruning. The same method, did not improve the classification accuracy of the trained tree for the glass data. In this case data were weak relative to the complex underlying model. Such a result was the best with respect to other pruning methods that even decreased the predictive accuracy.

Future work should consider both a more extensive experimentation in which more databases are considered. Moreover, since the iterative growing and pruning algorithm is affected by the random splitting of the training set, it would be better to evaluate the performance of the method with respect to several random partitioning of the training set, in order to reduce its variance in the corresponding results.

Finally, future research on decision tree pruning should address the problem of defining a less biased evaluation function f to use in a more informed search strategy, since the introduction of the state space has shown that very simple strategies are used by the well-known post-pruning methods.

184

Acknowledgments

Thanks to M. Pazzani, L. Saitta and A. Giordana for their helpful comments on earlier drafts of the paper.

References

1. L. Breiman, J. Friedman, R. Olshen, C. Stone: Classification and regression trees. Belmont, CA: Wadsworth International 1984
2. J. R. Quinlan: Induction of decision trees. Machine Learning 1, 81-106 (1986)
3. J. R. Quinlan: Simplifying decision trees. International Journal of Man-Machine Studies 27, 221-234 (1987) (also appeared in: B. R. Gaines, J. H. Boose (eds.): Knowledge Acquisition for Knowledge-Based Systems. Academic Press 1988)
4. M. Gams, N. Lavrac: Review of five empirical learning systems within a proposed schemata. In: I. Bratko, N. Lavrac (eds.): Progress in Machine Learning. Wilmslow: Sigma Press 1987
5. J. Mingers: An empirical comparison of selection measures for decision-tree induction. Machine Learning 3, 319 - 342 (1989)
6. J. Mingers: An empirical comparison of pruning methods for decision tree induction. Machine Learning 4, 227 - 243 (1989)
7. B. Cestnik, I. Kononenko, I. Bratko: ASSISTANT 86: A knowledge-elicitation tool for sophisticated users. In: I. Bratko, N. Lavrac (eds.): Progress in Machine Learning. Wilmslow: Sigma Press 1987
8. J. R. Quinlan: Determinate literals in inductive logic programming. Proceedings of the IJCAI 91. San Mateo, CA: Morgan Kaufmann 1991, pp. 746-750
9. T. Niblett: Constructing decision trees in noisy domains. In: I. Bratko, N. Lavrac (eds.): Progress in Machine Learning. Wilmslow: Sigma Press 1987
10. A. V. Aho, J. E. Hopcroft, J. D. Ullman: The design and analysis of computer algorithms. Reading, MA: Addison Wesley 1974
11. F. Esposito, D. Malerba, G. Semeraro: Pruning methods in decision tree induction: a unifying view. Technical report (1992)
12. T. Niblett, I. Bratko: Learning decision rules in noisy domains. Proceedings of Expert Systems 86. Cambridge: University Press 1986
13. B. Cestnik, I. Bratko: On estimating probabilities in tree pruning. Proceedings of the EWSL -91. Berlin: Springer-Verlag 1991, pp. 138-150
14. A. Barr, E. Feigenbaum: The handbook of artificial intelligence, (Vol. 1). Reading, MA: Addison Wesley 1981
15. S. B. Gelfand, C. S. Ravishankar, E. J. Delp: An iterative growing and pruning algorithm for classification tree design. IEEE Transactions on Pattern Analysis and Machine Intelligence PAMI-13, 2, 163-174 (1991)
16. W. Buntine, T. Niblett: A further comparison of splitting rules for decision-tree induction. Machine Learning 8, 75-85 (1992)
17. C. Schaffer: Deconstructing the digit recognition problem. In: Machine Learning: Proceedings of the Ninth International Workshop (ML92). San Mateo, CA: Morgan Kaufmann (1992), pp. 394-399

Controlled Redundancy
in
Incremental Rule Learning

Luis Torgo

LIACC
R.Campo Alegre, 823 - 2o.
4100 PORTO
PORTUGAL
Telf. : (+351) 2 600 16 72 - Ext. 115
e-mail : ltorgo@ciup1.ncc.up.pt

Abstract. This paper introduces a new concept learning system. Its main features are presented and discussed. The controlled use of redundancy is one of the main characteristics of the program. Redundancy, in this system, is used to deal with several types of uncertainty existing in real domains. The problem of the use of redundancy is addressed, namely its influence on accuracy and comprehensibility. Extensive experiments were carried out on three real world domains. These experiments showed clearly the advantages of the use of redundancy.

1   Introduction

This paper presents the learning system YAILS capable of obtaining high accuracy in noisy domains. One of the novel features of the program is its controlled use of redundancy. Several authors ([5, 7, 2]) reported experiments that clearly show an increase in accuracy when multiple sources of knowledge are used. On the other hand, the existence of redundancy decreases the comprehensibility of learned theories. The controlled use of redundancy enables YAILS to better solve problems of uncertainty common in real world domains. Another important feature of the system is its mechanism of weighted flexible matching. This feature also contributes for the better handling of noisy domains. In terms of learning procedures the system uses a bi-directional search procedure opposed to the traditional bottom-up or top-down search common in other systems.

The next section gives a description of some of the main issues on the YAILS learning algorithm. The following section describes the classification strategies used by YAILS. Finally, section 4 describes several experiments carried out with YAILS that show the effect of redundancy on both accuracy and comprehensibility.

2   YAILS Learning Strategies

YAILS belongs to the attribute-based family of learning programs. It is an incremental rule learning system capable of dealing with numerical attributes and unknown information (unknown attribute values or missing attribute information).

YAILS search procedure is bi-directional including both specialisation and generalisation operators.

This section gives some details on the search mechanisms of YAILS as well as on the treatment of uncertainty.

2.1   Basic Search Procedures

YAILS algorithm involves two major steps. Given a new example to learn, the first step consists of modifying the current theory (possibly empty) in order to adapt it to the example. If it does not succeed it starts the second step which tries to invent a new rule that covers the example.

Learning of this type of systems can be seen as a search over a space of all possible conjunctions within the language of the problem. In YAILS the search is guided by an evaluation function and employs two types of search transformations: specialisation and generalisation (fig.1). YAILS has two specialisation (and generalisation) operators.

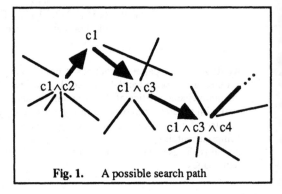

Fig. 1.   A possible search path

The first is adding (removing) one condition to a rule. The second is the restriction (enlargement) of a numerical interval within a rule.

YAILS uses exactly the same search mechanism when inventing a new rule while its goal is also to cover a particular example. For this purpose the specialisation operators are restricted in order to satisfy this goal. The restriction consists of adding only conditions present in the example being covered.

2.2   The Evaluation Function

The goal of the evaluation function is to assess the quality (Q) of some tentative rule. YAILS uses an evaluation function which relates two properties of a conjunction of conditions : consistency and completeness [8]. The value of quality is obtained by the following weighted sum of these two properties :

$$\text{Quality}(R) = [0.5 + \text{Wcons}(R)] \times \text{Cons}(R) + [0.5 - \text{Wcons}(R)] \times \text{Compl}(R) \qquad (1)$$

where

$$\text{Cons}(R) = \frac{\#\{\text{correctly covered exs.}\}}{\#\{\text{covered exs.}\}} \qquad \text{Compl}(R) = \frac{\#\{\text{correctly covered exs.}\}}{\#\{\text{exs. of same class as R}\}}$$

$$W_{\text{cons}}(R) = \frac{\text{Cons}(R)}{4}$$

This formula is a heuristic one, resulting from experiments and observations made with YAILS in real world domains. The formula weighs two properties according to the value of consistency (which is judged to be more important). Making the weights dependent on consistency is a way of introducing some flexibility into to the formula thus coping with different situations (such as rules covering rare cases or very general rules). Many other possible combinations of these and other properties are possible (see for instance [1,11]), and YAILS is in itself very easily changed in order to use another quality formula.

2.3 Unknown Information

The problem of unknown information is twofold. It raises problems during the learning phase and also in classification. The latter point is discussed in section 3.

YAILS system deals with two types of unknown information. The first arises when the value of some attribute is "unknown" and the second when the value is irrelevant. While the first case is interpreted as a kind of noise (thus presenting a problem) the second one is treated as a "don't care" situation (the human expert which has provided the examples to the system, may state that the attribute is irrelevant).

Before modifying the current theory to incorporate a new example, YAILS verifies whether the example is already covered. Both kinds of unknowns referred above may present some difficulties. These arise if one (or more) conditions of a rule tests an attribute for which the example has an "unknown" value. YAILS adopts a probabilistic strategy when dealing with this situation. A conditional probability is calculated as follows :.

$$P(A_i = V_i \mid A_j = V_j \wedge ... \wedge A_k = V_k) \tag{2}$$

where $A_j = V_j \wedge ... \wedge A_k = V_k$ are the conditions satisfied by the example
and $A_i = V_i$ is the condition of the rule for which the example has an "unknown" value.

Example :
Rule $\equiv$ colour = red $\wedge$ temperature > 37 $\wedge$ hair = dark

Example $\equiv$ colour = ? $\wedge$ temperature = 43 $\wedge$ hair = dark $\wedge$ ....
In this example the calculated probability would be
P(colour = red | temperature > 37 $\wedge$ hair = dark)

This probability estimate is used to decide whether the example satisfies the rule. The decision requires a threshold that is user-definable.

The case when there is no information about some attribute is in fact stating that any rule with a condition with that attribute is not satisfied by the example.

3   YAILS Classification Strategies

YAILS uses mechanisms like the controlled use of redundancy and weighted flexible matching in order to achieve high accuracy but still keeping simple the used theory. The system is able to use different set ups of these mechanisms which contributes to the good flexibility of the program. The following sections explain these two strategies in more detail.

3.1   Redundancy

Most existing algorithms like for instance, AQ [10] and CN2 [4], use a covering strategy during learning. This means that the algorithm attempts to cover all known examples and that whenever some example has been covered it is removed. These systems would consider a rule useless if it covered examples that are already covered by other rules. AQ16 [15] uses a set of weights to remove this type of rules (considered *redundant* rules). This method is able to produce simpler theories than if the redundant rules were left in.

YAILS does not follow this method. Whenever the current theory does not cover a new example, new rules are created. The goal of this procedure is to find a "good" rule that covers the example. However the introduced rule may cover examples already covered by other rules. The only criterion used to consider a rule is its quality (see 2.2). Thank to this strategy, YAILS usually generates more rules than other systems.

The utility of such redundant rules can be questioned. The problem becomes even more relevant if we are concerned with comprehensibility. Nevertheless, there are several advantages on using these rules. YAILS is an incremental learning system and so what may seem a redundant rule may become useful in future. This implies that by not discarding some redundant rules the system can save learning time. In addition hand we can look at redundancy as a way of dealing with certain types of uncertainty that arise during classification. Suppose that we have a rule that cannot be used to classify an example because it tests attributes whose values are unknown in the example. If redundant rules are admitted, it is possible that one such rule can be found to classify the example. The advantages of redundancy are in efficiency and accuracy. The disadvantage is the number of rules (comprehensibility) of the theory.

YAILS uses a simple mechanism to control redundancy. Our goal is obtain the advantages of redundancy but at the same time minimise the number of rules used for classification. This mechanism consists on splitting the learned rules in two sets :- the *foreground* rules and the *background* rules. This split is guided by a user-definable parameter (minimal utility) which acts as a way of controlling redundancy. The utility of one rule is calculated as the ratio of the number of examples uniquely covered by the rule, divided by the total number of examples covered by the rule (this measure is basically the same as the u-weights used in [15]). Given a value of minimal utility YAILS performs the following iterative process :

```
Let the initial set of Learned Rules be the Candidate Foreground (CF)
REPEAT
    Calculate the utility of each rule in the CF
    IF the lowest utility rule in CF has utility less than the minimal utility THEN
        Remove it from CF and put it on the Background Set of Rules
UNTIL no rule was put on the Background
Foreground Set is the final CF
```

The higher the minimal utility threshold the less redundant is the theory in the foreground. The redundancy present in the foreground set of rules is called here *static redundancy*. YAILS uses only the foreground set of rules (FS) during classification. Only when it is not able to classify one example, it tries to find one rule in the background set (BS). If such rule is found the system transfers it from the BS to the FS so that in the end FS contains the rules used during the classification of the examples. This latter type of redundancy is called *dynamic redundancy*. The advantage of this strategy is to minimise the introduction of redundant rules.

YAILS can use different types of classification strategies. The "normal" strategy includes both static and dynamic redundancy. Other possibility is to use only static redundancy disabling thus the use of the BS. Finally it is also possible to use all the rules learned disregarding the splitting referred above. This latter strategy corresponds to the maximum level of redundancy. Notice that for the two first strategies is always possible to state the level of static redundancy through the minimal utility parameter. Section 4 presents the results obtained with several datasets using different classification strategies showing the effect of redundancy on both accuracy and comprehensibility.

3.2   Weighted Flexible Matching

Systems like AQ16 [15] that strive to eliminate redundancy become more sensitive to uncertainty inherent in real world domains. A small number of rules means that few alternatives exist when classifying the examples. If some condition of those rules is not satisfied the rule can not be used and the system is unable to classify the example. To minimise this undesirable effect these systems use flexible matching. This mechanism consists basically of allowing rules to be used to classify examples even though some of their conditions are not satisfied. With this strategy the systems are capable of improving performance but keeping the theory simple. Nevertheless, flexible matching does not solve some types of problems. If we have very simple rules (one or two conditions) and an example with an unknown value, then flexible matching is not sufficiently reliable. Small rules are in fact quite frequent. When using for instance the "Lymphography" medical dataset the resulting theory can have on average 2 to 3 conditions per rule. Flexible matching may fail to help in these situations. That is the reason why YAILS uses both redundancy and flexible matching during classification.

To explain flexible matching in YAILS, we need to describe the notion of weights associated with all conditions in each rule. These are generated by YAILS in the learning phase. The aim of these values is to express the relative importance of a particular condition with respect to the conclusion of the rule. YAILS uses the decrease of entropy originated by the addition of the condition as the measure of this weight:

$$\text{Weight}(c) = H(R\text{-}c) - H(R) \tag{3}$$

where
c is a condition belonging to the conditional part of rule R,
R-c is the conjunction resulting from eliminating the condition c from the conditional part of R, and H(x) is the entropy of event x.

These values play an important role in flexible matching. Given an example to classify, YAILS calculates the value of its Matching Score (MS) for each rule. This value is 1 if the example completely satisfies all the conditions of the rule, and a value between 0 and 1 otherwise. In effect it is a ratio of the conditions matched by the example. These conditions are weigh using (3). On the other hand if the example has some unknown value, equation (2) is used as an approximation. The general formula to calculate MS values is the following :

$$MS(Ex,R) = \frac{\sum_{c_i \in R} [\, m_i \times \text{Weight}(c_i)\,]}{\sum_{c_i \in R} \text{Weight}(c_i)} \tag{4}$$

where

$$m_i = \begin{cases} 0 & \text{if the example doesn't satisfy condition } c_i \\ 1 & \text{if the example satisfies condition } c_i \\ \text{Probability as in (2)} & \text{if the example has an unknown value on } c_i\text{'s attribute} \end{cases}$$

Just to better illustrate the idea observe the following example (between brackets the condition weights) :

Ex $\quad \equiv a=a_3 \wedge b=37 \wedge c=? \wedge e=e_6 \wedge \dots.$

Rule $\quad \equiv a=a_3(0.343) \wedge c=c_4(0.105) \wedge e=e_6(0.65) \wedge f>32(0.04) \Rightarrow X$

Supposing that $P(c=c_4|a=a_3 \wedge e=e_6) = 0.654$

$$MS(Ex,Rule) = \frac{1 \times 0.343 + 0.654 \times 0.105 + 1 \times 0.65 + 0 \times 0.04}{0.343 + 0.105 + 0.65 + 0.04} \approx 0.9327$$

That is the matching score of the example relative to the rule is 93.27%.

Having calculated this value for all rules YAILS disregards those whose MS is less than some threshold. The remaining set of rules are the candidates for the classification of the example. For those rules the system calculates the Opinion Value (OV) of each rule which is the product of the MS times the rule quality (Q) obtained during the learning phase. The classification of the example is the classification of the rule with highest OV. Note that if this latter set of rules is empty this means that there was no rule in FS able to classify the example. In that case the next step would be to apply the same procedure in the background set.

The mechanisms of redundancy and weighted flexible matching are interconnected in YAILS. The user can control this mechanisms through the minimal utility parameter as well as the threshold referred to above. These two values enable YAILS to exhibit different behaviours. For instance, if you are interested in very simple theories then the minimal utility should be set near 1 and the flexible matching threshold to the lowest possible value but be careful not to deteriorate accuracy. On the other hand, if you are interested only in accuracy you could set the minimal utility to a value near 0 and raise the strictness of the flexible matching mechanism. Of course all these parameter settings are dependent on the type of domain. Section 4.1 shows some experiments with these parameters and their effect on accuracy and comprehensibility.

4 Experiments

Several experiments with YAILS were performed on real world domains. The three medical domains chosen were obtained from the Jozef Stefan Institute, Ljubljana. This choice enables comparisons with other systems as these datasets are very often used to test learning algorithms. On the other hand, the datasets offer different characteristics thus enabling the test to be more thorough. Table 1 shows the main characteristics of the datasets :

Table 1. Main characteristics of the datasets.

	Lymphography	Breast Cancer	Primary Tumour
Dimension	148 exs./9 attrs. 4 classes	288 exs./10attrs. 2 classes	339 exs./17attrs. 22 classes
Attributes	Symbolic	Symbolic + numeric	Symbolic
Noise	Low level	Noisy	Very noisy
Unknowns	No	Yes	Yes

The experiments carried out had the following structure: each time 70% of examples where randomly chosen for training and the remaining left for testing; all tests were repeated 10 times and averages calculated.

Table 2 presents a summary of the results obtained on the 3 datasets (standard deviations are between brackets).

Table 2. Results of the experiments.

	Lymphography	Breast Cancer	Primary Tumour
Accuracy	85% (5%)	80% (3%)	34% (6%)
No. of Used Rules	14 (2.7)	13.9 (5.6)	37.2 (2.8)
Aver. Conditions /Rule	1.86 (0.2)	1.94 (0.13)	1.96 (0.22)

The results are very good on two of the datasets and the theories are sufficiently simple (see table 3 for a comparison with other systems). This gives a clear indication of the advantages of redundancy. We should take into account that YAILS is an incremental system which means that all decisions are made sin a step-wise fashion and not with a general overview of all the data as in non-incremental systems. Because of this, a lower performance is generally accepted. This is not the case with YAILS (with exception to primary tumour) as we can see from the following table :

Table 3. Comparative results.

	Lymphog raphy		Breast Cancer		Primary Tumour	
System	Accuracy	Complexity	Accuracy	Complexity	Accuracy	Complexity
YAILS	85%	14 cpxs.	80%	13.9 cpxs.	34%	37.2 cpxs.
Assistant	78%	21 leaves	77%	8 leaves	42%	27 leaves
AQ15	82%	4 cpxs.	68%	2 cpxs.	41%	42 cpxs.
CN2	82%	8 cpxs.	71%	4 cpxs.	37%	33 cpxs.

The results presented in table 3 do not establish any ranking of the systems as this requires that tests of significance are carried out. As no results concerning standard deviations are given in the papers of the other systems and the number of repetitions of the tests is also different, the table is merely informative. It should also be noted that AQ15 uses VL-1 descriptive language that includes internal disjunctions in each selector. This means that, for instance, the 4 complexes obtained with AQ15 are much more complex than 4 complexes in the language used by YAILS (which does not allow internal disjunction).

4.1 The Effect of Redundancy

The controlled use of redundancy is one of the novel features we have explored. Although before redundancy affects positively accuracy it has a negative effect on comprehensibility. This section presents a set of experiments carried out in order to observe these effects of redundancy.

The experiments consisted on varying the level of "unknown" values in the examples given for classification. For instance a level of unknowns equal to 2 means that all the examples used in classification had 2 of their attributes with their values changed into "unknown". The choice of the 2 attributes was made at random for each example. Having the examples changed in that way three classification strategies (with different levels of redundancy) were tried and the results observed. The results presented below are all averages of 10 runs.

The three different classification strategies tested are labelled in the graphs below as "Redund.+", "Redund." and "Redund.-", respectively. The first consists on using all the learned rules thus not making any splitting between the foreground and the background set of rules (c.f. section 3.1). The second is the normal classification strategy of YAILS, with some level of static redundancy and dynamic redundancy. The last corresponds to a minimal amount of static redundancy and no dynamic redundancy. The accuracy results are given in figure 2.

Significant differences were observed. Redundancy certainly affects accuracy. With respect to the Breast Cancer dataset the advantage of redundancy is quite significant whenever the number of unknowns is increased. The advantages are not so marked on the Lymphography dataset.

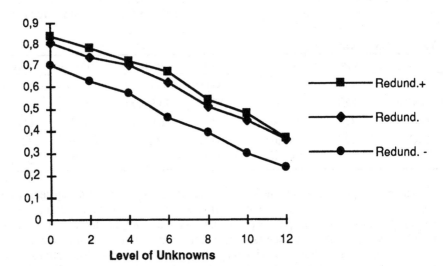

Fig.2.a -   Accuracy on the Lymphography dataset

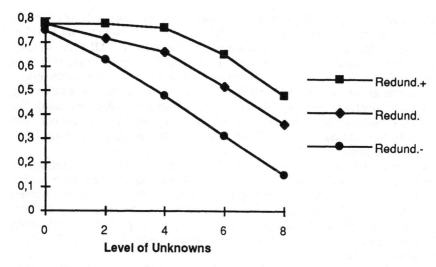

Fig. 2.b -   Accuracy on the Breast Cancer dataset

Redundancy has a negative effect on simplicity. The decision of what tradeoff should be between accuracy and comprehensibility is made by the user. The cost can be high in terms of number of rules. For instance in the Lymphography experiment the "Redund.+" strategy used a theory consisting of 28, rules while the "Redund.-" used only 6 rules. The "Redund." strategy is in between, but as the level of unknowns grows, it approaches the level of "Redund.+" thanks to dynamic redundancy. The gap is not so wide in the Breast Cancer experiment but still, there is a significant difference.

In summary, these experiments show the advantage of redundancy in terms of accuracy. This gain is sometimes related to the amount of "unknown" values present in the examples, but not always. Redundancy can be a good method to fight the problem of "unknowns", but the success depends also on other characteristics of the dataset.

5   Relations to other work

YAILS differs from the AQ-family [10] programs in several aspects. AQ-type algorithms perform unidirectional search. In general they start with an empty complex and proceed by adding conditions. YAILS uses a bi-directional search. AQ-type programs use a covering search strategy. This means that they start with a set of uncovered examples and each time an example is covered by some rule the example is removed from the set. Their goal is to make this set empty. In YAILS this is not the case thus enabling the production of redundant rules.

The main differences stated between YAILS and AQ-type programs also hold in comparison to CN2 [4] with the addition that CN2 is non-incremental. In effect CN2 has a search strategy that is similar to AQ with the difference of using ID3-like information measures to find the attributes to use in specialisation.

STAGGER [14] system uses weights to characterise its concept descriptions. In STAGGER each condition has two weights attached to it. These weights are a kind of counters of correct and incorrect matching of the condition. In YAILS, the weights represent the decrease of entropy obtained by the addition of each condition. This means that the weights express the information content of the condition with respect to the conclusion of the rule. STAGGER also performs bi-directional search using three types of operators: specialisation, generalisation and inversion (negation). The main differences are that STAGGER learns only one concept (ex. rain / not rain) and uses only boolean attributes. YAILS differs from STAGGER in that it uses redundancy and flexible matching.

The work of Gams [6] on redundancy clearly showed the advantages of redundancy. In his work Gams used several knowledge bases which were used in parallel to obtain the classification of new instances. This type of redundancy demands a good conflict resolution strategy in order to take advantage of the diversity of opinions. The same point could be raised in YAILS with respect to the combination of different rules. In [13] we present an experimental analysis of several different combination strategies.

The work by Brazdil and Torgo [2] is also related to this. It consisted of combining several knowledge bases obtained by different algorithms into one knowledge base. Significant increase in performance was observed showing the benefits of multiple sources of knowledge.

6   Conclusions

A new incremental concept learning system was presented with novel characteristics such as the controlled use of redundancy, weighted flexible matching and a bi-directional search strategy.

YAILS uses redundancy to achieve higher accuracy. The system uses a simple mechanism to control the introduction of new rules. The experiments carried out revealed that accuracy can be increased this manner with a small cost in terms of number of rules.

The use of a bi-directional search mechanism was an important characteristic in order to make YAILS incremental. The heuristic quality formula used to guide this search gave good results.

The rules learned by YAILS are characterised by a set of weights associated with their conditions. The role of these weights is to characterise the importance of each condition.

Several experiments were carried out in order to quantify the gains in accuracy obtained as a result of redundancy. Different setups of parameters were tried showing that redundancy usually pays off. Further experiments are needed to clearly identify the causes for the observed gains. We think that the level of "unknown" values affects the results. Redundancy can help to solve this problem.

Future work could exploit redundancy in other types of learning methods. It is also important to extend the experiments to other datasets and compare YAILS to other systems. It should be investigated what are the causes for the relatively poor results obtained on the Primary Tumour dataset. It seems that the systems is not producing as many redundant rules as on the other datasets. This can be deduced from the number of rules per class in the different experiments. In the Lymphography dataset there are about 3.5 rules per class and in Breast Cancer 6.9, but in the Primary

Tumour YAILS generates only 1.6 rules per class. This apparent lack of redundancy could be the cause of the problem on this dataset.

Acknowledgements

I would like to thank Pavel Brazdil for his comments on early drafts of the paper.

REFERENCES

1. Bergadano, F., Matwin,S., Michalski,R., Zhang,J. : "Measuring Quality of Concept Descriptions", in *EWSL88 - European Working Session on Learning*, Pitman, 1988.
2. Brazdil, P., Torgo, L. : "Knowledge Acquisition via Knowledge Integration", in *Current Trends in Knowledge Acquisition*, IOS Press, 1990.
3. Cestnik,B., Kononenko,I., Bratko,I.,: "ASSISTANT 86: A Knowledge-Elicitation Tool for Sophisticated Users", in *Proc. of the 2th European Working Session on Learning* , Bratko, I. and Lavrac, N. (eds.), Sigma Press, Wilmslow.
4. Clark, P., Niblett, T. : "Induction in noisy domains", in *Proc. of the 2th European Working Session on Learning* , Bratko,I. and Lavrac,N. (eds.), Sigma Press, Wilmslow, 1987.
5. Gams, M. : "New Measurements that Highlight the Importance of Redundant Knowledge", in *Proc. of the 4th European Working Session on Learning* , Morik,K. (ed.), Montpellier, Pitman-Morgan Kaufmann, 1989.
6. Gams,M. : "The Principle of Multiple Knowledge", Josef Stefan Institute, 1991.
7. Gams,M., Bohanec,M., Cestnik,B. : "A Schema for Using Multiple Knowledge", Josef Stefan Institute, 1991.
8. Michalski, R.S. : "A Theory and Methodology of Inductive Learning", in *Machine Learning - an artificial approach*, Michalski et. al (Eds), Tioga Publishing, Palo Alto, 1983.
9. Michalski, R.S. , Mozetic, I. , Hong, J., Lavrac, N. : "The multi-purpose incremental learning system AQ15 and its testing application to three medical domains", in *Proceedings of AAAI-86*, 1986.
10. Michalski, R.S. , Larson, J.B. : "Selection of most representative training examples and incremental generation of VL1 hypothesis: the underlying methodology and description of programs ESEL and AQ11", Report 867, University of Illinois, 1978.
11. Nunez,M.. : "Decision Tree Induction using Domain Knowledge", in *Current Trends in Knowledge Acquisition*, IOS Press, 1990.
12. Quinlan, J.R. : "Discovering rules by induction from large collections of examples", in *Expert Systems in the Micro-electronic Age*, Michie,D. (ed.), Edinburgh University Press, 1979.
13. Torgo, L. : "Rule Combination in Inductive Learning", in this volume.
14. Schlimmer,J., Granger,R. : "Incremental Learning from Noisy Data", in *Machine Learning* (1), pp.317-354, Kluwer Academic Publishers, 1986.
15. Zhang, J., Michalski, R.S. : "Rule Optimization via SG-TRUNC method", in *Proc. of the 4th European Working Session on Learning*, Morik, K. (ed.), Montpellier, 1989.

Getting Order Independence

in Incremental Learning

Antoine Cornuéjols

Equipe Inférence et Apprentissage
Laboratoire de Recherche en Informatique (LRI), UA 410 du CNRS
Université de Paris-sud, Orsay
Bâtiment 490, 91405 ORSAY (France)
email (UUCP) : antoine@lri.lri.fr

Abstract. It is empirically known that most incremental learning systems are order dependent, i.e. provide results that depend on the particular order of the data presentation. This paper aims at uncovering the reasons behind this, and at specifying the conditions that would guarantee order independence. It is shown that both an optimality and a storage criteria are sufficient for ensuring order independence. Given that these correspond to very strong requirements however, it is interesting to study necessary, hopefully less stringent, conditions. The results obtained prove that these necessary conditions are equally difficult to meet in practice.

Besides its main outcome, this paper provides an interesting method to transform an history dependent bias into an history independent one.

1   Introduction

Ordering effects in Incremental Learning have been widely mentioned in the literature without, however, being the subject of much specific study except for some rare pioneering works [1,4,9, and, incidentally, in 2][1]. In short, ordering effects are observed when, given a collection of data (e.g. examples in inductive concept learning), different ordered sequences of these data lead to different learning results. In this respect, ordering of data therefore seems to be equivalent to a preference bias that makes a choice among all the models or hypotheses that the learning system could reach given the collection of data (that is the models that would be obtained had the

---

[1] See also the AAAI Technical Report corresponding to the recent AAAI Spring Symposium (March 23-25, 1993, Stanford University) devoted to "Training Issues in Incremental Learning".

collection of data been presented in every possible orders). Hence, ordering undoubtedly amounts to some additional knowledge supplied to the system. This is why teachers have some value: by selecting suitable pedagogical presentations of the material to be learned they provide further knowledge that hopefully helps the learning process.

Learning without some bias that allows the reduction of the search space for the target concept or model is impossible except in the crudest form of rote learning. When looking more closely, it is usual to distinguish between :

- *representation bias* : where the search space is constrained because all partitions of the example space can not be expressed in the hypothesis space considered by the system (this is the basis for inductive generalization and is the main topic of current Machine Learning theory [12]), and

- *preference bias* : which dictates which subspace should be preferred in the search space (e.g. prefer simple hypotheses over more complex ones) (this type of bias has been much less studied because it touches on procedural aspects instead of declarative ones only).

Because ordering of inputs allows one to favor some models over some others, it seems to amount to a preference bias that chooses between competing hypotheses. In spite of this resemblance however, there is a deep difference with the biases generally discussed in Machine Learning. Indeed, with ordering effects, one *observes* the preference but cannot pinpoint directly where in the learning system it lies and how it works. This is in contrast with what is considered classically as a bias, where one can identify *operational* constraints _e.g. isolate representation constraints or procedures for choice between hypotheses. Thus we use the term global preference bias to denote preference among models due to ordering effects *after* a sequence of inputs has been observed, and the term local preference bias to denote the local choice strategy followed by the system when at each learning step it must choose to follow some paths and discard others.

Two questions then immediately come up :

1- *What is the relationship between a global preference bias and a local one ?*

2- *What is the relationship between a global preference bias that is observed or aimed at and a corresponding teaching strategy that specifies the order of inputs ? In other words, how to design a teaching strategy so as to get a certain global preference bias ?*

The second question is related to the recently introduced concept of teachability [5,8,15,16,17] and the not so recent concern for good training sequences [19,20].

However, it differs in a fundamental point in that, in the former the problem is essentially the determination of good examples to speed up learning, whereas in our setting we assume that the collection of instances is given a priori and our only degree of freedom lies in the choice of a good ordering. Additionally, researchers in the teachability concept have not been interested with the idea of guiding the learner toward some preferred model and away from others, they seek to characterize the learnability of concept classes irrelevant of particular preferences within the classes. Keeping in mind these differences, the emphasis on providing additional knowledge to the learner through an educational strategy is the same.

In order to answer these questions, and particularly the first one, it is necessary to determine the causes of the ordering effects.

2 Causes of ordering effects

It is instructive to look at incremental learners that are NOT order dependent, like the candidate elimination (CE) algorithm in Version Space [10,11], ID5R [18], or systems that are not usually considered as learning systems but could be, such as TMS [3] or some versions of the Bayesian Inference nets of Pearl [13]. They all have in common that they do not forget any information present in the input data. Thus, even when they make a choice between alternative hypotheses, like ID5 or TMS and unlike the CE algorithm, they keep enough information to be able to compare all potential competing models so as to select the best one at any moment, and change their mind if needed. They are therefore equivalent to non-incremental learning systems that get all the data at once and focus on the best hypothesis given the information supplied.

To sum up, order independent incremental learners *(i)* are able to focus on a optimal hypothesis when they have to choose among the current potential ones; and *(ii)* they do keep enough informations so as to not forget any potential hypothesis. If one or both of these properties is lacking, then incremental learning is prone to be order dependent. A closer look at each of these property in turn will help to see why.

(i) Optimality vs. non optimality.

Since the influential thesis and papers of Mitchell [10,11], is has become commonplace to consider learning as a search process in a concept or solution space. Whatever the form (generalization, explanation,...) and the constraints on the hypothesis space (e.g. representation language bias), the learner is searching the best solution in this space given the data at hand. In order to compare the solutions in the search space, it is possible to imagine that the learner evaluates and grades each one of them and then chooses the top one. Of course, the grade and therefore the rank of these solutions can be modified if the data are changed.

Because incremental learners usually function by adapting a current solution (or a small solution set) to cope with new informations, they proceed typically in a hill-climbing fashion (see figure 1) open to the draw-back of missing the global optimum solution in favor of local ones.

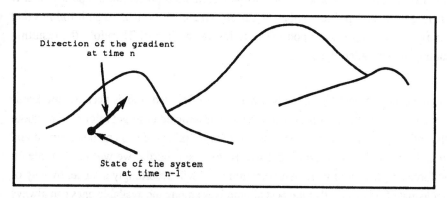

Fig. 1. At time n-1, the system is in a state corresponding to a given hypothesis. At time n, with a new arriving piece of data, the value of each hypothesis is re-evaluated and the system follows the direction of greatest gradient to reach a new state.

As underlined above, one must realize that in contrast to the common optimization problems where the optimums and the whole topology of the search space are set once and for all before the search starts, in incremental learning the topology is changed with each new input and the solutions in the hypothesis space are therefore open to re-evaluation, new optimums replacing old ones. Because of this, incremental learning wandering from one local and temporary optimum to the next can be order dependent unless it reaches the global current optimum at each step that is with each arriving data[2]. In that case of course, at the end of the training period and given that all the training data have been observed, the system would reach the global optimum for this set of data regardless of its ordering during learning.

In fact, it is easy to see that there is a second caveat in addition to the requirement of finding the global optimum at each time.

---

[2] Finding the global optimum at each step requires either to keep in memory all possible hypotheses, re-evaluate them and take the best one, or, short to this memory intensive method, to be able to re-construct any possible hypothesis with enough accuracy and keep track to the best one so far. This latter method is closed in spirit to Simulated Annealing or to Genetic Algorithms. In mathematics, this corresponds to ergodic systems.

(ii) To forget or not to forget.

Finding the optimal solution at each step is operating only to the extent that the set of all possible solutions is brought to consideration; if only part of it is available then the whole optimization process is bound to be sub-optimal. Now, beside adapting the current solution to new constraints expressed under the form of new data, incremental learners because they entertain only some preferred hypothesis or model, can also discard in the process part of the information present in the past inputs. If this forgetting is dependent upon the current state of the system, then it follows that it may also be dependent upon the ordering of the inputs. Therefore the resulting learning may be order dependent.

It is important to note that these two reasons if often tied (this is because one keeps only a current solution for adaptation that one is tempted to forget informations about other possibilities) are nonetheless independent in principle and can be observed and studied separately. For reasons that will be exposed shortly, we will concentrate on the forgetting aspect of incremental learning and will accordingly assume, by way of an adequate framework, that the best alternatives among the available ones can always be chosen by the learner.

Forgetting of information lies therefore at the heart of order dependence in incremental learning. But *forgetting can take two faces*. In the first one, information present in the input data is lost, meaning that the current hypothesis space considered by the learner is underconstrained. In the second one, by contrast, what is lost are potential alternatives to the current preferred hypotheses, which amounts to overconstraining the space of possibilities. *This last form of forgetting is equivalent to a local preference bias* which chooses among competing hypotheses which ones to pursue.

This raises then a more specific question than the aforementioned ones, but which contributes to the same overall goal :

3. *In which case an incremental learner can be order independent ? Or,*
   in other words, which information can be safely forgotten without
   altering the result of learning whatever is the ordering of inputs ?

It is this last question that this paper focuses on. It must be kept in mind that it is equivalent to the question : what local preference bias leads to a null global preference bias (i.e. to order independence) ?

In the following of the paper, **we will restrict ourselves to a simple concept learning model** in which the learner attempts to infer an unknown target concept f, chosen from a known concept class F of $\{0,1\}$-valued functions over an instance space X. This framework allows us, in the next section, to define a measure of the information gained by the learning system and of the effect of a local bias on this information. This measure naturally suggests an equivalence relation between local preference bias and additional instances, which is detailed in section 4. Then, in section 5, it becomes a relatively simple matter to answer question 3 above. The conclusion compares the framework adopted here with the emerging one of teachability and discusses the results obtained.

3   Information measure and local preference bias

In this section, we are interested in formalizing and quantifying the effect of a local preference bias on what is learned by the system. For this, we first define a characterization of the information maintained by a learner.

Let F be a concept class over the instance space X, and $f \in F$ be a target concept. The teacher has a collection of examples $EX=\{x_i, f(x_i)\}$ at his disposal, and makes a sequence $x=x_1, x_2, ..., x_m, x_{m+1}, ...$ with $x_m \in EX$ for all m. The learner receives information about f incrementally via the label sequence $f(x_1), ..., f(x_m), f(x_{m+1}), ...$ For any $m \geq 1$, we define (with respect to x,f) the mth *version space* :

$$F_m(x,f) = \{\hat{f} \in F : \hat{f}(x_1) = f(x_1), ..., \hat{f}(x_m) = f(x_m)\}$$

The version space at time m is simply the class of all concepts in F consistent with the first m labels of f (with respect to x). $F_m(x,f)$ will serve as a **characterization of what is known to the learner at time m about the target concept f.**

We know from Mitchell [10] that the version space can be economically represented and stored using the boundary sets S-set (set of the most general hypotheses that are more specific than the concepts in the version space), and G-set (set of the most specific hypotheses that are more general than the concepts in the version space)[3]. Each new example $(x_m, f(x_m))$ provides new information if it allows to reduce the version space by modifying, through the CE algorithm, either one of the boundary sets. Generally, the S-set and the G-set contain many elements, and in worst cases, they can grow exponentially over some sequences of examples [6].

A **local preference bias** is a choice strategy which, at any time m, discards parts of the current version space, generally in order to keep the boundary sets manageable.

---

[3] To be exact, a subset of the concept space can be represented by its S-set and G-set if and only if it is closed under the partial order of generality of the description language and bounded. This is the case for most learning tasks and concept representations and particularly when the description language consists in the set of all conjunctive expressions over a finite set of boolean features. See [7] for more details.

In this way, it reduces the version space and acts as if there had been some additional information that had allowed to constrain the space of hypotheses. The next section gives a closer look at this equivalence.

4 Bias and additional instances

We assume that the incremental learner maintains a version space of potential concepts by keeping the boundary sets. We assume further that the local preference bias, if any, acts by removing elements of the S-set and/or of the G-set, thus reducing the version space. Indeed, in so doing, it removes from the version space all concepts or hypotheses that are no longer more general than some element of the S-set and more specific than some element of the G-set. Besides, the resulting version space keeps its consistency since, in this operation, no element of the resulting S-set become more general than other elements of the S-set or of the G-set, and vice-versa, no element of the G-set can become more specific than other elements of the G-set or of the S-set.

To sum up, we now have a learning system that forgets pieces of information during learning by discarding potential hypotheses, but at the same time is optimal since, in principle, by keeping the set of all the remaining hypotheses, it could select the best among them. In that way, we isolate the effect of forgetting without intermingling with non optimality effects.

We are interested in studying the action of a local preference bias (which has been shown to be equivalent to the forgetting of potential hypotheses) along all possible sequences of data. More specifically, we want to find what type of local bias (or forgetting strategy) leads to no ordering effects, that is for which all training sequences conduct to the same resulting state.

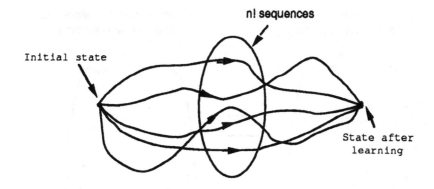

Fig. 2. For n instances, there are $n!$ possible training sequences. We look for conditions under which all sequences would result in the same state.

What makes this problem difficult is that the action of the local preference bias depends on which state the system is in, and therefore depends on the training sequence followed. This implies in turn that all training sequences should be compared in order to find conditions on the local bias.

A very simple but very important idea will allow to circumvent this obstacle. It has three parts :

(i) forgetting hypotheses amounts to overconstrain the search space

(ii) extra instances to an order independent learning algorithm would result in constraining the search space

(iii) if an incremental learner using a local bias b_1 (leading to forgetting of hypotheses) could be made equivalent to an order independent incremental learner using bias b_2, (leading to the consideration of extra instances) then, finding conditions on the local bias b_1 would be the same as finding conditions on the bias b_2, only this time irrelevant of the training sequence (since b_2 is used by an order independent learner).

(i) and *(ii)* allow to realize *(iii)* if it can be shown that the effect of the local bias b_1 is the same as the effect of additional instances given by an oracle or bias b_2 to an order independent learner. In other words, if it can be proved that any forgetting of hypothesis is equivalent to observing extra instances, then, conditions on b_1 will amount to conditions on the addition of fictitious instances to an order independent learning algorithm.

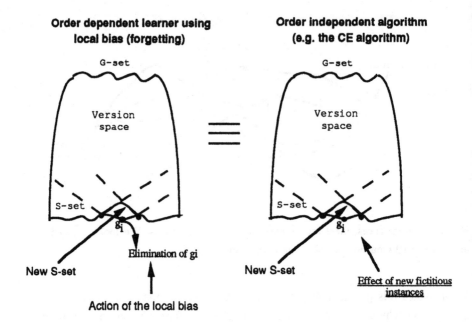

Order dependent learner using local bias (forgetting)

Order independent algorithm (e.g. the CE algorithm)

Fig. 3. The equivalence needed to allow the study of conditions on the local bias. The effect of the local bias (forgetting of some element of the S-set or G-set) is the same as the effect of additional instances made available to an order independent algorithm such as the CE algorithm.

Of this powerful idea, we will make a theorem.

Theorem 1 : *With each choice it makes, the local preference bias acts as if additional examples had been known to an order independent learner.*

<u>Proof</u> : (i) Case of the reduction of the S-set. For each element g_i of the S-set it is possible to find additional fictitious examples which, if considered by the CE algorithm, would lead to its elimination of the S-set. It suffices to take the <u>positive instances covered by</u> (or more specific than) <u>all g_j such that</u> ($g_j \in$ S-set and $j{\neq}i$) <u>and not covered by g_i or excluded by the G-set</u>. As a result, the CE algorithm would not have to modify the G-set nor the g_j such that ($g_j \in$ S-set and $j{\neq}i$) and it would generalize g_i just enough to cover the new instances. But since $\{g_j \,/\, (g_j \in$ S-set and $j{\neq}i)\}$ is the S-set of all past instances plus the new fictitious ones, g_i can only become more general than one or several g_j, and hence will be eliminated of the new S-set.

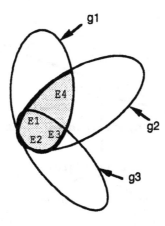

Fig. 4. In this figure, {g1,g2,g3} are assumed to be the S-set of the positive instances (E1,E2,E3). If E4 is observed, then neither g1 nor g2 need to be modified. In fact {g1,g2} is the S-set of all positive instances that belong to the gray area. g3 will need to be generalized just enough to cover E4, and this will make it more general than g1 and g2, hence it will be eliminated from the S-set.

(ii) Case of the reduction of the G-set. In the same way, in order to eliminate an element g_i of the G-set through the CE algorithm, it suffices to provide the negative instances covered by g_i but not covered by the other elements of the G-set and by the S-set. As for (i) above, the CE algorithm would then specialize g_i just enough to exclude the negative instances, and this would result in an element of the G-set that would be more specific than others, hence eliminated. □

The following **example** will help to understand this.

Let us assume that we present positive and negative instances of scenes made of several objects each one described by a conjunction of attribute-values, and that we use three families of attributes, each one organized as a tree with increasing order of generality toward the root.

Sizes

Shapes

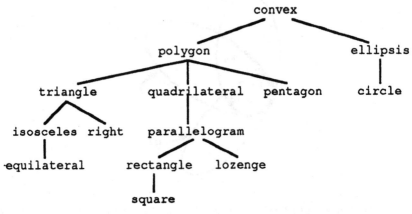

Colors

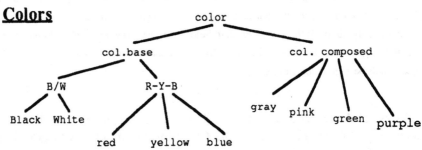

In the following, we show how an element of the S-set could be removed by observing more instances.

Let us suppose that we observe the following sequence of positive instances :

```
-E1:  +  {(large red square) & (small white lozenge)}
```

→ <u>S-set-1</u> = {(large red square) & (small white lozenge)}

```
-E2:  +  {(large   red   parallelogram)   &   (small   blue
equilateral)}
```

→ <u>S-set-2</u> = {(large red parallelogram) & (small col.-base polygon),

(? R-Y-B polygon) & (? col.-base parallelogram)}

```
-E3:  +  {(large yellow right) & (small blue rectangle)}
```

→ <u>S-set-3</u> = {(large R-Y-B polygon) & (small col.-base polygon),   ← g1

(? R-Y-B parallelogram) & (? col.-base polygon),   ← g2

(? R-Y-B polygon) & (? col.-base parallelogram)}   ← g3

Let us assume that at this point the local bias for some reasons decides to discard g3 from the S-set. This would result in

   S-set-4 = {(large R-Y-B polygon) & (small col.-base polygon),

        (? R-Y-B parallelogram) & (? col.-base polygon)}.

The very same S-set would be obtained if the learning algorithm was the CE algorithm that after E1, E2 and E3 observed a new instance covered by g1 and by g2 and not by g3 such as :

```
- E4: +   {(large yellow parallelogram) & (small black pentagon)}
```

5   Bias and order independence

What we have seen so far is that a local preference bias (forgetting hypotheses) can be made equivalent to another bias that would throw in chosen extra instances for the learner to observe. Thanks to this we can now tackle the main topic of this paper, namely what kind of local preference bias a learner can implement so as to stay order independent. Indeed, instead of studying a strategy of forgetting of hypotheses that depend on the current version space, and therefore on the past history, we now study addition of extra fictitious instances to the CE algorithm that is order independent. In other words, we are now in a position to specify conditions on the local preference bias by stating to which extra instances it should amount to.

We assume that the teacher has a set of n examples EX, and draws a sequence x of these according to her requirements.

Furthermore, we assume order independence, i.e. :

   (1) $\forall x, F_n^{LB}(x,f) = VS_{wb}$,   where VS_{wb} is constant.

(We use the notation F_n^{LB} to differentiate a learner implementing a local bias (LB) from one that does not and only implements the CE algorithm noted $F_n(x,f)$ in section 3. VS_{wb} means the version space obtained with bias).

Theorem 2 : *An incremental learner implementing a local preference bias is order independent for a collection EX of instances if the action of this bias is equivalent for all possible sequences x of elements of EX to the supply of the same set of additional instances.*

Proof : It follows immediately from theorem 1. ◻

Now, we want to enlarge theorem 2, and give conditions upon the set of fictitious examples that the local bias acting as an oracle can provide to the learner so that the learner be order independent and reach VS_{wb} possibly different from VS_{nb}.

The CE algorithm without bias would reach the state VS_{nb} (Version Space with no bias). If $VS_{wb} \neq VS_{nb}$, then it follows that extra instances should be provided to the CE algorithm so that it reaches VS_{wb}. Theorem 3 states which ones.

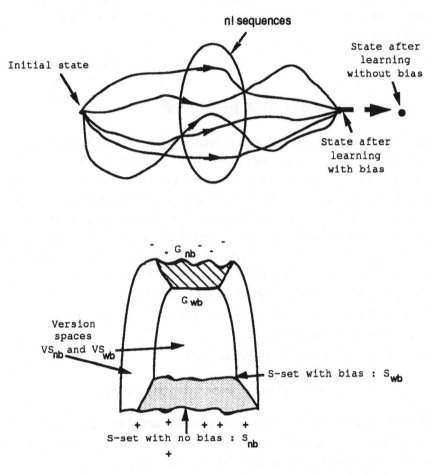

Fig. 5. Which fictitious instances should the oracle corresponding to the local bias provide to the CE algorithm so that it get to the version space VS_{wb} ? Answering this question amounts to give conditions on the local bias that would conduct a learner using it to VS_{wb} irrespective of the training sequence followed. The answer is that fictitious positive instances should be drawn from the gray array, whereas fictitious negative instances should be drawn from the stripped array. The '+' and '-' figure the real instances that conduct the CE algorithm to the VS_{nb} version space.

Let S_{nb} and G_{nb} be respectively the S-set and the G-set that the CE algorithm would obtain from the collection of instances EX, and let S_{wb} and G_{wb} be respectively the S-set and the G-set of VS_{wb} in (1) (the version space obtained on any sequence x of EX by the learner implementing the local preference bias).

Theorem 3 : *For an incremental learner implementing a local preference bias to be order independent for EX leading to the version space C, it is necessary that the action of this bias be equivalent to the supply of :*

- a set of fictitious positive instances such that they together with the real positive instances are covered and bounded by S_{wb}, and,

- a set of fictitious negative instances such that they together with the real negative ones are excluded and bounded by G_{wb}.

Proof : Self-evident. ◻

The next theorem is the application of theorem 3 to the case where $VS_{wb} = F_n(EX,f) = VS_{nb}$, that is the case where the local preference bias leads to the null global preference bias, i.e. has no effect. Such a local bias can be seen as eliminating options judiciously since the result obtained after any sequence x of EX is the same as what the CE algorithm would get on EX. In this case S_{nb} and S_{wb} are one and the same as are G_{nb} and G_{wb}.

Theorem 4 : *For an incremental learner implementing a local preference bias leading to the same result as an incremental learner without a local bias, it is necessary that the action of this bias be equivalent to the supply of :*

- a set of positive instances such that each one is covered by elements of S_{nb}, and ,

- a set of negative instances such that each one is covering all elements of G_{nb}.

It is as if this local preference bias knew "in advance" the collection EX of instances, and eliminated elements of the S-set and of the G-set judiciously. This leads to the final theorem.

Theorem 5 : *It is not possible for a local deterministic preference bias to lead to a null global preference bias for any arbitrary collection EX of examples.*

Proof : Indeed, at each step, the action of the local bias can only depend on the past training instances and the current state. In order to lead to order independence it would have to be equivalent to an oracle that provides instances drawn from an array of the instance space that can be defined only with respect to all the training instances. This would mean that the learner, through its preference bias, was always perfectly informed in advance on the collection EX of examples held by the teacher. □

6 Conclusion

In this research, we are interested in the following **general question** : *given a collection of examples (or data in general), how can a teacher, a priori, best put them in sequence so that the learner, a deterministic incremental learning system that does not ask questions during learning, can acquire some target concept (or knowledge)?*

This question, that corresponds to situations where the teacher does not have the choice of the examples and can not interpret the progress made by the student until the end of the learning period, leads to the study of incremental learning per se, independently of any particular system. The solution to this general interrogation could be of some use to several realistic settings where a teacher has an incremental learning system and a collection of data, or when data arrive sequentially but time allows to keep them in small buffers that can be ordered before being processed.

This framework is **to be compared with** the recent surge of interest for "teaching strategies" that allow to optimally teach a concept to a learner, thus providing lower bounds on learnability complexity [5,17]. The difference with the former framework is that in one case the teacher can only play on the order of the sequence of inputs, whether in the other case, the teacher chooses the most informative ideal examples but does not look for the best order (there are some exceptions such as [13]).

This paper has outlined some first results concerning order sensitivity in supervised conceptual incremental learning. The most important ones are :

(i) that order dependence is due non-optimality and/or to forgetting of possibilities corresponding to a local preference bias that heuristically selects the most promising hypotheses,

(ii) that this bias can be seen as the result of additional instances given to the learner (i.e. prior knowledge built into the system),

(iii) that (ii) allows to replace the difficult problem of determining the action of the local bias along different sequences of instances by a problem of addition (which is commutative, i.e. order independent) of instances to an order independent learner, which leads to

(iv) that there are strong contingencies for an incremental learner to be order independent on some collections of instances (either the corresponding prior knowledge is well-tailored to the future potential collections of inputs, or there is no prior knowledge, thus no reduction of storage and computational complexity).

In this study, we have given sufficient conditions only on the fictitious examples that should be provided by an oracle equivalent to a local preference bias. It would be nice to obtain necessary conditions that state which instances should necessarily be given by the oracle to get order independence. We are currently working on this question.

It should be clear that the problem of noisy data is of no concern to us here. We characterize through the version space what is known to the learner irrespective of the quality of the data. Noise would become an important issue if it was dependent on the ordering of the data (e.g. a sensor equipment that would degrade with time).

Issues for future research include : are these results extensible to more general learning situations (e.g. unsupervised) ? given a local preference bias, how to determine a good sequence ordering so as to best guide the system towards the target knowledge ?

Acknowledgments : I thank all the members of the Equipe Inference et Apprentisssage, and particularly Yves Kodratoff, for the good humored and research conducive atmosphere so beneficial to intellectual work. Comments from the reviewers helped to make this paper clearer.

References

1. **Cornuéjols A.** (1989) : *"An Exploration into Incremental Learning : the INFLUENCE System"*, in Proc.of the 6th Intl. Conf. on Machine Learning, Ithaca, June 29- July 1, 1989, pp.383-386.

2. **Daley & Smith** (1986) : *"On the Complexity of Inductive Inference"*. Information and Control, 69, pp.12-40, 1986.

3. **Doyle J.** (1979) : *"A truth maintenance system"*. Artificial Intelligence, 12, 231-272, 1979.

4. **Fisher, Xu & Zard** (1992) : *"Ordering Effects in COBWEB and an Order-Independent Method"*. To appear in Proc. of the 9th Int. Conf. on Machine Learning, Aberdeen, June 29-July 1st, 1992.

5. **Goldman & Kearns** (1991) : *"On the Complexity of Teaching"*. Proc. of COLT'91, Santa Cruz, Aug. 5-7 1991, pp.303-314.

6. **Haussler** D. (1988) : *"Quantifying inductive bias: AI learning algorithms and Valiant's learning framework"*. Artificial Intelligence, 36, 177-222.

7. **Hirsh** H. (1990) : *"Incremental Version-Space Merging"*. Proc. of the 7th Int. Conf. on Machine Learning. Univ. of Austin, Texas, June 21-23, 1990, pp.330-338.

8. **Ling** (1991) : *"Inductive Learning from Good Examples"*. In Proc. of the 12th Int. Joint Conf. on Artif. Intel. (IJCAI-91), pp.751-756.

9. **MacGregor** J. (1988) : *"The Effects of Order on Learning Classifications by Example: Heuristics for Finding the Optimal Order"*, Artificial Intelligence, vol.34, pp.361-370, 1988.

10. **Mitchell** T. (1978) : *Version Spaces : an Approach to Concept Learning*. PhD Thesis, Stanford, December 1978.

11. **Mitchell** T. (1982) : *"Generalization as Search"*, Artificial Intelligence, vol.18, pp.203-226, 1982.

12. **Natarajan** B. (1991) : *Machine Learning. A Theoretical Approach*. Morgan Kaufmann, 1991.

13. **Pearl** J. (1988) : *Probabilistic Reasoning in Intelligent Systems: Networks of Plausible Inference*. Morgan Kaufmann, 1988.

14. **Porat & Feldman** (1991) : *"Learning Automata from Ordered Examples"*. Machine Learning,7, pp.109-138, 1991.

15. **Rivest & Sloan** (1988) : *"Learning Complicated Concepts Reliably and Usefully"*. In Proc. of COLT'88 (Workshop on Computational Learning Theory), Cambridge 1988, pp.69-79.

16. **Shinohara & Miyano** (1990) : *"Teachability in Computational Learning"*, in Proc. of the Workshop on Algorithmic Learning Theory, 1990, pp.247-255.

17. **Salzberg, Delcher, Heath & Kasif** (1991) : *"Learning with a helpful teacher"*. Proc. of the IJCAI-91, pp.705-711.

18. **Utgoff** P. (1989) : *"Incremental Induction of Decision Trees"*. Machine Learning, 4,161-186,(1989).

19. **Van Lehn** (1987) : *"Learning one subprocedure per lesson"*. Artificial Intelligence, 31 (1), pp.1-40, january 1987.

20. **Winston** (1970) : *"Learning structural descriptions from examples"*, AI-TR-231, MIT, Artificial Intelligence Laboratory, Cambridge, MA, 1970.

Feature Selection
Using Rough Sets Theory

Maciej Modrzejewski

Institute of Computer Science, WUT
Nowowiejska 15/19
00-665 Warsaw, Poland

Abstract. The paper is related to one of the aspects of learning from examples, namely learning how to identify a class of objects a given object instance belongs to. In the paper a method of generating sequence of features allowing such identification is presented. In this approach examples are represented in the form of attribute-value table with binary values of attributes. The main assumption is that one feature sequence is determined for all possible object instances, that is next feature in the order does not depend on values of the previous features. The algorithm is given generating a sequence under these conditions. Theoretical background of the proposed method is rough sets theory. Some generalizations of this theory are introduced in the paper. Finally, a discussion of the presented approach is provided and results of functioning of the proposed algorithm are summarized. Direction of further research is also indicated.

1. Introduction.

One of the most important aspects of artificial intelligence (AI) is machine learning. During the last several years many methods and approaches have been proposed for this problem. Research in this field embraces inductive learning based on examples or on observations, discovery systems, neural nets learning, genetic algorithms learning and others [Mich91].

In our paper we deal with the inductive inference technique called learning from examples, more precisely with its subarea, from instance to class. The goal of learning is in this case identifying the class of objects to which a given instance of object belongs. The input data is a number of examples. In most applications examples are given as an attribute-value table. Attributes describe objects and directly reflect questions about object properties, which may be asked during process of object classification. Learning system must generate and represent somehow a way of making decisions concerning object class. The decisions, obviously, must be consistent with the provided examples.

There are two general methods of representing information related to decision making - a decision tree and a set of decision rules. For both representation methods many algorithms have been proposed. The problem of generating minimal decision tree has received especially large attention. From the algorithms dealing with this problem the most notable is Quinlan's ID3 algorithm [Quin79] and its mutations. The common feature of the algorithms is that they produce trees in which query to be currently asked depends on the response to the preceding queries. We call such tree adaptive. Concerning the second representation, a well known algorithm of generating a set of decision rules from examples is e.g. AQ15 [HoMM86].

In both representations sequence of queries asked to classify object depends on the object instance. This means that generally it is different for different instances. In decision tree the sequence results directly from the tree and in the set of decision rules it depends on the algorithm of searching the set.

We investigate another possibility - generating "as good as possible" sequence of attributes, which would be applicable for all object instances. In this approach the features order is predetermined and questions are asked according to this order regardless of previous responses. This method may be related to the decision tree representation, however in this case a decision tree has specific properties. All nodes of a given level of the tree are assigned the same feature. Such tree will be called preset tree. To store a preset decision tree it is only necessary to store the set of attributes along with the information when to stop. This is an advantage over adaptive tree for which all possible paths must be stored. If the number of attributes and possible decisions is large, the number of paths in adaptive decision tree may be enormous and amount of memory needed to store all nodes of the tree may be prohibitively large. Then the adaptive method becomes inapplicable.

The above observation and the fact that the size of preset decision tree depends on the order of attributes motivate more thorough studying the possibility of generating an optimal order. In the following sections we present our considerations related to this problem. We present algorithm PRESET generating sequence of attributes. We propose an effective method of representing and storing a preset decision tree. Results of experiments of PRESET algorithm functioning are presented as well.

As a theoretical background we use the rough set theory, introduced by Pawlak [Pawl82]. The theory is suitable for the problem since it allows processing knowledge represented in a data table form, where objects are characterized by attributes. We use several notions of rough sets theory and operation of reduction of knowledge. This operation allows extracting most important properties which make different two objects belonging to two different classes. We also introduce some theoretical enhancements necessary to deal with our problem.

In the section 2 we present basics of the rough sets theory and in the section 3 our enhancements of this theory. The section 4 contains the algorithm for ordering attributes and in the section 5 we discuss the proposed method.

2. Main concepts of the rough sets theory.

Before presenting our investigations we first review basics of the rough sets theory, following [Pawl91].

Information systems.
Rough sets theory allows dealing with some type of knowledge related to a set of objects. In this approach the knowledge is a collection of facts concerning objects. The facts are represented in a data table form. Rows of the table correspond to the objects and columns to attributes describing the objects. Entries in a row represent knowledge about object corresponding to that row. The knowledge is expressed by values of attributes. A data table as above is called an *information system.*
Formally, an information system S is a 4-tuple $S = (U, Q, V, f)$, where

U - is a nonempty, finite set of objects, called the universe;

Q - is a finite set of attributes;

$V = \bigcup V_q$, where V_q is a domain of attribute q;

f - is an information function assigning a value of attribute for every object
and every attribute, i.e.

$\qquad f : U \times Q \to V$, such that
for every $x \in U$ and for every $q \in Q$ $f(x,q) \in V$.

Indiscernibility relation.
For any set $P \subseteq Q$ of attributes a relation, called *indiscernibility relation* and denoted *IND* is defined as follows:

$\qquad IND(P) = \{(x,y) \in U \times U : f(x,a) = f(y,a) \text{ for every } a \in P\}.$

If $(x,y) \in IND(P)$, then x and y are called indiscernible with respect to P.
The indiscernibility relation is an equivalence relation over U. Hence, it partitions U into equivalence classes - sets of objects indiscernible with respect to P. Such partition (classification) is denoted by $U/IND(P)$.

Approximations of sets.
For any subset of objects $X \subseteq U$ and subset of attributes $P \subseteq Q$ the P-lower (denoted $\underline{P}X$) and P-upper (denoted $\overline{P}X$) *approximations* of X are defined as follows:

$\qquad \underline{P}X = \bigcup \{ Y \in U/IND(P) : Y \subseteq X \} ;$

$\qquad \overline{P}X = \bigcup \{ Y \in U/IND(P) : Y \cap X \neq \varnothing \} .$

A set for which $\underline{P}X = \overline{P}X$ is called an exact set, otherwise it is called rough (with respect to P).

Dependency of attributes.
A measure of dependency of two sets of attributes $P, R \subseteq Q$ is introduced in rough sets theory. The measure is called a *degree of dependency* of P on R and denoted $\gamma_R(P)$. It is defined as

$$\gamma_R(P) = \frac{card(POS_R(P))}{card(U)}, \text{ where}$$

$$POS_R(P) = \bigcup_{X \in U/IND(P)} \underline{R}X.$$

The set $POS_R(P)$ is called a positive region of classification $U/IND(P)$ (or in short a positive region of P) for the set of attributes R. Informally speaking, the set $POS_R(P)$ contains those objects of U which may be classified as belonging to one of the equivalence classes of $IND(P)$, employing attributes from the set R. The coefficient $\gamma_R(P)$ expresses numerically the percentage of objects which can be properly classified. For any two sets of attributes $P, R \subseteq Q$

$$0 \le \gamma_R(P) \le 1$$

and we say that P depends to degree $\gamma_R(P)$ on R.

Significance of attributes.
The coefficient γ is used to define an important for our investigations notion of *significance of an attribute*. The significance of an attribute $a \in R$, $R \subseteq Q$ is a measure expressing how important the attribute a is in R, regarding classification $U/IND(P)$. The significance is denoted σ_a^R and defined as follows:

$$\sigma_a^R(P) = \gamma_R(P) - \gamma_{R-\{a\}}(P).$$

Let us notice that such defined significance is relative in its nature since it depends on both set P and R. Therefore, an attribute may have different significance for different classifications and in different "contexts" (sets R in the definition above). However, we can also talk about an absolute significance of an attribute. For that purpose we take the whole set of attributes Q as the sets R and P in the definition. Then, i.e. for $R = P = Q$

$$\sigma_a^Q(Q) = \gamma_Q(Q) - \gamma_{Q-\{a\}}(Q),$$

and taking into account that $\gamma_Q(Q) = 1$,

$$\sigma_a^Q(Q) = 1 - \gamma_{Q-\{a\}}(Q).$$

Reduction of attributes.
Let $S = (U, Q, V, f)$ be an information system and let $P \subseteq Q$. Set P is called *independent* in S if for every $T \subset P$ $IND(P) \subset IND(T)$. Set $R \subseteq P \subseteq Q$ is a *reduct* of P if it is independent and $IND(R) = IND(P)$. This means that any reduct R of a set P classifies objects equally well as P does and attributes from $P-R$ are superfluous regarding distinguishing of objects.

Reducts are minimal in the sense that they cannot be reduced more (no attribute may be removed from a reduct without destroying its property of independence). The concept of reducts is one of the most important concepts in rough sets theory and it is used in most applications of the theory. There exist well defined and checked in practice algorithms which allow finding reducts effectively [SkRa91].

The example below illustrates the presented concepts.

Example 1.

Information system and indiscernibility relation.
An example information system is shown in Table 1 below.

	a	b	c	d
x_1	A	Z	4	4
x_2	B	X	3	2
x_3	C	X	2	2
x_4	C	Y	2	1
x_5	A	Y	4	1
x_6	B	Z	3	2
x_7	B	Y	3	3
x_8	C	Y	2	3

Table 1.

In this system:

$$U = \{x_1, \dots , x_8\}, \quad Q = \{a, b, c, d\},$$
$$(x_4, x_8) \in IND(\{a, b, c\}),$$
$$(x_2, x_3) \in IND(\{b, d\}),$$
$$(x_2, x_6) \in IND(\{a, d\}) \text{ and so on.}$$

Approximations.
Let us find the lower and upper approximations of set $X = \{x_1, x_2, x_4\}$ for $P = \{b, d\}$.
Since $U/IND(P) = \{ \{x_1\}, \{x_2,x_3\}, \{x_4,x_5\}, \{x_6\}, \{x_7\ x_8\} \}$, then $\underline{P}X = \{x_1\}$ and $\overline{P}X = \{x_1, x_2, x_3, x_4, x_5\}$.
Therefore X is rough with respect to P.

Dependency.
Let us compute $POS_R(Q)$ for $R = \{a, b, c\}$. In this case $U/IND(R) = \{ \{x_1\}, \{x_2\}, \{x_3\}, \{x_4,x_8\}, \{x_5\}, \{x_6\}, \{x_7\} \}$. Since $U/IND(Q) = \{ \{x_1\}, \dots , \{x_8\} \}$, then $POS_R(Q) = \{x_1, x_2, x_3, x_5, x_6, x_7\}$ and $\gamma_R(Q) = 0.75$.

Significance of attributes.
Using the above result we can conclude that
$$\sigma_d^Q(Q) = 1 - \gamma_{\{a,b,c\}}(Q) = 0.25.$$
Significance of other attributes in the system for $R = P = Q$ is given below:
$$\sigma_a^Q(Q) = \sigma_c^Q(Q) = 0,$$
$$\sigma_b^Q(Q) = 0.25.$$

Reducts.
There are two reducts of the set Q: $R_1 = \{a, b, d\}$ and $R_2 = \{b, c, d\}$. We can easily verify that both these sets and only they satisfy conditions stated in the definition of a reduct. To confirm that R_1 is a reduct we note that $U/IND(R_1) = U/IND(Q)$ and for every $q \in R$ $U/IND(R_1-\{q\}) \neq U/IND(R_1)$. After removing e.g. a we obtain $U/IND(\{b, d\}) \neq U/IND(Q)$.
□

3. Weighted information systems.

To solve the problem of ordering attributes, we introduce generalizations of some concepts of the rough sets theory. In this section we present notions used in further considerations.

We enhance modeling power of information systems by introducing weights of objects. To each object in a system its weight - a natural number - is assigned. The weights represent importance of objects in the system. Formally, in this case an information system becomes the *weighted information system* WS defined as follows:
$$WS = \langle U, Q, V, f, w \rangle,$$
where U, Q, V and f are defined in the same way as in the definition of information system and w is a complete function assigning weights to objects:
$$w : U \rightarrow \mathbf{N},$$
where $\mathbf{N}$ stands for the set of natural numbers.

We call w a *weighting function* and $w(x)$ - a *weight* of an object $x \in U$. Then we take into account the weights in considerations regarding the system. We introduce definitions reflecting the presence of the weights. They modify meaning of some notions in classical rough sets theory. The definitions are shown below:

Weighted quality of classification.
Having two sets of attributes P, $R \subseteq Q$ we denote the weighted quality of classification $U/IND(R)$ by the set P as $W\gamma_P(R)$ and define it as

$$W\gamma_P(R) = \frac{WPOS_P(R)}{WU}, \text{ where}$$

where $WPOS_P(R)$ is a sum of weights of objects constituting the positive region of classification $POS_P(R)$, i.e.
$$WPOS_P(R) = \Sigma \, (\, w(x) : x \in POS_P(R) \,)$$
and WU is a total sum of weights of objects in the system, i.e.
$$WU = \Sigma \, (\, w(x) : x \in U \,).$$

Weighted significance of an attribute.

Let $P, R \subseteq Q$ and $a \in P$. By a weighted significance $W\sigma_a^P(R)$ of an attribute a in P, with respect to the classification $U/IND(R)$, we mean the value

$$W\sigma_a^P(R) = W\gamma_P(R) - W\gamma_{P-\{a\}}(R).$$

Let us note that in the simplest case, when $P = R = Q$ in the definitions above, the following equalities hold:

i) $WPOS_Q(Q) = WU.$

ii) $W\gamma_Q(Q) = 1.$

iii) $W\sigma_a^Q(Q) = 1 - W\gamma_{Q-\{a\}}(Q)$ for each $a \in Q.$

We will call $W\sigma_a^Q(Q)$ the *absolute weighted significance* of an attribute. For the sake of simplicity we will denote it as $W\sigma_a$.

Using the above modified notions we may model frequent in real life situation when objects are not homogeneous. In such case the important fact may be not only how many objects but also which of them are becoming indistinguishable when removing attributes. Therefore the weights assigned to objects should be interpreted as an importance of distinguishing these objects from the others in the system. The weighted significance of an attribute expresses how much of such importance of objects we lose removing this attribute.

Example 2.

Let us modify the information system from Example 1 by adding weights to the objects. The new, weighted system is shown in Table 2 below:

	$w(x)$	a	b	c	d
x_1	1	A	Z	4	4
x_2	2	B	X	3	2
x_3	3	C	X	2	2
x_4	1	C	Y	2	1
x_5	2	A	Y	4	1
x_6	3	B	Z	3	2
x_7	1	B	Y	3	3
x_8	2	C	Y	2	3

Table 2.

Now we compute the absolute weighted significance of the attributes with weights of objects as shown in the column $w(u)$:

$$W\sigma_a = W\sigma_c = 0,$$
$$W\sigma_b = \frac{1}{2},$$
$$W\sigma_d = 0.2.$$

Comparing these values with results obtained in Example 1 we can notice that according to assigned weights attributes b and d are no longer equally significant. However loss of knowledge (expressed by unweighted significance) is the same for both of them, the loss of importance of objects (expressed by weighted significance) is higher for b and therefore removing this attribute is most "harmful" for the system. This results from the fact that without the attribute b objects x_2 and x_6 become indiscernible and we lose weights of total value 5, while without d weights of total value 3 are lost (sum of weights of x_4 and x_8, which become indiscernible in that case).

$\Box$

4. Algorithm to find sequence of attributes.

In this section we show a solution of the problem of ordering attributes to make the process of identifying objects most efficient. According to initial assumptions the problem is reduced to finding the proper permutation of attributes. This permutation should lead to minimal preset decision tree. A minimal tree is the one having minimal cost, i.e. sum of lengths of all paths from root to leaves.

We assume that the initial data provided is an information system of the form consistent with the definition given in the section 2. The other very important assumption is that attributes in the system have binary domain.

The first, preliminary step for generating an optimal sequence of attributes is determining a set of attributes which is to be ordered. In our approach this is achieved by identifying reducts of the set of all attributes. Then one reduct is chosen for the purpose of ordering attributes. Attributes not included in this reduct are removed from the system. The remaining attributes are independent, that is all of them are necessary for distinguishing objects.

The algorithm PRESET is proposed to solve the problem of ordering attributes. In view of the presented assumptions the initial point for the algorithm is an information system $S = \langle X, Q, V, p \rangle$ with independent set of attributes having binary domain. To find a sequence of attributes we construct weighted information system $WS = \langle U, Q, V, f, w \rangle$, in which

$U = X/IND(Q)$, i.e. objects in WS are equivalence classes of relation $IND(Q)$ in S; this means that no two objects in U are indiscernible or in other words $IND(Q)$ is empty over U,

Q is the set of attributes for which the order will be determined,

$V = \{\text{value\_0, value\_1}\}$, this means that attributes have binary domain; actual values depend on the system (these may be $\{0, 1\}$, $\{\text{TRUE, FALSE}\}$, $\{\text{yes, no}\}$ and so on),

f is a function with values equal to values of p:

$f : U \times Q \to V : f(u,q) = p(x,q)$, where x is an arbitrary object belonging to u,

$w(u) = 2$ for every $u \in U$.

Let us denote a sequence of attributes generated by the algorithm by $\mathscr{S}$. On the beginning the sequence $\mathscr{S}$ is empty.

The algorithm PRESET is as follows:

1.   Check cardinality of the set of attributes in WS.

1a. If the cardinality is 1, add the attribute to the sequence $\mathscr{S}$ and finish the algorithm, the sequence $\mathscr{S}$ is the sequence searched for, in the **reverse order**;

1b. Otherwise compute value of absolute weighted significance for each attribute in WS.
     Proceed to step 2.

2.   Choose the attribute having the lowest value of the significance (if there is one such attribute) or any attribute from the set of attributes having the lowest value (if there are more than one of them).
     Proceed to step 3.

3.   Add the chosen attribute (let it be q_i) to the sequence $\mathscr{S}$.
     Proceed to step 4.

4.   Construct diminished weighted system $WS' = <U', Q', V, f, w'>$, in which
     $Q' = Q - \{q_i\}$,
     $U' = U/IND(Q')$,
     $f : U' \times Q' \to V : f'(x',q') = f(x,q')$, where x is an arbitrary object belonging to u',

     $w' : U' \to \{1, 2\} : w'(u') = \begin{cases} 2 \text{ if } card(u') = 1 \text{ and } w(u) = 2 \text{ for } u \in u' \\ 1 \text{ otherwise} \end{cases}$

     Let $WS = WS'$, proceed to step 1.

∎

Example 3:

Consider information system representing knowledge about some animals. The system in its weighted form is shown in Table 3.

	w	Warm_Blood	Can_Fly	Has_Fur	Lives_in_Water
Elephant (E)	2	yes	no	no	no
Shark (S)	2	no	no	no	yes
Bat (B)	2	yes	yes	yes	no
Python (P)	2	no	no	no	no
Hawk (H)	2	yes	yes	no	no
Dolphin (D)	2	yes	no	no	yes

Table 3.

For the sake of simplicity we abbreviate the attributes in the system by single letters: B for Warm_Blood, C for Can_Fly, F for Has_Fur and W for Lives_in_Water.

The system from Table 3 satisfies initial conditions for the algorithm PRESET. We start with computing weighted absolute significance of all attributes:

$W\sigma_B = W\sigma_W = \frac{2}{3}$.

$W\sigma_C = W\sigma_F = \frac{1}{3}$.

Therefore in this stage we can choose either attribute C or F. Let choose attribute F: $\mathcal{S} = \langle F \rangle$.

Now we construct the new system with attribute F removed. It is shown in Table 4.

	w	B	C	W
{ E }	2	yes	no	no
{ S }	2	no	no	yes
{ B, H }	1	yes	yes	no
{ P }	2	no	no	no
{ D }	2	yes	no	yes

Table 4.

Absolute weighted significance of the attributes is now as follows:

$W\sigma_B = W\sigma_W = \frac{8}{9}$.

$W\sigma_C = \frac{1}{3}$.

Hence now we are obliged to attach attribute C to the sequence: $\mathcal{S} = \langle F, C \rangle$. The new form of the system is shown below, in the table 5.

	w	B	W
{ B, H, E }	1	yes	no
{ S }	2	no	yes
{ P }	2	no	no
{ D }	2	yes	yes

Table 5.

Significance of attributes:
$$W\sigma_B = W\sigma_W = 1.$$
Both attributes B and W are now equivalent. Let choose W: $\mathcal{S} = <F, C, W>$.
There remains only one attribute, which is added to the sequence, i.e.
$\mathcal{S} = <F, C, W, B>$ and the algorithm ends.

The order searched for is therefore $<B, W, C, F>$ and the sequence of questions to identify animal species should be as follows:
1. Is the animal warm-blooded?
2. Does the animal live in water?
3. Can the animal fly?
4. Does the animal have fur?

This sequence reflects the optimal strategy for reaching an answer about animal species, under condition that questions asked are always the same. Obviously, in three cases (Shark, Python and Dolphin) the answer is known already after two questions, case of Elephant requires three questions and in the case of Bat and Hawk all four questions are needed. The decision tree for the above sequence is shown in Figure 2.

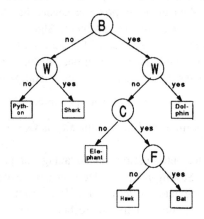

Figure 2.

Of 24 possibilities (all permutations of the four-element set of attributes) 4 produce minimal preset trees, i.e. trees with minimal sum of path lengths, which in this case is 17. We have found one of them. The remaining would have been obtained if we had made different choices in the first and third stages of the algorithm. More precisely, other sequences leading to minimal preset trees are: *<B, W, F, C>*, *<W, B, C, F>* and *<W, B, F, C>*.

□

5. Discussion of the proposed method.

A trivial solution of the problem of finding the optimal order of attributes is the exhaustive method, i.e. generating all possible permutations and selecting the best one. Nevertheless, it is impossible to use practically the exhaustive method since the number of permutations grows rapidly with the increase of number of attributes. Algorithm PRESET takes only a small fraction of time of exhaustive method.

However, our algorithm does not function well in all cases. In 100 experiments, when a set of examples has been generated randomly with various number of attributes (from 4 to 8) and objects, the algorithm arrived at correct result in 83 cases. We found that wrong results are obtained more probably if in early stage of the algorithm there are many attributes having the same value of significance and a decision must be made which one of them should be chosen. Error value, measured as the difference between generated and optimal tree costs did not exceed in conducted experiments 1.5% of the optimal tree cost.

The possible explanation of the above drawback is that the problem of finding optimal binary decision tree is known to be NP-complete [HyRi76]. Our problem, though formulated in different way, is similar, and is supposed to be of the class of NP-complete problems. We cannot yet prove or negate this statement, but if it is true, a polynomial algorithm cannot solve the problem. Algorithm PRESET is polynomial since amount of computation in each step of the algorithm depends on the number of object comparisons and significance evaluations. Assume that there are n objects (examples) and m attributes in a system. Number of comparisons needed to evaluate one significance is equal to the sum of all natural numbers from 1 to $n-1$, that is $\frac{n^2-n}{2}$. This must be repeated m times and the complexity is $O(\frac{m(n^2-n)}{2})$.

As was mentioned in the introduction, an advantage of preset decision tree is its memory requirements. Storing adaptive decision tree requires amount of memory needed to store all intermediate and terminal nodes. Assume that 4 memory units are devoted for an intermediate node (1 for an attribute, 2 for links to subtrees and 1 for node qualifier) and 2 units for a terminal node (1 for object identifier and 1 for node qualifier). Since there are as many terminal nodes as examples and the least number of intermediate nodes for binary tree is $n-1$, at least $6n-4$ memory units are needed to represent an adaptive tree.

In our approach we need to store attributes in appropriate order and information when to stop. Assuming that for storing an attribute we need 1 memory unit, the first part requires as many units as there are attributes. Since under our assumptions $n > m+1$, in the worst case $m = n-1$ and we need $n-1$ memory units for storing sequence of attributes (the best case would be $\log_2 n$). The method of representation of the second part is not obvious and we present it briefly below. Assume that tree root is placed at level 0. For each example we store the value 2^{m-l}, where l is a tree level of the terminal node respective to this example. In our example system describing animals, objects Shark, Python and Dolphin would be assigned value 4, object Elephant value 2 and objects Bat and Hawk value 1. This representation requires 2 memory units for each example (1 for the above value and 1 for example identifier) and $2n$ units for all examples. Therefore maximal amount of memory needed in our representation is $3n-1$ and is approximately twice less than the memory needed to represent the respective adaptive tree. The actual gain is in most cases higher since the number of attributes is less than $n-1$. There exists a simple algorithm for generating such representation as well as an algorithm of making questions using this information for stopping. Due to the lack of space they will not be presented here.

6. Conclusions.

In this paper we have studied a problem of sequencing attributes in a information system to obtain an optimal preset decision tree. We have presented a polynomial algorithm solving the problem in many cases. We find the results encouraging and justifying further research. In particular, we intend to enhance the algorithm PRESET for the case of multivalued attributes. We would also like to identify precisely the cases when the algorithm produces non-optimal sequences.

Our algorithm seems to have wide area of applications, spanning from building expert systems, querying databases etc. to testing combinational circuits.

We think that the approach of preset sequence of attributes can combine advantages of simplicity and unambiguity of decision procedure in tree representation with power, intuitiveness and representation efficiency of a set of decision rules.

Acknowledgment

The author wish to thank Prof. A. Skowron of Warsaw University and Prof. M. Moshkov of Nizhniy Novgorod Technical University for their valuable comments and inspiring suggestions.

References

[HyRi76] Hyafil L., Rivest R.L., *Constructing optimal binary decision trees is NP-complete*, Information Processing Letters, Vol. 5, No. 1,May 1976, pp. 15-17.

[HoMM86] Hong J., Mozetic I., Michalski R.S., *AQ-15: Incremental Learning of Attribute-Based Descriptions from Examples, The Method and User's Guide*, Report ISG 86-5, UIUCDCS-F-86-949, Dept. of Computer Science, University of Illinois, Urbana, 1986.

[Mich91] Michalski R.S., *Inferential Learning Theory: A Conceptual Framework for Characterizing Learning Processes*, Report P91-13 MLI 91-6, Center for Artificial Intelligence, George Mason University, Fairfax, 1991.

[Pawl82] Pawlak Z., *Rough Sets*, International Journal of Computer and Information Sciences, Vol. 11, No. 5, 1982, pp. 341-356.

[Pawl91] Pawlak Z., *Rough Sets, Theoretical Aspects of Reasoning about Data*, Kluwer Academic Publishers, 1991.

[Quin79] Quinlan R., *Discovering rules from large collection of examples*, in D. Mitchie (editor), *Expert systems in the microelectronic age*, Edinburgh University Press, Edinburgh 1979.

[SkRa91] Skowron A., Rauszer C., *The Discernibility Matrices and Functions in Information Systems*, ICS WUT Research Report 1/91, Warsaw, 1991.

Effective Learning in Dynamic Environments by Explicit Context Tracking

Gerhard Widmer[1] and Miroslav Kubat[2]

[1] Dept. of Medical Cybernetics and Artificial Intelligence, University of Vienna, and
Austrian Research Institute for Artificial Intelligence,
Schottengasse 3, A-1010 Vienna, Austria
e-mail: gerhard@ai.univie.ac.at
[2] Institute of Biomedical Engineering, Dept. for Medical Informatics,
Graz University of Technology
Brockmanngasse 41, A-8010 Graz, Austria
e-mail: mirek@fbmtds04.tu-graz.ac.at

Abstract. Daily experience shows that in the real world, the meaning of many concepts heavily depends on some implicit context, and changes in that context can cause radical changes in the concepts. This paper introduces a method for incremental concept learning in dynamic environments where the target concepts may be context-dependent and may change drastically over time. The method has been implemented in a system called *FLORA3*. *FLORA3* is very flexible in adapting to changes in the target concepts and tracking concept drift. Moreover, by explicitly storing old hypotheses and re-using them to bias learning in new contexts, it possesses the ability to utilize experience from previous learning. This greatly increases the system's effectiveness in environments where contexts can reoccur periodically. The paper describes the various algorithms that constitute the method and reports on several experiments that demonstrate the flexibility of *FLORA3* in dynamic environments.

1 Introduction

One of the basic tasks of Machine Learning is to provide methods for deriving descriptions of abstract concepts from their positive and negative examples. So far, many powerful algorithms have been suggested for various types of data, background knowledge, description languages, and some special 'complications' such as noise or incompleteness.

However, relatively little attention has been devoted to the influence of varying contexts. Daily experience shows that in the real world, the meaning of many concepts can heavily depend on some given context, such as season, weather, geographic coordinates, or simply the personality of the teacher. 'Ideal family' or 'affordable transportation' have different interpretations in poor countries and in the North, the meaning of 'nice weather' varies with season, and 'appropriate dress' depends on time of day, event, age, weather, and sex, among other things. So time-dependent changes in the context can induce changes in the meaning or definition of the concepts to be learned. Such changes in concept meaning are sometimes called *concept drift* (especially when they are gradual).

To discover concept drift, the learner needs feedback from its classification attempts, to update the internal concept description whenever the prediction accuracy decreases. This was the experimental setting of the system *FLORA*, which was first published in Kubat (1989), with a theoretical analysis in Kubat (1991). The system, though very simple, was successfuly applied in an expert-system-driven control mechanism for load re-distribution in computer networks (Kubat, 1992).

Frankly spoken, the original program *FLORA* was not very sophisticated from the machine learning (ML) point of view because it did not contain such common ML mechanisms as explicit generalization operators or search heuristics. These came later, in the frame of *FLORA2* (Widmer & Kubat, 1992) where some kind of intelligence was implemented (generalization, check for subsumption, and flexible reaction to the speed of drift).

Still, even this later version lacked an important attribute of intelligent behavior: the ability to use experience from previous learning. Whenever an old context reoccured, the system just blindly tried to re-learn it, waiving any previous experience. The consequence was that even if the same context re-appeared a thousand times, the system always needed, on average, the same number of examples to modify the concept description. This shortcoming motivated another upgrade of the system, *FLORA3*, which is able to adapt to concept drift while utilizing past experience and deals with recurring contexts much more effectively.

The next section discusses, in more detail, the issues of hidden contexts and concept drift, and the relevance of this problem in real-world applications. Then, the system *FLORA2* is described. Section 4 is dedicated to the main contribution of this paper, the algorithm for context tracking, which differentiates *FLORA3* from her predecessors. Section 5 reports on experimental results demonstrating the utility of the idea.

2 Dynamic environments, hidden contexts, and concept drift

When speaking about concept drift, one might distinguish two different types of drift (though they are not always clearly separable): *Real* concept drift reflects real changes in the world and can be exemplified by the changes in fashion— 'fancy skirt' or 'modern music'—or language—the semantic variation of such words as left-wing policy, conservatism, or liberalism.

Virtual concept drift, on the other hand, does not occur in reality but, rather, in the computer model reflecting this reality. In a practical setting, this kind of effect can emerge when the representation language is poor and fails to identify all relevant features, or when the order of training examples for learning is skewed, so that different types of instances are not evenly distributed over the training sequence.

Many potential sources of virtual concept drift can be identified. Most typically, the teacher is to blame, having only a particular context in mind and considering only the related pieces of information to be relevant; or the teacher's knowledge is limited. Also, the teacher may have good knowledge but some of the features may depend on values that cannot be measured, or the measurements are too expensive.

Sometimes, the agent learns by experimentation and simply does not come across all reasonable examples. For illustration, consider an autonomous agent or robot moving through a foreign world and trying to induce rules to survive (see the experiments reported in Section 5). In a complex world where not all relevant features are explicit, there is no choice but to put up with variables and predicates that can be acquired by the robot's devices. Their number is of course limited. Obviously, slightly different laws are valid in different parts of the world. If you want to grow a palm tree, you will surely apply different techniques in Africa and on the Arctic Circle.

Another aspect of the problem is that the agent does not a priori know how many contexts exist in the world, how to discern them, what their ordering is, and what impact they excercise on the concept drift. Sometimes, the drift consists in changed values of some variables, sometimes also the relevance of individual variables or predicates can dramatically change. Moreover, the transition is usually only gradual with rather fuzzy boundaries between two different concept interpretations. All this must be taken into account when building a flexible learning system.

The core idea underlying the philosophy of *FLORA* is that more recent pieces of information should receive higher levels of trust, in the belief that the older the examples, the higher the danger that they relate to an outdated context (the agent has meanwhile moved from the Arctic Circle to the Equator). The system always maintains a set of current (positive and negative) examples that represent its current world and that should be correctly described by the current concept hypothesis. The set of these examples is called window (*FLORA*, sitting in a coach, observes through it the world passing by). One by one, new examples are encountered and used to update the internal knowledge structures; at the same time, however, older examples are distrusted and deleted from the window. This, too, causes changes to the concept description. In this way, the current context is approximated—the system trusts only those examples that are currently inside the window. That enables *FLORA* to recognize a concept drift and adjust itself to it.

The latest descendant of the family, *FLORA3*, possesses the ability to store encountered contexts for future use, and to re-examine them whenever it discovers (or suspects) drift. Evidently, this makes sense only if the same (or similar) contexts reappear in the future, which is certainly the case in many realistic applications where the number of possible contexts is *finite*. For instance, there are four seasons that follow one by one in a cyclic order and cause regular changes in many natural phenomena. The specific environment where a robot is expected to work might consist of several rooms, each with its own characteristics. Even in fashion we can see that some phenomena reappear periodically, among them short skirts, preferred dress fabrics, or hair style. The same goes for contexts in political life—autocracy versus oligarchy versus democracy, lesser or greater influence of the church, and the like. Each of them implies different heuristics for defining law, guidelines for everyday life, and morale (these reappear, too).

3   The basic *FLORA* framework: learning and forgetting

In this section we briefly review the basic learning mechanism in the *FLORA* framework, as it was already realized in *FLORA2* (Widmer & Kubat, 1992). The following section will then describe the more advanced features of *FLORA3*.

The principle of the *FLORA* algorithm is shown in Figure 1. The rectangle 'knowledge' stands for the current concept description, the rectangle 'window' contains the currently trusted examples. Each time a new example arrives, it is added to the window; from time to time, the oldest or, alternatively, least relevant example is deleted from the window. Both events necessitate updates to the concept description.

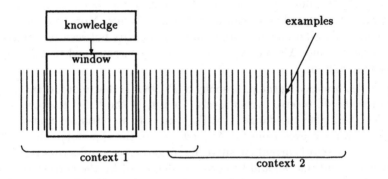

Fig. 1. The window of the system FLORA moving across the stream of examples.

The concept description is represented by three description sets, *ADES*, *PDES*, and *NDES*. The description sets are collections of *description items*— conjunctions of attribute-value pairs. Thus a description set can be interpreted as a *DNF* expression. *ADES* is a set of 'accepted' description items (*DI*s) covering only positive examples in the window (not necessarily all of them) and no negative examples; *PDES* is a set of 'potential' *DI*s, covering both positive and negative examples; *NDES* is a set of 'negative' *DI*s, covering only negative examples. Any *DI* for which we cannot find at least one example in the window is deleted. (Widmer & Kubat, 1992) gives an intuitive motivation for these three sets.

Obviously, each example that is being added to or deleted from the window may be described by a number of *DI*s. This entails the following consequences:

Adding a *positive* example to the window can cause new description items to be included in *ADES*, or some existing items to be 'confirmed,' or existing items to be transferred from *NDES* to *PDES*.

Adding a *negative* example to the window can cause new description items to be included in *NDES*, or some existing items to be 'reinforced,' or existing items to be transferred from *ADES* to *PDES*.

Forgetting an example can cause existing description items to be 'weakened,' or even deleted from the current description set, or moved from *PDES* to *ADES* (if the example was negative) or to *NDES* (if the example was positive).

Figure 2 summarizes these updates. The arrows indicate possible migrations of description items between sets after learning (L) or forgetting (F) from a positive (+) or negative (−) instance, respectively.

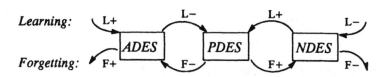

Fig. 2. Transitions among the description sets.

To operationalize this learning schema, let us recapitulate the learning algorithm of *FLORA2* as it was presented in Widmer and Kubat (1992). Assume that the three description sets already exist (at the beginning they might also be empty) and that they are encoded in the following form:

$$ADES = \{ADes_1/AP_1, ADes_2/AP_2, \ldots\}$$
$$PDES = \{PDes_1/PP_1/PN_1, \ldots\} \qquad (1)$$
$$NDES = \{NDes_1/NN_1, \ldots\}$$

where $ADes_i$ ($PDes_i$, $NDes_i$) are description items; AP_i and PP_i represent the number of positive examples matching the respective DIs; and PN_i and NN_i represent the number of negative examples matching the respective DIs. The counters AP_i, PP_i, PN_i, and NN_i help to decide whether to move the respective item to another description set, or, if it is equal to zero, whether to drop it altogether.

In order to prevent combinatorial explosion, the sizes of these description sets must somehow be restricted. In *FLORA2*, the set *ADES* is not a set of all possible description items. It is constructed by stepwise careful generalization (see below) and, in effect, represents one non-redundant DNF formula that expresses the current concept hypothesis. The same holds for *NDES*. *Redundancy* is eliminated by checking for subsumption *within* description sets: *ADES* is kept maximally general (that is, if some description item $ADes_i$ subsumes some $ADes_j$, only $ADes_i$ is kept in *ADES*). In *PDES*, only the most specific descriptions are kept, and *NDES* is again maintained maximally general. *Inconsistency* is avoided by checking for subsumption *between* description sets. In this way, for instance, over-generalization of *ADES* is avoided by checking it against *PDES* and *NDES*. These conditions are tested whenever one of the description sets is modified. The algorithms for incremental learning and forgetting then proceed as follows:

Incremental learning:

Assume that the system is presented with a new training instance, with given classification $C \in \{positive, negative\}$. Then the description sets are updated as follows (see also Figure 2):

If classification C is **positive**:

For all $ADes_i/AP_i$ in *ADES*:
  if $match(instance, ADes_i)$ then $AP_i := AP_i + 1$;
For all $PDes_i/PP_i/PN_i$ in *PDES*:
  if $match(instance, PDes_i)$ then $PP_i := PP_i + 1$;
For all $NDes_i/NN_i$ in *NDES*:
  if $match(instance, NDes_i)$ then remove $NDes_i$ from *NDES* and include it into *PDES* as a triple $NDes_i/1/NN_i$ and check the updated *PDES* for subsumptions;
If there is no $ADes_i$ in *ADES* that matches the new instance, then find a generalization of one of the $ADes_i \in ADES$ such that (1) the generalization covers the new instance; (2) the required degree of generalization is *minimal* and (3) the generalization does not subsume any descriptions in *PDES* or *NDES* (this ensures consistency against negative instances); as an extreme case, the description of the instance itself may be added to *ADES*; then check *ADES* for subsumptions (remove redundant descriptions);

If classification C is **negative**, the algorithm works analogously (just exchange *ADES* and *NDES* in the above algorithm).

Incremental forgetting:

When an old instance is dropped from the current window and 'forgotten,' the description sets are updated as follows (again, see Figure 2):

If the instance was a **positive** one:

For all $ADes_i/AP_i$ in *ADES*:
  if $match(instance, ADes_i)$ then $AP_i := AP_i - 1$;
  if $AP_i = 0$ then remove $ADes_i$ from *ADES*;
For all $PDes_i/PP_i/PN_i$ in *PDES*:
  if $match(instance, PDes_i)$ then $PP_i := PP_i - 1$;
  if $PP_i = 0$ then remove $PDes_i$ from *PDES* and include it into *NDES* as a pair $PDes_i/PN_i$ and check the updated *NDES* for subsumptions;

If the instance was a **negative** one, the algorithm works analogously (just exchange *ADES* and *NDES* in the above algorithm).

This algorithm provides the basis for learning in dynamic environments. However, more is needed to achieve really flexible and effective learning behaviour in domains with substantial concept drift.

4   *FLORA3*: Explicit context tracking

The ability to *forget*, as described in the previous section, provides the fundamental basis for the system's ability to adapt to concepts that change over time. Eventually, old instances will drop out of the window and be forgotten. However, this will work well only in domains where changes in the concepts are almost imperceptibly slow. When dramatic or sudden concept shifts occur, the fixed window size prevents the system from reacting flexibly. Ideally, when the system notices (or suspects) a beginning concept drift, it should shrink the window in order to discard old instances that now contradict the new concept. *FLORA3* includes a heuristic to automatically adjust the size of its window during learning. This is the subject of the next section.

Also, in environments where contexts can re-occur (periodically or randomly), the system would have to re-learn concepts that it had already learned at some earlier time. In such environments it would be advantageous to keep old, outdated concepts around for possible use in the future. In *FLORA3*, a mechanism for doing this has been developed. It is tightly coupled to the window adjustment algorithm and will be described in the section after next.

4.1   Automatic adjustment of window size

The behaviour of a *FLORA*-type system depends crucially on the size of the window. Too narrow a window will cause relevant instances and information to be forgotten too early; and when the window is too wide, the system will be very reluctant to follow a concept drift: it will hang on to noisy or outdated instances and hypotheses too long. The optimal window size, then, is a function of the current learning situation and should not be fixed beforehand. Rather, the learning system should be intelligent enough to automatically adjust its window size to the current demands. These demands are, of course, not clearly definable; the adjustment decisions can be made on a heuristic basis only.

We have experimented with many different heuristics for automatic window adjustment. The latest version takes into account both the complexity of the current hypothesis (vis-a-vis the number of instances covered) and the current estimated predictive accuracy of the hypothesis, which is constantly monitored by the system. The heuristic depends on three parameters which must be set by the user: lc (= threshold for low coverage of *ADES*); hc (= threshold for high coverage of *ADES*); and p (= threshold for acceptable predictive accuracy). Given these three parameters, the *window adjustment heuristic (WAH)* is defined as follows:

Let N = number of (positive) instances covered by $ADES$ and
S = size of $ADES$ (in terms of number of literals)
Then:
If $N/S < lc$ (coverage of $ADES$ is low)
   or the current predictive accuracy is bad ($< p$ and falling)
   and if $PDES$ is not empty (there are alternative hypotheses)
   then decrease window size by 20% and forget the oldest instances
else if $N/S > 2 * hc$ (coverage extremely high)
   and the current predictive accuracy is good ($> p$)
   then reduce the window size by 1
else if $N/S > hc$ (coverage high)
   and the current predictive accuracy is good ($> p$)
   then freeze the current window size (i.e., forget one example each time a new
   one is added)
else grow window by 1 (accommodate new instance without forgetting the oldest
   one)

where the *predictive accuracy* is an incrementally computed and updated measure of how well the current hypothesis fits the data: before learning from a new training instance, $FLORA3$ first tries to classify the instance on the basis of its current hypothesis; the *predictive accuracy* measure is the ratio, over the last 20 instances, of correctly classified instances.

In more colloquial terms, the window adjustment heuristic operationalizes the idea that the window should *shrink* (and old, now possibly outdated examples should be forgotten) when a concept drift seems to occur, and should be kept *fixed* when the concept seems stable enough. (When the concept is extremely stable, the window is even reduced stepwise by 1, in order to avoid keeping in memory unnecessarily large numbers of instances.) Otherwise the window should gradually *grow* until a stable concept description can be formed. The occurrence of a concept drift can only be guessed at by the learner, and the two heuristic indicators of such a drift used by $FLORA3$ are (1) the complexity of the descriptions in the set $ADES$ (where the intuition is that during the time of occurrence of a concept drift, it will be difficult to find a concise concept description that is consistent with all the examples), and (2) drops in the predictive accuracy, which is constantly monitored.

The ideal parameter settings will vary from one domain to the next. In all our experiments, we used $lc = 1.2$, $hc = 4$ and $p = 70\%$. Given that the heuristic is (necessarily) very syntactically oriented and is thus very sensitive to the description language used, it seems hopeless to try to find a completely general heuristic that would not depend on any parameters. (Widmer & Kubat, 1992) discusses in more detail the effects of this heuristic on the learning process.

4.2   Storage and re-use of old contexts

As already noted, there are many natural domains where there is a finite number of hidden contexts that may reappear, either cyclically or in an unordered fashion. In such domains, it would be a waste of effort to re-learn an old concept from scratch when it reappears. Instead, concepts or hypotheses should be saved so that they can be re-examined at some later time, when there are indications that they might be relevant again. The effect should be faster convergence if the concept (or some similar one) has already occurred. *FLORA3* includes a mechanism for doing just this. In designing this mechanism, several questions had to be answered:

1) Which parts of a hypothesis should be stored?
2) Which hypotheses are worth saving?
3) When should old hypotheses/concepts be reconsidered?
4) How can the adequacy or 'degree of fit' of an old concept be measured in a new situation?
5) How is an old hypothesis/concept to be used in a new situation?

The answer to question 1) is quite simple: the concept description/hypothesis is a triple {*ADES, PDES, NDES*} and is saved as such, because these sets summarize the current state of affairs. The match counts associated with the description items in the sets are not stored, because they will not be meaningful in some new situation.

In designing a solution to question 5), we note that when an old concept is retrieved at some later point in time, it finds itself in a new context: it will not agree with all the training instances in the current window; some items in the concept's description sets will be too specific, and others will be inconsistent with the data. Thus, it is not enough just to recompute the counts for the various description items. Instead, all the instances in the current window must be re-generalized. The retrieved concept is used as a *model* in this re-generalization process: the counts associated with all the items in the description sets are set to zero, and then the regular *FLORA* learning algorithm is invoked for every training instance in the current window. Instances that fit items already in the concept's description sets will confirm these items, and generally, those partial generalizations in the old concept that are in accordance with the new data will be used in the re-generalization process. Others will not be confirmed by the new instances and thus their counts will remain at zero. After re-generalizing all instances in the window, all those description items that still have counts of zero are removed as incorrect or irrelevant from the updated concept.

As for questions 2) - 4) — which hypotheses deserve to be saved, and when; when should old concepts be reconsidered; how is the appropriateness of an old concept to a new situation measured — the criteria that can be used to make these decisions can only be of a heuristic nature. Intuitively, only stable hypotheses/concepts should be saved, and the system should reconsider some old concepts whenever it perceives some substantial concept drift. It is the *window adjustment heuristic (WAH)* that tries to determine precisely these circumstances. So in *FLORA3*, storage and re-examination of old hypotheses are tightly linked to changes in the window size.

The complete algorithm for handling old contexts works as follows:

- When the current concept is *stable* (according to the WAH - see section 4.1): save the current hypothesis (unless there is already a stored concept with the same set of *ADES* descriptions).
- When *FLORA3* suspects a *concept drift*, i.e., when the WAH enforces a *narrowing of the window*: reconsider old, saved concepts and compare them to the current hypothesis. This is done in three steps:
  1) *Find the best candidate* among the stored concepts: an old concept becomes a *candidate* if it is consistent with the current example. All the candidates are evaluated with respect to the ratio of the numbers of positive and negative instances that they match (from the current window). The best candidate according to this measure is chosen.
  2) *Update the best candidate* w.r.t. the current data: the retrieved concept description is updated by setting all the counts in the description sets to 0 and then re-processing all the instances in the window according to this hypothesis (see the above discussion).
  3) *Compare the updated best candidate to the current hypothesis*: use some 'measure of fit' to decide whether the updated candidate (= old concept) is better than the current hypothesis; if so, replace the current hypothesis with the updated old concept. In the current version of *FLORA3*, the measure of fit is simply the relative *complexity* of the description, as it is used also in the window adjustment heuristic: a hypothesis is considered better if its *ADES* set is more concise. (Remember that *ADES* covers all positive and no negative instances, so the number of instances covered is the same for the *ADES* sets in both the current hypothesis and the updated best candidate.)

As one possible class of application domains for the *FLORA* systems is flexible control in real time systems (cf. Kubat, 1992), *efficiency* of the learning algorithm is an important criterion. The above algorithm tries to maintain efficiency by limiting the number of expensive re-processing episodes. First, old concepts are not reconsidered after every new training instance; they are only retrieved when the window adjustment heuristic suspects that a concept drift is taking place. And second, the expensive part of reconsidering an old concept—the re-generalization of all the instances in the window—is done only for one of them – the best candidate. Which old concept is the best candidate is determined through a simple heuristic measure, the number of positive and negative matches (see above). This is a very weak measure, of course, and can sometimes lead to an inappropriate candidate being chosen. Thus, efficiency is achieved at the possible expense of quality.

It seems worth pointing out once more exactly what the role of old concepts/hypotheses is in this process: at the time of a suspected concept shift, an old concept is used to *bias* the re-generalization of the examples in the window. It is not just retrieved and used as the current concept hypothesis. Instead, the old concept is used as a *model* for the re-generalization of the instances: it simply provides a list of generalizations that were useful in the past and that might, at least in part, also be useful in the new context. This reflects the insight that when an old hidden context reappears, the target concepts will tend to be *similar*, but not necessarily *identical* to how they appeared in the old context. [3]

5 Experimental results

In (Widmer & Kubat, 1992) it was shown that *FLORA2* (i.e., the basic learning algorithm plus automatic window adjustment) compares very favourably with systems like *STAGGER* (Schlimmer & Granger, 1986), which was also designed to deal with problems of concept drift. Here, we will concentrate on demonstrating that in domains with recurring hidden contexts, learning can still be considerably improved by explicitly storing and re-using old concepts.

We have done extensive experiments with *FLORA3* in various artificial domains, where we had full control over the rate and strength of concept drift. [4] In each case, we contrasted two versions of *FLORA3*, one with and one without the algorithm for re-examining old concepts (the latter one will be called *FLORA2* here, as it corresponds essentially to the system described in (Widmer & Kubat, 1992)).

For reasons of comparability, the first set of experiments used the same kind of data and concepts that were originally introduced in (Schlimmer & Granger, 1986) and then also used in (Widmer & Kubat, 1992), namely, a sequence of three (rather different) target concepts: (1) *size = small ∧ color = red*, (2) *color = green ∨ shape = circular* and (3) *size = (medium ∨ large)* in a simple blocks world. Training instances were generated randomly according to the hidden concept, and after processing each instance, the predictive accuracy was tested on 40 test instances (also generated randomly, according to the same underlying concept). The underlying concept was made to change after every 40 training instance, in the cyclic order 1-2-3-1-2-3-1-2-3. Thus, we created a situation of recurring concepts. This experiment was repeated several times. In the following plots, the solid line represents the results achieved by *FLORA3*, and the dashed line gives the results for *FLORA2*. Figure 3 displays the results of two typical individual runs, and Figure 4 shows the averaged results of 10 runs. The dotted vertical lines indicate where the underlying concept changes.

In interpreting these results, we first note that both systems do recover very quickly (in most cases) from changes in the underlying hidden concept. This is due to the basic learning and forgetting operators and to the window adjustment heuristic. This was discussed already in our previous publication on *FLORA2*.

---

[3] Fashion certainly is a prime example of this phenomenon.

[4] We also did experiments with 'real world' data, namely, the well-known *lymphography* data from Ljubljana. Ivan Bratko (personal communication) had suggested that there might be some perceptible concept drift in this data set. However, when analyzing *FLORA3*'s behaviour on these data, we could not discern any noticeable drift, and in comparative learning experiments, *FLORA3*'s performance on these data lagged behind that of a non-incremental learner like *CN2* (Clark & Niblett, 1989), so we concluded that the lymphography data were not appropriate for studying issues of concept drift.

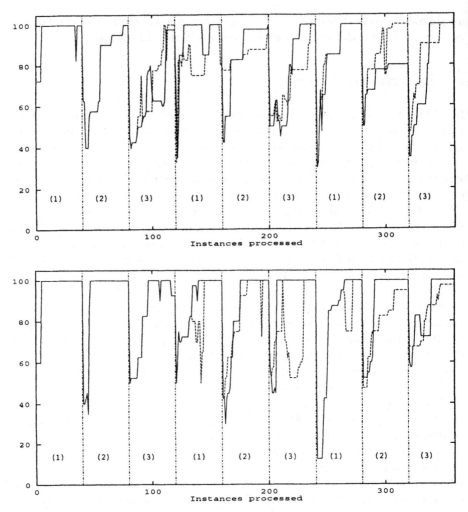

Fig. 3. Predictive accuracy in two individual runs (experiment 1).

What is more interesting here is that in situations where a concept re-occurs after a few cycles, there is a marked superiority of *FLORA3* over *FLORA2* in re-adjusting to this old concept. This can be seen most clearly from the two single-run plots, where *FLORA3* returns to the 100% mark much faster than does *FLORA2*. This strongly confirms the utility and importance of the context tracking mechanism in domains with recurring contexts.

The superiority of *FLORA3* can also be seen in the averaged plot in Figure 4, albeit less clearly. In the particular experiment summarized in this figure, it happened that in 2 out of the 10 random runs, *FLORA3* performed worse than *FLORA2* on the third concept – in fact, very much worse (which caused the average to be pushed below the curve for *FLORA2*). In both cases, the

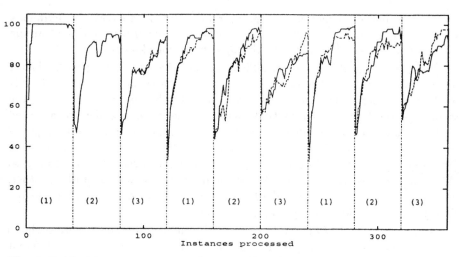

Instances processed

Fig. 4. Predictive accuracy, averaged over 10 runs (experiment 1).

reason was that *FLORA3* stored some overly general hypotheses during the first occurrence of concept 3, which caused it to go astray in subsequent occurrences of this same concept. As the context-tracking mechanisms of *FLORA3* are very heuristic in nature, irregularities like this are unavoidable.

Note that at the beginning (during the first occurrence of each concept, i.e, when no context recurrence happens), *FLORA3*, with its explicit reconsideration of saved hypotheses, actually seems to perform a bit worse than the simpler *FLORA2* (see the first plot in Figure 3). This has happened quite frequently in our experiments. There is a simple explanation for this. The availability of stored contexts may in fact sometimes lead the learning process astray: due to the heuristic nature of the context retrieval decisions, some context may erroneously be selected because it seems to be better than the current hypothesis. So the context tracking mechanism adds another degree of freedom - or source of potential errors, if you will - to the learning algorithm. However, when old contexts actually do reappear, the advantages of the context tracking approach begin to outweigh the disadvantages, as can be seen from the following phases in the experiment.

In a second set of experiments, we started from a fictitious scenario of an autonomous agent by the name of *FLORA3* exploring some unknown territory (planet), searching for food and trying to predict where food might be found. On this planet, food can be found in containers distributed throughout the country, and these containers are characterized by many attributes (such as their shape, color, size, weight, material, whether they hang from trees or bushes, . . .). Some containers do contain food, others don't. Now this particular planet is divided into several kingdoms, and the rules determining whether a container holds food are different in every kingdom.[5][6] Again, training data for this set of experiments were generated randomly – in this case, not only the descriptions of the training instances, but also *FLORA*'s path through the various kingdoms.

This learning problem is more difficult not only because it deals with a larger description space, but also because we introduced two sources of *noise* into this world: the borders of the kingdoms were designed to be imprecise, that is, in the vicinity of the border between two kingdoms, the instance generator assumed that with a certain probability, concepts (food containers) from both kingdoms could occur. And the second source of noise was the fact that *FLORA3*'s path (as a sequence of moves in arbitrary direction) was also generated randomly, so there was, in most cases, no clear transition from one context to another; rather, *FLORA3* would sometimes wander back and forth between two kingdoms before finally venturing more deeply into one of them.

As an example of *FLORA3*'s performance in this domain, Figure 5 shows the result of one random run. The planet in this experiment had 6 different kingdoms arranged in a circle, and *FLORA3* wandered through this circle twice. Note that in this figure there are no vertical lines to indicate the precise points where the underlying context changes, because the two types of noise mentioned above make it difficult to determine precisely when *FLORA3* is in a new context. (However, the reader is encouraged to examine the plot and try to guess where *FLORA3* is deeply in a particular kingdom.)

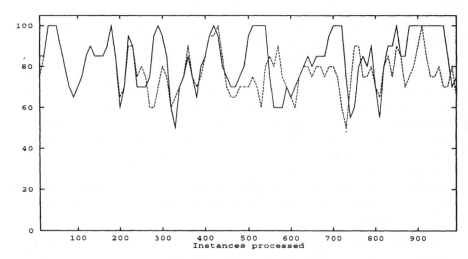

Fig. 5. Predictive accuracy on strange planet (experiment 2).

---

[5] Miroslav Kubat has a more elaborate story around this scenario, but space does not permit us to repeat it here.

[6] Readers less inclined towards fairytales might simply imagine a robot in a complex building with different types of rooms, where each room presents the robot with different operating conditions.

Basically, the results in this set of experiments confirmed our expectations. The systems' behaviour is again characterized by quite flexible adjustment to new contexts, with *FLORA3* markedly better in situations where old contexts reoccur. Due to the noise in the training data and the larger hypothesis space, convergence was, of course, slower than in the first type of experiments, and not always perfect, but our preliminary experience is that *FLORA3* seems to handle limited amounts of noise quite well.

6 Discussion and related work

To recapitulate briefly, the two basic ideas that contributed to the success of *FLORA3* are (1) recognizing and 'forgetting' old, harmful knowledge, and (2) explicitly storing old concepts and re-using them when a context transition seems to take place.

The idea of using forgetting to improve learning may seem counter-intuitive at first sight, but it has been suggested in the literature by a number of authors. Indeed, a kind of forgetting was implemented already in (Samuel, 1959) with the objective of avoiding the danger of storing prohibitively many pieces of experience in the memory. Samuel used *refreshing* (reinforcement) when a description item was utilized. The algorithm is very simple: After regular intervals, the item's age is incremented by 1. If the age exceeds a prespecified threshold, the item is deleted—forgotten. Reinforcement, in turn, consists in decrementing the age. Also Fikes, Hart, and Nilsson (1972) suggested that some sort of forgetting should be considered to prevent an unmanageably large store of experience. For some other considerations on forgetting, see Markovitch and Scott (1988), Torgo and Kubat (1991), or Kubat and Krizakova (1992).

In the above references, forgetting was understood mainly as a measure to prevent uncontrolled growth of the occupied memory, with the subsequent problem of computational tractability. Another motivation can be selection or filtering of the most useful knowledge to get rid of noise—this is the rationale behind pruning mechanisms in decision trees (Niblett, 1987), which also represent a kind of forgetting.

To a limited extent, the idea of tracking concept drift in the incremental learning paradigm has been studied in the context of unsupervised learning, especially in concept formation. In the systems *COBWEB* (Fisher, 1987) and *CLASSIT* (Gennari et al., 1989), the dynamic modification of the concept description is facilitated by two complementary operators *merge* and *split*. These perform generalization of two existing concepts into one (merge) and specialization of a concept into two subconcepts (split). Similar recovery operators are available also in *UNIMEM* (Lebowitz, 1987). But none of these systems can actually discard old, harmful information, and none of them explicitly stores previous concept descriptions. However, recent work on modified versions of *COBWEB* (Kilander & Jansson, 1993) is very much related to our approach and seems to yield very promising results.

The closest relative to our program is perhaps *STAGGER* (Schlimmer & Granger, 1986), because that system was designed explicitly to deal with concept drift. We showed already in (Widmer & Kubat, 1992) that *FLORA2* compared very favourably with *STAGGER* in terms of adjustment to concept drift. *FLORA3*'s added capability to use experience from past learning in new contexts leads to even more effective learning in environments with recurring contexts.

Schlimmer and Granger mention as one of *STAGGER*'s assets that it is sensitive to the amount of previous training, that is, the longer it has been trained on some concept, the more deeply ingrained will the concept be, and the more hesitant will *STAGGER* be to abandon it and adjust to a new context. This seems to mirror some results from the psychology of learning.

FLORA3 does not exhibit this type of behaviour: once a concept is deemed stable, *FLORA3* freezes the window size, which prevents the concept from becoming too deeply ingrained. This allows the system to quickly follow radical concept shifts, no matter how stable the previous hypothesis was thought to be. We regard this as an advantage of our approach. *FLORA3* is not meant to be a psychologically valid model of learning. Our interests are in practical applications, such as robotics and control in dynamic environments with limited information. There *flexibility* seems to be of prime importance. The system should be quick in adjusting to changes in the world. A related requirement is that the learning algorithm be *efficient*. And that is clearly the case. The basic learning and forgetting operators are very simple, and also the method for reassessing old concepts has been designed so as to keep the computational overhead small (see section 4.2).

One of the goals of our future work is a better formalization of the method and a more thorough theoretical analysis of its convergence properties. For simplicity reasons, we have so far relied on a very simple representation language. Once we have a better theoretical framework, we hope to be able to extend the system so that it can deal also with more complicated description languages, e.g., some subset of first order logic as it is used in systems like *FOIL* (Quinlan, 1990) or *LINUS* (Lavrač et al, 1991).

Acknowledgments

Thanks to Bernhard Pfahringer for very helpful comments on a first draft of this paper. We also wish to thank Ivan Bratko for supplying the lymphography data. Support for the Austrian Research Institute for Artificial Intelligence is provided by the Austrian Federal Ministry for Science and Research. The second author was partially supported by the Austrian *Fonds zur Förderung der Wissenschaftlichen Forschung* under grant no. M003-MED.

References

Clark, P. and Niblett, T. (1989). The CN2 induction algorithm. *Machine Learning Journal 3(4)* (1989), 261–283.

Fikes, R.E., Hart, P.E., and Nilsson, N. (1972). Learning and Executing Generalized Robot Plans. *Artificial Intelligence 3*, 251–288.

Fisher, D. (1987). Knowledge Acquisition via Incremental Conceptual Clustering. *Machine Learning 2*, 139–172.

Gennari, J., Langley, P., and Fisher, D. (1989). Models of Incremental Concept Formation. *Artificial Intelligence 40*, 11–61.

Kilander, F. and Jansson, C.G. (1993). COBBIT - A Control Procedure for COBWEB in the Presence of Concept Drift. *Proceedings of the European Conference on Machine Learning (ECML-93)*. Vienna, Austria.

Kubat, M. (1989). Floating Approximation in Time-Varying Knowledge Bases. *Pattern Recognition Letters 10*, 223–227.

Kubat, M. (1991). Conceptual Inductive Learning: The Case of Unreliable Teachers. *Artificial Intelligence 52*, 169–182.

Kubat, M. (1992). A Machine Learning Based Approach to Load Balancing in Computer Networks. *Cybernetics and Systems 23*, 389–400.

Kubat, M. and Krizakova, I. (1992). Forgetting and Ageing of Knowledge in Concept Formation. *Applied Artificial Intelligence 6*, pp. 193–204.

Lavrač, N., Džeroski, S. and Grobelnik, M. (1991). Learning Nonrecursive Definitions of Relations with Linus. *Proceedings of the 5th European Working Session on Learning (EWSL-91)*, Porto.

Lebowitz, M. (1987). Experiments with Incremental Concept Formation. *Machine Learning 2*, 103–138.

Markowitch, S. and Scott, P.D. (1988). The Role of Forgetting in Learning. *Proceedings of the 5th International Conference on Machine Learning*, Ann Arbor, MI, 450–465.

Niblett, T. (1987). Constructing Decision Trees in Noisy Domains. In Bratko, I.–Lavrač, N. (eds.) *Progress in Machine Learning*. Sigma Press, Wilmslow.

Quinlan, J.R. (1990). Learning Logical Definitions from Relations. *Machine Learning 5(3)*, 239–266.

Samuel, A.L. (1959). Some Studies in Machine Learning Using the Game of Checkers. *IBM Journal 3*, No.3.

Schlimmer, J.C. and Granger, R.H. (1986). Beyond Incremental Processing: Tracking Concept Drift. *Proceedings of the AAAI'86 Conference*, Philadelphia, 502–507.

Schlimmer, J.C. and Granger, R.H. (1986). Incremental Learning from Noisy Data. *Machine Learning 1*, 317–354.

Torgo, L. and Kubat, M. (1991). Knowledge Integration and Forgetting. *Proceedings of the Czechoslovak Conference on Artificial Intelligence*, Prague, Czechoslovakia, June 25–27.

Widmer, G. and Kubat, M. (1992). Learning Flexible Concepts from Streams of Examples: FLORA2. *Proceedings of the 10th European Conference on Artificial Intelligence (ECAI-92)*, Vienna, 363–367.

COBBIT—A Control Procedure for COBWEB in the Presence of Concept Drift

Fredrik Kilander and Carl Gustaf Jansson

Department of Computer and Systems Sciences
Royal Institute of Technology and Stockholm University
Sweden

Abstract. This paper is concerned with the robustness of concept formation systems in the presence of concept drift. By concept drift is meant that the intension of a concept is not stable during the period of learning, a restriction which is otherwise often imposed. The work is based upon the architecture of COBWEB, an incremental, probabilistic conceptual clustering system. When incrementally and sequentially exposed to the extensions of a set of concepts, COBWEB retains all examples, disregards the age of a concept and may create different conceptual structures dependent on the order of examples. These three characteristics make COBWEB sensitive to the effects of concept drift. Six mechanisms that can detect concept drift and adjust the conceptual structure are proposed. A variant of one of these mechanisms: dynamic deletion of old examples, is implemented in a modified COBWEB system called COBBIT. The relative performance of COBWEB and COBBIT in the presence of concept drift is evaluated. In the experiment the error index, i.e. the average of the ability to predict each attribute is used as the major instrument. The experiment is performed in a synthetical domain and indicates that COBBIT regain performance faster after a discrete concept shift.

1   Introduction

With a given data set, incremental or batch learning is a matter of taste. Because the data is given, it is finite and therefore available for scrutiny by any available mode of preparation, clustering and post-processing. Such is the state of much scientific data: collected, stored, processed and analyzed at length.

Reality throws a wild and evolving environment at us; dependencies between observable and non-observable features change over time. The ability to accurately categorize and associate phenomenon is highly valued in both people and machines, but there is a danger in the complacency that follows seemingly unshakable competence. Knowledge that is not regularly confirmed runs the risk of becoming obsolete when concepts surreptitiously drift, nurturing a creeping knowledge rot. A carefully captured flow of experience may be invalidated by a sudden, single blow of altered environmental conditions.

The problem of concept drift in the context of this paper is characterized by a change in the environment observed by an incremental machine learning system. The machine collects a number of samples from the environment and builds a tree over the conditional probabilities that relate smaller groups of observations. Each such group represents a concept.

Concept drift occurs when the environment change. The conditional probabilities reflected by the new observations change too and are no longer accurately represented by the concepts in the machine learning system. The occurence counts on which the probability estimates are based, include observations that the environment no longer can provide.

Programs and systems that continuously updates their view of the world fall into two groups. In the first are those for which the tracking of concept drift follows involuntarily from the basic architecture of the system. In the second are the programs designed to behave like concept trackers.

Common to the former kind of systems is their limited amount of storage for concepts or learned structures. Their ability to stay alert with recent trends is a side-effect of old knowledge being deleted. The deletion occurs simply because a section of storage used by old knowledge, is claimed for more recent data. Examples of such architectures are neural network models and genetic algorithms.

The group of systems designed to track concept drift include STAGGER [20, 19], FLORA [13], FLORA3 [21], FAVORIT [12] and RL [3]. These supervised learning systems focus on the ability to deal with training sequences involving concept drift. The FLORA system, for instance, employs a queue of recent training examples. When the oldest example leave the queue, FLORA updates its set of induced classification rules to be consistent with the contents of the queue. Discarded rules are kept suspended, awaiting future rehabilitation.

A shared behaviour of the systems that track concepts intentionally is that they maintain generalizations under a notion of recency and non-monotonicity. Objects that once supported general structures may be withdrawn, and the corresponding generalization diminished or made impotent. The difference these systems display from those that track concepts inadvertently, is that the decision to delete or inactivate old knowledge is conscious.

This paper is concerned with concept drift in unsupervised learning and is based on Douglas Fisher's COBWEB [6], an incremental, probabilistic, conceptual clustering system. COBWEB is designed to work under a condition of concept constancy, just as most other machine learning systems. The presentation sequences created by the temporal ordering of examples while allowing a change of concepts over time (concept drift), coincide with those orderings that are least suitable for COBWEB. The concept hierarchy becomes skewed, in that a concept node is found to be subordinate to the node that optimally is its peer. For a recent treatment of ordering effects in COBWEB, see Fisher, Xu and Zard [5].

The experiments with COBWEB were performed on COBBIT, Kilander's implementation of COBWEB in C. The COBBIT system is an extension to the control system in COBWEB. COBBIT uses a queue of training instances just as FLORA3 does and dynamically alters the size of the queue depending on its performance. This behaviour is intended to remove old knowledge from the hierarchy, leaving room for new, updated concepts.

2 Noise and Concept Drift

The term concept drift is more easily defined in terms of incremental, supervised learning. The learning situation there is equipped with a strong source of feedback on performance; the class label. The learning program creates a concept for each class, separating instances. If the program receives an object with a class label that is not what the concept assigns, the contradiction can be attributed either to noise (the label is wrong) or misconception of the concept (the induced concept is wrong).

If previous training instances are stored by the system (or implicitly trusted through the concepts they generate) it is possible to find an old training object which is identical to the disturbing one, save for the class label. Noise must then be the problem, and the system can deal with it in several ways, for instance by rejecting the contradicting instances. If the source of the misclassification cannot be established the system's only recourse is to modify its concept description, in the hope that the concept definition is improved.

The assumption that underlies the above incremental learning method is that the domain which is approximated by the concepts in the learning systems is fixed; that all examples are equally important regardless of when they were observed. The concepts in the domain are assumed to be eternal and stable. Removing this assumption allows for the possibility that a recent observation appears to contradict an earlier one, but the early observation can no longer be made and concepts built upon it are indeed wrong. Concept drift is present.

Removing the constancy assumption introduces another restriction; if any distinction in temporal terms is to be meaningful, the examples must be presented in the order they were labelled.

In supervised learning concept drift can be seen as a change in the process that labels examples. In unsupervised learning (clustering) there is of course no explicit class labelling. However, there is a similar process which can be thought of as the assignment of attribute values to objects. Only certain combinations of attribute values can be observered at any one time, and it is this set of dependencies between attributes and their values that a clustering systems attempts to approximate by forming groups of objects.

3 Cobweb

COBWEB is an incremental, probabilistic, conceptual clustering system [6]. COBWEB is discussed both as an incremental learning system as well as a potential model for basic level effects in an indexed memory. This work concentrates on the former aspect of COBWEB's capabilities.

From a stream of object instances, COBWEB creates and maintains a hierarchy, each level of which partitions the objects in an optimal way. Instances form the leafs of the hierarchy, the generalizations above form the concepts. The incremental nature of the system allows it to learn and perform at the same time. As expected, performance is limited until a representative sample of the domain has been acquired, but the prediction of a missing piece of information may be attempted from the start.

COBWEB is suitable as a normative system because it:

1. is well known
2. is easy to understand
3. is fairly easy to implement
4. is a foundation for other systems
5. is susceptible to concept drift, and
6. does not require parameters.

The closest rival to COBWEB is CLASSIT [7] but CLASSIT only accepts linear attributes. Other conceptual clustering systems to choose from are not lacking; UNIMEM by Michael Lebowitz [14, 15], WITT by Hanson and Bauer [9, 10], INC by Hadzikadic and Yun [8], OPUS by Bernd Nordhausen [18] and the works of Ryszard Michalski and Robert Stepp with the CLUSTER systems [16, 17].

UNIMEM is a forerunner of COBWEB but requires parameters. INC is a system very similar to COBWEB but it also needs parameters. WITT, OPUS and CLUSTER are batch clusterers. WITT can be set to learn incrementally using a series of smaller batches, but it still involves too many parameters.

Recent COBWEB descendants that should be mentioned but has escaped evaluation due to time-constraints are: ITERATE by Biswas et al. [2] and COBWEB$_R$, a system by Allen and Thompson [1].

The emerging qualities of COBWEB are that it is *incremental* and that it *lacks parameters* which constrains an otherwise unwieldy number of examination and experiment dimensions. The fact that COBBIT reintroduces a number of parameters is lamentable but impossible to avoid. Hopefully further research will be able to advise automatic settings for them.

The following problems appear in various degrees of severity when COBWEB is used on material which is subject to concept drift.

1. COBWEB does not distinguish between new and old training examples. New features must therefore appear in ever larger numbers if they are to replace their predecessors.
2. COBWEB retains every training example. Learning must therefore eventually stop at the limits of the computational or practical resources.
3. COBWEB may create different concept hierarchies depending on the input ordering. The input ordering found in material affected by concept drift is among the worst.

4   Cobbit

COBBIT is built around an implementation of COBWEB which for the larger part duplicates the original. No significant extensions have been applied to the COBWEB model of storing nodes and concepts in the concept hierarchy, the classification or prediction algorithms.

4.1 Detecting Concept Drift

In applications where COBWEB is used to make predictions about unseen objects one would certainly want the prediction mechanism to pay greater attention to recent information than to old and early one (unless a static domain is ensured). Mechanisms capable of detecting changes in concept stability are interesting because they may serve as triggers of automatic actions; relearning or adjustment of the internal structure.

Here follows six algorithmic devices to survey changes in the COBWEB hierarchy, two of which are strategies to deactivate undesirable objects:

1. **Trends in past preference counters.** For each attribute, past preference [4] will be established at the node where the most common value of the attribute is the majority value averaged over all examples beneath the node. If extra disjunctive structure is imposed on the category (i.e. novel data coming from changes) the level of past preference is expected to drop to a lower node, or even be split among several nodes. This can be monitored by following the development of the *correct-at-node* and *correct-at-descendant* counts. A major change in majority values among nodes beneath the node under surveillance can be suspected if the latter counter is increasing faster than the former. An immediate application of this is with the prediction mechanism which upon detecting this kind of phenomenon should ignore a higher *correct-at-node* count in favour of a prediction further down.

2. **Operators used to classify a new example.** In a well established hierarchy most of the domain can be expected to have been observed. The presence of a new example can therefore signal either change or a very rare event. The example will be placed by itself at some level as its own category. The level (relative the size of the hierarchy) is an indication of novelty. This only works for true novelty, a cyclic reoccurrence will not be noticed.

3. **Update frequency and its correlation to expected relative frequency.** If the domain is changing one can expect differences in the relative frequencies between two time periods. Although a possible case of the gambler's fallacy, one may expect certain observations to appear with a rate that corresponds to their previous exposure. If this frequency distribution is changing more than is likely to be attributed to random variation, one can suspect that it is an effect of an altered domain.

4. **Continuous monitoring of performance.** As each example is presented to COBBIT, it attempts to predict each and every attribute that has a known value. The percentage of correctly predicted attributes is output as the current *performance index*. The trend of this index allows for corrective action as soon as a drop in performance is observed.

5. **Monotonic deletion.** Its a simple matter to modify COBWEB and obtain the kind of short term memory used in FLORA. A first-in-first-out (FIFO) queue facilitates subtraction of each example after a suitable time.

6. **Dynamic deletion.** The insensitive nature of the previous approach can be cushioned by using one or more of the detection mechanisms outlined

above. The idea is that a concept suspected to be no longer present in the domain is to be removed. The motive for removing the object is in this case based on more than simply the time spent within the system, and there is an ambition to retain objects that are beneficial.

Deletion of an object can be achieved by marking it as *inactive*, or subtracting it from the hierarchy. Removal from the central concept hierarchy does not necessarily imply ejection from the system; several schemes of retaining objects backstage are plausible.

4.2   Cobweb Modified

This section deals with the consequences of equipping COBWEB with a version of the sixth device, dynamic deletion of old examples. This is implemented in COBBIT with a queue of examples and continuous monitoring of performance (device 4). Together they uphold an interval of examples; when an example leaves the queue it is subtracted from the hierarchy. The performance index is used to determine the size of the queue (within certain boundaries).

It can be expected (assuming a fair description language and input ordering) that a basic hierarchy is established and that further input either confirms what is already learned or is one of the following two cases: a new example that adds knowledge, because there is still more to learn or a new example that replaces old knowledge, because the domain is evolving.

Both cases contain new knowledge, and both cases should be added to the knowledge structure. So the problem is really one of identifying *old* knowledge and data structures. The simplest way to do this is using a queue, which assumes that the oldest example no longer can be trusted and ejects it, using a FIFO-strategy for deletion. If the features represented by a deleted node are still active in the domain, then they will manifest themselves again soon, if not already present in the queue.

Another approach is to remove concepts that have not been referenced or reinforced by the domain within a *reasonable* time. This is the least-recently-used (LRU) strategy for selecting a node to be deleted. However, under LRU the property of the queue (and the hierarchy) being a proper statistical sample of the domain is lost. LRU favours rare but regularly recurring events and disfavours short manifestations.

COBBIT's modification to COBWEB resides in the *control system*, the way learning, predictive performance and training are combined to a complete system. The following implements have been produced:

1. A procedure to subtract nodes from the COBWEB concept hierarchy.
2. A function that samples the the predictive performance of the concept hierarchy and COBWEB's prediction algorithm.
3. A function that provides a mapping from performance (as measured by the function in item 2) to a target size of the COBWEB concept hierarchy. The size is expressed as the number of training examples found at leaf level of the concept hierarchy.

4. A FIFO queue for training examples.
5. An extended control algorithm. The COBWEB standard control loop (*read-learn*, see table 2) has been extended to *read-evaluate-learn-trim* by using the queue in item 4.

Table 1. The Extract_Object procedure.

```
Extract_Object(object)
begin
    P = ParentOf(object).
    While P ≠ NULL do
    begin
        P = P - object
        R = ParentOf(P)
        If P is empty then delete P
        P = R
    end
end
```

Table 2. Control loop in COBWEB.

```
While not eof do
begin
    object = the next object from the input.
    If object is a training instance then
        root = Cobweb(object, root)
    else
        predict missing values and report.
end
```

4.3 Cobbit's Control Algorithm

The algorithm used to classify new examples in COBBIT is the same as in COBWEB. The change is introduced in the next upper level of the control hierarchy.

A new procedure that extracts objects from the hierarchy is shown in table 1. An *empty* node occurs when all its children have been subtracted from under

Table 3. Control loop in COBBIT.

```
While not eof do
begin
    object = the next instance from the input.
    IF object is a training instance then
    begin
        Error = PredictionError(object).
        root = Cobweb(object, root).
        Queue = Queue + object.
        MaxQSize = ((1 − Error) * (u − l)) + l.
        IF Length(Queue) > MaxQSize then
        begin
```
$$N = 1 + \frac{(Length(Queue) - MaxQSize)}{4}.$$
```
            While N > 0 do
            begin
                Extract_Object(Head(Queue)).
                Queue = Queue − Head(Queue).
                N = N − 1.
            end
        end
    end
    else
        predict missing values and report.
end
```

a generalization. All counters in the empty node are zero, but it still occupies space in the concept hierarchy and is therefore deleted from the tree.

The idealized control loop of COBBIT is described in table 3. The parameters u and l control the upper and lower bounds on the number of elements in the queue at any time. The queue can only grow one instance at a time, but it can shrink faster. The division by 4 when determining the number of objects to be ejected (N), dampens the effect of noisy examples which otherwise may cause an overly rapid depletion of objects. The quantity 4 was chosen arbitrarily— the effect of other values is not evaluated. Notice also the call to $Cobweb()$, COBWEB's classification procedure.

5 Experiments

Kibler and Langley [11] suggests several ways to measure performance. One is the general measure of *"the ability to predict a missing attribute's value, aver-aged across all attributes"*. For incremental systems, they suggest that learning is turned off every nth instance for testing against a test set of examples. Al-ternatively, every instance is treated as both a test and training object. This is the major instrument of measurement in these experiments. For each training example an error index is calculated thus:

$$1 - \frac{\text{nof correctly predicted attributes}}{\text{nof attributes}}.$$

This averages the ability to predict each attribute, and uses every example for both testing and training.

Kibler and Langley continues to remark that the learning curve (resulting from such a performance measure) can be informative, but that the information can be condensed into the asymptotic performance and the number of examples required to reach it. This fails to be immediately applicable under concept drift as the asymptotic target constantly is redefined.

It should be pointed out the concept trees generated by COBWEB are not evaluated in terms of cluster analysis. The interest is focussed on the system's ability to predict missing attribute values.

5.1 Experiment Design

The synthetic domain which provides the training examples is designed to condition its concept drift on a particular attribute, the *cue* attribute. When this attribute is active the language is complete and concept drift not present (although ordering effects remain). Holding the value of the cue attribute fixed, it can no longer be used to predict the values of the other attributes and concept drift can be simulated.

The first experiment shows the effect on COBWEB when the cue attribute is locked. There is no concept drift in the data—the next state of the domain is chosen at random. Even so, one could view this as a demonstration of a situation where the rate of concept drift is beyond the sampling rate of the input collectors.

The second experiment intends to show COBWEB's behaviour when the rate of concept drift is sufficiently slow to follow. The data provides a single alteration of state at the 11th example.

The third experiment is in two parts. It shows the effect of applying COBBIT's queue mechanism on the same data sets as in the second experiment. Variation of the lower and upper queue size parameters shows the effect of the queue device on performance.

The fourth experiment compares COBWEB and COBBIT on a complex domain with six independent substates, altering their state cyclically and each at a different rate. The interference of state changes is intended to stress the performance capacity of both systems, and give an indication of what performance can be expected under complicated input.

Finally a comparison is provided which reflects the cost of assimilation for the next example. As expected, COBWEB needs more and more time while COBBIT stays bounded by the size of the queue.

The primary sources of evaluation are the graphs over prediction error and queue sizes, as presented later in this section. In most instances the graphs display averages from 10 data-sets. The fraction of error used as a measure of performance quality, is a sum over several attributes.

5.2 Description Language

The domain used is *equal–not equal*. It corresponds to an ideal situation using three binary attributes. Attributes A_1 and A_2 are regular attributes. They take their values from $0, 1$. Attribute A_0 is the *cue* attribute, it supplies information about the state of the domain, the state that will be changed during learning. Table 4 gives all combinations of values. Since the complete set of possible examples quickly is exhausted, examples are repeated many times during learning.

Table 4. Domain *equal–not equal*.

A_0	A_1	A_2
0	0	1
	1	0
1	0	0
	1	1

5.3 Cobweb with and without Cue

Figure 1 shows the effect of hiding the cue attribute. The domain consists of three binary attributes from the *equal–not equal* domain. Each line represents the performance index averaged over 10 independent data sets, with 30 examples in each data set.

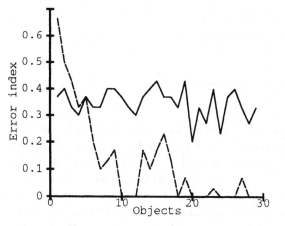

Fig. 1. Errors with visible and locked cue attributes.

The dotted line is the domain where the cue attribute reveals the state of the two other attributes. The state shifts randomly, but COBWEB quickly acquires the pattern. The solid line shows the performance when the cue attribute is set to zero, regardless of the state of the domain. COBWEB has no way to discern between the two states and prediction does not improve as more examples are seen. Note that the with-cue line begins at a higher level of error than without cue. The reason for this is that with the cue is always set to zero, it cannot be mispredicted. The resulting error average is kept around 50 % of 2/3.

5.4 Single Shift at Example 11—Cobweb

This domain consists of three binary attributes from the *equal—not equal* domain. The training sequence begins in the unequal state and shifts to the equal state at the 11th example. It then holds that state to the end. The graph in figure 2 is an average of 10 independent data sets, with 30 examples in each data set. With the cue attribute locked the maximum error is 2/3.

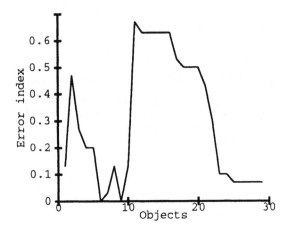

Fig. 2. Error for a single state, shifting at example 11.

Competence is gained as COBWEB begins to process the training set and the error level is low at the 10th example. When the domain changes, prediction suffers and the error soars to the maximum level. It takes another 11 examples before the error drops in earnest, but perfect performance as shown before the shift appears less likely.

The training instances in this run are identical to those in section 5.3, where COBWEB failed to learn (the solid line). The difference between the two experiments is that in the previous one the two states were randomly mingled. Here the states are sequentially separated, and COBWEB has time to accumulate conditional probabilities. After the shift has occurred, it takes almost the same number of examples to turn the accumulated counts the other way and perform well in the new state of the domain.

5.5 Single Shift at ex. 11—Cobbit Varying Queue Size

The graph in figure 3 is composed from four independent runs of COBBIT, using the queue mechanism. The data sets are in each case identical with the one used in the previous experiment, section 5.4. The parameter that is varied between each run is u, the upper limit of queue size. The lower limit l, was fixed at a size of 5 in all four runs.

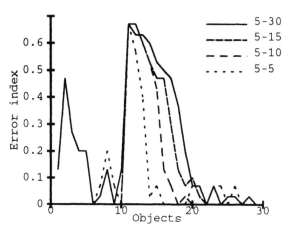

Fig. 3. Errors when varying the queue's upper limit.

The lines show the different settings of the u parameter; 5 (dotted), 10 (wide dash), 15 (long dash) and 30 (solid). Settings 20 and 25 are omitted but their positions are easily interpolated.

The graph shows how performance is regained must faster when the older examples (and their associated probabilities) are removed from the classification tree by the queue. Notice also that the difference between $u = 5$ and $u = 10$ is much larger than between $u = 15$ and $u = 30$. The reason for this is the simple domain; the short queue will flush out the old objects much faster. One should not be deceived into believing that a small value of u is beneficial under all circumstances; that would imply that all knowledge is harmful.

The queues for the four runs (figure 4) grows linearly until the shift occurs (with the exception of $u = 5$ and $u = 10$). At this point they level out and delay further growth of the queue until the error peak has diminished. When performance again is improving (error lessening) the queue again is allowed to grow.

A second collection of curves in figure 5 shows the behaviour when the queue's lower limit (l) is varied between 5 (dotted), 10 (wide dash), 15 (long dash) and 30 (solid). The upper limit was fixed at 30 in each instance.

The first striking difference is that all curves (except for $l = 5$) indicates a *worse* performance compared to figure 3. The curve for $l = 30, u = 30$ coincides

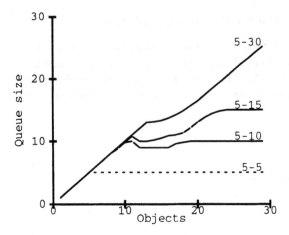

Fig. 4. Queue sizes when varying the queue's upper limit.

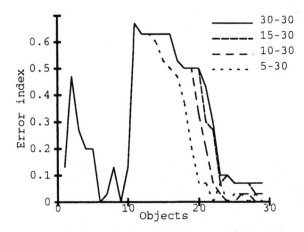

Fig. 5. Errors when varying the queue's lower limit.

with the performance for COBWEB as there are only 30 thirty examples and the queue never overflows. When the difference between the upper and lower limits is increased, COBBIT's control algorithm can, and does, use the queue to delete early examples.

The curve with the greatest range, 5-30 ($l = 5, u = 30$), is common to figures 3 and 5 both. It also appears to be the pivot point between the two graphs; in the former it appears as the worst case and in the latter as the best. Although the figures appear to advocate small settings of l and u this will only facilitate swift adaptation in the most trivial of cases.

Comparing the graphs that shows the evolution of the queue-size, a similar pivotal property is evident: in figure 4 the $l = 5, u = 30$ settings displays the queue with the most examples, in figure 6 it is the one with the fewest.

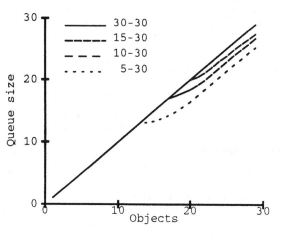

Fig. 6. Queue sizes when varying the queue's lower limit.

The queue must give the best performance for the most complex throughput and there is no simple strategy to guide the settings of the l and u parameters. A compromise appears unavoidable. If both parameters are set to similar values, the scope for dynamic behaviour lessens. Therefore is appears better to set u high, and provide COBBIT with the ability to exercise various queue sizes. The setting of l should be regarded as a minimal number of examples, beneath which generalization and induction becomes meaningless.

5.6 Complex Domain, Multiple Shifts

This test features a complex domain consisting of six concatenated attribute triplets from the equal—not equal domain. This yields a description language consisting of $6*3 = 18$ attributes. Each triplet is set up to alter its state cyclically, but the cycles are tuned to be out of phase so the resulting input data is shifting fast. The cycles used are 7, 15, 19, 29, 33 and 39. The resulting behaviour is that the three attributes $\{A_0, A_1, A_2\}$ alter their state every 7th example; attributes $\{A_3, A_4, A_5\}$ alter their state every fifteenth example, and so on. All cue attributes $\{A_0, A_3, A_6, A_9, A_{12}, A_{15}\}$ are locked to the value zero, giving a maximum error of $2/3$. COBBIT's queues are set to $l = 10, u = 40$.

Figure 7 gives the performance graphs for COBWEB (dotted) and COBBIT (solid). The origin of each data point is an average from 10 runs, but the graph shows rolling averages over 10 adjacent data points. The purpose of this is to clearly show the trend in the material.

Both systems behave almost identically up to the 29th example where the projected limit on the queue is reached (see figure 8). COBBIT begins to eject old

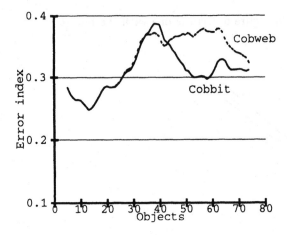

Fig. 7. Errors from Cobweb and Cobbit in the complex domain.

material, some of which apparently was important for prediction at this stage, since the level of error rise above COBWEB's . But COBBIT regains competence and displays a lower prediction error than COBWEB in the region of the 42nd example and onwards.

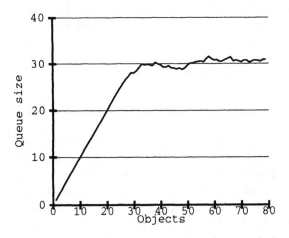

Fig. 8. Cobbit's queue size in the complex domain.

Also obvious in the graph is that COBWEB's error level also is dropping. This is because the number of possible examples in the domain are limited and COBWEB's collection of training examples is swelling. Should the run be extended, COBWEB will match COBBIT in predictive performance, because previous input will return. But the point is that COBBIT reacquires predictive performance *faster* than does COBWEB, and that COBWEB makes no difference between $P(A) = 100/1000$ and $P(A) = 1/10$.

The final graph (figure 9) compares COBWEB and COBBIT on the cost of assimilating an object into the hierarchy. The absolute times per object are not interesting here; the curves show rolling averages of 10 adjacent data points, each of which is an average from 10 independent runs. The input data is the same as in figure 7. Note how COBBIT requires *more* processing time per example from (approximately) 20 to 36 objects. After that break-even is achieved and COBWEB continues to increase, while COBBIT stays behind.

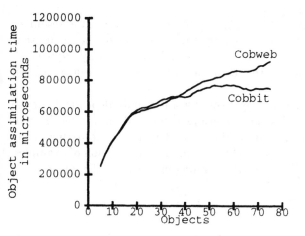

Fig. 9. COBWEB and COBBIT's object assimilation times.

6   Summary

The **desirable** properties of COBBIT include:

1. Predictions are based on recent input.
2. It is not burdened by lingering base rates.
3. Update time is bounded by a parameter.
4. It requires no change to COBWEBS classification procedure.

The experiments confirm that COBBIT recovers faster than COBWEB from drastic concept drift. The experiments also confirm that COBBIT in the long run require less processing time than COBWEB, due to COBWEB's monotonic accumulation of training examples, a behaviour avoided in COBBIT.

Among the **undesirable** properties of COBBIT are found:

1. Training examples and induced knowledge is lost (thrown away).

2. Examples are discarded indiscriminately, without regard for informative content.
3. It introduces two parameters, l and u which must be set by the user.

Section 3 provided a list of problems that appeared when COBWEB was used on data with concept drift. The COBBIT system introduce a list of devices: the two lists relate to each other in the following way.

COBWEB does not distinguish between new and old material, requiring new features to replace previous ones by quantity. In COBBIT, old instances are subtracted from the concept hierarchy when they reach the end of the queue. Their statistics are subtracted from all parents and they are effectively *unlearned*, using the *Extract_Object()* procedure.

COBWEB retains every training example and must stop when the resources for further learning are exhausted. In COBBIT it is the size of the queue that controls the number of examples retained. The size is continuously adjusted to approach a number determined by the recent performance, in the range between the l and u parameters.

The concept hierarchies created by COBWEB are usually dependent on the ordering of the training examples. The orderings found in data affected by concept drift are especially difficult. COBBIT does not alter the input ordering in any way. However, because of the queue mechanism and the subtraction of examples, ordering effects are only applicable to the training instances in the queue.

Acknowledgement

Thanks to our collegues in the Stockholm Machine Learning Group (ILP project members and others). This research was funded by the Swedish National Board for Industrial and Technical development under grant no. 9001734.

References

1. John A. Allen and Kevin Thompson. Probabilistic concept formation in relational domains. In *Machine Learning—Proceedings of the Eighth International Workshop (ML91)*, pages 375–379. Morgan Kaufmann Publishers, Inc, 1991.
2. Gautam Biswas, Jerry Weinberg, Qun Yang, and Glenn R. Koller. Conceptual clustering and exploratory data analysis. In *Machine Learning—Proceedings of the Eighth International Workshop (ML91)*, pages 591–595. Morgan Kaufmann Publishers, Inc, 1991.
3. Scott Clearwater, Tze-Pin Cheng, Haym Hirsch, and Bruce Buchanan. Incremental batch learning. In *Proceedings of the Sixth International Workshop on Machine Learning*, pages 366–370. Morgan Kaufmann Publishers, Inc, 1989.
4. Douglas Fisher. Noise-tolerant conceptual clustering. In *Proceedings of the Eleventh International Joint Conference on Artificial Intelligence*, volume 1, pages 825–830. Morgan Kaufmann Publishers, Inc, 1989.
5. Douglas Fisher, Ling Xu, and Nazih Zard. Ordering effects in clustering. In *Machine Learning: Proceedings of the Ninth International Workshop (ML92)*, pages 163–168. Morgan Kaufmann Publishers, Inc, 1992.

6. Douglas Hayes Fisher. *Knowledge Acquisition via Incremental Conceptual Clustering*. PhD thesis, University of California, Irvine, 1987.
7. John Gennari, Pat Langley, and Doug Fisher. Models of incremental concept formation. *Artificial Intelligence*, (40):11–61, 1989.
8. Mirsad Hadzikadic and David Y. Y. Yun. Concept formation by incremental conceptual clustering. In *Proceedings of the Eleventh International Joint Conference on Artificial Intelligence*, pages 831–836, 1989.
9. Stephen José Hanson and Malcolm Bauer. Machine learning, clustering and polymorphy. In *Uncertainty in artificial intelligence*, pages 415–428. Elsevier Science Publishers, 1986.
10. Stephen José Hanson and Malcolm Bauer. Conceptual clustering, categorization and polymorphy. *Machine Learning*, (3):343–372, 1989.
11. Dennis Kibler and Pat Langley. Machine learning as an experimental science. In *Proceedings of the Third European Working Session on Learning*. Morgan Kaufmann Publishers, Inc, 1988.
12. Miroslav Kubat and Ivana Krizakova. Forgetting and ageing of knowledge in concept formation. Technical report, Computer Centre, Brno Technical University, Udolni 19, 60200 Brno, 1989.
13. Miroslav Kubat and Jirina Pavlickova. System flora: Learning from time-varying training sets. In Yves Kodratoff, editor, *Machine Learning—EWSL-91*, number 482 in Lecture Notes in Artificial Intelligence. Springer-Verlag, 1991.
14. Michael Lebowitz. Concept learning in a rich input domain: Generalization-based memory. Technical report, Department of Computer Science, Columbia University, New York, 1984.
15. Michael Lebowitz. Experiments with incremental concept formation: Unimem. *Machine Learning*, (2):103–138, 1987.
16. Ryszard S. Michalski and Robert E. Stepp. Learning from observation: Conceptual clustering. In Jaime G. Carbonell, Ryszard S. Michalski, and Tom M. Mitchell, editors, *Machine Learning: An Artificial Intelligence Approach*, pages 331–363. Tioga publishing company, 1983.
17. Ryszard S. Michalski and Robert E. Stepp. A theory and methodology of inductive learning. In Jaime G. Carbonell, Ryszard S. Michalski, and Tom M. Mitchell, editors, *Machine Learning: An Artificial Intelligence Approach*, pages 83–129. Tioga publishing company, 1983.
18. Bernd Nordhausen. Conceptual clustering using relational information. In *Proceedings aaai-86 Fifth National Conference on Artificial intelligence*, pages 508–512, 1986.
19. Jeffrey Schlimmer and Richard Granger, Junior. Beyond incremental processing: Tracking concept drift. In *Proceedings aaai-86 Fifth National Conference on Artificial intelligence*, pages 502–507, 1986.
20. Jeffrey Schlimmer and Richard Granger, Junior. Incremental learning from noisy data. *Machine Learning*, 1(3):317–354, 1986.
21. Gerhard Widmer and Miroslav Kubat. Effective learning in dynamic environments by explicit context tracking. In *Proceedings of the European Conference on Machine Learning (ECML-93*, Vienna, Austria, 1993.

Genetic Algorithms for Protein Tertiary Structure Prediction

Steffen Schulze-Kremer

Brainware GmbH, Gustav-Meyer Allee 25, D-1000 Berlin 65 and Free University Berlin,
Institute of Crystallography, Takustraße 6, D-1000 Berlin 33, Germany
email STEFFEN@KRISTALL.CHEMIE.FU-BERLIN.DE

Abstract

This article describes the application of genetic algorithms to the problem of
protein tertiary structure prediction. The genetic algorithm is used to search a
set of energetically sub-optimal conformations. A hybrid representation of
proteins, three operators MUTATE, SELECT and CROSSOVER and a fitness
function, that consists of a simple force field were used. The prototype was
applied to the *ab initio* prediction of Crambin. None of the conformations
generated by the genetic algorithm are similar to the native conformation, but
all show much lower energy than the native structure on the same force field.
This means the genetic algorithm's search was successful but the fitness
function was not a good indicator for native structure. In another experiment,
the backbone was held constant in the native state and only side chains were
allowed to move. For Crambin, this produced an alignment of 1.86 Å r.m.s.
from the native structure.

Keywords

genetic algorithm / protein tertiary structure / *ab initio* prediction

1. Introduction

The work presented in this article concerns the application of genetic algorithms
[Holland, 1975] to the problem of protein structure prediction [Schulz & Schirmer,
1979; Lesk, 1991; Branden & Tooze, 1991]. Genetic algorithms in computer science
are heuristic methods that operate on pieces of information like nature does with
genes during evolution. Individuals, represented by a linear string of letters of an
alphabet (in nature nucleotides, in genetic algorithms bits, strings or numbers) are
allowed to mutate, crossover and reproduce. Members of a new generation and
their parents are then evaluated by a fitness function. Only the best individuals
enter the next reproduction cycle. After a given number of cycles, the population
consists of well adapted individuals that each represent a solution for the problem
of optimizing the given fitness function. Although it cannot be proven that the final

individuals contain the optimal solution it can be mathematically shown that the overall effort is maximised during a run [Holland, 1975]. In some applications, where the search space was too large for other heuristic or analytic methods, genetic algorithms produced better solutions than those known before [Davis, 1991].

In this work, the individuals are conformations of a protein and the fitness function is a simple force field. What follows is a description of the representation formalism, the fitness function and the operators used. The results of a run on Crambin are then presented and finally, the results of an experiment for side chain placement are shown.

2. Protein Representation

For any application of a genetic algorithm a choice has to be made on the representation of the "genes". In the present work, the so-called hybrid approach was taken [Davis, 1991]. This means, that the objects the genetic algorithm processes are encoded by numbers instead of bit strings, which were used in the original genetic algorithm [Holland, 1975]. A hybrid representation is usually easier to implement and also facilitates the use of operators. However, three potential disadvantages are encountered: strictly speaking, the mathematical foundation of genetic algorithms holds only for binary representations; binary representations run faster in many applications; and an additional encoding / decoding process may be required. For a hybrid representation of proteins there are at least two immediately intuitive choices, one being Cartesian coordinates, the other torsion angles.

2.1 Cartesian Coordinates

In this representation, the coordinates of all atoms of a protein are stored in a fixed order, i.e. the nth number always refers to the same component of the 3D coordinate of a particular atom. This representation has the advantage of being easily converted to and from the conformation of a protein. However, it faces the disadvantage that the use of a random mutation operator would most of the time create invalid instances, where atoms lie too far apart or collide. To prevent this from happening, a filter which eliminates invalid individuals had to be installed between the operator and the fitness function. This would be a rather time consuming process, especially when a large percentage of the individuals had to be sorted out. Therefore, the representation in Cartesian coordinates would considerably slow down the progress of the genetic algorithm. These considerations have led to another model.

2.2 Torsion Angles

In this representation a protein is described by a set of non-redundant torsion angles. This can be done under the assumption of constant standard binding geometries. Bond lengths and bond angles are taken to be constant and cannot be changed by the genetic algorithm. This assumption is a simplification of the real situation where bond length and bond angle depend on the environment of an atom within a protein. However, a set of non-redundant torsion angles allows enough degrees of freedom and therefore enough variability to represent any native conformation with only small spatial differences when superimposed on the original structure (i.e. small root mean square deviations, abbrev. r.m.s.)

The following diagram illustrates the use of torsion angles. A small fragment from a hypothetical protein is shown. Two basic building blocks, i.e. the amino acids phenyalanine (Phe) and glycine (Gly), are drawn as wire frame models. Atoms are described by their chemical symbols. The thicker bonds indicate the backbone. Main chain torsion angles phi, psi and omega are indicated next to their rotatable bond.

Special to the representation by torsion angles is the fact that small changes in the φ (phi) / ψ (psi) angles can induce large changes in the overall conformation. This is of advantage when creating variability through genetic operators. Also, as a consequence of this representation, one can get relative large r.m.s. differences when comparing a native conformation with a reconstruction of the same molecule under the assumption of constant standard bonding geometries. This difference can be minimized by slight changes in the torsion angles.

In the present work, the representation by torsion angles was used. The torsion angles of 129 proteins from the Brookhaven database [Bernstein et al, 1977] were statistically analyzed. The ten most frequently occurring values for each nonredundant torsion angle were collected in 10° intervals. At the beginning of the run, individuals were intitialized with either complete extended conformations, where all torsion angles are 180°, or with a random selection of the ten most frequent intervals for each torsion angle. For the ω (omega) torsion angle the constant value of 180° was used because of the rigidness of the double bond between the atoms C_{2i} and N_{i+1}. An evaluation of ω angles shows that with the exception of prolin average deviations of 5° occur from the mean of 180°, in rare cases 15°.

The genetic operators work on the torsional representation. For the application of the fitness function, it is necessary to translate proteins represented in torsion angles into Cartesian coordinates. Two programs have been written to carry out the conversion of one representation into another. The binding geometries were taken from the molecular modelling package Alchemy [Vinter et al, 1987] and the bond lengths from the program Charmm [Brooks et al, 1983]. Either a complete form with explicit hydrogen atoms or the so-called extended atom representation can be calculated.

Next to the calculation of the fitness of an individual, the conversion of the Cartesian representation into the torsional representation is the second most time consuming step. The torsion angle of each bond that extends to at least one other atom is calculated. In the reverse process, atoms with standard binding geometries are added to the molecule one by one according to residue type. Then, they are rotated by the amount of their torsion angle. This operation can be replaced by the addition of two vectors because both torsion angle and radius are known. The translation programs were successfully tested by comparison of native and reconstructed conformations. A native structure was translated into its torsion angle representation and back into a Cartesian representation. The native and reconstructed conformations were then superimposed with the FIT routine in the program Alchemy.

2.3 Format of Genes

Genes are stored one conformation in one ASCII file. The number of records per file equals the number of residues of the protein. Each record starts with a three letter identifier of the residue type. Ten floating point numbers in the format -xxx.xx follow, which stand for the torsion angles φ, ψ, ω, $χ1$, $χ2$, $χ3$, $χ4$, $χ5$, $χ6$, $χ7$, in this order. For residues with less than seven side chain torsion angles the extra fields carry the value 999.99. The ω angle was kept at the constant value of 180° in most applications.

3. Fitness Function

The fitness function in a genetic algorithm represents the "environment" of all individuals. In order to "survive" an individual has to perform better than its competitors in terms of the fitness function. In the present work, a simple steric potential energy function was chosen as the fitness function.

3.1 Motivation

The main reason for the choice of a simple steric potential energy function as the fitness function of the genetic algorithm was the observation, that up to date it has not been possible to develop a method to efficiently search the conformation space spanned by a force field for its global optimum. The problem with this task lies in the large number of degrees of freedom for a protein of average size. In general, molecules with n atoms have $3n$-6 degrees of freedom. This amounts in the case of proteins with about 100 residues to ((100 residues · approx. 20 atoms per residue) · 3) - 6 = 5994 degrees of freedom. Systems of equations with this number of variables are analytically intractable today [Gunsteren & Berendsen, 1990].

Efforts to empirically find the optimal solution are equally difficult. If there are no constraints for the conformation of a protein and only its primary structure given, then the number of conformations for a protein of medium size (100 residues) can be estimated to be (approx. 5 torsion angles per residue · approx. 5 likely values per torsion angle)^{100} = 25^{100}. Because potential energy function is not monotonous, in the worst case 25 to the power of 100 conformations had to be evaluated to find the global optimum. This is clearly beyond capacity of today's and tomorrow's super computers.

As can be seen from a number of previous applications, genetic algorithms were able to find sub-optimal solutions to problems of equally large search space [Davis, 1991; Lucasius & Kateman, 1989; Tuffery et al, 1991]. Sub-optimal in this context means, that it cannot be proven that the solutions generated by the genetic algorithm are in fact the optimum but they were in many cases better than any previously known solution. This can be of much help in n.p.-complete domains, where analytical solutions of the problem are not available. Therefore, it was attempted to apply the genetic algorithm to the *ab initio* protein structure prediction problem.

3.2 Conformational Energy

The steric potential energy function was taken from the program Charmm [Brooks et al, 1983]. It is the sum of the expressions for E_{bond} (bond length potential), E_{phi} (bond angle potential), E_{tor} (torsion angle potential), E_{impr} (improper torsion angle potential), E_{vdW} (van der Waals pair interactions), E_{el} (electrostatic potential), E_H (hydrogen bonds), and of two expressions for solvent interaction, E_{cr} and E_{cphi}

$$E = E(bond) + E(phi) + E(tor) + E(impr) + E(vdW) + E(el) + E(H) + E(cr) + E(cphi).$$

As constant bond lengths and bond angles were assumed, the expressions for E_{bond}, E_{phi} and E_{impr} are constant for each protein. The expression E_H was omitted because it would have required to exclude the effect of hydrogen bonds from the expressions for E_{vdW} and E_{el}. This, however, was not done by the authors of Charmm. In all runs, folding was simulated in vacuum with no ligands or solvent, i.e. E_{cr} and E_{cphi} are constant. This is certainly a crude simplification which will have to be extended in future. Thus, the potential energy function simplifies to:

$$E = E(tor) + E(vdW) + E(el).$$

If only the three expressions E_{tor}, E_{vdW} and E_{el} were calculated, there would be no force to drive the protein to a compact folded state. An exact solution to this problem is the inclusion of entropy. Unfortunately, measuring the difference in entropy between folded and unfolded state requires taking into account interactions of the protein with solvent. This cannot be done in a simple way. To have a running prototype, it was therefore decided to introduce *ad hoc* a pseudo entropic force, that drives the protein to a globular state. Analysis of a number of globular proteins reveals the following empirical relation between the number of residues and the diameter:

$$\text{expected diameter} = 8 \cdot \text{length}^{1/3} \text{ Å}$$

The pseudo entropic potential for a conformation is a function of its actual diameter. The diameter is defined to be the largest distance between any C_α atoms in a given conformation. A positive exponential of the difference between expected and the actual diameter E_{pe} is added to the potential energy, if that difference is less than 15 Å. If the difference is greater than 15 Å a fixed amount of energy is added (10^{10} kcal/mol). If the actual diameter is smaller than the expected diameter, E_{pe} is zero. This has the effect, that more extended conformations have more positive potential energy values and are therefore less fit for reproduction.

$$E_{pe} = 4^{(\text{actual diameter - expected diameter})} \text{ kcal/mol}$$

Occasionally, if two atoms are very close, the E_{vdW} can become very large. The maximum value for E_{vdW} in this case is 10^{10} kcal/mol and the expressions for E_{el} and E_{tor} are not calculated.

Runs have been performed with the potential energy function E as described above, where lower values mean fitter individuals and with a variant, where the four expressions E_{tor}, E_{vdW}, E_{el} and E_{pe} were given individual weights. The results were similar in all cases. Especially, scaling down the dominant effect of electrostatic interactions did not improve the results.

4. Operators

In order to combine individuals of one generation to produce new offspring, nature as well as genetic algorithms apply several operators. In the present work, individuals are protein conformations in their torsion angle representation under the assumption of constant standard binding geometries (see above). Three operators were invented to process these individuals: SELECT, MUTATE and CROSSOVER. The decision about the application of one operator is made at run time and can be controlled by various parameters.

4.1 SELECT

The first operator is the SELECT operator. If SELECT gets activated for a particular torsion angle, this angle will be replaced by a random choice of one of its ten most frequently occurring values. The decision, whether a torsion angle will be modified by SELECT is made independently for each torsion angle in a protein. A random number between 0 and 1 is generated and if this number is greater than the SELECT parameter at that time, SELECT is triggered. The SELECT parameter can change dynamically during the run. The values for SELECT to choose from are from a statistical analysis of 129 proteins from the PDB database. The number of values occurring in each of the 36 10°-intervals for that torsion angle was counted. The ten most frequent intervals, each represented by its left boundary, are available for substitution.

4.2 MUTATE

The MUTATE operator consists of three components: the 1°, 5° and 10° operator. After application of the SELECT operator and independently from it, for each torsion angle in a protein two decisions are made; first, whether a MUTATE operator will be applied and second, if the first decision was in favor of the

MUTATE operator, which of the three components will be carried out. Mutation is done by incrementing or decrementing (always an independent random chance of 1:1) the torsion angle by 1°, 5° or 10°. Care is taken that the range of torsion angle values is always in the [-180°, 180°] interval. The probability of applying the MUTATE operator is controlled by the MUTATE parameter, which can change dynamically during the run. Similarly, three additional parameters control the probability for choosing among the three components.

4.3 CROSSOVER

The CROSSOVER operator has two components: the two point crossover and the uniform crossover. It is applied to two genes (individuals) independently of the SELECT and MUTATE operators. First, the parent generation of individuals, possibly modified by SELECT and MUTATE, are randomly grouped pairwise. For each pair, an independent decision is made whether or not to apply the CROSSOVER operator. The probability for this is controlled by the CROSSOVER parameter, which can change dynamically during the run. If the decision is "no", the two individuals are not further modified and added to the list of offspring. If the decision is "yes", a choice between the two point crossover and the uniform crossover has to be made. This decision is controlled by two other parameters, that also can change dynamically during the run.

The two point crossover selects randomly two sites (residues) on one of the individuals. Then, the fragment between the two residues is exchanged with the corresponding fragment of the second individual. The uniform crossover decides independently for each residue, whether or not to exchange the torsion angles of that residue. The chance for exchange is always 1:1.

4.4 Parameterization

As indicated in the previous sections, there are a number of parameters to control the run of a genetic algorithm on protein conformations. The parameter values which were used for the runs presented in the results section are summarized in the following table. The ω torsion angle was kept constant at 180°. The intitial generation was created by a random selection of the torsion angles from the list of the ten most frequently occurring values for each angle. There were ten individuals in one generation. The genetic algorithm terminated after 1000 generations. At the start of the run, the chance for a torsion angle to be modified by the SELECT operator is 80%, at the end of the run 20%. The probability decreases linearly with the number of generations. In contrast, the chance of applying the MUTATE operator increases from 20% at the start to 70% at the end of the run. The 10°

component of the MUTATE operator is dominant at the start of the run (60%), whereas it is the 1˚ component at the end (80%). Likewise, the chance of performing the CROSSOVER operator rises from 10% to 70%. At the beginning of the run mainly uniform CROSSOVER is done (90%), at the end mainly two point CROSSOVER (90%).

This parameter setting has a small number of individuals but a large number of generations. This was chosen to keep cpu time low while allowing a maximum number of crossover events. This run took about 12 hours on a SUN SPARC station. At the beginning of the run, SELECT and uniform CROSSOVER are applied most of the time. This is to create some variety in the population. At the end of the run, the 1˚ component of the MUTATE operator dominates the scene. This is intended for fine tuning the conformations that have survived the fitness pressure so far.

Parameter	Value
ω angle constant 180˚:	on
initialize start generation:	random torsion angels
number of individuals:	10
number of generations:	1000
SELECT (start)	80%
SELECT (end)	20%
MUTATE (start)	20%
MUTATE (end)	70%
MUTATE (start 10˚)	60%
MUTATE (end 10˚)	0%
MUTATE (start 5˚)	30%
MUTATE (end 5˚)	20%
MUTATE (start 1˚)	10%
MUTATE (end 1˚)	80%
CROSSOVER (start)	70%
CROSSOVER (end)	10%
CROSSOVER (start uniform)	90%
CROSSOVER (end uniform)	10%
CROSSOVER (start two point)	10%
CROSSOVER (end two point)	90%

4.5 Generational Replacement

There are a number of ways of how to select from the individuals of one generation and its offspring the parents for the next generation. Given the constraint, that the number of individuals should remain constant, inevitably, some individuals have to be discarded. Two ways of controlling the transition are complete replacement and elitistic replacement. In the first case, all offspring become parents in the next generation. The parents of the old generation are completely discarded. This has the disadvantage, that a fit parent can be lost, if it only once produces bad offspring. With elitistic replacement all parents and offspring of one generation are sorted according their fitness. If the size of the population is n, then the n fittest individuals are selected as parents for the following generation. This mode has been used in the present work.

5. *Ab initio* Prediction Results

A prototype of a genetic algorithm with the representation, fitness function and operators as described above has been implemented. For *ab initio* prediction the sequence of Crambin was given to the program. Crambin is a plant seed protein from the cabbage *Crambe Abyssinica*. The structure was determined by W.A. Hendrickson and M.M. Teeter up to a resolution of 1.5 Å [Hendrickson & Teeter, 1981]. Crambin has a strong amphiphilic character, which makes it especially difficult to predict its tertiary structure with a simple force field. Because of its good resolution and its small size of 46 residues it was decided to use Crambin as a first candidate to start with. Independently from this work Scott Le Grand in the laboratory of Prof. Karplus at MIT did similar experiments, using a GA and a different force field. The results were basically the same as those presented here [Le Grand & Merz 1991]. The following structures are displayed in stereo projection. If the observer manages to look cross eyed at the picture in a way that superimposes both halves, a three dimensional impression can be perceived.

Crambin with side chains

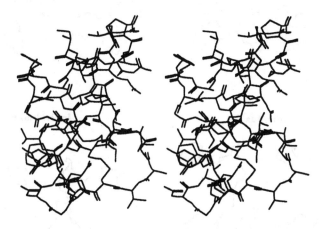

5.1 Conformations

In the following, the backbone structure of the ten best individuals generated by the genetic algorithm are shown in stereo projection.

Crambin, native

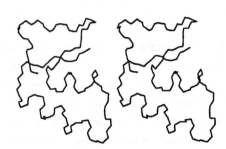

Individual P1

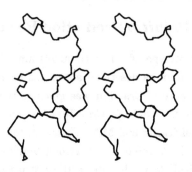

Individual P2

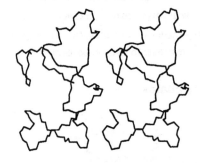

Individual P3

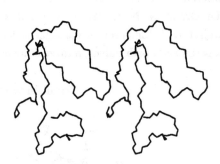

Individual P4

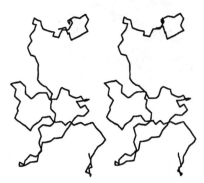

Individual P5

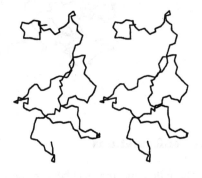

Crambin, native

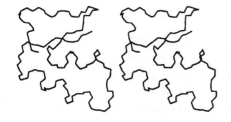

Individual P6

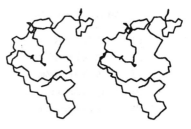

Individual P7

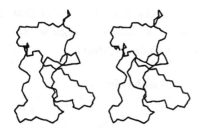

Individual P8

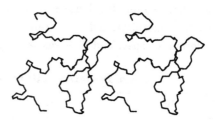

Individual P9

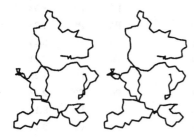

Individual P10

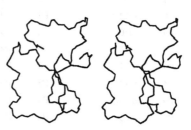

It can be seen from the graphs that none of the individuals generated show significant structural similarity to the native Crambin conformation. This can be confirmed by superpositioning the generated structures with the native conformation. The following table shows the r.m.s. differences between individuals

P1 to P10 and the native conformation. All values are in the range of 9 Ångström, which rejects any structural homology.

r.m.s. Deviation to Native Crambin

P1	10.07 Ångström	P6	10.31 Ångström
P2	9.74 Ångström	P7	9.45 Ångström
P3	9.15 Ångström	P8	10.18 Ångström
P4	10.14 Ångström	P9	9.37 Ångström
P5	9.95 Ångström	P10	8.84 Ångström

The following table shows the r.m.s. differences between the generated individuals. They can be grouped into two classes. The members within each class are similar, whereas structures from both classes have no similarity. One class holds the individuals P1, P2, P4, P5, P6, P8 and P9. The other class has P3, P7 and P10. The fact, that two unrelated classes of conformations were generated, means that the genetic algorithm did simultaneously search in different regions of the conformation space and thus was *not trapped in one a local optimum*.

r.m.s. Deviation within Generated Individuals

P1	P10	8.40	P10	P8	8.57	P4	P5	1.10
P1	P2	1.73	P10	P9	7.30	P4	P6	0.71
P1	P3	9.52	P2	P3	8.96	P4	P7	8.71
P1	P4	0.86	P2	P4	1.44	P4	P8	0.93
P1	P5	1.43	P2	P5	1.13	P4	P9	2.15
P1	P6	1.20	P2	P6	1.63	P5	P6	1.28
P1	P7	9.03	P2	P7	8.46	P5	P7	8.98
P1	P8	0.58	P2	P8	2.12	P5	P8	1.75
P1	P9	2.30	P2	P9	1.15	P5	P9	2.04
P10	P2	7.75	P3	P4	9.24	P6	P7	8.71
P10	P3	1.57	P3	P5	9.52	P6	P8	1.28
P10	P4	8.18	P3	P6	9.23	P6	P9	2.44
P10	P5	8.39	P3	P7	1.13	P7	P8	9.11
P10	P6	8.15	P3	P8	9.61	P7	P9	8.21
P10	P7	1.74	P3	P9	8.57	P8	P9	2.68

5.2 Energies

The following table lists the values of the four contributions to the potential energy function for the ten individuals generated. The total energy of all individuals is much lower than the energy for the native conformation of Crambin: E(vdW) -12.8 kcal/mol, E(el) 11.4 kcal/mol, E(tor) 60.9 kcal/mol, E(pe) 1.7 kcal/mol and E(total)

61.2 kcal/mol. It is obvious, that the largest contribution comes from electrostatic interactions. This is due to the six partial charges in Crambin. For a more elaborate force field these charges have to be neutralized.

Energy Contributions of the Generated Individuals

Individual	E_{vdw}	E_{el}	E_{tor}	E_{pe}	E_{total}
P1	-14.9	-2434.5	74.1	75.2	-2336.5
P2	-2.9	-2431.6	76.3	77.4	-2320.8
P3	78.5	-2447.4	79.6	80.7	-2316.1
P4	-11.1	-2409.7	81.8	82.9	-2313.7
P5	83.0	-2440.6	84.1	85.2	-2308.5
P6	-12.3	-2403.8	86.1	87.2	-2303.7
P7	88.3	-2470.8	89.4	90.5	-2297.6
P8	-12.2	-2401.0	91.6	92.7	-2293.7
P9	93.7	-2404.5	94.8	95.9	-2289.1
P10	96.0	-2462.8	97.1	98.2	-2287.5

6. Side Chain Placement Results

Crystallographers often face the problem of positioning the side chains when the primary structure and the conformation of the backbone is known. At present, there is no method that automatically does side chain placement with sufficient fidelity for routine, practical use. The side chain placement problem is much easier than *ab initio* prediction but still too complex for analytical treatment.

The genetic algorithm approach, as described above, can also be used for side chain placement. The torsion angles φ, ψ, and ω are kept constant at the values for the given backbone. Side chain placement by the genetic algorithm was done for Crambin. For each five residues, a superposition of the native and the predicted conformation was done. This is shown in stereo projection graphs on the following pages.

As can be seen, the predictions are quite well in agreement with the native conformation in most of the cases. The overall r.m.s. difference in this example is 1.86 Å. This is comparable to the results from a simulated annealing approach (1.65 Å) [Lee & Subbiah, 1991] and a heuristic approach (1.48 Å) [Tuffery et al, 1991].

Superposition of Residues 1-5

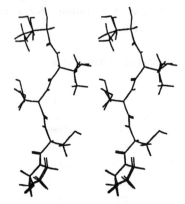

Superposition of Residues 6-10

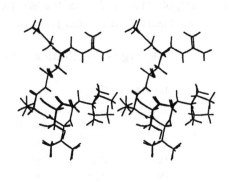

Superposition of Residues 11-15

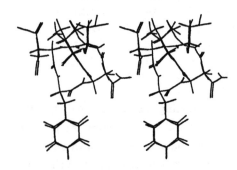

Superposition of Residues 16-20

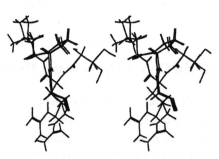

Superposition of Residues 21-25

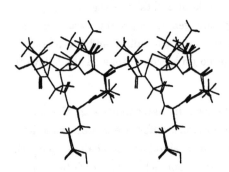

Superposition of Residues 26-30

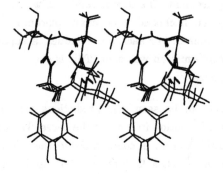

Superposition of Residues 31-35   **Superposition of Residues 36-40**

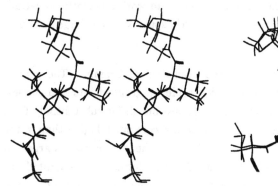 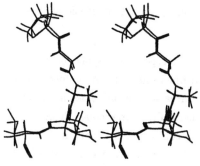

Superposition of Residues 41-46

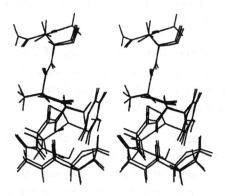

7. Discussion and Conclusion

A prototype for the application of a genetic algorithm to the problem of protein tertiary structure prediction is presented. The genetic algorithm searches for energetically favorable conformations. A hybrid representation of proteins and three operators MUTATE, SELECT and CROSSOVER to manipulate the "genes" of a genetic algorithm were developed together with a fitness function, that consists of a simple force field. The work was motivated by the fact that present attempts to find *ab initio* an energetically optimal conformation of a protein face the problem of a very large search space. If no constraints are given, it is virtually impossible to systematically evaluate all valid conformations in order to find the one with the lowest energy. Genetic algorithms have been shown to work efficiently on certain function optimization problems, where the search space was too large for other methods.

The prototype was applied on the *ab initio* prediction of Crambin. The genetic algorithm produced ten conformations, which could be grouped into two classes. Structures within one class are similar in structure but differ substantially from members of the other class. Electrostatic interactions were much higher than in the native conformation. This is likely to result from the six partial charges in Crambin, which were not neutralized. None of the conformations generated are similar to the native conformation. However, all conformations generated by the genetic algorithm show much lower energy than the native structure on the same force field. This means, that the genetic algorithm's search was successful as it produced "good" structures in terms of the fitness function and was *not trapped in one local minimum* but also that the *fitness function was not a good indicator for native structure*. Crambin has a strong amphiphilic character whereas the simple force field used is more suitable for globular, cytosolic proteins. Work has started to improve the model at this point.

In a side chain placement experiment, the backbone of Crambin was held constant in the native state and only side chains were allowed to move. The genetic algorithm produced an alignment of 1.86 Å r.m.s. from the native structure, which is reasonable when compared with other methods.

The results indicate, that in the domain of *ab initio* prediction of protein conformation the genetic algorithm could be an efficient instrument to produce likely candidates for sub-optimal solutions. Certainly, the algorithm cannot do better than the fitness function given to it. It seems therefore possible that with a fitness function that is a good indicator of native structure *ab initio* prediction might become feasible on present day computers.

8. Acknowledgments

This work was supported by the Bundesminister für Forschung und Technologie, grant number BEO 21 / 17405 A.

9. References

[Bernstein *et al*, 1977] F. C. Bernstein, T. F. Koetzle, G. J. B. Williams, E. F. Meyer Jr., M. D. Brice, J. R. Rodgers, O. Kennard, T. Shimanouchi, M. Tasumi, *The Protein Data*

Bank: A Computer-based Archival File for Macromolecular Structures, Journal of Molecular Biology, 112, pp. 535-542, 1977

[Branden & Tooze, 1991] C. Branden, J. Tooze, *Introduction to Protein Structure*, Garland Publishing New York, 1991

[Brooks *et al*, 1983] B. R. Brooks, R. E. Bruccoleri, B. D. Olafson, D. J. States, S. Swaminathan, M. Karplus, *Charmm: A program for Macromolecular Energy, Minimization and Dynamics Calculations*, J. Comp. Chem., vol 4, no 2, pp. 187-217, 1983

[Davis, 1991] L. Davis, (ed.) *Handbook of Genetic Algorithms*, New York, 1991

[Gunsteren & Berendsen, 1990] W. F. Gunsteren, H. J. C. Berendsen, *Computer Simulation of Molecular Dynamics: Methodology, Applications and Perspectives in Chemistry*, Angew. Chem. Int. Ed. Engl., vol 29, pp. 992-1023, 1990

[Hendrickson & Teeter, 1981] W. A. Hendrickson, M. M. Teeter, *Structure of the Hydrophobic Protein Crambin Determined directly from the Anomalous Scattering of Sulphur*, Nature, vol 290, pp. 107, 1981

[Holland, 1975] J. H. Holland, *Adaptation in Natural and Artificial Systems*, University of Michigan Press, Ann Arbor, 1975

[Le Grand & Merz 1991] S. M. Le Grand, K. M. Merz, *The Application of the Genetic Algorithm to the Minimization of Potential Energy Functions*, submitted to The Journal of Global Optimization, 1991

[Lee & Subbiah, 1991] C. Lee, S. Subbiah, *Prediction of protein side chain conformation by packing optimization*, J. Mol. Biol., no 217, pp. 373-388, 1991

[Lesk, 1991] A. M. Lesk, *Protein Architecture - A Practical Approach*, IRL Press, 1991

[Lucasius & Kateman, 1989] C. B. Lucasius, G. Kateman, *Application of Genetic Algorithms to Chemometrics*, Proceedings 3rd International Conference on Genetic Algorithms, George Mason University, 1989

[Schulz & Schirmer, 1979] G. E. Schulz, R. H. Schirmer, Principles of Protein Structure, Springer Verlag, 1979

[Tuffery *et al*, 1991] P. Tuffery, C. Etchebest, S. Hazout, R. Lavery, *A new approach to the rapid determination of protein side chain conformations*, J. Biomol. Struct. Dyn., vol 8, no 6, pp. 1267-1289, 1991

[Vinter *et al*, 1987] J. G. Vinter, A. Davis, M. R. Saunders, *Strategic approaches to drug design. An integrated software framework for molecular modelling*, J. Comput.-Aided Mol. Des., no 1, pp. 31-51, 1987

SIA: a Supervised Inductive Algorithm with Genetic Search for Learning Attributes based Concepts

Gilles Venturini

Equipe Inférence et Apprentissage
Laboratoire de Recherche en Informatique, bat. 490
Université de Paris-Sud
91405 Orsay Cedex, FRANCE.
email: venturi@lri.lri.fr

Abstract. This paper describes a genetic learning system called SIA, which learns attributes based rules from a set of preclassified examples. Examples may be described with a variable number of attributes, which can be numeric or symbolic, and examples may belong to several classes. SIA algorithm is somewhat similar to the AQ algorithm because it takes an example as a seed and generalizes it, using a genetic process, to find a rule maximizing a noise tolerant rule evaluation criterion. The SIA approach to supervised rule learning reduces greatly the possible rule search space when compared to the genetic Michigan and Pitt approaches. SIA is comparable to AQ and decision trees algorithms on two learning tasks. Furthermore, it has been designed for a data analysis task in a large and complex justice domain.

1 Introduction

Learning rules in propositional logic from a set of preclassified examples described in an attribute/value based language is a problem well known and studied in Machine Learning (Gams and Lavrac 1987). One reason for that is the fact that in many domains, events or experiences can be easily described using a set of variables or attributes.

Among the many existing algorithms that solve this problem, one can point out, on one hand, some methods that use heuristics to search the rule space. For instance, the ID3-based algorithms learn decision trees involving attributes which are relevant from an information theory point of view (Quinlan 1986). Rules can then be extracted from decision trees, a process which usually increases the system classification accuracy (Quinlan 1987). Another example is the AQ algorithms, which learn rules using the heuristic star algorithm (Michalski et al 1986) (Wnek and Michalski 1991).

On the other hand, some methods use stochastic algorithms (Kononenko and Kovacic 1992) or genetic algorithms (Holland 1975) to find optimal rules.

Examples of such algorithms are the classifier systems, which usually learn rules (classifiers) from examples that are not preclassified (Goldberg 1989) (Wilson 1987) (Venturini 1992), but which can also learn from preclassified examples (McCallum and Spackman 1990) (Bonelli and Parodi 1991). Other algorithms, for instance, are the GABIL system (De Jong and Spears 1991) which learns rules incrementally and the SAMUEL system (Grefenstette 1989)

Finally, some algorithms use a multistrategic search, combining heuristic and probabilistic algorithms. For instance, genetic algorithms, denoted GAs in the following, can discover important attributes in cooperation with an AQ based algorithm (Vafaie and DeJong 1991), or, GAs can improve and refine rules learned by an AQ algorithm, using a subpart of the set of examples (Bala, DeJong and Pachowicz 1991).

The genetic based rule searching algorithms mentioned above have a longer execution time than the heuristics methods. They also have fewer learning abilities: for instance, they do not handle easily numeric attributes because the classifier system rule description language is too simple, or because the GABIL method of encoding all possible values would lead to very long rules in the case of real-valued attributes. Furthermore, it has been recently shown (Wnek and Michalski 1991) that a genetic rule learning system, namely the classifier system CFS of Riolo, obtains the lowest performances among other learning methods, on a simple, noise free learning task.

Thus, one motivation for this work is the building of a GA based learning method that would be globally equivalent, with respect to performances and learning abilities, to the heuristic based methods mentioned above. Furthermore, this work is also motivated by a real world data analysis task in a complex domain which would not be easily handled by the methods mentioned above. The main reasons for this are that attributes are numeric or symbolic, examples are described using a variable number of attributes (mainly because some attributes may be undefined for some examples), and may belong to several classes.

In the following, section 2 describes SIA example and rule representations. Section 3 describes the main learning algorithm, the rule filtering algorithm, the classification procedure chosen and their main properties. Section 4 shows two evaluations of SIA on common learning tasks and section 5 describes the real task for which SIA has been designed. Section 6 concludes on this and future work.

2 Example and Rule Representation

2.1 Examples with Undefined Attributes, Multiple Classes and Weights

SIA learns production rules from a set Ex of examples of events in a given domain. An example ex is described using n attributes $A_1, ..., A_n$, which can be either numeric (real-valued for instance) or symbolic (with discrete values).

Firstly, it is considered that k attributes are defined for all examples and that the remaining $n - k$ attributes may be *undefined* for some examples. For instance, suppose that cars are being described using the attributes *number* −

of − accidents and *date − of − last − accident*. The attribute *date − of − last − accident* is undefined for cars that were never crashed. This notion of undefined attributes includes not only logical cases of undefined values (as in the car example), but also the noisy cases of missing or unknown attributes values, and systematic missing values (Weinberg, Biswas and Koller 1992).

Secondly, an example *ex* may belong to several classes among a set $C = \{C_1, ..., C_k\}$ of possible classes. For instance, the description of an animal can belong to the class "*dog*" and to the class "*mammal*". SIA learns a separated definition of each class.

Finally, examples can be weighted in order to create artificial examples distributions in *Ex*. For example, let us suppose that the learning task is to learn rules about cars. These rules should conclude that a car is *safe* or *unsafe*. Let us suppose that $\frac{9}{10}$ of the cars are safe. In order to learn reliable rules, many car examples must be recorded. Thus, a hundred of safe cars and a hundred of unsafe cars examples are recorded in *Ex*. The probability, in *Ex*, of a car to be safe is now $\frac{1}{2}$, instead of $\frac{9}{10}$ in the real domain. To recreate the examples original distribution in *Ex*, a weight $w = 9$ should be assigned to safe cars examples, and a weight $w = 1$ to unsafe cars examples. These weights introduce biases in the learning process by making some examples more important than others.

Thus, an example *ex* is represented as

$$(e, C_L, w)$$

where $e = \{e_1, ..., e_n\}$ is a vector of attributes values, among which some values may be undefined, C_L is the list of classes *ex* belongs to, and w is the example weight.

2.2 Attributes based Rule Representation

SIA learns a representation of each class in $\{C_1, ..., C_k\}$. For a class C_i, the representation learned is a set of rules R of the form

$$R \ : \ IF \ \underbrace{cond_1 \wedge ... \wedge cond_n}_{Condition\,part} \ THEN \ \underbrace{Class = C_i}_{Conclusion\,part} \ , \ \underbrace{Strength}_{Strength\,part}$$

In R condition part, *cond*$_i$ involves attribute A_i and equals either:

- "$\star$", meaning that A_i is not taken into account (the condition is always true), or

- "$A_i = value$", where A_i is a symbolic attribute and *value* is an observed value of A_i, or

- "$B \leq A_i \leq B'$", where A_i is a numeric attribute and where the lower and upper bounds B and B' are such that $B' \geq B$ (B and B' computation is detailed in the following).

An example of such a rule is

$R1$: IF $\star \wedge$ date $-$ of $-$ last $-$ accident $=$ yesterday THEN Class $=$ unsafe

Using this rule condition format, a matching operator between a rule R and an example ex can be defined: R matches the example $ex = (e, C_L, w)$ if all R conditions are true for vector e. If ex has an undefined or missing value for an attribute A_i, it can be matched by R only if A_i is not taken into account by R conditions ($cond_i = \star$). For instance, the event "$number - of - accidents = 0 \wedge date - of - last - accident = undefined$" can not be matched by $R1$.

The conclusion part concludes that an example $ex = (e, C_L, w)$, matched by R, belongs to class C_i. If ex really belongs to class C_i (i.e. $C_i \in C_L$), then ex is said to be correctly classified by R, else ex is misclassified.

The strength part of R is a set of coefficients that are used to measure the quality of R by computing a quality criterion $C_q(R)$ (see section 3). The higher $C_q(R)$ is, the more interesting R is. The value of this criterion represents the genetic strength of the rule that the genetic search will try to maximize.

This rule description language is thus slightly less powerful than the one use in AQ, because, for instance, a disjunction of conditions for the same class, is coded by several rules rather than by just one rule.

Possible Bounds for Numeric Conditions. When a numeric attribute A_i is involved in the condition $cond_i$ of the condition part of a rule, one must define what possible values the bounds B and B' described above can take. Let us suppose that A_i has m distinct ordered values $v_1, ..., v_m$ observed in Ex. One solution, similar to one used in AQ, is to define the possible set B_i of bounds for $cond_i$ as $B_i = \{v_1, ..., v_m\}$.

Another solution, which has been used in the following, is to define B_i as

$$B_i = \{-\infty, \frac{v_1 + v_2}{2}, ..., \frac{v_{m-1} + v_m}{2}, +\infty\}$$

which is similar to one approach used for finding thresholds in decision trees algorithms, but here, no statistical techniques are used: the learning process will select itself the proper bounds in B_i.

3 SIA Main Algorithms

3.1 Learning Algorithm Overview

The SIA basic learning algorithm is somewhat similar to the AQ algorithm because it uses a seed example ex as a start point, and tries to find the most optimal rule that covers this example using generalization. One important difference between the two methods is that SIA uses a genetic based search:

1. Let $\mathcal{R}$ be an empty set of rules,

2. Label "uncovered" all classes in the class lists of all examples in Ex,

3. Let $ex = (e, C_L, w)$ be an example of Ex such that there exists a class $C_i \in C_L$ labelled "uncovered".

4. Let R_{init} be the most specific rule that matches ex and concludes "$Class = C_i$",

5. Using a GA, generalize the condition part of R_{init} to find the optimal rule(s) R^* that match(es) ex (rules that maximize the rule evaluation criterion $C_q(R)$),

6. Label "covered" all classes C_i in the class list of examples matched by R^* rule(s),

7. Add R^* to $\mathcal{R}$,

8. If some examples remain such that a class in their class list is labelled "uncovered", then go to 3,

9. Possibly, eliminate rules in $\mathcal{R}$ using the rule filtering algorithm,

10. Ouput $\mathcal{R}$

In step 4, the R_{init} rule is computed as follows: the symbolic conditions of R_{init} are of the form "$A_i = e_i$". The numeric conditions are of the form "$B \leq A_i \leq B'''$" where B and B' are the closest lower and upper bounds to e_i in B_i. However, if the value of A_i is undefined for ex, the corresponding condition $cond_i$ in R_{init} is set to "$\star$": the algorithm must learn a rule that classifies ex without using the missing attribute A_i.

The behavior of the algorithm is illustrated in a simple case on figure 1: two attributes A_1 and A_2 define an example space where the examples can belong to the classes "+" or "-".

This algorithm ensures the completeness of $\mathcal{R}$ over Ex, if the rule filtering step 9 is ommitted. No mechanism is used to choose the seed example in step 3: SIA is sensitive to the order of the examples, unless every example is selected as a seed in steps 3 and 8.

3.2 Genetic based Rule Discovery Process: SIA approach

The genetic search process of step 5 in the SIA main algorithm tries to find rules that maximize $C_q(R)$ by generalizing the condition part of the starting rule R_{init}. According to the GA principles (Holland 1975), this process uses a population P of rules to perform a probabilistic parallel search in the rule space. The search process generates rules using genetic operators, which here are based on generalization. The population P is initially empty and has a maximum size of 50 rules. The search process is the following one:

1. Let $P = \emptyset$,

2. Generate one or two rules by choosing an operator to apply among:

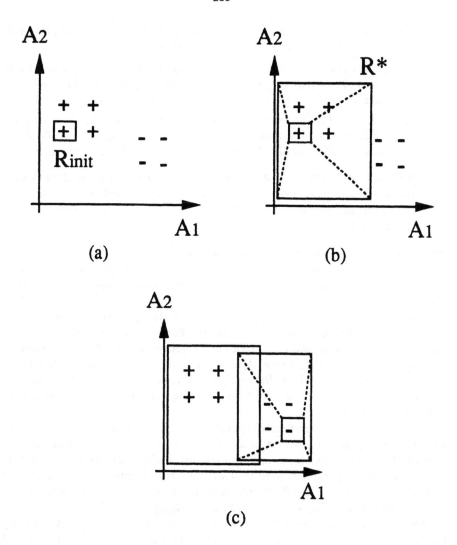

Figure 1: (a) SIA chooses an initial example of class "+", and (b) generalizes R_{init} to find R^*. Then (c), it starts on again with another uncovered example of class "-".

(a) creation (probability of 10 %): generalize R_{init} into an offspring rule R'. Evaluate $C_q(R')$. Apply the insertion operator to R'.

(b) generalization (80 %): select randomly one rule R in P and generalize its condition part to generate R'. Evaluate $C_q(R')$. If $C_q(R') > C_q(R)$ then R' replaces R in P, else apply the insertion operator to R'.

(c) crossover (10 %): select randomly two rules R_1 and R_2 in P. Apply a uniform crossover operator to obtain two offsprings R'_1 and R'_2. Evaluate $C_q(R'_1)$ and $C_q(R'_2)$, and apply to them the insertion operator.

3. Termination criterion: if step 2 has been repeated for more than Nb_{max} times without generating a better rule R' than the best rule in $P \cup R_{init}$, then Stop and output the rule(s) R^* of $P \cup R_{init}$ that maximize(s) $C_q(R)$, else go to 2.

where Nb_{max} is given by the domain expert or user.

The creation operator (point 2a) introduces new start points in the search space and is applied with a probability greater than 10% at the beginning of the search.

The generalization operator (point 2b and partially in 2a) generalizes randomly some conditions of a selected rule R. For instance, a condition "$A_i = value$", where A_i is a symbolic attribute, is generalized to "$\star$". A condition "$B_k \leq A_i \leq B_l$", $k < l$, where A_i is a numerical attribute is generalized to "$B_{k-k'} \leq A_i \leq B_{l+l'}$" where $B_{k-k'}, B_{l+l'} \in B_i$, or can also be generalized to "$\star$". R' may replace R in order to avoid following too many times the same path in the search space.

The uniform crossover operator (point 2c) exchanges conditions between two selected rule R_1 and R_2, with a probability $p_c = 0.5$, which generates two offsprings. The aim of the crossover is to exchange building blocks between rules.

The insertion operator is used to insert an offspring rule R' in P: if $R' \in P$ then R' is not inserted. If $|P| < 50$ then R' is added to P, else R' replaces the lowest strength rule R_{low} in P if $C_q(R') > C_q(R_{low})$.

This optimization process stops when no better rules where generated during the last Nb_{max} rule generations. It may find multiple (and different) optimal rules because SIA has no way to choose between several optimal rules (unless the expert gives a more precise criterion). The search may be intensive if Nb_{max} is high. Generated rules always match the seed example ex and have the same conclusion part as R_{init}.

Rule Evaluation Criterion C_q. Each rule R is assigned a quality or strength value $C_q(R)$ which evaluates R quality in the following way:

$$\begin{cases} C_q(R) = \frac{c - \alpha nc + \beta g}{csize} \\ C_q(R) \geq 0 \end{cases}$$

where $\alpha \geq 0$, $\beta = 0 \, or - 0.001 \, or + 0.001$ and where

- c is the total weight of the examples that R classifies correctly,

- nc is the total weight of the examples that R misclassifies,

- g is an abstract measure of R generality, which takes values between 0 and 1: 0 means that R is very specific, 1 that R is very general. Intermediate values of g are computed by measuring the proportion of attributes not taken into account in R condition part,

- $csize$ is the total weight of the examples in Ex that belong to class C_i (the concept total weight or size).

The strength of a rule is high if this rule classifies correctly many examples and misclassifies as few examples as possible.

This evaluation criterion has several interesting properties:

1. it ensures the expert that learned rules accuracies ($\frac{c}{c+nc}$), if there are no missing values introducing irreductible errors, is above $\frac{\alpha}{1+\alpha}$. A short proof of this is the following one: the rule R_{init} has a strength above 0 because it classifies (correctly) one example only. Thus, succeeding optimal rules will have a strength above $C_q(R_{init})$, and also greater than 0. This implies, as β is chosen small enough so that βg is negligible compared to $c - \alpha nc$, that these rules will verify $c - \alpha nc \geq 0$, which can be rewritten as follows:

$$Accuracy(R) = \frac{c}{c+nc} \geq \frac{\alpha}{1+\alpha}$$

The domain expert can thus ask SIA for consistent rules ($\alpha > |Ex|$), or relax this constraint by asking for rules with, for instance, a minimum of 98% accuracy (with $\alpha = 50$). To deal efficiently with noise and find a good value for α, the expert should have a rough idea of the noise percentage in its data.

2. it can guide the search process either towards specific or general rules expressions with $\beta = -0.001$ or $\beta = +0.001$ respectively (see figure 2). If the expert wants to favor the generality of the learned rules instead of their consistency, β can be increased, but the property described above may not hold any more.

3. it makes a difference between noise and concept boundaries : in the situation (a) of figure 3, the "-" example is considered like noise and SIA, with $\alpha = 1$ for instance, learns R_1 because $C_q(R_1) > C_q(R_2)$. In situation (b), the "-" example is not considered like noisy but like belonging to the concept boundary, and SIA learns R_1 and not R_2.

This criteria can also be customized.

SIA Versus Michigan and Pitt Approaches. Two approaches to genetic based rule learning exist, known as the Michigan and Pitt approaches. In the Pitt approach (Grefenstette 1989) (Janikow 1992), a genetic entity of the population is a rule set of N rules, which strength is a measure of the N rules performance.

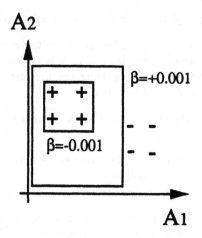

Figure 2: SIA can learn rules with most specific ($\beta = -0.001$) or most general ($\beta = +0.001$) expression.

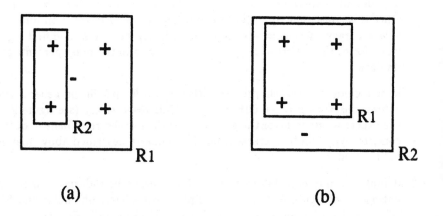

Figure 3: The rule evaluation criterion $C_q(R)$ makes a difference between noise (a) (see the position of the "-" example) and concept boundary (b). SIA learns R_1 and not R_2 (for $\alpha = 1$) in both cases.

Genetic approaches	Search space size
Pitt	$N^{k(val+1)^n}$
Michigan	$k(val+1)^n$
SIA	2^n

Table 1: Search space size for different genetic learning approaches, where N is the number of rules per entity in the Pitt approach, k the number of classes, n the number of attributes and val the number of values per attributes (for symbolic attributes and one class per example).

Thus, this approach performs a global optimization of a set of N rules, and learns a set of well co-adapted rules. However, the genetic search space is very large and the value of N must be known in advance.

In the Michigan approach, a genetic entity is one rule, and the GA searches for a subpopulation of efficient rules (Wilson 1987). The genetic search space is thus reduced.

In the SIA approach, a genetic entity is a rule, but the GA searches for one rule only among the possible generalizations of an example. Thus, in the case of supervised learning, the most positive aspect of the SIA approach, compared to the Michigan and Pitt approaches, is that it reduces drastically the genetic search space (see table 1), even if several searches must be performed if several rules are to be learned.

3.3 Rule Filtering Algorithm

This algorithm is a kind of rules postprocessing method which eliminates fastly some redundant rules in a set of rules $\mathcal{R}$. For every rule $R \in \mathcal{R}$, it computes R internal strength (Venturini 1992), denoted $strength_I(R)$, which measures how useful R is with respect to the other rules of $\mathcal{R}$. Then, rules with an internal strength below a given threshold T_{str} can be deleted:

1. Let $strength_I(R) = 0$ for all rules $R \in \mathcal{R}$,

2. For every example $ex = (e, \mathcal{C}_L, w)$ of Ex do

   (a) Let M be the set of rules that matches ex and R^* the subset of rules in M that have the highest strength $C_q(R^*)$

   (b) Let $strength_I(R) = strength_I(R) + w$ for rules R of R^*.

3. Let $strength_I(R) = \frac{strength_I(R)}{c+nc}$ for all rules R, ($c + nc$ is the total weight of the examples that R matches)

4. Remove every rule R from $\mathcal{R}$ such that $strength_I(R) \leq T_{str}$, where T_{str} is given by the expert.

If $T_{str} = 0$, $\mathcal{R}$ completeness over Ex is kept. If $T_{str} > 0$, this completeness constraint may be relaxed.

One interesting property of this algorithm is that its complexity is linear with the number of rules and examples. The experimental results of section 4 show that it reduces significantly the number of rules, and most of the time, increases the rules classification accuracy on unseen cases.

Several other methods could be used as well, like the rule elimination algorithm Quinlan uses when extracting rules from decision trees (Quinlan 1987).

3.4 Classification Procedure

The aim of the classification procedure is to decide, with a set of rules $\mathcal{R}$, to which classes a new unseen example $ex = (e, ?, w)$ belongs to.

Firstly, a rule-example distance $d(R, ex)$, similar to the one used in (Salzberg 1991), is defined in the following way

$$d(R, ex) = \frac{1}{n(R)} \sqrt{\sum_{i=1}^{n} d_i^2}$$

where:

- for a symbolic attribute A_i, $d_i = 0$ if the condition $cond_i$ of R is true for e, else $d_i = 1$,

- for a numeric attribute A_i, $d_i = 0$ if the condition $cond_i$ of R is true else:
  - if $e_i > B'$ then $d_i = \frac{e_i - B'}{max_i - min_i}$
  - else if $e_i < B$ then $d_i = \frac{B - e_i}{max_i - min_i}$

  where $cond_i = "B \leq A_i \leq B'"$, min_i and max_i are the minimum and maximum values of A_i in Ex (if $d_i > 1$ then $d_i = 1$)

- $n(R)$ is the number of conditions in R which are different than $"\star"$

If $d(R, ex) = 0$ then R matches ex (as explained in section 2.2.1), else $d(R, ex)$ computes a partial match score between R and ex.

The decision procedure computes this distance for every rules of $\mathcal{R}$. Let d_{min} be the minimal distance measured. Let R^* be the set of rules such that $d(R^*, ex) = d_{min}$ and which have the highest value of $C_q(R)$: ex belongs to the classes on which R^* rules conclude. This measure separates the example space with boundaries made of straight lines and parabols (see Salzberg work). Here, several classes can be given to an example, like "dog" and "mammal" for instance.

3.5 Complexity

Giving an interesting and useful bound for the time complexity of SIA genetic search process is difficult. The worst case analysis (for symbolic attributes and example belonging to several classes) supposes that the search process, starting from the rule R_{init}, generates the 2^n possible rules. Further more, it supposes that better rules appear only at the cycle before the deadline of Nb_{max} cycles, which give a maximum of $2^n Nb_{max}$ rule evaluations. It then supposes that a new search process starts for every example of Ex and for every classes it belongs to, which gives a worst case complexity of $2^n Nb_{max}|Ex|k$ rule evaluations, or $2^n Nb_{max}|Ex|^2 nk$ tests of the form "$A_i = value$" (where k is the number of classes, n the number of attributes).

However, for learning the $F20$ problem described in the next section with 800 examples, the worst number of rule evaluations would be 10^{12}, and in reality, SIA evaluates $1.3\,10^5$ rules which is about $7.7\,10^6$ times less.

4 Evaluations

Two evaluations have been performed with $\alpha > |Ex|$, $T_{str} = 0$, $\beta = +0.001$ (consistent, complete and most general rules), and $Nb_{max} = 600$ cycles.

4.1 Robots Domain

This learning task comes from (Wnek and Michalski 1991). It consists of learning independently five different concepts (robot descriptions) from 6 attributes taking less than 4 values each. The number of all possible robot descriptions is 432 and the concepts to be learned are described in a logic way: for instance, concept $C1$ is "head is round and jacket is red or head is square and is holding a balloon", where "head", "jacket" and "holding" are attributes. Thus, the learning task is easier for systems that learn rules described in the same language as the concept description language like AQ15, AQ17-HCI or SIA, than for systems like CFS (a classifier system), neural networks or decision trees (C4.5), which use a different representation. The experiment starts with a training set containing 6% of the whole set of positive examples and 3% of the whole set of negative examples of concept C1, and goes up to (100%,10%). This process is repeated from concept C2 to C5. SIA learns rules for the positive class only, which is an ability common to AQ15 and AQ17-HCI. The evalution procedure evaluates the learned rules with an exact error rate on the whole set of possible descriptions. Results obtained without the rule filtering algorithm are given in table 2.

SIA performances, which were averaged over five runs, are comparable to or even higher than AQ17-HCI performances for this learning task.

4.2 $F20$ Multipexor Learning Task

This task is a boolean function learning task. The first n bits of a boolean input vector are used to select one of the 2^n remaining bits of the vector. If the selected

	percentage of pos. and neg. training examples				
	(6%,3%)	(10%,10%)	(15%,10%)	(25%,10%)	(100%,10%)
CFS	21.3%	20.3%	22.5%	19.7 %	16.3%
NNets	9.7%	6.3 %	4.7 %	7.8%	4.8 %
C4.5	9.7%	8.3 %	1.3 %	2.5%	1.6 %
AQ15	22.8%	5.0 %	4.8 %	1.2%	0.0%
AQ17-HCI	4.8 %	1.2 %	0.0%	0.0%	0.0%
SIA	7.8 %	0.4 %	0.0%	0.0%	0.0%

Table 2: Robots domain: average error rate for different learning methods from (Wnek and Michalski 1991) and SIA error rate

bit equals 0 then, the vector class is 0, else it is 1. The problem studied here is $F20$ where 4 bits select one of the 16 remaining bits, for a total of 20 boolean attributes. The learning and evaluation methodologies used are the same as those used by Quinlan for C4.5 (Quinlan 1988): a training set of examples is randomly generated with a test set of 1000 unseen cases. The evaluation of the learned rules is performed with these unseen cases and all runs are repeated five times. The averaged results are reported on table 3.

Above 400 examples, SIA outperforms the decision tree algorithm, but not the rule extraction procedure associated to it. SIA learns much more rules than C4.5, firstly because, unlike C4.5, SIA learns classes 0 and 1 (which doubles at least the number of rules), and secondly because the multiplexor learning task has the characteristic that several rules with equal generality can represent the same portion of the examples space. As mentioned before, SIA discovers all possible (among the most general and consistent) concept descriptions, and the postprocessing algorithm does not eliminate all redundancy in rules, even if it may improve globally their performances. For 800 examples, SIA learned rules are comparable to the rules extracted from C4.5 decision trees. When searching for one rule (for 800 examples), SIA explores about 0.13 % of the possible 2^{20} generalizations.

However, the execution time is one hour on a Sun Sparc Elc (for 800 examples), which is certainly much longer than what C4.5 and the rule extraction procedure would need.

5 Application

SIA has been initially designed for a data analysis task in the french justice domain. A domain expert, Bruno Aubusson de Cavarlay[1], has described 1250 french justice files using 100 attributes. These files have a variable length (some

---

[1] Bruno Aubusson de Cavarlay works at the Centre de Recherches Sociologiques sur le Droit et les Institutions Pénales (CESDIP), URA 313 du CNRS, Ministère de la Justice, 4 rue de Mondonvi, 75001 Paris FRANCE

	C4.5			
	D. Trees		Rules	
# ex.	# nodes	% accu.	# rules	% accu.
200	49.0	68.8 %	8.6	69.2 %
400	95.8	82.1 %	14.4	88.0 %
600	121.0	87.4 %	16.2	97.4 %
800	171.4	92.4 %	18.4	98.3 %

	SIA			
		before filt.		After filt.
# ex.	# eval.	# rules	% accu.	# rules	% accu.
200	90000	62	60.7 %	53.6	60.4 %
400	131000	93.8	78.8 %	78.4	79.2 %
600	160000	95.2	90.8 %	73.8	91 %
800	130000	89.4	97.1 %	66.2	98.3 %

Table 3: Results for $F20$: "# ex." is the number of training examples, "% accu." is the learned rule accuracy (percentage of correctly classified unseen examples), "# eval" is the mean number of rules SIA has evaluated

attributes are undefined), because, for instance, no culprit may be found for a given file, and thus the attributes about culprits are undefined for these files. The aim of the expert is, for instance, to analyse how the french law is applied in reality (Aubusson de Cavarlay 1987a) (Aubusson de Cavarlay 1987b). Each attribute has roughly 20 values. The rule space is thus very large (at least 21^{100}). Examples are weighted to recreate the real domain probabilites. This task is currently under study and several problems appear, like for instance: some concepts are described with a very small number of examples (2 or 3 for instance) in a huge description space, or, some attributes values are redundant (they code differently the same information), which leads SIA to find rules that underline these dependancies instead of some more interesting ones.

6 Conclusion

This study has tried to show that genetic algorithms can be useful tools for supervised inductive learning. The resulting algorithm, SIA, reduces the rule search space by searching rules one at a time. It can learned rules from examples that may be described with a variable number of attributes and that may have multiple classes. SIA learning abilities are comparable to those of other heuristic based algorithms, as well as the experimental results obtained on two learning tasks. However, SIA learning times are still important compared to the decision trees or AQ based methods. SIA is currently applied to the analysis of the complex french justice domain.

The work presented here is a beginning. Many theoretical points must be studied such as incrementality, introduction of more background knowledge and learnability results. Also, further evaluations and comparisons are needed in order to evaluate all properties of SIA, like dealing with noisy data and missing values.

Acknowledgements

I would like to thank Janusz Wnek for providing robots domain data and Bruno Aubusson de Cavarlay, the french justice expert. I would also like to thank Yves Kodratoff and the Inference and Learning group for providing useful comments on this work.

References

Aubusson de Cavarlay B. (1987a), La diversité du traitement pénal, *Données sociales 19*, 589-593.

Aubusson de Cavarlay B. (1987b), *Les filières pénales*, CESDIP, Déviance et Contrôle Social 43.

Bala J., De Jong K.A. and Pachowicz P. (1991), Learning noise tolerant classification procedures by integrating inductive learning and genetic algorithms, Proceedings of the First International Workshop on Multistrategy Learning 1991, R.S. Michalski and G. Tecuci (Eds), 316-323.

Bonelli P. and Parodi A. (1991), An efficient classifier system and its experimental comparison with two representative learning methods on three medical domains, Proceedings of the Fourth International Conference on Genetic Algorithms, R.K. Belew and L.B. Booker (Eds), 288-295, Morgan Kaufmann.

De Jong K. (1988). Learning with Genetic Algorithms: An overview. Machine Learning 3, 121-138: Kluwer Academic.

De Jong K. and Spears W.M. (1991), Learning concept classification rules using genetic algorithms, Proceedings of the 12th International Joint Conference on Artificial Intelligence 1991, J. Mylopoulos and R. Reiter (Eds), 651-656, Morgan Kaufmann.

Gams M. and Lavrac N. (1987), Review of five empirical learning systems within a proposed schemata, Progress in Machine Learning, I. Bratko and N. Lavrac (Eds), 46-66, Sigma Press.

Goldberg D.E. (1989). *Genetic Algorithms in Search, Optimization and Machine Learning*: Addison Wesley.

Grefenstette J.J. (1989), A system for learning control strategies with genetic algorithms. In Proceedings of the third International Conference on Genetic Algorithms, J.D. Schaffer (Ed), 183-190, Morgan Kaufmann.

Holland J.H. (1975). *Adaptation in natural and artificial systems*. Ann Arbor: University of Michigan Press.

Janikow C.Z. (1992), Combining competition and cooperation in supervised inductive learning, Proceedings of the Ninth International Workshop on Machine Learning 1992, D. Sleeman and P. Edwards (Eds), 241-248 , Morgan Kaufmann.

Kononenko I. and Kovacic M. (1992), Learning as optimization: stochastic generation of multiple knowledge, Proceedings of the Ninth International Workshop on Machine Learning 1992, D. Sleeman and P. Edwards (Eds), 257-262 , Morgan Kaufmann.

McCallum J.H. and Spackman K.A. (1990), Using genetic algorithms to learn disjunctive rules from examples, Proceedings of the Seventh International Conference on Machine Learning 1990, B.W. Porter and R.J. Mooney (Eds.), 153-159, Morgan Kaufmann.

Michalski R.S., Mozetic I., Hong J. and Lavrac N. (1986), The multi-purpose incremental learning system AQ15 and its testing application to three medical domains, Proceedings of AAAI-86 Fifth National Conference on Artificial Intelligence, 1041-1045, Morgan Kaufmann.

Quinlan J.R. (1986), Induction of decision trees, Machine Learning 1,1.

Quinlan J.R. (1987), Generating production rules from decision trees, Proceedings of the Tenth International Joint Conference on Artificial Intelligence 1987, J. McDermott (Ed), 304-307, Morgan Kaufmann.

Quinlan J.R. (1988), An empirical comparison of genetic and decision trees classifiers, Proceedings of the Fifth International Conference on Machine Learning 1988, J. Laird (Eds), 135-141, Morgan Kaufmann.

Salzberg S. (1991), A nearest hyperrectangle learning method, Machine Learning 6, 251-276.

Vafaie H. and De Jong K. (1991), Improving the performance of a rule induction system using genetic algorithms, Proceedings of the First International Workshop on Multistrategy Learning 1991, R.S. Michalski and G. Tecuci (Eds), 305-315.

Venturini G. (1992), AGIL: solving the exploration versus exploitation dilemma in a simple classifier system applied to simulated robotics, Proceedings of the Ninth International Workshop on Machine Learning 1992, D. Sleeman and P. Edwards (Eds), 458-463 , Morgan Kaufmann.

Weinberg J.B., Biswas G. and Koller G.R. (1992), Conceptual clustering with systematic missing values, Proceedings of the Ninth International Workshop on Machine Learning 1992, D. Sleeman and P. Edwards (Eds), 464-469, Morgan Kaufmann.

Wilson S.W. (1987), Quasi-Darwinian Learning in a Classifier System, Proceeding of the Fourth International Workshop on Machine Learning 1987, P. Langley (Ed), 59-65, Morgan Kaufmann.

Wnek J. and Michalski R.S. (1991), An experimental comparison of symbolic and subsymbolic learning paradigms: phase I - learning logic-style concepts, Proceedings of the First International Workshop on Multistrategy Learning 1991, R.S. Michalski and G. Tecuci (Eds), 324-339.

SAMIA : A BOTTOM-UP LEARNING METHOD USING A SIMULATED ANNEALING ALGORITHM

Pierre Brézellec & Henri Soldano

LIPN (CNRS/URA 1507) Université Paris Nord
Avenue Jean-Baptiste Clément 93430 Villetaneuse
e-mail : brezel@lipn.univ-paris13.fr

&

Institut Curie, section Physique-Chimie, A.B.I
11, rue Pierre et Marie Curie 75005 Paris.

Abstract. This paper presents a description and an experimental evaluation of SAMIA, a learning system which induces characteristic concept descriptions from positive instances, negative instances and a background knowledge theory. The resulting concept description is expressed as a disjunction of conjunctive terms in a propositional language. SAMIA works in three steps. The first step consists in an exhaustive use of the theory in order to extend the instances representation. Then the learning component combines a bottom-up induction process and a simulated annealing strategy which performs a search through the concept description space. During the final step, the theory is used again in order to reduce each conjunctive term of the resulting formula to a minimal representation. The paper reports the results of several experiments and compares the performance of SAMIA with two other learning methods, namely ID and CN. Accuracies on test instances and concept description sizes are compared. The experiments indicate that SAMIA's classification accuracy is roughly equivalent to the two previous systems. Morever, as the results of the learning algorithms can be expressed as a set of rules, one can notice that the number of rules of SAMIA's concept descriptions is lower than both ID's and CN's one.

Keywords. Bottom-Up Algorithms, Characteristic Descriptions, Concept Learning, Simulated Annealing.

I Introduction

During the past few years various systems have been proposed to perform concept learning from examples in the following situation : The goal is to learn concept representations allowing an accurate classification of test sets of objects in two or more classes - Object representation is at propositional level, consisting generally in an attribute-value list - Various kinds of noise can corrupt the data, such as misclassification of examples and random errors on attribute values of examples ; such types of noise are viewed as simple models for difficulties encountered in natural domain learning problems - Concept representations searched for are supposed to be disjunctive ones , i.e., constituted of several conjunctive terms - Both learning set size and object description size can be large.

These systems perform a partial exploration of the concept space to be searched, using various heuristics and some statistical criteria (CN2 [Clark & Niblett 89], ID3 [Quinlan 86]) or truncation and flexible matching (AQ [Zhang & Michalski 89]). The concept representations used are either decision trees (ID3), decision lists (CN2) or disjunctive formulas (AQ). The search is performed by a top-down generate and test procedure (though AQ uses a data-driven mixed strategy) using specialization operators. For this class of learning problems, little attention has been paid to bottom-up strategies which were considered as inefficient. However, bottom-up techniques have been previously applied to other learning problems concerning noncorrupted data, conjunctive concept representation and first-order object representation ([Mitchell 82], [Kodratoff & Ganascia 86], [Bisson 92]). In bottom-up methods, the concept representation space is generally restricted to particular conjunctive terms. More precisely, given a concept C and a set of positive instances of C, a conjunctive term may appear in a formula only if it is obtained by maximal specific generalization of a subset of the positive instances.

The system we propose here is devoted to concept acquisition from positive and negative instances. It describes instances as conjunctions of literals and uses a theory composed of a set of production rules. The theory is used during a preprocessing step in order to extend the description of instances. During the learning step a disjunctive formula is searched for using a simulated annealing optimization procedure. A postprocessing step is then performed in order to obtain minimal representations of the conjunctive terms of the formula. This formula is a characteristic representation of the concept (and not a discriminant one as in top-down methods previously mentioned).

Section 2 presents knowledge representation, properties of the concept representation space, the preprocessing and postprocessing steps and some issues about the learning bias. Section 3 is devoted to the learning component and its simulated annealing algorithm. Section 4 presents experiments on one artificial domain and two natural domains in which SAMIA is compared to CN and ID. The section 5 reviews related works. The paper ends with a summary and outline of our projects.

II   Presentation of the System

Let A be the set of atoms of a given propositional language. A is divided into a set P of primitive atoms and a set S of non primitive atoms. Moreover a theory T is given expressed as an unordered set of rules. The left part of each rule is a conjunction of literals of A, and the right part (i.e., the conclusion) is a literal of A. As usual, an instance is defined by the assignation of the values True or False to every atom of A. However each instance is initially described as the conjunction of the corresponding literals of P. The first step of the overall learning mechanism consists of a saturation of every instance with respect to the theory T. After the preprocessing step, each instance is represented as the conjunction of the positive literals, where a positive literal is a primitive or a non primitive atom whose value is True. Then, the second step consists in searching for a concept representation f from a set E_p of positive instances and a set E_n of negative instances. Each element of the search space is a disjunction of conjunctive terms. However only particular conjunctive terms, hereafter denoted as prototypes, are considered. Such terms are maximal specific generalizations of subsets of the set E_p of positive instances. In our framework prototypes are recursively defined by an instance or the result of the maximal specific generalization (msg for short) of two prototypes using an intersection operator msg. Let e_1 and e_2

be two prototypes, then $msg(e_1,e_2)$ is defined as the conjunction of positive literals[1] belonging to both e_1 and e_2. The justification of the restriction of conjunctive terms to maximal specific generalizations relies on the following property :

Proposition 1 : For any term t (i.e., any conjunction of positive literals of A), there exists a prototype p such that p covers[2] exactly the positive instances covered by t and a subset of the negatives instances covered by t.

The prototype p is simply the maximal specific generalization of the positive instances covered by t, and thus is more specific than t. This prototype space, together with the general-to-specific partial ordering, defines a "Galois lattice" (E_p, A) (Algebraic structure [Ganter, Rindefrey & Skorsky 86]). Another useful property of the prototypes is related to the logical dependencies between atoms. Such relations may be either explicit ones (i.e., represented inside the theory T) or implicit ones.

Proposition 2 : Let a_1 ,..., a_k be atoms of A, and assume that the following implication '$a_1 \wedge ... \wedge a_{k-1} ---> a_k$' holds for a subset E of the positive instances. Then if a prototype, resulting from the maximal specific generalization of a subset of E, contains a_1 ,..., a_{k-1}, then it contains a_k.

Notice that if $E = E_p$, then a_k belongs to any prototype containing a_1 ,..., a_{k-1}. As a consequence of the last proposition, we have the following corollary :

Corollary : Let us consider a rule of T containing only positive literals. If the left part of this rule belongs to a given prototype, then its conclusion also belongs to it.

The property described by the last corollary is the basis of the last step of the learning mechanism. Let f be the formula resulting from the search through the concept representation space. During the postprocessing step, each prototype p of f is rewritten as a conjunctive term with a minimum size and logically equivalent to p. This is simply performed by removing from p every atom which is logically deduced from other atoms of p and rules of the theory. This process has been designed for theories seen as acyclic AND/OR graphs as in [Drastal, Czako & Raatz 89]. A simple example is used in order to illustrate the whole learning mechanism :

Example :

P={triangle, square, circle, color_black, color_red},

S={polygon, ellipse},

T={triangle --> polygon, square --> polygon, circle --> ellipse}

E_p={i_1=(triangle, color_red), i_2=(square, color_red), i_3=(square, color_black)}

E_n is not represented here.

1. Preprocessing step : Both positive and negative instances are extended. E_p={i_1=(triangle, polygon, color_red),i_2=(square, polygon, color_red),i_3=(square, polygon, color_black)}.

2. Searching for a concept representation : Let us suppose that the result f is as follows : f=$e_1 \vee e_2$, e_1=$msg(i_1,i_2)$ = (polygon, color_red), e_2=$msg(i_2,i_3)$ = (square, polygon).

---

[1]We will give hereafter a detailed explanation of why negative literals are not allowed in generalizations (It is related to the flexibility of the concept representation).

[2]A prototype p covers an instance e iff $e \supseteq p$ (i.e., p is more general than e).

3. Postprocessing step : Prototypes are reduced to a minimal form. "e_1" is unchanged, but 'polygon' is removed from e_2 since 'polygon' follows from 'square' and 'square --> polygon'. So, we obtain : f = (polygon, color_red) ∨ (square).

Finally, let us remark that when a new instance is processed for a classification purpose, the instance has to be preprocessed in order to be described using the whole language, before it is compared to the prototypes. Another way to check that a prototype p covers an instance e is to use the initial description of e together with the theory, and to make attempts to prove p.

Negative literals, inductive bias and general attribute-value representation.

In concept learning problems instances are often represented as attribute-value lists such that for each attribute corresponds a value domain D. Various types of attributes are defined, each corresponding to a particular structure of D [Michalsky 84]. Thus for some element of the concept representation space, a given attribute is constrained to a subset of D. The space of allowed constraints on D is usually defined through a generalization operator and represents a form of inductive bias. In our framework each attribute is associated with a set of atoms each corresponding to some subset of D. Then the space of constraints is defined as the space of conjunctions of atomic constraints. As a first example we will consider a non structured value domain D. In this case, when no bias is defined, any subset of D is allowed as a constraint and each value x of D is associated with an atom X representing the subset D-{x}. Such a representation is a minimal coding of the attribute and has been used in our experiments on natural domain problems with D={A,T,G,C} (cf section 4.2 and 4.3). Negative literals are clearly useless here. Moreover some restricted constraint spaces cannot be defined when negative literals are allowed. As an example let us suppose that the user defines a constraint space reduced to the simple subset {A,T}. Then allowing negative literals forces us to add {G,C} to the constraints space. A second example is boolean functions learning. Here negative literals are necessary, so they are explicitly represented as new atoms of A. The 11-multiplexer function has been processed this way, using a language containing 22 atoms (cf section 4.1). Considering now structured attributes, the structure may be represented as a part of the theory T. This has been shortly exemplified before in the case of a hierarchy. Here again the restriction to positive literals allows more flexibility in defining the constraints space : as an example let us suppose a shape attribute whose value domain D is structured as follows :

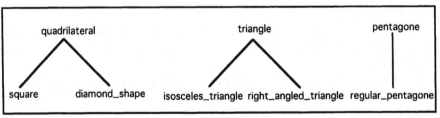

Here the theory is represented as a set of rules. If the negative literals are not allowed, the theory may be restricted to a set of rules 'x --> y' where x is a node of the hierarchy and y is its parent node. However, if negative literals are allowed, the rules that correspond to the contrapositive (i.e. '¬y --> ¬x' rules) must be added to the theory, together with rules that link roots of the hierarchy as 'quadrilateral -->

¬pentagone' and rules expressing constraints as '¬square ∧ ¬diamond_shape -->
¬quadrilateral'.

Now, let us consider the generalization of the pair of instances ((isosceles_triangle),
(square)). When no new atoms are added, the generalization leads to the *null*
prototype. This corresponds to the usual bias on hierarchies [Michalski 84]. On the
other hand, if all negative literals are represented as new atoms, after preprocessing
msg returns (not_diamond_shape, not_right_angled_triangle, not_regular_pentagone,
not_pentagone) which is reduced after the postprocessing step to (not_diamond_shape,
not_right_angled_triangle, not_pentagone). A third bias may be considered here by
only adding new atoms that correspond to the negation of atoms which are not leaves
of the hierarchy. In this case the whole process leads to the prototype
(not_pentagone).

Finally defining prototypes as conjunction of positive literals, adding negative literals
as new atoms when necessary, and using a theory in order to extend the language,
allows a user-defined flexible handling of inductive bias (it has been shown here for
the general attribute-value representation case). Furthermore it should be pointed out
that the *msg* operator clearly has linear computational complexity relatively to the
size of the language A. As a consequence the size of the language may be as large as
necessary.

III   The Learning Component

Simulated Annealing is a method which was proved to be useful in the search of near-
optimal solutions for NP-complete optimization problems [Collins, Eglese & Golden
88]. This method performs a search for the optimum state of a system according to a
given cost function referred to as the energy of the system. A move modifies the
current state and then the variation of energy of the system is evaluated. If the move
decreases the energy of the system, the new state becomes the current state as in hill-
climbing methods ; on the other hand, if the move increases the energy of the system,
the new state may become the current state with a probability which depends on the
value of a control parameter, denoted as temperature, which decreases slowly during
the search.

More precisely, let E be a finite space of states, H a cost function of states whose
values are positive real numbers, T the temperature, S and S' states of E. Then, our
version of the basic sequential simulated annealing algorithm is as follows :

```
Basic Sequential Simulated Annealing Algorithm
1. S <-- compute an arbitrary initial state
2. T <-- choose the initial temperature
3. Repeat N times
            3.1. Repeat L times
                    3.1.1. Compute at random a neighboring state S' of S
                    3.1.2. ΔH <-- H(S')-H(S)
                    3.1.3. If ΔH≤0 then S  <-- S'
                    3.1.4. If ΔH>0 ther S  <-- S' with a probability e^(-ΔH/T)
            3.2. Let T decrease as T <-- a * T
4. Return S.
```

The learning component of SAMIA performs a bottom-up search defined as follows :

E is the space of disjunctive formulas whose conjunctive terms are prototypes. A state S of E is a disjunction of at most NTMAX[3] terms.

H(S), which represents the cost of a state S of E, is defined as the probability of misclassification, and is estimated using examples and counter-examples :

$$H(S) = p_{ex} * \frac{\Sigma errors_{ex}}{|Ex|} + p_{cex} * \frac{\Sigma errors_{cex}}{|Cex|}$$

where,

• p_{ex} (resp. p_{cex}) is the probability of a given object to be a positive instance (resp. negative instance) of the concept,

• $\Sigma errors_{ex}$ is the number of positive instances not covered by S,

• $\Sigma errors_{cex}$ is the number of negative instances covered by S.

When p_{ex} and p_{cex} are defined as the proportions of positive and negative instances used for learning, we have :

H(S) = 1 - Accuracy(S)

where Accuracy is defined as usual (cf section 4).

The initial value of the state S is a disjunctive formula of NTI[4] terms. NTI is strictly greater than 1 and lower or equal to NTMAX. The terms of the initial state are randomly selected positive instances.

A neighbor S' of a state S results from the application of a randomly selected operator to S. Let n be the number of terms of S. Then the operators used here are defined as follows :

1°) *Extension operator* : If n is strictly lower than NTMAX, the *extension operator* appends a new term to S ; this term is a randomly selected positive instance,

2°) *Contraction operator* : The contraction operator removes a randomly selected term from S,

3°) *Generalization operator* : The *generalization operator* randomly selects a term t of S and performs the maximal specific generalization of t with a randomly selected positive instance e. If the resulting term *msg*(t,e) covers a ratio of negative instances smaller than a consistency threshold value PCEX[5], then a new state is generated by replacing the term t by *msg*(t,e). Checking consistency of the new term is useful since no specialization operator is available.

Finally, before returning the result S, SAMIA discards each term more specific than at least one other term. This step eliminates redundancies.

Before describing the experiments, we give below an example of a curve which shows the behavior of SAMIA (i.e., its accuracy on the learning set) with respect to N (i.e., the number of iterations, here set up to 2600) during the learning step of the concept "11-multiplexer" :

---

[3]NTMAX is a user parameter.

[4]NTI is a user parameter.

[5]PCEX is a user parameter.

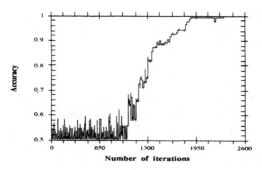

Number of iterations

IV Experiments

The learning component of SAMIA together with ID and CN[6] have been tested on one artificial domain problem, the 11-multiplexer problem, and two natural domain problems issued from DNA sequence analysis (learning of promoters and 5'-splice sites). This twofold evaluation is motivated by considering that 1) Artificial domains let us control the environment of the experiments. Thus, it is easy to introduce varying degrees of corruption of attributes values or of class membership values, 2) Generally, in natural domain such as experimental data classification or pattern recognition problems, neither the relevant object description nor the proper form of an accurate concept description are known.

Two aspects of the algorithms' behavior have been used to assess them :

1°) *Classification accuracy* : Given a set of instances where true classification is known, the accuracy of a concept description is the estimated percentage of correct classification (i.e., ACC is the number of correct classifications divided by the number of instances tested).

2°) *Syntactic complexity of the concept representations [Zhang & Michalski 89]* : SAMIA, ID and CN have different concept description languages. These are the Disjunctive Formulas, Decision Trees, and Decision Lists. The syntactic complexity of the descriptions are computed as follows :

-The syntactic complexity of a disjunctive formula is NT*ANS where NT is the number of terms of the disjunctive formula and ANS is the average number of literals in the conjunctive terms,

-The syntactic complexity of a decision tree is NN where NN is the number of its nodes (including leaves) ; NL is the number of the leaves of the decision tree,

-The syntactic complexity of a decision list is NR*ANS where NR is the number of rules of the decision list and ANS is the average number of selectors in the rules.

We enumerate below ID's (with and without pruning), CN's and SAMIA's user-variable parameters which are used in our experiments.

-ID without pruning (see [Quinlan 86]) : Prune threshold=0%, Variance termination threshold=10%,

-ID with pruning : Prune threshold=10%, Variance termination threshold=10%,

---

[6]ID and CN [Boswell 90ab] are respectively Boswell's implementations of the ID3 [Quinlan 86] and CN2 [Clark & Niblett 89] algorithms.

-CN (see [Clark & Niblett 89]) : Threshold of significance=1, Star size=5,
-SAMIA : N=2600, L=8, a=0.996, NTMAX=20, NTI=2, PCEX=0.02, except in the
"5'-splice" sites problem where it is set up to 0.0.

4.1 The 11-multiplexer Problem

The 11-multiplexer boolean function has often been used to evaluate learning methods
([Wilson 87], [Quinlan 88], [Van de Velde 89], [Zhang & Michalski 89]). Each object
is a boolean vector divided into 3 address bits and 2^3 data bits. An object is a positive
instance of the 11-multiplexer function if the data bit whose index in the vector
corresponds to the address bits has value 1. The 11-multiplexer function can be
represented as a normal disjunctive form (8 terms of 4 literals each (i.e., $(x_1=0 \wedge$
$x_2=0 \wedge x_3=0 \wedge x_4=1) \vee ... \vee (x_1=1 \wedge x_2=1 \wedge x_3=1 \wedge x_{11}=1)))$.

In order to evaluate SAMIA, ID and CN in noisy environments, two kinds of noise
have been introduced :

1°) *Noise of level n on class membership values* : n percent of the positive instances
and n percent of the negative instances are randomly selected ; then, the value of the
class of each selected instance is modified.

2°) *Noise of level n on attribute values* : n percent of the positive instances and n
percent of the negative instances are randomly selected ; then, the value of a randomly
chosen attribute of each selected instance is modified.

The instances of the test sets are not corrupted ([Clark & Niblett 89], [Rendell & Cho
90]).

The experimental design is defined as follows :

Step-1 : Random selection of 200 positive learning instances and 200 negative
learning instances of the 11-multiplexer function.

Step-2 : Corruption of the learning sets according to the kind and level of noise.

Step-3 : Learning using SAMIA, ID (with and without pruning) and CN.

Step-4 : Classification of test instances (the 1648 positive and negative instances left
out in step 1).

This procedure is repeated 40 times.

Table 1 presents the results of each algorithm for varying degrees of corruption of
class membership values (the attribute value corruption level is 0). In each case, we
present the average accuracy on the test data and the average syntactic complexity of
the resulting concept descriptions.

| table 1 |

class error	SAMIA PCEX 0.02			ID with pruning			ID without pruning			CN		
	ACC	NT	ANS	ACC	NL	NN	ACC	NL	NN	ACC	NR	ANS
0	0.959	11.5	4.3	0.921	83.8	166.7	0.904	78.3	155.7	0.986	18.7	2.8
5	0.907	16.9	4.9	0.841	119.6	238.3	0.84	104	207.4	0.873	41.4	3.4
10	0.809	19.3	4.9	0.762	145.5	290	0.77	132.6	264.3	0.79	51.8	3.6
15	0.765	19.4	5	0.725	167.3	333.6	0.733	154.7	308.5	0.742	59.2	3.8
20	0.702	19.8	5	0.678	183.7	366.4	0.685	174.4	347.9	0.695	65.5	3.9

Table 2 presents the results of each algorithm for varying degrees of corruption of attribute values (class membership corruption level is 0).

table 2

attribute error	SAMIA PCEX 0.02			ID without pruning			ID with pruning			CN		
	ACC	NT	ANS	ACC	NL	NN	ACC	NL	NN	ACC	NR	ANS
5	0.95	12.9	4.6	0.883	97.5	194	0.87	85.8	170.6	0.959	25.2	2.8
10	0.939	13.9	4.6	0.866	108.4	215.9	0.86	93	185	0.933	31.3	2.9
15	0.917	15.7	4.8	0.869	103.8	206.7	0.873	81.9	163	0.898	37.7	3.2
20	0.929	15.8	5	0.838	112.7	224.4	0.841	85.4	170.3	0.883	39.3	3.4

4.2   The "Promoter" Problem

The genome of the Prokaryotes, i.e., bacteria for instance, can be considered as a string which is composed of coding regions -i.e., genes- and non coding regions. A promoter is a particular region which initiates the first step in the expression of an adjacent gene. The set of positive and negative instances of promoters of the Escherichia Coli bacteria that we use in our experiment is described in [Towell, Shavlik & Noordewier 90]. It contains 53 positive instances and 53 negative instances. Each instance is composed of 57 attribute-value pairs whose value domains are {A,T,G,C}. A standard leave-one-out method has been used in this experiment. Let N be the total number of instances, then the training is performed using N-1 instances, and the remaining instance is classified. This procedure is repeated N times, so that each instance is excluded once from the training set. The whole procedure was repeated 10 times for SAMIA whose results are non-deterministic, and an average accuracy was computed.

Table 3 summarizes the experimental results.

table 3

promoter problem	SAMIA PCEX 0.02			ID without pruning			ID with pruning			CN		
	ACC	NT	ANS	ACC	NL	NN	ACC	NL	NN	ACC	NR	ANS
	0.814	3.6	10.92	0.773	30.9	40.8	0.792	24.8	32.7	0.83	9.1	1.2

In this problem, as in the next one, in order to allow fair comparison of syntactic complexities, SAMIA's prototypes are translated from the propositional language to constraints on the value domain of the attributes. Then a prototype is a conjunction of constraints ($a_i \in S_i$), where S_i denotes a subset of {A,T,G,C}, and a_i the ith attribute. Comparison with ID is still unfair since each node is associated with four possible outcomes, namely {A}, {T}, {G}, {C}.

4.3 The "5'-splice site" Problem

The genes of the Eukaryotes (i.e humans and leeks for instance) are split. Thus, these genes are composed of coding regions -called exons- and non coding regions -called introns-. A "5'-splice site" is a region that directs the excision of the introns [Brunak,

Engelbrecht & Knudsen 91]. The training set used here contains 302 positive instances and 600 negative instances of 5'-splice sites. A test set containing 118 positive instances and 600 negative instances is also provided. Each instance is described using 18 attribute-value pairs whose value domains are {A,T,G,C}. The procedure is repeated 40 times for SAMIA.

Table 4 summarizes the experimental results.

table 4

5'-splice site problem	SAMIA PCEX 0.0			ID without pruning			ID with pruning			CN		
	ACC	NT	ANS	ACC	NL	NN	ACC	NL	NN	ACC	NR	ANS
	0.88	19.8	12.4	0.84	214	285	0.89	89	121	0.88	64	2.3

4.4 Discussion

The first comment is that, roughly speaking, the accuracies of the three systems are equivalent. This is interesting since the three problems are very different. The concept representation space of the 11-multiplexer is rather small and the concept is highly disjunctive. Many useless attributes are used to describe the promoter problem and few instances are provided. "5'-splice sites" are described with a relatively small number of attributes and many instances are provided. Comparing the sizes of the concept representation learned by the three systems, it should be noticed that SAMIA produces less rules ; in the case of the noise free 11-multiplexer problem SAMIA is closed to the optimal solution regarding both the number of rules and the average rule length. Moreover, it should be pointed out that SAMIA seems to slightly better handle misclassification noise. Concerning the two other experiments, full comparison of syntactic complexities is difficult. However, the average number of components in SAMIA's rules is larger than CN's one. This is not surprising since SAMIA searches for characteristic concept descriptions.

Finally, the table bellow reports the average elapsed cpu time (seconds), during learning[7] :

cpu time	11-multi.	Promoter	5'-splices
ID	1.92	2	4
CN	20	90	101
SAMIA	350	433	1922

The run times reveal that SAMIA is the slowest of the three algorithms. This is mainly due to the simulated annealing search strategy that requires more computation time to solve complex problems. However, a large research effort focuses on parallel implementations of this strategy [Roussel-Ragot 90].

---

[7]SAMIA, ID, and CN were run on a SUN/Sparc 1.

V Related Works

Concerning the concept representation space, our approach is close to the work of [Kudo & Shimbo 89]. In this work the authors search for all maximal subsets of the positive instances whose maximal specific generalizations cover no negative instances. Their algorithm seems efficient but still has exponential complexity with the number of positive instances since it performs an exhaustive search. In another related work, learning is performed by constructing a Gallois lattice [Liquière & Méphu Nguifo 90]. The construction is only partial thanks to the use of a consistency criterion. As a matter of fact the nodes of the lattice represent prototypes as defined here. Unfortunately, here again exhaustive search leads to intractable computational complexity. From this point of view the simulated annealing strategy seems to limite the following shortcoming of bottom-up methods : although the concept representation space is restricted, the space which is practically searched may be much larger, since search is performed in a space whose elements are subsets of instances. Finally, one can note that the redundancies of the description language, which are unavoidable when using background knowledge in order to perform an exhaustive deductive step, have only limited effect in such methods, since the computational complexity of the generalization operator is linear with the size of the language.

Concerning the use of background knowledge, and the control of learning bias, full evaluation of our method has not yet been performed. In the future, we intend to compare our system to MIRO [Drastal, Czako & Raatz 89] in which the theory is used to move the description language toward a more abstract one, rather than extending the language as it is done here.

VI   Conclusion

The most significant aspects of our method is that 1) it combines a bottom-up approach and simulated annealing search strategy, 2) it uses background knowledge in a preprocessing level in order to extend instance description as do various other learning systems ([Rouveirol 90], [Brézellec & Champesme 91], [Bisson 92]), 3) it uses background knowledge in a postprocessing level in order to obtain a minimal representation of the conjunctive terms of the concept description.

The experiments we have conducted show that ID, CN and SAMIA have comparable performance. Moreover, since SAMIA's $smsg$ operator has linear computational complexity relatively to the size of the language, we think that it will be well suited to situations in which an exhaustive deductive step is applied to the learning instances.

At present, we plan to add other operators to SAMIA. For instance, we think that an operator that will undo a generalization step is necessary to improve SAMIA's efficiency. Indeed, such an operator will decrease the "gap" between a state and its neighborhood, and therefore the search space will be "smoother".

Finally, we intend to examine other optimization algorithms ("Taboo search" for instance) and their relations to learning. As in this work, it will require some ideas to fit a learning problem to an optimization one.

Acknowledgments

We thank the LRI of Orsay (France) for giving us ID and CN, and the "UCI Repository Of Machine Learning Databases and Domain Theories" for supplying the "promoter" data set. Special thanks go to Alain Viari (Institut Curie/CNRS) for his invaluable assistance in understanding the two biological problems and to Alex Simionovici for correcting various syntactical english errors of our paper. This work has been supported by a grant from ORGANIBIO (Cm2aO program).

References

[Bisson 92] Gilles Bisson, "Conceptual Clustering in a First Order Logic Representation", Tenth European Conference on Artificial Intelligence, Vienna 92, Bernd Neumann, pp 458-468.

[Boswell 90a] J. Boswell, "Manual for NewID version 2.1", The Turing Institute, January 1990.

[Boswell 90b] J. Boswell, "Manual for CN2", The Turing Institute, January 1990.

[Brunak, Engelbrecht & Knudsen 91] Soren Brunak, Jacob Engelbrecht, Steen Knudsen, "Prediction of Human mRNA Donor and Acceptor Sites from the DNA Sequence", Journal of Molecular Biology (n° 220, 1991), pp 49-65.

[Brézellec & Champesme 92] Pierre Brézellec, Marc Champesme, "Vers un système d'apprentissage moins sensible au bruit, et aux descriptions et théories initiales", Huitième Congrès Reconnaissance des Formes et Intelligence Artificielle, Lyon-Villeurbanne 91, pp 945-952.

[Collins, Eglese & Golden 88] N.E. Collins, R.W. Eglese, B.L. Golden, "Simulated annealing - An annotated bibliography", American journal of mathematical and management sciences 8, pp 209-307.

[Clark & Niblett 89] Peter Clark, Tim Niblett, "The CN2 Induction Algorithm", Machine Learning (volume 3, number 4, March 89), Kluwer Academic Publishers, pp 261-283.

[Drastal, Czako & Raatz 89] G. Drastal, R. Czako, S. Raatz, "Induction in an abstraction space : A form of constructive induction", Proceedings of the Eleventh International Joint Conference on Artificial Intelligence, Detroit 89, Morgan Kaufmann, pp 708-712.

[4] Ganter B., Rindefrey K., Skorsky M. "Software for a formal concept analysis", Classification as a tool of Research, North Holland 1986.

[Liquière & Méphu Nguifo 90] Michel Liquière, Engelbert Méphu Nguifo, "LEarning with GAlois Lattice : Un système d'apprentissage de concepts à partir d'exemples", Cinquièmes Journées Françaises d'Apprentissage, Lanion 90, pp 93-113.

[Kodratoff & Ganascia 86] Yves Kodratoff, Jean-Gabriel Ganascia, "Improving the generalization step in Learning", Machine Learning, An Artificial Approach (volume II), Morgan Kaufman (1986), pp 215-244.

[Kudo & Shimbo 89] Mineichi Kudo, Masaru Shimbo, "Optimal subclasses with dichotomous variables for features selection and discirmination", IEEE Trans. Systems, Man, Cybern., 19, pp 1194-1199.

[Michalski 84] R.S. Michalski, "A Theory and Methodology of Inductive Learning", Machine Learning : An Artificial Approach (volume I), Springer Verlag (1984), pp 83-129.

[Michalski & al 86] Ryszard S. Michalski, Igor Mozetic, Jiarong Hong, Nada Lavrac, "The multi-purpose incremental learning system AQ15 and its testing application to three medical domains", Proceedings of the Fifth National Conference on Artificial Intelligence, Morgan Kaufman, pp 1041-1045.

[Quinlan 86] J.R. Quinlan, "Induction of Decision Trees", Machine Learning (volume 1, number 1, 1986), Kluwer Academic Publishers, pp 81-106.

[Quinlan 88] J.R. Quinlan, "An Empirical Comparison of Genetic and Decision-Tree Classifier", Proceedings of the Fifth International Conference on Machine Learning, Ann Arbor 88, pp 135-141.

[Rendell & Cho 90] Larry Rendell, Howard Cho, "Empirical Learning as a Function of Concept Character", Machine Learning (volume 5, number 3, August 90), Kluwer Academic Publishers, pp 267-298.

[Roussel-Ragot 90] P. Rousel-Ragot, "La méthode du recuit simulé : Accélération et parallélisation", Thèse de doctorat de l'Université Paris 6.

[Rouveirol 90] Celine Rouveirol, "Saturation : Postponing Choices when Inverting Resolution", Seventh International Conference on Machine Learning, Austin 90, pp 557-562.

[Towell, Shavlik & Noordewier 90] Geoffrey G. Towell, Jude W. Shavlik, Michiel O. Noordewier, "Refinement of Approximate Domains Theories by Knowledge-Based Neural Networks", AAAI 90, pp 861-866.

[Van de Velde 89] Walter Van de Velde, "IDL, or Taming the Multiplexer", Proceedings of the Fourth European Working Session on Learning, Montpellier 89, Morgan Kaufmann, pp 211-225.

[Wilson 87] S. W. Wilson, "Classifier Systems and the Animat Problem", Machine Learning (volume 2, number 4, 1987), Kluwer Academic Publishers, pp 199-226.

[Zhang & Michalski 89] Jianping Zhang, Rysard S. Michalski, "Rule Optimization Via SG-Trunc Method", Proceedings of the Fourth European Working Session on Learning, Montpellier 89, Morgan Kaufmann, pp 251-262.

Chapter 3:

Position Papers

Predicate Invention in ILP – an Overview

Irene Stahl*

Fakultät Informatik, Universität Stuttgart, Breitwiesenstr. 20-22,
D-7000 Stuttgart 80

Abstract. Inductive Logic Programming (ILP) is a subfield of machine learning dealing with inductive inference in a first order Horn clause framework. A problem in ILP is how to extend the hypotheses language in the case that the vocabulary given initially is insufficient. One way to adapt the vocabulary is to introduce *new predicates*.

In this paper, we give an overview of different approaches to *predicate invention* in ILP. We discuss theoretical results concerning the introduction of new predicates, and ILP-systems capable of inventing predicates.

1 Introduction

Inductive inference aims to construct a theory covering given facts. More formally, given a set of positive examples $E^{\oplus}$, a set of negative examples $E^{\ominus}$ and a theory T, the system is to find a theory T' such that $T' \vdash E^{\oplus}$ and $T' \not\vdash E^{\ominus}$. That is, T' has to be consistent with the examples.

Inductive Logic Programming (ILP) [Mug92] is inductive inference in a restricted first order logic framework: both the given theory T and the target theory T' are restricted to Horn clause theories. Using that framework as opposed to propositional calculi, ILP belongs to the most powerful inductive inference paradigms.

In order to restrict the generally infinite search space for T', ILP systems impose a bias on the hypotheses. This bias includes the vocabulary for the hypotheses, i.e. the available predicate, function and constant symbols. If the search space does not include a hypothesis that is consistent with the examples, an ILP system should shift its bias. This can be done by introducing *new predicates* in the hypotheses language such that the extended vocabulary is sufficient for the induction task.

This operation is referred to as *Predicate Invention*. The paper aims to discuss theoretical and practical aspects of predicate invention in ILP.

2 Two Theoretical Results

Inductive inference is based on examples true or false in an intended model. The system is expected to produce a finite set of formulas in a language $\mathcal{L}$ explaining the positive and excluding the negative examples.

---

* This work has been supported by the European Community ESPRIT project ILP (Inductive Logic Programming).

More formally, let $\mathcal{M}$ be the intended model and $\mathcal{L}_0$ the language of ground facts over the predicate, function and constant symbols in $\mathcal{M}$. A *complete presentation* of $\mathcal{M}$ consists of

$$E^{\oplus} = \{\phi \in \mathcal{L}_o \mid \mathcal{M} \models \phi\} \quad \text{and} \quad E^{\ominus} = \{\phi \in \mathcal{L}_o \mid \phi \notin E^{\oplus}\}.$$

For the following proofs, we assume $E^{\oplus}$ to be recursively enumerable.

The positive and negative example sets inductive inference systems are supplied with are - in practice finite - subsets of $E^{\oplus}$ and $E^{\ominus}$. However, for finite example sets there is no need to invent new predicates, as the positive example set can always be used as correct result of inductive inference. Therefore, we consider the limit case that a complete, possibly infinite presentation of $\mathcal{M}$ is given.

The goal of inductive inference in this setting is to find a *finite set of formulas* T in $\mathcal{L} \supseteq \mathcal{L}_0$ such that

$$T \vdash E^{\oplus} \wedge T \not\vdash E^{\ominus}$$
$$\equiv \forall \phi \in \mathcal{L}_0 \, ((\phi \in E^{\oplus} \to T \vdash \phi) \wedge (\phi \notin E^{\oplus} \to T \not\vdash \phi))$$
$$\equiv \forall \phi \in \mathcal{L} \, (T \vdash \phi \leftrightarrow \phi \in E^{\oplus})$$

The last formula with finite T is exactly the definition of T being a *finite axiomatization* of $E^{\oplus}$. Therefore, the problem of inductive inference is in the limit the problem of finding a finite axiomatization for a given model. If the intended model is *not finitely axiomatizable* within a language $\mathcal{L}$, inductive inference can not succeed. Furthermore, it is not even *decidable* whether the set $E^{\oplus}$ of ground facts valid in $\mathcal{M}$ is finitely axiomatizable within the language $\mathcal{L}$.

Theorem 1. *Given a recursively enumerable set of ground facts $E^{\oplus}$ in a language $\mathcal{L}_0$ it is undecidable whether $E^{\oplus}$ is finitely axiomatizable in $\mathcal{L} \supseteq \mathcal{L}_0$.*

Proof. We omitt the application of Rice's Theorem on the undecidability of nontrivial index sets [Ric53].

Thus an inductive inference system can not decide whether its vocabulary is sufficient for axiomatizing the intended model. Only finite, decidable hypotheses languages $\mathcal{L}$ as e.g. CLINT's language series [Rae92] or RDT's rule schemata [KW91] allow a decision by enumerating all possible hypotheses. If none of them is consistent with the examples, the intended model is not finitely axiomatizable within $\mathcal{L}$. For infinite or undecidable languages $\mathcal{L}$ as e.g. first order Horn logic, the insufficiency for axiomatizing the intended model has to be assumed heuristically.

If the hypotheses language $\mathcal{L}$ is not sufficient, the inductive inference system may try to extend $\mathcal{L}$ by a new predicate. The introduction of a new predicate is useful for finding a finite axiomatization, as Kleene proved [Kle52]:

Theorem 2. *Any recursively enumerable set C of formulas in a first order language $\mathcal{L}_0$ is finitely axiomatizable in a first order language $\mathcal{L}$ using additional predicate symbols except from those in $\mathcal{L}_0$.*

For our purpose, the set C is the presentation $E^{\oplus}$ of the intended model. Kleene's theorem assures that inductive inference will *always succeed* provided the system invents the appropriate new predicates.

The practical application of Kleene's result faces some problems. Though Kleene's proof of the theorem is constructive, it gives no practicable method for constructing a finite axiomatization. In the course of his proof Kleene introduces new predicates regardless of whether they are really necessary for finite

axiomatizability. In contrast, inductive inference systems should introduce new predicates only if they are needed.
This capability involves dealing with the following problems:

1. *when* to introduce a new predicate. It is undecidable whether a new predicate is necessary for finitely axiomatizing the intended model.
2. *how* to induce a definition for the new predicate and *what* to use as base for that induction process. The intended model provides no direct information about the new predicate.
3. *how* to determine the arity and the argument terms of the new predicate.

In the following, we are going to discuss the two main approaches to predicate invention, *reformulation* and *demand driven approaches*.

3 Reformulation Approaches and Inverse Resolution

Reformulation approaches introduce new intermediate predicates as a reformulation of an already existing theory in order to express it more compact and concise. This is done without direct reference to the goal of learning a specific concept.

The introduction of intermediate predicates is a kind of reversal of explanation based learning which deductively replaces intermediate predicates by their definition. *Inverse resolution systems* directly explore the idea of inverting deductive resolution steps. *Scheme-driven* approaches define new intermediate predicates as combinations of known predicate literals that match one of the schemes for useful literal combinations given initially.

3.1 Inverse Resolution Systems

The inverse resolution operator that introduces a new predicate is often called *W-operator* or *intraconstruction*. Given a set of clauses $\{B_1, ..., B_n\}$ it constructs a set of clauses $\{C_1, ..., C_n\}$ and a clause A such that B_i results from resolving A with C_i on a fixed literal $L \in A$. Since L is resolved away in B_i and nothing is known about its predicate symbol, a new predicate is invented.

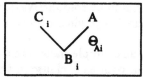

The intraconstruction operator we are going to use throughout the following discussion is the G_2-operator [Wir88]. It sets A to $lgg(\{B_1, ..., B_n\}) \cup \{L\}$, where lgg is the least general generalisation [Plo70] of the input clauses and L is a new predicate. L is negative only if $lgg(\{B_1, ..., B_n\})$ already contains a positive head literal. The clauses C_i are set to $\{L\}\Theta_{A_i} \cup (B_i - lgg(\{B_1, ..., B_n\})\Theta_{A_i})$.

The crucial problems are the arguments of the new predicate literal and the application criteria for the operator.

CIGOL [MB88] uses a restricted form of G_2. The new predicate literal in A must be negative, i.e. all clauses B_i must have the same head predicate. The clauses C_i are restricted to unit clauses such that the equation simplifies to $C_i = \{\overline{L}\}\Theta_{A_i}$.

For determining the arguments of the new predicate, the substitutions Θ_{A_i} are considered. If a substitution for a variable in Θ_{A_i} has no variables in common with substitutions for other variables in Θ_{A_i} it is irrelevant and must not appear as argument of the new predicate.

The operator is applied whenever it results in a reduction of the size of the knowledge base.

LFP2 [Wir88] employs the unrestricted G_2-operator described above. In contrast to CIGOL, argument terms are considered to be relevant for the new predicate if they occur in the remaining as well as in the omitted parts of the B_i. The arguments of the new predicate L are set to

$$\{ t \in args(lgg(\{B_1, .., B_n\})) | \ \forall i \in \{1, .., n\}$$
$$t\Theta_{A_i} \in args(B_i - lgg(\{B_1, .., B_n\})\Theta_{A_i}) \}$$

where $args(C)$ are the argument terms of the literals in clause C. As in CIGOL the operator is triggered by the minimum size of the knowledge base.

ITOU The intraconstruction operator of ITOU [Rou91] applies only to flattened, i.e. function free, Horn clauses. It is a slight modification of G_2.

First, the new predicate literal L in A must be negative. Secondly, the operator is applied only to two clauses B_1 and B_2 such that the new predicate describes the variation of B_1 and B_2 relatively to their common generalisation. The last modification concerns the definition of C_i:

$$C_i = \{\overline{L}\} \cup (B_i\Theta_{A_i}^{-1} - lgg(\{B_1, ..., B_n\})).$$

Because of the lack of structured terms, the inverse substitution $\theta_{A_i}^{-1}$ is a variable renaming and can be simply determined from B_i and A. Similar as in LFP2, the variables of the new predicate L are defined to

$$\{ x \in var(lgg(\{B_1, B_2\})) \ | \ x\Theta_{A_1} \in var(B_1 - lgg(\{B_1, B_2\})\Theta_{A_i}) \ \vee$$
$$x\Theta_{A_1} \in var(B_2 - lgg(\{B_1, B_2\})\Theta_{A_i}) \ \}$$

Intraconstruction in ITOU is triggered by a user request.

RINCON [WL89] tries to improve the efficiency of its theory by introducing intermediate predicates. It restricts G_2 to two input clauses B_1 and B_2. As the definition of the new predicate is to be conjunctive, it must be the positive head literal in A. As arguments of the new predicate all variables within $lgg(\{B_1, B_2\})$ are used.

The process is triggered by an example clause the theory does not explain yet. RINCON tries intraconstruction with each clause in the background theory and choses the one that can be used for rewriting the most rules if several possible reformulations exist.

Banerji's System The peculiarity of the intraconstruction operator DREAM is that the two input clauses B_1 and B_2 must have an identical head P and a nonempty set C of common identical body literals. Then, without use of lgg A is set to $(P \leftarrow C, L)$ where L is a new predicate literal. As arguments of L, the most complex terms common to the remaining parts of B_1 and B_2 are taken. If L is $D(t_1, ..., t_n)$, DREAM produces as definition of D the sentences

$$D(x_1, ..., x_n) \leftarrow P_i' \text{ where } P_i'[x_1/t_1, ..., x_n/t_n] = B_i - \{P \leftarrow C\}$$

Banerji's system revises incrementally a theory based on examples. After each revision, it tries to apply DREAM on every pair of clauses within the revised theory.

3.2 Scheme-driven Systems

Scheme-driven systems define new predicates as combinations of known predicate literals. In order to restrict the space of possible combinations, they use *schemes* describing useful literal combinations at an abstract level. If an instantiation of a scheme with known predicate literals proved useful during learning, an oracle is asked to approve it as definition of a new predicate.

CIA [Rae92] is used together with the example driven learner CLINT [Rae92]. It uses *higher order schemes* for predicate invention.

A higher order scheme S is a Horn clause with existentially quantified predicate variables. A Horn clause c *matches* S if there exists a substitution Θ for the predicate variables in S and a substitution ρ for the variables in S such that $head(S)\Theta\rho = head(c)$ and $body(S)\Theta\rho \subseteq body(c)$. It matches S *partially* if only the second condition holds, i.e. if the head predicate in S remains variable.

Given a positive example, CLINT generates a starting clause. CIA matches this clause against all schemes available in the data base. If it matches a scheme, the resulting clause is proposed to the oracle. If it matches only partially a scheme the oracle is requested to approve or reject the partial clause as a new predicate definition. In the former case, the oracle names the variable head predicate.

The same method is applied on the generalised starting clause produced by CLINT. In a last step, all new rules are transformed into schemes to be used in subsequent learning steps. Thus, the space of new predicate definitions CIA considers depends on the theory induced so far.

FOCL [SP91] is an extenstion of Quinlan's FOIL [Qui90]. Both systems induce Horn clauses from general to specific by successively adding body literals to the target clauses according to the maximum information gain.

As FOIL adds literals one at a time, it overlooks the possibility that a combination of literals may have a large information gain whereas the single literals have zero or less gain. To overcome this limitation, FOCL considers combinations of literals restricted by *relational clichés*. Relational clichés are schemes that restrict the number of literals in a combination, the predicates used to fill the single literal positions and the variables the literals should share.

If no literals with positive gain exist to be added to the clause, the instantiation of the relational clichés with maximum gain is added and cached for later reuse. After the system completed its learning, the cached instantiations of relational clichés are proposed to the user to be named and adapted in the background theory.

As in CIA, the new predicates FOCL induces depend strongly on the available clichés. Directly recursive defined new predicates can not be found.

4 Demand-driven Approaches

As opposed to reformulation approaches, demand-driven systems try to discover situations where the given vocabulary is not sufficient for finitely axiomatizing the intended model. Then, a new predicate is invented. The decision about introducing a new predicate is done heuristically, as an exact decision can not be done in general.

MENDEL [Lin91] is an inverse resolution system that differs from the reformulating systems mainly in the control of intraconstruction. Only if the theory grows beyond a fixed bound, the intraconstruction operator EXTRACT is applied. In that case MENDEL assumes that the current theory is not finitely axiomatizable within the given vocabulary, and introduces a new predicate.

EXTRACT is a nondeterministic G_2-operator as it sets A instead of the unique

$$lgg(\{B_1, ..., B_n\}) \cup \{L\} \text{ to } g(\{B_1, ..., B_n\}) \cup \{L\}$$

where g may be any common generalisation of $\{B_1, ..., B_n\}$. Thus, MENDEL has to cope with an additional nondeterministic choice apart from which clauses $\{B_1, ..., B_n\}$ to use. The arguments of the new predicate literal L are the variables in Θ_{A_i}.

The clauses generated for the new predicate L are subject to further generalisation steps. Only if they result in a directly recursive clause for L, the new predicate is accepted.

SIERES [WO91] starts with the least general generalisation of the examples as clause head and specialises this clause by successively adding literals to its body until the output of each example is computed correctly by the clause.

The space of Horn clauses SIERES searches is constrained by *argument dependency graphs* specifying the number of literals within a clause and the argument dependencies between them. The arguments of possible body literals are restricted further by the preference for *critical terms*, i.e. unused input- or unbound output terms. Only if not enough of them exist, uncritical terms or new variables are used as arguments.

If none of the existing predicates yields a correct extension of the clause, a new predicate is invented. A minimal selection of critical terms is taken as arguments such that the resulting clause contains no more critical terms. A definition of the new predicate is determined by a recursive call of SIERES on the example set defined by the bindings of the chosen argument terms for all examples. The criterion for inventing a new predicate is applicable only because SIERES searches a finite subset of Horn logic as hypotheses space.

There are some restrictions and difficulties with this approach. First, a new predicate can only be invented at the end of a clause. A second problem is that sparse examples for the new predicate may cause the induction process to fail. A more complex problem is that the recursive call of the system on the examples of the new predicate may not terminate, but lead to an infinite chain of new predicates.

DBC (Discrimination-Based Constructive Induction) [KNS92b] proceeds similar to SIERES. An overgeneral clause is completed with a new predicate such that all negative examples are excluded from being covered. Instead of using critical terms for determining the arguments of the new predicate, DBC searches for a minimal relevant variable set that discriminates between positive and negative examples.

First, all variables of the clause are used as arguments of the new predicate. Its instantiations according to the examples for the clause constitute its preliminary definition. This definition corrects the overgeneral clause but may contain irrelevant terms. DBC tests greedily for each variable whether the variable and its instantiations can be omitted from the new predicate and its definition without sacrificing correctness. The resulting reduced new predicate is added to the overgeneral clause, and its instantiations for the positive and negative examples of the clause are used as positive and negative examples for the new predicate in the subsequent induction process.

DBC is used with the top-down heuristically guided learner CHAM [KNS92a]. A new predicate is constructed whenever there are no correct clauses fullfilling the encoding length restriction [Qui90]. The clauses to be specialized by new predicates are chosen heuristically among the overgeneral clauses.

The system stops predicate invention when the whole theory violates the encoding length restriction, or when the instances of the new predicate are the same as the examples of the clause except for the name of the predicate. Thus, it avoids heuristically the looping problem of SIERES.

MOBAL/CLT [Mor91, Wro92] is a knowledge acquisition system that helps creating a model for an application domain. The domain model of MOBAL consists of function free Horn clauses, where each rule has an attached *support set* listing exceptions and examples for the applicability of that rule. An exception is an instantiation of the rule it must not be applied with, whereas an example is a successful instantiation.

If a new fact contradicts the latest theory, the knowledge revision module KRT selects in a first step the rule to be specialised among those responsible for the inconsistency. In the second step the selected rule is minimally specialised by adding the wrong instantiation to its exception set. Then reformulation operators are tried that aim to replace the extensional exception list with an intensional description.

If a known predicate discriminates the positive examples of the rule from its exceptions, it is added to the rule definition. Otherwise the concept learning tool CLT [Wro92] invents a new predicate c for that purpose. As arguments of the new predicate c a subset of the rule variables is taken. The values of those variables in the support set yield the positive and negative examples of c. Based on them, the learning module RDT [KW91] tries to induce an intensional definition of the new concept c. If RDT succeeds, c is added to the body of the incorrect rule. Else the search for a definition is postponed until further exceptions occur. As the grouping of exceptions resembles concept formation, this approach to predicate invention is called a *concept formation approach*.

RDT is capable of inducing rules both with c as head and c within the body. This is important for the evaluation criterion of CLT. A new concept is accepted if at least two sufficient conditions were found about c, i.e. rules with c as head, *and* at least two necessary conditions, i.e. rules with c as only body literal, or at least one rule that uses c in its body among other literals. The acceptance criterion demands that the new predicate can be used for rewriting a minimum number of rules in the knowledge base.

Non-Monotonic Learning A special case of predicate invention is closed world specialisation [BM92]. Given a clause covering negative examples, it is specialised by the negation of a new exception predicate, i.e. negative examples are treated as exceptions of the rule applicability. As negation by failure is used, all previously covered examples are still covered.

5 Comparison and Evaluation

5.1 Decision Criteria for Introducing a New Predicate

The decision criteria for introducing a new predicate can be classified in *demand-driven* and *goal-free* methods.

Demand-driven approaches decide heuristically on their vocabulary being insufficient for finitely axiomatizing the intended model. That is, new predicate invention is triggered whenever the system fails in expressing the target theory within the given vocabulary. Using a finite hypotheses language as in SIERES, this may be decided by checking all hypotheses on consistency. For infinite hypotheses languages, the decision about the fail of the system has to be done heuristically. MENDEL assumes the vocabulary being insufficient whenever the hypotheses grows too large. Similarly, DBC uses the encoding length restriction. MOBAL introduces a new predicate if none of the existing predicates characterizes a rule's exception set.

Goal-free approaches introduce new predicates without a direct reference to the goal of learning a specific concept. Nevertheless, due to the constraints systems impose on new predicates, they are very likely to be useful for finitely axiomatizing the intended model either. One constraint used by CIGOL, LFP2 and RINCON is *knowledge base compression*. Among the possible reformulations of the knowledge base the one that reduces the size of the theory most is chosen. This is closely connected to MENDEL's decision criterion and to MOBAL's acceptance criterion.

Another goal-free constraint on new predicates is imposed by *schemes*. If scheme-driven systems observe a literal combination they assume to be useful and interesting according to their schemes, they propose it as new predicate definition to the oracle.

5.2 Evaluation of the Different Approaches

The *evaluation* of the different approaches to predicate invention is difficult. There are only sparse theoretical and empirical results concerning the quality of the new predicates introduced by the systems. Wrobel [Wro92] and Ling [Lin91] propose a set of *quality dimensions* along which the new predicates could be measured.

Though we were not able to do any experimental tests on the systems we discussed, in table 1 we try to give an assessment of the systems according to Wrobels and Lings quality dimensions:

1. Is the *learnability* of the desired target concepts improved by means of predicate invention? For most systems this is - at least possibly - the case. Only in RINCON it is not improved as it uses new predicates as a mere reformulation of the theory.

2. Is the system capable of inducing *directly recursive defined new predicates*? Only those *could* be necessary for finite axiomatizability, but need not necessarily be. Non-recursively defined new predicates are eliminable by unfolding and therefore not necessary. Most systems except RINCON and FOCL allow for inducing recursive new predicates. However, this may require further learning steps.

3. Is the *classification accuracy* of the resulting axiomatization improved by the use of new predicates? For inverse resolution and scheme-driven systems it is

	learn-ability	recursive definitions	accuracy	efficiency	structure
CIGOL	possibly	yes	?	decreases	
LFP2	possibly	yes	?	decreases	more
ITOU	possibly	yes	?	decreases	compact
RINCON	no	no	same	better	theory
Banerji	yes	yes	?	decreases	
CIA	possibly	yes	?	decreases	theory size
FOCL	yes	no	same	decreases	increases
MENDEL	yes	yes	?	decreases	
SIERES	yes	yes	at least not worse	decreases	more compact theory
DBC	yes	yes	at least not worse	decreases	
MOBAL	possibly	yes	at least not worse	decreases	

Table 1. Evaluation

unclear how new predicates affect classification accuracy. The operators themselves as pure reformulations have of course no effect. But if the new predicate definitions are subject to further learning steps, there is the danger of overgeneralisation or -specialisation and therefore less accuracy.

4. Does the *efficiency* of the resulting axiomatization improve or decrease? Usually, efficiency should decrease as additional resolution steps are necessary to apply the new predicates. Only RINCON produces a more efficient theory. However, this is mostly due to the fact that RINCON's rules are organized in a kind of Rete-net.

5. Does *structure* and *understandability* of the resulting knowledge base improve? The problem is how to measure structure or understandability. Most systems aim to produce smaller, more compact theories. Only for CIA and FOCL new predicates increase the theory size as they are not used to rewrite the theory.

Table 1 shows only weak results about the properties of predicate invention operators. This may be due to the fact that some properties, e.g. learnability, are undecidable, whereas others, e.g. knowledge base understandability, can not be properly quantified. Additionally, the experimental evaluation of systems performing predicate invention in ILP is almost lacking.

6 Conclusions

In this paper, we have discussed different approaches to predicate invention in ILP. There are only few systems able to invent new predicates and only weak or no results about the properties of their operators. The crucial problems concerning the introduction of new predicates, have not yet been solved satisfactorily. Nevertheless, the *need* for predicate invention is undoubted.

322

References

[BM92]   Bain, M., Muggleton, S. (1992): *Non-Monotonic Learing* in S. Muggleton (ed): Inductive Logic Programming, Academic Press

[Ban92] Banerji, R. B. (1992): *Learning Theoretical Terms* in S. Muggleton (ed): Inductive Logic Programming, Academic Press

[KW91]   Kietz, J., Wrobel, S. (1991): *Controlling the Complexity of Learning in Logic through Syntactic and Task-Oriented Models* in S. Muggleton (ed): Inductive Logic Programming, Academic Press

[KNS92a] Kijsirikul, B., Numao, M., Shimura, M. (1992): *Efficient Learning of Logic Programs with Non-determinate, Non-dicriminating Literals* in S. Muggleton (ed): Inductive Logic Programming, Academic Press

[KNS92b] Kijsirikul, B., Numao, M., Shimura, M. (1992): *Discrimination-Based Constructive Induction of Logic Programs*, Proc. of the 10th Nat. Conf. on AI, San Jose, CA

[Kle52] Kleene, S. C. (1952): *Finite Axiomatizability of Theories in the Predicate Calculus Using Additional Predicate Symbols* in S. C. Kleene: Two Papers on the Predicate Calculus, Memoirs of the American Mathematical Society No. 10, Providence, RI

[Lin91] Ling, C. X. (1991): *Inventing Necessary Theoretical Terms in Scientific Discovery and Inductive Logic Programming*, Report No. 302, Dept. of Computer Science, University of Western Ontario, London, Ontario

[Mor91] Morik, K. (1991): *Balanced Cooperative Modeling*, in R. S. Michalsky, G. Tecuci (eds): Proc. First Int. Workshop on Multistrategy Learning, 65 – 80

[MB88]   Muggleton, S., Buntine, W. (1988): *Machine Invention of First-Order Predicates by Inverting Resolution*, Proc. of the 5th Int. ML Workshop, Morgan Kaufman

[Mug92] Muggleton, S. (1992): *Inductive Logic Programming*, in S. Muggleton (ed): Inductive Logic Programming, Academic Press

[Plo70] Plotkin, G. D. (1970): *A Note on Inductive Generalisation* in: B. Meltzer, D. Mitchie (eds): Machine Intelligence 5, Edinburgh University Press

[Qui90] Quinlan, J. R. (1990): *Learning Logical Definitions from Relations*, Machine Learning 5, 239 – 266

[Rae92] De Raedt, L., Bruynooghe, M. (1992): *Interactive Concept-Learning and Constructive Induction by Analogy*, Machine Learning 8(2), 107-150

[Ric53] Rice, H. G. (1953): *Classes of Recursively Enumerable Sets and their Decision problems*, Trans. AMS 89

[Rou91] Rouveirol, C. (1991): *Extensions of Inversion of Resolution Applied to Theory Completion* in S. Muggleton (ed): Inductive Logic Programming, Academic Press

[SP91]   Silverstein, G., Pazzani, M. J. (1991): *Relational Cliches: Constraining Constructive Induction During Relational Learning*, Proc. MLW 91

[Wir88] Wirth, R. (1988): *Learning by Failure to Prove*, Proceeding of EWSL 88, Pitman, 237 – 251

[WO91]   Wirth, R., O'Rorke, P. (1991): *Constraints on Predicate Invention* in Proc. of the 8th Int. Workshop on ML, Morgan Kaufmann

[WL89]   Wogulis, J., Langley, P. (1989): *Improving Efficiency by Learning Intermediate Concepts*, Proc. of the 11th IJCAI, Detroit

[Wro92] Wrobel, S. (1992): *Exploiting a Problem-Solving Context to Focus Concept Formation*, to appear in Machine Learning journal

Functional Inductive Logic Programming with Queries to the User

F. Bergadano[1] and D. Gunetti[2]

[1]University of Catania, via A. Doria 6/A,
95100 Catania, Italy, bergadan@mathct.cineca.it

[2]University of Torino, corso Svizzera 185,
10149 Torino, Italy, gunetti@di.unito.it

Abstract

The FILP learning system induces functional logic programs from positive examples. For every predicate P, the user is asked to provide a mode (input or output) for each of its argument, and the system assumes that the mode corresponds to a total function, i.e., for a given input there is one and only one corresponding output that makes the predicate true. Functionality serves two goals: it restricts the hypothesis space and it allows the system to ask existential queries to the user. By means of these queries, missing examples can be added to the ones given initially, and this makes the learned programs complete and consistent and the system adequate for learning multiple predicates and recursive clauses in a reliable manner.

1 Introduction

Recently there has been a growing interest, within the Machine Learning community, in the problem of learning logic programs from positive and negative examples in the form of ground literals. The obtained results should naturally be communicated and proposed as important tools for Logic Programming and even for Software Engineering at large. However, this has not yet happened. The reason is, we think, twofold.

First, learning logic programs is difficult, and systems tend to be slow and do not always terminate successfully, even when a solution program exists. A common way to handle this problem consists in restricting the hypothesis space by means of strong constraints of various kinds. In this paper we follow the same idea, and restrict the inductive hypotheses to logic programs that are *functional*, i.e. such that each n-ary predicate can be associated to a total function as follows: m of its arguments are labeled as input, while the remaining n-m are labeled as output, and for every given sequence of input values, there

Acknowledgement: This work was partially supported by ESPRIT project BRA 6020 on Inductive Logic Programming.

is one and only one sequence of output values that makes the predicate true. Functionality constraints have been used before [9, 7, 6, 3]; in the present paper we employ them to query the user for missing examples and explicitly address the problem of consistency and completeness.

Second, the kinds of programs that are learned are usually very simple and often limited to clauses defining just one predicate. Few systems [8, 2, 5] are able to learn programs for multiple predicates, while even beginning Prolog programmers write programs with different clause consequents. This is due, in part, to the need of learning clauses one at a time and independently of each other. If we want to learn a program for predicates P and Q, and we try to construct a clause antecedent for P where Q occurs, then Q must have been defined by the user, or determined extensionally, by means of all of its relevant examples. Something similar occurs with recursion, i.e. for the case when Q=P. We will show in this paper that, as a consequence of the extensional interpretation of recursion and sub-predicates, systems may be unable to learn a program, even when an allowed inductive hypothesis that is consistent with the examples exists. Even worse, it may happen that a program is learned that computes wrong outputs even for the *given* examples.

The FILP system, presented here, solves this problem by querying the user for any example that may be missing, depending on the hypothesis space that has been defined. The queries that are asked to the user are of the type of the existential queries of CLINT [5] and MIS [8], because they contain unbound variables. However, in FILP learning is one-step and example completion is done in a preprocessing phase.

2   The FILP System

Since FILP learns functional relations, it really only needs positive examples. Negative examples are implicitly assumed to be all the ones having the same input values as the positive examples but different output values. In the sequel, by *example* we usually mean *positive example*, while α and γ represent generic conjunctions of literals.

It is well known that in logic programming variables have not a fixed role: they can act as input or output variables as desired. For example, the predicate $append(X,Y,Z)$ can be used with mode $append(in,in,out)$ to append two lists, or with mode $append(out,out,in)$ to split a list in two sublists.

On the other hand, if we want to learn functional logic programs (logic programs whose input-output behavior is functional) we need to specify a (functional) mode for every variable of every literal used in the learning task, in order to employ and learn only functional relations. For example $append(in,in,out)$ would be a legal way to use append, but $append(out,out,in)$ would not, because it does not represent a function. On this ground, in our system we ask the user to provide a functional mode for all predicates, and then we use it for constraining the allowed clauses as follows:

1) Suppose Q and P have mode Q(in,out) and P(in,out); the literal Q(W,Z) can

occur in an intermediate clause P(X,Y) :- α, Q(W,Z), γ iff either (a) W=X (i.e., the input is bound because it is passed as input in the head of the clause) or (b) W occurs in α (i.e., it is computed before Q is called) [10];
2) A clause is in an acceptable final form only if the output variables of its head occur in the body, i.e., only if the output is not left unbound.

Moreover, all clauses are required to be function-free. This can be achieved by means of a flattening procedure [7]. A basic version of FILP without queries (BFILP) follows the algorithmic scheme of FOIL [4]:

Basic FILP:
For all inductive predicates P do
while examples(P) $\neq \emptyset$ do
    Generate one clause "P($\vec{X}$) :- α"
    examples(P) $\leftarrow$ examples(P) $-$ covered(α)

Generate one clause:
$\alpha \leftarrow$ true
while covered(α) $\neq \emptyset$ do
    if consistent(α) then return(P($\vec{X}$) :- α)
        else choose a predicate Q and its arguments Args
            such that the functionality constraint is satisfied
            if no such Q is found then backtrack
            $\alpha \leftarrow \alpha \wedge$ Q(Args)

Where every predicate Q can be defined by the user (intensionally) by means of logical rules or (extensionally) simply giving some examples of its input-output behavior. In particular, clauses can be recursive and, in this case, Q = P, and its truth value can only be determined by the available examples.

Definition 1: We say that the clause P(X,Y) :- α(X,Y) *extensionally covers* P(a,b) iff α(a,Y) *extensionally computes* Y = b, where extensional computation is defined as follows:

- α = Q(a,Y) with functional mode Q(in,out). Then Q(a,Y) *extensionally computes* Y = b iff Q(a,b) is derivable from the definition of Q or is a given example of Q.
- $\alpha = \gamma$(X,T), Q(T,Y) with functional mode γ(in,out) and Q(in,out). Then γ(a,T), Q(T,Y) *extensionally computes* Y = b iff γ(a,T) *extensionally computes* T = e and Q(e,b) is derivable from the definition of Q or is a given example of Q.

In the algorithm, an example P(a,b) belongs to covered(α) iff α(a,Y) extensionally computes Y=b, and consistent(α) is true iff, for no such example, α(a,Y) extensionally computes Y=c and c$\neq$b. The choice of the literal Q(Args) to be added to the partial antecedent α of the clause being generated is guided by heuristic information. It might nevertheless be a wrong choice in some cases, in the sense that it causes the procedure "Generate one clause" to fail by exiting the while loop without returning any clause. This problem is remedied by making the choice of Q(Args) a backtracking point.

In the worst case, all possible literals will be tried every time, and the complexity is exponential in the number of these literals. We view this problem as intrinsic of induction and unavoidable - the only thing we can do is reduce the number of possible clauses by means of strong constraints given a priori by the user. An advantage of extensional methods is that clauses are generated independently of each other. As a consequence we must search the space of possible clauses (exponential in the number of possible literals), not the space of possible logic programs (= *sets* of possible clauses). This independence of the clauses is made possible by the extensional interpretation of recursion and of the other inductive relations: when a predicate Q corresponding to an inductive relation occurs in a clause antecedent α, it is evaluated as true when the arguments match one of the positive examples. The method leads to a fundamental property of extensional methods (proofs are found in [1]).

Definition 2: A program P is *complete* w.r.t. the examples E iff ($\forall$ Q(i,o) $\in$ E) P $\vdash$ Q(i,o). A program P is *consistent* w.r.t. the examples E iff ($\nexists$ Q(i,o) $\in$ E) P $\vdash$ Q(i,o') and o$\neq$o'.

Lemma 1: Suppose BFILP successfully exits its main loop and outputs a logic program P, that always terminates (w.r.t. SLD-resolution) for the given examples. Let Q(X,Y) :- α(X,Y) be any clause of P, then
($\forall$Q(a,b)$\in$Examples(Q)) α(a,Y) ext. computes Y=b $\rightarrow$ P $\vdash$ Q(a,b).

Theorem 1: If BFILP terminates successfully, then it outputs a complete program P.

The above proof is also valid for systems such as FOIL, and is a partial justification of the extensional evaluation of the generated clauses. However, extensionality forces us to include many examples, which would otherwise be unnecessary. In fact other desirable properties, similar to the one given by Theorem 1, are not true:

1) For a complete and consistent logic program P, it may happen that P $\vdash$ Q(a,b), but none of its clauses extensionally cover Q(a,b). As a consequence BFILP would be unable to generate P, and would not terminate successfully. Consider this program P:

reverse(X,Y) :- *null*(Y), *null*(X).
reverse(X,Y) :- *head*(X,H), *tail*(X,T), *reverse*(T,W), *append*(W,[H],Y).

Let *reverse*([a,b],[b,a]) be the only given example. This example follows from P (P $\vdash$ *reverse*([a,b],[b,a])) but is not extensionally covered: the first clause does not cover it because *null*([a,b]) is false, and the second clause does not cover it extensionally because *head*([a,b],a) and *tail*([a,b],[b]) are true, but *reverse*([b],[b]) is not in examples(*reverse*).

2) Let P be a program to compute a function Q and Q(i,o) ∈ examples(Q). Even if, for all clauses Q :- α in P, consistent(α) is true, it may still happen that P ⊢ Q(i,o') with o ≠ o'. In other words BFILP might generate a program that is not consistent even for the given examples. Consider the following program P:

reverse(X,Y) :- *head*(X,H), *tail*(X,T1), *head*(Y,H), *tail*(Y,T2), *reverse*(T1,T2).
reverse(X,Y) :- *null*(X), *null*(Y).
reverse([X,Y,Z],[Z,Y,X]).

which can be learned by BFILP with this set of examples:
reverse([],[]), *reverse*([1],[1]), *reverse*([3,2,1],[1,2,3]).
Then P ⊢ *reverse*([3,2,1],[3,2,1]). Nevertheless, *reverse*([3,2,1],[3,2,1]) is not extensionally covered by the first clause. In fact, *reverse*([2,1],[2,1]) is not given as an example. In order to prevent BFILP from generating that inconsistent program, in this case we must tell the system that *reverse*([2,1],[2,1]) is wrong. This is done by adding a positive example, namely *reverse*([2,1],[1,2]).

To overcome the above problems, FILP queries the user for some of the missing examples. Every legal clause (= permitted by the constraints) of the type "P(X,Y) :- A(X,W), Q(X,W,Z), α." where Q is an inductive predicate with mode Q(in,in,out), is processed with the following procedure:

for every example P(a,b) do
    extensionally compute A(a,W), obtaining a value W = c
    ask the user for the value Z computed by Q(a,c,Z)
    add this example to examples(Q)

This procedure must be repeated for every clause, again and again, until no more examples are added for the inductive predicates. Both for making the above procedure terminate and for guaranteeing the termination of learned programs, we require that any recursive call within a generated clause matches the following pattern: "P(X_1, ..., X_i, ..., X_n) :- ..., Q(X_i,Y), ..., P(X_1, ..., Y, ..., X_n), ..." where Q(X,Y) is known to define a well ordering between Y and X ($Y < X$). A similar technique is found in [4], but does not guarantee termination on new examples. It is possible to show that, if every recursive clause in P satisfies the above constraint, then the example completion procedure terminates.

As an instance, suppose that we want to learn *reverse*. Consider the clause *reverse*(X,Y) :- *tail*(X,T), *reverse*(T,W). It satisfies the constraint on recursive calls because, when *tail*(X,T) is true, then T is a shorter list than X and this is a well order relation. Consider the example *reverse*([a,b,c],[c,b,a]). By using the clause, the user is queried for the value of *reverse*([b,c],W), and this is added to examples(*reverse*). This new example causes the repetition of the procedure, and the user is queried for *reverse*([c],W), and at the next step for *reverse*([],W).

Lemma 2: Suppose the examples given to an extensional learning system are completed with the above completion procedure. Suppose also that some pro-

gram P belongs to the hypothesis space and Q(a,b)∈examples(Q) after the completion.
If P ⊢ Q(a,b) then the first clause in P resolved against Q(a,b) extensionally covers Q(a,b).

Theorem 2: If a complete and consistent program P exists, then FILP will terminate successfully.

Theorem 3: If FILP terminates successfully, then it outputs a consistent program P.

By virtue of Theorem 1, this program will also be complete.

References

[1] F. Bergadano and D. Gunetti. Sufficient and Correct Induction of Functional Logic Programs. *Tech. Rep. 92.9.2, CS Dept., Univ. of Torino*, 1992.

[2] J. U. Kietz and S. Wrobel. Controlling the Complexity of Learning in Logic through Syntactic and Task-Oriented Models. In *Proc. Workshop on Inductive Logic Programming*, pages 107–126, 1991.

[3] N. Lavrac, S. Dzeroski, and M. Grobelnik. Learning nonrecursive definitions of relations with linus. In Y. Kodratoff, editor, *Proc. of the Machine Learning-EWSL 91*, pages 265–281, Porto, Portugal, 1991. Springer-Verlag.

[4] R. Quinlan. Knowledge Acquisition from Structured Data. *IEEE Expert*, 6(6):32–37, 1991.

[5] L. De Raedt and M. Bruynooghe. CLINT: a Multistrategy Interactive Concept-Learner and Theory Revision System. In *Proc. Workshop on Multistrategy Learning*, pages 175–190, 1991.

[6] L. De Raedt and Maurice Bruynooghe. Belief Updating from Integrity Constraints and Queries. *Artificial Intelligence*, 53:291–307, 1992.

[7] C. Rouveirol. Flattening: a Representation Change for Generalization. *Machine Learning*, 1993. Special issue on Evaluating and Changing Representation, K. Morik, F. Bergadano and W. Buntine (Eds.).

[8] E. Y. Shapiro. *Algorithmic Program Debugging*. MIT Press, 1983.

[9] I. Stahl, B. Tausend, and R. Wirth. General-to-specific learning of horn clauses from positive examples. In P. Dewilde and J. Vanderwalle, editors, *Proc. of the CompEuro, 1992*, pages 436–441, The Hague, Netherlands, 1992. IEEE Comp. Soc. Press.

[10] R. Wirth and P. O'Rorke. Constraints on predicate invention. In L. A. Birnbaum and G. C. Collins, editors, *Proc. of the 8th Int. Workshop on ML*, pages 457–461, Evanston, Illinois, 1991. Morgan Kaufmann.

A note on refinement operators

Tim Niblett *(tim@turing.com)*
The Turing Institute
36 North Hanover Street
Glasgow G1 2AD, Scotland

Abstract

The top down induction of logic programs is faced with the problem of ensuring
that the search space includes all the desired hypotheses. The conventional way of
of organizing the search space is via *refinement* of clauses. Within this context the
existence of a well behaved refinement operator complete for Horn clause logic is
desirable.

We show that there is no natural way in which a complete refinement operator
can be defined which avoids the production of non-reduced clauses. Consideration
is given to subsets of full Horn clause logic for which more efficient refinement
operators can be constructed.

Category: Short Paper

1 Introduction

The Model Inference System (MIS) was developed by Shapiro ([6], [7]) drawing from
theoretical studies by (among others) Gold ([1]), and Plotkin ([3], [5], [4]).

Plotkin studied the basis of generalization mechanisms within first order logic and
characterized the notion of generalization as θ-subsumption. It is difficult to ensure
that an inductive learning system based on subsumption is complete since subsumption
is not well behaved. The contribution of MIS is that it provides a framework for a
complete learning system, capable of learning any finitely axiomatizable clausal theory
up to a given level of complexity. The search space is organized as a *refinement
graph*, which is generated by a *refinement operator*. Shapiro claims in [7] that there
is a most general refinement operator, complete for clausal logic. The purpose of this
note is to demonstrate that the most general refinement operator described by Shapiro
is not complete. In addition it is shown that there there is no "natural" refinement
operator which does not introduce non-reduced refinements. This raises doubts about
the efficiency of top down methods of inferring logic programs.

1.1 Organization of this note

The central result is straightforward to prove and is found in Section 5. The material
before that is a review of supporting concepts. In Section 2 we review the concept of

subsumption and explain why a naive approach to top-down learning does not work. In Section 3 we outline the model inference problem in the framework created by Shapiro, and explain the role of refinement operators. Refinement operators and their properties are described in Section 4. The most general refinement operator is explained and the central result proven in Section 5. In Section 6 a complete refinement operator which introduces redundant clauses is described. Finally, in Section 7 we discuss the implications of the negative result we have uncovered.

Throughout this note we restrict attention to Horn clause logic, rather than the full clausal logic considered by Shapiro. It does not affect the principal result which holds *a fortiori* for full clausal logic, simplifies the presentation, and is consistent with practical uses of the MIS architecture.

2   Subsumption

A Horn clause $B_0 \leftarrow B_1, \ldots, B_n$ is equivalent to the set $\{B_0, \bar{B}_1, \ldots, \bar{B}_n\}$, where the B_i and $\bar{B}_i$ are atoms and negated atoms respectively, in what follows.

A substitution σ of terms for variables, is written $\{t_1/x_1, \ldots, t_n/x_n\}$. If C is a clause, then $C\sigma$ is the result of substituting the t_i in σ for the corresponding x_i.

We say that clause C θ-subsumes clause D if $C\sigma \subseteq D$ for some substitution σ. We write this as $C \leq D$. In what follows θ-subsumption is simply called subsumption.

The *size* of a clause C is the number of symbol occurrences in C (excluding punctuation) minus the number of distinct variables occurring in C. If every model of a set of sentences Σ is also a model of clause C we say that $\Sigma \models C$ We assume a complete derivation procedure for Horn clause logic and write $\Sigma \vdash C$ to show that C is derivable from Σ.

Given two clauses C and D we write $C \cong D$ when C subsumes D and D subsumes C. This is an equivalence relation. Two properties of subsumption are of interest to us. If $C \leq D$ then $C \vdash D$, although the reverse is not true. If $C \leq D$ then it is *not* true that $size(C) \leq size(D)$, hence subsumption cannot itself function as a refinement operator. Plotkin ([3]) gives examples of infinite strictly descending chains under subsumption. Plotkin also defines the notion of reduction. A clause C is *reduced* if there is no clause D such that $D \subset C$ and $D \cong C$. If two clauses are reduced then they are equivalent up to renaming of variables. We say that a substitution θ *decreases* clause C if $|C\theta| < |C|$, where $|C|$ is the number of elements in C interpreted as a set.

3   The model inference problem

The language $\mathcal{L}$ is the set of Horn clause sentences constructed from a finite number of function and predicate symbols. We consider two clauses C and D to be equivalent if they are alphabetic variants, that is if there exists a substitution $\tau = \{y_1/x_1, \ldots, y_n/x_n\}$ where the y_i are distinct and $C\tau = D$.

The sentences of $\mathcal{L}$ are of the form

$$b_0 \leftarrow b_1 \wedge \ldots \wedge b_n (n \geq 0)$$

```
T = {}
repeat
      read the next fact
      repeat
            while T is too strong do
                  apply the contradiction backtracing algorithm,
                  and remove from T the refuted clause.
            while T is too weak do
                  add to T refinements of previously refuted hypotheses.
      until T is neither too strong nor too weak with respect
            to the facts read so far
forever
```

Figure 1: The MIS framework

where the b_i are atoms.

Two subsets of $\mathcal{L}$ are distinguished. $\mathcal{L}_o$ the observational language, and $\mathcal{L}_h$ the hypothesis language. We assume $\mathcal{L}_o \subset \mathcal{L}_h \subseteq L$. Both sublanguages are decidable.

The domain of enquiry is a model M of $\mathcal{L}$ and we assume an oracle for M which given $\alpha \in \mathcal{L}_o$ returns true iff α is true in M. The set of observational sentences true in M is $\mathcal{L}_o^M$.

A set of sentences $\Sigma \subset \mathcal{L}_h$ is an $\mathcal{L}_o$-complete axiomatization for M iff Σ is true in M and $\Sigma \vdash \mathcal{L}_o^M$ The Model Inference problem is to find a finite $\mathcal{L}_o$-complete axiomatization for M.

3.1 Admissibility requirements

$\mathcal{L}_o$ should contain enough information to refute any false theory. $\langle \mathcal{L}_o, \mathcal{L}_h \rangle$ is admissible if for every model M of $\mathcal{L}$ and every $\Sigma \subset \mathcal{L}_h$ the set $\{\alpha \in \mathcal{L}_o \mid \Sigma \vdash \alpha\} = \mathcal{L}_o^M$ implies that Σ is true in M.

Shapiro ([6]) shows that the observational language of ground literals of $\mathcal{L}$ with hypothesis language $\mathcal{L}$ itself is complete.

3.2 The incremental algorithm

The MIS framework is shown in Figure 1. It is intended to identify finitely axiomatizable theories in the limit. To ensure termination, it is important to note that all proof attempts are done modulo a total recursive function h which provides a limit on the complexity of the proof for any literal. In general the value of h should depend on the syntactic complexity of the goal to be proved.

The efficiency of this algorithm depends on two things, the contradiction backtracing algorithm (see [8]), and the structure of refinements. For completeness it is essential that the refinement generation process be complete. We now turn our attention to this.

4 Refinement operators

We first consider refinement operators. From a technical point of view a refinement operator is a specialization of subsumption, introduced to ensure that there are no infinite descending chains. In general we assume that there is a measure (*size*) of the structural complexity of clauses which maps to the natural numbers. We insist that for any natural number $n(\geq 0)$, the set of clauses of size n (modulo alphabetic variants) is finite.

Definition 1 *Clause D is a refinement of clause C if $C \vdash D$ and* size(C) < size(D).

Definition 2 *A refinement operator ρ is a mapping from clauses to subsets of their refinements, such that for any $C \in \mathcal{L}$ and any $n > 0$ the set $\rho(C)(n)$ (the set $\rho(C)$ restricted to clauses of size $\leq n$) is recursively enumerable.*

A refinement operator ρ induces a partial order $\leq_\rho$ with the empty clause $\Box$ as (unique) minimal element. We say that $C \leq_\rho D$ if there is a chain $C = C_0, \ldots C_n = D$ such that $C_{i+1} \in \rho(C_i), 0 \leq i \leq n$. We write $C <_\rho D$ if $C \leq_\rho D$ and $\neg(D \leq_\rho C)$.
For any clause C the set $\{D \in \mathcal{L} \mid C \leq_\rho D\}$ is written as $\rho^\star(C)$.

Definition 3 *A refinement operator ρ is complete for $\mathcal{L}$ if $\rho^\star(\Box) = \mathcal{L}$.*

We now turn to a consideration of Shapiro's most general refinement operator ρ_o which was claimed in [6] to be complete for $\mathcal{L}$. A most general refinement operator is simply a refinement operator which is complete for $\mathcal{L}$.

5 Shapiro's most general operator

If X and Y are atoms and C a clause we say that X *is more general than Y with respect to C* if there is a substitution θ such that $X\theta = Y$ and $C\theta = C$. If $H \leftarrow B$ is a reduced clause then X *is a most general atom such that $H \leftarrow B \wedge X$ is reduced* if for any atom Y such that Y is more general than X with respect to $H \leftarrow B$, the clause $H \leftarrow B \wedge Y$ is not reduced.

Definition 4 *Let $C = H \leftarrow B$ be a reduced Horn clause. Then $D \in \rho_o(C)$ if exactly one of the following holds:*

1. $D = C\theta$, where $\theta = \{V/W\}$ does not decrease C and both V and W occur in C.

2. $D = C\theta$, where $\theta = \{f(X_1, \ldots, X_n)/W\}$ does not decrease C, f is an n-ary ($n \geq 0$) function symbol, W occurs in C and each $X_i, 1 \leq i \leq n$, is a distinct variable not occurring in C.

3. $D = H \leftarrow B \wedge P$, where P is a most general atom with respect to C for which $H \leftarrow B \wedge P$ is reduced.

Note that for any clause C there are at most a finite number of applications of (1) and (2), but an infinite number of applications of (3) since in general there are infinitely many atoms most general with respect to C. Shapiro [7] shows that these refinements can be enumerated by *size*.

Theorem 1 ρ_o *is not complete for* $\mathcal{L}$.

Proof We exhibit a counterexample. Consider the reduced clause $C = a \leftarrow p(A, B, C) \wedge p(D, E, C) \wedge p(F, G, E) \wedge p(F, B, H)$. Assume that $C \in \rho_o^\star(\Box)$. There must exist a reduced clause D such that $C \in \rho_o(D)$, obtained by an application of (1), (2) or (3) in the definition of ρ_o. Assume that C was obtained by (3). Removing any of the goals in the body produces a clause that is not reduced, counter to assumption. Clause C cannot have been obtained by (2) since it contains no function symbols. It cannot have been obtained by (1), since the replacement of a single occurrence of B, C, E or F leads to a reduced clause, counter to assumption. Since C cannot have been obtained by an application of (1), (2) or (3) it has no predecessor in ρ_0. ∎

6 A most general refinement operator

The above proof shows that if a refinement operator adds at most one literal at a time to a reduced clause, then it is impossible to construct a most general refinement operator, none of whose refinements will be reducible. This is a potentially serious problem for top down inductive systems since the introduction of non-reduced clauses into a refinement operator will lead to greatly reduced efficiency.

For the sake of completeness we produce a most general refinement operator (ρ_1), based on Shapiro's, which is complete for $\mathcal{L}$.

Definition 5 *Let $C = H \leftarrow B$ be a Horn clause. Then $D \in \rho_1(C)$ if exactly one of the following holds:*

1. *$D = C\theta$, where $\theta = \{V/W\}$ does not decrease C and both V and W occur in C.*

2. *$D = C\theta$, where $\theta = \{f(X_1, \ldots, X_n)/W\}$ does not decrease C, f is an n-ary $(n \geq 0)$ function symbol, W occurs in C and each $X_i, 1 \leq i \leq n$, is a distinct variable not occurring in C.*

3. *$D = H \leftarrow B \wedge P(X_1, \ldots, X_n)$, where P is a predicate symbol of arity n, and where the X_i are new variables not occurring in H or B.*

The proof that this refinement operator is complete is straightforward. Given a non-null clause $C = H \leftarrow B$ with B possibly empty we can show that C has a predecessor C' such that $C' \in \rho_1(C)$. If any literal $t \in B$ is of the form $p(X_1, \ldots, X_n)$ where the X_i are distinct variables not occurring elsewhere in C then $C' = C - \{t\}$ is a predecessor. Similarly if there is a term $t = f(X_1, \ldots, X_n)(n \geq 0)$ occurring one or more times in any place in any of the literals of C, and the X_i are distinct variables not occurring elsewhere in C then $C' = C\theta$ where $\theta = \{f(X_1, \ldots, X_n)/W\}$ and W does not occur in C is a predecessor. Otherwise if X is any variable occurring more than once in C, then replacing a single occurrence of X by W, where W is a variable not occurring in C provides a predecessor C'. Finally, if $C = p(X_1, \ldots, X_n) \leftarrow$ where the X_i are distinct variables, then the predecessor is $\square$. As each application of of ρ_1 increases *size* by 1 and since there a finite number of clauses of any given size n it follows that ρ_1 is a most general refinement operator for $\mathcal{L}$.

7 Conclusion

It seems that any top-down structuring of the Hypothesis space for Horn clause programs will suffer from the problem of redundant hypotheses. This leaves us in the position of having to make a tradeoff between efficiency and completeness, or of having to focus on restrictions of full Horn clause logic if we want to learn top down.

It is an open questions as to which restrictions on full first order logic are compatible with complete non-redundant refinement operators. Shapiro ([7]) illustrates a non-redundant refinement operator for the class of context-free transformations. We mention one additional subset here.

An interesting semantic restriction is to ij-determinate clauses [2]. With the restriction to ij-determinate clauses it is possible to show given a non-reduced clause correct with respect to the intended interpretation that any extension of this clause is equivalent with respect to the intended interpretation to a non-reduced clause. This means that redundant (ie. non-reduced) clauses need never be generated, and hence there is a most general refinement operator for ij-determinate clauses which does not generate redundant clauses.

The result suggests that it may be possible to learn ij-determinate programs efficiently within the MIS framework.

Acknowledgements

My thanks to Wray Buntine who pointed out a flaw in the proof that ρ_0 is a most general refinement operator. This work was partially supported by the European Community Esprit Programme under contract P2154, MLT.

References

[1] E.M. Gold. Language identification in the limit. *Information and Control*, 10:447–474, 1967.

[2] S. Muggleton and C. Feng. Efficient induction of logic programs. In S. Muggleton, editor, *Inductive Logic Programming*, pages 281–298. Academic Press, London, 1992.

[3] G.D. Plotkin. A note on inductive generalisation. In B. Meltzer and D. Michie, editors, *Machine Intelligence 5*, pages 153-163. Elsevier North-Holland, New York, 1970.

[4] G.D. Plotkin. *Automatic Methods of Inductive Inference*. PhD thesis, Edinburgh University, August 1971.

[5] G.D. Plotkin. A further note on inductive generalisation. In B. Meltzer and D. Michie, editors, *Machine Intelligence 6*, pages 101-124. Elsevier North-Holland, New York, 1971.

[6] E. Y. Shapiro. An algorithm that infers theories from facts. In *Proceedings of IJCAI-81*, pages 446-451. Kaufmann, Los Altos, CA, 1981.

[7] E.Y. Shapiro. Inductive inference of theories from facts. TR 192, Dept. Comp. Sc., Yale University, Connecticut, 1981.

[8] E.Y. Shapiro. *Algorithmic Program Debugging*. MIT Press, 1983.

An Iterative and Bottom-up Procedure for Proving-by-Example

Masami Hagiya

Department of Information Science, University of Tokyo
Hongo 7-3-1, Bunkyo-ku, Tokyo 113, JAPAN
hagiya@is.s.u-tokyo.ac.jp

Abstract. We give a procedure for generalizing a proof of a concrete instance of a theorem by recovering inductions that have been expanded in the concrete proof. It consists of three operations *introduction, extension* and *propagation,* and by iterating these operations in a bottom-up fashion, it can reconstruct nested inductions. We discuss how to use EBG for identifying the induction formula, and how EBG must be modified so that nested inductions can be reconstructed.

1 Introduction

When a teacher explains a theorem in mathematics to a student, he often picks up an appropriate instance of the theorem and explains why the theorem is true using that instance. In other words, he gives a proof of an instance of a theorem instead of proving its general case. A proof of a concrete instance often contains enough information to reconstruct a proof of the general case.

Explanation-based generalization (*EBG* for short), which has been formulated in the field of *deductive learning* or *explanation-based learning,* is a method for generalizing a proof as discussed above [2], though pure EBG generalizes a proof by simply replacing a term in a proof with a variable.

The problem we study in this paper, on the other hand, is that of generalizing a proof of an instance of a theorem and obtaining an inductive proof of the general case of the theorem by automatically recovering inductions that have been expanded in a proof of an instance. Some researchers in the field of explanation-based learning have also studied this problem under the name of *generalizing number* [?, 5], but there can be found very few foundational studies on the method that are based on formal logic except those by the author [3, 4].

Assume that we are given a concrete proof, i.e., a proof of a concrete instance of a theorem, as depicted in the left-hand side of Figure 1. In the figure, $P(i)$ denotes a proposition on natural number i, Π a proof of $P(0)$, Φ_0 a proof of $P(1)$ from $P(0)$, and Φ_1 a proof of $P(2)$ from $P(1)$.

If one can generalize proofs Φ_0 and Φ_1 to a single general proof Φ of $\forall i(P(i) \rightarrow P(S(i)))$, then one can obtain an inductive proof as depicted in the right-hand side of Figure 1. Note that S denotes the successor function and numerals 1, 2, etc. are considered as abbreviations of terms $S(0)$, $S(S(0))$, etc. The conclusion

$$\begin{array}{c} \Pi \\ P(0) \\ \Phi_0 \\ P(1) \\ \Phi_1 \\ P(2) \end{array}$$

$$\frac{\Pi \qquad\qquad \Phi}{P(0) \quad \forall i(P(i) \to P(S(i)))}{P(2)}$$

Fig. 1. A Concrete Proof and an Inductive Proof

$P(2)$ is considered to be derived from the universal formula $\forall i P(i)$. In proof Φ, $P(i)$ is called the *induction formula* and i the *induction variable*.

The procedure for generalizing a concrete proof as explained above must consist of those steps of finding the parts Π, Φ_0 and Φ_1, fixing the induction formula $P(i)$ and generalizing Φ_0 and Φ_1 to Φ.

The purpose of this paper is to formulate a generalization procedure that can iterate the above steps and reconstruct inductions that are nested within one another. We discuss how to use EBG for identifying the induction formula, and how EBG must be modified so that nested inductions can be reconstructed.

In this paper, we do not care whether a concrete proof is written by hand or automatically generated by a theorem prover. An SLD-trace of a logic program is a typical example of the latter case. As is explained in the next section, our procedure can reconstruct inductions whose induction formula $P(i)$ is of form $\exists x Q(i, x)$. By applying it to an SLD-trace of a logic program, one can obtain a proof that guarantees the existence of x for any i such that $Q(i, x)$ holds, i.e., the termination of the logic program with respect to the input-output relation $Q(i, x)$, where i is an input and x is an output.

In the deductive approach for program synthesis, the relation $Q(i, x)$ is given in advance and then the formula $\forall i \exists x Q(i, x)$ is proved. The generalization procedure of this paper, on the other hand, is given an SLD-trace of a logic program, and generalizes the trace to an inductive proof. The relation $Q(i, x)$ is not given in advance but is identified during generalization.

Bruynooghe, De Raedt and De Schreye in [1] use a concrete proof to guide unfold/fold program transformation, but a concrete proof is not directly generalized to an inductive proof.

In the next section, we introduce the recursion operator and formulate the induction schema. We then describe the operations of the generalization procedure. The extension of EBG is finally discussed.

2 Generalization Procedure

The generalization procedure of this paper reconstructs inductions whose induction formula $P(i)$ is of form $\exists x Q(i, x)$, where $Q(i, x)$ is an atomic formula. In general, x is a vector of variables, but for simplicity we assume that x is a single variable in this paper.

Formulas of form $\forall i \exists x Q(i, x)$ are called $\forall \exists$-*specifications,* and (constructively) proving a formula of this kind corresponds to synthesizing a program satisfying the input-output relation $Q(i, x)$, where i is considered as an input and x an output.

Since it is not easy to directly handle the existential quantifier $\exists$, we introduce the *recursion operator,* denoted by r, and express the output explicitly in term of the input and r. If n is a term denoting a natural number, $f(i, x)$ is a function whose first argument i is a natural number, and t is a term, then $r(n, f, t)$ is also a term. The operator r satisfies the following reduction rules.

$$r(0, f, t) = t$$
$$r(S(n), f, t) = f(n, r(n, f, t))$$

After introducing r, we can formulate the following inference rule, which we call Σ_1-*induction.*

$$\frac{\overset{\Pi}{P(0,t)} \qquad \overset{\Phi}{\forall i \forall x (P(i, x) \to P(S(i), f(i, x)))}}{P(n, r(n, f, t))}$$

This rule says that if Π is a proof of $P(0, t)$ and Φ is a proof of $\forall i \forall x (P(i, x) \to P(S(i), f(i, x)))$, then one can conclude $P(n, r(n, f, t))$ for any integer n. We also write the above inductive proof as $R(n, f, \Phi, t, \Pi)$, i.e., $R(n, f, \Phi, t, \Pi)$ is a proof of $P(n, r(n, f, t))$. In Φ, i is called the induction variable, $P(i, x)$ the induction formula and $f(i, x)$ the induction term.

The generalization procedure consists of the following three operations.

- Introducing an induction — If a proof of $P(1, u)$ from $P(0, t)$ can be generalized to an induction, replace it with an inductive proof.
- Extending an induction — If $P(S(n), v)$ is derived from $P(n, u)$ whose proof is inductive, extend the induction to $P(S(n), v)$.
- Propagating an induction — If there has been obtained an inductive proof of $P(n, u)$ and there exists a proof of $P(0, t)$ elsewhere, replace the latter with the inductive proof.

The procedure iteratively applies these operations from the inner subproofs to the outer ones, i.e., it applies the operations in a bottom-up fashion.

2.1 Introducing Inductions

In order to obtain a Σ_1-induction by generalization, we first search in the given concrete proof for a subproof of the following form.

$$\begin{array}{c} \Pi \\ A_0 \\ \Phi_0 \\ A_1 \end{array}$$

A_0 and A_1 are atomic formulas sharing the same predicate symbol. Π is a proof of A_0, and Φ_0 is a proof of A_1 from A_0, where the assumption A_0 is used exactly once in Φ_0.

The identification of the induction formula $P(i, x)$ and the induction term $f(i, x)$ is the most difficult step of this operation. Here is one of the possible methods.

We first apply the following EBG procedure on Φ_0, where A_0 is considered as the only *operational* atom.

1. For each maximal term appearing in Φ_0 (except those appearing in the axioms), introduce a new variable and replace the term with the new variable.
2. Do unification in each inference step of Φ_0 so that the inference step becomes valid.

By the second step, we obtain the most general substitution for the newly introduced variables such that the result is a valid proof.

Assume that by EBG, we have obtained a proof Φ'_0 of A'_1 from A'_0. Since Φ_0 is an instance of Φ'_0, there exists a substitution θ for the newly introduced variables such that $\theta(\Phi'_0) = \Phi_0$. Let A'_0 be of form $P(x_1, \cdots, x_n)$, where $x_1, \cdots, x_n$ are newly introduced variables that were not instantiated during EBG. We then check the following condition: A'_1 *is an instance of* $P(x_1, \cdots, x_n)$, *i.e., there exist terms* $u_1, \cdots, u_n$ *such that* $A'_1 = P(u_1, \cdots, u_n)$.

If the above condition is satisfied, we divide the variables $x_1, \cdots, x_n$ into the following three sets:

1. the set of x_j such that $u_j = S(x_j)$ and $\theta(x_j) = 0$.
2. the set of x_j such that $u_j = x_j$, and
3. the set of others.

We then introduce a new variable i, which is intended to become the induction variable, and replace each variable x_j in Set 1 with i. Each variable x_j in Set 2 is instantiated simply with $\theta(x_j)$. Each variable z that is not among $x_1, \cdots, x_n$ is also instantiated with $\theta(z)$.

In the following explanation, we assume that Set 3 consists of a single variable x and u is the corresponding term. We then define the function f by $f(i, x) = u$. As a result, we obtain a proof Φ of $P(S(i), f(i, x))$ from $P(i, x)$. Since i and x are arbitrary, it can be considered as a proof of $\forall i \forall x (P(i, x) \rightarrow P(S(i), f(i, x)))$.

We can finally obtain the inductive proof $R(1, f, \Phi, t, \Pi)$ of $P(1, f(0, t))$, because $A_0 = P(0, t)$ for some term t. The original proof of A_1 is then replaced with $R(1, f, \Phi, t, \Pi)$.

Let us give a simple example. Assume that we have the following axioms for the predicates add and mul. These axioms are exactly the definite clauses of the logic program defining add and mul.

$$\forall i\ \text{add}(0, i, i)$$
$$\forall i \forall j \forall k (\text{add}(i, j, k) \rightarrow \text{add}(S(i), j, S(k)))$$
$$\forall i\ \text{mul}(0, i, 0)$$
$$\forall i \forall j \forall k \forall l (\text{mul}(i, j, k) \wedge \text{add}(k, j, l) \rightarrow \text{mul}(S(i), j, l))$$

The proof of mul(2,2,4), which uses these axioms, takes the form of the tree in the following figure.

```
                           add(0,2,2)
                              |
  mul(0,2,0)    add(0,2,2)   add(1,2,3)
          \      /              |
          mul(1,2,2)           add(2,2,4)
                  \             /
                  mul(2,2,4)
```

The proof can be considered as an SLD-trace of the logic program.

The operation explained so far can be applied on the subproof whose conclusion is add(1,2,3). Applying EBG on the proof of add(1,2,3) from add(0,2,2), we obtain a proof of add($S(i), y, S(x)$) from add(i, y, x). By the above method, y is instantiated with 2, and we obtain the induction formula add($i, 2, x$), and the induction term $S(x)$. Function f is defined by $f(i, x) = S(x)$. We finally obtain the proof $R(1, f, \Phi, 2, \Pi)$ of add(1,2,3), where Π is the proof of add(0,2,2) and Φ is the proof of $\forall i \forall x(\text{add}(i, 2, x) \rightarrow \text{add}(S(i), 2, S(x)))$.

2.2 Extending Inductions

If n is a numeral and $P(S(n), f(n, u))$ is proved from $P(n, u)$, whose proof is of form $R(n, f, \Phi, t, \Pi)$, then one can extend the inductive proof $R(n, f, \Phi, t, \Pi)$ to $R(S(n), f, \Phi, t, \Pi)$, because $u = r(n, f, t)$.

In the previous example, this operation can be applied on the subproof of add(2,2,4). As a result, we obtain the proof $R(2, f, \Phi, 2, \Pi)$ of add(2,2,4) from the inductive proof $R(1, f, \Phi, 2, \Pi)$ of add(1,2,3).

2.3 Propagating Inductions

Assume that there exists a proof $R(n, f, \Phi, t, \Pi)$ of $P(n, u)$, where Φ is a proof of $P(S(i), f(i, x))$ from $P(i, x)$. Assume also that there exists a proof of $P(0, t')$ somewhere else. Then one can replace the proof of $P(0, t')$ with $R(0, f, \Phi, t', \Pi)$. We call this operation *propagation* of an induction.

This operation can be applied on add(0,2,2) above mul(1,2,2). As a result, the proof of add(0,2,2) is replaced with the inductive proof $R(0, f, \Phi, 2, \Pi)$.

One may generalize $R(n, f, \Phi, t, \Pi)$ before applying propagation. This makes the generalization procedure more complete.

2.4 EBG on Inductions

Since the procedure is iterated to reconstruct nested inductions, EBG may be applied on an inductive proof of form $R(n, f, \Phi, t, \Pi)$. Special care must be taken when applying EBG on Φ because Φ is a proof of $P(S(i), f(i, x)))$ from $P(i, x)$. Since i and x are universal variables, terms containing i or x must not be replaced

341

with a new variable during EBG. This means that terms that are maximal among those that do not contain i or x are replaced with new variables.

If the result of generalizing Φ is a proof Φ' of $P'(S(i), f'(i,x))$ from $P'(i,x)$ and that of generalizing Π is a proof Π' of P'', then one must introduce another new variable y and unify $P'(0,y)$ and P'' to make the induction valid.

In the previous example, EBG is applied on an inductive proof while the following subproof is being generalized.

```
mul(0,2,0)      add(0,2,2)
        \       /
        mul(1,2,2)
```

The proof $R(0, f, \Phi, 2, \Pi)$ of $\text{add}(0,2,2)$, which was obtained by propagation, is generalized to the proof $R(y, f, \Phi', z, \Pi')$, whose conclusion is $\text{add}(y, z, r(y, f, z))$. Therefore we obtain a proof of $\text{mul}(S(i), 2, r(x, f, 2))$ from $\text{mul}(i, 2, x)$. Thus we can introduce an induction by the introduction operation and reconstruct a nested induction. Note that the induction term of the outer induction is $r(x, f, 2)$.

Since the conclusion of an induction contains the recursion operator r, one must in general do unification between terms containing r during EBG. The details are not discussed here due to the space limitation.

References

1. Bruynooghe,M., De Raedt,L., De Schreye,D.: Explanation based program transformation, *Proceedings of IJCAI 89*, 1989, pp.407-412.
2. Ellman,T.: Explanation-based learning: A survey of programs and perspectives, *ACM Computing Surveys*, Vol.21, No.2 (1989), pp.163-221.
3. Hagiya,M.: Programming by example and proving by example using higher-order unification, *10th International Conference on Automated Deduction* (Stickel,M., ed.), Lecture Notes in Artificial Intelligence, Vol.449 (1990), pp.588-602.
4. Hagiya,M.: From programming-by-example to proving-by-example, *Theoretical Aspects of Computer Software* (Ito, T., Meyer,A.R., eds.), Lecture Notes in Computer Science, Vol.526 (1991), pp.387-419.
5. Shavlik,J.W., DeJong,G.F.: An explanation-based approach to generalizing number, *Proceedings of IJCAI 87*, 1987, pp.236-238.
6. Shavlik,J.W., DeJong,G.F.: Acquiring general iterative concepts by reformulating explanations of observed examples, *Machine Learning Volume III* (Kodratoff,Y., Michalski,R., eds.), 1990, pp.302-350.

Learnability of Constrained Logic Programs

Sašo Džeroski[1], Stephen Muggleton[2], Stuart Russell[3]

[1] Institut Jožef Stefan, Jamova 39, 61111 Ljubljana, Slovenia
[2] Oxford University Computing Laboratory, 11 Keble Road, Oxford OX1 3QD, UK
[3] Computer Science Division, University of California, Berkeley, CA94720, USA

Abstract. The field of *Inductive Logic Programming* (ILP) is concerned with inducing logic programs from examples in the presence of background knowledge. This paper defines the ILP problem and describes several syntactic restrictions that are often used in ILP. We then derive some positive results concerning the learnability of these restricted classes of logic programs, by reduction to a standard propositional learning problem. More specifically, k-literal predicate definitions consisting of constrained, function-free, nonrecursive program clauses are polynomially PAC-learnable under arbitrary distributions.

1 Introduction

The theory of Probably Approximately Correct (PAC) learning has been applied principally to propositional concept classes. Despite their successes, propositional learning approaches suffer from the limited expressiveness of their hypothesis language. Learning systems that use more expressive languages, have recently attracted a substantial amount of research in the machine learning community. As the learned hypothesis most often takes the form of a logic program, the field has been named Inductive Logic Programming (ILP) [10].

In this paper we will concentrate on the problem of learning a single concept or *target predicate*. Other work in ILP has focussed on learning several, possibly interdependent, concepts [14, 2]. Few PAC-learnability results have been established for either case (see Section 2), although the multiple-concept learning methods of [14] and [2] identify the correct concept in the limit.

Some ILP systems, such as LINUS [7], FOIL [12], and mFOIL [3], work by extending propositional approaches to a first-order framework. While FOIL and mFOIL use heuristic search techniques from propositional learning to construct first-order clauses directly, LINUS explicitly converts the first-order representation to a propositional one by defining an appropriate set of Boolean features.

In the paper, we use the transformation approach to obtain learnability results for logic programs by direct application of existing propositional PAC-learnability results. Section 2 defines the ILP problem and some syntactic restrictions, illustrating them in the context of a simple example. Section 3 shows how an ILP problem can be transformed to a propositional problem, and Section 4 gives the principal results. Section 5 discusses ways in which the imposed restrictions might be relaxed and suggests topics for further research.

2   Inductive Logic Programming

In the rest of this paper, we will assume that the reader is familiar with logic programming terminology as defined in the standard textbook of Lloyd [8]. In the logical framework we have adopted, a concept is a predicate. When expressed as a logic program, a concept (predicate) definition is a set of clauses, each having the same (target) predicate in its head.

The task of ILP is defined as follows. Given is a set $\mathcal{E} = \mathcal{E}^+ \cup \mathcal{E}^-$ of positive $\mathcal{E}^+$ and negative $\mathcal{E}^-$ examples of a target predicate, represented as ground literals. Background knowledge $\mathcal{B}$, a set of normal program clauses, typically including further facts describing the examples in $\mathcal{E}^+$ and $\mathcal{E}^-$, is also given. The task is to find a hypothesis $\mathcal{H}$, also a set of normal program clauses, such that $\mathcal{B} \wedge \mathcal{H} \models \mathcal{E}^+$ (where $\models$ is the relation of logical entailment), and $\forall e \in \mathcal{E}^- : \mathcal{B} \wedge \mathcal{H} \not\models e$. We define l to be the number of distinct predicates $p_1 \ldots p_l$ in $\mathcal{B}$, and n to be the arity (number of arguments) of the target predicate q.

In practice, ILP systems work within various syntactic restrictions in order to limit the complexity of the problem. In a *k-literal predicate definition* each clause has at most k literals in its body. A *k-clause predicate definition* consists of up to k clauses. A k-clause definition corresponds to a first-order k-term DNF formula and a k-literal definition to a first-order k-DNF formula.

Several additional restrictions are defined below. First of all, we assume an integer constant j is given. We consider only problems where all predicates in $\mathcal{B}$ are of arity not greater than j. We also require the background knowledge $\mathcal{B}$ to be efficient. We call $\mathcal{B}$ *efficient* if all atomic queries to it can be answered in time polynomial in the arity of the query predicate.

Several types of restrictions can be imposed on the clauses that form the hypothesis. A clause is *constrained* if all variables in its body also appear in the head. A clause is *function-free* if it mentions no function symbols. A clause is *nonrecursive* if the predicate symbol in its head does not appear in any of the literals in its body. A predicate definition is constrained/function-free/nonrecursive if all the clauses in it are constrained/function-free/nonrecursive. Although mutually recursive predicate definitions are not considered recursive above, this causes no problems as we are concerned with learning a definition of a single predicate, given definitions of some other predicates.

Let us illustrate the above definitions on the ILP problem of learning the *daughter* relationship. The task is to define the target relation $daughter(X, Y)$, which states that person X is a daughter of person Y, in terms of the background knowledge predicates *female* and *parent*, the latter being defined in terms of the relations *mother* and *father*. All these relations are given in Table 1. There are two positive and two negative examples of the target relation.

A 1-*clause* definition of the target predicate in terms of the specified background knowledge predicates is: $daughter(X, Y) \leftarrow female(X), parent(Y, X)$. In the above terminology, this hypothesis is nonrecursive, constrained and function-free. It is also a 2-literal definition, where the maximum arity of background knowledge predicates is 2 ($k = 2, j = 2$).

Training examples	Background knowledge		
$daughter(sue, ann)$. $\oplus$	$mother(ann, sue)$.	$parent(X, Y) \leftarrow$	$female(ann)$.
$daughter(eve, tom)$. $\oplus$	$mother(ann, tom)$.	$mother(X, Y)$.	$female(eve)$.
$daughter(tom, ann)$. $\ominus$	$father(tom, eve)$.	$parent(X, Y) \leftarrow$	$female(sue)$.
$daughter(eve, ann)$. $\ominus$	$father(tom, jim)$.	$father(X, Y)$.	

Table 1. A simple ILP problem: learning family relationships.

Given the above definitions, we can state the following prior results. Page and Frisch [11] have shown that a single constrained, nonrecursive definite program clause is PAC-learnable. Džeroski and Lavrač [4] have shown that the problem of learning constrained nonrecursive function-free program clauses can be transformed into a propositional learning problem. Džeroski et al. [5] prove that k-clause determinate function-free nonrecursive definitions are PAC-learnable under simple distributions.

The work reported here is based on the latter results, and extends the former, replacing the single constrained nonrecursive definite clause with a set of nonrecursive constrained function-free program clauses. The class of constrained programs considered in this paper is a proper subset of the class of determinate programs considered in [5]. However, the learnability results for determinate programs are *distribution-dependent*, i.e., they hold for the class of simple distributions only, whereas the results presented here are *distribution-free*.

3 Transforming ILP problems to propositional form

Our learnability results are based on transforming an ILP problem to a propositional form, then using propositional learnability results. We consider only the problem of learning nonrecursive constrained function-free program clauses. To solve the problem of constructing a definition for the target predicate $q(X_1, X_2, ..., X_n)$ by transforming it to propositional form proceed as follows.

Algorithm 1

Input: *Examples for target predicate $q(X_1, X_2, \ldots, X_n)$ and definitions of predicates $p_1, p_2, ..., p_l$.*

Output: *A propositional learning task, i.e., a set of features and a set of examples (vectors of feature values).*

1. *$F = \{ p_r(Y_1, Y_2, ..., Y_{r_j}) | p_r \in \{p_1, ..., p_l\}, Y_i \in \{X_1, ..., X_n\}\}$*
2. *for each $q(a_1, a_2, ..., a_n) \in \mathcal{E}^+$ and each $\neg q(a_1, a_2, ..., a_n) \in \mathcal{E}^-$ do*
   - *set the values of $X_1, ..., X_n$ to $a_1, ..., a_n$,*
   - *determine f, the vector of truth values of the literals in F, by posing the corresponding ground queries from F to the background knowledge,*
   - *f is an example of a propositional concept c (positive if $q(a_1, a_2, ..., a_n)$ or negative if $\neg q(a_1, a_2, ..., a_n)$)*

First, construct a list F of all literals that use predicates from the background knowledge and variables from the set $\{X_1, X_2, ..., X_n\}$. This is the list of features used for propositional learning. Second, transform the examples to propositional form. For each example, the truth value of each of the propositional features is determined by calls (queries) to the background knowledge. These two steps are done by Algorithm 1.

Next, apply a propositional learning algorithm to the propositional version of the problem. Finally, transform the induced propositional concept definition to program clause form. In this step, each feature in the propositional description is replaced with the corresponding literal.

The background knowledge $\mathcal{B}$ may take the form of a set of ground facts or a nonground logic program. Only ground (membership) queries have to be posed to $\mathcal{B}$. (NB: These are not queries to the example distribution!) The arguments of the target and background knowledge predicates may be sorted (or typed), as in LINUS [7], in which case the number of propositional features involved is greatly reduced [4].

To illustrate the transformation process, Table 2 gives the propositional version of the ILP problem from Table 1. In Table 2, d, f and p stand for $daughter$, $female$ and $parent$, respectively. To outline the transformation from a propositional DNF formula to a predicate definition, suppose a propositional learner induces the concept $c \leftrightarrow x_1 \wedge x_5$ from the examples in Table 2. The feature x_1 is replaced with the literal $female(X)$, the feature x_5 with the literal $parent(Y, X)$ and the definition obtained is: $daughter(X, Y) \leftarrow female(X), parent(Y, X)$.

$d(X,Y)$	X	Y	Propositional features					
			$f(X)$	$f(Y)$	$p(X,X)$	$p(X,Y)$	$p(Y,X)$	$p(Y,Y)$
c			x_1	x_2	x_3	x_4	x_5	x_6
1	sue	ann	1	1	0	0	1	0
1	eve	tom	1	0	0	0	1	0
0	tom	ann	0	1	0	0	1	0
0	eve	ann	1	1	0	0	0	0

Table 2. Propositional form of the *daughter* relationship problem.

4 Results

Theorem 1. *Algorithm 1 transforms the ILP problem of learning a set of constrained nonrecursive function-free program clauses defined by a set of m examples $\mathcal{E}$ of the target predicate $q(X_1, X_2, ..., X_n)$, and background predicates $p_1, p_2, ..., p_l$ of maximum arity j, to a propositional form in $\mathcal{O}(poly(j)mln^j)$, time, if each query to the background knowledge takes $\mathcal{O}(poly(j))$ to answer.*

Proof: The number of features in F (step 1 of the algorithm) is bounded by $N = ln^j$, as the arity of the background predicates is bounded by j, and for each of the l background predicate there can be at most n^j features. The transformation of a single example to propositional form takes $\mathcal{O}(poly(j)N)$ time to determine the truth values of features in F. For m examples, the transformation process takes $\mathcal{O}(poly(j)mln^j)$ time. $\square$

Theorem 2. *k-literal nonrecursive predicate definitions consisting of constrained function-free normal program clauses are polynomially PAC-learnable under arbitrary distributions.*

Proof: After transforming the problem to a propositional form, we use the algorithm for learning k-DNF outlined in [6]. The transformation from propositional k-DNF to a k-literal definition takes $\mathcal{O}(h)$ time, where h is the size of the induced propositional formula, which is at most $\mathcal{O}((2N)^{k+1})$ time. The learnability under arbitrary distributions of k-literal predicate definitions consisting of nonrecursive constrained function-free program clauses then follows from the polynomial PAC-learnability of k-DNF. $\square$

5 Discussion and further work

We have proved a positive learnability result for a restricted class of logic programs. The complexity analysis indicates that our approach would scale well with the arity of the target predicate and the number of predicates in the background knowledge, but not with the maximum number of literals in a clause and the maximum arity of background knowledge predicates.

Despite the imposed restrictions, the considered class of logic programs includes many interesting and nontrivial concept definitions. These include concepts from chess, such as position illegality in a chess endgame [12, 7, 3], and qualitative models of dynamic systems [3]. Such concepts have been successfully induced by existing ILP systems.

Let us now discuss how these restrictions can be removed. Removal of the function-free restriction is straightforward, because any clause containing function symbols can be *flattened*, that is, rewritten in function-free form with the addition of one background clause per function symbol [13]. However, a constrained clause with function symbols can yield a flattened clause with new variables. Thus, the restrictions to constrained and function-free clauses are tightly coupled. Fortunately, the new variables introduced by the flattening process are determinate, i.e., have uniquely determined values, given the values of the old variables.

In a separate paper [5], we relax both restrictions and prove that k-clause function-free determinate predicate definitions are learnable under a broad class of distributions, called simple distributions [9]. However, the learnability results for the determinate (possibly recursive) case, require sampling according to the noncomputable universal distribution m [9], or its polynomial-time version, whereas the results presented here are distribution-free.

The restriction to non-recursive clauses is a more fundamental one. It can be relaxed if we allow the use of queries [5] about the target predicate. These results are also derived for simple distributions under the assumption of sampling according to the universal distribution m. Further research should concentrate on removing the determinacy restriction and the restriction to simple distributions. Only positive results can be obtained using our transformation approach. Namely, the hardness of a transformed propositional problem does not guarantee that the original first-order problem cannot be solved efficiently by some other means. Page and Frisch [11] show positive results for constrained clauses, also showing negative results for sorted theories. An advantage of our approach, however, is that new propositional PAC-learnability results, such as [1], can be transferred to the ILP framework.

Acknowledgements

The work reported in this paper is part of the ESPRIT BRA Project 6020 Inductive Logic Programming. Thanks to Luc De Raedt for his comments on the paper.

References

1. D. Angluin, M. Frazier and L. Pitt. Learning conjunctions of Horn clauses. *Machine Learning*, 9(2): 147–164, 1992.
2. L. De Raedt. *Interactive Theory Revision: An Inductive Logic Programming Approach*. Academic Press, London, 1992.
3. S. Džeroski and I. Bratko. Handling noise in inductive logic programming. In *Proc. Second International Workshop on Inductive Logic Programming*. ICOT TM-1182, Tokyo, 1992.
4. S. Džeroski and N. Lavrač. Refinement graphs for FOIL and LINUS. In S.H. Muggleton, editor, *Inductive Logic Programming*, pages 319–333, Academic Press, London, 1992.
5. S. Džeroski, S. Muggleton and S. Russell. PAC-learnability of determinate logic programs. In *Proc. Fifth ACM Workshop on Computational Learning Theory*, pages 128–135, ACM Press, Baltimore, MD, 1992.
6. D. Haussler. Quantifying inductive bias: AI learning algorithms and Valiant's model. *Artificial Intelligence*, 36(2): 177–221, 1988.
7. N. Lavrač, S. Džeroski and M. Grobelnik. Learning nonrecursive definitions of relations with LINUS. In *Proc. Fifth European Working Session on Learning*, pages 265–281, Springer, Berlin, 1991.
8. J. W. Lloyd. *Foundations of Logic Programming* (2nd edn), Springer, Berlin, 1987.
9. M. Li and P. Vitányi. Learning simple concepts under simple distributions. *SIAM Journal of Computing*, 20(5): 911–935, 1991.
10. S. H. Muggleton. *Inductive Logic Programming*, Academic Press, London, 1992.
11. C. D. Page and A. M. Frisch. Generalization and learnability: a study of constrained atoms. In S. H. Muggleton, editor, *Inductive Logic Programming*, pages 29–61, Academic Press, London, 1992.
12. J. R. Quinlan. Learning logical definitions from relations. *Machine Learning*, 5(3): 239–266, 1990.
13. C. Rouveirol. Extensions of inversion of resolution applied to theory completion. In S.H. Muggleton, editor, *Inductive Logic Programming*, pages 63–92, Academic Press, London, 1992.
14. E. Y. Shapiro. *Algorithmic Program Debugging*, The MIT Press, Cambridge, MA, 1983.

Complexity Dimensions and Learnability

S.H. Nienhuys-Cheng and M. Polman

Dept. of Computer Science,
Erasmus University of Rotterdam,
The Netherlands,
Email: cheng@cs.few.eur.nl

Abstract. In a discussion of the *Vapnik Chervonenkis* (VC) *dimension* ([7]), which is closely related to the learnability of concept classes in Valiant's PAC-model ([6]), we will give an algorithm to compute it. Furthermore, we will take Natarajan's equivalent dimension for *well-ordered* classes into a more general scheme, by showing that these well-ordered classes happen to satisfy some general condition, which makes it possible to construct for a class a number of equivalent dimensions. We will give this condition, as well as a relatively efficient algorithm for the calculation of one such dimension for well-ordered classes.

1 Introduction

The PAC-model is concerned with learning concepts f (sets of strings from some domain X), grouped together in a concept class F. F is called PAC-learnable if, globally, an algorithm exists that reads in examples (pairs x, y where $x \in X$ and $y = 0$ if $x \notin f$ and $y = 1$ if $x \in f$) for some *target* concept $f \in F$, and outputs a concept $g \in F$ that is with tunable probability tunably close to f. We are interested in the number of examples needed to PAC-learn F; we call F *polynomial sample learnable* (PSL) if, globally, the number of examples needed to learn any $f \in F$ is bounded by a polynomial in the input parameters of a PAC-algorithm, among which is n, the maximum length of the example strings. For formal definitions of the above notions, we refer to [2] and [4]. For the proofs omitted in this article, regarding a number of results, we refer to our research report ([4]).

2 Shattering and the VC-Dimension

An important notion in PAC-learning is *shattering*.

Definition. A class of concepts F on X *shatters* a set $S \subseteq X$ if the set given by $\{f \cap S | f \in F\}$ is the power set of S (denoted by 2^S).

Definition. The *VC-dimension* of a concept class F on X is the greatest integer d such that there exists a set $S \subseteq X$ of cardinality d that is shattered by F. It is denoted by $D_{\text{vc}}(F)$. If no greatest d exists, $D_{\text{vc}}(F)$ is infinite.

We can think of a set S, shattered by class F, *partitioning* F: $f, g \in F$ are equivalent if $f \cap S = g \cap S$, which gives a total of $2^{|S|}$ equivalence classes.

Our objective is to find an algorithm for the computation of $D_{vc}(F)$, where $|\cup F|$ is finite. Consider the following:

Definition. Let F shatter S. We call $x \in \cup F - S$ an *extending* element of S if for every $A \subseteq S$, we can split the equivalence class (denoted by $F_{S,A}$) into two nonempty subclasses: the concepts that contain x, and the ones that do not.

Lemma 1. *Let F shatter S. Then $T = S \cup \{x\}$ is shattered by F iff x is an extending element for S. (If no extending element exists, S is called maximal.)*

Notice that for a maximal set S, $|S|$ does not always equal D_{vc}.

The algorithm we constructed computes $D_{vc}(F)$ by expanding in each iteration the shattered sets found in previous iterations. This is done by adding to these sets an extending element, if possible, until no extending element can be found for any generated set. Extending elements for previously found shattered sets are found by splitting the equivalence classes as in the definition.

Algorithm:
1. Let $d = 0$. Start with the empty set $\emptyset$ and its equivalence class $F_{\emptyset,\emptyset} = F$.
2. Suppose $d = n$. Suppose also that we have constructed $S_1, ..., S_k$ where every S_i is shattered by F and $|S_i| = n$. For all $x \in \cup F - S_i$ check if every $F_{S_i,A}$ (found in the previous iteration) can be divided into $F_{S_i \cup \{x\}, A \cup \{x\}}$ and $F_{S_i \cup \{x\}, A}$, both nonempty. If yes, then let $d = n+1$. Every $S_i \cup \{x\}$ is a shattered set of $n+1$ elements.
3. Repeat step 2 until no extending element exists for any S_i: $D_{vc}(F) = d$.

Example 1. Consider class F: $f_1 = \{0, 2, 3\}$, $f_2 = \{0, 3, 4\}$, $f_3 = \{1, 2, 3\}$, $f_{4,} = \{0, 1, 3, 4\}$, $f_5 = \{0, 1, 2, 3\}$, $f_6 = \{2, 3, 5\}$, $f_7 = \{1, 3, 4\}$, $f_8 = \{3, 4\}$.
$D_{vc}(F)$ can be found in the following way (we will only follow one "track"): $\emptyset$ can be extended to $\{0\}$ because F can be divided into: $F_1 = \{f_1, f_2, f_4, f_5\}$ and $F_2 = \{f_3, f_6, f_7, f_8\}$. $\{0\}$ can be extended to $\{0, 1\}$ because F_1 can be divided into: $F_3 = \{f_4, f_5\}$ and $F_4 = \{f_1, f_2\}$. Similarly $\{0, 1\}$ can be extended to $\{0, 1, 2\}$. No 4-element shattered set can be found, so $D_{vc}(F) = 3$.

We proceed with a number of definitions and results, important for the following sections:

Definition. Let X_n be the set of strings in domain X of length $\leq n$. The class of *projections* F_n over X_n is the set given by $\{f \cap X_n | f \in F\}$.
A concept class F is said to be of *polynomial* VC-dimension if $D_{vc}(F_n)$ is $O(p(n))$ for some polynomial p.

Theorem 2 [1]. *A class of concepts F is PSL if and only if F is of polynomial VC-dimension.*

Lemma 3 [3]. *Let F be a class of concepts on some finite domain X. Then $2^{d_{vc}} \leq |F| \leq (|X| + 1)^{d_{vc}}$, where $d_{vc} = D_{vc}(F)$.*

3 Alternative Dimension

Besides PSL another learnability criterion exists, called PSL with omission-only error from positive examples: only positive examples are given to the algorithm and its output concept should always be a subset of the target concept. For a class F to be thus learnable, it has to be *well-ordered* and have a polynomial VC-dimension *or* a polynomial *dimension* (see [2]). We will need the following definitions:

Definition. Let $f \in F$. $graph(f)$ is the set of all examples for f. We call f *consistent* with a set of examples S if $S \subseteq graph(f)$. A class F is called *well-ordered* if, for any set of positive examples S for some concept f in F, there exists a concept $g \in F$ such that g is consistent with S and g is a subset of any concept in F consistent with S. (We call g the *least concept consistent with S*, denoted by $M(S)$.)

Definition dimension ([2]). The *dimension* of a well-ordered class F of concepts, $dim(F)$, is the least integer d such that for every concept $f \in F$, there exists a set S_f, $|S_f| \leq d$, such that $f = M(S_f)$.

In [2] it is proved that a well-ordered class is PSL with omission only error iff $dim(F_n)$ is $O(p(n))$ for some polynomial p. To find $dim(F)$ we consider the sets S of elements in every f such that f is $M(S)$. Any such S of minimal cardinality may be chosen as S_f. Then we have: $dim(F) = max\{|S_f| \, | f \in F\}$. We will proceed with a number of propositions concerning well-ordered classes.

Proposition 4 ([2]). *A finite class of concepts F is well-ordered iff for any $f, g \in F$, there exists an $h \in F$ such that $h = f \cap g$.*

Proposition 5 ([2]). *Let F be well-ordered. Let A and B be two sets of elements. Then $M(A \cup B) = M(M(A) \cup M(B))$*

Proposition 6. *Let F be well-ordered. Then $f \in F$ is the least concept consistent with a set $S \subset f$ iff there is no $g \in F$ such that $S \subseteq g \subset f$. Also, let f be $M(S)$ and let $S' \supset S$, $S' \subseteq f$. Then $f = M(S')$.*

With these propositions the following (essential) theorem can be proved

Theorem 7. *Let F be a well-ordered class over domain X. If $f \in F$ and S is any set such that:*
1. $f = M(S)$
2. there is no $S' \subset S$ such that $f = M(S')$
Then S is shattered by F and has no extending elements within f. (We call S a minimal set of f.)

Proof. f is not the least concept consistent with any proper subset of S. Suppose F does not shatter S. Then there exists a set $S' \subset S$ such that there is no concept $g \in F$ with $g \cap S = S'$. Let $h = M(S')$ and $T = h \cap S$. Then $T \neq S'$, so $T \cap (S - S')$

is nonempty and $|T| > |S'|$. Since $S = (S-T) \cup S' \cup T$, it follows from Proposition 5 that:

$$M(S) = M(M(S-T) \cup M(S') \cup M(T)) .$$

Now, from Proposition 6 it follows that $M(S')$ is the same concept as $M(T)$. Therefore, and by Proposition 5:

$$M(S) = M(M(S-T) \cup M(S')) = M((S-T) \cup S') .$$

So, $f = M(S) = M((S-T) \cup S')$, but $|S| > |(S-T) \cup S'|$: f is the least concept consistent with a subset of S, which gives us a contradiction: $h \cap S = S'$. We conclude that S is shattered by F. After this it is easily verifiable that S has no extending elements within f.

4 Equivalent Dimensions

We will define a more general property for concept classes than that of well-orderedness; for classes having this property, a number of alternative dimensions (among which dim), all equivalent to D_{vc}, can be constructed.

Consider this: let F be a concept class over finite domain X, such that there exists an injective function $\mu : F \to 2^X$, where $|\mu(f)| \le D_{vc}(F)$ for every $f \in F$. If we associate with μ a number $D_\mu(F) = max\{|\mu(f)| \mid f \in F\}$, then

Theorem 8. $d_\mu \le d_{vc} \le d_\mu \, ^2\log(|X|+1)$, where $d_\mu = D_\mu(F)$ and $d_{vc} = D_{vc}(F)$.

The essence of the above is this: suppose that F is such, that for each $f \in F$, there is a set S, $|S| \le D_{vc}(F)$, somehow uniquely related to f. Then, if the function μ gives one such set for every f, $D_\mu(F)$ gives us a dimension with the properties of Theorem 8. Now suppose that F is such, that a μ exists, which generates (for every $n \in N$) for every $f_n \in F_n$ a set of elements from X_n smaller than $D_{vc}(F_n)$. Then our result would change to:

$$D_\mu(F_n) \le D_{vc}(F_n) \le D_\mu(F_n) \, ^2\log(|X_n| + 1) .$$

Since $^2\log(|X_n|+1)$ grows only polynomially in n, $D_{vc}(F_n)$ is $O(p(n))$ iff $D_\mu(F_n)$ is $O(q(n))$, where p and q are polynomials in n: D_μ is *equivalent* to D_{vc}.

Thus, the property we were looking for is the existence of a function μ as specified above. With any such μ we can associate a new dimension equivalent to the VC-dimension. Clearly, well-ordered classes are an example of classes having this general property: μ could be such that $\mu(f_n) = S_{f_n}$. Then $D_\mu(F_n) = dim(F_n)$, which is equivalent to $D_{vc}(F_n)$.

5 An Algorithm For An Alternative Dimension

We have constructed an algorithm to find, for any concept f in a well-ordered class F over domain X, a set R_f, such that f is $M(R_f)$. Any subset R_f^- of R_f, that is a minimal set (as in Theorem 7) of f, is shattered by F. Furthermore, if we define a new dimension as the cardinality of the greatest R_f^- for all f, then this dimension is equivalent to the VC-dimension (just as $dim(F)$). We need the following definitions:

Definition. $\emptyset$ is said to have 0 layers. $f \in F$ is said to have k *layers* if every $g \subset f$ has less than k layers and there is at least one $g \subset f$ that has $k-1$ layers. For every $f \in F$, a *representation set* R_f is defined as follows:
1. If f is $\emptyset$, then $R_f = \emptyset$.
2. Suppose R_g is defined for every concept g with less than k layers. Consider the set H, being $\{h| \not\exists g, f \supset g \supset h\}$. Let $H = \{h_1, ..., h_n\}$. If $f \neq \cup h_i$, then pick any $a \in f - \cup h_i$ and let $R_f = \{a\}$. If $f = \cup h_i$, then define $R_f = \cup R_{h_i}$.

Example 2. Consider Fig. 1a: In this figure concepts in a concept class over the integer domain are represented by Venn-diagrams. A representation set for the 3-layer concept $\{1, 2, 3, 4\}$ is $\{2, 3, 4\}$. A representation set for the most outer concept is $\{9\}$.

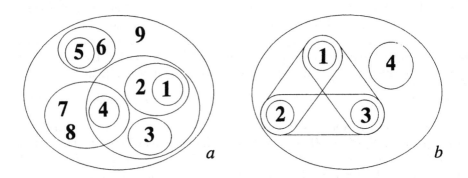

Fig. 1. Concept classes over the integer domain

Proposition 9. *For any $f \in F$, $\not\exists g \in F$, with $R_f \subseteq g \subset f$. So f is the least concept consistent with R_f.*

From Theorem 7 of Sect. 3, it follows that any minimal set $R_f^- \subseteq R_f$ is shattered by F. Proposition 9 guarantees that such an R_f^- exists. Suppose that F_n is well-ordered for each n. If we choose for every $f_n \in F$ an R_{f_n} and if $\mu(f_n)$ is any $R_{f_n}^-$, then we have:

Theorem 10. *Let $D(F_n) = max\{|R_{f_n}^-| | f_n \in F_n\}$ for each n. Then D is a dimension equivalent to D_{vc}.*

All of the above leads immediately to an algorithm to find an R_f for every $f \in F$: first construct representative sets of the 1-layer concepts, then the 2-layer concepts, etc. until every $f \in F$ has an R_f. The efficiency lies in the fact that every R_f is built up from at most $|H|$ (as in the definition of R_f) sets of elements, which are already known by the time R_f is being calculated. Furthermore, the total number of elements involved in the calculation never exceeds $|F|$. The next thing to be done is to find a set $R_f^- \subseteq R_f$, that is a minimal set of f. The largest such R_f^- gives us our dimension.

Example 3. Consider Fig. 1b, where the representative set of the most outer concept is $\{1, 2, 3, 4\}$. Minimal subsets of it are $\{1, 2, 3\}$ and $\{1, 4\}$.

6 Conclusion

If a concept class F fulfils the required properties, we can define new dimensions, equivalent to D_{vc}, with respect to functions over F. After proving that a minimal set for some concept in a well-ordered class is shattered, we can compute such a dimension by a relatively efficient algorithm, using a representation set R_f for every concept f and a minimal subset $R_f^- \subseteq R_f$ of f.

7 Future Work

Since we find a strong correspondence between concepts in PAC-learning and models in first order logic, we are currently working on applying complexity dimension theory to classes of models. More about this can be found in [5].

References

1. Blumer, A., Ehrenfeucht, A., Haussler, D., Warmuth, M.: Learnability and the Vapnik-Chervonenkis Dimension. Journal of the Association for Computing Machinery **36** No. **4** (1989) 929-965
2. Natarajan, B.: On Learning Boolean Functions. Proceedings of the 19th Annual ACM Symposium on Theory of Computation 269-304
3. Natarajan, B.: Machine Learning, a Theoretical Approach. Morgan Kaufman Publishers, Inc (1991)
4. Nienhuys-Cheng, S.H., Polman, M.: Complexity Dimensions and Learnability. Research Report EUR-CS-92-06 (1992)
5. Polman, M., Nienhuys-Cheng, S.H.: Some Topics Related to PAC-Learning. Proceedings of CSN'92, Utrecht, Netherlands, (nov. 1992)
6. Valiant, L.G.: A theory of the learnable. Communications of the ACM **27** No. **11** (1984) 1134-1142
7. Vapnik, V., and Chervonenkis, A.: On the uniform convergence of relative frequencies of events to their probabilities. Theory of Probability and its Applications **16** No. **2** (1971) 264-280

Can Complexity Theory Benefit from Learning Theory?

Tibor Hegedűs

Department of Computer Science
Comenius University, 84215 Bratislava, Slovakia
hegedus@mff.uniba.cs

We show that the results achieved within the framework of Computational Learning Theory are relevant enough to have non-trivial applications in other areas of Computer Science, namely in Complexity Theory. Using known results on efficient query-learnability of some Boolean concept classes, we prove several (co-NP-completeness) results on the complexity of certain decision problems concerning representability of general Boolean functions in special forms.

1. Introduction

The seminal paper of Valiant [11] initiated a considerable amount of research in Computational Learning Theory. The goal of the field is to "give a rigorous, computationally
detailed and plausible account of how learning can be done" [2]. This characterizatio
indicates a close relationship to Complexity Theory. In fact, the considered mode
and criteria of successful learning are all in the spirit of traditional Complexity Theor
In addition to this methodological contribution, it turned out to be the case [10] th
complexity-theoretic results can be applied directly to show non-learnability results i
the standard PAC model. More precisely, if the CONSISTENCY problem for a class
Boolean functions (deciding whether there is a function in the class consistent with give
data) is NP-hard, then that class is not PAC -learnable in a representation-depende
sense (if RP≠NP), *i.e.*, Learning Theory also benefits from some particular results
Complexity Theory.

However, in this paper we show that the cooperation between the two fields is n
necessarily destined to be a one-way traffic. To do this, we use a recent result of [5] whi
says that if a class of Boolean functions is learnable using equivalence and membershi
queries (again in a representation-dependent sense), then the MEMBERSHIP proble
for that class (deciding whether a function given, say, in DNF, belongs to that class
is in co-NP. MEMBERSHIP is essentially the problem of deciding whether a gener
Boolean function is representable in a special form. Because a number of classes ha

been shown to be query-learnable, we obtain several non-trivial inclusions in co-NP for decision problems which are intuitively only in Σ_2^p. In fact, in most cases we prove that the considered problems are co-NP-complete. This is the case of linearly separable functions (functions computable by a single neuron - the basic component of neural networks), threshold functions of order at most k (for any fixed $k \geq 0$), n-dimensional balls, k-DNF and k-CNF functions (for any fixed $k \geq 1$), read-once and read-twice DNF formulas, and k-term DNF (k-clause CNF) formulas for any fixed $k \geq 1$ (using the last result, some progress on the complexity of the MINIMAL DNF EXPRESSION problem [4] is also achieved). As far as the corresponding search problems (find a special representation of a function given in DNF if one exists) are concerned, using query-learnability they can be solved in time $2^{O(nm)}$ (n is the number of variables and m the number of terms in the input).

All these results suggest that Computational Learning Theory is a mature field and its results are relevant enough to have non-trivial applications in other areas of Computer Science.

2. Definitions and models

We denote (for $n \geq 1$) $X_n = \{0,1\}^n$, $F_n = \{ f \mid f : X_n \to \{0,1\} \}$. For a function (concept) $f \in F_n$, $\mathrm{POS}(f) = \{ x \mid x \in X_n \text{ and } f(x) = 1 \}$. A concept class is a sequence $C = \{C_n\}_{n\geq 1}$, $C_n \subseteq F_n$ for all $n \geq 1$.

Informally, learning a concept is equivalent to identifying it from a given class of possibilities (concept class). The formal models of concept learning are further specified by determining what is a learning algorithm and what are the criteria of succesful identification.

A concept class C is PAC-learnable if there is a polynomial algorithm A and a polynomial p such that for every $n \geq 1$, every target concept $f \in C_n$, every probability distribution D_n on X_n, and every ϵ, δ ($0 < \epsilon, \delta < 1$) the following holds: if A is given a sample of $p(n, \frac{1}{\epsilon}, \frac{1}{\delta})$ pairs $(x, f(x))$ selected from X_n according to D_n, then it outputs a representation of a hypothesis $h \in C_n$ such that with probability at least $1 - \delta$, the error of h (the probability that a randomly selected point $x \in X_n$ is classified differently by the target function and the final hypothesis) is at most ϵ (this is the original model introduced by Valiant [11]; see [2, 3] for more details).

If exact, on-line learning is considered, we will say that C is query-learnable if for every $n \geq 1$ each concept $f \in C_n$ is exactly identifiable by a polynomial time (in n) algorithm using equivalence queries from C_n and membership queries. An equivalence query is a question of the type "Does the concept $f \in C_n$ equal to the target concept?" (if not, we are given a counterexample); a membership query is a question like "Does the value of the target concept on $x \in X_n$ equal to 1?" (see [2] for details).

3. Results

The basic idea of [10] in using complexity-theoretic results within the framework of Learning Theory is based on a correspondence between PAC-learnability of a concept class C and the complexity of the decision problem CONSISTENCY for C.

> CONSISTENCY for C
> Instance: POS, $NEG \subseteq \{0,1\}^n$ (for some $n \geq 1$).
> Question: Is there a function $f \in C_n$ such that $f(x) = 1$ for all $x \in POS$ and $f(x) = 0$ for all $x \in NEG$?.

Pitt and Valiant [10] showed that if a class C is PAC-learnable then CONSISTENCY for C is in RP (see [4] for details on RP and other notions of Complexity Theory used in the paper). It follows that to obtain a non-learnability result for a class C (assuming RP$\neq$NP), it suffices to show that CONSISTENCY for C is NP-hard (results of this type are given in [10]; see also [5]). That is, one can make use of pure complexity-theoretic results within the framework of Learning Theory. Unfortunately, the only currently known way to prove that a class C is PAC-learnable is using the inclusion of CONSISTENCY for C in P (or at least in RP), hence one cannot expect that Learning Theory could contribute to Complexity Theory in proving new inclusion results in RP. That is, the approach of [10] establishes a quite one-sided cooperation between the two fields.

However, it is not the case that this cooperation is destined to be a one-way traffic. To see this, we use a recent result of [5] which relates another decision problem to learning tasks.

> MEMBERSHIP for C
> Instance: A Boolean function f given in DNF.
> Question: Is $f \in C$?

The basic argument, due to [5], is the following.

Theorem 3.1. *If a class C is query-learnable, then* MEMBERSHIP *for C is in* co-NP.

Once again, NP-hardness of MEMBERSHIP for a class C establishes that C is not query-learnable (if NP$\neq$co-NP). Results along this line are given in [5] for unions (intersections) of k halfspaces (for any fixed $k \geq 2$), corresponding to simple 2-layer neural network architectures (see [5] for details).

Conversely, for classes which are known to be query-learnable, we have that the corresponding MEMBERSHIP problems belong to co-NP. Usually these inclusion results are not obvious; for "reasonable" classes MEMBERSHIP is - intuitively - in Σ_2^p, but its inclusion in NP or co-NP is much less trivial. Of course, we do not claim that our inclusion proofs based on query-learnability are "nice" or "instructive", but once you know that some result holds true, you can try to find a more instructive proof.

To sum up, now it suffices to list the known positive results on query-learnability to obtain interesting contributions to Complexity Theory.

First, consider some geometrically defined classes of functions corresponding to natural learning systems like neural networks. A Boolean function $f \in F_n$ is *linearly separable* if there exist real weights $w_1, \ldots, w_n$ and a real threshold t such that $POS(f) = \{ x \mid x \in X_n$ and $\sum_{i=1}^n w_i x_i \geq t \}$. *Threshold functions of order at most k* (for any fixed $k \geq 0$) mean a generalization of linear separability: weights are assigned to all monomials $x_{i_1} x_{i_2} \ldots x_{i_l}$ of the input attributes, $0 \leq l \leq k$; n-dimensional balls are defined analogously. All the described concept classes are query-learnable (even without membership queries) [7, 8, 9], hence the following results can be obtained.

Theorem 3.2. *It is* co-NP-*complete to decide whether a Boolean function given in* DNF *is*

(1) *linearly separable;*

(2) *of threshold order at most k;*

(3) *an n-dimensional ball.*

Proof: The inclusions in co-NP follow from the query-learnability of the listed classes; the co-NP-hardness results are proved by reduction from the DNF-TAUTOLOGY problem (given a Boolean function f in DNF, does f equal to the constant *one* function?). See [6] for details, where direct proofs of inclusions in co-NP are given using a result from combinatorial geometry (Helly's theorem) and a linear programming approach (parts (1) and (2) correct some mistakes in the literature, where the considered decision problems were claimed to be NP-complete). ∎

A further class which is query-learnable without membership queries is k-DNF (k-CNF) for any fixed $k \geq 1$ [11]. These are Boolean functions representable as DNF (CNF) expressions with at most k literals in each term (clause).

Theorem 3.3. *For any fixed $k \geq 1$, it is* co-NP-*complete to decide whether a Boolean function given in* DNF (CNF) *belongs to k-DNF (k-CNF).*

Proof: We only have to prove co-NP-hardness. Let k be fixed, $k \geq 1$, and consider the following reduction from DNF-TAUTOLOGY: given $f \in F_n$ in DNF, construct a DNF for the function $g(x, y_1, \ldots, y_{k+1}) = f(x) \vee y_1 \ldots y_{k+1}$. One can show that $f \equiv 1$ if and only if g is in k-DNF; the result for k-CNF follows. ∎

Some concept classes are known to be not query-learnable without membership queries (if RP$\neq$NP), but they become learnable if membership queries are allowed. However, we can make use of these learnability results in exactly the same way as above.

The class *k-term* DNF (*k-clause* CNF) - for any fixed $k \geq 1$ - is the class of Boolean functions representable by DNF (CNF) expressions with at most k terms (clauses). It is known that for any fixed $k \geq 1$ *k*-term DNF (*k*-clause CNF) is query-learnable [1], hence we easily obtain the following.

Theorem 3.4. *For any fixed $k \geq 1$, it is* co-NP-*complete to decide whether*

(1) *a Boolean function (given in DNF) has a DNF with at most k terms;*

(2) *a Boolean function (given in CNF) has a CNF with at most k clauses.*

Proof: To prove co-NP-hardness for (1), use the following reduction from DNF-TAUTOLOGY: for $f \in F_n$ in DNF, construct a DNF representation for the function $g(x, y_1, \ldots, y_{k+1}) = f(x) \vee y_1 \vee \ldots \vee y_{k+1}$; clearly, $f \equiv 1$ if and only if g can be expressed as a DNF with at most k terms; part (2) follows from part (1). ∎

As a by-product, some progress on the complexity of the famous MINIMAL DNF EXPRESSION [4] problem is achieved.

MINIMAL DNF EXPRESSION
Instance: A Boolean function f in DNF and an integer $K \geq 1$.
Question: Has f a DNF representation with at most K terms?

Theorem 3.5. *The* MINIMAL DNF EXPRESSION *problem is* NP-hard, co-NP-hard, *and belongs to* Σ_2^p.

Proof: The NP-hardness result is given in [4], the co-NP-hardness follows from our previous arguments, and the inclusion in Σ_2^p is straightforward. ∎

Further examples of query-learnable classes are *read-once* and *read-twice* DNF formulas [2]. These are Boolean functions representable by DNF formulas where each variable appears at most once (twice). For this class we can prove the following.

Theorem 3.6. *It is* co-NP-*complete to decide whether a Boolean function (given in DNF) is a read-once (read-twice) DNF formula.*

Proof: It suffices to use the following reduction from DNF-TAUTOLOGY: given a function $f \in F_n$ in DNF, construct a DNF representation for the function $g(x, y_1, y_2) =$

$f(x) \vee y_1 y_2 \vee \bar{y}_1 \bar{y}_2$. One can show that $f \equiv 1$ if and only if g can be expressed as a read-once DNF. The case of read-twice DNF formulas is handled analogously. ∎

Finally, consider the search version of the above problems: given a Boolean function $f \in F_n$ in DNF (with m terms), construct a special representation of f if one exists (say, find the weights and the threshold of a neuron computing the given function if one exists). A simple simulation of a query learning algorithm gives the following result.

Theorem 3.7. *If a class C is query-learnable, then the corresponding search problem for C can be solved in time $2^{O(nm)}$.*

References

[1] D. Angluin, "Learning k-term DNF Formulas Using Queries and Counterexamples", Technical Report, Yale University, YALE/DCS/RR-559, 1987.

[2] D. Angluin, "Computational Learning Theory: Survey and Selected Bibliography", in: *Proceedings of the 24th Annual ACM Symposium on the Theory of Computing*, 1992, pp. 351–369.

[3] M. Anthony and N. Biggs, *Computational Learning Theory*, Cambridge University Press, Cambridge, 1992.

[4] M. R. Garey and D. S. Johnson, *Computers and Intractability: A Guide to the Theory of NP-Completeness*, Freeman, San Francisco, 1979.

[5] T. Hegedűs, "Computational Limitations on PAC and On-Line Learning over the Boolean Domain: a Comparison", submitted for publication.

[6] T. Hegedűs and N. Megiddo, "On the Geometric Separability of Boolean Functions", submitted for publication.

[7] W. Maass and Gy. Turán, "On the Complexity of Learning from Counterexamples", in: *Proceedings of the 30th Annual IEEE Symposium on Foundations of Computer Science*, IEEE Computer Society Press, Los Angeles, 1989, pp. 262–267.

[8] W. Maass and Gy. Turán, "Algorithms and Lower Bounds for On-Line Learning of Geometrical Concepts", Report 316, IIG-Report Series, Graz University of Technology, 1991.

[9] W. Maass and Gy. Turán, "How Fast can a Threshold Gate Learn?" Report 321, IIG-Report Series, Graz University of Technology, 1991.

[10] L. Pitt and L. Valiant, "Computational Limitations on Learning from Examples", *Journal of the ACM* **35** (1988) 965–984.

[11] L. Valiant, "A Theory of the Learnable", *Communications of the ACM* **27** (1984) 1134–1142.

Learning Domain Theories using Abstract Background Knowledge

Peter Clark*
Knowledge Systems Laboratory
National Research Council
Ottawa, Canada
pete@ai.iit.nrc.ca

Stan Matwin
Ottawa Machine Learning Group
Computer Science
University of Ottawa, Ottawa, Canada
stan@csi.uottawa.ca

Abstract. Substantial machine learning research has addressed the task of learning new knowledge given a (possibly incomplete or incorrect) domain theory, but leaves open the question of where such domain theories originate. In this paper we address the problem of constructing a domain theory from more general, abstract knowledge which may be available. The basis of our method is to first assume a structure for the target domain theory, and second to view background knowledge as constraints on components of that structure. This enables a focusing of search during learning, and also produces a domain theory which is explainable with respect to the background knowledge. We evaluate an instance of this methodology applied to the domain of economics, where background knowledge is represented as a qualitative model.

1 Introduction

It is now well recognised that to learn all but the simplest domain theories from examples, background knowledge is required to constrain search. While several recent learning systems use background knowledge to extend the theory language (e.g. by introducing new terms [1]), the use of background knowledge to constrain search in a domain-specific fashion is still a relatively unexplored area. This paper presents and evaluates a simple methodology for doing this. An extended version of this paper is available as [2].

We define a **domain theory** to be a system of knowledge for solving some specific target task, and **background knowledge** more generally to refer to arbitrary available knowledge. We thus view an idealised domain theory as task-specific, coherent and non-redundant (avoiding details irrelevant to the task). In contrast, background knowledge may be over-general (for the performance task), ambiguous and contain inconsistencies.

1.1 A Simple Methodology

Our general methodology is to decompose the learning task as follows:

1. assume a domain-independent *structure* for the learned domain theory.
2. view background knowledge as specifying *constraints on components* of this structure.

By assuming a domain theory structure, the learning problem can be decomposed into sub-problems, and by interpreting background knowledge as constraints on components we can define restricted search spaces for solving each sub-problem. Domain knowledge is thus used to extract a domain-specific subset of each space.

---

* This research was primarily conducted while at University of Ottawa, supported by NSERC strategic grants.

1.2 An Instance of this Approach

For the rest of this paper we work with a particular instance of this approach, designed to account for a *language gap* between the terminology of the background knowledge and the terminology used to describe examples. For example, in the economics application considered later, background knowledge is expressed using qualitative terms while the raw data is numeric, and no well-defined mapping exists between the two. This language gap problem is common in AI (e.g. [3]).

Applying the methodology, we assume a 'two-layer' structure for the target domain theory, in which the top layer uses the abstract terminology of the background knowledge and the bottom layer relates this terminology to the basic facts known about examples. Thus we assume a complete domain theory is a set of clauses of the form $P_1 \wedge ... \wedge P_i \rightarrow Q$, consisting of the union of two clause sets as follows:

Prediction rules: A set of clauses of the form

$$T_1 \wedge ... \wedge T_i \rightarrow C_j \qquad (1)$$

where the $T_i \in T$ are abstract terms used to express background knowledge and C_j is a class prediction.

Term Definitions: A set of clauses of the form

$$F_1 \wedge ... \wedge F_i \wedge G_1 \wedge ... \wedge G_j \rightarrow T_k \qquad (2)$$

where $F_i \in F$ are literals whose truth value on examples is known and $G_i \in G$ are other literals with known definitions (e.g. arithmetic tests).

The T_i can be described as ill-defined 'theoretical' terms, and the F_i as 'observational' terms [4], the two-layer structure distinguishing between these two vocabularies of background knowledge and observation. We call a clause of type (1) a **rule**, and a clause of type (2) a **definition**. A domain theory thus consists of a set of rules and set of definitions, which we will refer to as *RSet* and *DSet* respectively. This 'two layer' structure is depicted in Figure 1.

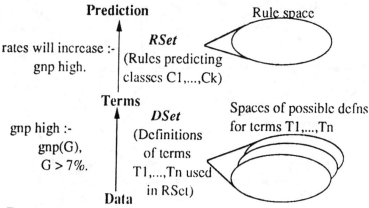

Fig. 1. The Two-Layered Theory Structure and Search Problem.

1.3 Issues for a Learning System

Two key issues must be addressed to conduct learning within this structure. First, a suitable representation of background knowledge must be designed, and a mapping from it to the search spaces defined (specifying which parts of the spaces should be searched and which can be ignored). Second, the interdependence between the different searches must be addressed. In the two layer structure depicted in Figure 1, the two searches are not independent: to search for a good rule set, we need to know the definitions of the terms in those rules so that their accuracy on training data can be computed; however to evaluate which definition of a term maximises a rule set's accuracy, we need to already have that rule set selected. The learning algorithm must address this problem.

2 Application to the Domain of Economics

2.1 Data and Learning Task

We now describe the application of this framework to the economics domain.

The **raw economic data** consist of the numeric values of 10 economic parameters $P_i \in P$ for a particular country at a particular time, taken from an economic magazine (the Economist). The ten parameters are the boxed items shown in Figure 2. Bi-annual values for 10 countries over 8 years were used.

The **learning task** is to predict (for some country) the direction of change (increase or decrease) of each parameter P_i in year $Y + 1$ given values of all parameters P in years up to and including Y.

For each parameter P_i, positive and negative **training examples** are extracted from the raw data by choosing a year Y, observing whether P_i increases or decreases in year Y+1 (the target class), and recording the values of all parameters P for year Y and previous years (the attributes). To constrain the task, we only look two years back in the past. Ten training sets are extracted from the raw data in this way, one for each P_i.

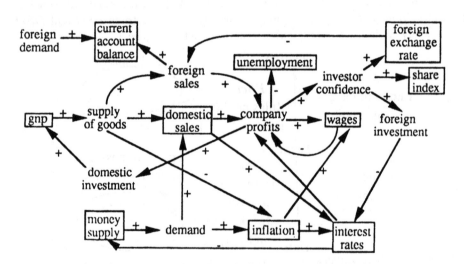

Fig. 2. The Economic Qualitative Model used as Background Knowledge.

2.2 Specifying the Rule Space using a QM

While we do not have enough economic knowledge for parameter prediction independent of the data, we do have *some* knowledge of the relationships among economic parameters. Some potential rules are plausible according to this naive knowledge, whereas others are not. For example, the rule

"**if** interest rates high **then** GNP will decrease."

has a plausible explanation: high interest rates reduce companies' profits, reducing future investment and eventually reducing productivity and GNP.

We capture this naive knowledge in the form of a **qualitative model** (QM), in a similar way to [5]. The QM expresses the believed relations between the 10 parameters P and an additional 8 unmeasurable parameters Q (the unboxed items in Figure 2). The model can be depicted as a network of nodes and directed arcs, each node representing one of these parameters and each arc representing a qualitative influence of one parameter on another. Each parameter has an associated numeric value (for a given country and year), but in the model we use just two qualitative values, high or low. As in Qualitative Process Theory [6], we label the arcs Q+ to denote a positive influence and Q− a negative influence. If we can find a path from one parameter P_i to another P_j, then we say there is a plausible relationship between P_i and P_j, explainable by the path, which can be used to form a rule in the domain theory. The complete model thus specifies the space of rules *RSpace* from which a 'concrete' domain theory can be extracted, each path in the model corresponding to a different rule.

The model we use is depicted in Figure 2, constructed manually by the authors in the style of Charniak's economic model [7]. A rule extraction algorithm is used to extract plausible rules from the model: a rule corresponds to a subgraph which has exactly one node reachable from every other node. This node forms the rule's <conclusion> and the other nodes (discounting those representing the Q_i) form the rule's <condition>, and with values high and low assigned to the nodes consistent with the Q+ and Q− labels in the subgraph.

2.3 Specifying the Definition Space

While our qualitative model looks similar to the QMs of Qualitative Process Theory, it differs in one important respect: we do not assume a particular mapping from qualitative values onto quantitative values. For example, what should the definition be of "high GNP"? (e.g. GNP > some constant? GNP > previous year's GNP? etc.). However, while we do not know which definitions of these terms are most suitable, we *do* know some constraints on their form. For example, a definition of "high GNP" should at least test whether the current GNP is greater than some other value, and (to a first approximation) probably should not refer to data from other countries or data several years old.

This sort of knowledge constitutes the second part of the background knowledge, namely a specification of the space of plausible definitions of terms in the model. We express this by constraining definitions in *DSet* to have the form:

$$v_{iy} \geq f(v_{iy-1}, v_{iy-2}, K) \longrightarrow P_i = \text{high} \qquad (3)$$

where v_{iy}, v_{iy-1} and v_{iy-2} are the numeric values of parameter P_i in years Y, Y-1 and Y-2 respectively, K is a constant and $f()$ is an arithmetic expression using operators $\{+,-,/,*\}$, and in which v_{iy-1}, v_{iy-2} and K appear at most once.

3 Learning Algorithms

To overcome the 'bootstrapping problem' of mutual dependence of the two searches (Section 1.3), we proceed as follows:

1. Assume the 10 qualitative terms to be defined as $(v_{iy} \geq v_{iy-1}) \rightarrow P_i = \text{high}$, i.e. assume an initial $DSet$.
2. Given these definitions, induce rules $RSet$ using the training data. This is done using a greedy set covering algorithm, and performing a standard general-to-specific beam search for a good rule at each iteration of the covering algorithm (the same algorithm used in CN2 for propositional learning [8]). The space searched is the QM-constrained space of rules (Section 2.2).
3. Keeping $RSet$ fixed, use a hill-climbing algorithm to search for an improved $DSet$, by trying alternative definitions for individual terms according to eqn (3). Hill-climb until a local optimum is reached.

4 Empirical Investigation

We applied these learning algorithms and the background knowledge to the economics data, using a random 2:1 train:test split of the dataset and averaging over five trials. The purposes of the experiments were three-fold: first, to illustrate the methodology and show that a domain theory can be learned which is both predictive and explainable with respect to the background knowledge; second, to examine the applicability of the suggested algorithms to the problem; and third, as a side issue, to comment on how good our qualitative model is as a source of background knowledge for this task. The QM dramatically reduces the size of the rule space from 90,000 rules to 1666 rules [2]. We hope that these 'explainable' rules will be adequate for constructing a predictive domain theory. We also hope that the background knowledge will focus search on the 'best' rules on the space, rules which a heuristic search of the entire rule space might otherwise miss, and thus outperform an unconstrained search.

RSpace to search:	Accuracy (%)		runtime (sec)
	Train	Test	
(i) search entire rulespace (90,000 rules)	94.2 ±0.1	53.9 ±1.2	5141 ±318
(ii) search QM-space (1666 rules)	60.3 ±0.4	54.5 ±0.6	510 ±81
(iii) search QM-space + optimise $DSet$	62.3 ±0.3	54.7 ±0.9	(n/a)

Table 1. Comparison of learning with and without the QM as background knowledge.

We compared three learning scenarios: (i) assume a fixed $DSet$ then search the entire rule space, (ii) assume a fixed $DSet$ then search the QM-constrained rule space (steps 1 and 2 in Section 3), (iii) same, then try to improve the initial term definitions using the optimiser (steps 1-3 in Section 3). Our results (Table 1) were somewhat surprising, in that no significant accuracy difference was found. The main contribution of the background knowledge, in this case, is thus to provide 'explainable' rules (i.e. compatible with background knowledge) and to reduce learning time. The results, only slightly better than the default accuracy of 50%, also reflect the substantial difficulties of predicting purely from sparse economic data, ignoring major factors such as politics, industrial infrastructure etc. Further analyses of this data set using a variety of other algorithms suggest the data is highly impoverished, on its own, as a basis for prediction, and suggest further experiments with a richer dataset would be useful.

5 Discussion and Conclusion

From the methodology's point of view, the most important point we have illustrated is that it can be applied to efficiently learn a domain theory which is structured and explainable with respect to the available background knowledge. All the rules 'make sense', i.e. are explainable in the same style as the example in Section 2.2, while non-sensical rules have been naturally excluded as a consequence of our approach. This explainability aspect is particularly significant if the learned knowledge is to be incorporated within a body of existing knowledge, as is becoming increasingly the case in machine learning research. It also offers significant potential for assisting in the labour-intensive task of post-learning rule engineering, an essential part of commercial application of machine learning, in which non-sensical rules have to be identified, removed or edited, and the training data modified.

Our particular results in this economics domain were also surprising, in that the background knowledge had little impact on predictive accuracy, its main advantage instead being explainability. This suggests that the information content of our particular qualitative model, for prediction purposes, was more limited than we originally expected, and also reflects the inherent limits in predicting from sparse economic data. Results of the evaluation also suggest the obvious and exciting extension to allow feedback from the results of learning to improve the background knowledge itself.

Acknowledgements: We are particularly grateful to Rob Holte and Peter Turney for their insightful comments on earlier drafts of this paper, and to Peter Turney for his additional analyses of the economic dataset.

References

1. S. Muggleton and C. Feng. Efficient induction of logic programs. In *First International Conference on Algorithmic Learning Theory*, pages 369–381, Tokyo, Japan, 1990. Japanese Society for Artificial Intellligence.
2. Peter Clark and Stan Matwin. Learning domain theories using abstract background knowledge. Tech. Report TR-92-35, Dept CS, Univ. Ottawa, May 1992.
3. Bruce W. Porter, Ray Bareiss, and Robert C. Holte. Concept learning and heuristic classification in weak-theory domains. *Artificial Intelligence*, 45:229–263, 1990.
4. Ranan B. Banerji. Learning theoretical terms. In Stephen Muggleton, editor, *Inductive Logic Programming*. 1992.
5. Gerald DeJong. Explanation-based learning with plausible inferencing. In *Proc. 4th European Machine Learning Conference (EWSL-89)*, pages 1–10, 1989.
6. Kenneth D. Forbus. Qualitative process theory. *AI Journal*, 24:85–168, 1984.
7. James C. Spohrer and Christopher K. Riesbeck. Reasoning-driven memory modification in the economics domain. Technical Report YALEU/DCS/RR-308, Yale University, May 1984.
8. Peter Clark and Robin Boswell. Rule induction with CN2: Some recent improvements. In Yves Kodratoff, editor, *Machine Learning – EWSL-91*, pages 151–163, Berlin, 1991. Springer-Verlag.

Discovering Patterns in EEG-Signals: Comparative Study of a Few Methods

Miroslav Kubat[1], Doris Flotzinger[2], and Gert Pfurtscheller[1]

[1] Ludwig-Boltzmann Institute of Medical Informatics and Neuroinformatics
Graz University of Technology, Brockmanngasse 41, 8010 Graz
e-mail mirek@fbmtds04.tu-graz.ac.at
[2] Department of Medical Informatics, Institute of Biomedical Engineering
Graz University of Technology, Brockmanngasse 41, 8010 Graz

Abstract. The objective of this paper is to draw the attention of the *ML*-researchers to the domain of data analysis. The issue is illustrated by an attractive case study—automatic classification of non-averaged *EEG*-signals. We applied several approaches and obtained best results from a combination of an *ID3*-like program with Bayesian learning.

1 Introduction

The general task of machine learning applied to data analysis is to facilitate the classification of unseen examples, to extract relevant information from the data, and to provide intelligent interpretation of the classification scheme.

The research reported here relates to a broader project, aiming at the development of a Brain-Computer Interface (*BCI*), a direct link between the brain and an electronic device. The objective is to discover typical patterns in the measured *EEG*-signals in order to recognise simple commands such as 'move right,' 'move left,' 'move up,' or 'move down.' A description of the *BCI* with first results are published in (Pfurtscheller, Flotzinger & Kalcher, 1992).

Each example submitted to the learner represents a single *EEG*-measurement consisting of 70 numerical values, and is classified so that each class stands for one command. We started with the simple task of discerning 'move left' from 'move right.' Detailed discussion of the data acquisition and preprocessing would go beyond the scope of this paper. Suffice it to say that, for each learning example, potentials were measured on 14 electrodes placed on an intact scalp of a test person, in the frequency band of 8-12 Hz in 5 time-slices preceding the movement of the left or right hand. Thus we had 70 real-valued attributes and two classification classes.

We applied several techniques to the analysis of three sets of examples. Each of these sets was obtained from a different test person. The sizes of the sets were 213, 140, and 246 examples, respectively. For each person, we used 60% of the examples for learning and the rest for testing. All results were averaged over 10 different random selections of learning examples. (In the *BCI*-project, the machine is always trained for one particular person.)

Two phenomena characterized the data: they were sparse and of low quality. *Sparseness* relates to the vast number of all possible combinations of attribute values, from which only tens or hundreds are available as learning examples, without any guarantee of representativeness. The *low quality* of the data is caused by the different degree of attention of the tested persons, by changes in vigilance, by artefacts during recording, by not using the optimal frequency band, and by other factors. The examples are noisy, and perhaps do not contain the expected information altogether, because waves measured on a single frequency band of 14 electrodes are certainly insufficient for 'reading thoughts.' Also, there is a high probability that most of the attributes are irrelevant.

In the search for the best suited data-analysis method, we postulated three minimum requirements:

1) The inferred pattern must be maximally *accurate* so as to enable sufficiently precise classifications;

2) The results must be as *stable* as possible—i.e. the classification accuracy must be about the same on each of the data sets;

3) The method should enable *interpretation*, so that the researchers can use the results for further improvement of the experimental setting.

2 Brief Outline of the Applied Methods

We have applied two subsymbolic methods (Multilayer Perceptron and Learning Vector Quantizer), and three symbolic methods (Bayesian Classifier, Induction of Decision Trees, and a combination of these two).

Multi-Layer Perceptron (*MLP*)

The *MLP* is a traditional neural network whose topology builds on a few layers of processing units—an *input* layer consisting of d nodes, where d is the number of attributes or the dimension of the input vector (in our case $d = 70$); a *hidden* layer whose size is user-defined; and an *output* layer consisting of c nodes, where c is the number of classes (two, in our case). Inputs to the individual units are weighted. The output of each unit (except for the input layer) is a function of the weighted sum of its inputs: we applied the common sigmoid *activation* function. For more detailes, see (Rumelhart, Hinton, & Williams, 1989).

In the *classification* phase, the values of each individual attribute are propagated through the network. The class assigned to the output node with the highest value of the activation function is used as the classification value.

Learning is carried out by error propagation from the output to the input layer. The difference between desired and actual output of the network is used to correct the weights at each layer. Usually a predetermined number of runs through the training set is performed. The initial weights are set to small random values.

We experimented with several topologies of the *MLP* and achieved the best results for one hidden layer with ten units.

Learning Vector Quantizer (*LVQ*)

The essence of the *LVQ* (Kohonen, 1990) is in dividing the d-dimensional space into a predefined number of regions. Each region is represented by a so called *reproduction* vector which is assigned a classification value.

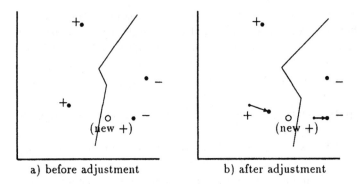

a) before adjustment   b) after adjustment

Fig. 1. *LVQ:* two closest reproduction vectors adapt to the new arrival.

In the *classification* phase, the new example is assigned the classification value of the closest reproduction vector.

The *learning* scheme consists of two parts: (1) *initialization* defines the initial boundaries of the regions and the respective reproduction vectors; (2) *tuning* is a trial-and-error mechanism: the system takes the examples one by one and tries to classify them. If the classification attempt is wrong, the reproduction vector is pushed slightly away (in the d-dimensional learning space) from the example, and the second closest reproduction vector, if it is of the same class as the example, is pulled closer to the example. These adjustments are performed for a predetermined number of runs through the whole training set.

For the initialization, we followed the recommendation of (Peltoranta, 1992) to use k-means. The parameter k determines the ideal number of reproduction vectors. The best results were achieved for $k = 2$ and 3.

Conversion to Symbolic Values

Any transformation from numeric to symbolic values entails information loss. However, it can significantly reduce the learning space and stress 'regularities' in the data. The conversion algorithm we have implemented is based on entropy minimization. For each attribute, the following procedure was applied:

1) Find the minimum and maximum value of the attribute. Compute the entropy of the whole interval by $H_{initial} = \Sigma_{i=1}^{c} p_i \log p_i$, where c is the number of classes (here, $c = 2$), and p_i is the probability of the i-th class;

2) Find the optimal split of the interval into subintervals minimizing the overall entropy $H = H_1 + H_2$, where H_1 and H_2 are entropies of the individual intervals;

3) If the difference between the previous entropy and the new entropy is less then p_{min} percent, then *stop*. Otherwise, pick the interval with the highest entropy and find its ideal split, maximizing the overall entropy;

4) Repeat the previous step until either the algorithm fails to improve the overall entropy by at least p_{min} percent or the number of intervals has reached the user-specified maximum.

Typical number of intervals per attribute was 4. Typical value for p_{min} was 5%.

Bayesian Classifier B

This simple approach gives surprisingly good results even if the general requirement of the pairwise independency among the attributes is not satisfied.

In the *classification* phase, the example is assigned the class C_i for which the following formula has the maximum value:

$$P(C_i \mid v_1, \ldots, v_d) = P(C_i) \cdot \Pi_{k=1}^d P(v_k \mid C_i)$$

where d is the number of attributes, $v_1, \ldots, v_d$ are the attribute values of the example to be classified, $P(C_i)$ is the a priori probability of the occurence of class C_i, and $P(v_k \mid C_i)$ is the a priori probability of the k-th attribute value in class C_i. The probabilities are calculated as relative frequencies in the data (even though they may not be well statistically grounded for rare values v_i).

Induction of Decision Trees IDT

The *learning* principle of the algorithm for the induction of decision trees consists of growing the tree and pruning the tree. Growing is carried out by the following procedure:

Find the attribute with the maximal information content and place it at the root of the tree. The n distinct values of the attribute divide the data set into n subsets. If all examples of a subset belong to a single class, then make the subset a leaf assigned a label of this class. Otherwise, find in each of the subsets the best attribute, splitting the subset into 'subsubsets,' and so on until either all of the remaining subsets are empty or assigned a label, or until there is no unused attribute left (in the last case, the final subset will be assigned more than one class). For a formula deciding which attribute is best, see (Quinlan, 1986).

When the tree is constructed, the next step is its pruning to avoid overspecialized descriptions and to discard noise (Niblett, 1987). Pruning consists in cutting off those branches that are not well statistically grounded.

The *classification* procedure consists in propagating the example through the tree starting from the root and testing at each node the respective attribute value. Depending on its value, the branch leading to the next node is selected. When a leaf is reached, then its class is assigned to the example.

IDT initializing Bayes

IDT is used to reduce the dimension of the learning space which is then analyzed with the Bayesian Classifier. The procedure consists of the following three steps:

1) Run *IDT* on the d-dimensional data and build a decision tree;
2) Discard all attributes that have not appeared in the decision tree. The new dimension of the space is $d1 \leq d$;
3) Determine a priori probabilities (in the $d1$-dimensional space) to serve the Bayesian Classifier.

3 Experimental Results

The most general results in *accuracy* are summarized in Table 1. As expected, the Bayesian Classifier, if run on all 70 attributes, is the clear loser because it lacks any ability to discern between relevant and irrelevant information. The subsymbolic approaches scored better. However, they were not very stable on data files of different quality—*MLP* achieved the absolutely best score on C87B but was practically useless on C05B because 50% accuracy can be achieved by mere tossing a coin. Hence, the subsymbolic methods are more sensitive to the quality of the learning data. The favourable results of *IDT* can be explained by its ability to assess the relevance of the individual attributes.

Table 1. Accuracy of the predictions of the side of hand movement from *EEG* data recorded prior to the actual movement.

	C05B	C16B	C87B	Average	st.dev.
MLP	49.7	72.1	84.1	68.6	14.3
LVQ	51.6	71.6	82.2	68.5	12.7
Bs	60.7	59.3	70.9	63.6	5.2
IDT	71.3	73.6	79.3	74.7	3.4
IDT-Bs	70.5	77.3	79.9	75.9	3.9

The absolute winner is the method that extracts the most significant attributes by means of *IDT* and then runs Bayes on them. The reason is that the ordering imposed by the decision tree is too rigid. Instead of a precise ordering of the attribute tests, Bayes supplies conditional probabilities and thus allows for more flexibility. The results of this approach are also relatively *stable*.

Apart from accuracy and stability, the Introduction postulated also the important requirement of *interpretability*. Though it *is* possible to extract knowledge from Neural Networks (Towell, Craven & Shavlik, 1991), the process is far from being easy and straightforward. The results from *IDT*, in turn, can immediately be interpreted, for instance, 'most important is the potential on electrodes 5 and 10 in time slice 2, and then the potential on electrode 14 in time slice 4.' This helps the user to develop a deeper understanding of the results of the analysis and supply guidelines for further experiments.

4 Conclusion

For data analysis in vast learning spaces, the analyst must be acquainted with a rich repertoir of methods with their pros and cons, and be able to apply them in a flexible manner. To deal only with numeric data is an oversimplification of a real-world task. In our future research, we want to enrich the original data so that they contain also results of measurements at other frequency bands and predicates such as 'activation on right hemisphere precedes activation on the frontal electrodes.' It is encouraging to know that the combination *IDT*–Bayes worked well because this will work even if Boolean variables are added. Also, the experience saying that symbolic analysis tends to produce better results than numerical is positive because symbolic analysis is usually much faster than numerical.

Acknowledgements

Thanks are due to Wolfgang Mohl for data recording and preprocessing. The research was sponsored by grants from 'Fonds zur Förderung der wissenschaftlichen Forschung' (Project $S49/02$ and Lisa-Meitner fellowship $M003\ MED$ for M.Kubat) and from the Austrian Federal Ministery of Science and Research ($Gz5.167/2 - 27b/91$)

References

Kohonen, T. (1990). The Self-Organizing Map. *Proceedings of the IEEE*, Vol.78, No.9, pp. 1464–1480

Niblett, T. (1987). Constructing Decision Trees in Noisy Domains. In Bratko,I.-Lavrač,N. (eds.) *Progress in Machine Learning*. Sigma Press, Wilmslow

Peltoranta M. (1992). Methods for Classification of Non-Averaged *EEG* Responces using Autoregressive Model Based Features. PhD-thesis. Graz University of Technology.

Pfurtscheller, G., Flotzinger, D., and Kalcher, J. (1992). Brain-Computer Interface—A New Communication Device for Handicapped Persons. In: Zagler,W. (ed): *Computer for Handicapped Persons: Proceedings of the 3rd International Conference*, Vienna, 409–415

Quinlan, J.R. (1986). Induction of Decision Trees. In: *Machine Learning 1*, 81–106

Rumelhart, D.E., Hinton, G.E., and Williams, R.J. (1989). Learning Internal Representations by Error Propagation. In: Rumelhart,D.E. et al. (eds.): *Parallel Distributed Processing*, MIT Press, Cambridge, MA, Vol.1, pp.318–362

Towell, G.G., Craven, M.W. and Shavlik.J. (1991). Constructive Induction in Knowledge-Based Neural Networks. *Proceedings of the 8th International Workshop on Machine Learning*, Morgan Kaufmann, San Mateo

Learning to Control Dynamic Systems with Automatic Quantization

Charles X. Ling*   Ralph Buchal[†]

Abstract

Reinforcement learning is often used in learning to control dynamic systems, which are described by *quantitative* state variables. Most previous work that learns *qualitative* (symbolic) control rules cannot construct symbols themselves. That is, a correct partition of the state variables, or a correct set of qualitative symbols, is given to the learning program.

We do not make this assumption in our work of learning to control dynamic systems. The learning task is divided into two phases. The first phase is to extract symbols from quantitative inputs. This process is also commonly called quantization. The second phase is to evaluate the symbols obtained in the first phase and to induce the best possible symbolic rules based on those symbols. These two phases interact with each other and thus make the whole learning task very difficult. We demonstrate that our new method, called STAQ (Set Training with Automatic Quantization), can aggressively partition the input variables to a finer resolution until the correct control rules based on these partitions (symbols) are learned. In particular, we use STAQ to solve the well-known cart-pole balancing problem.

1   Introduction

In a dynamic and interactive environment, an agent (or robot) receives inputs fr⟨ the environment via sensors, makes decisions, and transmits outputs to the envir⟨ ment via effectors, in order to achieve a certain goal. If the dynamic behavior known completely or partially to the agent, traditional control methods (such as P control, model identification) may be used to determine the appropriate control rul However, in *unknown* dynamic systems (such as exploration in a new environmen or in *very complicated* dynamic systems (such as temperature control in a buildir an economics system, weather etc.) whose behaviour is completely unknown or fil⟨ with noise, traditional control methods cannot solve the problem effectively. If t⟨ agent is *adaptive*, it can *learn* control rules gradually based on past experience, l⟨

---

*Department of Computer Science, University of Western Ontario, London, Ontario, Canada N 5B7. Email: ling@csd.uwo.ca

[†]Department of Mechanical Engineering, University of Western Ontario, London, Onta⟨ Canada N6A 5B7.

intelligent human beings. That is, the goal of the agent can be achieved by acquiring a set of control rules without identifying the dynamic equations of the system. Thus, the learning is *model free*. Automating the acquisition of control rules for general dynamic systems requires a robust and reliable learning mechanism, and therefore poses a major challenge for machine learning.

Interactive learning in a dynamic environment with weak feedback on how the goal is achieved is often called *reinforcement learning*. From the machine learning point of view, reinforcement learning is usually regarded as unsupervised learning, because no external teacher is available to guide the system completely for every action the system takes. The system only receives weak feedback indicating the status of the system, and the feedback from the actions is often *delayed or cumulative*. The agent's learning task is to construct a function (called a *policy* or a *strategy*), mapping from the current state and the current sensory inputs to actions so as to maximize the *discounted cumulative reinforcements* or *goal* [Sutton, 1984; Watkins, 1989; Lin, 1990].

Model-free learning to control dynamic systems is conceptually possible. Since control rules based on dynamic equations can be expanded to a set of rules in the form of "**if** situation **then** action", model free learning acquires this set of rules directly. Although the system is described at any point in time quantitatively by a set of real numbers, usually the state-space can be grouped into several regions, and it suffices to apply a *singular* action in each region (situation) to achieve the goal. Therefore, model-free learning includes two subtasks: one is to group the state-space into regions appropriately, and the second is to learn the appropriate control rules (actions) for all regions.

We introduce a new algorithm called STAQ, an acronym for *Set Training with Automatic Quantization*, that learns qualitative rules via automatic quantization. The STAQ algorithm is applied to the well-known pole-balancing task. We show that STAQ is general and robust since the learned control rules can balance the cart-pole for an extended period of time starting from *any* random position. STAQ is applicable to other dynamic systems of the *same class*: that is, any dynamic system with a finite number of real number sensory inputs, a finite number of output effectors, and delayed feedback. In contrast with previous methods which use predefined partitions of the state-space (fixed bias), the STAQ program employs a technique called the *progressive splitting algorithm* (PSA) to partition the state space dynamically, starting from a a very coarse partition, until enough resolution is reached and a set of control rules achieving the goal is learned.

2 The Pole-Balancing Problem

Cart-pole balancing is a very typical dynamic system. Learning to balance the cart-pole was the subject of one of the earliest experiments done in machine learning, and is the learning task studied in this paper. In the definition, "A rigid pole is hinged to a cart, which is free to move within the limits of a track. The learning system attempts to keep the pole balanced and the cart within its limits by applying a force of fixed magnitude to the cart, either to the left or to the right." [Selfridge *et al.*,

1985] The *goal* is to balance the cart-pole for a certain period of time. Failure is reported when the angle of the pole or the position of the cart exceeds certain limits defined by the users. In the cart-pole system, we define that the control strategy fails to balance the cart-pole if $|x| > 2.4$ meters (the cart bumps against the ends of the track) or $|\theta| \geq 12°$. All non-failure states are treated equally well. Thus, stability, for example, is not included as part of the goal. Failure is the *only* feedback received by the learner. This means that the learning program is given a very weak guidance. A bad action may cause failure long after the action is applied. Thus, the evaluation of the decisions (credit assignment) can be a long process requiring many trials.

The learning algorithm is model free: it uses the simulator merely as a *black box* and refrains from using any knowledge embedded in the simulator. No qualitative model of the system, even the symmetric property, is available to the learning program. The *only* information the learner receives is the vectors of these four real number sensory inputs $(x, \dot{x}, \theta, \dot{\theta})$ at every sampling, and the failure signal when the system fails.

The pole-balancing problem has been chosen as a model for machine learning task by many researchers. It was first studied by Michie and Chambers [Michie and Chambers, 1968] in 1968, and more recently by Anderson, Barto, Selfridge, Sutton, Sammut and so on (cf [Anderson, 1986; Barto *et al.*, 1983; Selfridge *et al.*, 1985; Sammut and Cribb, 1990]). However, almost all of the previous work which learns the symbolic control rules requires pre-partitions of the state-space.

3   The STAQ Algorithm

Since the task includes both quantization and induction of symbolic rules, the learning algorithm is divided into two phases. The first phase creates better symbols based on the suggestions of inductive learning and evaluation of bias in the second phase. More specifically, the first phase extracts symbols, or partitions the real number state variables into ranges. The problem to be solved is how many ranges are sufficient for each variable and what are the end points of the ranges. The second phase is an inductive learning process that induces the best possible rules based on the current set of symbols. The learning process also evaluates the symbols constructed in the first phase. If the best symbolic rules learned cannot satisfy the success criterion, refinement of certain partitions is needed. Suggestions on how and where refinements of partitions are needed are also proposed in the learning process. The STAQ algorithm then returns to the first phase, in which these ranges are split into two – a refined set of symbols is constructed. Starting with a very coarse partition, these two phases iterate until enough resolution of state variables is obtained such that rules based on these symbols are learned to pass the success criterion.

A new algorithm, called *set training* is designed for inductive learning of robust rules based on a *given* partition. An evaluation of the current partition, i.e. *halting criterion*, is conducted during set training. The halting criterion is true if the best set of control rules has been found. If the best results so far still do not pass the success criterion, PSA (Progressive Splitting Algorithm) partitions the state space further based on the suggestion (high flip count) given in the evaluation. The success criterion for the learning task is that the *average* balancing time for 12 initial cases (see later) is greater than 10,000 time steps.

The STAQ algorithm is outlined in Figure 1.

Read 12 Initial Cases
L1: **repeat**
        Apply Set Training Algorithm
        {* To induce the best rules based on current partition*}
        until (Halting Criterion = true)
        if Best Average Balancing Time < 10,000)
            then Apply Progressive Splitting Algorithm. **goto** L1
            else Succeed!
        Perform 100 tests with random initial positions

Figure 1: The STAQ Algorithm

4   Results of the STAQ

Using the standard parameters of the cart-pole, STAQ splits 6 times before it learns a control strategy that produces an average balancing time over 10,000 steps. Figure 2 shows the learning curve after the 4th, 5th, and 6th splits. As expected, before the 6th split the partitions obtained do not provide with enough resolution (symbols) for representing/learning good control rules, so the performance during set training is very poor. After the 6th split however, enough resolution is achieved, good control rules are learned, and the success criterion is satisfied. Notice that the fluctuation still exists since set training is non-monotonic, and all the boxes are coupled. The result is summarised in Table 1. As shown in this table (and other tables), very good and robust results are produced in the 100 random tests whose initial positions are drawn randomly from $|x| < 2.4$ and $|\theta| < 12°$. The balancing time of the random test is obtained using the set of boxes when maximum average balancing time is reached.

It is interesting to examine the partitions obtained by STAQ. The algorithm actually produces fewer number of boxes than the original BOXES (144 versus 162) as shown in Table 1. Observe that the acquired partition is not symmetric. The learning program has no knowledge of the symmetry property of the cart-pole system. In fact, symmetric partition is *not* needed to achieve the goal: one could balance the cart-pole within one side of the track only.

4.1   Evaluation of STAQ

To determine how well the STAQ programs could cope with altered conditions, the simulation parameters are changed. Again, STAQ is not informed of *any* knowledge about the dynamic system, except the vectors of four real number state variables at

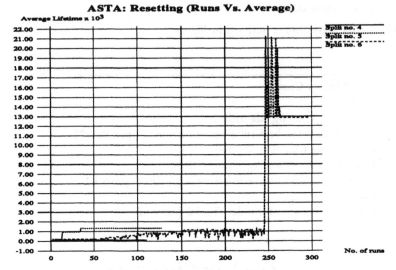

Figure 2: STAQ: Learning Curve after 4th, 5th, 6th Splitting.

sampling. This tests if STAQ can develop *different* sets of qualitative symbols for *different* cart-pole systems. Since STAQ does not take any knowledge of the dynamic system, this also tests if STAQ is general and powerful for learning to control general dynamic systems.

Variations of the simulator include reducing the force pushing right to 5 Newtons, increasing the length of the pole to 1.5 m, and changing all the parameters except the pole length. STAQ is able to develop *different* partitions in all of these new environments. To summarize, variations in dynamic systems can be *well sustained* by the STAQ algorithm without any significant changes in results, except different qualitative symbols are constructed. Thus, STAQ is able to construct both symbols and symbolic control rules for general dynamic systems. STAQ realizes the automatic transformation from quantitative representation to qualitative representation.

5 Conclusions

Learning in an unknown dynamic and interactive environment with weak feedback can be very difficult. Since the sensory inputs are quantitative, both symbol construction, symbolic rule learning, and symbol evaluation are parts of the learning task. We have demonstrated that our learning algorithm STAQ accomplishes these tasks for the general dynamic systems.

References

[Anderson, 1986] Charles W. Anderson. *Learning and problem solving with multilayer con-*

STAQ	Maximum average of 12 initial cases	Maximum lifetime of individuals	Average lifetime of 100 random tests
After split no.	6	6	
After No. of runs	247	247	
Balancing time (in time steps)	21 k	> 100 k	17 k
State variables	Partitions (New ones inserted by SPA shown bold)		
x	$-2.40\ldots0.00\ldots\mathbf{1.20}\ldots2.40$		
$\dot{x}$	$-6.00\ldots\mathbf{-3.00}\ldots\mathbf{-1.50}\ldots0.00\ldots6.00$		
θ	$-0.20\ldots0.00\ldots\mathbf{0.10}\ldots0.20$		
$\dot{\theta}$	$-4.00\ldots\mathbf{-2.00}\ldots\mathbf{-1.00}\ldots0.00\ldots4.00$		

Table 1: Results of STAQ with the Standard Simulator

nectionist systems. PhD thesis, University of Massachusetts, Amherst, 1986.

[Barto et al., 1983] Andrew G. Barto, Richard S. Sutton, and Charles W. Anderson. Neuron-like elements that can solve difficult learning control problems. *IEEE Trans. on Systems, Man, and Cybernetics*, SMC-13(5):834–846, 1983.

[Lin, 1990] Long-Ji Lin. Self-improving reactive agents: Case studies of reinforcement learning frameworks. In *Proceedings of the First International Conference on the Simulation of Adaptive Behavior*, September 1990.

[Michie and Chambers, 1968] D. Michie and R. Chambers. Boxes: An experiment in adaptive control. In *Machine Intelligence 2 (E. Dale and D. Michie, Eds.)*, pages 137–152. Oliver and Boyd, Edinburgh, 1968.

[Sammut and Cribb, 1990] Claude Sammut and James Cribb. Is learning rate a good performance criterion for learning. In *Proceedings of the Seventh International Workshop on Machine Learning*. Morgan Kaufmann, 1990.

[Selfridge et al., 1985] Selfridge, Richard Sutton, and Andrew Barto. Training and tracking in roboltics. In *Proceedings of the Ninth International Joint Conference on Artificial Intelligence*, Los Angeles, CA, 1985.

[Sutton, 1984] Richard S. Sutton. *Temporal Credit Assignment In Reinforcement Learning*. PhD thesis, University of Massachusetts at Amherst, 1984. (Also COINS Tech Report 84-02).

[Watkins, 1989] Chris Watkins. *Learning from delayed rewards*. PhD thesis, Cambridge University, 1989.

Refinement of Rule Sets with JoJo

Dieter Fensel and Markus Wiese

Institut für Angewandte Informatik und Formale Beschreibungsverfahren,
University of Karlsruhe, P.O. Box 6980, 7500 Karlsruhe, Germany
e-mail: fensel@aifb.uni-karlsruhe.de

Abstract. In the paper we discuss a new approach for learning classification rules from examples. We sketch out the algorithm JoJo and its extension to a four step procedure which can be used to incrementally refine a set of classification rules. Incorrect rules are refined, the entire rule set is completed, redundant rules are deleted and the rule set can be minimized. The first two steps are done by applying JoJo which searches through the lattice of rules by generalization and specialization.

1 Introduction

Learning from examples deals with the task of learning general descriptions (decision trees or rules) from examples. In the paper we discuss a four step procedure which can be used to refine a set of classification rules. First, the rules which become incorrect because of new negative examples are refined. Each incorrect rule is replaced by a set of rules which covers the positive examples but not the new negative ones. In a second step, the rule set is extended to cover the new positive examples. Third, redundancy of the rule set is corrected by deleting rules. In a fourth step, a minimal subset can be computed which covers all positive examples. Steps one and two are carried out by applying the JoJo-algorithm. The main feature of JoJo is that it integrates generalization and specialization into one heuristic search procedure.

The *version space* algorithm is one of the earliest algorithms which obtained classification rules from a set of examples [13]. It applies a dual search strategy in the lattice of possible rules. If a negative example is given, all general rules which cover it are specialized. If a positive example is given, all special rules which do not cover it are generalized. The search procedure starts at the top and the bottom of the lattice and converges to the final rule which covers all positive and no negative examples. The version space algorithm performs a complete search and can therefore only be applied to small data sets because it is impossible to find the minimal hypothesis (Occam´s Razor) consistent with the given examples in polynomial time [1].

Heuristic (i.e. incomplete) search procedures like *AQ* [14], *C4* [17], *CN2* [3], *CABRO* [11], *FOIL* [16], and *PRISM* [2] work by *specialization* only. They start with very general descriptions and specialize them until they are correct. This is done by adding additional premises to the rule or by restricting the range of an attribute which is used in a premise.

In [5] we discussed the heuristic search procedure *RELAX* which works by *generalization* only. It starts with very special descriptions and generalizes them as long as they are not incorrect. It regards every example as a very specific rule which is generalized. This is done by deleting premises from the rule. The motivation for this procedure are algorithms used for minimizing electronic circuits [12].

Algorithms which use specialization as search strategy generally have the problem of overspecialization. In an i-th specialization step, a specialization can be performed which possibly makes an earlier specialization unnecessary. If, for example, three premises are added to a rule in three steps, it could be that the premises which were added in the second and third step make the premise of the first step unnecessary (cf. [6] for an example).[1] The rule could be made more general by deleting the first premise without decreasing its correctness. Therefore, when using specialization as a search direction it cannot be guaranteed that the result is really a maximal-general description. This problem does not arise when using generalization as search strategy. In every step, one unnecessary premise is deleted, if possible. The procedure stops if no such premises exist anymore. Therefore, it is guaranteed that the final rule is a most-general description, i.e. no other more general rule is correct. On the other hand, learning most-specific descriptions with generalization as a search direction would have the dual problem that one cannot be sure that the final result is really most-specific.[2]

The problem of rules which are constructed by specialization is discussed by [15] as necessity to *prune* rules. Rules which are constructed by specialization are pruned in a second step. It is determined whether they can be generalized without changing their correctness. Therefore, [15] proposes a specific combination of both search paradigms. First, rules are constructed by specialization and then, in a second step, it is determined whether they can be generalized.

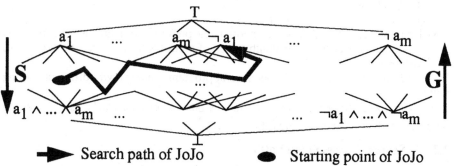

Figure 1. Specialization and generalization as different search directions in the lattice of conjunctions.

Because in general it cannot be determined which search direction is the better one, we developed the algorithm JoJo which integrates both search directions into one procedure similar to the version space algorithm.[3] The next chapter sketches the main ideas of JoJo and in chapter three we characterize the four-step procedure which can be used to refine a given rule set according to new examples.

2 The Main Ideas of JoJo

JoJo is a procedure which learns rules from examples. It integrates generalization and specialization into one heuristic search process. The procedure starts at an arbitrary point in the lattice of complexes and generalizes or specializes as long as the quality or correctness of the descriptions regarded can be improved, i.e. until a local optimum can be found, or the search resources (e.g., computation time) are not yet consumed.

2.1 Choice of the Starting Points

---

1. The problem can be compared with the problem of multi-colinearity of some variables.
2. This is a simple consequence of the duality principle of lattices.
3. The two search directions and their advantages and disadvantages are discussed in [7].

Procedures which can only specialize have a predefined starting point for the search. They must start as generally as possible, because a possible solution could not be found if it is more general than the starting point. Similiarly, procedures working only with specialization must start as specifically as possible. JoJo is able to start at an arbitrary point in the lattice because both search directions are used.

A starting point can be described by two parameters, the vertical position (the length of the description) and the horizontal position (the chosen attributes).

Criteria for choosing a vertical position

- An expert can estimate the possible length of the rules or has some experience from earlier program runnings.
- Rules are produced randomly for every length and the distribution of their quality[1] is used to decide the position.
- The procedure starts with a small sample or very limited resources and arbitrary positions in order to find a good starting point.
- The starting point is randomly chosen. In the average case this is not worse than always starting with the bottom or top element like other procedures do.
- Heuristic: Few positive examples and most-specific descriptions as a target indicate long rules, whereas few negative examples and most-general descriptions as a target indicate short rules.

Criteria for choosing a horizontal position

- If the vertical position has been chosen, the premises with the highest correlation to the goal concept (or the combination of premises if this is not too expensive) can be selected.

In general, it is possible to carry out several program runnings with different starting points.

Rules which were already produced by JoJo or other algorithms can be used as starting points for further refinement and improvement.[2]

2.2 Search Process in the Lattice

The gist of JoJo consists of three components: a *generalizer*, a *specializer*, and a *scheduler*.

The *generalizer* computes, validates and orders the descriptions which can be reached by the next generalization step using a predefined generalization strategy and a predefined preference criterion (g-preference). An example of a simple generalizer is H-RE-LAX [6]:

- Conjunctions are generalized by deleting a premise.
- The g-preference applied is:[3]

$$1 - \frac{\text{number of covered negative examples} + 0.5}{\text{number of all covered examples} + 0.5}$$

The *specializer* computes, validates and orders the descriptions which can be reached by the next specialization step using a predefined specialization strategy and a predefined preference criterion (s-preference). An example of a simple specializer is:

- Conjunctions are specialized by adding a premise.

---

1. A possible quality criterion is the average correctness of the rules with the same length.

2. It is possible to check rules for overspecialization when that rules are produced by an algorithm using specialization only as search direction.

3. 0,5 is added in order to prevent division by zero and to favor rules which cover more examples when several rules do not cover any negative example.

- The s-preference applied is equal to the g-preference.

It is evident that other generalizers or specializers with different strategies and preference criteria are possible.

The *scheduler* selects the next description out of the set of all possible generalizations and specializations by using a predefined (total) t-preference. An example of a simple scheduler is:

- Specialize, if the error rate of the rule is higher than a specified threshold.
- Otherwise, choose the best generalization if a possible generalization exists, i.e. a generalization with allowable error rate.
- Otherwise stop.

The scheduler would prefer maximal general (but correct) descriptions.[1]

2.3 Creating a Rule Set with JoJo

Given is a set of positive and negative examples. JoJo searches for a first general and correct rule "r". Then the covered positive examples are removed and the procedure is repeated until the number of remaining positive examples is less than a specified threshold. Instead of searching only one time per rule, JoJo can perform several runs using different starting points for every rule.

3 Incremental Refinement of Rules with JoJo

In the following we extend the ideas presented above to form a learning procedure which works incrementally (cf. [10], [4]). It modifies given rules according to additional given examples. The input is a set of rules describing a hypothesis and a set of old and new positive and negative examples for the hypothesis described by the rules. Its task is to transform the set of rules so that it covers all positive, but no negative examples. Alternatively, some lower thresholds for errors of the rules can be given to the algorithm. The output of the algorithm are the refined rules and the example set. Additional examples can lead to a further application of JoJo. JoJo searches for a new set of rules which is *correct, complete, non-redundant*, and (if necessary) *minimal*.

3.1 Correctness

The *first* step modifies overly general rules, i.e. rules which cover too many negative examples. An incorrect rule is replaced by a set of rules covering all positive examples covered by the incorrect rule, but not covering the negative ones.

One possibility to refine an incorrect rule is to specialize the given rules as long as they do not cover the new negative examples. A rule could be specialized by adding a new premise to its premises. The problem of this approach is that the addition of one attribute involves a minor syntactical but a major semantical change of the rule. In the case of boolean attributes the number of the covered cases are halved. In the case of non-boolean attributes, the change is even much more drastic.[2] In addition, each specialization procedure deals with the problem of overspecialization. A specialization in an i-th step can allow some previous specializations to be undone. Therefore, each learning procedure applying specialization requires additional pruning of its results to prevent overspecialization.

---

1. Depending on the chosen preferences and strategies, there is the danger that loops arise. If the value of the preference criterion has to increase for every step completed this danger does not exist.

2. The ratio of the new and old cover of the rule is (Cartinality of the range of the attribute)$^{-1}$

Alternatively, a rule can be replaced by a set of rules which covers a subset of the examples which were covered by the old rule. Therefore, we apply JoJo for the sub-space which is defined by the incorrect rule.

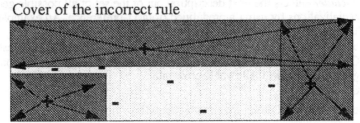

Cover of the incorrect rule

■■■■■ Cover of the new rule set

- Covered negative examples   + Covered positive examples

Figure 2. Specializing an incorrect rule by a set of rules.

This is done for each incorrect rule. Then the incorrect rules are replaced by the corresponding rule sets.

3.2   Completeness

After the last step every rule is correct in the sense that no rule covers more negative examples than is specified by a threshold. In a *second* step, the set of rules must be completed. This is done by applying JoJo to the set of still uncovered positive examples and all negative examples. JoJo computes new rules which are correct. These rules are computed as long as the number of positive examples which remain uncovered is larger than that what is specified by a threshold.

3.3   Non-Redundancy and Minimality

In this step, rules are deleted which are more special than other rules. This is done by checking the subset relation between the sets of premises of the rules. A rule is more special than a second one if its set of premises is a superset of the second one. In a fourth (optional) step a *minimal set of rules* is computed. A minimized set of rules has the same cover as the original one but consists of a minimal number of complexes. Because this problem is NP-complete we apply the following heuristic search:

1. Look for the best rule of the rule set (i.e. the one which covers the most examples).
2. Remove all positive examples which are covered by this rule.
3. Add the best rule to the final rule set.
4. If more positive examples remain than are specified by a threshold go to step 1.

4   Implementation and Empirical Evaluation of JoJo

JoJo is implemented in C and available under Sun-Unix and MS-DOS. It is integrated into the RJ-environment [9] which preprocesses unknown-values, ordinal, multi-valued, and continuous attributes. It has been tested with several data sets of the machine learning library and with data sets of the ESPRIT project StatLog (data sets with more than 10.000 objects and 40 attributes). The major result of these tests is its ability to learn very brief, i.e. general, descriptions of classes (cf. [8]) compared with results of algorithms like CN2 or C4.

5 Conclusion

The paper introduced a new approach for learning rules by examples which uses a more flexible heuristic search strategy than other algorithms which only generalize very specific or specialize very general descriptions. JoJo can start with arbitrary rules and generalizes or specializes them as long as the quality of the rule which is being regarded is improved. The algorithm JoJo is extended to a four-step closed-loop learning procedure which allows the stepwise refinement of given rule sets according to new examples.

Acknowledgement

We thank Jörg Klein and Monika Zickwolff for helpful and fruitful discussions and Jefferey Butler for correcting our English.

References

1. A. Blumer, A. Ehrenfeucht, D. Haussler, and M. K. Warmuth: Ocam´s Razor, In Information Processing Letters, vol 24, 1987, pp. 377-380.
2. J. Cendrowska: PRISM: An algorithm for inducing modular rules. In *Int. J. Man-Machine Studies*, vol. 27, 1987, pp. 349-370.
3. P. Clark and R. Boswell: Rule Induction with CN2: Some recent Improvements. In *Proceedings of the European Workshop on Machine Learning (EWSL'91)*, March 6-8, Porto, Portugal, 1991, pp. 151-163.
4. C. Decaesteckert: Incremental Classification: A multidisciplinary viewpoint. In *Proceedings of the Conference Symbolic-Numeric Data Analysis and Learning*, Versailles, September 18-20, 1991, pp. 283-295.
5. D. Fensel and J. Klein: A new approach to rule induction and pruning. In *Proceedings of the 3rd International Conference on Tools for Artificial Intelligence (ICTAI'91)*, Palo Alto, November 11-13, 1991.
6. D. Fensel and J. Klein: Solving a Generalization Task by Generalization: RELAX, H-RELAX, and I-RELAX. Three Algorithms for Rule Induction and Pruning. In Forschungsbericht des Institut für Angewandte Informatik und Formale Beschreibungsverfahren der Universität Karlsruhe (TH), no 235, Januar 1992.
7. D. Fensel: JoJo. In research report, Institut für Angewandte Informatik und Formale Beschreibungsverfahren, University of Karlsruhe, no 254, January 1993.
8. D. Fensel and M. Pechowski: An Evaluation of B-RELAX and JoJo. In research report, Institut für Angewandte Informatik und Formale Beschreibungsverfahren, University of Karlsruhe, March 1993.
9. D. Fensel, J. Klein, and U. Neubronner: RJ - An Environment for Learning from Example. In research report, Institut für Angewandte Informatik und Formale Beschreibungsverfahren, University of Karlsruhe, February 1993.
10. J. H. Gennari, P. Langley, and D. Fisher: Model of Incremental Concept Formation. In *Artificial Intelligence*, vol. 40, no. 1-3, September, 1989, pp. 11-62.
11. T.T.T. Huyen and H.T. Bao: A method for generating rules from examples and its application. *In Proceedings of the Conference Symbolic-Numeric Data Analysis and Learning*, Versailles, September 18-20, 1991, pp.493-504.
12. E. J. McCluskey: Minimizing of Boolean Functions. In *Bell System Tech. Journal*, vol. 35, no. 5, November 1956, pp. 1417-1444.
13. T.M. Mitchell: Generalization as Search. In B. Webber et.al. (eds), *Readings in Artificial Intelligence*, Tioga Publishinh Co., Palo Alto, 1981.
14. R. S. Michalski, I. Mozetic, J. Hong and N. Lavrac: The Multi-Purpose Incremental Learning System AQ15 and its Testing Application to Three Medical Domains. In *Proceedings of the 5th National Conference on AI (AAAI-86)*, Philadelphia, PA, August 11-15, pp. 1041-1045, 1986.
15. J.R. Quinlan: Simplifying decision trees. In Gaines et.al. (eds.), *Knowledge-Based Systems*, vol. 1, Academic Press Ltd, London, 1988, pp. 239-252.
16. J. R. Quinlan: Learning Logical Definitions from Relations. In *Machine Learning*, vol 5, no 3, 1990, pp. 239-266.
17. J.R. Quinlan: Probabilistic Decision Trees. In *Machine Learning. An Artificial Intelligence Approach*, vol. *III*, Y. Kodratoff et.al. (eds.), Morgan Kaufmann Publisher, San Mateo, CA, 1990.

Rule Combination
in
Inductive Learning

Luis Torgo

LIACC
R.Campo Alegre, 823 - 2º.
4100 PORTO
PORTUGAL
Telf. : (+351) 2 600 16 72 - Ext. 115
Fax : (+351) 2 600 3654
e-mail : ltorgo@ciup1.ncc.up.pt

Abstract. This paper describes the work on methods for combining rules obtained by machine learning systems. Three methods for obtaining the classification of examples with those rules are compared. The advantages and disadvantages of each method are discussed and the results obtained on three real world domains are commented. The methods compared are: selection of the *best* rule; PROSPECTOR-like probabilistic approximation for rule combination; and MYCIN-like approximation. Results show significant differences between methods indicating that the problem-solving strategy is important for accuracy oflearning systems.

1 Introduction

Most work in inductive learning tends to discuss the learning method details, but little attention is paid to the problem of how the learned rules are used. This paper shows that different problem solving strategies can lead to very different accuracy results. This clearly indicates the importance of these strategies when comparing performance of learning systems.

Our experiments used an attribute-based learning system to generate theories which were then tested with different problem-solving strategies. This problem is however extensible to other types of learning systems. In general, whenever different sources of knowledge are used (including in multi-strategy learning systems) we need a method for conflict resolution.

Experiments were made on three real world domains. Their goal was to observe if different classification strategies could lead to different results. The following strategies were used : two well known expert systems approaches, MYCIN [11] certainty factors and PROSPECTOR's [5] odds), together with the *best rule* strategy.

The next section describes briefly the inductive system used in the experiments. Section 3 presents the different strategies and section 4 the experiments carried out.

2 The Inductive Engine

In the context of this work the inductive system is used only as generator of rules. The system used for learning those rules was YAILS [12,13]. YAILS system belongs to the attribute-based family of learning programs. It is an incremental rule learning system capable of dealing with numerical attributes and noisy domains. It uses a kind of hill-climbing search strategy with different types of generalisation and specialisation operators. This bi-directional search is guided by an evaluation function which is described in section 3.3.

3 Strategies for Classifying Examples

The goal of inductive learning systems is to generate rules for later use. Application of rules may present some problems, however. We are concerned with the problem of several rules covering an example to be classified. We need a way for deciding which rule is to be followed. This is often referred as the conflict resolution strategy. Alternatively, we may decide to combine different opinions. Several methodologies exist to solve these problems. In the following sections three different strategies are presented. Each strategy attempts to deal with the problem of uncertainty caused, for instance, by unknown attribute values or incomplete description of examples.

3.1 Using Certainty Factors (MYCIN)

MYCIN [11] is one of the best known expert systems. MYCIN uses certainty factors (CF) as a way of modelling reasoning under uncertainty. A certainty factor is a number between -1 and 1 that represents the change in our belief on some hypothesis. A positive number means an increase in the belief and a negative number the contrary. A value of 0 means that there is no change in our belief on the hypothesis. In this work we are particularly interested in the parallel combination of rules, i.e. given $E_1 \Rightarrow H$ and $E_2 \Rightarrow H$ together with their respective confidence factors we are interested on the confidence factor of H given that E_1 and E_2 are true. The formulas used for rule combination in MYCIN are the following :

If CF(H,E1) and CF(H,E2) have opposite signs :

$$CF(H,E_1E_2) = \frac{CF(H,E1)+CF(H,E2)}{1-\min[|CF(H,E1)|,|CF(H,E2)|]} \qquad (1)$$

If CF(H,E1) and CF(H,E2) are both greater or equal to zero :

$$CF(H,E_1E_2) = CF(H,E_1)+CF(H,E_2)-CF(H,E_1)\times CF(H,E_2) \qquad (2)$$

If CF(H,E1) and CF(H,E2) are both less than zero :

$$CF(H,E_1E_2) = CF(H,E_1)+CF(H,E_2)+CF(H,E_1)\times CF(H,E_2) \qquad (3)$$

For the probabilistic definition of CF's we use the following [7] :

$$CF(H,E) = \begin{cases} \dfrac{\lambda(H,E)-1}{\lambda(H,E)} & \text{if } \lambda(H,E) \geq 1 \\[2mm] \lambda(H,E)-1 & \text{if } 0 \leq \lambda(H,E) \leq 1 \end{cases} \qquad (4)$$

where

$$\lambda(H,E) = \frac{P(E|H)}{P(E \mid \overline{H})}$$

This formalisation is derived from a set of axioms [7] which imply that the rules must be conditionally independent given the hypothesis and its negation [9]. This assumption does not hold in general. Nevertheless, this approach has been widely used and achieved good practical results.

3.2 Using Degree of Sufficiency and Necessity (PROSPECTOR)

PROSPECTOR [5] can be considered another successful expert system. In PROSPECTOR the uncertainty associated with a rule is described by two values (LS and LN) which express the degree of sufficiency and necessity with which the conditional part of a rule (E) implies the conclusion (H):

$$LS = \frac{P(E \mid H)}{P(E \mid \overline{H})} \quad \text{and} \quad LN = \frac{P(\overline{E} \mid H)}{P(\overline{E} \mid \overline{H})} \tag{5}$$

If we define the prior and posterior odds on H given E respectively as

$$O(H) = \frac{P(H)}{P(\overline{H})} \quad \text{and} \quad O(H/E) = \frac{P(H \mid E)}{P(\overline{H} \mid E)} \tag{6}$$

we obtain the following definition

$$O(H \mid E) = LS \times O(H) \quad \text{and} \quad O(H \mid \overline{E}) = LN \times O(H) \tag{7}$$

The formula used in PROSPECTOR for rule combination is as follows :

$$O(H \mid E_1^*, \dots, E_n^*) = \prod_{i=1}^{n} L_i^* \times O(H) \tag{8}$$

where

$$L_i^* = \begin{cases} LS_i & \text{if } E_i^* = E_i \\ LN_i & \text{if } E_i^* = \overline{E_i} \\ 1 & \text{if } E_i^* \text{ is unknown} \end{cases}$$

This approach also assumes conditional independence on all E_i 's.

3.3 Using *Best Rule* Strategy

This strategy represents a very simple but efficient way of producing the classification of an example given a set of potentially conflicting rules. It assumes that each rule is characterised by a value which expresses its "quality". When rules are generated by an inductive system this is easily obtained during the learning phase. Here we use a measure of quality provided by YAILS which is a function of two properties: its consistency and completeness. Rule quality is calculated as follows:

$$\text{Quality}(R) = [0.5 + W_{cons}(R)] \times \text{Cons}(R) + [0.5 - W_{cons}(R)] \times \text{Compl}(R) \tag{9}$$

where

$$Cons(R) = \frac{\#\{correctly\ covered\ exs.\}}{\#\{covered\ exs.\}} \qquad Compl(R) = \frac{\#\{correctly\ covered\ exs.\}}{\#\{exs.\ of\ same\ class\ as\ R\}}$$

$$W_{cons}(R) = \frac{Cons(R)}{4}$$

The notion of quality used here is a weighted sum of the consistency and completeness of the rule. The weights are proportional to the value of consistency giving thus some degree of flexibility (see [12, 13] for more details). Our formula for the calculation of quality is a heuristic one. Many other possibilities exist for evaluating a composite effect of various rule properties (see for instance [1] for a function which also includes simplicity).

Let us now come back to the *best rule* strategy. All rules applicable to a given example form a candidate set. After the candidate set has been formed, the rule with the highest quality value is chosen. The conclusion of this rule is followed.

4 Experiments

The experiments performed consisted of comparisons of the classification accuracies obtained by the three approaches described earlier. The same data was used in all experiments. Three medical domain datasets (obtained from Ljubljana) -Lymphography, Breast Cancer and Primary Tumour were used in these comparisons. Each of the datasets was divided in two subsets, one for learning and other for testing (70% for learning and 30% for testing). The three classification strategies were tried using the same learned theory. Table 1 presents the average of ten repetitions of these experiments (standard deviations are between brackets). In order to examine the differences, t-tests with a 95% confidence level were performed. The values which represented a significant difference are in italics on the table.

Table 1. Results of experiments.

	MYCIN-like	PROSPECTOR-like	Best Quality
Lymphography	78% (5%)	63% (9%)	81% (3%)
Breast Cancer	67% (6%)	78% (3%)	77% (4%)
Primary Tumour	23% (4%)	33% (6%)	32% (7%)

The results of table 1 were quite surprising. The best rule strategy was expected to be the worst since it does not take into account combinations of opinions. MYCIN's certainty factors performed worse than the others, with the exception of Lymphography dataset. PROSPECTOR's approach performed quite badly on Lymphography dataset. Both Breast Cancer and Primary Tumour datasets are known to be rather noisy. In this context the results suggest that the degree of uncertainty of the dataset counteracts in some way the advantages of combination of rules (at least for PROSPECTOR's approach as MYCIN's approach is always bad).

These differences show that the classification strategy can significantly affect the accuracy obtained by learning systems. These experiments seem to indicate that the *best rule* strategy can be a good strategy especially if we take in to account its simplicity when compared to other methods.

5   Relations to other work

Recently several people have studied the effects of multiple sources of knowledge (see [2] for a survey). All approaches share the problem of conflict resolution which is one of the issues tackled by the two probabilistic approaches examined in this paper.

Gams et al., [6] made several experiments with several knowledge bases when classifying new instances. They tried two different strategies to obtain the classification : *best-one* which uses the opinion with highest confidence factor (this is a strategy similar to ours) and the *majority* strategy where confidence factors add up in order to reach a conclusion. This latter strategy represents a kind of combination of different opinions. The authors made extensive experiments on artificial domains and the results showed that the *best-one* strategy scored better whenever few knowledge bases were used. When the number of knowledge bases increased the majority strategy was tbetter. These results seem to suggest that if flexible matching were introduced (which would increase the potential number of opinions) the probabilistic combination strategies examined in this paper might perform better.

Brazdil and Torgo [3] used different learning algorithms to generate several knowledge bases which were combined into one using a kind of best quality strategy. This work suggested that good results could be obtained with this simple strategy, but no comparisons were made with other possible combination strategies.

6   Future Work

The experiments carried out did not admit rules whose conditional parts were not completely satisfied (i.e. flexible matching). It would be interesting to see how accuracy would be affected if flexible matching were used.

The experiments could be extended to other datasets and other learning systems. Experiments with some existing ILP systems are under consideration. This later extension requires not only parallel evidence combination methods (as presented in the paper), but also sequential combination methods to cover the case of rule chaining.

The main extension should be to broaden the range of methods used to combine rules. Some effort could be invested towards the use of a model which does not exhibit the limitations of conditional independence [8] that both certainty factors and degrees of sufficiency and necessity suffer from. Some experiments could be done with Dempster-Shaffer [4] theory of evidence and Pearl's belief networks [10].

7   Conclusions

The experiments carried out in this paper suggest that a simple and quite naive *best rule* strategy performs quite well in comparison with the two other more complex strategies tested. As for PROSPECTOR-like approach, the results on Lymphography were quite bad, and similar to the *best rule* on the other datasets. With respect to MYCIN's certainty factors the performance was quite disappointing altogether.

The results did not show a clear advantage of the two traditional methods which combine different opinions. A possible cause for this could be a small number of rules to combine. This could perhaps improve if flexible matching were used. The differences in classification accuracy observed between three different combination strategies indicate that more care should be taken when discussing the performance of learning systems. A great deal of work done in the area of approximate reasoning and uncertainty management could be exploited by the ML community.

Acknowledgements
I would like to thank both Pavel Brazdil and Zdenek Kouba for their help and comments.

REFERENCES

1. Bergadano, F., Matwin,S., Michalski,R., Zhang,J. : "Measuring Quality of Concept Descriptions", in *EWSL88 - European Working Session on Learning*, Pitman, 1988.
2. Brazdil,P., Gams,M., Sian,S., Torgo,L., Van de Velde,W. : "Learning in Distributed Systems and Multi-Agent Environments", in *Machine Learning - EWSL91 ,European Working Session on Learning*, Kodratoff,Y. (Ed), Lecture Notes on Artificial Intelligence, Springer Verlag, 1991.
3. Brazdil,P., Torgo,L. : "Knowledge Acquisition via Knowledge Integration", in *Current Trends in Knowledge Acquisition*, IOS Press, 1990.
4. Shafer, G. : *A Mathematical Theory of Evidence*, Priceton University Press, Princeton, 1976.
5. Duda,R., Hart,P., Nilsson,N. : "Subjective Bayesian methods for rule-based inference systems", in Proceedings of the AFIPS National Computer Conference, vol. 47, pp. 1075-1082.
6. Gams,M., Bohanec,M., Cestnik,B. : "A Schema for Using Multiple Knowledge", Josef Stefan Institute, 1991.
7. Heckerman,D. :"Probabilistic interpretation for MYCIN's certainty factors", in *Uncertainty in Artificial Intelligence*, Kanal,L. et al.(eds.), North-Holland, 1986.
8. Kouba,Z. : "Data Analysis and Uncertainty Processing", in *Advanced Topics in Artificial Intelligence*, Marik,V. et al. (eds.), Lectures Notes in Artificial Intelligence, Springer-Verlag, 1992.
9. Mántaras,R., : *Approximate Reasoning Methods*, Ellis Howood Limited, 1990.
10. Pearl, J. : *Probabilistic Reasoning in Intelligent Systems: Networks of Plausible Inference*, Morgan Kaufmann Publishers, 1988.
11. Shortliffe,E., Buchanan,B., "A Model of Inexact Reasoning in Medicine", in *Mathematical Biosciences*, 23, 1975.
12. Torgo,L. : YAILS an incremental learning program, LIACC-ML Group, Internal report nº 92.1, 1992.
13. Torgo,L. : "Controlled Redundancy in Incremtnal Rule Learning", in this volume.

Using Heuristics to Speed up Induction on Continuous-Valued Attributes

Günter Seidelmann

Hahn-Meitner-Institut Berlin GmbH
Bereich Datenverarbeitung und Elektronik
Glienicker Str. 100, W-1000 Berlin 39, Germany
Email: seidelmann@vax.hmi.dbp.de

Abstract. Induction of decision trees in domains with continuous-valued attributes is computationally expensive due to the evaluation of every possible test on these attributes. As the number of tests to be considered grows linearly with the number of examples, this poses a problem for induction on large databases. Two variants of a heuristic, based on the possible difference of the entropy-minimization selection-criterion between two tests, are proposed and compared to a previously known heuristic. Empirical results with real-world data confirm that the heuristics can reduce the computational effort significantly without any change in the induced decision trees.

1 Introduction

Learning from examples has been recognized as a promising way of acquiring knowledge for classification purposes. Especially top-down induction of decision trees (TDIDT) has been used successfully in a number of applications (see e. g. [2], [3], [5]).

Early TDIDT-methods are restricted to nominal attributes. But in many applications, e. g. in process control, which include sensory data, continuous-valued attributes are predominant and should be treated adequately. A straightforward extension, as briefly mentioned in [4], leads to good results, but has the disadvantage of a rather high computational effort, which increases with the number of examples. On large data bases the runtime of the induction can therefore become inacceptable. This aspect has not found much attention until Fayyad and Irani [1] recently proposed a heuristic to reduce the average complexity while preserving the induced trees.

This paper describes two versions of a supplementary heuristic and argues that a combination with the one developed by Fayyad and Irani can reduce the computational effort significantly. The characteristics of the heuristics are discussed and their payoff is tested on different sets of real-world data.

Sect. 2 briefly describes the *ID3* algorithm and the results of Fayyad and Irani. In Sect. 3 another approach is motivated and two variants of a new heuristic are given. The results of empirical comparisons are presented in Sect. 4. Finally, conclusions can be found in Sect. 5.

2 Induction on Continuous-Valued Attributes

Induction of decision trees typically expects the examples to be represented as a set of attribute-value pairs with respect to a common set of attributes with each example belonging to one of a disjoint set of classes. In general, the algorithms select a test on one or more of the attributes to partition the set of examples into subsets, which are further divided recursively until a termination criterion is met. The generated tree consists of the selected tests at the inner nodes with subtrees for each possible outcome. The leaves are marked with the predominant class of the corresponding subset.

The well-known *ID3* [3] selects the test which minimizes the average entropy $E(T)$ in the resulting subsets. Let $C_1, \ldots, C_k$ be the classes occuring in the example set, $P(C_i)$ the corresponding probabilities, T a test on the examples which partitions the set into subsets $T_1, \ldots, T_m$, $P(T_j)$ the probability of an example to fall into the subset T_j and let $P(C_i \mid T_j)$ denote the conditional probability of an example out of T_j belonging to class C_i. The remaining average entropy $E(T)$ after the evaluation of a test T is then given by:

$$E(T) = -\sum_{j=1}^{m}\sum_{i=1}^{k} P(T_j)P(C_i \mid T_j)\log_2(P(C_i \mid T_j)) \tag{1}$$

For continuous-valued attributes tests of the form $A(x) < V$, with $A(x)$ denoting the attribute value of an example x, are generated by varying the threshold value V. This can be done efficiently by ordering the examples according to their attribute values and representing the tests as a splitting of this list (see Fig. 1). This admits an incremental computation of the probabilities needed in (1).

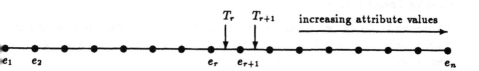

Fig. 1. Tests splitting the ordered list of examples

The number of possible tests $A(x) < V$ is linear in the number of examples[1], whereas only one test needs to be evaluated for a nominal attribute. Therefore the runtime of TDIDT- algorithms grows significantly in the presence of continuous-valued attributes, so that induction on large data bases becomes a time-consuming effort.

Not every possible test needs to be evaluated, however. In the ordered list of examples (see Fig. 1) two adjacent examples e_r and e_{r+1} often belong to

---

[1] If different examples have the same attribute value, the number of tests is, of course, sublinear.

the same class. Intuitively, it does not seem to make sense to divide the set of examples between them. Fayyad and Irani prove that in terms of the entropy-minimization selection criterion used in *ID3* either the division before example e_r or after example e_{r+1} is indeed superior to the one between them. They introduce the term *boundary point* for those thresholds whose constituting examples e_r and e_{r+1} belong to different classes.

As tests between boundary points are always inferior to at least one of their neighbouring tests, the following heuristic can be used:

Heuristic 1. *In the test selection process only those tests need to be evaluated which fall on boundary points.*

The achievable reduction in the number of test evaluations depends heavily on the data. Given n examples out of k different classes, a perfectly predicting attribute yields only $k - 1$ boundary points, whereas a totally uncorrelated attribute can be expected to result in $(n-1)\frac{k-1}{k}$ boundary points. This indicates that Heuristic 1 will work particularly well on data sets which contain few classes.

3 Heuristics Based on the Maximum Difference

In order to select a test at a node during the induction, the algorithm has to generate and evaluate the possible tests on all available attributes. The test yielding the minimum remaining entropy (1) is selected. If there are many examples and a continuous-valued attribute is considered, two successive tests T_r and T_{r+1} (see Fig. 1) have a very small difference in their rating by the selection criterion. With an estimation of this difference the evaluation of test T_{r+1} can safely be omitted if test T_r is sufficiently inferior to a previously found one.

Hence an upper bound is needed for the difference between $E(T_{r+1})$ and $E(T_r)$ with the two tests differing only in the example e_{r+1}. Such a bound is given in Theorem 1.

Theorem 1. *Given n examples $e_1, \ldots, e_r, e_{r+1}, \ldots, e_n$ and two successive tests T_r and T_{r+1} which split the examples after e_r and e_{r+1} (resp.) the following holds:*

$$E(T_r) - E(T_{r+1}) \leq \frac{2\log_2(n+1) - \log_2 r}{n} = \text{max-diff}(T_r) \qquad (2)$$

Let now E_{min} be the minimum remaining entropy reached so far by a test during the test selection. If a test T_r results in an entropy $E(T_r)$ such that $E(T_r) - \text{max-diff}(T_r) > E_{min}$, the following test T_{r+1} does not have to be considered. Furthermore, as the function max-diff(T_r) decreases strictly monotonously in r, even more tests can eventually be eliminated. This leads to:

Heuristic 2. *If the minimal remaining entropy reached so far is given by E_{min}, the next test to be evaluated after test T_r is $T_{r+\Delta}$ with:*

$$\Delta = \max\left(1, \left\lceil \frac{E(T_r) - E_{min}}{\text{max-diff}(T_r)} \right\rceil\right) \qquad (3)$$

On close examination the heuristic shows the following properties:

- As Δ depends on E_{min}, the number of tests to be omitted is influenced by the order in which the attributes are processed. To achieve high savings the most relevant attribute should be chosen first.
- Since max-diff(T_r) is monotonously decreasing in r, the Δ-values are higher in the second half of the list.
- In general, Heuristic 2 will be more effective on irrelevant attributes than on relevant ones, provided a relevant attribute has been processed previously.

The following extension takes advantage of some of these properties. As higher benefits are obtained in the second half of the lists, it can be useful to start with a test in the middle of the list of examples and to proceed successively to the borders, using Heuristic 2.

Now the first test to be evaluated for an attribute is the one which splits the set of examples in the middle. These tests will have different entropy measures depending on the class distribution in the two subsets. Their entropy measures can be used to estimate the relevance of the attributes. By processing those attributes first that yield low entropy measures, an optimal order of the attributes can be approximated. This method is stated in the following heuristic:

Heuristic 3. *For each attribute A_i the examples are partitioned at the median into two roughly equally large sets by a test T_{m_i}. The examples in the set with attribute values below or above the median are ordered by decreasing or increasing attribute values resp. These lists are ordered by increasing values of $E(T_{m_i})$ and processed according to Heuristic 2.*

4 An Empirical Comparison

As the efficiency of the heuristics discussed depends heavily on the characteristics of the data, an evaluation using real-world data is needed. In these experiments the heuristics are used on their own as well as in combinations.

The data sets used are listed in Table 1 together with a brief description. Except for the solar data all of them are publicly available; as far as training and test sets are supplied separately, they were joined for the following experiments. Examples with values missing were removed.

As the heuristics aim for a reduction in the number of tests to be evaluated by the entropy-minimization selection-criterion, the number of tests actually considered during the induction gives a first metric for comparison. It is a machine- and implementation-independent efficiency measure of the heuristics, which ignores the overhead associated with them. The results for different data sets are given in Fig. 2.

Some observations should be discussed:

- The heuristics based on the max-diff bound perform poorly on the medical domains cleve1, cleve2 and pima. These domains contain many examples with identical attribute values, thus reducing the number of possible tests that are to be omitted despite high Δ-values.

Table 1. Brief description of the data sets

Domain	Name	Examples	Attributes	Classes
Heart-diseases	cleve1	297	13	2
Same as above, but 5 classes	cleve2	297	13	5
Glass types	glass	214	9	6
Diabetes	pima	768	8	2
Semiconductor films	solar	540	10	4
Sonar signals	sonar	208	60	2
Vowel recognition	vowel	990	10	11

- Heuristic 1 is more efficient on data sets with few classes. It yields exceptionally high reductions on the sonar data and performs better on the cleve1 data with 2 classes than on the corresponding set cleve2 with 5 classes.
- Only on the vowel data the more sophisticated Heuristic 3 performs considerably better than Heuristic 2, where obviously a more suitable order of attributes is found.
- The combinations of two heuristics consistently achieve good results. They reduce the number of test evaluations by at least 43 % on the cleve2 data up to 83% on the vowel data.

Reductions in the number of test evaluations are achieved at the expense of the computational overhead associated with each heuristic. From a practical point of view the only interesting metric is reduction in total runtime. As expected, no substantial reductions are attained in the medical domains cleve1[2], cleve2 and pima. However, in most cases the overhead of the heuristics is compensated by reductions in the number of test evaluations; only the large overhead of Heuristic 3 did not pay off.

Especially the combinations work reliably on the other data sets. The combination of Heuristic 1 with Heuristic 2 results in a speed-up between 20% (sonar data) and 30% (vowel data); the combination with Heuristic 3 saves between 10% (glass data) and 39% (vowel data).

5 Conclusion

When decision trees are induced by means of the entropy-minimization selection-criterion, the number of tests to be evaluated can be reduced by using simple heuristics. This result has been confirmed by empirical experiments. As the heuristics exploit different characteristics of the data, a combination of them will work reliably for a wide variety of applications.

The heuristics apply first of all to the entropy-minimization selection-criterion. In [1] Fayyad and Irani mention that their heuristic (Heuristic 1 in this paper) can be used with other selection measures as well. It should be possible to derive

---

[2] In [1] Fayyad and Irani report a runtime reduction of more than 15% for their heuristic on this data set.

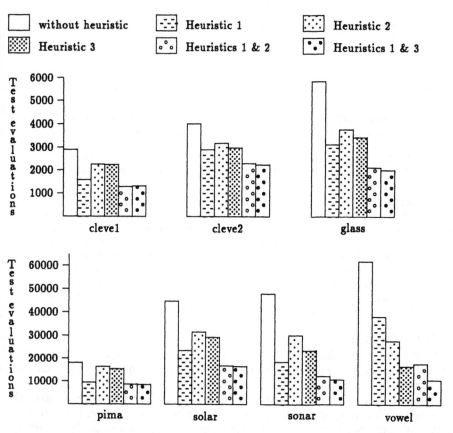

Fig. 2. Number of tests evaluated

bounds – similar to the one found for the entropy measure – for other selection criteria, so that Heuristics 2 and 3 could be applied to them as well.

References

1. U. M. Fayyad and K. B. Irani. On the handling of continuous-valued attributes in decision tree generation. *Machine Learning*, 8(1):87–102, 1992.
2. W. J. Leech. A rule-based process control method with feedback. *ISA Transactions*, 26(2):73–80, 1987.
3. J. R. Quinlan. Learning efficient classification procedures and their application to chess end games. In *Machine Learning: An Artificial Intelligence Approach*, pages 463–482. Tioga Press, 1983.
4. J. R. Quinlan. Simplifying decision trees. *International Journal on Man-Machine Studies*, 27:221–234, 1987.
5. J. C. Schlimmer. Learning meta knowledge for database checking. In *Proceedings of the Ninth National Conference on Artificial Intelligence*, pages 335–340. AAAI Press / The MIT Press, 1991.

Integrating Models of Knowledge and Machine Learning

Jean-Gabriel GANASCIA[2]   Jérôme THOMAS[1-2]   Philippe LAUBLET[1]

[1]ONERA, DMI, GIA
29, av. de la division Leclerc
BP 72
92322 Chatillon Cedex
e-mail:{laublet thomas}@onera.fr

[2]LAFORIA-CNRS
Université Pierre et Marie Curie
Tour 46-0, 4 place Jussieu
75252 Paris Cedex
e-mail:{ganascia thomas}@laforia.ibp.fr

Abstract: We propose a framework allowing a real integration of Machine Learning and Knowledge acquisition. This paper shows how the input of a Machine Learning system can be mapped to the model of expertise as it is used in KADS methodology. The notion of learning bias will play a central role. We shall see that parts of it can be identified to what KADS's people call the inference and the task models. Doing this conceptual mapping, we give a semantics to most of the inputs of Machine Learning programs in terms of knowledge acquisition models. The ENIGME system which implements this work will be presented

1. Introduction

In the classical view, the goals of machine learning are to develop computational theories of learning and to build learning machines. From this last point, machine learning can be seen as a process of transforming source data (observations, traces of computation, teachers' remarks...) into organized and usable knowledge. Among all the inputs of ML programs, some are easily identified, for instance, the notion of sources of data. But, there are many other inputs which are not so easily identified. They correspond to the notion of learning bias whose role has been emphasized by many authors in the past [Mitchell 82, Utgoff 86, Ganascia 88, Russel 90,...]. Without going into details, it appears that, since induction can be seen as a search process, and since the space of possible generalizations is huge, it is necessary to introduce many heuristics and constraints to guide the search.

For us, the process of knowledge acquisition can be seen as an interactive process with a machine learning program where the source data and the different parts of the bias must be progressively refined. In this process, the role of the expert will be to teach the learner when it makes a mistake and to give it a way to modify its behaviour. Hence, it is really useful for the apprentice to be able to explain, in an understandable way, the false reasoning to allow the expert to isolate one or more false steps in it. A first way to modify the behaviour of the system is to give a counter-example of the false rule to the learner. But this way of proceeding can be a little tedious especially if we don't have a great number of examples or if we have given too weak a bias. A better way to modify the behaviour of the learner is to modify its exploration constraints. Thus, these constraints and their use by the learning tool must make sense for the expert.

To fulfil these objectives, the solution proposed is to constrain the apprentice during the induction phase with kinds of knowledge that are issued from the KADS knowledge acquisition methodology. Such constraints have several points of interest. First, the learning bias will be knowledge which comes from the knowledge acquisition framework, thus, its acquisition may be done by the tools developed in this area. Second, the same models, with the same semantics, will be used by all the knowledge acquisition actors, i.e., the learning tool, the knowledge engineer, the expert and the inference engine. We think that this point is really important because it allows the expert to foretell the effects of a constraint on the rule system produced.

In the course of this paper, we will use an example related to the first bid of the card game of bridge. Thus, as a preliminary step, let us explain the main features of this problem. The goal is, knowing the hand, to choose an opening. In this example, in order to simplify, we will only choose a suit and no level of opening. It is obviously a classification problem, but the expert uses several intermediate concepts (between the observables and the opening) to reach the solution. An expert resolution will roughly follow the reasoning: to value the hand, if the valuation is sufficient then pass else, the next step is to abstract the kind-of-distribution from the distribution and the strong-suit to see if we have a normal hand or an extraordinary one. Indeed, there are two different ways to solve the problem, if it's an extraordinary hand, we will follow a convention otherwise we will abstract the kind of hand from the observables, then we will compute the solution.

The next section will present the notion of learning bias as it is classically understood in the Machine Learning community. Then we shall provide some information concerning the CHARADE learning system and the notion of model of expertise in the KADS methodology. Finally, we shall present the role for learning of the inference structure and the task structure in sections four and five.

2. Learning bias

According to [Russel 90] one distinguishes three kinds of bias: the *domain bias*, the *restriction type bias* and the *preference type bias*.

A) The domain bias contains the attributes, their syntax, hierarchies of descriptors, axioms expressing properties of attributes (as total order among the possible values, ...) and so on. It corresponds to a part of the *domain knowledge* in the KADS terminology.

B) So, the domain bias defines a structured hypothesis space which is the set of the candidate theories that the program could propose for any possible set of observation sentences. If the expert already has knowledge which allows to prune some parts of this space, it may be useful to provide the system with. According to [Russel 90], we will call such a knowledge the *restriction type bias*. This information is implicit in most of the learning systems. Making it explicit allows more flexibility in the use of an apprentice.

C) The third kind of bias is what [Russel 90] names the *preference type bias*. It provides the system with a preference ordering which allows the learner to choose between of the possible relations.

Our aim is to express all the learning bias as parts of the knowledge and to acquire it. Historically, designing the CHARADE system [Ganascia 87, 88], the aim was to provide some semantics for informations required as input to a learning system. Therefore, some of those inputs were related to the operationality of the induced knowledge, i.e., to the goal of the learned knowledge. We now pursue this work and for that we choose to provide some explicit links with the KADS methodology.

3. Background

The CHARADE system generates knowledge bases automatically from examples by detecting correlations in a training set of examples. It is based on the use of two distributive lattices, one for the learning set, i.e., the set of examples, and one for the description space. The properties of the lattices are used in the learning process to facilitate the detection of similarities and to limit the search cost. Concretely, a similarity corresponds to a correlation empirically observed in the learning set. If all the examples that have a conjunction of descriptors D1 in their description, also have the descriptor d2, it's possible to induce that D1 implies d2 in the learning set. The principle of induction used in symbolic learning consists in a generalization of these relations to the whole description space.

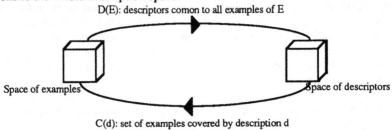

D(E): descriptors comon to all examples of E

Space of examples   Space of descriptors

C(d): set of examples covered by description d

Fig. 1. The C and D functions between the two spaces

The main difficulty consists in the large number of potential regularities that are useless. It is important to note that the CHARADE system makes use of logical constraints to restrict the logical implications it generates, to useful ones.

For KADS [Wielinga 92], the model of expertise produced during the analysis phase allows the specification of the expertise that the future system has to use to perform the problem-solving tasks. It consists of four layers: the *domain layer*, the *inference layer*, the *task layer* and the *strategy layer*. In this paper, we are only interested in the first three.

* The domain layer describes the concepts, the relations and the different properties of the domain. For instance, in the bridge example, the domain layer will include all the concepts' descriptions (possible values, type,...) the relations between these concepts, semantic networks linking them,...

* The inference layer is the description of the possible inference steps that are considered as primitive ones at the abstraction level of expertise model. An inference step (or a fragment) consists of a *knowledge source* that describes the type of inference (e.g.: classify, abstract ...)., and of *metaclasses* as inputs and outputs of the knowledge source. A metaclass (or a role) describes the *role* of domain entities in the problem-solving process and it is linked to the domain concepts which fulfil this role. The inference structure network gives a visual representation of dependencies between the different inference steps (see figure 2 for the example).

* In the task layer, it is possible to define composite tasks recursively and the ordering of the tasks (simple or composite) is described in a textual form with selection and iteration operators. This task structure gives the way to go through the inference structure (see figure 3 for the example).

In the following sections of this paper, we suppose that it is possible to build this problem solving method by a process similar to those of [McDermott 88, Wielinga 92,...]. Then, we emphasize how this model can be useful not only to elicit new domain knowledge as in the previously mentioned approaches, but also to learn this knowledge inductively from examples.

4. The Inference Structure

In ENIGME, the general idea is to learn only relations which follow the primitive inference steps of this structure. Indeed, as it has been asserted before, this structure gives the dependencies between the different concepts involved in a resolution process. Since the purpose of the produced rules is to accomplish such a resolution, the only useful relations are those which link concepts following these dependencies. For instance, once the inference structure (see figure 2) of the bridge example has been acquired, if ENIGME has to learn the relations of the select_conv knowledge source it will learn the relations between concepts involved in the roles: *valuation, syndrome1, solution classes* and *convention*.

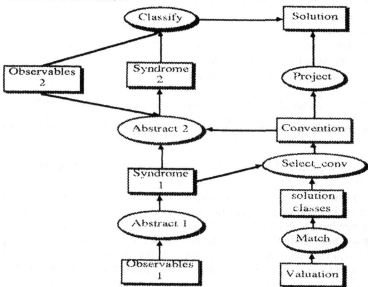

Fig. 2. The inference structure of the bridge example.

Thus, from the search point of view, the inference structure allows the learner to consider only the parts of the search space whose elements are conjunctions of concepts involved in the input roles of a fragment. Since the dimension of this space is exponential with the number of attributes, if all the concepts are not involved in the same fragment, the gain will be significant. In the example, the search space is reduced by a factor of roughly 10^9. Moreover, since it restricts the search space to consider only the rules following the reasoning given by this expert, it reduces the set of all the possible generalizations, thus the role of the preference bias will be strongly limited by this structure.

But with only this structure, the apprentice doesn't know the context of the fragment in the resolution process. This context is composed of the place of the fragment in the resolution process (i.e., what has be done, what will be done) and the control on this process. In the KADS model, this context is described in the task layer, and its use by ENIGME is the subject of the next part

5. The Task Structure

This structure is used to describe the chaining of the steps in the resolution process and the control on this chaining (see the figure 3 for the bridge example). The language used by the KADS formalism has one ground instruction: the fragment. A fragment matches one step of the problem solving method. For instance, the fragment *select_conv (syndrome1 valuation solution-classes) -> convention* (see figure 3) corresponds to the step of the resolution which decides if this resolution will use a convention. The other instructions describe the control over the resolution process. This control is mainly expressed through two features: the conditional instructions and the loops. ENIGME uses this control to discover which examples match which step of the resolution process.

Task {
    match (valuation) -> solution-classes
    If opening = yes[1] *Then {*
        abstract1 (observables1) -> syndrome1
        select_conv (syndrome1 valuation solution-classes) -> convention
        If conventional-opening = club *Or*
            conventional-opening = no-trump *then*
                project (convention) -> solution
        Else { abstract2 (syndrome1 observables2 convention) -> syndrome2
                classify (syndrome2 observables2) -> solution   *}}*

Fig. 3. The task structure of the bridge example.

The first consequence of the use of such a structure is on the examples' description. Indeed, they have to represent an experience of the problem's resolution. Thus, their description must include all the concepts involved in all the roles of the inference structure their resolution goes through. Then if these examples come from a database, we can have to complete these examples with all the intermediate concepts (like the abstractions,...). On the other hand, if there are several ways to solve the problem, the examples can have different descriptions. For instance, in the bridge example, there are two ways to reach the solution. If the hand is normal, we will follow the left branch of the inference structure and, so, an example of a normal hand will be described with the concepts involved in the roles: *valuation, observables1&2, syndrome1&2, solution-classes, convention and solution*. On the other hand, if the hand is an extraordinary one, we will follow the right branch of the inference structure and, so, the example will be described with the concepts involved in the roles: *valuation, observables1, syndrome1, solution-classes, convention and solution*[2].

Another major consequence of the use of task structure is the possible reasoning done by the produced rules. Indeed, in most of the current machine learning tools, this reasoning is, implicitly, done with one inference step which associates directly the solution with the description of the case. In this tool, thanks to these structures, the produced rules belong to a complete rule system. For instance, with the bridge

---

[1] In this version of ENIGME, the tests in the instructions are expressed with domain concepts. It may be useful (and more in the KADS spirit) for this control to be expressed in more abstract terms.

[2] In this example, the second description language is included in the first one, but, it is not necessary.

example, a resolution process may have up to four inference steps. The expert is much more confident with this kind of rule system than with a single rule which associates, directely, the observables to the solution.

6. Conclusion

The aim of this paper is to provide some basis for a real integration of Machine Learning and Knowledge Acquisition which could not just be reduced to a juxtaposition. To achieve this integration, we have developed a parallel among the Knowledge Acquisition models and the inputs of Machine Learning tools. It helps to establish that some parts of the learning bias can use some parts of the structured model of expertise, as it is presented in the KADS methodology, efficiently. As a conclusion, we want to draw attention to three points.

In the first place, the positive result of this work is the achievement of an integrated system named ENIGME which strongly couples Knowledge Acquisition and Machine Learning. It was empirically tested on a non trivial problem which is presented in the paper. We shall pursue its development by inserting it in an existing Knowledge Acquisition environment in the VITAL project.

In the second place, we have to note that we strongly coupled Knowledge Acquisition and Machine Learning. This strong couple is based on the fact that most of the inputs of the learning algorithms could be interpreted both in terms of their role in Machine Learning and in terms of problem solving models. This result is very significant by itself.

Lastly, the positive results we obtained need to be tempered since we did not succeed in assimilating all the learning bias to components of problem solving models: the preference-type bias has no interpretation in terms of Knowledge Acquisition models. Up to now, it only has some sense in terms of Machine Learning algorithms, its main role being to order the generalization space. In the future, we shall examine deeply the exact role of the preference-type bias and its meaning.

We thank the whole machine learning and knowledge acquisition team at the LAFORIA, particularly Karine Causse and Bernard Le Roux. The research reported here was carried out in the course of the VITAL project P5365 partially funded by the ESPRIT II program of the Commission of the European Communities.

[Ganascia 88]   Jean-Gabriel Ganascia, *Improvement and refinement of the learning bias semantic.*, ECAI 88

[Mitchell 82]   Tom M. Mitchell, *Generalization as Search.*, Artificial Intelligence V18 N°2 March 1982

[McDemott 88] John McDermott, *Preliminary steps toward a taxonomy of problem solving methods.*, In Automating KA for expert systems ed. by S. Marcus

[Russel 90]   Stuart J. Russel and Benjamin N. Grosof, *Declarative Bias: An Overview.*, in Change of representation and inductive bias. ed. by P. Benjamin

[Utgoff 86]   Paul E. Utgoff, *Shift the bias for inductive concept learning,* Machine learning: An Artificial Intelligence approach V. 1

[Wielinga 92]   B.J. Wielinga, A.Th. Schreiber and J.A. Breuker, *KADS: A Modelling Approach to Knowledge Engineering.*, Knowledge Acquisition volume 4, number 1, march 1992.

Exploiting Context When Learning to Classify

Peter D. Turney

Knowledge Systems Laboratory, Institute for Information Technology
National Research Council Canada, Ottawa, Ontario, Canada, K1A 0R6
turney@ai.iit.nrc.ca

Abstract. This paper addresses the problem of classifying observations when features are context-sensitive, specifically when the testing set involves a context that is different from the training set. The paper begins with a precise definition of the problem, then general strategies are presented for enhancing the performance of classification algorithms on this type of problem. These strategies are tested on two domains. The first domain is the diagnosis of gas turbine engines. The problem is to diagnose a faulty engine in one context, such as warm weather, when the fault has previously been seen only in another context, such as cold weather. The second domain is speech recognition. The problem is to recognize words spoken by a new speaker, not represented in the training set. For both domains, exploiting context results in substantially more accurate classification.

1 Introduction

A large body of research in machine learning is concerned with algorithms for classifying observations, where the observations are described by vectors in a multidimensional space of features. It often happens that a feature is context-sensitive. For example, when diagnosing spinal diseases, the significance of a certain level of flexibility in the spine depends on the age of the patient. This paper addresses the classification of observations when the features are context-sensitive.

In empirical studies of classification algorithms, it is common to randomly divide a set of data into a testing set and a training set. In this paper, the testing set and the training set have been deliberately chosen so that the contextual features range over values in the training set that are different from the values in the testing set. This adds an extra level of difficulty to the classification problem.

Section 2 presents a precise definition of context. General strategies for exploiting contextual information are given in Section 3. The strategies are tested on two domains. Section 4 shows how contextual information can improve the diagnosis of faults in an aircraft gas turbine engine. The classification algorithms used on the engine data were instance-based learning (IBL) [1, 2, 3] and multivariate linear regression (MLR) [4]. Both algorithms benefit from contextual information. Section 5 shows how context can be used to improve speech recognition. The speech recognition data were classified using IBL and cascade-correlation [5]. Again, both algorithms benefit from exploiting context. The work presented here is compared with related work by other researchers in Section 6. Future work is discussed in Section 7. Finally, Section 8 presents the conclusion. For the two domains and three classification algorithms studied here, exploiting contextual information results in a significant increase in accuracy.

2 Definition of Context

This section presents a precise definition of context. Let C be a finite set of classes. Let F be an n-dimensional feature space. Let $\dot{x} = (x_0, x_1, ..., x_n)$ be a member of $C \times F$; that is, $(x_1, ..., x_n) \in F$ and $x_0 \in C$. We will use $\dot{x}$ to represent a variable and $\dot{a} = (a_0, a_1, ..., a_n)$ to represent a constant in $C \times F$. Let p be a probability distribution defined on $C \times F$. In the definitions that follow, we will assume that p is a discrete distribution. It is easy to extend these definitions for the continuous case.

Primary Feature: Feature x_i (where $1 \leq i \leq n$) is a *primary feature* for predicting the class x_0 when there is a value a_i of x_i and there is a value a_0 of x_0 such that:

$$p(x_0 = a_0 | x_i = a_i) \neq p(x_0 = a_0) \tag{1}$$

In other words, the probability that $x_0 = a_0$, given $x_i = a_i$, is different from the probability that $x_0 = a_0$.

Contextual Feature: Feature x_i (where $1 \leq i \leq n$) is a *contextual feature* for predicting the class x_0 when x_i is *not* a primary feature for predicting the class x_0 and there is a value $\hat{a}$ of $\hat{x}$ such that:

$$p(x_0 = a_0 | x_1 = a_1, ..., x_n = a_n)$$
$$\neq p(x_0 = a_0 | x_1 = a_1, ..., x_{i-1} = a_{i-1}, x_{i+1} = a_{i+1}, ..., x_n = a_n) \tag{2}$$

In other words, if x_i is a contextual feature, then we can make a better prediction when we know the value a_i of x_i than we can make when the value is unknown, assuming that we know the values of the other features, $x_1, ..., x_{i-1}, x_{i+1}, ..., x_n$.

The definitions above refer to the class x_0. In the following, we will assume that the class is fixed, so that we do not need to explicitly mention the class.

Irrelevant Feature: Feature x_i (where $1 \leq i \leq n$) is an *irrelevant feature* when x_i is *neither* a primary feature *nor* a contextual feature.

Context-Sensitive Feature: A primary feature x_i is *context-sensitive* to a contextual feature x_j when there are values a_0, a_i, and a_j, such that:

$$p(x_0 = a_0 | x_i = a_i, x_j = a_j) \neq p(x_0 = a_0 | x_i = a_i) \tag{3}$$

The primary concern here is strategies for handling context-sensitive features.

When p is unknown, it is often possible to use background knowledge to distinguish primary, contextual, and irrelevant features. Examples of this use of background knowledge will be presented later in the paper.

3 Strategies for Exploiting Context

Katz *et al.* [6] list four strategies for using contextual information when classifying:

1. **Contextual normalization:** The contextual features can be used to normalize the context-sensitive primary features, prior to classification. The intent is to process context-sensitive features in a way that reduces their sensitivity to the context.

2. **Contextual expansion:** A feature space composed of primary features can be expanded with contextual features. The contextual features can be treated by the classifier in the same manner as the primary features.

3. **Contextual classifier selection:** Classification can proceed in two steps: First select a specialized classifier from a set of classifiers, based on the contextual features. Then apply the specialized classifier to the primary features.

4. **Contextual classification adjustment:** The two steps in strategy 3 can be reversed: First classify, using only the primary features. Then make an adjustment to the classification, based on the contextual features.

This paper examines strategies 1 and 2 (see Sections 4 and 5). A fifth strategy is also investigated:

5. **Contextual weighting:** The contextual features can be used to weight the primary features, prior to classification. The intent of weighting is to assign more importance to features that, in a given context, are more useful for classification.

The purpose of contextual normalization is to treat all features equally, by removing the affects of context and measurement scale. Contextual weighting has a different purpose: to prefer some features over other features, if they may improve accuracy.

4 Gas Turbine Engine Diagnosis

This section compares contextual normalization (strategy 1) with other popular forms of normalization. Strategies 2 to 5 are not examined in this section. The application is fault diagnosis of an aircraft gas turbine engine. The feature space consists of about 100 continuous primary features (engine performance parameters, such as thrust, fuel flow, and temperature) and 5 continuous contextual features (ambient weather conditions, such as external air temperature, barometric pressure, and humidity). The observations fall in eight classes: seven classes of deliberately implanted faults and a healthy class [7].

The amount of thrust produced by an engine is a primary feature for diagnosing faults in the engine. The exterior air temperature is a contextual feature, since the engine's performance is sensitive to the exterior air temperature. Exterior air temperature is not a primary feature, since knowing the exterior air temperature, *by itself*, does not help us to make a diagnosis. This background knowledge lets us distinguish primary and contextual features, without having to determine the probability distribution.

The data consist of 242 observations, divided into two sets of roughly the same size. One set of observations was collected during warmer weather and the second set was collected during cooler weather. One set was used as the training set and the other as the testing set, then the sets were swapped and the process was repeated. Thus the sample size for testing purposes is 242.

The data were analyzed using two classification algorithms, a form of instance-based learning (IBL) [1, 2, 3] and multivariate linear regression (MLR) [4]. IBL and MLR were also used to preprocess the data by contextual normalization [7].

The following methods for normalization were experimentally evaluated:

1. no normalization (use raw feature data)
2. normalization without context, using
    a. normalization by minimum and maximum value in the training set (the minimum is normalized to 0 and the maximum is normalized to 1)
    b. normalization by average and standard deviation in the training set (subtract the average and divide by the standard deviation)
    c. normalization by percentile in the training set (if 10% of the values of a feature are below a certain level, then that level is normalized to 0.1)
    d. normalization by average and standard deviation in a set of healthy baseline observations (chosen to span a range of ambient conditions)
3. contextual normalization (strategy 1), using
    a. IBL (trained with healthy baseline observations)
    b. MLR (trained with healthy baseline observations)

Contextual normalization was done as follows. Let $\hat{x}$ be a vector of primary features and let $\hat{c}$ be a vector of contextual features. Contextual normalization transforms $\hat{x}$ to a vector $\hat{v}$ of normalized features, using the context $\hat{c}$. We used the following formula for contextual normalization:

$$v_i = (x_i - \mu_i(\hat{c})) / \sigma_i(\hat{c}) \qquad (4)$$

In (4), $\mu_i(\hat{c})$ is the expected value of x_i and $\sigma_i(\hat{c})$ is the expected variation of x_i, as a function of the context $\hat{c}$. The values of $\mu_i(\hat{c})$ and $\sigma_i(\hat{c})$ were estimated using IBL and MLR, trained with healthy observations (spanning a range of ambient conditions) [7]. Table 1 (derived from Table 5 in [7]) shows the results of this experiment.

Table 1: A comparison of various methods of normalization.

Classifier	Normalization	no. correct	percent correct
IBL	none	102	42
IBL	min/max train	101	42
IBL	avg/dev train	97	40
IBL	percentile train	92	38
IBL	avg/dev baseline	111	46
IBL	IBL	139	57
IBL	MLR	128	53
MLR	none	100	41
MLR	min/max train	100	41
MLR	avg/dev train	100	41
MLR	percentile train	74	31
MLR	avg/dev baseline	100	41
MLR	IBL	103	43
MLR	MLR	119	49

For IBL, the average score without contextual normalization is 42% and the average score with contextual normalization is 55%, an improvement of 13%. For MLR, the improvement is 7%. According to the Student t-test, contextual normalization is significantly better than all of the alternatives that were examined [7].

5 Speech Recognition

This section examines strategies 1, 2, and 5: contextual normalization, contextual expansion, and contextual weighting. The problem is to recognize a vowel spoken by an arbitrary speaker. There are ten continuous primary features (derived from spectral data) and two discrete contextual features (the speaker's identity and sex). The observations fall in eleven classes (eleven different vowels) [8].

For speech recognition, spectral data is a primary feature for recognizing a vowel. The sex of the speaker is a contextual feature, since we can achieve better recognition by exploiting the fact that a man's voice tends to sound different from a woman's voice. Sex is not a primary feature, since knowing the speaker's sex, *by itself*, does not help us to recognize a vowel. This background knowledge lets us distinguish primary and contextual features, without having to determine the probability distribution.

The data are divided into a training set and a testing set. Each of the eleven vowels is spoken six times by each speaker. The training set is from four male and four female speakers ($11 \times 6 \times 8 = 528$ observations). The testing set is from four new male and three new female speakers ($11 \times 6 \times 7 = 462$ observations). Using a wide variety of neural network algorithms, Robinson [9] achieved accuracies ranging from 33% to 55% correct on the testing set. The mean score was 49%, with a standard deviation of 6%.

Three of the five strategies in Section 3 were applied to the data:

Contextual normalization: Each feature was normalized by equation (4), where the context vector $\hat{c}$ is simply the speaker's identity. The values of $\mu_i(\hat{c})$ and $\sigma_i(\hat{c})$ are estimated simply by taking the average and standard deviation of x_i for the speaker $\hat{c}$. In a practical application, this will require storing speech samples from a new speaker in a buffer, until enough data are collected to calculate the average and standard deviation.

Contextual expansion: The sex of the speaker was treated as another feature. This strategy is not applicable to the speaker's identity, since the speakers in the testing set are distinct from the speakers in the training set.

Contextual weighting: The features were multiplied by weights, where the weight for a feature was the ratio of inter-class deviation to intra-class deviation. The inter-class deviation of a feature indicates the variation in a feature's value, across class boundaries. It is the average, for all speakers in the training set, of the standard deviation of the feature, across all classes (all vowels), for a given speaker. The intra-class deviation of a feature indicates the variation in a feature's value, within a class boundary. It is the average, for all speakers in the training set and all classes, of the standard deviation of the feature, for a given speaker and a given class. The ratio of inter-class deviation to intra-class deviation is high when a feature varies greatly across class boundaries, but varies little within a class. A high weight (a high ratio) suggests that the feature will be useful for classification. This is a form of contextual weighting, because the weight is calculated on the basis of the speaker's identity, which is a contextual feature.

Table 2 shows the results of using different combinations of these three strategies with IBL. These results show that there is a form of synergy here, since the sum of the improvements of each strategy used separately is less than the improvement of the three strategies used together ($(58 - 56) + (55 - 56) + (58 - 56) = 3\%$ vs. $66 - 56 = 10\%$).

Table 2: The three strategies applied to the vowel data.

strategy 1: contextual normalization	strategy 2: contextual expansion	strategy 5: contextual weighting	no. correct	percent correct
No	No	No	258	56
No	No	Yes	269	58
No	Yes	No	253	55
No	Yes	Yes	272	59
Yes	No	No	267	58
Yes	No	Yes	295	64
Yes	Yes	No	273	59
Yes	Yes	Yes	305	66

The three strategies were also tested with cascade-correlation [5]. Because of the time required for training the cascade-correlation algorithm, results were gathered for only two cases: With no preprocessing, cascade-correlation correctly classified 216 observations (47%). With preprocessing by all three strategies, cascade-correlation correctly classified 236 observations (51%). This shows that contextual information can be of benefit for both neural networks and nearest neighbor pattern recognition.

6 Related Work

The work described here is most closely related to [6]. However, [6] did not give a precise definition of the distinction between contextual features (their terminology: parameters or global features) and primary features (their terminology: features). They examined only contextual classifier selection, using neural networks to classify images, with context such as lighting. They found that contextual classifier selection resulted in increased accuracy and efficiency. They did not address the difficulties that arise when the context in the testing set is different from the context in the training set.

This work is also related to work in speech recognition on speaker normalization [8]. However, the work on speaker normalization tends to be specific to speech recognition. Here, the concern is with general-purpose strategies for exploiting context.

7 Future Work

Future work will extend the list of strategies, the list of domains that have been examined, and the list of classification algorithms that have been tested. It may also be possible and interesting to develop a general theory of strategies for exploiting context.

8 Conclusion

The general problem examined here is to accurately classify observations that have context-sensitive features. Examples are: the diagnosis of spinal problems, given that spinal tests are sensitive to the age of the patient; the diagnosis of gas turbine engine faults, given that engine performance is sensitive to ambient weather conditions; the recognition of speech, given that different speakers have different voices; the classification of images, given varying lighting conditions. There is clearly a need for general strategies for exploiting contextual information. The results presented here demonstrate that contextual information can be used to increase the accuracy of classifiers, particularly when the context in the testing set is different from the context in the training set.

Acknowledgments

The gas turbine engine data and engine expertise were provided by the Engine Laboratory of the NRC, with funding from DND. The vowel data were obtained from the University of California data repository (ftp ics.uci.edu, directory /pub/machine-learning-databases) [10]. The cascade-correlation [5] software was obtained from Carnegie-Mellon University (ftp pt.cs.cmu.edu, directory /afs/cs/project/connect/code). The author wishes to thank Rob Wylie and Peter Clark of the NRC and two anonymous referees of ECML-93 for their helpful comments on this paper.

References

1. D.W. Aha, D. Kibler, and M.K. Albert: Instance-based learning algorithms, *Machine Learning*, 6, 37-66, 1991.

2. D. Kibler, D.W. Aha, and M.K. Albert: Instance-based prediction of real-valued attributes, *Computational Intelligence*, 5, 51-57, 1989.

3. B.V. Dasarathy: *Nearest Neighbor Pattern Classification Techniques*, (edited collection), Los Alamitos, CA: IEEE Press, 1991.

4. N.R. Draper and H. Smith: *Applied Regression Analysis*, (second edition), New York, NY: John Wiley & Sons, 1981.

5. S.E. Fahlman and C. Lebiere: *The Cascade-Correlation Learning Architecture*, (technical report), CMU-CS-90-100, Pittsburgh, PA: Carnegie-Mellon University, 1991.

6. A.J. Katz, M.T. Gately, and D.R. Collins: Robust classifiers without robust features, *Neural Computation*, 2, 472-479, 1990.

7. P.D. Turney and M. Halasz: Contextual normalization applied to aircraft gas turbine engine diagnosis, (in press), *Journal of Applied Intelligence*, 1993.

8. D. Deterding: *Speaker Normalization for Automatic Speech Recognition*, (Ph.D. thesis), Cambridge, UK: University of Cambridge, Department of Engineering, 1989.

9. A.J. Robinson: *Dynamic Error Propagation Networks*, (Ph.D. thesis), Cambridge, UK: University of Cambridge, Department of Engineering, 1989.

10. P.M. Murphy and D.W. Aha: *UCI Repository of Machine Learning Databases*, Irvine, CA: University of California, Department of Information and Computer Science, 1991.

IDDD: An Inductive, Domain Dependent Decision Algorithm

L. Gaga[1,2], *V. Moustakis*[1,3], *G. Charissis*[4] *and S. Orphanoudakis*[1,2]

[1]Institute of Computer Science, Foundation of Research and Technology - Hellas (FORTH), Heraklion, Crete, Greece

[2]Department of Computer Science, University of Crete, Heraklion, Crete, Greece

[3]Department of Production and Management Engineering, Technical University of Crete, Chania, Crete, Greece

[4]Director, Pediatric Surgery Clinic, University Hospital, Heraklion, Crete, Greece

Abstract. Decision tree induction, as supported by ID3, is a well known approach of heuristic classification. In this paper we introduce *mother-child* relationships to model dependencies between attributes which are used to represent training examples. Such relationships are implemented via IDDD which extends the original ID3 algorithm. The application of IDDD is demonstrated via a series of concept acquisition experiments using a 'real-world' medical domain. Results demonstrate that the application of IDDD contributes to the acquisition of more domain relevant knowledge as compared to knowledge induced by ID3 itself.

1 Introduction

The ability to classify objects or events as members of known classes is a very common task for learning systems. A well known approach to heuristic classification is decision tree induction. An alternative to decision tree induction is given by ID3, an algorithm described in [1]. ID3 uses a heuristic search process to find a set of discriminant descriptions between classes, given: (1) A set of observational statements each of which is assigned to a certain class and (2) a universe of classes.

Working in a recursive manner, the algorithm selects the most discriminant attribute maximizing an information gain function at each step. The result is a tree in which nodes represent tests on attributes, while branches are possible values of the corresponding attributes.

In this paper we present IDDD, which extends ID3 using dependency relationships, between attributes, as domain knowledge agents. IDDD is based on *NewId*, an enhanced implementation of ID3, developed by the Turing Institute, [2]. In section 2 we present IDDD and the definition of the dependency relationships. In section 3, we present experimental results from a 'real-world' medical application. These results show the value of domain knowledge in decision tree induction, which is further discussed in section 4.

2 IDDD

The basic premise of IDDD lies in the deployment of domain knowledge in the induction process. We introduce dependency relationships between attributes that provide some structure over the rather 'flat' data representation used by *NewId*. A *simple* dependency, *B depends_on A*, states that information represented by *B* is useful only when it is combined with information represented by *A*. *A* is identified as a *mother* and *B* as a *child* attribute.

Another form of the relation defined above is the exclusion of an attribute when a specific value has already been assigned to another attribute. We call this dependency *exclusive* and its definition is the following: *B depends_on A* : $a_i, \ldots, a_j$, where $a_i, \ldots, a_j$ represent distinctive values if mother is nominal and the interval $[a_i, a_j]$ when mother is a linear attribute. We should note here that any *child* attribute may have only one *mother*, while this restriction does not apply to a *mother* attribute.

NewId is able to 'handle' relationships such as the ones defined above, yet this is not based on explicit modeling of domain knowledge. However, when the value of a *mother* is unknown, *NewId* may drift into irrelevant attribute selection. Furthermore, when both *A* and *B* score equally in information gain, *NewId* may select *B* instead of *A*. The outcome is a set of rules which may be accurate, from the point of view of classification accuracy but meaningless from the expert's point of view.

One approach to addressing this problem is suggested by van Someren [3]. A preprocessing system for reconstructing the attribute set is elaborated. For instance, attribute *A* valued in V_A and *B* valued in V_B are replaced by an attribute *F* valued in $V_A \times V_B$. It can be readily seen that such an approach can lead to an enormous increase in the number of attribute values, which may 'bias' tree induction in favor of *F* [1]. Also, this approach does not address linear attributes. In IDDD, instead of reformulating the attribute set, we modify the node selection process. This work is also related to that of Manago [4], who proposed a frame-based language to represent training examples.

2.1 Simple Dependency

This dependency can also be defined in *NewId* using its *ordering* mechanism. To express the above dependency with *NewId* we must define the ordering relationship: *A BEFORE B*. The imposition of order among attributes affects the procedure via which the most discriminant attribute is selected. If *A* has not been selected splitting on *B* is prevented. The approach taken in IDDD is different. We distinguish between two cases:

Case I: *A* emerges as the most discriminant attribute. The dependency mechanism is not triggered but the information that *A* has been used is recorded to allow further selection of attribute *B* along the current branch.

Case II: *B* emerges as the most discriminant attribute. Selection of *B* is prevented but the algorithm is forced to establish a node for *A*.

2.2 Exclusive Dependency

This dependency is not handled by *NewId*. Yet, exclusive dependencies are able to represent complex attribute relationships. By stating that, *B DEPENDS_ON A: $a_i, \cdots a_k$* we can prevent selection of *B* when *A* is valued in the $a_i \cdots a_k$ subset.

When *A* is valued in a nominal set, handling of the exclusive dependency is similar with the case of the simple dependency.

When *A* is linear, the selection of a split point is determined by the knowledge embodied in the dependency relationship. In dealing with linear attributes, *NewId* uses a statistical procedure to determine a point to split. In IDDD, instead of relying on 'domain independent' statistical metrics, we assume that the presence of a specific value in a dependency relationship means that this value is important to the domain and use this value to split. Thus, when *A* is linear, we distinguish among three types of the exclusive dependency, namely:

Case III: B DEPENDS_ON A: $\leq a_i$.
Case IV: B DEPENDS_ON A: $> a_i$
Case V: B DEPENDS_ON A: $a_i \cdots a_j$.

Each of the expressions defined above implies a different approach both to the determination of a split value and to decision tree construction. In cases III and IV splitting is done at the a_i point and selection of attribute *B* is restricted to branches where the value of *A* is either 'less than or equal to', or 'greater than', a_i respectively. In case V, we first split on a_i and then again on a_j. The path defined over the $a > a_i$ & $a \leq a_j$ values restricts *B* selection.

3 Experimental Results

In the framework of the MLT (ESPRIT P2154) project, we developed a real-world medical application, involving the therapeutic decision procedure of Maldescensus Testis. Maldescensus Testis refers to a pathological state where one, or both testicles are not properly descending from their inner-body positions after birth. If untreated, this leads to non- functional (atrophied) testicles that may even become malignant (cancerous) in adulthood [5]. The classification task is to assign a case to one of the following therapeutic *classes*: Follow up, Hormonal Treatment, Surgical.

Attributes used to represent case data are (attribute names are enclosed in parentheses): visit (visit), age (age), etiology (etiology), status of one testicle (one-t), status of the other testicle (two-t), size of one testicle (size-of-one), size of the other testicle (size-of-two). To capture the fact that treatment occurs over several visits of the patient, the following attributes were added to link the previous visit and the current one: previous status of one testicle (pre-one-t), previous status of the other testicle (pre-two-t), previous treatment (treatment).

NewId provides a 'don't care' value for attributes that are not applicable under certain circumstances. For example, when visit = 'first', attributes pre-one-t, pre-two-t and treatment are not applicable. However, *NewId* induces rules like:

IF (pre-two-t=normal) & (two-t=normal) & (visit=first) THEN follow up.

In another instance, *Newld* misses the fact that a 'pre' status is not self contained. It has meaning only when combined with a 'current' status.

IF (one-t=inguinal) & (visit=third) & (pre-two-t=normal) THEN surgical

Finally, when a testicle's pathology is 'not palpable', size cannot be measured. Although in such cases size was valued as 'don't care', rules like the following one were induced by *Newld*:

IF (size-of-two>0.60) & (two-t=not palpable) THEN hormonal

Correction and/or elimination of such rules should lead to a more domain meaningful set.

To evaluate possible improvements in the rules induced by IDDD, three rule acquisition experiments were carried out. In the first experiment, *Newld* is used to induce rules without any domain knowledge. We name the set of induced rules as '*original*'. The three rules cited above belong to this set.

A different order in attribute selection might have prevented *Newld* from inducing rules like those included in the '*original*' set. Thus, we placed some structure on domain attributes by using the *Newld's* "ordering" definition facility [2]. Accordingly, the following attribute ordering scheme was defined:

(1) visit BEFORE pre-one-t, visit BEFORE pre-two-t
(2) one-t BEFORE pre-one-t, two-t BEFORE pre-two-t
(3) one-t BEFORE size-of-one, two-t BEFORE size-of-two

This constitutes the second experiment; we shall refer to it as '*ordering*'. Although, '*ordering*' improved the '*original*' set of rules, induction of meaningless rules continued. One such rule is listed below:

IF (one-t=not palpable) & (size-of-one $\leq$ 0.60) THEN surgical

Finally, a third experiment was also conducted in which full *mother/child* dependencies were implemented; a 'pre' status attribute (pre-one-t, pre-two-t) depends on both 'current' status (one-t,two-t) and visit attributes. Since in IDDD a *child* may only possess one *mother*, the relationship "visit BEFORE 'pre' status" was maintained. Thus, the third experiment ('*dependency*') was conducted using the following attribute dependency and order relationships:

(1) size-of-one DEPENDS_ON one-t:not palpable
(2) size-of-two DEPENDS_ON two-t:not palpable
(3) pre-one-t DEPENDS_ON one-t, pre-two-t DEPENDS_ON two-t
(4) visit BEFORE pre-one-t, visit BEFORE pre-two-t

3.1 Results

Each experiment constitutes a specific domain description. For each domain description, the average number of rules induced and average classification accuracy was estimated by applying case data to a ($V = 8$) cross validation process [6]. The results listed in Table 1 clearly indicate that use of domain knowledge decreases classification accuracy but contributes to the induction of considerably reduced rule sets. *Newld* tries to cover as many examples as possible. However, in the specific application domain, the class of an example may depend on the occurrence of extraneous factors which are not recorded. In these cases, the assignment of examples to classes is not compatible to the pure medical knowledge. Thus, *NewId* induces rules which are meaningless from the expert's point of view. Since IDDD tries to produce a more domain meaningful set of rules, it is expected that it will not cover cases like the ones mentioned above, resulting in a decreased classification accuracy. Furthermore, 'ordering' is also responsible for the decrease in accuracy. Use of 'ordering' affects classification accuracy because it forces *NewId* to discard attributes even when these emerge as the most discriminant ones. This fact is inherited by the *'dependency'* domain description.

Average	original	ordering	dependency
Number of Rules	146	84	84.5
Classification Accuracy	76.9	67.4	68.4

Table 1: ($V = 8$) fold evaluation results

Our goal was to produce a more domain meaningful set of rules. We attempted the validation of results with the participation of four medical experts. Each one assigned one of the following labels to each rule:

Valuable. A rule that exactly matches with clinical decision procedures.

Over-General. A rule that fails to consider specific clinical evidence.

Over-Specific. A rule which represents more knowledge than necessary.

Useless. A rule perceived as meaningless by the expert.

'Ordering' alone does not improve rule quality. Table 2 indicates that the percentage of valuable rules in both domain descriptions is the same. Yet, the percentage of useless rules was improved and the number of rules covering negative examples was decreased. A rule covers a negative example when it is capable of classifying a case which belongs to a class different from the one implied by the rule. Rule sets are identified as distinctive. This means that we focused on rules belonging to one domain and not to the other. In Table 2 we also present the results of a cross *'dependency'*, *'original'* assessment. Notice the improvement in all rule quality aspects; the percentage of useless rules decreases significantly while more than 50% of the rules were assessed as valuable.

	orig.	order.	orig.	depend.
Useless	117 (66%)	31 (49%)	110 (59%)	6 (8%)
Over-General	34 (19%)	15 (24%)	42 (22%)	23 (31%)
Over-Specific	16 (9%)	14 (22%)	18 (10%)	6 (8%)
Valuable	9 (5%)	3 (5%)	9 (5%)	38 (52%)
Distinctive Rules	176	63	188	73
Rules Covering Negative Ex.	28 (16%)	8 (13%)	28 (15%)	7 (10%)

Table 2: *'original'* vs *'ordering'* and *'original'* vs *'dependency'*

4   Conclusions

Attributes used to describe a real world application are often interrelated. These relationships are characteristics of the application domain. Their formal definition can facilitate the rule learning process leading to the acquisition of more qualitatively and domain relevant rules. IDDD proved effective in introducing to the tree induction process domain dependent knowledge via explicit definition of attribute dependency relationships. However, a shortcoming of the IDDD dependencies is the fact that definition is restricted to 'single mother multiple children' cases. That is, a child is not allowed to possess multiple mothers. Thus, multiple dependencies of the same attribute cannot be expressed.

This paper constitutes a contribution towards the formal use of domain dependent knowledge in induction. Use of *NewId* was only indicative and/or demonstrative. Dependency relationships can be readily represented and used in conjunction with other inductive learning algorithms, for instance with CN2 [7]. The effectiveness of dependency relationships defined in IDDD indicates that further work is necessary towards the investigation, formal definition, and handling of domain knowledge in the inductive process.

Acknowledgements

Work reported in this paper was partially supported via CEC contracts MLT (ESPRIT, P2154) and GAMES-II (AIM, A2034). The authors would like to thank Drs. Yannopoulos and Vlachakis of the Pediatric Surgery Clinic, University of Crete, and Ms. Natassa Papageorgiou for evaluating rule sets. The comments of the three anonymous reviewers helped considerably in improving an earlier draft; we gratefully acknowledge their work.

References

[1] J.R. Quinlan. Induction of Decision Trees. *Machine Learning*, 1.1:81–106, 1986.

[2] R.A. Boswell. Manual for Newid version 2.0. *Technical Report*, January 1990.

[3] M.W van Someren. Using Attribute Dependencies for Rule Learning. In K. Morik, editor, *Knowledge Representation and Organization in Machine Learning*, pages 192–210. Springer-Verlag, Berlin, 1989.

[4] Michel Manago. Knowledge Intensive Induction. In *Proceedings of the Sixth International Workshop on Machine Learning*, pages 151–155, Cornell Univercity, 1989. Morgan Kaufmann.

[5] W.E Grupe. Abnormalities of the Genital Tract. In M.E Avery and H.W Taeusch Jr., editors, *Schaffer's Diseases of the Newborn*, pages 401–411. W.B Saunders Company, Philadelphia, 1984.

[6] L. Breiman, J.H Friedman, R.A Olshen, and C.J Stone. *Classification and Regression Trees*. Wadsworth International, 1984.

[7] Peter Clark and Tim Niblett. The CN2 Induction Algorithm. *Machine Learning*, 3:261–283, 1989.

An Application of Machine Learning in the Domain of Loan Analysis[1]

José Ferreira*   Joaquim Correia*   Thomas Jamet**   Ernesto Costa*
joseferreira@uc.pt   quim@lia.uc.pt   thomas@isoft.fr   ernesto@uc.pt

* Lab. de Informática e Sistemas, Universidade de Coimbra, 3000 COIMBRA, PORTUGAL
**Isoft, Chemin du Moulin, 91400 ORSAY, FRANCE

Abstract: Making decisions on whether to give or not a financial support to an industrial project is a very common and yet very complex task. Financial institutions need much expertise to deal with the large amount of information that has to be considered for this process. An expert system based approach seems to be an interesting solution to the problems raised by this type of application. Knowledge acquisition is, however, a very time consuming task. We have used APT, a multistrategy learning system, as a knowledge elicitation tool in the domain of loan decision. We describe the process of building and refining a knowledge base and compare the results of our approach to a conventional expert system.

Keywords: generalization, knowledge acquisition, machine learning applications

1 Introduction

The analysis of large scale projects that ask for financial support is a regular activity in banking institutions. A loan process comprises five steps: proposal, proposal analysis, decision, contract and amortization.

The most important step is the decision one, since the others are mostly administrative steps. The decision process begins with an analysis of the documentation provided by the project's promoter, involving an economist and an engineer that are responsible for the first appreciation of the loan request. Then, experts will visit the plant, if the enterprise exists. Finally, the decision is taken. All these activities involve high costs and require a lot of expertise. To deal with these needs in expertise, an expert system, SPAC [5], has been developed at Bank Caixa Geral de Depósitos, in collaboration with the University of Lisbon.

As usual in the process of building knowledge based systems, acquiring the knowledge for SPAC was the toughest and longest task. To overcome these difficulties, we have used APT [4] as an automatic knowledge base builder. We wanted to test APT's applicability in this domain and verify if there could be significant gains in time and in the dimension of the knowledge base.

To implement this application, we have had the collaboration of the experts from the Bank that provided SPAC and gave some information regarding the domain in hand. They also have validated the results obtained after we have used APT.

In this paper we present the results of our experiment. We begin with brief descriptions of both SPAC and APT. Next, we describe the domain. We then present

---

[1]This work was partially supported by CEC, through ESPRIT-2 contract 2154 - MLT

APT at work and conclude with a summary of the results and some comments on the validity of the approach.

2 The SPAC Expert System

SPAC is a standard forward chaining rule based system. It took about two years to develop to the current state, it currently contains about 450 rules and is now being tested at the bank.
Several sources were used for knowledge elicitation:
- readings on loan guide books and loan processes;
- structured and unstructured interviews;
- responses given by experts to elicitation grids for uncertainty coefficients.
Rules in SPAC are of the form:

MakeRule(decision20,   ((enterprise:value #= existing) AND
(promoter_profile:value #= weak) AND
(project_quality:value #= satisfactory) AND
(econ_financ_feasibility:value #= weak) AND
(guarantees:value #= good),
{decision:value = no; decision:certainty = 1.0;}));

The meaning of the rule above is: when promoter's profile is weak, project's quality is satisfactory, economic and financial feasibility is weak, guarantees of payment are good and the enterprise exists, the decision to financially support the project is *no* with a certainty value of 1.0.

3 APT

APT is a multistrategy learning system that is able to learn general problem solving rules from one single example given by one expert, provided it has some initial knowledge of the domain. For a complete description of the system see [4].
APT uses a domain theory, in the form of hierarchies of concepts, some of them having relations associated to other concepts in the theory and properties associated to values (numerical ones, for example). We show in figure 1 a partial representation of some of the concepts that are considered in the session we present next. Due to the extension, we do not present the complete hierarchy.
The expert initially proposes a problem. If there are any rules applicable to the problem, they are presented. If there are no rules, or the user rejects the proposed ones, he is asked for a particular solution for the problem. The solution is normally a decomposition of the problem into simpler ones. We call this a reduction. Once this is given, APT looks for relations among the concepts appearing in the problem and in the reduction. These are proposed as explanations, in the sense of causal justifications of why the reduction is suitable for the problem. The explanations accepted by the expert provide a lower bound for a rule that APT will try to generalize. It will then propose a set of examples, following a smallest generalization step strategy [2], allowing to generalize one concept at a time and verifying that any further generalization is justified by the preceding steps. At the end, one or more rules will be learned. The expert accepts, rejects or adjusts them. If adjustment has to take place, APT enters a phase that allows for guided refinement of the domain theory [4]. As a

result, one or more rules will be learned and the domain theory will incrementally be refined and completed.

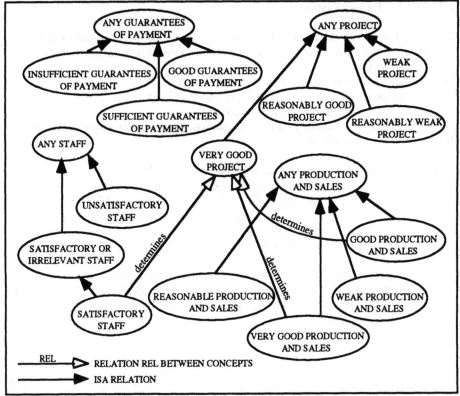

Fig. 1. Part of the initial domain theory.

4 Loan Analysis And Decision

In figure 2, we present a partial taxonomy of the problems in the domain. Square boxes are filled with non-elementary problems, whereas elliptical delimiters with elementary problems. As shown in the figure, several sub-problems are not elementary, but due to its extension we do not present the complete hierarchy of problems.

Making decisions on loan support involves several uncertainties, even for the experts in the domain. Deciding on the leadership capacity of a project's promoter is rather fuzzy and necessarily introduces uncertainty in the results. SPAC accounts for this fuzziness by using certainty factors associated to each rule. APT however, can not use this type of information. The rules acquired by APT will, therefore, disregard this incertitude. Nevertheless, APT's results are quite satisfactory. We justify this statement by noticing that in SPAC, certainty factors are propagated over the rules involved in a decision process and assign a confidence degree to the result. They are never used to inhibit or emphasize the applicability of a rule, which means that every applicable rule will be considered, regardless its results. So, for both SPAC and APT, the final decision is the same, differing only in the confidence degree.

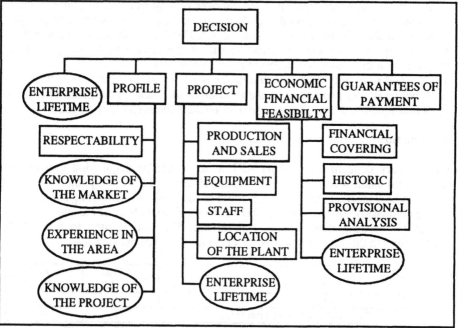

Fig. 2. Partial taxonomy of problems in the domain of loan decision.

5 APT At Work

We can not show the session with APT, because it is very long. See [1] for a detailed description. We will summarize some aspects of the interaction with APT.

Consider the problem of *evaluating* the quality of a project, in the case of a *new enterprise* with a *very good production and sales* policy, considering the plant has a *good location* and *suitable equipment* and *staff* is *satisfactory*.

As there are no rules for solving the proposed problem, the user is asked for a solution. He said that his particular *project* can be classified as *very good*.

APT now tries to establish causal relations between the concepts in the problem and those in the solution. It finds the relation *determines* between the considered concepts and builds explanations for the problem/solution pair around this relation. All proposed explanations were accepted in this session. Starting with the problem, the solution and the explanations, a rule is created. The explanations define the applicability condition for the rule, which can thus only be applied to the particular problem. The generalization process now begins. It is considered that the problem given by the user is an instance of a more general class of problems. It is this class of problems that we are trying to learn how to solve. APT builds a generalization lattice, that defines the generalization possibilities for each concept in the rule. It will then walk through the lattice, one step at a time, generating and proposing more general examples. For a complete description of the generalization process see [2]. The user classifies the proposed examples as valid or invalid instances of the class of examples he wants APT to learn. For this particular problem, 18 examples were proposed, 15 of them accepted and the other 3 rejected.

At the end of the generalization phase, an over general rule was acquired, because one concept was over generalized. Some of its sub concepts produce positive instances of the class of problems, others don't. The domain theory has to be refined by grouping the "positive concepts" as sub concepts of a new concept and the "negative concepts" as sub concepts of a different new one.

The learned rule said: when the *enterprise* is *new* or *existing*, the *production and sales* policy is *very good* or *good*, the *location* of the plant is *good*, with *suitable* or *irrelevant equipment*, *satisfactory* or *irrelevant staff*, the *project* is *very good*.

6 Evaluation

Our primary concern when using APT as a knowledge acquisition tool in this particular domain was to observe the results in terms of how many rules we would have and how much of the application could be modeled. We had strong expectations on the comparison between the number of rules we would have at the end and those in SPAC, because these are very particular. We also wanted to test APT's applicability to this kind of domains, specially involving decision tasks.

PROBLEM	# SPAC RULES	# APT RULES
DECISION	44	5
PROFILE OF A NEW PROMOTER	17	10
PROFILE OF EXISTING PROMOTER	18	6
PROJECT EVALUATION	48	11
ECONOMIC AND FINANCIAL FEASIBILITY	34	6
GUARANTEES OF PAYMENT	15	(*)
RESPECTABILITY OF NEW PROMOTER	3	2
RESPECTABILITY OF EXISTING PROMOTER	4	3
MANAGEMENT CAPACITY	26	9
PRODUCTION AND SALES	38	14
LOCATION OF THE PLANT	36	9
EQUIPMENT	37	9
STAFF	15	6
COMMERCIALIZATION	40	4
RAW MATERIAL	22	5
PRODUCT-MARKET RELATION	58	26

(*) It was not possible to execute the sessions regarding this particular sub-problem, because the evaluation of the guarantees for payment was not provided by the bank. Formulas for this evaluation are secret.

APT has proved its capabilities as a knowledge elicitation tool in the domain. Because it allows for incremental refinement of the domain theory, it avoids the necessity of a complete formulation of a domain theory right from the beginning. It is normally very difficult to produce such complete, error-free formulation. The strategy used by APT, generalizing one concept at a time is a very friendly one. It prevents for extraneous generalizations due to the incapacity of classifying very general examples. We have noticed that the number of rules learned by APT is much lesser than those in SPAC, as shown in the table. More important than the number is the quality of the rules. Experts from the bank have validated the resulting rules. They agreed on their quality and, moreover, they realized that SPAC would profit if the domain could be structured as APT's domain theory was. This is now being done. We have also noticed that the deeper the hierarchies of concepts involved in one problem are, the greater the difference between the number of rules of APT and the number of rules in SPAC. This is because we can generalize further in the hierarchies, so each APT rule covers more SPAC rules.

Comparison of the time spent to build the application could not be considered, because we already had a knowledge base. But, since we began with no knowledge about the application domain, we have had some of the problems that knowledge engineers normally have to face when eliciting knowledge. We "interviewed" the SPAC rules to build the domain theory and we used SPAC itself to classify the examples proposed by APT.

7 Conclusions

We found that the use of learning systems as APT for knowledge elicitation can be a very interesting way to overcome the problem of extracting knowledge from experts. The improvements achieved with such learning systems can be of several types:

- the initial domain theory does not need to be complete, since the learning sessions will be responsible for the detection of missing knowledge, and will automatically correct it, with the guidance of the user;
- the expert (or the knowledge engineer) does not have to think of all cases at once, only a few examples of the classes of cases he can have in the domain, since the system will generate the others, by looking for analogous examples;
- the interactive characteristic of the system makes it friendly and easy to understand.

References

1. Coimbra, Isoft, and LRI: Case Study on Loan Analysis. Technical Report, MLT ESPRIT Project P2154, November 1992.

2. NEDELLEC C.: A Smallest Generalization Step Strategy. In: Proceedings of the Eighth International Workshop on Machine Learning, pp 529-533, June 1991.

3. NEDELLEC C.: How to Specialize by Theory Refinement. In: Proceedings of Tenth European Conference on Artificial Intelligence, August 1992.

4. Isoft, LRI, and Coimbra: User's guide to APT. Deliverable 4.2, MLT ESPRIT Project P2154, September 1991.

5. P. J. XARDONÉ and E. P. LEITÃO: SPAC - Sistema Pericial para Análise de Crédito. Faculdade de Ciências, Universidade de Lisboa, 1989.

Extraction of Knowledge from Data Using Constrained Neural Networks

Raqui Kane[1], Irina Tchoumatchenko[2], Maurice Milgram[1] *

[1] LRP-CNRS, Université Paris-VI, 4 Place Jussieu, 75252 Paris, CEDEX 05 France
[2] ACASA, LAFORIA-CNRS, Université Paris-VI, 4 Place Jussieu, 75252 Paris, CEDEX 05 France

Abstract. This paper deals with two complementary problems: the problem of extracting knowledge from neural networks and the problem of inserting knowledge into neural networks. Our approach to the extraction of knowledge is essentially constraints-based. Local constraints are imposed on the neural network's weights and activities to make neural networkunits work as logical operators. We have modified two well-known learning algorithms, namely the simulated annealing and the backpropagation, with respect to imposed constraints. In the case of the non-empty domain theory, the knowledge insertion technique is used to impose global constraints to determine the neural network's topology and initialization according to a priori knowledge about the problem under study. The knowledge to be inserted can be expressed as a set of propositional rules. We report simulation results obtained by running our algorithms to extract boolean formulae.

1 Introduction

Last decade artificial neural networks have demonstrated capabilities as efficient mapping devices. The criticism usually made about neural networks is that the way work has little explanation in humanly comprehensible terms. Despite a growing number of research efforts to interpret trained neural networks in logical terms, a general method for the extraction of logical rulesfrom *arbitrary* neural networks has not yet been found. Both propositional [4] [1] and fuzzy [2] logic approaches were used for extracting knowledge from a trained neural network. The main difference between the extraction method presented in this paper and the previously developed ones is the intensive use of constraints. To facilitate knowledge extraction as well as to bias neural learning to explore the most interesting part of a weight space, we adapt the knowledge insertion technique. Some logical formalisms have been mapped into neural networks [4] [3]. Unfortunately, the expressive power of neurally-mapped logic is restricted, as a satisfactory decision for variables handling has not been found.

---

* This work is supported by a grant from the DRET

2 Our Approach to Knowledge Extraction

Extracting knowledge from an arbitrary neural network is recognized as a complex task. One possible approach to the extraction problem is to constrain appropriately a neural network making it logically-interpretable. Naturally, neural network learning algorithm should be modified with respect to the imposed constraints. We use symmetric sigmoid function $f(x) = tanh(kx)$, where the steepness parameter k is chosen appropriately to allow both a step function approximation and a reasonable time convergency. This choice of a steepness parameter realizes the first constraint on the unitsáctivities, namely the unitsáctivities are arbitrarily close to -1 or 1. We call such a unit a *logical unit*. Let i be a logical unit with n inputs $x_1^i \cdots x_n^i$. The output of the unit is defined by the following equation:

$$o^i = f(\sum_{j=1}^{n} w_{ij} \star x_j^i - \theta_i)$$

Let's impose the constraint on the neural network's weights to be in the finite set of values $\{-1, 0, 1\}$. As it directly follows from the conjunction (disjunction) truth table analysis, a so-constrained unit i realizes conjunction (disjunction) from its inputs if and only if $\theta_i = \epsilon \sum_{j=1}^{n} w_{ij}^2 - 1$ and $\epsilon = 1$ ($\epsilon = -1$), where $\sum_{j=1}^{n} w_{ij}^2$ represents a number of non-zero unit inputs. To summarize, we impose the following constraints:

1. $\forall x_j^i, \ x_j^i \in \{-1, 1\}$
2. $\forall w_{ij}, \ w_{ij} \in \{-1, 0, 1\}$
3. $\theta_i = \epsilon \sum_{j=1}^{n} w_{ij}^2 - 1$, where $\epsilon = 1$ ($\epsilon = -1$) if unit i realizes a conjunctive (disjunctive) operator.

So, we can formulate the following recursive method for extracting logical rules:

- For each hidden (output) unit i:
  - Analyse the bias of the unit:
    * *If* its bias is positive, *Then* unit realizes a conjunction of its inputs
    * *If* its bias is negative, *Then* unit realizes a disjunction of its inputs
    * *If* its bias is null, *Then* unit is inactive
  - For each weight coming to the unit:
    * *If* weight w_{ij} from unit j to unit i is negative, *Then* the logical operator realized by unit i is applied to $\neg x_j^i$
    * *If* weight w_{ij} from unit j to unit i is positive, *Then* the logical operator realized by unit i is applied to x_j^i
    * *If* weight w_{ij} from unit j to unit i is null, *Then* x_j^i is not considered

Example 1. Given the simple one-hidden-layer neural network presented in Fig.1. Running recursively our algorithm, we will obtain:

- for the first layer:
  - the bias of unit 1 is positive, so unit 1 realizes the conjunction of its inputs $\neg x_1 \wedge \neg x_2 \wedge x_3$, where $\neg x_1$ and $\neg x_2$ result from the negative weights

- • the bias of unit 2 is negative, so unit 2 realizes the disjunction of its inputs $x_1 \lor \neg x_3$, where $\neg x_3$ results from the negative weight and x_2 is not included due to its zero weight
- for the second layer:
  - • the bias of unit 3 is negative, so unit 2 realizes the disjunction of its inputs $(\neg x_1 \land \neg x_2 \land x_3) \lor \neg (x_1 \lor \neg x_3)$ and, after transformations, we obtain $\neg x_1 \land x_3$

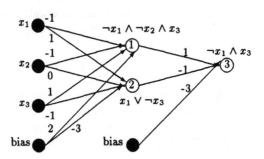

Fig. 1. Extracting rules from a sample constrained neural network

3 Modifications of the Learning Algorithm

The main problem for extracting logical rules using the proposed constrained-based method is to modify a standard neural network learning algorithm to keep the neural network's weights into a finite set of values $\{-1, 0, 1\}$. In this section, we propose two minor, but efficient modifications of the simulated annealing learning algorithm and the penalty function modification for the back-propagation. To validate each method, we have trained networks with different architectures to learn boolean formulae.

3.1 Modifications of the Simulated Annealing Algorithm

- *Modification1.* To force a neural network to respect the imposed constraints, we change the initialization and the update steps of the standard simulated annealing learning algorithm as follows:

  - *Initialization:* Select randomly initial weights in $\{-1, 0, 1\}$. Compute the resulting biases $\theta_i = \epsilon \sum_{j=1}^{n} w_{ij}^2 - 1$, where ϵ is randomly chosen in $\{-1, 1\}$.
  - *Update:* A fixed number of values is randomly chosen in the set of weights and biases. If a bias is chosen, we change its sign. If a weight is chosen, we randomly change its value in $\{-1, 0, 1\}$ and then compute the resulting bias.

– *Modification2 (simulated annealing controled by gradient)*. Changes of weights can be controled by the sign of the gradient. For the weights from $\{-1, 0, 1\}$, the variation can be performed in two cases:
  - the gradient is positive and the initial weight is -1 or 0
  - the gradient is negative and the initial weight is 1 or 0

Thermal equilibrium is reached if there are no more changes possible when computing the gradients of the weights.

Example 2. The one-hidden-layer neural network $3 - 3 - 1$ with 3 input units, 3 hidden units and 1 output unit, was trained to learn the boolean formula $(x_1 \wedge x_2) \vee \neg x_3$ using the above-described modifications of the simulated annealing. Both algorithms have achieved the desired results, namely the weights were kept in $\{-1, 0, 1\}$. The first algorithm converged in about 2000 iterations, while the second one converged in about 1000 iterations. The neural network's state after training and its interpretation in logical terms using our extraction method are presented in Table 1.

Table 1. Extraction of a boolean formula from the $3 - 3 - 1$ neural network trained with the modified simulated annealing algorithms

Links from First To Second Layer	Links from Second to Third Layer	Extracted Formula
$w_{11}^{(1)} = $ -1.000000 $w_{12}^{(1)} = $ -1.000000 $\neg x_1 \vee \neg x_2$ $w_{13}^{(1)} = $ 0.000000 $\theta_1^{(1)} = $ -3.000000	$w_{11}^{(2)} = $ -1.000000	
$w_{21}^{(1)} = $ 0.000000 $w_{22}^{(1)} = $ 1.000000 x_2 $w_{23}^{(1)} = $ 0.000000 $\theta_2^{(1)} = $ 1.000000	$w_{12}^{(2)} = $ 0.000000 $\neg x_1 \vee x_3$ $w_{13}^{(2)} = $ 1.000000	$(x_1 \wedge x_2) \vee \neg x_3$
$w_{31(1)} = $ 0.000000 $\neg x_3$ $w_{32}^{(1)} = $ 0.000000 $w_{33}^{(1)} = $ -1.000000 $\theta_3^{(1)} = $ 1.000000	$\theta_1^{(2)} = $ -3.000000	

3.2 Modification of the Backpropagation Algorithm

We have found that the following modification of the backpropagation algorithm provides both better performance and flexibility. We penalize any unwanted weight changes during training by adding an extra term $P(W)$ to the standard error function $E(W)$. The penalty term $P(W)$ will force weights to approach -1 or 0 or 1 during training. Thus, the function to minimize using the standard gradient descent method becomes $E(W) + \lambda P(W)$, where λ is an adjustable parameter to get the best convergence properties ($\lambda = 0.01$). We have chose $P(W)$ to be a differentiable juxtaposition of 5 paraboles:

$$P(x) = 8(x+1)^2 \mathbb{1}(x)_{]-\infty;-\frac{3}{4}]} + (1 - 8(x+\frac{1}{2})^2)\mathbb{1}(x)_{[-\frac{3}{4};-\frac{1}{4}]} + 8x^2\mathbb{1}(x)_{[-\frac{1}{4};\frac{1}{4}]} +$$
$$(1 - 8(x-\frac{1}{2})^2)\mathbb{1}(x)_{[\frac{1}{4};\frac{3}{4}]} + 8(x-1)^2\mathbb{1}(x)_{[\frac{3}{4};\infty[}$$

Example 3. The $3 - 2 - 1$ neural network was trained by the modified back-propagation algorithm to learn boolean formula $(x_1 \wedge x_2) \vee \neg x_3$. Convergence was reached as fast as with standard backpropagation. The neural network's state after training and its iterpretation in logical terms according to our extraction method are presented in Table 2.

Table 2. Extraction of a boolean formula from the $3 - 2 - 1$ neural network trained with the modified backpropagation

Links from First To Second Layer		Links from Second to Third Layer		Extracted Formula
$w_{11}^{(1)} = 1.083391$		$w_{11}^{(2)} = 0.813960$		
$w_{12}^{(1)} = -0.063624$	$x_1 \vee \neg x_3$			
$w_{13}^{(1)} = -1.143470$				$(x_1 \wedge x_2) \vee \neg x_3$
$\theta_1^{(1)} = -1.0$		$w_{12}^{(2)} = 0.920622$	$x1 \wedge x_2$	
$w_{21}^{(1)} = 0.0430180$				
$w_{22}^{(1)} = 0.920361$		$\theta_1^{(2)} = 1.0$		
$w_{23}^{(1)} = -0.822301$	$x_2 \vee \neg x_3$			
$\theta_2^{(1)} = -1.0$				

Remark. We encountered the problem of tautologically true rule extraction after training the network both by the modified simulated annealing algorithms and by the modified backpropagation. This problem is related to the initialization of the neural network and the local mimina problem. The lowest rate of tautologically true rule extraction was obtained for computational experiments with the modified backpropagation.

4   Inserting Rules into a Constrained Neural Network

Inserting a logical rule into a neural network means building a neural network which realizes the same input-output mapping as the rule to be inserted. Below, we propose a method for inserting simple propositional rules into constrained . This method is based on the truth-table analysis of the rule to be inserted.

– *Inserting conjunctive rules.* Using logical units with weights into $\{-1,1\}$, it is straightforward to put a logical rule

$$A : -B_1 \wedge \cdots \wedge B_p \wedge \neg C_1 \wedge \cdots \wedge \neg C_n$$

with p positive and n negative literals into correspondance with a logical unit realizing the same mapping. This rule is translated into a neural network unit by setting weights on all links corresponding to positive literals to 1 and weights on all links corresponding to negative literals to -1. Analysing the truth table of a conjunctive logical rule, it is easy to see that for the ideal step function the bias of the unit corresponding to the rule's consequent can be chosen from $[p - n - 2; p - n]$. Practically, to insure good convergence properties, we use a quasi-step function; hence it is reasonable to set the bias equal to $p - n - 1$.

– *Inserting disjunctive rules.* Mapping of disjunctive logical rule with p positive and n negative literals

$$A : -B_1 \vee \cdots \vee B_p \vee \neg C_1 \vee \cdots \vee \neg C_n$$

is done as follows. Weights on all links corresponding to positive literals are equal to 1, weights on all links corresponding to negative literals are equal to -1 and the bias can be set to any values from $[-p - n; -p - n + 2]$. We set it equal to $-p - n + 1$ to provide better convergence properties.

Using this approach based on the thruth table analysis, we are able to insert any propositional rule into our constrained neural network.

5 Conclusion

The method for knowledge extraction from strongly constrained neural networks is presented and validated on the simple problem of boolean formulae extraction. Two widely used learning algorithms were modified with respect to the imposed constraints. It was found that though slightly modified simulated annealing learning algorithm works reasonably well, the proposed penalty function modification for standard backpropagation provides both better performance and flexibility. To facilitate neural learning as well as further rule extraction for a given problem the propositional rule insertion technique was proposed. Currently we are working on validation of our extraction/insertion method on the real–world problem of the protein secondary structure prediction. A constraints-based method for numerical dependencies extraction is under study.

References

1. Bochereau, L., Bourgine, P.: Extraction of semantic features from a multilayer neural network, Proceedings of the IJCNN90, Washington DC.
2. Masuoka, R., Watanabe, N., Kawamura, A.: Neuro-fuzzy system - fuzzy inference using a structured neural network. In Proc. of the International Conference on Fuzzy Logic and Neural Networks, 173–177, 1990.
3. Sethi, I.K.: Entropy nets: From decision trees to neural networks. Proc. of the IEEE, vol.78, No.10, 1990.
4. Towell,G.G., Shavlik, J.W.: The extraction of refined rules from knowledge-based neural networks. Submitted to Machine Learning (8/91).

This article was processed using the LaTeX macro package with LLNCS style

Chapter 4:

Workshop and Panel Overview Papers

Integrated Learning Architectures

E. Plaza[1], A. Aamodt[2], A. Ram[3],
W. van de Velde[4], M. van Someren[5]

[1] Institut d'Investigació en Intel·ligència Artificial (CEAB-CSIC),
Camí de Santa Bàrbara, 17300 Blanes, Catalunya, Spain.   plaza@ceab.es
[2] University of Throndheim (Norway).   agnar@ifi.unit.no
[3] Georgia Institute of Technology (USA).   ashwin@cc.gatech.edu
[4] AI-Lab, Vrije Universiteit Brussels (Belgium).   walter@arti.vub.ac.be
[5] Universiteit van Amsterdam (Netherlands).   maarten@swi.psy.uva.nl

Abstract. Research in systems where learning is integrated to other components like problem solving, vision, or natural language is becoming an important topic for Machine Learning. Situations where learning methods are embedded or integrated into broader systems offers new theoretical challenges to ML and enlarge the potential range of ML applications. In this position paper we propose the research topic of integrated learning architectures as an initial discussion of the role of learning in intelligent systems. We review the current state of the art and characterise several dimensions along which integrated learning architectures may vary. This paper has been prepared as a position paper with the purpose of providing an initial common ground for discussion in the ECML-93 Workshop on Integrated Learning Architectures. The paper has been edited by E Plaza on the basis of the individual contributions of the authors.

Over the years, AI has divided itself into a number of research areas: planning, learning, vision, knowledge representation etc. Moreover, a multiplicity of learning methods and systems have been developed in the last decade in Machine Learning. There are currently more and more advocates both in ML and AI in general that invite the research community to think about our current situation and re-think our research strategies keeping in mind the long-range goal of a theoretical comprehension and a computational integration of present and future work. In the ML community, a growing trend exists today towards theoretical and implementational integration of the ML methods already developed. We want to bring together in the Integrated Learning Architectures workshop this growing research lines that integrate different ML methods with each other and ML with problem solving. In this paper, we will initiate the discussion of the role of learning in intelligent systems as a key issue on the research agenda on integrated systems.

1. Background

One of the main issues in AI is that of the adaptation of a system to its environment: hardly any system that systematically behaves identically during its interactions with the environment could be considered intelligent. The lack to adequately cope with the adaptation issue has been 'explained' in different ways: lack of flexibility or adaptability, lack of graceful degradation (brittleness), etc. From the beginning of AI, research on learning processes coped with these problems, from adapting to the environment and learning through practice to learning from observation and discovery.

Machine Learning developed into an active field in these last years, and therefore developed its owns goals, techniques, research programmes and paradigmatic achievements. Nevertheless, the necessity of understanding the role of learning processes in intelligent systems remains an open issue.

On the more technical side, building AI systems, both research and commercial, have also suffered from a number of problems, particularly the knowledge acquisition bottleneck and the fragility issue. Machine Learning has been mainly applied to the first problem as an aid to synthesis of new knowledge. Ideally, learning has been viewed, in this paradigm, as a process that from examples (and maybe interactions with some expert users) 'generates' a complete delivery system capable of solving a range of tasks: e. g. use a learning program to build and deliver a rule-based expert system. This approach has a modularity advantage: it is easier (or not much more difficult) in principle to connect ML techniques and AI problem solving techniques when kept both separate. However, an ML-generated delivery system will most likely suffer the same adaptability deficiencies as any other AI system. Yet it is manifest that a lot of flexibility and adaptability can be gained if an AI system, working in a task environment, would be capable of learning from practice, from experience, or from observation, depending on the task at hand (or from all of them). Therefore we have arrived again at the issue of integrating learning with task performance.

The integration of learning into a broader framework is a decisive strategic decision in ML research, from which scientific and technical advances can be gained. Integration issues can establish the nature and goals of learning in the framework of global goals or concerns (e.g. adaptation to environment, routine task speed-up, theory revision, etc.) In fact, it is difficult to conceive how learning can make any sense in complex domains without constraints external to the learning process itself.

Research in ML addresses specific learning tasks in the context of specific problem solvers. In particular the complexity of the full scope of intelligent learning and problem solving is sometimes narrowed down by:

- Assuming a single, uniform task for the performance component. Apart from systems that learn declarative knowledge bases, most systems involve performance tasks that are defined by data and solutions and that have no internal structure.
- Focusing on learning at a single dimension of the performance knowledge (e.g. generalisation, speed up or compression)
- Presenting relevant input data for the learning process in the right form, indicating the role of the data in the learning task. It may not be obvious if and how knowledge is relevant for learning. For example, if we learn to drive a car, it may not be clear if understanding the mechanics of the car is relevant and if so, how this can be used to learn to drive.

Although these simplifications are inevitable in early stages of the research, the limits of this approach are becoming visible. There has also been work in AI generally, and in ML specifically, that is directly concerned with the issues mentioned. All of this deals, in some way or other, with the integration of learning into a more broad architecture. We can arrange them into three main research strategies: cognitive architectures (e.g. SOAR [Newell 90], ACT* [Anderson 83], PI [Holland et al], etc), architectures integrating learning and problem solving (integrated architectures like THEO [Mitchell et al 91], ICARUS [Langley et al], PRODIGY [Carbonell et al], and case-based reasoning systems like JULIA [Kolodner 87], PROTOS [Porter 90]), and multistrategy learning [MSL-91].

The broader framework in which learning takes place in integrated architectures opens a new spectrum of opportunities for ML research and application. For instance, some issues that were implicit in ML systems need now to be dealt with explicitly. In current research on multistrategy systems, the issue of selecting one learning method among several alternatives is now addressed, and also the criteria that may be used to direct such a selection. In an integrated architecture it is required that the situations that offer opportunities for learning are clearly stated: which kind of situations (failures, success, impasses, etc. and their types) can be exploited by learning, and how? Different options have been explored: impasse-driven learning in Soar, architecture-specific axioms in EBL-Prodigy, etc. These are some of the goals we addressed in the following section.

2. What is an Integrated Learning Architecture?

To qualify as an Integrated Learning Architecture (ILA), a system must be able to learn and to perform at least one problem solving task, and either learning and problem solving must be flexibly integrated in a single control structure, or learning and problem solving must flexibly use the same knowledge structures. The main point here is distinguishing learning embedded in a global system from mere usage of learning methods instrumental to (but external to) build, say, an expert system.

An ILA can be characterised as an architecture for tasks with three different life cycles: simple problem solving, interactive problem solving and learning. These systems can be characterised in terms of their architecture.

Problem Solving	Data	Knowledge	Architecture
Simple PS	presented once & forgotten	stable	stable
Interactive PS	increasing/ being replaced/ forgotten	stable	stable
Learning	increasing/ being replaced/ forgotten	changing	stable

Some tasks are "instantaneous": data are presented and a solution is requested. For other tasks, part of the knowledge remains valid and potentially applicable but other information (data) may change. This is the case in interactive consultation, monitoring systems, etc. Learning systems (in particular incremental learning systems) perform tasks at two levels of scope/time span: (a) the "problem" level (where only *data* change with a new problem) and (b) the "task" or "domain" level: they acquire *knowledge* for performing a particular range of tasks (in addition to type (a) problem solving with changing *data*). Our interest is in systems or methods that perform tasks involving both problem solving and learning and that are "architectures" in the sense that they are described in terms of components which can be configured in different ways. In particular we want to explore systems performing tasks with both learning and problem solving subtasks.

ILA's define a framework in which a number of new problems can be investigated:

(a) Selecting a learning method

For instance, some issues that were implicit in ML systems need now to be dealt with explicitly. In current research on multistrategy systems, the issue of selecting one learning method among several alternatives is now addressed, and also the criteria that may be used to direct such a selection.

(b) Learning from different types of data

A characteristic of integrated learning architectures is that learning is experiential, i.e. it occurs incrementally through the performance of some reasoning task. Situations that offer opportunities for learning are clearly stated: which of situations (failures, success, impasses, etc. and their types) can be exploited by learning, and how? Different options have been explored: impasse-driven learning in Soar, architecture-specific axioms in EBL- Prodigy, etc.

(c) Selecting data for learning

Planning to learn, detecting opportunities to learn, and selecting learning methods to solve errors of other components of the architecture or improve their performance. The label of "active learning" is used to stress the importance of learning processes in natural intelligent systems, and to emphasise the relevance of learning process in AI systems.

(d) Goal directed learning and problem solving

An ILA has a flexible if not opportunistic learning strategy, in the sense that learning goals that are not immediately satisfiable are remembered so that the reasoner can recognise and use opportunities to pursue them. The learning goals in a ILA can be explicitly represented (e.g. the concepts of SUCCEEDS, FAILS, SOLE-ALTERNATIVE in EBL-Prodigy) or can be implicitly established in the implementation of the architecture.

This raises the following questions:
- What is the goal(s) of learning?
- How learning goals are generated and selected?
- What knowledge of another component does a learning method require in order to be able to learn?
- How do learning and problem solving constrain each other?
- How can they support each other?
- How the results of learning are integrated into the overall architecture?

(e) Which knowledge is needed to perform integrated learning and problem solving?

What knowledge of another component does a learning method require in order to be able to learn? How is that knowledge represented and used?

One approach is to use a *self-model* of the architecture. Self-model(s) is(are) required because of the integration of learning method(s). In general, a learning method has to have a model of *what are* "successes" and "failures" in the architecture, and of other relevant concepts for learning (e. g. the SOLE-ALTERNATIVE concept in EBL-PRODIGY). These concepts are part of the learning *self-model* of the ILA. Again, the self-model (the definitions of these concepts) can be explicit (as in the architecture axioms of EBL-Prodigy[1]) or can be implicitly established in the implementation of the architecture. These models are method-specific, i.e. they are different for different learning methods (this is called "white-box requirement" of Prodigy in [Carbonell et al], meaning that any ML method has to be able to view and represent what it requires of the system).

Moreover, the learning method needs to be able to effectively inspect part of the structure and behavior (state) of the architecture, and interpret that into its method-specific model. Therefore, *learning is a type of meta-level inference.* A meta-level inference is a kind of inference able to inspect (to have a model of) the object level, infer some new decision, and modify the object-level in such a way that it complies to that decision [Smith 86]. For instance, in EBL-PRODIGY, the architecture has to be able to analyse its behavior, detect situations that involve a failure, select and apply the EBS method, and include the result in its knowledge-base. Meta-level inference in learning has been acknowledged in the literature as the introspective [Ram et al 92] or reflective [Plaza 92] characteristic of embedded learning.

Some examples may clarify this point. Meta-XP in Meta-AQUA [Ram et al 92] record a declarative model of the AQUA system problem solving, determine the blame assignment and selects the adequate method (EBG, index specialisation, etc.) the execution of which transforms the system's knowledge such that its behavior is improved. Another example is the Massive Memory Architecture [Plaza 92], where decisions, successes and failures are declaratively recorded in the system's memory of cases and search control in problem solving is guided (when lacking specific domain knowledge) by analogical transfer of past decisions in similar situations to the current problem.

The meta-level issue is also implicit in the inferential learning theory [Michalski 91]. In ILT learning methods are analysed as higher-level inference patterns the result of which are "knowledge transmutations", i.e. the modification of the system's knowledge as mandated by the inference performed by the learning method.

(f) Theoretical integration: learning and problem solving as inference

Inevitably the issues of integrating learning with different types of problem solving into a coherent whole (an ILA) arises as a necessary element both for ML research specifically, and for the role of learning in AI more broadly. These topics will shape the discussion and understanding of integrating learning, in a principled and comprehensive way, with other kinds of architecture components. Our approach to this is architectural, viewing learning as problem solving, rather than "inference based" as in the work by Michalski [Michalski 91] and inductive logic programming.

---

[1] At least conceptually, architecture axioms are explicit in EBL-Prodigy. However, computationally, the architecture has those axioms implicitly included into the implementation (Alicia Pérez, personal communication).

There are different dimensions along which ILAs may be at variance. One is the typology of opportunities for learning that are established in an architecture. This is part of the method-specific self-model, as for example in EBL-PRODIGY the typology is composed of the following types of learning opportunities SUCCEEDS, FAILS, SOLE-ALTERNATIVE, and GOAL-INTERFERENCE. Another dimension ranges from the fixed attachment of particular learning methods to specific types of situations vs. the dynamic selection of methods in multistrategy learning systems. Prodigy is an example of the fixed attachment of a learning method: only one of the existing methods (EBS, STATIC, derivational analogy, etc.) is used; while Meta-AQUA [Cox et al] selects a learning method according to the type of situation encountered.

A third dimension corresponds to the spontaneous/deliberate occurrence of learning. SOAR and the Massive Memory Architecture are examples of spontaneous learning in the sense that learning taking place automatically and not after an explicit system decision. PRODIGY and Meta-AQUA on the other hand are both examples of deliberate learning because both apply a learning method as an explicit decision resulting from an assessment of the utility of applying a particular learning method to a concrete situation.

3. A Framework for Describing ILAs

In this section we outline a framework for describing integrated learning architectures and propose our research strategy based on that framework. An *integrated architecture* is the computational realisation of a theory in terms of a fixed form, variable contents program that can be instantiated in a systematic and predictable way to achieve a range of systems the behavior of which exhibits a range of aspects of intelligence. Well known integrated architctures are SOAR [Newell 90], ACT* [Anderson 83], PI [Holland et al], etc), THEO [Mitchell et al 91], ICARUS [Langley et al] and PRODIGY [Carbonell et al].

We propose that there are three distinct architectural levels that are meaningful, and useful, to talk about and that correspond roughly to a *why*, *how* and *what* descriptions. These are the knowledge level, the functional (symbol) level and the behavior level.

- The behavioral description describes the observable behavior exhibited by a system when it is being applied or executed. This is a *what* model of system behaviour (i.e., a series of episodes of the system's activities) and it is created by an act of *observation*.

- The functional description describes a system in terms of its representational and computational primitives that together constitute the architectural primitives. The functional description is a *how* model of system behaviour and created by an act of *mechanisation*.

- The knowledge level description describes a system in terms of the knowledge of the world and the principles that are applied when using that knowledge (principles of rationality). It is a 'why' model of system behaviour and created by an act of *rationalisation*.

For example a re-implementation of Mycin in SOAR has a behavioral description in terms of consultation episodes, a functional description describing how these consultations are realised as a search in a problem space using certain operators and preference rules, and a knowledge level description that explains the system behavior in terms of the medical and patient knowledge that it is assumed to embody.

These three perspectives can be used as follows. An integrated architecture is, basically, described at the functional level. That is, it provides one with classes of structures (e.g., state-space, rule, knowledge source, blackboard) and mechanisms (e.g., state-space search, chunking, unification) interconnected and controlled in a fixed way. These structures and mechanisms are the architectural primitives that must be used in order to realise a system behavior. This system behavior, once exhibited, can be described either at the behavioral level or at the knowledge level. Thus, and this is crucial, a single functional architecture is used to implement a range of knowledge level and behavioral descriptions. This makes an architecture a computational theory with "fixed form" but "variable contents" that is targeted towards implementing a range of knowledge level and behavioral descriptions in a controlled and predictable way.

Knowledge level descriptions are, typically, in terms of goals, tasks, methods and models [Steels 90]. Descriptions in these terms capture not only the actual knowledge that is being used, but also the structure that emerges when the knowledge is being put to use in a class of situations. This structure can be called a knowledge level architecture, i.e., a use-specific window on the knowledge. For example, the model of heuristic classification is visible in a pattern of inferences that contribute to abstract, heuristic match and refinement steps in reasoning [Clancey 85]. The model is not visible at the functional level, but it is the recurrent structure for knowledge level descriptions of behavioral episodes exhibited by the system.

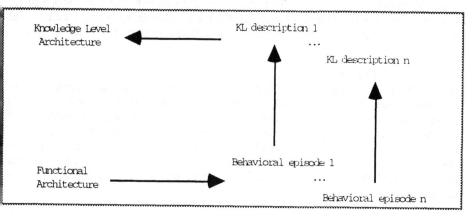

We propose to compare architectures by the range of knowledge level architectures that they can realise. Integrated learning architectures will include in their knowledge level architecture, at least one learning goal. Learning goals, tasks and methods are described in exactly the same way as the reasoning aspects. The problem solving aspects of a diagnostic application might be roughly described as follows:

Goal: diagnosis of a car
Task: identify smallest component with functional discrepancy
Method: try shortcut rules, otherwise hierarchical decomposition and testing
Models: heuristic symptom-fault associations, structural model,
expected behavior of components, tests.

The same system could exhibit learning behavior along the following lines:

Goal: reduce number of tests required
Task: acquire shortcut rules from successful episodes
Method: learning through progressive refinement
Models: causal model of component behavior

Implicit in this description is a decision on when to learn (after success), how to learn and what knowledge to use. This is the knowledge level equivalent of the architecture axioms (section 2), and we call them *integration principles*. In other words, an integration principle is a paradigmatic way to interconnect problem solving and learning in order to achieve a learning goal. Note that learning through progressive refinement is not the computational learning technique but an indication of the fact that the system behaves as if it uses such a technique. Whether this is the case or not depends on the functional architecture and as shown in the previous figure, there is no direct mapping from functional architecture to knowledge level architecture.

The above description in terms of goals tasks and methods, without the actual knowledge statements is the knowledge level architecture of the system. In this case it is likely to be fixed. It is however, perfectly possible that the same functional architecture could be used to realise other knowledge level architectures. For example the system might be able to learn from failures as well and maybe include a learning goal of limiting memory overhead which it realises by a task of forgetting infrequently used rules. It may exhibit pursue different learning goals depending on circumstances. In that case it will implement different knowledge level architectures (or a more sophisticated one). For example, the functional architecture of SOAR provides a single learning mechanism (chunking) that can realise a multiplicity of knowledge level learning goals (speedup, increasing goal directedness, smoother interaction, and so forth).

A similar role can be given to the behavior description, though it is typically less central. We propose that classes of behaviors can be described qualitatively to capture behavioral characteristics that make no difference from a rational (knowledge level) point of view but imply different pragmatic constraints. For example the ordering of questions in an interaction episode may be important to determine the practical usability of a system. Behaviors could be characterised as smooth, erratic, aggressive and so forth to describe pragmatic aspects of architectures. These are more prominent for physically behaving systems like robots, and we will not treat this issue further in this paper.

The above scheme is the basis for a research strategy on integrated learning architectures. We propose to analyse functional architectures in terms of the knowledge level architectures that they can realise and, the other way around, to derive ways in which a desired knowledge level architecture can be realised in a given functional architecture. This requires the investigation of knowledge level descriptions of learning goals, tasks and methods in addition to problem solving, and the development of integration principles and architectural axioms that can realise knowledge level architectures in functional architectures.

The framework could be used to describe existing architectures. Here is an initial description of SOAR [Newell 90] and CREEK [Aamodt] architectures. The descriptions are highly incomplete, both in depth and breadth and are intended to serve as an example of characterisations of well-known systems, as well as a proposal to further discussions and eventually to sum up the architectures presented at the workshop.

3.1 Knowledge Level Description

A knowledge level description of an architecture is a description in terms of the purpose of the architecture and how this purpose is fulfilled by a task decomposition, methods and knowledge. At this level, a system's behaviour in terms of what it intends to do, and what it brings to bear in order to be able to do it, can be explained. The potential and limitations of the system's capabilities can be predicted.

Knowledge-level description of SOAR:

Goal:	Unified cognitive behaviour.
Subtasks:	Solve problem
	Learn during problem solving
Methods:	Problem solving by state-space search, states are existing or created goals.
	Learning by chunking.
Knowledge:	Domain knowledge as productions.
	Strategic knowledge as preferences.

Knowledge-level description of CREEK

Goal:	Problem solving in real world, open domains.
Subtasks:	Solve problem.
	Learn after each problem solving session.
Methods:	Problem solving by combined case-based and generalisation-based reasoning.
	Learning by retaining cases.
Knowledge:	Domain knowledge as a dense semantic net, with cases integrated into it.
	Strategic knowledge as heuristics.

Description items: Goal hierarchy. Tasks assigned to goals. Methods to achieve tasks. Knowledge needed by the methods. A method is applied to a task. This will either lead to an achievement of the task or a decomposition of it into subtasks[2].

3.2 Symbol Level Description

A symbol level description of an architecture is a description in terms of its knowledge representation language, the inference methods of the language, and how these combine into specific reasoning and learning methods. At this level, it can be explained how a system is able to achieve its goals through its methods and its knowledge, by referring

---

[2] See [Steels 90] on knowledge-level descriptions of expert systems and [van de Velde 90] for an application to learning systems.

to the underlying functions that are executed. Predictions can be made about a system's problem solving competence, what it is able to learn, its ability to interact with the external world, etc.

<u>Description items</u>: Knowledge representation language, operations on the representation - in terms of input/output descriptions. A symbol level description, not getting into the actual computational mechanisms.

Symbol-level description of SOAR:

```
Representation:  Problem spaces represents tasks
                 Productions represent all knowledge
                 Attribute-value pair is the representational
                 unit
Functions
   - probl.solv: Decision cycle: Elaborate, Decide
                        Decide: Evaluate preferences, Detect impasse,
                              Create subgoal
   - learning:      Create chunk after each impasse/subgoaling
   - primitive:   Select problem space, Select state, Select
                        operator, Apply operator to state.
```

Symbol-level description of CREEK:

```
Representation:  Single semantic network holds all knowledge
                 Frames represent all concept types
                 Frame-slot-facet-value quadruple
                 (Concept-relation-relation_type-value)
                 is the representational unit
Functions
   - probl.solv: Main cycle: Understand-Generate-Select
                        Subcycle for each main function: Activate-
                        Explain-Focus
   - learning:      Main cycle for case-learning:
                        • Extract-Construct-Evaluate-Store
   - primitive:   Spread activation, Determine context, Retrieve
                        cases, Derive plausible hypotheses, Select
                        best hypothesis, Extract relevant case info,
                        Index case
```

4. Conclusion

Although there is already some experience in the embedding of learning methods into integrated architectures, most of the crucial issues remain open nowadays. Some of the open issues are general to any computational system that integrates several components, from hybrid representation languages to integrated cognitive architectures. These issues includes the uniform vs. hybrid approaches discussion, and the tight/loose integration spectrum. Uniform approaches like Theo and Soar achieve integration by having all components represented in the same language. Introspective systems like Meta-AQUA and the Massive Memory Architecture achieve integration having a self-model of the system used for learning purposes. Still, other systems like Prodigy have several learning methods that have different models of the problem solving component and thus are separately integrated with the same problem solver but no further integration among them is achieved.

More specifically, embedding learning arises some crucial issues for ML, as we discussed in §2: What knowledge of another component does a learning method require in order to be able to learn? What is(are) the goal(s) of learning? How learning goals are generated and selected in the integrated architecture? How the results of learning are integrated into the overall architecture? Furthermore, the necessity of a comprehensive theory for analysing and comparing different learning and problem solving components arises. One candidate is the Inferential Learning Theory [Michalski 91], another one is using a knowledge-level description like the Components of Expertise [Steels 90] for describing both learning and problem solving components [van de Velde 90], [Plaza 92].

There are also following are some long term research objectives:

- categorisation of learning goals of agents, either as individual [Mitchell 90] or as a group [Brazdil et al 92].

- study of integration principles (architecture axioms) and their applicability conditions. Associated methods for flexible and dynamic (re-)configuration of learning task and methods within problem solving to deal with varying learning goals imposed by the environment.

- techniques for the genuine combination of learning methods, rather than treating them as alternatives to be selected or, alternatively, techniques for the unification of learning methods in a single approach.

- learning beyond domain knowledge, for example of new tasks or methods. Learning about learning (about why, when, what and how to learn).

- learning under resource limitations (anytime learning, memory management, role of forgetting).

- are the processes of learning and problem solving really different van de Velde 90]? Are learning and adaptation really different [Maturana and Varela]?

- integration with physical behaving systems, robots [van de Velde 92] while taking into account recent results from robotics [Maes 90], biology [Maturana and Varela] and epistemology [Clancey 85].

The ultimate goal, of course, is to construct an architecture that embodies the answers to all of these questions. The research strategy outlined above is an approach toward this goal. It is our feeling that work on isolated learning can not yield significant new insights and that now is the time to try the integration of the results from Machine Learning and other disciplines in a unifying theory and architecture of reasoning, behavior and learning.

Advances in the direction of ILA's will be both of theoretical and practical interest. We expect that it will integrate research on learning and problem solving, increasing our understanding of intelligence. On the other hand it will teach us how to apply learning in the context of intelligent systems, even where these are based on a wide variety of problem solving architectures. This will broaden the range of possible applications of ML techniques.

Acknowledgements

Enric Plaza acknowledges the support of the Massive Memory Project funded by the PRONTIC 90/801 project grant at the IIIA. Ashwin Ram acknowledges the support of the National Science Foundation under grant IRI-9009710 and of the Georgia Institute of Technology. Walter Van de Velde acknowledges the support of the Belgian Ministry of Scientific Research under grant ADIOS (IT/IF/18).

References

[Aamodt 90] Aamodt, A (1990), Knowledge-intensive case-based reasoning and sustained learning. *Proc. ECAI-90*, Stockholm.

[Anderson 83] Anderson, J R (1983), *The Architecture of Cognition.* Harvard University Press: Cambridge.

[Brazdil et al 92] Brazdil, P, et al (1992), Multi-agent learning. In *Proc. EWSL-92.* Speringer Verlag.

[Carbonell et al] Carbonell, J G, Knoblock, C A, Minton, S, (1992), PRODIGY: An integrated architecture for planning and learning. In K VanLehn (Ed), *Architectures for Intelligence*, p. 241-278.

[Clancey 85] Clancey, W (1985), Heuristic classification, *Artificial Intelligence* 27, p. 289-350. North-Holland, Amsterdam.

[Clancey 90] Clancey, W (1990), The frame reference problem in the design of intelligent machines. In Van Lehn and Newell, A (Eds.) *Architectures for Intelligence.* Erlsbaum: Hillsdale, NJ.

[Cox et al] Cox, M T, Ram, A (1991), Using introspective reasoning to select learning strategies. In R Michalski and G Tecuci (Eds.) *Proc. Int. Work. on Multistrategy Learning*, p. 217-230.

[Holland et al] Holland, J H, Holyoak, K J, Nisbett, R E, Thagart, P R (1986), *Induction: Processes of Inference, Learning and Discovery.* The MIT Press: Cambridge, MA.

[Kolodner 87] Janet Kolodner: Extending problem solver capabilities through case-based inference. *Proc. 4th Workshop on Machine Learning*, UC-Irvine, June 22-25 1987. pp 167-178.

[Langley et al] P Langley, K Thompson, W F Iba, J Gennari, J A Allen (in press), An Integrated Cognitive Architecture for Autonomous Agents. In W van de Velde (in press), Editor, *Towards Learning Robots*, MIT Press.

[Maes 90] Maes, P (Ed.) (1990) Special Issue on Designing Autonomous Agents. *Robotics and Autonomous Systems*, 6(1-2). North-Holland, Amsterdam.

[Maturana and Varela] Maturana, H R , and Varela, F J (1992), *The Tree of Knowledge: the biological roots of human understanding*. Shambala: Boston.

[Michalski 91] Michalski, R S (1991), Inferential learning theory as a basis for multistrategy task-adaptive learning. In R Michalski and G Tecuci (Eds.) *Proc. Int. Work. on Multistrategy Learning*, p. 3-18.

[Mitchell 90] Mitchell, Y (1990), Becoming increasingly reactive. In *Proc. AAAI-90*, p. 1051-1058.

[Mitchell et al 91] Mitchell, T M, Allen, J, Chalasani, P, Cheng, J, Etzioni, O, Ringuette, M, Schlimmer, J C (1991), Theo: a framework for self-improving systems. In K Van Lenhn (Ed.) *Architectures for Intelligence*. Laurence Erlbaum.

[MSL-91] R Michalski and G Tecuci (Eds.) *Proc. Int. Work. on Multistrategy Learning*, p. 217-230. Harpers Ferry, November 7-9, 1991.

[Newell 90] A Newell (1990), *Unified Theories of Cognition*. Cambridge MA: Harvard UniversityPress

[Plaza 92] Plaza, E (1992), Reflection for analogy: Inference-level-reflection in an architetcure for analogical reasoning. *Proc. IMSA'92 Workshop on Reflection and Metalevel Architectures*, Tokyo, November 1992, p. 166-171.

[Porter 90] Bruce Porter, Ray Bareiss, Robert Holte: Concept learning and heuristic classification in weak theory domains. Artificial Intelligence, vol. 45, no. 1-2, September 1990. pp 229-263.

[Ram et al 92] Ram, A, Cox, M T, Narayanan, S. (1992), An architecture for integrated introspective learning. *Proc. ML'92 Workshop on Computational Architectures for Machine Learning and Knowledge Acquisition*.

[Smith 86] Smith, B C, (1986), Varieties of self-reference. In *Theoretical Aspects of Reasoning about Knowledge*, p. 19-43, Morgan Kaufmann, Los Altos, CA.

[Steels 90] L Steels (1990), The Components of Expertise, *AI Magazine*, August 1990.

[van de Velde 90] W --van de Velde, W (1990), Reasoning, Behavior and learning: A knowledge-level perspective . *Proc. of Cognitiva 90*, pp. 451-463. Madrid 20-23 Nov. 1990.

[van de Velde 92] van de Velde, W (Ed.) (1992), Toward Learning Robots.Special Issue of *Robotics and Autonomous Systems*, 8(1-2). North-Holland, Amsterdam.

An Overview of Evolutionary Computation

William M. Spears †
Kenneth A. De Jong
Thomas Bäck
David B. Fogel
Hugo de Garis

Abstract. Evolutionary computation uses computational models of evolutionary processes as key elements in the design and implementation of computer-based problem solving systems. In this paper we provide an overview of evolutionary computation, and describe several evolutionary algorithms that are currently of interest. Important similarities and differences are noted, which lead to a discussion of important issues that need to be resolved, and items for future research.

1 Introduction

Evolutionary computation uses computational models of evolutionary processes as key elements in the design and implementation of computer-based problem solving systems. There are a variety of evolutionary computational models that have been proposed and studied which we will refer to as evolutionary algorithms. They share a common conceptual base of simulating the evolution of individual structures via processes of selection and reproduction. These processes depend on the perceived performance (fitness) of the individual structures as defined by an environment.

More precisely, evolutionary algorithms maintain a population of structures that evolve according to rules of selection and other operators, such as recombination and mutation. Each individual in the population receives a measure of its fitness in the environment. Selection focuses attention on high fitness individuals, thus exploiting the available fitness information. Recombination and mutation perturb those individuals, providing general heuristics for exploration. Although simplistic from a biologist's viewpoint, these algorithms are sufficiently complex to provide robust and powerful adaptive search mechanisms.

Figure 1 outlines a typical evolutionary algorithm (EA). A population of individual structures is initialized and then evolved from generation to generation by repeated applications of evaluation, selection, recombination, and mutation. The population size N is generally constant in an evolutionary algorithm, although there is no *a priori* reason (other than convenience) to make this assumption. We will

---

† The first author is affiliated with the AI Center of the Naval Research Laboratory in Washington, DC 20375 USA. His email address is spears@aic.nrl.navy.mil

```
procedure EA; {
t = 0;
initialize population P(t);
evaluate P(t);
until (done) {
        t = t + 1;
        parent_selection P(t);
        recombine P(t);
        mutate P(t);
        evaluate P(t);
        survive P(t);
}       }
```

Fig. 1. A typical evolutionary algorithm

discuss the issue of a dynamic population size later in this paper.

An evolutionary algorithm typically initializes its population randomly, although domain specific knowledge can also be used to bias the search. Evaluation measures the fitness of each individual according to its worth in some environment. Evaluation may be as simple as computing a fitness function or as complex as running an elaborate simulation. Selection is often performed in two steps, parent selection and survival. Parent selection decides who becomes parents and how many children the parents have. Children are created via recombination, which exchanges information between parents, and mutation, which further perturbs the children. The children are then evaluated. Finally, the survival step decides who survives in the population.

Let us illustrate an evolutionary algorithm with a simple example. Suppose an automotive manufacturer wishes to design a new engine and fuel system in order to maximize performance, reliability, and gas-mileage, while minimizing emissions. Let us further suppose that an engine simulation unit can test various engines and return a single value indicating the fitness score of the engine. However, the number of possible engines is large and there is insufficient time to test them all. How would one attack such a problem with an evolutionary algorithm?

First, we define each individual to represent a specific engine. For example, suppose the cubic inch displacement (CID), fuel system, number of valves, cylinders, and presence of turbo-charging are all engine variables. The initialization step would create an initial population of possible engines. For the sake of simplicity, let us assume a (very small) population of size four. Here is an example initial population:

Individual	CID	Fuel System	Turbo	Valves	Cylinders
1	350	4 Barrels	Yes	16	8
2	250	Mech. Inject.	No	12	6
3	150	Elect. Inject.	Yes	12	4
4	200	2 Barrels	No	8	4

We now evaluate each individual with the engine simulator. Each individual receives a fitness score (the higher the better):

Individual	CID	Fuel System	Turbo	Valves	Cylinders	Score
1	350	4 Barrels	Yes	16	8	50
2	250	Mech. Inject.	No	12	6	100
3	150	Elect. Inject.	Yes	12	4	300
4	200	2 Barrels	No	8	4	150

Parent selection decides who has children and how many to have. For example, we could decide that individual 3 deserves two children, because it is so much better than the other individuals. Children are created through recombination and mutation. As mentioned above, recombination exchanges information between individuals, while mutation perturbs individuals, thereby increasing diversity. For example, recombination of individuals 3 and 4 could produce the two children:

Individual	CID	Fuel System	Turbo	Valves	Cylinders
3'	200	Elect. Inject.	Yes	8	4
4'	150	2 Barrels	No	12	4

Note that the children are composed of elements of the two parents. Further note that the number of cylinders must be four, because individuals 3 and 4 both had four cylinders. Mutation might further perturb these children, yielding:

Individual	CID	Fuel System	Turbo	Valves	Cylinders
3'	250	Elect. Inject.	Yes	8	4
4'	150	2 Barrels	No	12	6

We now evaluate the children, giving perhaps:

Individual	CID	Fuel System	Turbo	Valves	Cylinders	Score
3'	250	Elect. Inject.	Yes	8	4	250
4'	150	2 Barrels	No	12	6	350

Finally we decide who will survive. In our constant population size example, which is typical of most EAs, we need to select four individuals to survive. How this is accomplished varies considerably in different EAs. If, for example, only the best individuals survive, our population would become:

Individual	CID	Fuel System	Turbo	Valves	Cylinders	Score
3	150	Elect. Inject.	Yes	12	4	300
4	200	2 Barrels	No	8	4	150
3'	250	Elect. Inject.	Yes	8	4	250
4'	150	2 Barrels	No	12	6	350

This cycle of evaluation, selection, recombination, mutation, and survival continues until some termination criterion is met.

This simple example serves to illustrate the flavor of an evolutionary algorithm. It is important to point out that although the basic conceptual framework of all EAs is similar, their particular implementations differ in many details. For example, there are a wide variety of selection mechanisms. The representations of individuals ranges from bit-strings to real-valued vectors, Lisp expressions, and neural networks. Finally, the relative importance of mutation and crossover (recombination), as well as their particular implementations, differs widely across evolutionary algorithms.

The remainder of this paper is organized into three sections. First, we will continue our introduction to evolutionary algorithms by describing at a high level a variety of implementations. Second, we will discuss the issues underlying the differences between the implementations, taking the opportunity to provide comparisons at a finer level of detail. Finally we will discuss how these issues might be resolved and summarize recent work in this area. Our goal is to encourage increased discussion, with the eventual hope for more powerful and robust evolutionary algorithms.

2 Varieties of Evolutionary Algorithms

The origins of evolutionary algorithms can be traced to at least the 1950's (e.g., Fraser, 1957; Box, 1957). For the sake of brevity we will not concentrate on this early work but will discuss in some detail three methodologies that have emerged in the last few decades: "evolutionary programming" (Fogel et al., 1966), "evolution strategies" (Rechenberg, 1973), and "genetic algorithms" (Holland, 1975).

Although similar at the highest level, each of these varieties implements an evolutionary algorithm in a different manner. The differences touch upon almost all aspects of evolutionary algorithms, including the choices of representation for the individual structures, types of selection mechanism used, forms of genetic operators, and measures of performance. We will highlight the important differences (and similarities) in the following sections, by examining some of the variety represented by the current family of evolutionary algorithms.

These approaches in turn have inspired the development of additional evolutionary algorithms such as "classifier systems" (Holland, 1986), the LS systems (Smith, 1983), "adaptive operator" systems (Davis, 1989), GENITOR (Whitley, 1989), SAMUEL (Grefenstette, 1989), "genetic programming" (de Garis, 1990; Koza, 1991), "messy GAs" (Goldberg, 1991), and the CHC approach (Eshelman, 1991). We will not attempt to survey this broad range of activities here. The interested reader is encouraged to peruse the recent literature for more details (e.g., Belew and Booker, 1991; Fogel and Atmar, 1992; Whitley, 1992; Männer and Manderick, 1992).

2.1 Evolutionary Programming

Evolutionary programming (EP), developed by Fogel et al. (1966) traditionally has used representations that are tailored to the problem domain. For example, in real-valued optimization problems, the individuals within the population are real-valued vectors. Similarly, ordered lists are used for traveling salesman problems, and graphs for applications with finite state machines. EP is often used as an optimizer, although it arose from the desire to generate machine intelligence.

The outline of the evolutionary programming algorithm is shown in Figure 2. After initialization, all N individuals are selected to be parents, and then are mutated,

```
procedure EP; {
t = 0;
initialize population P(t);
evaluate P(t);
until (done) {
        t = t + 1;
        parent_selection P(t);
        mutate P(t);
        evaluate P(t);
        survive P(t);
}        }
```

Fig. 2. The evolutionary programming algorithm

producing N children. These children are evaluated and N survivors are chosen from the $2N$ individuals, using a probabilistic function based on fitness. In other words, individuals with a greater fitness have a higher chance of survival. The form of mutation is based on the representation used, and is often adaptive (see Section 3.2). For example, when using a real-valued vector, each variable within an individual may have an adaptive mutation rate that is normally distributed with a zero expectation. Recombination is not generally performed since the forms of mutation used are quite flexible and can produce perturbations similar to recombination, if desired. As discussed in a later section, one of the interesting and open issues is the extent to which an EA is affected by its choice of the operators used to produce variability and novelty in evolving populations.

2.2 Evolution Strategies

Evolution strategies (ESs) were independently developed by Rechenberg (1973), with selection, mutation, and a population of size one. Schwefel (1981) introduced recombination and populations with more than one individual, and provided a nice comparison of ESs with more traditional optimization techniques. Due to initial interest in hydrodynamic optimization problems, evolution strategies typically use real-valued vector representations.

Figure 3 outlines a typical evolution strategy (ES). After initialization and evaluation, individuals are selected uniformly randomly to be parents. In the standard recombinative ES, pairs of parents produces children via recombination, which are further perturbed via mutation. The number of children created is greater than N. Survival is deterministic and is implemented in one of two ways. The first allows the

```
procedure ES; {
t = 0;
initialize population P(t);
evaluate P(t);
until (done) {
        t = t + 1;
        parent_selection P(t);
        recombine P(t)
        mutate P(t);
        evaluate P(t);
        survive P(t);
}        }
```

Fig. 3. The evolution strategy algorithm

N best children to survive, and replaces the parents with these children. The second allows the *N* best children and parents to survive. Like EP, considerable effort has focused on adapting mutation as the algorithm runs by allowing each variable within an individual to have an adaptive mutation rate that is normally distributed with a zero expectation. Unlike EP, however, recombination does play an important role in evolution strategies, especially in adapting mutation.

2.3 Genetic Algorithms

Genetic algorithms (GAs), developed by Holland (1975), have traditionally used a more domain independent representation, namely, bit-strings. However, many recent applications of GAs have focused on other representations, such as graphs (neural networks), Lisp expressions, ordered lists, and real-valued vectors.

Figure 4 outlines a typical genetic algorithm (GA). After initialization parents are selected according to a probabilistic function based on relative fitness. In other words, those individuals with higher relative fitness are more likely to be selected as parents. *N* children are created via recombination from the *N* parents. The *N* children are mutated and survive, replacing the *N* parents in the population. It is interesting to note that the relative emphasis on mutation and crossover is opposite to that in EP. In a GA mutation flips bits with some small probability, and is often considered to be a background operator. Recombination, on the other hand, is emphasized as the primary search operator. GAs are often used as optimizers, although some researchers emphasize its general adaptive capabilities (De Jong, 1992).

```
procedure GA; {
t = 0;
initialize population P(t);
evaluate P(t);
until (done) {
        t = t + 1;
        parent_selection P(t);
        recombine P(t)
        mutate P(t);
        evaluate P(t);
        survive P(t);
}       }
```

Fig. 4. The genetic algorithm

2.4 Variations on these Themes

These three approaches (EP, ESs, and GAs) have served to inspire an increasing amount of research on and development of new forms of evolutionary algorithms for use in specific problem solving contexts. A few of these are briefly described below, selected primarily to give the reader a sense of the variety of directions being explored.

One of the most active areas of application of evolutionary algorithms is in solving complex function and combinatorial optimization problems. A variety of features are typically added to EAs in this context to improve both the speed and the precision of the results. Interested readers should review Davis' work on real-valued representations and adaptive operators (Davis, 1989), Whitley's GENITOR system incorporating ranking and "steady state" mechanisms (Whitley, 1989), Goldberg's "messy GAs", that involve adaptive representations (Goldberg, 1991), and Eshelman's high-powered CHC algorithm (Eshelman, 1991).

A second active area of application of EAs is in the design of robust rule learning systems. Holland's (1986) classifier systems were some of the early examples, followed by the LS systems of Smith (1983). More recent examples include the SAMUEL system developed by Grefenstette (1989), the GABIL system of De Jong and Spears (1991), and the GIL system of Janikow (1991). In each case, significant adaptations to the basic EAs have been made in order to effectively represent, evaluate, and evolve appropriate rule sets as defined by the environment.

One of the most fascinating recent developments is the use of EAs to evolve more complex structures such as neural networks and Lisp code. This has been dubbed "genetic programming", and is exemplified by the work of de Garis (1990), Fujiko and Dickinson (1987), and Koza (1991). de Garis evolves weights in neural networks, in an attempt to build complex behavior. Fujiko and Dickinson evolved Lisp expressions to solve the Prisoner's Dilemma. Koza also represents individuals using Lisp expressions and has solved a large number of optimization and machine learning tasks. One of the open questions here is precisely what changes to EAs need to be made in order to efficiently evolve such complex structures.

3 Issues

In the previous section we highlighted the similarities and differences of the various forms of evolutionary algorithms. The differences arise from a number of relevant issues. In this section we will explore these issues briefly, and take the opportunity to also define the algorithms above in greater detail.

3.1 Scaling, Selection and Fitness

Central to every evolutionary algorithm is the concept of fitness (i.e., evaluation). If we assume, without loss of generality, that we wish to maximize fitness, then we wish to concentrate search in those areas of higher fitness. This concentration of effort, commonly referred to by the term *exploitation*, is the task of selection. Each EA addresses this issue in a different manner.

Before we describe selection mechanisms further, it is also important to consider the issue of *scaling*. Suppose one has two search spaces. The first is described with a real-valued fitness function F. The second search space is described by a fitness function G that is equivalent to F^p, where p is some constant. The relative *positions* of peaks and valleys in the two search spaces correspond exactly. Only the relative *heights* differ (i.e., the vertical scale is different). Should our EA search both spaces in the same manner?

There is no right or wrong answer to this question, since it really depends on our goals and the problems to be solved. If we believe that the EA should search the two spaces in the same manner, then selection should only be based on the relative ordering of fitnesses. ESs, for example, use precisely this method. Parent selection is performed uniformly randomly, with no regard to fitness. Survival simply saves the N best individuals, which is only based on the relative ordering of fitnesses. This form of selection is often referred to as *ranking* selection, since only the rank of individuals is of importance. EP selection is similar to that of the ES algorithm. All individuals are selected to be parents. Each parent is mutated once, producing N children. A probabilistic ranking mechanism chooses the N best individuals for survival, from the union of the parents and children. Again, this is a selection mechanism based on rank.

The GA community has also advocated ranking for some situations, but by and large many members believe that F and G should be searched differently. Fitness proportional selection is the probabilistic selection mechanism of the traditional GA. Parent selection is performed based on how fit an individual is with respect to the population average. For example, an individual with fitness twice the population average will tend to have twice as many children as average individuals. Survival, though, is not based on fitness, since the parents are automatically replaced by the children.

One problem with this latter approach is that, as the search continues, more and more individuals receive fitnesses with small relative differences. This lessens the selection pressure, slowing the progress of the search. This effect, often referred to as "lacking the killer instinct", can be compensated somewhat by scaling mechanisms, that attempt to magnify relative differences as the search progresses. A number of scaling mechanisms exists, but their description is beyond the scope of this paper. The interested reader is urged to refer to Grefenstette and Baker (1989) for an investigation into the relationships between fitness, scaling, and selection.

3.2 Mutation and Adaptation

As mentioned earlier, selection serves to focus search into areas of high fitness. Of course, if selection were the only genetic operator, the population would never have any individuals other than those introduced in the initial population. Other genetic operators perturb these individuals, providing exploration in nearby areas. Although a number of operators are possible, we will concentrate on the two predominant operators, namely, mutation and recombination.

The importance of mutation in EAs varies widely. Koza (1991) does not use mutation at all. GAs typically use mutation as a simple background operator, to ensure that a particular bit value is not lost forever. Using our previous example, suppose every member of our engine population had four cylinders. Then mutation can reintroduce six and eight cylinder engines. Recall that GAs traditionally work on bit-strings. Under these conditions, mutation in GAs typically flips bits with a very low probability (e.g., 1 bit out of 1000).

Mutation is far more important in ESs and EP. Instead of a global mutation rate, mutation probability distributions can be maintained for every variable of every individual. Thus, each variable can be mutated according to a different probability distribution. More importantly, ESs and EP encode the probability distributions as extra information within each individual, and allow this information to evolve as well. What is achieved is the *self-adaptation* of mutation parameters, *while* the space is being searched. Again, full details of this are beyond the scope of this paper. The interested reader is encouraged to read Bäck et al. (1991), Bäck and Schwefel (1993), and Fogel (1992).

3.3 Recombination and Adaptation

Recombination is the other predominant genetic operator. Recombination merges variables from two parents to produce offspring that have variables from both parents. Like mutation, the relative importance of recombination in various EAs varies widely. EP does not make use of recombination. Koza (1991) only uses recombination to form new Lisp expressions.

ESs and GAs use both recombination and mutation. There are a number of recombination methods for ESs, all of which assume that the individuals are composed of real-valued variables. Either the values are exchanged (as in our "engine" example above), or they are averaged. For example, a four cylinder parent could recombine with an eight cylinder parent to produce a six cylinder child. Finally, the ES community has also considered multi-parent versions of these operators. Although the ES community places more emphasis on mutation, and does not adaptively modify crossover, they also feel crossover is essential for the proper adaptation of the mutation parameters.

The GA community places primary emphasis on crossover, and a number of recombination operators are widely used. Again, for the sake of brevity, we will only discuss the most popular, namely, *one-point, multi-point* and *uniform* recombination. One-point recombination inserts a *cut-point* within the two parents (e.g., between the 3rd and 4th variables, or bits). Then the information before the cut-point is swapped between the two parents. Multi-point recombination is a generalization of this idea, introducing a higher number of cut-points. Information is then swapped between pairs of cut-points. Uniform crossover, however, does not use cut-points, but simply uses a global parameter to indicate the likelihood that each variable should be exchanged between two parents. Considerable experimental and theoretical work has investigated the differences between these forms of recombination. Spears and De Jong (1992), Booker (1992), and Vose and Liepins (1991) provide theoretical comparisons.

Despite the emphasis on recombination within the GA community, interest in mutation has increased recently, partly due to the influence of the ES and EP communities. Schaffer and Eshelman (1991) have experimentally shown that mutation is a powerful search operator in its own right, while still maintaining the usefulness of crossover in certain situations. Spears (1992a) agrees with this view, and has theoretically shown some of the strengths and weakness of mutation and recombination. It is important to realize that recombination and mutation provide different search biases, which may or may not be appropriate for the task at hand. Since a priori appropriateness may be hard to determine, the key to more robust EA systems probably lies in the adaptive selection of such genetic operators. Unfortunately, very little has been done in the way of adaptive recombination. Schaffer and Morishima (1987) have experimented with *punctuation-marks* that indicate where good cut-points may exist. Davis (1989) has experimented with adapting the rate at which recombination is applied, given performance feedback. Finally, Spears (1992b) has shown that it is feasible for the GA to choose between two forms of recombination. Clearly, however, this is an area for further research.

3.4 Representation

Of course, any genetic operator such as mutation and recombination must be defined with a particular individual representation in mind. Again, the EA community differs widely in the representations used. Traditionally, GAs use bit strings. In theory, this representation makes the GA more problem independent, because once a bit string representation is found, standard bit-level mutation and recombination can often be used. We can also see this as a more genotypic level of representation, since the individual is in some sense encoded in the bit string. Recently, however, the GA community has investigated more phenotypic representations, including vectors of real values (Davis, 1989), ordered lists (Whitley et al., 1989), neural networks (Harp et. al, 1991), and Lisp expressions (Koza, 1991). For each of these representations, special mutation and recombination operators are introduced. The EP and ES communities are similar in this regard. The ES and EP communities focus on real-valued vector representations, although the EP community has also used ordered list and finite state automata representations, as suggested by the domain of the problem.

Although much has been done experimentally, very little has been said theoretically that helps one choose good representations, nor that explains what it *means* to have a good representation. Also, very little has been done in the way of adaptive representations, with the exception of messy GAs (Goldberg, 1991), Argot (Shaefer, 1987), the dynamic parameter encoding (DPE) scheme of Schraudolph and Belew

(1992), and the Delta coding of Whitley et al. (1991). Messy GAs, Argot, DPE, and Delta coding all attempt to manipulate the granularity of the representation, thus focusing search at the appropriate level. Despite some initial success in this area, it is clear that much more work needs to be done.

3.5 Adaptive EAs

Despite some work on adapting representation, mutation, and recombination within evolutionary algorithms, very little has been accomplished with respect to the adaptation of population sizes and selection mechanisms. One way to characterize selection is by the *strength* of the selection mechanism. Strong selection refers to a selection mechanism that concentrates quickly on the best individuals, while weaker selection mechanisms allow poor individuals to survive (and produce children) for a longer period of time. Similarly, the population can be thought of as having a certain *carrying capacity*, which refers to the amount of information that the population can usefully maintain. A small population has less carrying capacity, which is usually adequate for simple problems. Larger populations, with larger carrying capacities, are often better for more difficult problems. Although some work has attempted to characterize good population sizes (Goldberg, 1989a), more theory is needed. In lieu of theory, then, perhaps the evolutionary algorithm can adapt both selection pressure and the population size dynamically, as it solves problems.

3.6 Performance Measures, EA-Hardness, and Evolvability

Of course, one can not refer to adaptation without having a performance goal in mind. EP and ES usually have optimization for a goal. In other words, they are typically most interested in finding the best solution as quickly as possible. The GA community has often taken a similar stance, although there is also some concern that such a stance can be somewhat misleading. De Jong (1992) reminds us that GAs are *not* function optimizers per se, although they can be used as such. There is very little theory indicating how well GAs will perform optimization tasks. Instead, theory concentrates on what is referred to as *accumulated payoff*. The difference can be illustrated by considering financial investment planning over a period of time (e.g., you play the stock market). Instead of trying to find the *best* stock, you are trying to maximize your returns as the various stocks are sampled. Clearly the two goals are somewhat different, and maximizing the return may or may not also be a good heuristic for finding the best stock. This difference in emphasis clearly has implications for how an EA practitioner can (and should) measure performance, which will have further implications for how adaptation should be accomplished.

This difference also colors much of the discussion concerning the issue of problem difficulty. The GA community refers to hard problems as *GA-Hard*. Since we are now in the broader context of EAs, let us refer to hard problems as *EA-Hard*. Often, a problem is considered difficult if the EA can not find the optimum. Although this is a quite reasonable definition, difficult problems are often constructed by taking advantage of the EA in such a way that selection deliberately leads the search away from the optimum. Such problems are called *deceptive* (Goldberg, 1989b). From a function optimization point of view, the problem is indeed deceptive. However, the EA may nonetheless maximize accumulated payoff. Should we call a deceptive problem EA-Hard? The answer obviously depends on our goals.

It is clear, then, that problem difficulty is a function of the problem, the goal, and the algorithm used to solve that problem. Although deceptiveness is one possibility, other measures of problem difficulty are needed.† One possibility is *fitness correlation*, which appears to be a measure of EA-Hardness that places less emphasis on optimality (Manderick et al., 1991). Fitness correlation measures the correlation between the fitness of children and their parents. Manderick et al. found a strong relationship between GA performance and the strength of the correlations. Similarly, Lipsitch (1991) has also proposed examining fitness correlations. Another possibility is problem modality. Those problems that have many suboptimal solutions will, in general, be more difficult to search. Finally, this issue is also very related to a concern of de Garis, which he refers to as *evolvability*. de Garis notes that often his systems do not evolve at all, namely, that fitness does not increase over time. The reasons for this are not clear and remain an important research topic.

3.7 Distributed EAs

Because of the inherent natural parallelism within an EA, much recent work has concentrated on the implementation of EAs on parallel machines. Typically either one processor holds one individual (in SIMD machines), or a subpopulation (in MIMD machines). Clearly, such implementations hold promise of execution time decreases. More interestingly, though, for the topic of this paper, are the evolutionary effects that can be naturally illustrated with parallel machines, namely, speciation, nicheing, and punctuated equilibria. Belew and Booker (1991) contain many examples of the most current work in this area.

4 Current Trends

With a better understanding of the similarities and differences between various implementations of EAs, the community has begun to concentrate on generalizing results initially shown only for specific EAs. For example, Grefenstette and Baker (1989) illustrate that many features of EAs do not change when certain properties of selection and scaling are assumed. They also indicate when the features change, if the properties are not met. Although this work is preliminary, it helps explain why a wide variety of EAs have all met with success. Bäck is also investigating the differences between GAs and ESs and is attempting to merge the best features of each in order to have a more robust EA.

---

† For an analysis of deception, see Grefenstette (1992).

As we understand better the strengths and weaknesses of our current evolutionary models, it is also important to revisit the biological and evolutionary literature for new insights and inspirations for enhancements. Booker (1992) has recently pointed out the connections with GA recombination theory to the more general theory of population genetics recombination distributions. Mühlenbein (1993) has concentrated on EAs that are modeled after breeding practices. In the EP community, Atmar (1992) highlights some errors common to evolutionary theory and the EA community.

5 Summary

We have attempted to provide a brief overview of the field of evolutionary computation by describing three classes of evolutionary algorithms which have served to define and shape the field. By highlighting their similarities and differences, we have identified a number of important issues that suggest directions for future research.

With the rapid growth of the field, there is a particularly pressing need to extend existing and developing new analysis tools which allow us to better understand and evaluate the emerging varieties of EAs and their applications. We hope this paper will serve as a catalyst for such activities.

Affiliations

William M. Spears is affiliated with the Naval Research Laboratory (USA), Kenneth A. De Jong with George Mason University (USA), Thomas Bäck with the University of Dortmund (Germany), David B. Fogel with ORINCON Corporation (USA), and Hugo de Garis with the ATR Laboratory (Japan).

References

Atmar, W. (1992) The philosophical errors that plague both evolutionary theory and simulated evolutionary programming. *Proceedings of the First Annual Conference on Evolutionary Programming*, 27-34. San Diego, CA: Evolutionary Programming Society.

Bäck, T., Hoffmeister, F., & Schwefel, H.-P. (1991) A survey of evolution strategies. *Proceedings of the Fourth International Conference on Genetic Algorithms*, 2-9. La Jolla, CA: Morgan Kaufmann.

Bäck, T., & Schwefel, H.-P. (1993) An overview of evolutionary algorithms for parameter optimization. Submitted to the *Journal of Evolutionary Computation*.

Belew, R. K., & Booker, L. B. (eds.) (1991) *Proceedings of the Fourth International Conference on Genetic Algorithms*. La Jolla, CA: Morgan Kaufmann.

Booker, L. B. (1992) Recombination distributions for genetic algorithms. *Proceedings of the Foundations of Genetic Algorithms Workshop*. Vail, CO: Morgan Kaufmann.

Box, G. E. P. (1957) Evolutionary operation: a method of increasing industrial productivity. *Applied Statistics*, Vol. 6, 81-101.

Davis, L. (1989) Adapting operator probabilities in genetic algorithms. *Proceedings of the Third International Conference on Genetic Algorithms*, 60-69. La Jolla, CA: Morgan Kaufmann.

de Garis, H. (1990) Genetic programming: modular evolution for darwin machines. *Proceedings of the 1990 International Joint Conference on Neural Networks*, 194-197. Washington, DC: Lawrence Erlbaum.

De Jong, K. A. (1975) *An analysis of the behavior of a class of genetic adaptive systems*. Doctoral Thesis, Department of Computer and Communication Sciences. University of Michigan, Ann Arbor.

De Jong, K. & Spears, W. (1991) Learning concept classification rules using genetic algorithms. *Proceedings of the Twelfth International Joint Conference on Artificial Intelligence*, 651-656. Sydney, Australia: Morgan Kaufmann.

De Jong, K. A. (1992) Are genetic algorithms function optimizers? *Proceedings of the Second International Conference on Parallel Problem Solving from Nature.*

Eshelman, L. J., & Schaffer, J. D. (1991) Preventing premature convergence in genetic algorithms by preventing incest. *Proceedings of the Fourth International Conference on Genetic Algorithms*, 115-122. La Jolla, CA: Morgan Kaufmann.

Fogel, L. J., Owens, A. J., & Walsh, M. J. (1966) *Artificial Intelligence Through Simulated Evolution*. New York: Wiley Publishing.

Fogel, D. B. (1992) An analysis of evolutionary programming. *Proceedings of the First Annual Conference on Evolutionary Programming*, 43-51. La Jolla, CA: Evolutionary Programming Society.

Fogel, D. B., & Atmar, J. W. (eds.) (1992) *Proceedings of the First Annual Conference on Evolutionary Programming*. La Jolla, CA: Evolutionary Programming Society

Fraser, A. S. (1957) Simulation of genetic systems by automatic digital computers. *Australian Journal of Biological Science*, 10, 484-491.

Fujiko, C., & Dickinson, J. (1987) Using the genetic algorithm to generate LISP source code to solve the prisoner's dilemma. *Proceedings of the Second International Conference on Genetic Algorithms*, 236-240. Cambridge, MA: Lawrence Erlbaum.

Goldberg, D. E. (1989a) Sizing populations for serial and parallel genetic algorithms. *Proceedings of the Third International Conference on Genetic Algorithms*, 70-79. Fairfax, VA: Morgan Kaufmann.

Goldberg, D. E. (1989b) *Genetic Algorithms in Search, Optimization & Machine Learning*. Reading, MA: Addison-Wesley.

Goldberg, D. E., Deb, K., & Korb, B. (1991) Don't worry, be messy. *Proceedings of the Fourth International Conference on Genetic Algorithms*, 24-30. La Jolla, CA: Morgan Kaufmann.

Grefenstette, J. G., and Baker, J. E. (1989) How genetic algorithms work: a critical look at implicit parallelism. *Proceedings of the Third International Conference on Genetic Algorithms*, 20-27. Fairfax, VA: Morgan Kaufmann.

Grefenstette, John J. (1989) A system for learning control strategies with genetic algorithms. *Proceedings of the Third International Conference on Genetic Algorithms*, 183-190. Fairfax, VA: Morgan Kaufmann.

Grefenstette, J. G. (1992) Deception considered harmful. *Proceedings of the Foundations of Genetic Algorithms Workshop*. Vail, CO: Morgan Kaufmann.

Harp, S. A., Samad, T., & Guha, A. (1991) Towards the genetic synthesis of neural networks. *Proceedings of the Fourth International Conference on Genetic Algorithms*, 360-369. La Jolla, CA: Morgan Kaufmann.

Holland, J. H. (1975) *Adaptation in Natural and Artificial Systems*. Ann Arbor, Michigan: The University of Michigan Press.

Holland, J. (1986) Escaping brittleness: The possibilities of general-purpose learning algorithms applied to parallel rule-based systems. In R. Michalski, J. Carbonell, T. Mitchell (eds.), *Machine Learning: An Artificial Intelligence Approach*. Los Altos: Morgan Kaufmann.

Janikow, C. (1991) *Inductive learning of decision rules from attribute-based examples: A knowledge-intensive genetic algorithm approach*. TR91-030, The University of North Carolina at Chapel Hill, Dept. of Computer Science, Chapel Hill, NC.

Koza, J. R. (1991) Evolving a computer program to generate random numbers using the genetic programming paradigm. *Proceedings of the Fourth International Conference on Genetic Algorithms*, 37-44. La Jolla, CA: Morgan Kaufmann.

Lipsitch, M. (1991) Adaptation on rugged landscapes generated by iterated local interactions of neighboring genes. *Proceedings of the Fourth International Conference on Genetic Algorithms*, 128-135. La Jolla, CA: Morgan Kaufmann.

Manderick, B., de Weger, M., & Spiessens, P. (1991) The genetic algorithm and the structure of the fitness landscape. *Proceedings of the Fourth International Conference on Genetic Algorithms*, 143-149. La Jolla, CA: Morgan Kaufmann.

Männer, R., & Manderick, B. (1992) *Proceedings of the Second International Conference on Parallel Problem Solving from Nature*, Amsterdam: North Holland.

Mühlenbein, H., & Schlierkamp-Voosen, D. (1993) The distributed breeder genetic algorithm. Submitted to the *Journal of Evolutionary Computation*.

Rechenberg, I. (1973) *Evolutionsstrategie: Optimierung Technischer Systeme nach Prinzipien der Biologischen Evolution*. Frommann-Holzboog, Stuttgart.

Schaffer, J. D., Eshelman, L. J. (1991) On crossover as an evolutionarily viable strategy. *Proceedings of the Fourth International Conference on Genetic Algorithms*, 61-68. La Jolla, CA: Morgan Kaufmann.

Schaffer, J. D. & Morishima, A. (1987) An adaptive crossover distribution mechanisms for genetic algorithms. *Proceedings of the Second International Conference on Genetic Algorithms*, 36-40. Cambridge, MA: Lawrence Erlbaum.

Schraudolph, N. N., & Belew, R. K. (1992) Dynamic parameter encoding for genetic algorithms. *Machine Learning Journal*, Volume 9, Number 1, 9-22.

Schwefel, H.-P. (1981) *Numerical Optimization of Computer Models*. New York: John Wiley & Sons.

Shaefer, C. G. (1987) The ARGOT strategy: adaptive representation genetic optimizer technique. *Proceedings of the Second International Conference on Genetic Algorithms*, 50-58. Cambridge, MA: Lawrence Erlbaum.

Smith, S. (1983) Flexible learning of problem solving heuristics through adaptive search. *Proceedings of the Eighth International Joint Conference on Artificial Intelligence*, 422-425. Karlsruche, Germany: William Kaufmann.

Spears, W. M., and De Jong, K. A (1991) On the virtues of uniform crossover. *Proceedings of the Fourth International Conference on Genetic Algorithms,* 230-236. La Jolla, CA: Morgan Kaufmann.

Spears, W. M. (1992a) Crossover or mutation? *Proceedings of the Foundations of Genetic Algorithms Workshop,* Vail, Colorado: Morgan Kaufmann.

Spears, W. M. (1992b) Adapting crossover in a genetic algorithm. *Naval Research Laboratory AI Center Report AIC-92-025.* Washington, DC 20375 USA.

Vose, M. D., & Liepins, G. E. (1991) Schema disruption. *Proceedings of the Fourth International Conference on Genetic Algorithms,* 237-242. La Jolla, CA: Morgan Kaufmann.

Whitley, D. (1989) The GENITOR algorithm and selection pressure: why rank-based allocation of reproductive trials is best. *Proceedings of the Third International Conference on Genetic Algorithms,* 116-121. Fairfax, VA: Morgan Kaufmann.

Whitley, D., Starkweather, T., & Fuquay, D. (1989) Scheduling problems and traveling salesmen: the genetic edge recombination operator. *Proceedings of the Third International Conference on Genetic Algorithms,* 133-140. Fairfax, VA: Morgan Kaufmann.

Whitley, D., Mathias, K., & Fitzhorn, P. (1991) Delta coding: an iterative search strategy for genetic algorithms. *Proceedings of the Fourth International Conference on Genetic Algorithms,* 77-84. La Jolla, CA: Morgan Kaufmann.

Whitley, D. (ed.) (1992) *Proceedings of the Foundations of Genetic Algorithms Workshop.* Vail, CO: Morgan Kaufmann.

ML techniques and text analysis

Pieter Adriaans

Syllogic B.V.
Houten

Abstract

In this paper text analysis is presented as a special subdiscipline of automated language learning, which in itself is a subdiscipline of machine learning. A formal classification scheme for analysis of language learning algorithms in terms of abstract learners and speaker/authors is introduced. The inductive inference approach of Gold and successors is rejected as being of little practical value. The perspectives of this newly emerging field are discussed in the light of a number of exemplifying research projects.

1 Introduction

Although the ideal of a completely transparant natural language interface to a computer is still way out of reach, there is an abundance of interesting applications of ML techniques to text analysis. People are producing more and more texts at increasing speed. It is impossible to read everything. Therefore the need for automatic text analysis is growing rapidly.

The field of machine learning of language has witnessed substantial growth in interest and results in the past few years. Machine Learning techniques are in principle very useful in the context of language learning. Yet language learning has special problems of its own, that are not in the focus of interest of most researchers in the ML community, e.g.:

- The special algebraic structure of linguistic samples

- The highly structured and complex nature of language, and in particular the supposed irregularities, synonyms, metaphors etc.

- The complex interplay between the partial information about syntax and the lack of definition in the semantics of the samples.

- Special biases concerning the 'cooperativeness' of the author or speaker

These aspects call for another approach incorporating different algorithms, different complexity measures and different sampling techniques. At the moment contributions to this field tend to be scattered over various subfields (ML, AI, linguistics, psychology etc.). In this paper we will try to give an impression of this newly emerging field.

Before we proceed we wish to make two disclaimers. In the first place it is not possible to give a complete picture of the field within the limited space available. We will only touch upon developments that we think are important from our own limited point of view. Given the lack of a clearly defined research community it is possible that we overlook developments that are interesting. The fact that some research is not mentioned does not mean that we do not consider it to be important since the projects we discuss are only exemplifying. In the second place the explicit focus on text analysis does not imply that we are not interested in speech analysis. By excluding speech we hope to make life easier. There is an abundance of interesting applications of ML techniques in Text analysis. Incorporating speech seems to be much harder, although there are indications that interesting forms of cross fertilization between these two fields are possible.

The field of language learning has long been neglected in traditional linguistics. Learnability is an important criterion to judge the validity of any grammatical formalism aiming at explaining structures in natural language. One of the reasons interesting NL applications are still out of reach is the knowledge acquisition bottleneck in the definition of grammars and lexicons. ML techniques are beginning to be used to alleviate this problem.

1.1   A formal model

In [3] a formal model to study various forms of automated language learning is proposed. Language learning is seen as a process that involves at least two agents: a learner and a speaker (or author). Their interaction can be described in an operational setting in terms of rights and obligations in a language game. An abstract speaker/author is a mathematical formalisation of a certain kind of linguistic behaviour. It is a model of performance. In the general we can say that we can learn a language if we can deduce competence from performance. Consequently it is not possible to say something about the learnability of a language per se. We can only investigate learnability in relation to a certain kind of behaviour of a dialogue partner: i.e. a 'teacher' or an abstract opponent. Learnability therefore is not an abstract quality of a language. Our ability to learn a language may vary with ability or willingness of our teacher to adapt his behaviour. Learning a language is equal to getting to understand a speaker. We have learned (c.q. we understand) a language when we can predict (or imitate) the behaviour of a speaker based on information about his performance so far. The problem of learning a language is reduced to that of learning behaviour by observing behaviour.

The interactions in a pure linguistic rational dialogue presuppose that we are able to analyze the meaning of new concepts introduced by our opponent in pure operational terms. To do this we introduce the concept of an abstract speaker/author. An abstract speaker/author is a formal model of a speaker or author who is defending certain views. Formally an abstract speaker is a set $A = < D, L, S, E_P, O >$ where:

- D is a lexicon,

- L is a language which is a subset of the Kleene closure $D*$ of D,

- S is the set of true sentences of L,

- E_P is an examples routine that produces an element of S according to a mode of presentation P when called and

- O is an oracle routine that tells us whether or not a certain element of $D*$ is member of L and S.

The mode of presentation P is a formal notion corresponding to teacher behaviour. Various approaches to automated language learning can be modeled in relation to various definitions of abstract speakers. Different levels of supervision can be interpreted as different possibilites to influence the examples routine. An extreme form of unsupervised learning just discards the oracle routine. Different modes of presentation can be analysed to estimate their effect on the learnability of a language. This brings us to the following definition:

Learnable Abstract Linguistic Behaviour (LALB). Let $A = < D, L, S, E_P, O >$ be an abstract speaker of a language with a finite syntax and semantics. The behaviour of A is effectively learnable if there exists an algorithm that in time polynomial to a description of the language L and its semantics S constructs a function F that (with high probability) correctly predicts the behaviour of the oracle O.

It is clear that the learnability of behaviour in this sense depends on the mathematical properties of the lexicon D, the syntactic structure of the language L, the regularity of the semantics S and the mode of presentation P of the examples routine E. There is a whole four dimensional spectrum of possible learning situations. The definition of LALB can be relaxed to syntactic learning when we consider examples routines that produce wellformed sentences instead of only true sentences.

The formal concept of an abstract speaker/author can be used to model various interesting real life projects. It is not possible to go into formal details but examples of interesting applications are:

- Semantic and syntactic disambiguation of texts

- Text search algorithms for free text databases

- Automated document classification

- Automatic information/data extraction from text

- Adaptive NLP systems

- Automatic creation of dictionaries

- Automatic analysis of bi-lingual corpora

- Automatic creation of indexes

- Automatic acquisition of grammar rules

In the third part of this paper we will see that a number of these projects are currently being investigated.

1.2 Early attempts: Distributional analysis

The fact that it is fairly easy to recognize interesting syntactical patterns in texts using statistical techniques has been rediscovered over and over again ever since people began to analyse text with computers. Attempts have been made to construct algorithms that generate phrase structure grammars from the analysis of plain text. One early approach, advocated by Lamb, uses the distributional analysis of Harris and Hockett [15,16,17,19]. One defines phrase categories by associating phrase structures that are found in the same context. Contexts that share the same categories are considered to be equivalent. Complex phrase structure categories can be constructed by concatenation of simple categories. This approach has been criticised by Gold, who showed that even for the class of context free languages it is impossible to construct a learning algorithm that can learn a grammar from arbitrary free text. This means that we cannot learn a context free grammar by just listening to a speaker. The crux of the argument lies in the possibility to construct a teacher that for any learning algorithm constructs an example set that forces the learner to make an infinite number of wrong guesses. For a long time the criticism of Gold paralyzed serious research efforts in the field of automated text analysis so it is necessary to take a closer look at his results.

1.3 Gold's critique on unsupervised text analysis

In his landmark paper in 1967 Gold introduced the concept of identification in the limit [14]. The paper is important because it gives a conceptualization of the language learning problem that is mathematically feasible. First we specify a set of languages. Each language is taken to be a set of strings on the same finite alphabet. A teacher chooses a language from this set and a method of presentation. Every string in the language may only be presented once. The learner gets complete information if he gets positive as well as negative examples. Positive information means that he only gets positive examples. This equals the presentation of the language as plain text. The learning session starts at a certain moment of time t_0 and continues for ever. At each time t_n the learner receives a unit of information and is to make a guess as to the identity of the unknown language on the basis of the information received from the teacher sofar. The class of languages will be considered learnable with respect to the specified method of information presentation if there is a learning algorithm the learner can use to make his guesses and that has the following property: Given any language of the class there is some finite time after which the guesses will all be the same and they will be correct. One of the striking conclusions of this research was that context-free languages can not be identified on the basis of positive examples alone.

1.4   An evaluation of Gold's critique

What is the value of Gold's theories? We believe that the importance of Gold's work lies in the fact that he gave the theory of language learning a firm basis in recursion theory. His results however have a very limited practical value. They indicate extreme borderlines that only exist if we have infinite learning time. The concept is too abstract to give us any indication for the development of effective learning algorithms. The whole dimension of a systematic analysis of teacher behaviour and teacher-student interaction simply is not caught by the model of learning by enumeration. Therefore the most important question of finding effective practical heuristic strategies for language learning is not covered by Gold's research. It is exactly this dimension that we are interested in.

2   New developments from ML perspective

Although Gold's approach led to a number of interesting developments in the theory of inductive inference (See [6]) there has been very little progress in terms of practical applications of automated language learning. In the past few years however we have seen a number of developments that create a more promising perspective for language learning:

- Hardware with more power, e.g. cheap workstations and (massively) parallel architectures

- Better software tools, e.g. the general recognition of Prolog as implementation environment

- New ML paradigms, such as connectionist approaches, ILP and EBL

- New theoretical developments, such as Kolmogorov complexity and related concepts like the a priori probability of binary strings

- The availability of large text corpora on electronic media

Partly these developments are the same as those the ML community in general has benefited from, but there also has been a special impact on language learning research. In the following we will give an overview of some exemplary results.

2.1 Some current research

2.1.1 Inductive Inference, Complexity Theory and Information Compression

Some authors have deepened Gold's results in a more practical direction by formulating natural constraints that make certain types of grammar effectively learnable in certain circumstances. Theoretical results concerning constraints that make context-free languages effectively learnable are reported by Abe and Yokomori [33,1,2], although Abe's locality constraint seems rather artificial. Adriaans [5] has formulated 'Naturalness Constraints' that make context-free languages effectively learnable when sampling under the universal Solomonoff-Levin distribution [22].

In general minimum description length theory seems to be a promising approach to language learning. Powers for instance suggests that an unsupervised black-box approach based on information compression, could be most suitable for learning many structural properties exhibited by natural language [27].

In linguistic circles ideas concerning lexical cohesion of texts are beginning to emerge which suggest interesting approaches to automated language learning [25]. Also statistical approaches to parsing using socalled 'stochastic Context-Free Grammars' are promising in this respect [18].

2.2 Explanation-Based Learning (EBL)

Stan Matwin and Stan Szpakowicz (University of Ottawa) investigate methods to extract knowledge from expository texts. In such texts, examples are often introduced to show how to assemble rules acquired from the text into an operational concept or procedure. They apply EBL to accomplish this automatically [23]. Rey-Long Liu and Von-Wun Soo present a new language acquisition model to acquire parsing related knowledge via an EBL approach [21]. The domain theory in the model consists of two parts: a static part and a dynamic part. The static part consists of the universal linguistic principles proposed in the Generalized Phrase Structure Grammar (GPSG) formalism, while the dynamic part contains the context-free grammar rules as well as syntactic and thematic features of lexicons. In parsing both parts work together. Asker et al. describes a method for automatic lexical acquisition that extends an existing lexicon that, in addition to ordinary lexical entries, contains prototypical entries for various non-exclusive *paradigms* of open-class words [7]. This is done by reasoning about the constraints places on the unknown words in a text by *phrase templates* that have been abstracted from the grammar and domain specific texts using an explanation based learning method [29].

2.3 Connectionist approaches

Wellknown is the early research of Rumelhart and McClelland on learning the past tenses of english verbs [28]. St. John and McClelland present a parallel distributed processing model that learns to comprehend single clause sentences. The learning procedure allows the model to take a statistical approach to solving the bootstrapping problem of learning the syntax and semantics of a language from the same data [30]. In 1991 'Machine Learning' devoted a special issue to connectionist approaches to language learning [31], with special contributions on learning from ordered examples, inferring graded state machines and grammatical structure. The practical value of the proposals seems however limited.

2.4 Linguistic approaches

Valardi et al. observe that a poor encoding of the semantic lexicon is the bottleneck of many existing systems. To overcome these problems they propose an algorithm to learn syncategoremattical concepts from text examplars. Their knowledge acquisition method is based on learning by observations from examples of word co-occurrences (collocations) in a large corpus, detected by a morphosyntactical analyzer. Interactive human intervention is required in the training phase [32].

3 Conclusions: Directions for the future

These examples make clear that in different areas people from different disciplines are working on problems that have a close connection. It is the purpose of the workshop to bring these people together.

We conclude with a list of open problems that have to be solved before practical applications of ML in text analysis can be realized:

- Multi-layer learning, the combination of information on letter-, word-, sentence- or paragraph level in the learning process

- Ergonomic aspects of Text Analysis applications, i.e. batch analysis vs. on-line support

- Tractable practical complexity measures for various types of texts, i.e. a 'learnability' taxonomy

References

1. Abe, N., *Polynomial Learnability and Locality of Formal Grammars*, in Proceedings of the *26th Annual Meeting of the Association for Computational Linguistics*, ACL, 7-10 June 1988.

2. Abe, N. *Polynomial Learnability of Semilinear Sets*, Unpublished manuscript, 1988.

3. Adriaans, P.W., *A Domain Theory for Categorial Language Learning Algorithms*, in Proceedings of the Eighth Amsterdam Colloquium, P. Dekker and M. Stokhof (eds.), University of Amsterdam, 1992.

4. Adriaans, P.W., *Bias in Inductive Language Learning*, Proceedings of the ML92 Workshop on Biases in Inductive Language Learning, Abderdeen 1992.

5. Adriaans, P.W., *Language Learning from a categorial point of view*, Diss. Universiteit van Amsterdam, 1992.

6. Angluin, D., and C.H. Smith, *Inductive inference: Theory and Methods*, Computing Surveys, Vol 15, No. 3, pg. 237-269, 1983.

7. Asker, L., C. Samuelsson and B. Gambäck, *EBL²: An approach to automatic Lexical Acquisition* in Proceedings of the *14th International Conference on Computational Linguistics (COLING '92)*, Nantes, France.

8. Brent, M.R., *Automatic Acquisition of Subcategorization Frames from Untagged Text*, in Proceedings of the *29th Annual Meeting of the Assocation for Computational Linguistics*, pg. 209-214, ACL, 18-21 June 1991.

9. Brill, E., *Discovering the Lexical Features of a Language*, in Proceedings of the *29th Annual Meeting of the Association for Computational Linguistics*, pg. 339-340, ACL, 18-21 June 1991.

10. Cottrell, G.W., *A Connectionists Approach to Word Sense Disambiguation*, Morgan Kaufmann, 1989.

11. Daelemans, W. and D. Powers (eds.), *Background and Experiments in Machine Learning of Natural Language*, in *Proceedings First SHOE Workshop*, ITK, Tilburg University, 1992.

12. Dagan, I., *Lexical Disambiguation: Sources of Information and their Statistical Realization*, in Proceedings of the *29th Annual Meeting of the Association for Computational Linguistics*, pg. 341-342, ACL. 18-21 June 1991.

13. Finch, S. and N. Chater, *A Hybrid Approach to the Automatic Learning of Linguistic Categories*, University of Edinburgh, 1991.

14. Gold, E. M., *Language Identification in the Limit*, in *Information and Control*, Vol. 10, pg. 447-474. Academic Press, Inc., 1967.

15. Harris, Z.S., *Methods in Structural Linguistics*, Univ. of Chicago Press, Chicago, 1951.

16. Harris, Z.S., *Distributional Structure*, in *The Structure of Language*, J.A. Fodor and J.J. Katz (eds.), Prentice Hall, New York, 1964.

17. Hocket, C.F., *A Course in Modern Linguistics*, Macmillan, New York, 1958.

18. Jelinek, F. and J.D. Lafferty, *Computation of the Probability of Initial Substring Generation by Stochastic Context-Free Grammars*, in *Computational Linguistics*, Vol. 17, No. 3, pg. 315-324, MIT Press, 1991.

19. Lamb, S.M., *On the mechanization of syntactic analysis*, in *1961 Conference on Machine Translation of Languages and Applied Language Analysis*, (National Physical Laboratory Symposium No. 13), Vol. II, pg. 674-685, Her Majesty's Stationery Office, London, 1961.

20. Last, R.W., *Artificial Intelligence Techniques in Language Learning*, Ellis Horwood, 1989.

21. Liu, R.-L. and V.-W. Soo, *Augmenting and Efficiently Utilizing Domain Theory in Explanation-Based Natural Language Acquisition*, in *Machine Learning*, Proceedings of the Ninth International workshop (ML92), D. Sleeman and P. Edwards (Eds.), Morgan Kaufmann Publishers, San Mateo, 1992.

22. Li, M. and P.M.B. Vitányi, *Learning simple concepts under simple distributions*, SIAM Journal of Computing, pg. 911-935, 1991.

23. Matwin, S., and S. Szpakowicz, *Machine Learning Techniques in Knowledge Acquisition from Text*, in *Think*, Vol. 1, No. 2, pg. 37-50, ITK, 1992.

24. McClelland, J.L. and A.H. Kawamoto, *Mechanisms of Sentence processing; Assigning roles to Constituents of Sentences*, in *Parallel Distributed Processing, Explorations in the Microstructure of Cognition*, Volume 2: Psychological and Biological Models, J.L. McClelland , D.E. Rumelhart, and the PDP Research Group, MIT Press, Massachusetts, 1988.

25. Morris, J. and G. Hirst, *Lexical Cohesion Computed by Thesaural Relations as an Indicator of the Structure of Text*, in *Computational Linguistics*, Vol. 17, No. 1, pg. 21-48, MIT Press, 1991.

26. Powers, D.M.W. and W. Daelemans, *The extraction of hierachical structure for Machine Learing of natural language*, in Daelemans, W. and D. Powers (eds.), *Background and Experiments in Machine Learning of Natural Language*, in *Proceedings First SHOE Workshop*, ITK, Tilburg University, 1992.

27. Powers, D.M.W., *A Basis for Compact Distributional Extraction*, in *Think*, Vol. 1, No. 2, pg. 51-63, ITK, 1992.

28. Rumelhart, D.E. and J.L. McClelland, *On Learning the Past Tenses of English Verbs*, in *Parallel Distributed Processing, Explorations in the Microstructure of Cognition*, Volume 2: Psychological and Biological Models, J.L. McClelland, D.E. Rumelhart and the PDP Research Group, MIT Press, Massachusetts, 1988.

29. Samuelsson, C. and M. Rayner, *Quantitative evaluation f Explanation Based Learning as an Optimization Tool for a Large-scale Natural Language System*, in Proc. of the *12th International Joint Conference on Artificial Intelligence*, Sydney, Australia, pp 609-615.

30. St. John, M.F. and J.L. McClelland, *Learning and Applying Contextual Constraints in Sentence Comprehension*, in *Artificial Intelligence*, Vol. 46, No. 1-2, pg. 217-257, North-Holland, 1990.

31. Touretzky, D.S. (ed.), *Machine Learning, Special Issue on Connectionist Approaches to Language Learning*, Kluwer Academic Publishers, Vol. 7, no. 2/3, 1991.

32. Velardi, P., et al (eds.), *How to Encode Semantic Knowledge: A Method for Meaning Representation and Computer-Aided Acquisition*, in *Computational Linguistics*, Vol. 17, No. 2, pg. 153-170, MIT Press, 1991.

33. Yokomori, T., *Learning Context-Free Languages Efficiently, A Report on Recent Results in Japan*, in K.P. Jantke (ed.) *Proceedings Int. Workshop Analogical and Inductive Inference*, J. Siekmann (ed.), Lecture Notes in Artificial Intelligence, no. 397, pg. 104-123, October 1-6, 1989.

Authors Index

Springer-Verlag
and the Environment

We at Springer-Verlag firmly believe that an international science publisher has a special obligation to the environment, and our corporate policies consistently reflect this conviction.

We also expect our business partners – paper mills, printers, packaging manufacturers, etc. – to commit themselves to using environmentally friendly materials and production processes.

The paper in this book is made from low- or no-chlorine pulp and is acid free, in conformance with international standards for paper permanency.

ecture Notes in Artificial Intelligence (LNAI)

Lecture Notes in Computer Science

Vol. 631: M. Bruynooghe, M. Wirsing (Eds.), Programming Language Implementation and Logic Programming. Proceedings, 1992. XI, 492 pages. 1992.

Vol. 632: H. Kirchner, G. Levi (Eds.), Algebraic and Logic Programming. Proceedings, 1992. IX, 457 pages. 1992.

Vol. 633: D. Pearce, G. Wagner (Eds.), Logics in AI. Proceedings. VIII, 410 pages. 1992. (Subseries LNAI).

Vol. 634: L. Bougé, M. Cosnard, Y. Robert, D. Trystram (Eds.), Parallel Processing: CONPAR 92 – VAPP V. Proceedings. XVII, 853 pages. 1992.

Vol. 635: J. C. Derniame (Ed.), Software Process Technology. Proceedings, 1992. VIII, 253 pages. 1992.

Vol. 636: G. Comyn, N. E. Fuchs, M. J. Ratcliffe (Eds.), Logic Programming in Action. Proceedings, 1992. X, 324 pages. 1992. (Subseries LNAI).

Vol. 637: Y. Bekkers, J. Cohen (Eds.), Memory Management. Proceedings, 1992. XI, 525 pages. 1992.

Vol. 639: A. U. Frank, I. Campari, U. Formentini (Eds.), Theories and Methods of Spatio-Temporal Reasoning in Geographic Space. Proceedings, 1992. XI, 431 pages. 1992.

Vol. 640: C. Sledge (Ed.), Software Engineering Education. Proceedings, 1992. X, 451 pages. 1992.

Vol. 641: U. Kastens, P. Pfahler (Eds.), Compiler Construction. Proceedings, 1992. VIII, 320 pages. 1992.

Vol. 642: K. P. Jantke (Ed.), Analogical and Inductive Inference. Proceedings, 1992. VIII, 319 pages. 1992. (Subseries LNAI).

Vol. 643: A. Habel, Hyperedge Replacement: Grammars and Languages. X, 214 pages. 1992.

Vol. 644: A. Apostolico, M. Crochemore, Z. Galil, U. Manber (Eds.), Combinatorial Pattern Matching. Proceedings, 1992. X, 287 pages. 1992.

Vol. 645: G. Pernul, A M. Tjoa (Eds.), Entity-Relationship Approach – ER '92. Proceedings, 1992. XI, 439 pages, 1992.

Vol. 646: J. Biskup, R. Hull (Eds.), Database Theory – ICDT '92. Proceedings, 1992. IX, 449 pages. 1992.

Vol. 647: A. Segall, S. Zaks (Eds.), Distributed Algorithms. X, 380 pages. 1992.

Vol. 648: Y. Deswarte, G. Eizenberg, J.-J. Quisquater (Eds.), Computer Security – ESORICS 92. Proceedings. XI, 451 pages. 1992.

Vol. 649: A. Pettorossi (Ed.), Meta-Programming in Logic. Proceedings, 1992. XII, 535 pages. 1992.

Vol. 650: T. Ibaraki, Y. Inagaki, K. Iwama, T. Nishizeki, M. Yamashita (Eds.), Algorithms and Computation. Proceedings, 1992. XI, 510 pages. 1992.

Vol. 651: R. Koymans, Specifying Message Passing and Time-Critical Systems with Temporal Logic. IX, 164 pages. 1992.

Vol. 652: R. Shyamasundar (Ed.), Foundations of Software Technology and Theoretical Computer Science. Proceedings, 1992. XIII, 405 pages. 1992.

Vol. 653: A. Bensoussan, J.-P. Verjus (Eds.), Future Tendencies in Computer Science, Control and Applied Mathematics. Proceedings, 1992. XV, 371 pages. 1992.

Vol. 654: A. Nakamura, M. Nivat, A. Saoudi, P. S. P. Wang, K. Inoue (Eds.), Prallel Image Analysis. Proceedings, 1992. VIII, 312 pages. 1992.

Vol. 655: M. Bidoit, C. Choppy (Eds.), Recent Trends in Data Type Specification. X, 344 pages. 1993.

Vol. 656: M. Rusinowitch, J. L. Rémy (Eds.), Conditional Term Rewriting Systems. Proceedings, 1992. XI, 501 pages. 1993.

Vol. 657: E. W. Mayr (Ed.), Graph-Theoretic Concepts in Computer Science. Proceedings, 1992. VIII, 350 pages. 1993.

Vol. 658: R. A. Rueppel (Ed.), Advances in Cryptology – EUROCRYPT '92. Proceedings, 1992. X, 493 pages. 1993.

Vol. 659: G. Brewka, K. P. Jantke, P. H. Schmitt (Eds.), Nonmonotonic and Inductive Logic. Proceedings, 1991. VIII, 332 pages. 1993. (Subseries LNAI).

Vol. 660: E. Lamma, P. Mello (Eds.), Extensions of Logic Programming. Proceedings, 1992. VIII, 417 pages. 1993. (Subseries LNAI).

Vol. 661: S. J. Hanson, W. Remmele, R. L. Rivest (Eds.), Machine Learning: From Theory to Applications. VIII, 271 pages. 1993.

Vol. 662: M. Nitzberg, D. Mumford, T. Shiota, Filtering, Segmentation and Depth. VIII, 143 pages. 1993.

Vol. 663: G. v. Bochmann, D. K. Probst (Eds.), Computer Aided Verification. Proceedings, 1992. IX, 422 pages. 1993.

Vol. 664: M. Bezem, J. F. Groote (Eds.), Typed Lambda Calculi and Applications. Proceedings, 1993. VIII, 433 pages. 1993.

Vol. 665: P. Enjalbert, A. Finkel, K. W. Wagner (Eds.), STACS 93. Proceedings, 1993. XIV, 724 pages. 1993.

Vol. 666: J. W. de Bakker, W. P. de Roever, G. Rozenberg (Eds.), Semantics: Foundations and Applications. Proceedings, 1992. VIII, 659 pages. 1993.

Vol. 667: P. B. Brazdil (Ed.), Machine Learning: ECML – 93. Proceedings, 1993. XII, 471 pages. 1993. (Subseries LNAI).